THE GOOD GARDENER?

NATURE

HUMANITY

AND THE

GARDEN

Artifice
books on architecture

CONTENTS

4

For every gardener.

ACKNOWLEDGMENTS

In the summer of 2013, a remarkable collection of garden lovers gathered at the University of Delaware for a symposium titled *Earth Perfect? Nature, Utopia, and the Garden.* Inspired by our 2012 essay collection of the same title, the event brought gardening practitioners into heartfelt conversation with scholars and writers of the garden to consider certain fundamental questions: What constitutes a garden? Why did human beings begin to garden? How do we garden in this twenty-first century, and how should we garden in and for the future? Can a new ethos grounded in gardening lead us to a more sustainable relationship between humanity and the natural world? Is gardening indeed a utopian endeavor, the expression of an innate desire to perfect the Earth and of a hope that such perfection can be more nearly approached, if never fully achieved?

Over the course of four days the symposium participants shared their experience and ideas, and also enjoyed sustainability-themed tours of the magnificent public gardens at Winterthur, Longwood, Chanticleer, and Mt. Cuba Center, and of community gardens sponsored by the Delaware Center for Horticulture. The present collection, conceived as a companion to *Earth Perfect?*, is composed in large part of essays by these symposium participants and functions as an homage to the quality of engagement we enjoyed in those days together.

Neither this book nor the symposium would have been possible without the support of Ann Ardis, Director of the Interdisciplinary Humanities Research Center and Deputy Dean, College of Arts and Sciences; George Watson, Dean of the College of Arts and Sciences; and Matthew Kinservik, Associate Dean for the Humanities, all of University of Delaware; and Robbie and Wendy Richards. We also wish to thank the following: at Winterthur, David Roselle and Chris Strand; at Longwood, Paul Redman and Joan McClintock; at Chanticleer, Bill Thomas and Anne Sims; at Mt. Cuba Center, Eileen Boyle; at the Delaware Center for Horticulture, Pam Sapko and Lenny Wilson; at the Delaware Center for the Contemporary Arts, Maxine Gaiber and Maiza Hixson; Angela Treadwell Palmer of Millersville Native Plants; Timothy Murray and Mark Samuels Lasner from the University of Delaware Library, Special Collections; and, importantly, all whose participation helped to make the symposium so memorable.

Special debts of gratitude are owed to Jeffrey Chase for his symposium and website design, Jessica Henderson for her editorial assistance, and Donald Dunham for fielding myriad questions regarding content and style from the inception of the project. At Artifice books on architecture, we are grateful to Rachel Pfleger for designing another exquisite book and to publisher Duncan McCorquodale for embracing the project with such enthusiasm.

6 THE GOOD GARDENER: NATURE, HUMANITY, AND THE GARDEN

IRIS

I am from Puerto Rico, from Loíza, Puerto Rico, a very small town and near San Juan. So, when I came here to the United States I found out that I was supposed to be different than many other people because of my skin color. And I could not stand that because I came from a place where most of the people look like me, and that was fine, and we were having fun and celebrating and doing what was normal as a family and as a country. It really took me by surprise, and that gave me *coraje* — you know: I was sad, I was angry, I was mad, I was disappointed. It was frustrating that I have to act differently because people around me wanted me, or were telling me, that I was supposed to have like a little space where I could go and crawl away because of who I was. And I couldn't understand.

So when I started working on this Norris Square neighborhood project, I took every opportunity to present my country, Puerto Rico, as what it is. A US citizen place — you know, we are *Americanos*. And I started bringing in little pieces of culture through music, and through food, and through colors, and dance.

The gardens gave me that opportunity to really, really create these spaces that make me feel happy and comfortable, and I thought that many other people will feel the same way. This is a 2200 block of Palethorp Street, which was devastated by drugs. It was nuts in here, it was trashed. Before that, there were houses here, there were homes, there were people going to school and working, and having a normal life. But drugs destroyed all of that. And we end up with all these empty lots filled with trash.

The Pennsylvania Horticultural Society helped us to make these gardens, they gave us this opportunity. How do you do when the federal government takes 60 people from the community to federal prison? And the community is devastated because these people, they were mothers, and fathers, and brothers, and everything else. What do you do with a dirty space, with people very sad because they didn't have any contact with their loved ones? What do you do? Well, we take an empty lot and we turn that into a garden.

And with not a lot of resources, then you have to depend on recycling and using the 'Oops Paint'; they're only $6. And for some reason, these hideous colors that nobody wants — that's why they are called 'Oops Paint'. They are the wrong colors for people — those are the ones that I want and I get excited and happy, and that I put together. And this is what you see now. This is a place in the community. We don't have the community center, we don't have a theater, we don't have anything that we could walk to and have fun or gather.

So the gardens, specifically this one, Las Parcelas, has become that place where we get together as people and we celebrate. I started putting colors, and making curtains, and painting, and doing things like that, and the music. And then they asked me to coordinate the gardeners. I don't have any training in horticulture whatsoever, so that was another challenge and I took it as that, another challenge in life. Something else that life threw at me.

So I was planting hostas anywhere that I want to, that I thought they looked good. And then all the horticulturists, they come and say, "You know, do you know that this is a hosta?" "Yeah. I know it's a hosta." "Do you know that they like shade?" "Yes, I do but, in North Philly, they like sun." They didn't die and they were amazed that the hostas were doing so good in full sun. It shows adaptation, you know; as if they knew that's what we have and they perform for us.

So it was just like getting these plants. Whatever we get is what we planted because there were no resources. And what does this mean? We keep on planting. And what is this doing to us as people? It's not doing that much. So I started thinking, what if we build a *casita*, because that is something that will remind us of Puerto Rico — and stories, and grandmothers, and family, and life. And it was very tiny. It was *very* tiny and we have been adding through the years, every time that we get enough money.

So different people from the community, they have brought nails, pieces of wood, pieces of plywood, and for us, this was exciting. It's memories, it's family, it's life to be able to have the *casita*. And even if you are not a gardener here, people pass by and it's the jokes, and the stories, and everything. It has

Figure 1/ Iris. Photograph courtesy of GreenTreks Network, Inc.

brought people together. So I say that the program here that we're having is culture mixed with horticulture. But believe it or not, I put the culture first and then we add the 'h-o-r-t-i-'; that is how I would put it together: the culture with horticulture. And it has worked for us.[1]

JOE

I remember always having a garden from the age of around eight years old. Actually it was my mother's garden then. She loved roses and spent a lot of time tending to them. She would start another plant with a cutting from the old one. I watched her a lot when we were both outside in the garden.

The way I learned was to begin by taking a cutting a few inches long from new growth on the plant you want to duplicate. Then you take off the leaves that may be on the stem part that goes into the ground, just like you would do when you plant tomato plants in the spring. You then stick it in the ground where you want the plant to grow, water it good,

and put a big jar over it to help it begin growing. My mother said the jar helped the plant to grow. Well, she probably regretted showing me how to do it, and my father's giving me my own penknife, because every time I found an old jar, I would cut off some of her rosebush to start a new plant. Sometimes on my way home from school I would stop at some neighbor's yard to cut a piece of rosebush to make another. I remember one time there were more jars in her garden than there were rosebushes.

Being so young and learning things, I thought all bushes could be propagated that way. Whenever I saw a bush I liked, I would take out my knife and cut a piece to take home and plant. I never had any luck and so I guess I eventually gave up the practice.

It may have been when I was around ten years old when I learned a little about growing vegetables. A few relatives owned or rented ground for farming in New Jersey. They grew corn, tomatoes, potatoes, and squash among other things. My family spent a lot of time there just visiting. When

Figure 2/ Joe. Photograph by Phyllis D'Ambrosio.

it was planting time, I would ride up on the tractor and watch the seeds being planted. It was a funny-looking machine my uncle used to stick the seed into the ground. I think he made the machinery himself.

I was hardly ever there at planting time, but during the harvest I was there a lot. My uncle showed me how to drive the tractor, even though my mother didn't want me to learn. She didn't want me to do anything. If they were harvesting crops in the field when I was there, my uncle let me drive the tractor along as they loaded the produce or vegetables that had been picked and boxed onto the trailer and drive it to the barn to be unloaded and then drive it back out to the field.

When I was older, maybe around 12, my next foray into the garden was after Easter. We would always have plants around Easter. Tulips, hyacinths, lilies, and whatever else that someone gave us or my mother bought at the store. After the plants died in the house my mother would put them in the trash. That year I took them out of the trash and planted them in the garden. I got rid of the green wilted stems and covered them with dirt. I didn't tell my mother what I did because I didn't want to get hollered at for digging in the trash. Well, after a while nothing came up. I guess I thought they were like roses and were going to sprout soon, but nothing ever appeared and I forgot all about them.

The next year was surprising. My mother said there was something growing where nothing should have been. I went out to look. It was the plants from the trash that I planted. It was early spring with snow still on the ground and there were green things peeking out through the snow. A few weeks later it turned out to be the tulips, hyacinths, and daffodils. I told my mother I took them out of the trash and planted them last year after she threw them out. Do you know that she still hollered at me almost a year later for being in the trash? Mothers! That was my next learning experience. I learned about plants that grew from bulbs. I guess my mother learned about them, too, because after that, I never saw any more plants from Easter in the trash.

When I turned 14, I got a job at a steel fabrication shop painting steel. Wow, I was making 62 and a half cents an hour. The owner found out that I liked flowers and introduced me to his garden. It was all woody plants except for an area in front of his porch where there were flowers growing. It became my job for the next four years to plant his tulip and hyacinth bulbs every fall and dig them up every spring after they flowered. At times I would be tasked with cutting the lawn with a push-type mower. I was glad the lawn was not too big. He was an old Dutchman who didn't like to spend money.

The owner lived and worked in Philadelphia but had a large property in Pottsville, Pennsylvania. He drove me there one Saturday to paint his hairpin fence that faced the road in front of his house. That was where I learned about weeds. He didn't have a garden so to speak, but here and there along the fence were some plantings. There were weeds growing along the fence that needed to be pulled out in order to paint the fence. He didn't tell me which was which, but I soon learned which was which when he came out to check on my progress. He didn't rant and rave when he looked at the pile of what I thought were all weeds, but gave me a stern talking to. Anything else I pulled out went into a pile alongside the original pile, and then got covered with the original pile in case there were plants that should not have gotten 'the old heave-ho'.

It was off to high school next. Now I'm about 16. I sent for a flower catalogue from Burpee Seed Company. Wow, when it arrived I was so excited. I didn't know there were so many plants you could buy. I had money to buy plants because I had that part-time job. It was an interesting part of my life to be able to order plants from a catalogue and have them delivered to me by mail. When they came I would open the box and look at them wondering if they were going to grow, since many were bare root plants that I knew nothing about. There were also the iris-type plants that were grown from rootstock called rhizomes.

I was born and raised in Philadelphia. I lived in a row house with a backyard. It had dirt around the edges where the roses were growing. My father wouldn't let me break up the concrete for more flowers, so I scavenged bricks from wherever I could and accumulated enough to build a flowerbed on top of the concrete. My father bought me sand and cement and let me use his tools to build it. I didn't have gloves or think of wearing them. My fingers and hands had blisters, cuts, and calluses, and were always rough-feeling. I laugh to myself when I think of when that bed was finished. None of the bricks were too straight but it didn't fall apart. It lasted 30-some years. The dirt for the plants I had to get myself. My father told me that black-looking dirt was the best to use. I would take an empty bucket and put it in the basket on the front of my bike, pedal around to some fields and look for black dirt, fill the bucket and pedal back home with it. The bucket was big and when I filled it up it was heavy. Sometimes on the way home, I would fall over with the bike and spill the dirt. Then it would take me longer to get home and my mother would holler at me for being gone too long. It took a lot of bicycle rides to get enough dirt to fill the brick boxes for the flowers.

I ran out of room because I had so many flowers. I didn't know they got so big. I had to build two more beds with bricks to continue my endeavor. However, the next ones I built looked almost professional. I grew many plants from seed. I learned to save some seeds to plant the following year. I learned about annuals and perennials. I discovered that I liked perennials a lot more, since they came up every year without my help.

When I was out getting dirt with my bike I would see different flowers on plants. Sometimes I would dig the roots out and bring one or two home to plant in the garden. My mother would always ask me where I got the plant because they didn't sell that kind where we shopped. I think she may have been thinking I was stealing them.

My mother was getting exasperated because the flower locations were encroaching on her area to hang the clothes to dry. So I asked my aunt if I could plant some flowers in her yard. She said, "Of course you can." So I planted her yard also.

When I turned 18, I enlisted in the Army. I didn't find anything interesting with flowers there. When I was discharged three years later, my aunt, whose yard I had turned into a garden, called me up. She told me to get over to her house as soon as possible. She had an emergency only I could take care of. She wouldn't tell me what the emergency was but to hurry over.

It turned out to be a funny story. In the spring of the year before I went into the military, she had bought some pussy willows for decoration inside the house. They were quite tall for the vase and so she cut about a foot or so from the bottom of the stems so they fit where she wanted to show them. She threw the cut-off stem pieces into the trash. Well, me being a junk-picker, I just couldn't help myself, so I retrieved them out of the trash can and just stuck them into the ground to see if they would grow. They started to grow and I left for the military. They were in the ground for four years now and had gotten so tall and spread out over the clothes line that they just took up all the sun and she couldn't hang clothes out to dry anymore. I learned a lot about pussy willows that year. It was a tough job getting those roots out.

Off and on and here and there I fiddled with gardening for quite a few years. I finally got married in 1978. We lived in an apartment for a couple of years. There was a piece of ground adjacent to the building where we lived where we were allowed to have a garden. I thought it would be nice to just grow some vegetables for ourselves instead of flowers. We made some friends during that time. One family has now been our friends for the past 34 years. The ground wasn't too good for hand-tilling. It needed plenty of work. I borrowed my uncle's tiller to loosen up the soil and after I did my plot I loaned it to my new friend to do his plot. I mostly planted tomatoes and cucumbers. They are the best when they come right out of the garden. It took quite a bit of work to get the ground ready for planting. I dug some peat moss and fertilizer in and I was ready to go. What I didn't care for too much was the water. It had to be carried over in buckets, for the spigot was a good 200 feet away from the garden. The crops turned out fairly well. There were some veggies to give away.

One of the other plots was tended by a hired gardener. Two neighbors had hired him to do their work in their garden plots. He was a good worker. He had those plants looking really good. I'd swear he was out there day and night. Well, it was a hot summer. There wasn't too much rain and the plants seemed to dry out rather quickly. I think the gardener had to leave for some emergency and was gone for a while. Meanwhile the plot owners took care of the garden. Some of the tomatoes started to get blossom-end rot, but it wasn't really too bad. It looked as though just one of the varieties had it. One morning I awoke for work and went to water the garden. When I got there, the tomato plants of that two-person garden were decimated. The red tomatoes looked to be ok but all the green foliage on the plants was curling up and dying. It turned out that the two persons thought the tomatoes had some kind of fungus or disease and bought something to spray on them to help get rid of it. Whatever they bought and sprayed was killing the plants. The next morning the hired gardener returned to the garden and discovered his work deteriorating before his eyes. He was sort of an unhappy person to say the least. He quit that day and I never saw him again. I never did find out what was sprayed on those tomato plants and I'm very glad that the wind didn't carry it over to mine.

After two years in the apartment we purchased a house and moved. It was an end unit on a row of townhouses. It had a large side and rear lawn with a few small ash trees. The following spring I began a garden anew. I started a vegetable garden with tomatoes, cucumbers, peas, and peppers, both hot and sweet. It did rather well that year. The following year I added strawberries and raspberries. The strawberries were great but I never did get any raspberries. It seemed the birds really liked them, too, and got to them just before I would get to pick them. That went on for a couple of years till I decided the raspberries had to go.

I replaced them with pumpkins. I must admit, I didn't know how much room was needed for them. Those vines took over the garden. They grow up to six inches per day at their peak and grew 40 to 50 feet in length. Eventually the vines were growing close to the door. One morning when I opened the door, about two feet of the vine fell into the house. It had been windy the night before and I figured the wind blew the vine towards the door. It was as if the plants wanted to come in. That was my first and last experience with pumpkins. Too much work for the one pumpkin from the vines. It was good though. I think it made four pumpkin pies.

I wanted some trees on the property to shade some of the garden and house. I picked out a couple of birch trees. I began to dig a hole for them. The two ideal symmetrical places to put them had rocks a few inches beneath the soil. I may have been able to relocate them but this is where they would look the best. I borrowed a compressor and jackhammer from my pal and went to work on those rocks. Well, those rocks were granite. I heated and hammered and hardened those points I was using at least a half dozen times. Those rocks were hard. I finally got them out by drilling holes in them and driving a point in to break them apart. I spent a good four days on each hole. Finally the trees got planted. They really looked great and were getting big. I guess about five years later they got some kind of fungus and began to die. If I had caught it earlier I might have saved them but, alas, I was too late. They did make good firewood for the fireplace, though.

I put in some pussy willows along the side of the house where the birch trees came out. I would say about six feet from the curb. They grew and grew and grew. I liked them and they looked nice, especially in the spring. The only problem with them was that they liked growing toward the west, which is where the street was. After about ten years they came out, too.

In 1998 we purchased a single home across the street from where we lived for 18 years. It was time to start another garden. Instead of one large garden, I had three areas to garden. I heard there was a rock quarry in the area and I must have been right on it. Wherever I dug there was a rock. I had a couple of piles of them. One day my wife asked if she could have a few. I gave them all to her and she made borders around different plantings. I had to help her with some of the heavier ones that she couldn't lift. She did a great job. I think this year she is making a rock garden.

I continue putting in my regular vegetable garden plants. The flower garden is increasing in size every year. I usually purchase a plant or two that I do not have. I ran across some gladiolus bulbs last spring and stuck them in. It looked like thin long blades of grass that came up. I planted them deep enough to winter them over, so they should be coming stronger this year. While purchasing mine, I thought I'd get some for my cousin. I gave them to her and told her how to plant them. I kept asking her how they were doing and she told me that just some grass was growing where she planted the bulbs and she pulled out the grass. I laughed and told her that it was the gladiolus she pulled out. Now she is waiting to see this year if anything comes up. I also would like to plant a fig tree. I think I can put it close to the house on the leeward side so the winter wind doesn't have much effect on it. I have seen quite a few in this zone so I'm anticipating it will do well.

This year I'm becoming an arboriculturist. There are too many trees on my property that interfere with the sun falling on the vegetable garden areas, especially the high noon areas. I have been doing minor trimming over the years but it has been mainly on the lower branches. This year I'll have to rent a high reach and sharpen up my chain saws. I may even cut down the two trees I don't like and plant a couple of mountain ash trees.

My gardens pale in comparison with the ones I see in garden books. Anyone can come in and look at mine, so I guess they are public gardens. My gardens can all be seen from the street when cars or pedestrians pass by. The only section that is sort of walled off is what I call the nature section. It has some forsythia on the outside facing the street. It is shaded most of the day and has many a pretty weed growing there in the summer. They may be some type of flower but most of them I got from different fields when they were in bloom because I liked the flower. I just call them weeds because I have

never looked them up to see what they might be. I'm just content to look at them.

I don't really know when I started composting, but it was at an early age. It was one day when I was working, I glanced over at the neighbor digging a hole and putting some stuff in the ground and covering it with dirt. I went over to her and asked what she was planting. She told me it was just some vegetable scraps and instead of throwing them out, she buries the scraps in the garden because it is like fertilizer for the plants. Her garden looked nice and pretty so I started doing the same thing in my mother's garden. I now have a compost bin but I still, on occasion, dig a hole next to some plants and bury green waste. While I'm digging the hole I usually come across earthworms so it must be a healthy thing to do.

In the fall when the leaves are falling, I'll get out my lawn vacuum machine that sucks up and mulches the leaves into tiny pieces and gathers them in a bag and start cleaning off the lawn. I'll take those mulched leaves and spread them under the bushes to do whatever they do next. While I'm doing that, I look around at my neighbors' properties and see their bags of leaves out by the curb to be picked up by the trash men. I wonder why my neighbors don't do what I do. A few have told me that I could have their leaves if I want them. I told them politely, no thanks. I think they just wanted to get rid of their leaves for free. One also asked if I wanted his grass clippings since he bags his when he cuts his grass. I told him that I would take them if they didn't have chemicals sprayed on them. He wasn't aware that various chemicals aren't good for the garden or food grown there, but he knows it now.

Gardening has really changed over the years I have been on this earth. It seems as though there were more gardens back when I was growing up. Some gardens sprang up because of World War II. Back in the 1940s, many items were rationed, like butter, coffee, sugar, and flour, and many more items that I can't remember. Fruits and vegetables were hard to get, so many people had gardens to have fresh things to eat. Wherever you went, there they were full of vegetables that people liked to eat. As time progressed to the 1960s and 1970s, there were large farms producing lots of fruits and vegetables. The only problem was the farmers were now selling their stuff nationally and the fruits and vegetables had to have a longer shelf life to satisfy the customers. Eventually some of the fruits and vegetables started to taste different. The scientists, in breeding the fruits and vegetables to make them last longer, were causing them to lose their taste. Take for instance, the tomato. Back in the 1940s and 1950s, they tasted much better than they do today. Today it is quite hard to find a really good tomato the way they used to be, unless you grow it yourself. Back then they were picked when they were ripe. Today they are picked green and stored in a cooler and given a shot of ethylene gas to make them turn red, then sent right to the market. They sure last a long time on the shelf now, but their taste isn't too good.

In the late 1940s I remember hucksters used to come around with their horse and wagons selling fresh fruits and vegetables. It seemed like everyone on my block would buy something. When watermelons were in season the hucksters would cut a plug of the watermelon so you could taste for yourself just how sweet it was. I don't know of anyone doing that today. I can hear that refrain of theirs, "Waaaateermelon red ripe waaaateermelon, 75 cents apiece. Peaches, fresh peaches, four pounds for a dollar. Straaaawberries, red ripe straaaawberries." It seems like yesterday.

It's starting to come full circle now. People are starting to realize that things out of the garden have more taste and so more gardens are starting to spring up. So, if you don't have a garden, start one. See what happens![2]

DEREK

Gardeners are passionate about rakes and hoes. I've had my hoe cast in bronze and it sits on the windowsill at Pheonix House, one of the few objects that has passed the HB test. My earliest memories are of the old lawnmower with which we labored to cut the grass. I am so glad there are not lawns in Dungeness. The worst lawns, and for that matter the ugliest gardens, are along the coast in Bexhill — in Close and Crescent. These are the 'gardens' that would give Gertrude Jekyll a heart attack or turn her in her grave. Lawns, it seems to me, are against nature, barren and often threadbare — the enemy of a good garden. For the same trouble as mowing, you could have a year's vegetables, runner beans, cauliflowers and cabbages, mixes with pinks and peonies, shirley poppies and delphiniums; wouldn't that beautify the land and save us from the garden terrorism that prevails?

My first garden tool was a little trowel with which I kept the flowerbeds in front of the Nissen hut in order. When I left home in 1960 my parents kept my spades and rakes for me and after my father died I stored them behind a chest in my flat in London.

My precious hoe is worn down by work, its head held to the shaft by three rusty nails. The rake is even nearer my heart because its shaft broke and I put the whole thing in the bonfire to clean out the wood and replaced it with a very beautiful piece of driftwood.

Rake, hoe, shovel and trowel are the most useful tools here, and the secateurs to clip back the santolinas; spades and

Figure 3/ Derek, 1992. Photograph courtesy of REX, Geraint Lewis.

forks are of little use, except for shifting manure. The wood of the tools is polished by my hand; the rake, which is used most often, glitters a dull pewter.

There is a shop in Appledore which has wonderful garden tools and is very expensive. I bought a utility spade there, with its ace-of-spades shape for £7. Unlike woodworking tools, there isn't yet a market in garden tools which are objects of both practicality and great beauty.

I was always a passionate gardener — flowers sparkled in my childhood as they do in a medieval manuscript. I remember daisies — white and red — daisy chains on the lawn, fortresses of grass clippings, and of course the exquisite overgrown garden of Villa Zuassa, by Lake Maggiore, where in April 1946 my parents gave me my first grown-up book: *Beautiful Flowers and How to Grow Them*. The garden cascaded down to the lake, its paths banked by huge camellias. The beds were full of fiery scarlet pelargoniums — the scent of red. By the shore, lizards ran over a stone monument.

There were enormous pumpkins, and mulberry trees to feed the silkworms belonging to the little lady in black who lived in the lodge. The flowers in the beds along the rose pergola — lupins, peonies and shirley poppies — bloomed under the showers of petals from pink roses. The heady scent of privet and lime drifted into the walled garden.

I came home to my parents' married quarters and planted a purple iris. My father capitalized on my interest and was happy to let me mow the lawn, but my childhood passion was put to an end when I moved up to London at 18.

When I came to Dungeness in the mid-eighties, I had no thought of building a garden. It looked impossible: shingle with no soil supported a sparse vegetation. Outside the front door a bed had been built — a rockery of broken bricks and concrete: it fitted in well. One day, walking on the beach at low tide, I noticed a magnificent flint. I brought it back and pulled out one of the bricks. Soon I had replaced all the rubble with flints. They were hard to find, but after a storm a few more would appear. The bed looked great, like dragon's teeth — white and grey. My journey to the sea each morning had purpose.

I decided to stop there; after all, the bleakness of Prospect Cottage was what had made me fall in love with it. At the back I planted a dog rose. Then I found a curious piece of driftwood and used this, and one of the necklaces of holey stones that I hung on the wall, to stake the rose. The garden had begun.[3]

Figure 4/ Derek's garden, 2008. Prospect Cottage, back, Dungeness, Kent, UK. Photograph by Amanda White.

Figure 5/ Derek's garden, 2008. Prospect Cottage, front, Dungeness, Kent, UK. Photograph by Amanda White.

16

NATURE, HUMANITY, AND THE GARDEN

The Lord God planted a garden eastward in Eden, and there He put the man whom He had formed. And out of the ground the Lord God made to spring up every tree that is pleasant to the sight and good for food. The tree of life was in the midst of the garden, and the tree of the knowledge of good and evil. A river flowed out of Eden to water the garden, and there it divided and became four rivers…. Then the Lord God took the man and put him in the Garden of Eden to tend and keep it.[4]

(Genesis 2:8–10, 15)

In the Biblical tradition, the first human was a gardener, and after his expulsion from the Garden of Eden for eating the fruit of the Tree of Knowledge, his life as gardener would become one of hardship and toil as he coaxed an uncertain harvest from an unfamiliar, barren earth. While this gardener's story is linked specifically to the Judeo-Christian tradition, it is, nevertheless, the story of humanity more broadly. It is a universal tale. To be human is to be a gardener. But how is this so — and why?

Iris, Joe, and Derek, each in their own way, provide the answers. Their words reveal that their toilsome creations, their cherished gardens, are places of nourishment for the body and soul. They are places of healing, of self-discovery and self-expression, of political activism and social intercourse, and of environmental speculation and preservation efforts. They are the fundaments of culture and are simultaneously — what these gardeners have not overtly stated — the very guarantors of human life, a fact embedded deeply in the linguistic record. As Robert Finley in this collection reminds us, to garden is to cultivate, and to cultivate is both to 'dwell' or 'inhabit' and to 'till'.[5] These are all words derived from the Indo-European

————— **Figure 6/** Naturalists John Muir, on right, and John Burroughs, c. 1899. Photograph by Edward C. Curtis. John Muir Papers, Holt-Atherton —————
Special Collections, University of the Pacific Library. © 1984 Muir-Hanna Trust.

root $k^w el$-, revealing the deep truth that we must garden to live: we must clear or 'claim' a space in 'nature' to construct a dwelling, however humble, and we must cull the earth's bounty, even if indirectly, for our sustenance. Gardens, in all their myriad forms, define the nature of our relationship with the place — the Planet — we inhabit; and given that gardens are fundamental to human survival, the questions of how and why we garden should lie at the heart of all environmental discourse.

The essays gathered in this volume provide windows into gardens ranging from the palatial gardens of ancient Persia to the cemeteries of the American South, from the garbage dumps of Rio de Janeiro to the spiritual or 'cosmic' gardens of the Orient, from Aboriginal territories in Australia to the estates of Northern Ireland's landed gentry, and from Yellowstone National Park to the entire Earth. This volume was conceived as a companion to *Earth Perfect? Nature, Utopia, and the Garden*. Like its predecessor, it focuses on the garden as product of the innate human drive to perfect Earth and on the delicacy of this gardening venture. Being human, we are prone to error. That is the human condition. As gardeners, therefore, we are destined to err, so we would do well to tread lightly, to garden cautiously and gently. The seeds we plant may well yield fruit unimagined in scope and longevity.

John Muir spoke true when reflecting that "Going to the woods is going home."[6] Nature is our home, and this home is the garden.

Annette Giesecke, Naomi Jacobs.

In deepest gratitude to Iris Brown and Joe Wojciechowski, and in memory of Derek Jarman (1942–1994).

NOTES

1/ Interview with Iris Brown, lead gardener of Las Parcelas, and longtime resident of the Norris Square neighborhood, Philadelphia. PhilaPlace Collection [http://www.philaplace.org/media/742/], Historical Society of Pennsylvania. Transcription of the interview by permission of the Historical Society of Pennsylvania.

2/ Joe Wojciechowski, "My Life with Gardens", a presentation for the Earth Perfect? seminar at the University of Delaware, spring 2013, printed by permission of Joe Wojciechowski.

3/ Derek Jarman's words are excerpted from *Derek Jarman's Garden*, London: Thames & Hudson, 1995, pp. 7, 9, 11, 12, by permission.

4/ King James Version of the Bible.

5/ *The American Heritage Dictionary of Indo-European Roots*, Calvert Watkins rev. and ed., Boston: Houghton Mifflin Company, 1985, p. 33. For Robert Finley's essay, see pp. 162–171.

6/ Muir, John, *Our National Parks*, in *John Muir: Eight Wilderness-Discovery Books*, Terry Gifford intro., London: Diadem Books, 1991, p. 498. The location of Muir and Burroughs in Figure 6 is unknown. The John Muir Papers, Holt-Atherton Special Collections, University of the Pacific Library, state "probably Alaska" as location.

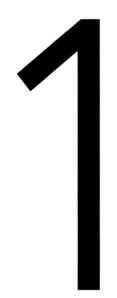

GARDENING

WITH

NATURE

20 /STEPHEN FORBES AND LEANNE LIDDLE

HIDDEN GARDENS: AUSTRALIAN ABORIGINAL PEOPLE AND COUNTRY

A song of the joy which lies in the land. Read it and feel humble at the greatness of humanity as a part of the world. 'The land is YOU'[1]

Gardening, as it is conventionally understood, has likely never been practiced in Aboriginal Australia. Millennia ago, domesticated plants and animals spread from south-eastern New Guinea to islands in the Torres Strait, lying between New Guinea and Australia, but stopped just short of the northern Australian coast. The historian Geoffrey Blainey considers this dramatic halt "one of the baffling questions in prehistory", but there may be a straightforward explanation. Aboriginal people may well have made a choice *not* to garden.[2] The Umpila people on the north east coast of Cape York, close to the Torres Strait, observe of gardening for food, "It is not our way. It is alright for other people. We get our food from the bush."[3] In 1977 the Yolngu elder Galarrwuy Yunupingu recalled his father's prohibition on unnecessarily disturbing the land:

> One day I went fishing with dad. As I was walking along behind him I was dragging my spear on the beach which was leaving a long line behind me. He told me to stop doing that. He continued telling me that if I make a mark or dig for no reason at all I've been hurting the bones of the traditional people of that land. We must only dig and make marks on the ground when we perform or gather food.[4]

This proscription might seem to disqualify Aboriginal land stewardship as garden cultivation. However, as we will demonstrate, the rigorous dialectic determining Aboriginal traditional law (the Law), the remarkable discipline and scope of the evolving curatorial practice in landscape management, the relationship with Country (the sum of the land and the sea, people, plants, and animals), and the deep understanding of place and plant materials evident in Aboriginal practice, art, and design all suggest a conception of gardening that cannot be said to be merely metaphorical.[5]

A garden may be the expression of our relationship with plants. That relationship, in turn, may be construed as a partnership rather than the exploitation characterizing horticultural and agricultural gardens. The nature of the partnership between people and plants expressed in the Aboriginal relationship with Country suggests a philosophy of cultivating a garden through the exercise of rights and responsibilities. Bill Gammage, a historian of Aboriginal land management, observes of Australia prior to 1788, when the British arrived: "There was no wilderness. The Law — an ecological philosophy enforced by religious sanction — compelled people to care for all their country. People lived and died to ensure this."[6]

Our success as a species is based on the role of plants as mediators between light and life and on the application of plants to human endeavor. Our relationship with plants represents our most profound and intimate relationship, after our relationships with one another and with the divine.

The search for knowledge, reconciliation, and even salvation through plants can be seen as a logical response to their transformative power.[7] An ideal garden, then, might better be better viewed in terms of a relationship and partnership than as the imposition of our will.

WHEN IS A PIECE OF LAND A GARDEN?

The definition of the word 'garden' has historically focused on an enclosure that protects a cultivated area from the wild. This emphasis is perhaps fitting, as enclosure may have been important to the survival of both cultivated plants and their cultivators.[8] The notion of cultivation, while significantly absent from the story of the Garden of Eden, has been integral to the idea of gardens.

Theophrastus, the ancient Greek philosopher and so-called father of botany, suggests in his *De causis plantarum* (*On the Causes of Plants*) two "great divisions" for the plant kingdom: spontaneous phenomena belonging either to the plant or to the country, and "phenomena initiated by human art, which either helps the nature of the plant achieve its goal or goes beyond it".[9] Essentially, Theophrastus distinguishes the natural expression of a plant's genotype (the nature of the plant) in its natural environment (the nature of the country) from the cultivated expression resulting from human art or intervention (presumably including enclosure). Although Theophrastus' "great divisions" are helpful in understanding our relationship with plants, the separation of humans from nature is largely misconceived, as the botanist David Mabberley has observed.[10]

Western gardens eventually dispensed with enclosures, and with that, the distinction between the garden and nature began to erode. The early eighteenth-century British landscape architect William Kent famously "leaped the fence and saw all Nature was a garden".[11] In the same leap, Western gardens dispensed with a straitened notion of cultivation.[12]

In our own century a British court considered whether land from which the owner had cleared trees constituted a garden (in which case the owner's action was legal) or not (in which case a license was required). In the 2008 decision, Lord Justice Moses found the *Oxford English Dictionary* definition of a garden as "an enclosed piece of ground devoted to the cultivation of flowers, fruit or vegetables" to be inadequate. Moses observed that "no description will categorically establish whether a piece of land is a garden or not. It is incumbent on the fact finder to determine its use." The definition of a garden, Moses ruled, lies in "the relationship between the owner and the land, and the history and character of the land and space".[13]

In contrast to Moses with his pragmatic, legalistic analysis, the garden scholar John Dixon Hunt defines gardens from the perspective of cultural history and landscape theory. A garden, says Hunt,

> will normally be out-of-doors, a relatively small space of ground (relative, usually to accompanying buildings or topographical surroundings). The specific area of the garden will be deliberately related through various means to the locality in which it is set: by the invocation of indigenous plant materials, by various modes of representation or other forms of reference (including association) to that larger territory. Either it will have some precise boundary, or it will be set apart by the greater extent, scope, and variety of its design and internal organization; more usually, both will serve to designate its space and its actual or implied enclosure. A combination of inorganic and organic materials are strategically invoked for a variety of usually interrelated reasons — practical, social, spiritual, aesthetic — all of which will be explicit or implicit expressions or performances of their local culture. The gardens will therefore take different forms and be subject to different uses.[14]

Hunt's detailed definition, writes the architect Donald Dunham, provides "a broader, more inclusive explanation as to what a garden is".[15] A perhaps more provocative definition of a garden, however, comes from Dunham himself — in the form of a question: "What then is the space ... between human intentions and nature? The garden?"[16]

Finally, we should consider the writer Robert Finley's meditations on the *Boreal Poetry Garden*, conceived in 2005 by the Canadian poet and artist Marlene Creates. On six acres of forest just outside St John's, Newfoundland, Creates has temporarily installed site-specific poems on card; Creates also presents live-arts events there, with walks and on-site poetry readings. In the absence of cultivation, Creates' garden is defined by her presence and by her relationship with the land, expressed through the site-specific poems. Finley suggests an alternative gardener's toolkit with which to tend Creates' garden: acknowledged transience, lightness of touch (or reticence), impressionability, and devotion to the ineffable qualities of places and their multiple histories. The contents of such a tool kit are determined by our relationship with a place rather than by the requirements of planting seeds and cultivation.

Finley reflects on the etymology of the word 'cultivate', which originates in "the Indo-European root $k^w el$- to revolve, circle, wheel, all of which we can see in the action of the plow or the spade on soil: a turning over".[17] But the word also means "to move around, sojourn, inhabit, and to dwell". Seeing gardens in spatial and temporal terms, from the multiple histories of viewers' perspectives, is important to our understanding of gardens [Figure 1]. Perhaps gardens are as much about our construction through our experience and memories as about the change through cultivation that

———— **Figure 1/** Danie Mellor's *Postcards from the edge (in search of living curiosities)* observes the assimilation of differing cultural influences ————
in merging colonial engraving and design with a European observer's naïve utopian (or paradisical) view of his own Aboriginal country.
Danie Mellor; Mamu, Ngagen and Ngajan people, Queensland. *Postcards from the edge (in search of living curiosities)*, 2011.
Mixed media on paper. Courtesy Art Gallery of South Australia.

can be documented and archived. Perhaps the nature of our relationship with the place we inhabit is as much a garden as is the physical act of cultivation.

THE DREAMING, LAW, AND COUNTRY

The "entire purpose" of Australian Aboriginal people, asserts the anthropologist Wade Davis, was "not to improve anything; it was to engage in the ritual and spiritual activities deemed to be essential for the maintenance of the world precisely as it was at the moment of creation". In Western terms, Davis says, this would be comparable to intellectuals' and scientists' having focused their efforts from the beginning of time on maintaining the Garden of Eden.[18]

Davis' claim that Australian Aboriginal people consciously sought "not to improve anything" is perhaps too stark — Aboriginal people certainly reimagined and redefined the Australian landscape. Their relationship with Country essentially defines an evolving curatorial practice in landscape management. Such curatorial practice, however, is certainly in marked contrast to the wholesale resetting of landscapes that characterizes farming of domesticated crops and that is encapsulated in the notion of the Neolithic Revolution (the apparently abrupt change from hunting and gathering to early agriculture) and the subsequent industrialization of modern agriculture. As the archaeologist Harry Lourandos suggests, Aboriginal people historically "resisted the direct imposition of food producing techniques" demonstrated by New Guineans, Torres Strait Islanders, and Macassans (trepang fishers from Indonesia).[19] In fact, even the presence on the Australian mainland of cultivated domesticates of species such as banana, taro, and greater yam provides no evidence of gardening, as these perhaps arrived when New Guinea and Australia were joined during the mid to late

Holocene 6,000 to 12,000 years ago. The distinctions among people, plants, and land inherent in agriculture are distant from holistic Aboriginal perceptions of caring for Country: agriculture, the anthropologist Athol Chase observes, "implies a radically different perception of the environment and its legitimate human occupants and … authorises a radically different manipulation of plants and their habitats".[20] The authorizing environment is a critical concept here — the relationship among people, plants, and land is rarely considered holistically in modern agriculture.

The authorizing environment and operating assumptions of European colonists in Australia were based on English climate, soils, and grasses. In 1785, prior to colonization of Australia by the British in 1788, President of the Royal Society and Australian botanical explorer Sir Joseph Banks expressed no doubt to the Committee on Transportation that "… the soil of many parts of the Eastern coast of New South Wales between the latitudes of 30 and 40 degrees is sufficiently fertile to support a considerable number of Europeans who would cultivate it in the ordinary modes used in England". While Banks' observation proved accurate, the change to the landscape as a result of expanding populations of sheep and cattle and changing fire regimes was rapid. Limited attention was paid to the variability of the Australian climate, the fragility of many Australian soils under the pressure of overgrazing by introduced hoofed animals, the ecology of native grasses, and the critical role of fire management — particularly, appropriate fire regimes. The result was a rapid decline in the sustainable productivity of the land. [21]

Aboriginal people, by contrast, have sought not to increase productivity but to stabilize the availability of resources. In the Australian environment, Lourandos submits, such an approach may well be the most sustainable.[22] Traditional Law provides the authorizing environment for Aboriginal peoples and determines the boundaries for an evolving curatorial practice in landscape management. The Law derives from Aboriginal understanding of the origin of Country. In English 'The Dreaming' (or 'Dreamtime') has fallen into common usage to encompass Aboriginal religion and to explain the origins of Country. The term appears to be based on the Arrernte word *altyjerre*, which refers both to the time of creation and to a dream (although *altyerr-iperre* has more recently been interpreted to mean "things that come into being as a result of events that happened in Story").[23] The anthropologist William Edward Hanley Stanner indicates the linguistic and cultural challenges here, as Aboriginal people in their own dialects "use terms like Alcheringa, mipuramibirina, boaradja — often almost untranslatable, or meaning literally something like 'men of old'".[24] For Anangu (Western Desert people including Pitjantjatjara and Yankunyjatjara people), the Law is embedded in the Tjukurrpa, a term Simon Forrest, a Wadjuk elder, defines as "a group's epistemology and cosmology

and their understanding of their place in the universe". Tjukurrpa also establishes "rules and laws for how people should act and behave within society and interact with the environment and natural phenomena", and it determines "an individual's responsibility and connectedness to all that surrounds life".[25] As the Yolngu elder Galarrwuy Yunupingu eloquently expressed:

> The land is my back-bone. I only stand straight, happy, proud and not ashamed about my colour because I still have land. The land is the art. I can paint, dance, create and sing as my ancestors did before me…. I think of the land as the history of my nation. It tells us how we came into being and [by] what system we must now live … my land is my foundation … without land I am nothing. [26]

The idea of Country resides within The Dreaming and the Law — a complex interlocking framework of social, cultural, spiritual, economic, and environmental dimensions. Aboriginal art perhaps provides the most accessible, though still powerful, interpretation of the relationship between people and The Dreaming, the Law, and Country. Bernard Tjalkuri's *Wati Punya* illustrates a narrative on Country as part of the Tjukurrpa around Watarru, on the Anangu Pitjantjatjara Yankunytjatjara (APY) lands in the north-west of South Australia [Figure 2]. Tjalkuri's work conveys a rich, multilayered, and continuing relationship with Country.[27] *Wati Punyu* tells the story of Country and of the punyu — a striking, largely black marsupial apparently now extinct that lived and nested in a burrow in spinifex grasslands.[28] Ginger Wikilyiri's *Kunumata*, 2008, and *Kunumata*, 2009, illustrate a narrative on Country as part of the Tjukurrpa around Kunumata, a sacred place near Nyapari on the APY lands [Figures 3, 4]. *Kunumata*, 2008, shows Kuniya kutu (carpet pythons) chasing mingkari (marsupial mice) in a landscape punctuated by many mice holes and rocky hills. The carpet pythons, through their presence at Kunumata, are

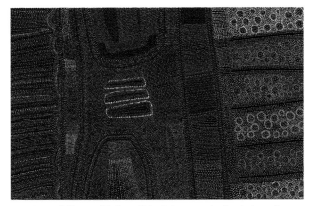

— **Figure 2/** Bernard Tjalkuri; Pitjantjatjara people, South Australia. —
Wati Punyu, 2009. Acrylic on canvas. Courtesy Art Gallery
of South Australia.

representative of actual carpet pythons and of mythic ancestral beings from the Tjukurrpa (The Dreamtime). *Kunumata*, 2009, shows the place of the Kuniya kutu: sacred hills and dunes that have strong Tjukurrpa and are connected with a network of Snake Dreaming stories stretching hundreds of kilometers (songlines) from Watarrka (Kings Canyon) to Kunumata. Kunumata is also close to sites important for ancestral 'ili' (native fig) beings and for the 'nyii nyii' (zebra finch) beings. The 'nyii nyii' beings' story stretches hundreds of kilometers south to the coast in the Great Australian Bight.[29]

Aboriginal art's evidence of relationship to Country and cultural protocols is vividly demonstrated in the Spinifex people's Native Title claim to 55,000 square kilometers of land, granted in the Federal Court of Australia in 2000.[30] The claim had been lodged in 1996, and a year later the Spinifex people began an arts project specifically to support it. The Spinifex people submitted to the court two paintings recording their link to the land; the paintings, collaborative artworks undertaken by men and women, were formally included in the preamble to the judgment.[31] The archaeologist and anthropologist Scott Cane describes the paintings of the Spinifex people as

Figure 5/ Simon Hogan; Pitjantjatjara people, Western Australia. *Tjitji Wirriryba*, 2009. Acrylic on linen. Courtesy Art Gallery of South Australia © the artist, courtesy Spinifex Arts Project.

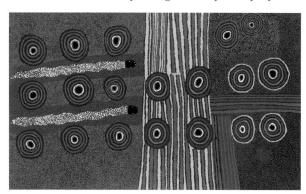

Figure 3/ Ginger Wikilyiri; Pitjantjatjara people, South Australia. *Kunumata*, 2008. Acrylic on canvas. Private Collection.

Figure 6/ Roy Underwood; Pitjantjatjara people, Western Australia. *Ungunkitji & Munparn*, 2009. Acrylic on linen. Courtesy Art Gallery of South Australia © the artist, courtesy Spinifex Arts Project.

Figure 4/ Ginger Wikilyiri; Pitjantjatjara people, South Australia. *Kunumata*, 2009. Synthetic polymer paint on canvas. Courtesy Art Gallery of South Australia.

expressions of "the grandeur of their law and the diversity and meaning of their country", and they helped to convince Chief Justice Michael Black that "the Spinifex People ... have a connection with the land and waters over which they claim native title."[32] These collaborative works marked the beginning of the continuing Spinifex Arts Project and the development of a substantial contribution to contemporary art that continues to describe the Spinifex people's deep connection to Country. Tjuntjuntjara community elder Simon Hogan's painting *Tjitji Wirriryba* utilizes the 'wanari' (mulga) tree and a series of rock holes to form the main design and to represent Walyuwalytjara, a place sacred for its connection to a creation time story about the 'minyma liru' (female snake)—an important element of the Tjukurrpa for the Spinifex people [Figure 5].[33]Another painting, Roy Underwood's *Ungunkitji & Munparn*, illustrates the Spinifex Country sandhills and waterholes, north-east of Ilkurlka, where water can be found year round due to the presence of highly revered powerful water snakes [Figure 6].[34] As Cane observes of the Spinifex people:

> Their world and their existence is a living metaphor of the mythology of the shadow in the sun. The Spinifex People live in a sheltered world known only to a few and protected from exposure by the desiccating remoteness of their life in the hardest landscape in the most arid continent on the face of the earth. Theirs is a secluded world, sequestered in the spinifex and sand, where drinkable water is hidden beneath the sand, food is camouflaged in arid gardens, raw materials are nowhere apparent, and the sacred realm is secret.[35]

ABORIGINAL GARDENS? TRADITIONAL OWNERSHIP, *TERRA NULLIUS*, AND GARDENS

A tacit assumption of land ownership runs through conventional notions of gardens. Such ownership is usually expressed through land title, perhaps less commonly through a formal lease or license, and less often again through more tenuous or ephemeral relationships such as squatting or so-called guerrilla gardening.[36] Owners of public gardens also frequently bear the responsibility for a garden's management, though not necessarily.

Land ownership among Aboriginal people is complex and generalizations can be unhelpful. However, in exploring land among the Pintupi people from the Western Desert, anthropologist Fred Meyers provides a useful shorthand: land ownership resides in the relationships a person can claim between himself and a place. Ownership consists "primarily in control over the stories, objects, and ritual associated with the mythological ancestors of The Dreaming at particular places". An individual's identification with Country "must be actualized and accepted by others through a process of negotiation", which "objectifies social relations among persons into an enduring arrangement of sharing an estate".[37] Among the Spinifex people, Scott Cane observes, knowledge of Tjukurrpa alone is not sufficient for claiming ownership of land. However, Tjukurrpa does figure as "a means for negotiating rights and interests in land". Cane writes: "One can speak for country—and thus assert rights and interest over it—if one is fully cognisant of the Tjukurrpa associated with it. Tjukurrpa provides, in this sense, a means for asserting a political interest in land."[38]

For two centuries recognition of Aboriginal ownership of land in Australia and Australian Torres Strait Islands was largely precluded by the conceit that Australia was, prior to European settlement in 1788, *terra nullius* (land belonging to no one). In 1992, however, in Mabo v. Queensland (No. 2), the Australian High Court rejected *terra nullius* and ruled that Australian common law recognized native title, which could be extinguished only by "a loss of connection to the land".[39] The case had been brought by the Meriam people of Murray Island, in the Torres Strait, against the state of Queensland, to which the island had been annexed in the nineteenth century. The decision, significant in terms of formal recognition of Aboriginal rights, is of peculiar interest in relation to the interpretation of gardens and gardening.

Unlike mainland Australian Aboriginal people, the Meriam people keep gardens, and those gardens were taken as evidence of the continuity of traditional law and customs that the High Court deemed the basis of native land entitlement. The court relied on a fact-finding report that had previously been prepared by Justice Martin Moynihan, a justice of the Supreme Court of Queensland. Moynihan reported that the Meriam people identified garden land "by reference to a named locality coupled with the name of relevant individuals if further differentiation is necessary" and that boundaries consisted of "known land marks such as specific trees or mounds of rocks". Gardening, he determined, was "of the most profound importance to the inhabitants of Murray Island at and prior to European contact", and it seemed to be more important than fishing. Gardening was not only a means of subsistence; it was the source of produce for consumption or exchange during community rituals such as marriage and adoption, cult rituals, and activities associated with death. Moynihan described how prestige among the Meriam people depended on gardening prowess "both in terms of the production of a sufficient surplus for ... social purposes ... and to be manifest in the show gardens and the cultivation of yams to a huge size". He noted that the Meriam associated "considerable ritual" with gardening, and that "gardening techniques were passed on and preserved by these rituals. Boys in particular worked with their fathers and by observations and imitations reinforced by the rituals and other aspects of the social fabric gardening practices were passed on."[40]

The fact that Aboriginal land rights were, at least initially, in no small measure dependent on the Meriam people's gardens—a construct absent from the Australian mainland—presents a remarkable historic irony. Early observers provided evidence of Aboriginal people's disdain for European agriculture as well as their apparent rejection both of gardens and cultivation. In 1828, for example, (writing as Dr. Roger Oldfield) the Rev. Ralph Mansfielld reported that "the interior tribes consider the whites, as a strange plodding race, for the greater part slaves, obliged to get their living by constant drudgery every day. Whereas, for themselves, their wants being easily supplied, 'they toil not, neither do they spin'."[41] The words of an Aboriginal woman from Arnhem Land, in northern Australia, (first quoted by anthropologists Ronald and Catherine Berndt in 1964) have often been re-quoted. To a Fijian missionary working in a mission garden she said: "You people go to all that trouble, working and planting seeds, but we don't have to do that. All these things are there for us, the Ancestral Beings left them for us. In the end, you depend on the sun and the rain just the same as we do, but the difference is that we just have to go and collect the food when it is ripe. We don't have all this other trouble."[42]

Even in contemporary Australia the idea of growing bush food as a horticultural crop can be anathema to Aboriginal people. Bush food wholesaler Peter Yates describes the sight of "bush tomatoes growing in neat horticultural rows" as "disturbing" to Aboriginal people, and explains why:

> Bush tomatoes, as with everything else in the world, are supposed to be made through ceremony, not grown by people.... These captive plants may have seemed to the women to challenge the proper order of the world; in short, to be sacrilegious.... These are not just foods: they are bound up in stories of creation, in kinship, and in multiple layers of personal and collective memory.... Bush foods are an inseparable part of themselves.[43]

CULTIVATION

The twentieth-century British archaeologist V. Gordon Childe (who was born in Australia) famously labeled two periods of momentous change in the history of Western culture as the Neolithic Revolution (the transition from hunting and gathering to agriculture) and the Urban Revolution (the switch from village-based societies to societies with towns and cities).[44] Although the concept of the Neolithic Revolution provides an invaluable analysis of and perspective for the development of agriculture and Western civilization, the idea is often seen to imply a hierarchy of progress in the history of culture.[45] This is perhaps no surprise, given that Childe was influenced by a Marxist analysis of human endeavor.[46] Childe's observations, while based on material culture, were utilized to reinforce nineteenth-century perspectives in social evolution and social Darwinism derived from thinkers such as Auguste Comte, Herbert Spencer, and Lewis Henry Morgan.[47] However, Childe's perspectives are not necessarily deterministic—as Childe himself observes: "Reality is an activity, a process that is neither repeating itself over and over again nor yet is approximating

to a pre-determined goal or the realization of a preconceived plan. It is on the contrary genuinely creative, constantly bringing forth what has never been produced before, genuine novelties."[48] Wade Davis' observation that culture is "simply a matter of choice and orientation, adaptive insights and cultural priorities" resonates with Childe's.

The drivers for the Neolithic Revolution in the West, in the so-called Fertile Crescent (stretching from the Tigris and the Euphrates, in Mesopotamia, to the Nile Valley), remain uncertain. The assumption that cultivation of crops (and domestication of animals) was more efficient than hunting and gathering, in terms of return for energy expended in seeking food, or was better able to counter the impacts of poor seasons is now viewed as unconvincing. Indeed, there is evidence to suggest that a hunter-gatherer lifestyle is a more energy-efficient choice than early agriculture.[49] Currently, the catalyst for the transition to agriculture is variously identified as: the adoption of slavery and a culture seeking the accumulation of material wealth; the establishment of a significant non-food-producing sector of specialists; the selection of plants and animals for domestication; the harnessing of yeasts for brewing beer and baking bread, and resulting improved nutritional outcomes; or a demand for fibers, among other factors.[50]

The notion that Australian Aboriginal culture was characterized by a total absence of agriculture is widespread and has been entrenched in a description of Aboriginal people as hunter-gatherers. Certainly there is no evidence in Australian Aboriginal culture of anything resembling Childe's Neolithic Revolution. The historical record does contain, however, numerous examples of Aboriginal plant cultivation, harvest, and storage, in the reports of early Australian explorers and settlers. These examples are routinely dismissed according to a definition of agriculture that assumes that particular technological innovations in sowing, harvesting, and cultivation are necessary preconditions for it. While utilized by archaeologist Ian Gilligan to dismiss Aboriginal agriculture, an alternative definition of agriculture — "to engage in agriculture is, by definition, to 'cultivate' a resource, meaning to take active measures to at least nurture and protect, if not modify, the resource in question" — might rather support such an argument.[51] The definition of agricultural practices can be stretched, Gilligan notes (though he does not concur), to include "hunter-gatherer strategies such as broadcast 'sowing' of wild seeds and intensive 'harvesting' of wild resources".[52] Despite the absence of domestic animals from grazing systems in Australia, the Aboriginal people's conscious, audacious, and disciplined approach to managing Australia might well satisfy definitions of agriculture, cultivation, and gardening.

In 1836, Sir Thomas Livingstone Mitchell, an explorer and surveyor, observed on the south-eastern Australian basalt plains "a vast extent of open downs — quite yellow with

Figure 7/ John Michael Skipper, *Rapid Bay, South Australia*, 1836. Watercolor on paper. Courtesy Art Gallery of South Australia.

Murnong", and "natives spread over the field, digging for roots".[53] In the same region, in 1841, George Augustus Robinson, who held the colonial office of protector of Aborigines, saw women "spread over the plains as far as [he] could see them — and each had a load as much as she could carry". The women burned the grass, Robinson noted, "the better to see these [murnong] roots". This crop and harvest was hardly accidental: the burn favored the murnong over the grass. In the same region (and likely within a decade of Mitchell and Robinson) colonist Isaac Batey described a slope of "rich basaltic clay, evidently well fitted for the production of myrnongs". He continued:

> On the spot are numerous mounds with short spaces between each, and as all these are at right angles to the ridge's slope, it is conclusive evidence that they were the work of human hands extending over a long series of years. The uprooting of the soil to apply the best term was accidental gardening, still it is reasonable to assume that the Aboriginals were quite aware of the fact that turning the earth over in search of yams instead of diminishing that form of food supply would have a tendency to increase it.[54]

In the early nineteenth century, tubers and plants were collected in Aboriginal camps and traded with other tribes and clans, according to William Buckley, an escaped British convict who lived with the Wathaurong from 1800 to 1835. The contemporary ethnobotanist Beth Gott cites Buckley's evidence and suggests that the Aboriginal "regime of firing, gathering and digging" documented by early colonial witnesses "bore sufficient resemblance to agriculture/horticulture to be regarded as a sort of natural gardening which ensured

the continued abundance of the important food plants of the plains".[55]

The archaeologist Rhys Jones' 1969 description of Aboriginal people's landscape management as "fire-stick farming" transformed perceptions of Aboriginal people's manipulation of Country.[56] More recently, the historian Bill Gammage's study of the importance of systematic and controlled burning of Australia by Aboriginal people (and this both on a scale and in a detail unimaginable to European colonists then and now) has significantly shifted the conversation about the nature of the relationship between Aboriginal people and Country. Importantly, his conclusions coincide with those of the nineteenth-century surveyor William Light, who considered South Australia "land already in the possession of persons of property [rather] than left to the course of nature alone".[57] A watercolor by J. M. Skipper (1836) illustrates Light's view of Rapid Bay en route to the establishment of Adelaide [Figure 7].

Eighteenth-century colonial paintings, as Gammage demonstrates, present an Australian landscape that bears a striking resemblance to the naturalistic English landscape garden of the eighteenth century. Such 'gardenless' gardens, synonymous with the landscape architect Capability Brown, were the height of fashion for English country houses and estates. Indeed, the resemblance between the gardens and the Australian landscape was much remarked on at the time. "In many places the trees are so sparingly, and I had almost said judiciously distributed", observed the explorer Charles Sturt, "as to resemble the park lands attached to a gentleman's residence in England."[58] These extensive expanses of grass in a park-like setting, of the type depicted in Martha Berkeley's *Mount Lofty, from The Terrace, Adelaide*, painted about 1840

[Figure 8], and Joseph Lycett's 1824–1825 engraving *View from Near the Top of Constitution Hill, Van Diemen's Land* [Figure 9], were viewed with enthusiasm, both for their beauty and for their economic potential.

Tellingly, Gammage uses the language of landscape gardeners in describing the vegetation produced by Aboriginal use of fire: belts (grass lanes in timber or timber lanes in grass); clumps or copses of trees or scrub; clearings of grass in forest, scrub, heath, or spinifex.[59] Templates for vegetation, Gammage suggests, had been established by Aboriginal people and carefully maintained across Australia, "where [they] best suited plant(s) and people". There were also templates for animals, which were "kept suitably apart but linked into mosaics ultimately continent wide". Individual templates, writes Gammage, "might have multiple uses or overlap, but together they rotated growth in planned sequences, some to harvest, some to lure and locate". Fire served as the Aboriginal people's chief "shepherd". The complex patterns Aboriginal people burned in the varied Australian terrain required, in Gammage's words, "intricate knowledge of plants and fire, visionary planning, and skill and patience greater than anything modern Australia has imagined".[60] Significantly, environmental change resulting from curtailment of Aboriginal burning practices on the part of the colonists to 'protect' property was rapid. Australian farmer-philosopher Eric Rolls' experience of the Pilliga Scrub in the New South Wales was in sharp contrast to that of explorer John Oxley's 1818 vista of "a forest of ironbarks and big white-barked cypress trees, three to four only to the hectare". Rolls suggests that a rapid invasion of trees onto these park lands followed the removal of traditional Aboriginal burning regimes despite the arrival of the colonists

and their stock: "Australia's dense forests are not remnants of 200 years of energetic clearing, they are the product of 100 years of energetic growth." While such an assertion is not without critics — for example the ecologists John Benson and Phil Redpath provide an alternative perspective suggesting climate as the key driver for vegetation in the Pilliga Scrub — Gammage defends Rolls' claim.[61]

Firing, gathering, and digging, then, would appear to be gardening practices, but in fact do not constitute the full range of these. For instance, The Dreaming requires ceremonies to ensure the continued existence of plants and animals. Such ceremonies are usually referred to as 'increase ceremonies' or 'increase rituals'. The botanist Peter Latz, who was raised in the Aboriginal community of Hermannsburg, dislikes those terms, which suggest a progressive unnatural increase in species, and proposes 'maintenance ceremony' as more apt. Deborah Bird Rose, a scholar of the Aboriginal relationship with Country, proposes the term 'rituals of well-being', to emphasize the rituals' purpose in maintaining particular species rather than fomenting uncontrolled increase: "These rituals are aimed to promote life but not to promote it promiscuously." Latz cautions that discussion of this complicated subject outside the context of the "complex religious life of Aboriginal people" can be "misleading".[62] Nevertheless, increase rituals (as we shall continue to call them here) suggest, as clearly as the literal act of cultivation, the existence of a garden. In the last century, Mick (Irinyili) MacLean, of the Wangkangurru people, worked with the linguist Luise Hercus to record a song, from Pulawani, in the Simpson Desert in South Australia, that was sung to increase acacia seeds.[63] The isolation of an increase ceremony from Country, language, and performance limits the power of the ritual. Nevertheless, the songs provide remarkable insights into the relationship between people, plants, and Country.[64] Thus, for example, the "Seed Song from Pulawani" commences with an evocation of the searing heat and desperate drought in the Simpson Desert: "Dry leaves everywhere, / Dry leaves fallen on the ground." Then, upon the utterance of a spell, what is dry becomes green: "Dry stump become light green / Dry stump grow green!" New leaves begin to show, and roots are growing. These spread further and swell with sap. "Tall trees are standing there. / Green, green colour all around / Green plants in vast numbers." The plants yield seeds, the seeds feed the populace, and so on. Beyond a doubt, cultivation is the theme of these mesmeric verses. Indeed, some increase rituals prescribe physical acts of cultivation such as the planting of seeds or tubers.[65]

Is the space between human intentions and nature not 'the garden'? Daphne Nash, who has worked among Aboriginal people of the Western Desert exploring their use of plants, reflects on the reluctance to describe Aboriginal engagement with plants as gardening:

Figure 8/ Martha Berkeley, *Mount Lofty from The Terrace, Adelaide,* c. 1840. Watercolor on paper. Courtesy Art Gallery of South Australia.

VIEW from near the TOP of CONSTITUTION HILL,
Van Diemens Land.

London Published Jan 1.1825. by J. Souter 73. St Pauls Church Yard.

Figure 9/ Joseph Lycett, *View from near the top of Constitution Hill, Van Diemen's Land*, 1824–1825. Aquatint, hand-colored. Published in *Views in Australia* (1925). Courtesy National Library of Australia, nla.pic-an7692946.

... the main difficulty in coming to this conclusion is that Aboriginal gardens are not recognizably European gardens. As a consequence of people's reluctance to recognize and apply a known term to a new situation, the real similarities and differences between Aboriginal gardening and European gardening are obscured.

Nash observes that Pintupi people continue to cultivate particular species (such as *Solanum* spp., pituri, bush potatoes, and yams). She further observes that Aboriginal people also cultivate plants for social and cultural reasons, notably for ceremony and keeping in touch with place and kin. Nash's work is well supported by the practices of Murinpatha and Jamandjung people in the Keep River district of North-Western Australia. Such active cultivation, as Bill Gammage suggests, is acceptable to Aboriginal people so long as cultivation is undertaken within the Law and not perceived as undermining plant associations or offending rules on fire, local control, or species diversity.[66] Indeed, the ethnobotanist

Glenn Wightman has heard contemporary Aboriginal land custodians in the Top End of the Northern Territory refer to their country as gardens (though other custodians have refuted this). Some Aboriginal people, according to Wightman, think that it is good to try to promote plants and animals to become more common — yet he also reports that others believe it is against The Dreamtime, or Creation-period, law.[67]

ART AND DESIGN

Contemporary Australian Aboriginal art is often viewed as the most vibrant art movement in the nation; it is "perhaps the greatest single cultural achievement of Australia's post-white settlement history", as cultural critic Paul Carter has claimed.[68] The works commonly illustrate aspects of Country and of spirituality associated with Country. Even the work of earlier artists such as the Arrernte elder Albert Namatjira — work that was once thought to reflect the imposition of a European picturesque genre on the central Australian landscape, for the sake of a tourist market — has been reevaluated, in art historian Howard Morphy's words, as "Aboriginal representations of land that challenged both European occupation and European preconceptions of the centre as an arid wasteland".[69] Indeed, the author and artist Paul Carter suggests that Namatjira's work "remained Aranda": "By interpreting the Western tradition of representation performatively, regarding it as a way of re-enacting the iconography of Biblical illustration, he could preserve an indigenous conviction that the landscape was the creative original and abiding presence that lent these representations their meaning."[70] Namatjira's *Waterhole, Macdonnell Ranges* illustrates the nature of his work [Figure 10], as does Wenten Rubuntja's *Landscape* [Figure 11], which was painted some 30 years later but conforms stylistically to the Hermannsburg School established by Namatjira. Significantly, Rubuntja observed of his own style and that of the Papunya Tula artists, whose dot paintings are created in the traditional style of ceremonial body and sand art: "Doesn't matter what

Figure 10/ Albert Namatjira; Western Arrernte people, Northern Territory. *Waterhole, MacDonnell Ranges*, c. 1950s. Watercolor on paper.
Courtesy Art Gallery of South Australia © Legend Press, Sydney, Australia.

Figure 11/ Wenten Rubuntja; Arrernte people, Northern Territory. *Landscape*, 1988. Watercolor on cardboard.
Courtesy Art Gallery of South Australia © estate of the artist licensed by Aboriginal Artists Agency Ltd.

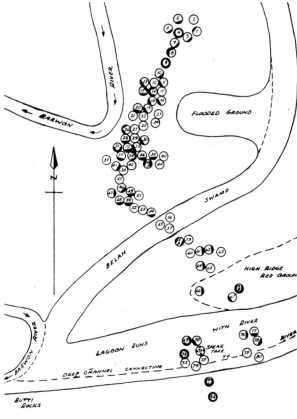

Figure 12/ Henry King (photographer), Taphoglyph (Aboriginal carved tree) near Dubbo, NSW, c. 1910. From C. C. Towle, *Album II, Photographs of Aboriginal rock art and stencil art, stone tools and landcsapes*, c. 1925–1944. Courtesy State Library of New South Wales (SPF/1153).

Figure 13/ Map diagram of the Collymongle bora ground drawn by Lindsay and Russell Black in 1944. The circles represent the exact position of the carved trees within the site. Lindsay and Russell Black, Map diagram of the Collymongle bora ground. Published in *The Bora Ground*, 1944. Courtesy State Library of New South Wales, ML 572.991/B.

sort of painting we do in this country, it still belongs to the people, all the people. This is worship, work, culture. It's all Dreaming. There are two ways of painting. Both ways are important, because that's culture."[71]

However, although the designs associated with works of Aboriginal art are celebrated, the design intent evident in the artworks, when performed through the rigorous discipline of an evolved curatorial practice in landscape management, is routinely dismissed as naturally occurring or of only limited consequence. The art of landscape stewardship—and also the epistemology and cosmology of The Dreaming expressed on Country that are fundamental to Aboriginal artworks—does not elicit the same recognition evident for the artworks that derive from such practice. Perhaps the most accessible evidence of a designed landscape is in the preparation of burial sites by the Gamilaroi people, of central-north-west New South Wales and south-west Queensland, and the Wiradjuri

people, of the Lachlan, Macquarie, and Murrumbidgee Rivers in central New South Wales. The carving of dendroglyphs to mark ceremonial sites of burial or initiation illustrates remarkable accomplishment in design and execution of land art, especially given the use of stone axes as the only available tool [Figures 12, 13]. The first European account of the carved trees was provided in the British explorer John Oxley's 1817 expedition journal, published in 1820, and was accompanied by an aquatint drawn originally by surveyor George Evans.[72]

The artist Brook Andrew, of the Wiradjuri people, revisits the nineteenth-century Prussian naturalist William Blandowski's album of photographs, *Australien in 142 photographischen Abbildungen* [Figures 14, 15].[73] In 1857 Blandowski collaborated with the Yarree Yarree (Nyeri Nyeri) people near the junction of the Murray and Darling Rivers in collecting and identifying botanical and zoological specimens, and made drawings of various Aboriginal practices. Andrew's

Figure 14/ Brook Andrew; Wiradjuri people, New South Wales. *The Island I*, 2008. Black ink, silver foil on linen. Courtesy Art Gallery of South Australia.

Figure 15/ William Blandowski, *Native Tomb on the Lachlan River.* Plate 107 from *Australien in 142 photographischen Abbildungen nach zehnjährigen Erfahrungen zusammengestellt*, 1862. Courtesy Cambridge University, Haddon Library.

manipulation of Blandowski's images exposes the romanticization of so-called primitive peoples and their cultural expressions. The University of Queensland Art Gallery observes, "Seen through twenty-first-century eyes, [Blandowski's images] are fantastical and utopian imaginings of Indigenous life that critically reflect on Australia's colonial past," for as the visual arts writer Laura Murray Cree suggests, Andrew's art challenges "the limitations imposed by power structures, historical amnesia, stereotyping and complicity".[74]

POISON COUNTRY OR PARADISE ?

Australian Aboriginal society in 1788 (the date of the first permanent European settlement) was regarded as primitive by the invaders. The assumption that particular technological innovations such as the use of fire and the working of metals, the domestication of plants and animals, and the adoption of writing represented progress toward a more advanced society was inherent in a perspective that imagined stages in a linear progression from savagery to barbarism to civilization. As Wade Davis observes, however, "There is no hierarchy of progress in the history of culture, no Social Darwinian ladder to success." Expression of the "raw genius" shared by all cultures "in stunning works of technological innovation, as has been the great historical achievement of the West, or through the untangling of the complex threads of memory inherent in a myth, a primary concern, for example, of the Aborigines of Australia", is, Davis asserts, "simply a matter of choice and orientation, adaptive insights and cultural priorities".[75]

Choice and cultural priorities make moot the objection that Australian Aboriginal people, as hunter-gatherers, had still to achieve a Neolithic Revolution. The Neolithic Revolution, the Urban Revolution, and the Industrial Revolution (a revolutionary desciptor *not* coined by V. Gordon Childe) might be interpreted simply as choices that led to modern agriculture organized along industrial lines to maximize yields and, ideally, return on investment. The industrial approach to modern agriculture is underwritten by additional direct inputs required for high yields — through irrigation, fertilizers, and agrichemicals, as well as fuel energy required for cultivation, sowing and harvesting, and the application of fertilizers and agrichemicals — together with indirect inputs such as plant breeding and research and the development of agricultural technologies. In a market-based economy, where short-run economic results might outweigh long-run environmental, social, and cultural concerns, such a perspective certainly has validity. However, the long-run outcomes remain a matter of conjecture. The long-run outcomes for Aboriginal Country are apparent over a 50,000-year tenure.[76]

It would be romantic to suppose that Aboriginal management of Country has delivered the most sustainable possible production of plants and animals. Indeed, there remains significant debate about the impact of Aboriginal people on the Australian environment.[77] There are also important reservations about how sustainability is interpreted in non-industrialized cultures.[78] However, the idea that Aboriginal people forged an evolving curatorial practice through a rigorous dialectic is hardly fanciful. It is worth reiterating here Davis' contention that Australian Aboriginal people's purpose was "to engage in the ritual and spiritual activities deemed to be essential for the maintenance of the world precisely as it was at the moment of creation".

In the Western creation story, Adam and Eve were expelled from the Garden of Eden for disobeying God and eating of the fruit of the Tree of the Knowledge of Good and Evil. And while Adam had been required only to "dress ... and to keep" the Garden of Eden, he and Eve were now required to go forth beyond the Garden "to till the ground". Cultivation of ground was required as a consequence of both Adam's new environment and God's curse. "Cursed is the ground for thy sake," God told Adam, "in sorrow shalt thou eat of it all the days of thy life; Thorns also and thistles shall it bring forth to thee; and thou shalt eat the herb of the field; In the sweat of thy face shalt thou eat bread, till thou return unto the ground." When Adam's son Cain murdered his brother, Abel, God punished Cain with a new curse: "When thou tillest the ground, it shall not henceforth yield unto thee her strength."[79] The shift from the Garden of Eden, without cultivation, to a new environment requiring cultivation and, then, to a blighted landscape, perhaps provides an allegory distinguishing Aboriginal "living on Country" from an unsustainable, post-lapsarian, Western-style exploitation of land. Renaissance humanists invoked the idea of the degree of human action on landscape to classify our relationship with Nature — wilderness being the first nature, agricultural lands second nature, and the garden, as a collaboration of art and nature, a third nature.[80] In Australia, as indeed everywhere, the relationship between nature and people is important; in this setting a wilderness is hardly the Garden of Eden, nor are blighted landscapes the waste places of the Bible.[81] Is first nature, then, both a divine garden and a wilderness? And is a blighted landscape a wilderness or a dystopian fourth nature?

British colonists endeavored to install European agriculture and pastoral systems in Australia without the benefit of either a rigorous dialectic or tens of thousands of years of Traditional Ecological Knowledge. The impact on the Australian continent has been catastrophic; the impact on the sustainability of land and water systems is still to be resolved. Likely the most catastrophic intervention was the British nuclear testing at Maralinga (now part of the Maralinga Tjarutja lands, in the far west of South Australia). In *Poison Country*, Jonathan Kumintjara Brown observes the obliteration of meaning in relation to Tjukurrpa and Law caused by the atomic testing in his people's Country at Maralinga in South Australia [Figure 16]. The testing included seven major atomic explosions in 1956 and 1957, and many smaller tests until 1963. In the context of a series of paintings entitled *Maralinga Nullius* describing the impact of the testing, Brown observed, "It is not a protest.... But I am asking: why did they do this damage to my grandfather's land?"[82] Nici Cumpston's work is equally haunting, illustrating the Ngarrindjeri camps now flooded under permanent impoundments at Lake Bonney, on

the Murray River in South Australia [Figure 17]. The Murray, Australia's longest river, now has severe environmental problems as a result of over-allocation of water and the imposition of regulators to control remaining flows.[83] How such environmental degradation is viewed by Aboriginal peoples is poignantly captured by Deborah Bird Rose, who memorializes the reaction of her teacher, Ngarinman elder Daly Pulkara from the Victoria River region in the Northern Territory, to a land scarred by gullies, dead trees, and scald areas — the effects of extreme erosion:

> I asked ... what he called this country and he looked at it deeply, and said in a heavy voice: 'It's the wild. It's just the wild.'... The wild, in Daly's terms, is a form of wilfulness gone crazy — a loss of connectivity. The 'wild' shows us that self without other is no self at all, but just a bare gully where life disappears and does not return.[84]

By way of stark contrast, Valerie Sparks' monumental print *The Organisation of the View* [Figure 18] illustrates, in the artist's

———— **Figure 16/** Jonathan Kumintjara Brown; Pitjantjatjara people, ———— South Australia. *Poison country*, 1995. Acrylic, natural ochres on canvas. Courtesy Art Gallery of South Australia.

Figure 17/ Nici Cumpston; Barkindji people, NSW. *Campsite, Nookamka Lake II*, 2008. Inkjet print on canvas, hand colored with watercolors and pencils. © the artist.

Figure 18/ Valerie Sparks, *The organisation of the view*, 2005. Computer generated color inkjet print on 3 sheets. National Gallery of Victoria, Melbourne.

words, "landscapes that appear to be so real that they should exist but are impossible at the same time" — composite landscapes that combine images of plants and landscapes from various locales in Australia and that are eerily reminiscent of the Australian landscape as witnessed by European colonists upon their arrival.[85] The perception of Europeans at settlement was that the Australian landscape was so finely 'shaped', such a 'real' reflection of their own garden aesthetic, that it could not have been created by Aboriginal people. However, the reality is a different one: "No chance of Nature, no careless hand, no random fire could make so rich a paradise."[86] The Land and the People are inseparable — in this context the space between the People and Nature is the Garden.

NOTES

1/ Yunupingu, James Galarrwuy, "A Letter from Black to White", *Aboriginal Child at School*, vol. 5, no. 1, 1977, p. 39.

2/ Blainey, Geoffrey, *Triumph of the Nomads: A History of Aboriginal Australia*, South Melbourne: Macmillan, 1976, pp. 236–237.

3/ Chase, A. K., "Domestication and Domiculture in Northern Australia: A Social Perspective", *Foraging and Farming*, David R. Harris and Gordon C. Hillman eds., London: Unwin Hyman, 1989, p. 52.

4/ Yunupingu, "A Letter from Black to White", p. 39.

5/ Country definition: Aboriginal communities' cultural associations with their Country may include or relate to languages, cultural practices, knowledge, songs, stories, art, paths, landforms, flora, fauna and minerals. These cultural associations may include custodial relationships with particular landscapes such as land, sea, sky, rivers as well as the intangible places associated with The Dreaming. Custodial relationships are extremely important in determining who may have the capacity to authentically speak for their Country, http://www.hsc.csu.edu.au/ab_studies/glossary/2236/glossary2.htm, accessed 14 March 2014. Country is multi-dimensional — it consists of people, animals, plants, Dreamings; underground, earth, soils, minerals and waters, surface water, and air. There is sea country and land country; in some areas people talk about sky country. Country has origins and a future; it exists both in and through time: Deborah B. Rose, *Nourishing Terrains: Australian Aboriginal Views of Landscape and Wilderness*, Canberra: Australian Heritage Commission, 1996, p. 8.

6/ Gammage, Bill, *The Biggest Estate on Earth: How Aborigines Made Australia*, Sydney: Allen & Unwin, 2011, p. 2.

7/ Forbes, Stephen, "Enquiry into Plants: Nature, Utopia and the Botanic Garden", *Earth Perfect? Nature, Utopia, and the Garden*, Annette Giesecke and Naomi Jacobs eds., London: Black Dog Publishing, pp. 220–241.

8/ Garden etymology: c. 1300, from Old North French *gardin* (thirteenth century, Modern French *jardin*), from Vulgar Latin *hortus gardinus* "enclosed garden", via Frankish *gardo, from Proto-Germanic *gardaz- (cognates: Old Frisian *garda*, Old Saxon *gardo*, Old High German *garto*, German *Garten* "garden", Old English *geard* "enclosure", see *yard* (n.1). Italian *giardino*, Spanish *jardin* are from French. See Anne von Erp-Houtepen, "The Etymological History of the Garden", *Journal of Garden History*, vol. 6, no. 3, 1986, pp. 227–231.

9/ Einerson, Benedict, "Introduction", *Theophrastus De Causis Plantarum, Volume I: Books 1–2*, Benedict Einarson and George K. K. Link trans., Loeb Classical Library 471, Cambridge, MA: Harvard University Press, 1975, p. xi.

10/ Mabberley, David J., "Where are the Wild Things", *Paradisus: Hawaiian Plant Watercolors by Geraldine King Tam*, Honolulu, Hawai'i: Honolulu Academy of Arts, 1999, pp. 1–11.

11/ Walpole, Horace, "The History of the Modern Taste in Gardening" (1770), *Anecdotes of painting in England: with some account of the principal artists; and incidental notes on other arts / collected by the late Mr. George Vertue; and now digested and published from his original mss. by Mr. Horace Walpole*, London: J. Dodslet, 1786, pp. 247–316.

12/ Forbes, Stephen J., David Cooper, and Tony Kendle, "The History of Development of Ecological Landscape Styles", *Urban Nature Conservation: Landscape Management in the Urban Countryside*, Tony Kendle and Stephen J. Forbes eds., London: Spon, 1997, pp. 69–113.

13/ http://www.dailymail.co.uk/news/article-1032112/When-garden-garden-Judges-better-definition.html#ixzz2d3ND8G46, accessed 14 March 2014.

14/ Hunt, John Dixon, *Greater Perfections: The Practice of Garden Theory*, Philadelphia: University of Pennsylvania Press, 2000, pp. 14–15.

15/ Dunham, "Architecture *Without* Nature?", p. 141.

16/ Dunham, "Architecture *Without* Nature?", p. 140.

17/ Finley, Robert, "Marlene Creates' Boreal Poetry Garden", published in this volume, pp. 162–171.

18/ Davis, Wade, "*The World Until Yesterday* by Jared Diamond"—review, *The Guardian*, Wednesday 9 January 2013, http://www.theguardian.com/books/2013/jan/09/history-society, accessed 14 March 2014.

19/ Lourandos, Harry, "Change or Stability?: Hydraulics, Hunter-gatherers and Population in Temperate Australia", *World Archaeology*, vol. 11, 1980, pp. 258–259.

20/ Chase, "Domestication and Domiculture", p. 51.

21/ Carter, Harold B., *Sir Joseph Banks 1743–1820*, London: British Museum, 1988, p. 214.

22/ Lourandos, "Change or Stability", p. 256.

23/ Wolfe, Patrick, "On Being Woken Up: The Dreamtime in Anthropology and in Australian Settler Culture", *Comparative Studies in Society and History*, vol. 33, no. 2, 1991, pp. 197–224; Rose, *Nourishing Terrains*, p. 26.

24/ Stanner, William E. H., *The Dreaming and Other Essays*, Melbourne: Black Ink, 2009, p. 51.

25/ Forrest, S., "Welcome", *Spinifex: People of the Sun and Shadow*, Bentley, W. Australia: John Curtin Gallery, 2012, p. iv.

26/ Yunupingu, *A letter from Black to White*, p. 39.

27/ Cumpston, Nici, *Desert Country*, Adelaide: Art Gallery of South Australia, 2010, p. 168.

28/ Robinson, A. C., P. Copley, P. Canty, L. Baker, and B. Nesbitt, *A Biological Survey of the Anangu Pitjantjatjara Lands, South Australia, 1991–2001*, South Australia: Department for Environment and Heritage, p. 206.

29/ Cumpston, *Desert Country*, p. 166.

30/ Federal Court of Australia, Mark Anderson on behalf of the Spinifex People v. State of Western Australia, http://www.austlii.edu.au/au/cases/cth/federal_ct/2000/1717.html, accessed 14 March 2014.

31/ Cane, Scott, *Pila Nguru: The Spinifex People*, Fremantle, W. Australia: Fremantle Press, 2002, p. 17.

32/ Cane, Scott, *Pila Nguru: Art and Song from the Spinifex People*, Semaphore, South Australia: Spinifex Arts Project, 1999, p. 7.

33/ Cumpston, *Desert Country*, p. 134.

34/ Cumpston, *Desert Country*, p. 136.

35/ Cane, Scott, quoted in Nicolas Rothwell, "Spinifex", *Tupun Nguranguru: People of the Sandhill Country—Spinifex Arts Project 15th Anniversary Exhibition*, exhibition catalogue, Melbourne: Vivien Anderson Gallery, 2012, pp. 7–9.

36/ Balmori, Diana, and Margaret Morton, *Transitory Gardens, Uprooted Lives*, New Haven: Yale University Press, 1993.

37/ Myers, Fred, *Pintupi Country, Pintupi Self*, Washington, DC: Smithsonian Institution Press and Canberra: Australian Institute of Aboriginal Studies, 1986, pp. 157–148.

38/ Cane, *Pila Nguru: The Spinifex People*, p. 112.

39/ http://en.wikipedia.org/wiki/Native_title_in_Australia, accessed 14 March 2014.

40/ http://www.austlii.edu.au/au/cases/cth/HCA/1992/23.html, accessed 14 March 2014, High Court of Australia—Mabo and others v. Queensland (No. 2).

41/ Oldfield, Roger, "An Account of the Aborigines of NSW, 1828", *Australian Reminiscences and Papers of L. E. Threlkeld, missionary to the Aborigines 1824–1859*, vol. 2, Neil Gunson ed., Canberra: Australian Institute of Aboriginal Studies, 1974, p. 354.

42/ Berndt, Ronald M., and Catherine H. Berndt, *The World of the First Australians*, Sydney: Ure Smith, 1964, p. 108.

43/ Yates, Peter, "The Bush Foods Industry and Poverty Alleviation in Central Australia", *Dialogue*, Academy of Social Sciences in Australia, vol. 28, no. 2, 2009, p. 49.

44/ Childe, V. Gordon, *Man Makes Himself*, London: Watts and Co., 1936; Childe, "The Urban Revolution", *Town Planning Review*, vol. 21, 1950, pp. 3–17.

45/ http://blogs.telegraph.co.uk/news/tomchiversscience/100198199/in-defence-of-jared-diamond-western-science-and-the-reality-of-human-progress/, accessed 31 January 2014.

46/ Greene, Kevin, "V. Gordon Childe and the Vocabulary of Revolutionary Change", *Antiquity*, vol. 73, 1999, pp. 97–109.

47/ http://en.wikipedia.org/wiki/Social_Darwinism, accessed 31 January 2013.

48/ Childe, V. Gordon, *Society and Knowledge*, New York: Harper, 1956, p. 123.

49/ Weisdorf, Jacob L., "From Foraging to Farming: Explaining the Neolithic Revolution", *Journal of Economic Surveys*, vol. 19, no. 4, 2005, pp. 561–586; Peregrine, Peter N., "What Happened in Prehistory?, *Faculty Monographs*, Book 1, Appleton, WI: Lawrence University, 2012, pp. 27–29, http://lux.lawrence.edu/faculty_monographs/1, accessed 31 January 2014.

50/ Katz, Solomon H., and Mary M. Voigt, "Bread and Beer: The Early Use of Cereals in the Human Diet", *Expedition*, vol. 28, 1986, pp. 23–34.

51/ Gilligan, Ian, "Agriculture in Aboriginal Australia: Why Not?", *Bulletin of the Indo-Pacific Prehistory Association*, vol. 30, 2010, p. 151.

52/ Gilligan, "Agriculture," p. 153.

53/ Gott, Beth, "Aboriginal Fire Management in Southeastern Australia: Aims and Frequency", *Journal of Biogeography*, vol. 32, p. 1204.

54/ Frankel, D., "An Account of the Aboriginal use of the yam-daisy". *The Artefact*, vol. 7, nos. 1–2, 1982, pp. 43–45; Batey, Isaac, *Reminiscences* [manuscript], Royal Historical Society of Victoria, n.d.

55/ Gott, Beth, "Koorie Use and Management of the Plains", *The Great Plains Crash. Proceedings of a Conference on the Grasslands and Grassy Woodlands of Victoria, Victorian Institute of Technology 2/3 October, 1992*, R. N. Jones ed., Melbourne: Indigenous Flora and Fauna Association and Victorian National Parks Association, 1999, pp. 41–45.

56/ Jones, Rhys, "Fire-stick Farming", *Australian Natural History*, vol. 16, 1969, pp. 224–228.

57/ Hylton, Jane, *South Australia Illustrated: Colonial painting in the Land of Promise*, Adelaide: Art Gallery of South Australia, 2012, p. 35; South Australian Company, *Supplement to the First Report of the South Australian Company's Directors 1837*, Colonel Light's letter to the Colonisation Commissioners, 1837, p. 20.

58/ Sturt, Charles, *Narrative of an expedition into central Australia,* vol. 2, London: T. & W. Boone, 1849, pp. 229–230.

59/ Gammage, *The Biggest Estate on Earth*, pp. 199–205.

60/ Gammage, *The Biggest Estate on Earth*, p. 211; Gammage, Bill, "The Adelaide District in 1836", *Turning Points: Chapters in South Australian History*, Robert Foster and Paul Sendziuk eds., Adelaide: Wakefield Press, 2012, p. 10.

61/ Rolls, Eric, *A Million Wild Acres*, Melbourne: Nelson, 1981, quoted in Gammage, *The Biggest Estate on Earth*, p. 317; Benson, John S., and Phil Redpath, "The Nature of Pre-European Native Vegetation in Australia: A critique of Ryan, D. G., Ryan, J. R. and Starr, B. J. (1995) *The Australian Landscape — Observations of Explorers and Early Settlers*", *Cunninghamia*, vol. 5, no. 2, 2011, pp. 314–316; Gammage, *The Biggest Estate on Earth*, pp. 339–340.

62/ Latz, Peter, *Bushfires and Bushtucker: Aboriginal Plant Use in Central Australia*, Alice Springs: IAD Press, 1995, p. 69.

63/ McLean, Mickin, R. M. W. Dixon, and M. Duwell eds., *The Honey-ant Men's Love Song and Other Aboriginal Song Poems*, St Lucia: University of Queensland Press, 1990, pp. 117–125.

64/ Strehlow, Ted G. H., *Songs of Central Australia*, Sydney: Angus & Robertson, 1971; *The Seed Song from Pulawani* (A description of the searing heat and desperate drought in the Simpson Desert) / Dry leaves everywhere, / Dry leaves fallen on the ground. (This verse is sung in a whisper, repeated five times, it is a spell to turn what is dry green) / Dry stump, become light green! /Dry stump, become light green! / Dry stump grow green! / Dry stump grow green! (The old dead stump begins to become green now) / Dry stumps, dry stumps becoming soft green. / Dry stumps, dry stumps becoming soft green. (New leaves are beginning to show and roots are growing) / Roots are growing / Roots are growing / Roots are swelling with sap. / Roots are spreading further / Roots are spreading further / Roots are growing. / Roots are spreading further / Roots are spreading further / Roots are swelling with sap. / The roots are growing big, huge, / Tall trees are standing there. / Green, green colour all around / Green plants in vast numbers / Are standing up straight. / Ripening plants with green colour all around / Green colour all around. / They put it by the tree. / yes, they put it by the tree. / The stone / They put a stone at the side of the tree. (They bury a stone at the butt of the tree) / The stone is by the tree, / Yes, the stone is put by the tree, / The stone is at the side. / They take the seed, with a stone they pound it. / They pound it, they smash it. (Now tomorrow we will eat them) / They grind the seed. / They grind the seed. / May that tree remain there, standing alone. / May that tree remain there, standing alone. / It stands there / A dark tree, /A dark tree alone. / Clover is growing there, clover. / They start cooking the dough. / They are painting themselves for a ceremony. / They are painting-up / For a ceremony. (Mick McLean said that this verse was 'right alongside my country', it referred to the Pulwani well itself, and to the ceremony which was to be held right there) / The handle, / The handle, / It is a stone-axe he looks at / It is a stone-axe he holds. (The large pounding slab, ngampa, used for cracking hard seed, is here being likened to a stone axe, and it is referred to by the Aranda term for stone axe in the following verses) / It is a stone axe, a stone / He looks at it, he picks it up, / It is a stone-axe, a stone. / They are pounding, / They are smashing up the seeds / With a stone they are smashing them up / With a stone. / They are breaking off the shell from the seeds to make food / They are breaking it off to the side / They are breaking and tossing away the shell. (Pulawani is in my country, a hundred miles east of Ilpura on the Finke River. That is the end of the story.)

65/ Rose, *Nourishing Terrains*, p. 54.

66/ Nash, Daphne, *Aboriginal Gardening: Plant Resource Management in Three Central Australian Communities*, Thesis (M.A.), Canberra: Australian National University, 1993, pp. 22, 149, 238, http://www.australianhumanitiesreview.org/archive/Issue-July-2005/02Gammage.html, accessed 13 March 2014; Head, L. M., J. M. Atchison, and R. L. Fullagar, "Country and Garden: Ethnobotany, Archaeobotany and Aboriginal Landscapes Near the Keep River, Northwestern Australia", *Journal of Social Archaeology*, vol. 2, 2002, pp. 73–196.

67/ Wightman, Glenn (Ethnobiologist, biocultural diversity, flora and fauna), Dept. of Land Resource Management, Northern Territory Government, pers. comm. email 31 December 2013.

68/ McLean, Ian, and the Institute of Modern Art, *How Aborigines Invented the Idea of Contemporary Art: Writings on Aboriginal Art / edited and introduced by Ian McLean*, Sydney: Institute of Modern Art and Power Publications, 2011, p. 17.

69/ Morphy, Howard, *Aboriginal Art*, London: Phaidon Press, 1998, p. 273.

70/ Carter, Paul, *The Lie of the Land*, London: Faber and Faber, 1996, p. 45.

71/ http://en.wikipedia.org/wiki/Wenten_Rubuntja, accessed 14 April 2014.

72/ Oxley, John, *Journal of Two Expeditions into the Interior of New South Wales Undertaken by Order of the British Government in the Years 1817–18*, London: John Murray, 1820.

73/ http://maa.cam.ac.uk/maa/the-island-catalogue/, accessed 14 March 2014.

74/ http://www.artmuseum.uq.edu.au/brook-andrew, accessed 14 March 2014; http://www.brookandrew.com/images/brook_andrew.pdf, accessed 14 March 2014; Cree, Laura M., "Brook Andrew", *Artist Profile*, issue 11, 2010, pp. 50–59; Allen, Harry, *Australia: William Blandowski's Illustrated Encyclopaedia of Aboriginal Australia*, Canberra: Aboriginal Studies Press, 2010.

75/ Davis, Wade, "*The World Until Yesterday* by Jared Diamond"—review, *The Guardian*, Wednesday 9 January 2013. Davis, *The Wayfinder: Why Ancient Wisdom Matters in the Modern World*, Toronto: House of Anansi Press, 2009.

76/ Rasmussen, M., et al., "An Aboriginal Australian Genome Reveals Separate Human Dispersals into Asia", *Science*, vol. 334, 2011, pp. 94–98.

77/ Flannery, Tim, *The Future Eaters*, Sydney: Reed, 1994; Latz, P., *The Flaming Desert: Arid Australia—A Fire Shaped Landscape*, Alice Springs: Peter Latz, 2007.

78/ Sveiby, Karl-Erik, "Aboriginal Principles for Sustainable Development as Told in Traditional Law Stories", *Sustainable Development*, vol. 17, 2009, pp. 341–356.

79/ The story of Adam and Eve is told in Genesis chapters 2 and 3 —specifically quoted here are verses 2:15, 3:17–19, 23, 4:12. Quotations here are from the King James Version of the Bible (KJV).

80/ Morgan, Luke, "Meaning", *A Cultural History of Gardens in the Renaissance*, E. Hyde ed., London: Bloomsbury, 2013, p. 127.

81/ See particularly KJV Isaiah 51:3, "For the LORD shall comfort Zion: he will comfort all her waste places; and he will make her wilderness like Eden, and her desert like the garden of the LORD."

82/ Cumpston, *Desert Country*, p. 128; Debelle, Penelope, "Eerie shapes in frog suits", *The Advertiser*, 15 June 1996, p. 27.

83/ http://guildhouse.org.au/member/nici-cumpston/, accessed 31 January 2014.

84/ http://www.ecologicalhumanities.org/rose.html, accessed 31 January 2014.

85/ http://valeriesparks.com.au/library/file/Proof%20Catalogue.pdf, accessed 31 January 2014.

86/ Gammage, *The Biggest Estate on Earth*, p. 238.

38 /DAVID E. COOPER

GARDENERS OF THE COSMOS: THE WAY OF THE GARDEN IN EAST ASIAN TRADITION

Friedrich Nietzsche complained that in European philosophies of art, attention focused too much on the spectators of art works and too little on the artists who created them. Art, he objected, has been envisaged primarily in terms of its products and not, as it should be, as an "activity" or "task" — the "highest task ... of this life", no less.[1] This is not a complaint and objection he could have raised against East Asian traditions of thought. Here, the arts are 'Ways' (Chinese *dao*, Japanese *dō*) — practices that, while they may produce works for people to appreciate, are essentially 'tasks' that belong to the endeavor to live well.

The value of an art or Way is not a simple function of the merit of its products. This is as true of gardening as it is of other activities classed as Ways in China, Japan, and Korea. One could, as in gardening magazines, understand the expression 'a good gardener' in purely technical terms, as referring to someone who makes gardens that are — by horticultural, aesthetic, ecological, or whatever criteria — successful. But this is a thin understanding that does not correspond to the rich East Asian conception of gardening's engagement with the good life. An important component in this conception is a perception of good gardening — and of Ways more generally — as nurturing a right relationship between human culture and the natural realm. In a volume devoted to exploring connections between gardening, nature, and humanity, it is a promising strategy to turn to those traditions in which these connections have been salient and accorded deep significance.

WAYS

The significance of gardening in these traditions is nicely hinted at in the words of my title. The phrase 'gardeners of the cosmos' is one I have borrowed from a recent book on Daoism whose author explains that a key metaphor in Daoist texts is that of cultivation. The model for Daoist sages or adepts is the responsible gardener who plants, nourishes, weeds, and then lets things grow according to nature. They may be called "gardeners of the cosmos", people who "slowly shape their life and environment" with a right appreciation of the relation between human activity and the order of nature.[2]

The metaphor of gardeners of the cosmos is not without earlier and close relatives. The eighteenth-century Chinese poet and painter, Cheng Hsieh, encouraged his readers to "regard the universe as a garden" [Figure 1].[3] Nor is the image confined to China and to Daoism. The distinguished Japanese garden designer and Zen Buddhist priest, Shunmyo Masuno, invites us to draw on the ancient idea of *tokikata*, which he characterizes as "the reading of the cosmos through the garden".[4] As the chosen profession of Shunmyo Masuno suggests, however, gardening does not provide simply a metaphor for human beings' place in the cosmos. Gardening, in the literal sense, is itself a way in which people shape their lives and their environments. Gardening itself is a Way, a *dao* or *dō*. It is difficult to exaggerate the importance of the idea of a Way in East Asian cultures, and difficult as well to articulate the idea succinctly. The term applies to a wide range of human practices — to those, like painting, that we call 'fine arts'; to 'martial arts', such as *judō* and *aikidō*; to crafts like flower arranging (*kadō* — 'the Way of flowers'); and to ones that belong in no such convenient categories of Western discourse, such as *chadō*, 'the Way of tea', and indeed gardening. Each Way requires training, apprenticeship, and the mastery of techniques. A Way, however, is much more than the exercise of a skill. For a true practitioner of a Way, it is "a way of life" and "self-development" or, to invoke the metaphor of gardening, "self-cultivation".[5] Ways have even been described as "forms of moving meditation" or "secular means of enlightenment".[6]

Expressions like 'self-cultivation' indicate that practitioners of Ways are engaged in care of the self — in the training and disciplining of emotions and desires that all too easily fracture or destabilize a person. The mindful or 'one-pointed' concentration required for successful practice counteracts the tendency to act capriciously and impulsively. Hence the many anecdotes of calligraphers or gardeners who spend long periods in poised attention before committing to a brush stroke or the placing of a stone. It would be wrong, however, to think of self-cultivation as directed solely at 'inner' processes — or, better, wrong to think that, in East Asian traditions, a sharp distinction can be maintained between 'inner' and 'outer'. Necessarily, a Confucian classic reminds us, "a man's heart will be shown in his outward appearance."[7] Daoists seek, in one commentator's words, "bio-spiritual cultivation" and, in another's, a "tuning of the body".[8] Bodily care and cleanliness, meanwhile, are imperatives for followers of Shinto.

Self-cultivation, then, is care of the person as a whole. A Way is an education in bodily discipline, demeanor, style, and comportment as much as in management of the soul. It is cultivation, as well, of the virtues. In fact, caring for the self — through attention to cleanliness, say — is already to be exercising virtues, for this contributes to a flourishing life. An example of a virtue both required for and reinforced by practicing Ways is a humility that ensures respect for the traditions, materials, and other sources that make achievements possible.

That there is cultivation of the body and of the virtues is sufficient to show that the meditation and enlightenment associated by some writers with Ways are not a form of inner navel-gazing. It should be emphasized, too, that the mindfulness and virtues to be cultivated necessarily entail engagement with the world. As the Confucian classic cited earlier puts it, virtue cannot help but show up — "shine" — in one's ways of dealing with family, friends, and the wider world.[9] Conscientious followers of Shinto, writes one author, aim to bring "purity, order ... cleanliness ... brightness — in a word, immaculate impeccability" into the world around them.[10] Confucius, his follower Xunzi, and the Daoist sage Zhuangzi, respectively, spoke of the consummate performer of music as helping to "bring things to completion", "serv[ing] heaven and earth", and allowing things "to accomplish their own mandates".[11]

Remarks like these reflect an ancient conviction that there are symmetries or correspondences between human affairs and the processes of nature that make it possible for

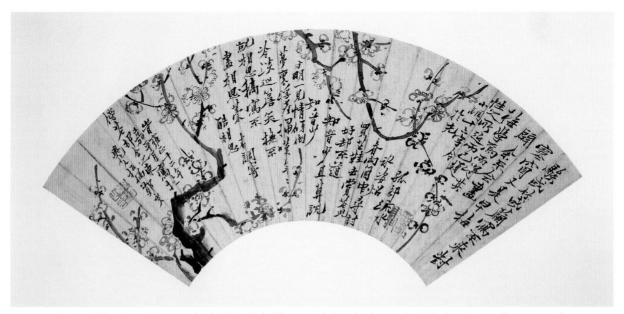

Figure 1/ The Way of Nature guides the Way of Life: "If untutored about bamboo and orchids, the paintings will not come....", Zheng Xie [Cheng Hsieh] (1693–1765), "Blossoming Plum" 1734. Folding fan, ink on paper, 19 x 56 cm (7 1/2 x 22 in). Artists' seals: Zheng Xie zhiyin and one other. Photograph courtesy of the Kaikodo Gallery, New York, NY.

the moral and cultural activities of people to influence the latter. This 'correlative thinking', as it is sometimes called, in turn reflects and reinforces the ambition that pervades East Asian teachings — to achieve harmony between one's own life and the wider reality to which it belongs. Through cultivating our own natures, says Zhuangzi, we become "blended with heaven and earth" and thereby are "in accord with the ultimate course" of things.[12] The self-cultivating Ways of human beings are, in effect, "forms of integration into some larger whole".[13] Human Ways, properly practiced, bring us into harmony with *the* Way (the *dao*).

The general thought here is not confined to traditions, like Daoism and Confucianism, that employ the explicit rhetoric of harmony with the *dao*. For Shintoists, respectful religious practice achieves "fellowship with the *kami*" the divine forces that hold sway over the world.[14] For Zen Buddhists, the Way of tea fosters a selflessness or 'emptiness' that emulates, at the human level, the emptiness of a reality where there is only 'not-self' (Pali *anatta*). A Way, thereby, is not just a means for bringing one's life into harmony with the truth of things, but an epitome of the proper relationship between human beings and the larger order. The practice of a Way exemplifies or manifests a relationship that may be impossible to articulate in literal language. This helps to explain why Ways are invested, in East Asian traditions, with profound significance. In Daoism, Zen Buddhism, Shinto, even Confucianism, there is a primacy of practice over theory or doctrine. Shinto, for example, has been described as "spirituality without an agenda", an "existential religiosity" whose vehicle is the various rituals, arts, and practices of adepts, and not a body of doctrine to which they must subscribe.[15] In none of these dispensations is the route to self-realization and virtue that of assenting to a set of propositions. Living well is not some extra bonus that right beliefs may bring. Rather it is in and through living well — through practicing a Way — that Daoist craftsmen, Confucian musicians, and Zen calligraphers know the way of things that cannot be said.

GARDENING AND SELF-CULTIVATION

"The garden", declared the twentieth-century Japanese philosopher Nishitani Keiji, "is my Zen master."[16] The remark dramatizes a conviction that many East Asian thinkers — and not just Buddhists — would endorse. Gardening enjoys a certain pre-eminence among the Ways through which human beings may come to lead fully realized lives. Each Way seeks to reflect or promote a balanced relationship between humanity and nature, and a practice so obviously engaged with natural processes as gardening would seem to be in a privileged position to achieve this. In good gardening, it has

been said, one discerns a "dialectic" of "cooperation between human beings and the natural world".[17] The garden is certainly regarded in the traditions that concern us as an arena for self-cultivation or care of the self. It is a place, for a start, where discipline and close attention to 'materials' — to the properties of a plant, say, or the quality of the soil — must replace whim and impulse. The famous advice of the eleventh-century Japanese treatise on gardening, the *Sakuteiki*, to "follow the request of the stone" can go proxy for countless injunctions in the literature to be mindful of and responsive to the natures of things and creatures in the garden, the character of its site, and the wider environment in which it is set.[18]

Such injunctions are found, for example, in the many 'Records' kept by Chinese literati that describe their experience of the gardens that they have made and in which they relax, meditate, and converse with friends. A prominent theme in works like Sima Guang's eleventh-century *Garden of Solitary Enjoyment* and Chen Fuyao's *Flower Mirror* some 600 years later is the power of the garden to afford protection from "the dust and grime of the city".[19] This is less a reference to urban pollution than a metaphor for a frenzied and convention-bound immersion in political affairs and business that allows no scope for self-reflection. In the garden, by contrast, a person is not governed by artificial regulations and has the time and the inspiration — from observing the lives of plants and birds — to reflect on "the principles of things" and on the direction that his or her own life should take.

One should not, perhaps, picture literati like Sima Guang as involved in muscular activities like digging soil or sawing branches. But elsewhere in the literature the role of gardening in disciplines of the body is certainly indicated. Zen Buddhist writers, for instance, emphasize the importance, in order to reduce self-centeredness, of absorption in routines of physical work — to the point, it has been joked, of holding that the very purpose of having a garden is to work in it. In Shinto, equally, an emphasis is placed on making the garden in which the shrine is set immaculate and clean — a fit precinct for people who are dressed in immaculate clothes and have purified themselves with water. For Shinto, as for Zen, the attention to bodily discipline that the garden invites is not disjoined from attention to mental and emotional discipline. They belong together in a wider economy of care for one's person. The same is true of the attention paid by Daoists to care of the body. Here there is an emphasis on a "tuning of the body" so that it chimes with the various rhythms that mark the processes of nature. One reason for the importance attached by Daoists to gardening is that it attunes people to the rhythms of the day and the seasons, and thereby promotes integration into the cosmos itself.[20]

Following a Way, we saw, is an education in virtue. Different Ways are no doubt especially suited to developing different virtues — courage in the case of *aikidō*, say, or courtesy and solicitude in that of *chadō*. The garden is regarded, certainly, as an arena in which to exercise and refine a number of virtues. We have, in fact, already mentioned some personal qualities manifested in good gardening—cleanliness and self-discipline, for example — that figure among the virtues (Chinese *de*) in East Asian traditions. Among the important and related virtues that the good gardeners must exercise if their enterprise is to flourish are humility, trust, and respect. Humility is primarily a sense of dependence, a modest appreciation that one's success is contingent on factors beyond one's control. Gardening is a Way that is especially apt to encourage this sense. A garden will not 'work', despite the gardener's best efforts, unless the soil is suitable, the rains come, and the rabbits stay away. Nor can the gardener even make these efforts except in a context where knowledge and skills have been developed and handed down by others. Even the most creative and original gardeners are in debt to traditions that stretch back centuries.

A humble appreciation of the need for the natural world to cooperate if the enterprise is to flourish merges with the virtue of trust. This is a precondition for engaging in any enterprise with a degree of confidence. For the gardener to make or tend the garden with the prospect that it will flourish, there must be trust in the benevolence of the *kami*, or in the continuance of the rhythms that regulate climates, seasons, growth, and decay, or in the responsiveness of the world to well-conceived projects. If the gardener's humility shades into the virtue of trust, so it does into those of care and respect. In a work compiled in its present form in the fifteenth century by Japanese Buddhist priests and landscape designers, the gardener is instructed "not to trample on the roots of [a] tree. When you make a landscape garden, maintain an attitude of reverence and respect, giving each aspect your full attention."[21] The virtuous gardener displays respect for plants not simply by desisting from wanton destruction of them and by treating them with protective care, but by attending to their nature and identifying what is good for them, what they need in order to flourish. Respect implies a refusal to regard things simply in terms of their use and a resolve, instead, to see and treat them for what they are.

Respect for natural things is an important component in the celebrated Daoist notion of *wu wei*. Literally, the words mean 'non-action', but refer, as an early commentator on the *Daodejing* put it, to "following what is spontaneous or natural", or to "taking no action contrary to nature", as a later commentator prefers.[22] The ideal of *wu wei*, crucially, is not simply cultivation of spontaneity in one's own person, but regard for and a resolve to foster the 'own nature' (*ziran*) of all other beings. The Daoist gardener will "support the own course of ... things", and "nourish" them through "following along with the way each thing is of itself".[23] This means that not only will a plant be allowed to grow as it should but that,

for example, it will be placed in the garden so as to bring out, rather than disguise, its distinctive nature.

Finally, one should not overlook the role attributed to the garden in several East Asian traditions as a place for educating and exercising various social virtues. For Confucian literati, the garden was not generally a place, despite the title of Sima Guang's work, just for 'solitary enjoyment'. Writings ranging from the celebrated fourth-century "Preface to the poems composed at the Orchid Pavilion" to Chen Fuyau's *Flower Mirror* emphasize the aptness of the garden as a setting for considerate behaviour, cultured conversation, and the promotion of friendship and social harmony [Figures 2, 3].[24] A similar theme is found in Daoist writings. In a fable composed early in the fifth century, the poet Tao Qian (aka Tao Yuanming) describes a Utopia, "Peach Blossom Land", almost inaccessible to outsiders, where people live in peace and harmony in an idyllic grove, ignorant of the violent, frenzied world beyond.[25]

The idea that pervades these texts is that it is only when insulated against 'worldly filth' or 'the dust and grime of the city' that human beings can authentically relate to one another. Lives immersed in worldly affairs are governed by regulations, external powers, and the imperatives of political and economic advancement. When so immersed, people are incapable of true friendship and mutual regard, of being natural and spontaneous in their treatment of one another. The garden is both a metaphor for, and an exemplar of, a place where human beings freely participate in a gathering of equals.

GARDENING, ENVIRONMENT, AND HARMONY

It is just possible that, from this account of the garden's role in self-cultivation, someone might form an image of the good gardener as a cultured scholar or serene monk enclosed in a garden, occasionally in the company of like-minded friends or fellow monks, but otherwise cut off from the wider world. The image is encouraged, perhaps, by a poem like that of the Zen priest, Ryōkan (d. 1831), in which he writes of his love of the seclusion and escape from worldliness that he finds in a friend's garden — one where he also finds "the spirit of Zen".[26] But the point made earlier about Ways in general applies to gardening as well: the good practitioner of a Way cannot help but have an engagement with the world. Indeed, the point applies with special force to a Way that requires such a direct contact with, and so decisive an impact on, the natural world. Charles Jencks wrote of the "resonance with outer nature" that, in Chinese tradition, the "life-breath" or inner power of a painter is deemed to have.[27] He could have said the same of the gardener with equal or greater validity.

Figure 2/ The garden as setting for cultured conversation. *Gathering At The Lanting Orchid Pavilion,* Chen Jiuru (Chinese), ink and color on satin, 40 x 196 cm (15 3/4 x 77 1/4 in). Indianapolis Museum of Art, John Herron Fund, 1990. 113. Photograph courtesy of the Indianapolis Museum of Art.

Let's begin by considering some connections between good gardening and natural environments that are indicated in East Asian literatures. Some of these, in fact, are indicated in the Ryōkan poem cited above. Secluded the garden may be, but the poet is acutely aware of its relationship to a larger environment — to the "cool, clear autumnal sky" and "the evening rain" that falls on the trees. The "spirit of Zen" that the garden evokes is, in part at least, the Buddhist sense of the world as an intimately interconnected whole. To be mindful of anything is to appreciate that it owes its identity to its place within an intricate web or net of relationships.

This holistic appreciation that the garden encourages has significant implications for the gardener's aesthetic engagement with the environment. Long before William Kent, inventor of the ha-ha that invited "all Nature" into the garden, Chinese and Japanese landscapers had become masters in the use of 'borrowed scenery' (Chinese *jeijing*, Japanese *shakkei*).[28] That a gardener should borrow scenery from the surrounding environment is an important precept both in the *Sakuteiki* and in the most celebrated of Chinese works on gardening, Ji Cheng's 1631 *Yuanye* (*The Craft of Gardens*). As this text explains, however, the gardener must be alert not only to how the scenery may enhance the experience of the garden, but to the "suitability" of the garden design to the surrounding environment.[29] A designer would be disrespectful towards nature by creating a garden that occluded, or jarred with, a beautiful natural prospect. There are other ways, too, in which a design by a gardener properly attuned to nature will be aesthetically influenced by knowledge of natural environments. The design may, as in many Japanese gardens, represent some famously beautiful scene, and materials — rocks, say, or sand — taken from the location depicted may be incorporated into the garden. Rather like a tailor's swatch, parts of the garden actually exemplify what they represent.

If the art of gardening has aesthetic implications for the relationship between gardens and natural environments, so too do the virtues required for good gardening. The exercise of cleanliness, care, humility, and other virtues extends beyond the confines of the garden. Care and respect for what grows in a garden, for example, carries over into the wider environment. Among the *One Hundred and Eighty Precepts* of the Daoist Celestial Masters (second or third century CE) there are around 20 that enjoin respectful treatment of environments. Rivers should not be contaminated, trees not wantonly felled, and so on. It is important to appreciate that these precepts do not reflect an ideal of untouched wilderness. Typically, the places where rivers and trees are to be respected are sacred spaces, frequented by people, and often in the vicinity of temples.[30] Care for such environments is comparable to the concern, in Shinto, to ensure that sites are protected and kept pure as fit places for the *kami* to dwell.

Respect for animals is especially urged in some classic Daoist texts — a respect that carefully negotiates between protecting animals (not least, from human predation) and 'letting them be', allowing them to follow their own nature, their own course. Several of the remarks and anecdotes associated with the sage Liezi (fl. fourth century BCE) attest to this respect. It is said that he treated his own animals, including pigs, "as equally his own kin", and he was dismissive of the view

that animals were placed on earth to satisfy our needs and appetites. Animals have a nature and purpose of their own, and it is important that we try to understand these and interpret the creatures' behavior rightly. Again, it is not a wildlife ideal that Liezi is promulgating. Indeed, he hopes that the many animals that he welcomes into his garden to be fed will lose their desire to live "deep in the mountains and hidden away in the valleys". The aim, instead, should be to return to the days, before human beings terrorized and exploited them, when beasts and birds lived together with us in peaceful proximity.[31]

An important topic of discussion in ancient China — unsurprisingly, given the immense scale of its agriculture — was farming. In a manner somewhat prescient of contemporary debates about organic farming and intensive production, the focus was not simply on matters of cost-effectiveness and nutrition, but also on ethical aspects of farming. Especially in Confucian writings, attention was paid to the social virtues that a good agricultural system should encourage. Indeed, the main value of agriculture, according to one text, resides in the virtuous qualities of the life led by simple and unselfish farmers — one very different from the contrived and self-seeking life of merchants in the cities.[32] Several of these virtues are natural extensions, beyond the garden wall, of those cultivated in the garden. The well-field system described by Mencius sounds, in fact, like one of a community of small-scale kitchen gardens. What makes it the best system, for Mencius, is not primarily its efficiency, but its capacity to promote friendship, mutual help, solicitude, love and harmony among the farmers and their families.[33]

Qualities needed for good gardening, then, manifest themselves in engagement with the larger natural world. But we know that gardening, as a Way, must have the further ambition of achieving and exemplifying harmony with the order of things — with *the* Way. Indeed, the aspects of self-cultivation and the various virtues identified over the last few pages have only a provisional status. For them to be genuine excellences of a human life, they must be shown to contribute to and reflect this harmony. This is precisely what many texts in several East Asian traditions attempt to show.

Very large claims, we saw, were made about the capacity of human beings to influence the cosmos, to "bring things to completion". According to the Eastern Han dynasty Daoist text, *The Scripture of the Great Peace*, it is, in one commentator's words, "the great responsibility of humankind to maintain harmonious communication with Heaven and Earth in order to bring about cosmic harmony".[34] With its special relationship to the earth, gardening was unsurprisingly credited with helping humankind in this monumental task. But it was also assigned important, if less cosmically decisive, roles in both enabling and epitomizing harmony between human beings and reality.

Ways exist in East Asian traditions in part, I suggested, because they are vehicles of an implicit knowledge of truths that cannot be fully articulated. It is in and through such practices that people understand the way of things and conduct their lives in harmony with it. Gardening is an especially apt vehicle of this understanding. Despite differences in their metaphysical conceptions of reality, there is broad agreement among the East Asian traditions on the holistic character of the world, the

Figure 3/ The garden as setting also for the promotion of social harmony. *Poetry Gathering at the Orchid Pavilion*. Nakabayashi Chikkei (Japanese,1816–1867). Ink, color and gofun on silk, 149.5 x 57 cm (58 7/8 x 22 3/8 in) (image); 217 x 76 cm (85 1/2 x 30 in) (overall). Indianapolis Museum of Art, Mr. and Mrs. Richard Crane Fund, 2000.21. Photograph courtesy of the Indianapolis Museum of Art.

transience or impermanence of all phenomena, the spontaneity of the source of the world we experience, and the mystery of this source. Working in gardens is peculiarly suited to evoking a sense of each of these dimensions of the way of things. To begin with, it is work that, sensitive to the seasons, the life-cycles of plants and insects, and other rhythms in nature, encourages a sense of "integration into the cosmic rhythm" of the universe at large.[35] At the same time, the gardener becomes acutely aware of the interconnectedness of things within a whole process. In the garden, an eighteenth-century poet and painter wrote, it is as if flowers are inviting butterflies, rocks inviting clouds, pine trees inviting the wind, banana trees inviting the rain, and so on.[36] Butterflies, the wind rustling through the branches, and much else that the gardener experiences are likely, of course, to induce in addition an impression of the ephemeral character of phenomena. "Impermanency", one of Lafcadio Hearn's Buddhist interlocutors reminded him, "is the nature of our life" — recalling perhaps the days when the refined inhabitants of Heian-kyō (Kyoto) would stroll in gardens in search of the pathos of the transience of things that falling blossoms or dissolving mists evoked.[37] The idea that we should be sensitive to impermanence is not peculiar to Buddhism. It is there in Daoist texts and is reflected in the Shinto practice of dismantling and rebuilding shrines at relatively short intervals.

The ephemeral nature of events in the garden is one reason why it is essential for gardeners to be spontaneous — to remain alert, flexible, and responsive to changing circumstances. The garden is an education in spontaneity, not only because it teaches the need for this flexibility but because gardeners must also be responsive to "the request of the stone" and of plants, trees, and other components of the garden. There must be no attachment, in other words, to rigid plans that impose on things what is alien to their nature. In exercising spontaneity and naturalness, the gardener is in effect emulating the workings of reality. People follow "the way of the earth", explains the *Daodejing*, and thereby follow the way of the *dao*. This is because the *dao* in its turn "follows the way of spontaneity".[38] The *dao* does not "contend" or enforce, for there is nothing outside of it to contend against and force itself upon. While it is responsible for there being things at all, these are not created or manufactured by the *dao* according to some purpose or plan. Comparable conceptions are found in other traditions. In simple activities like hoeing, writes a Japanese philosopher, people are brought into a "face-to-face relation with the absolute" that Zen Buddhists call "emptiness" — an ineffable source of the world of experience that, like the *dao*, has no plan and imposes nothing on that world.[39]

This last remark leads to a final respect in which gardening is a form of implicit knowledge of the way of things. In her elegant and acute book on *ikebana*, Gustie Herrigel wrote that, while much can be said about flower-setting, there stands "behind everything that can be represented …

waiting to be experienced … the mystery and deep ground of existence".[40] Herrigel, one feels, would be happy to apply her words as well to flower-growing, to gardening more generally. In doing so, she would be echoing claims about the power of gardening to evoke a sense of mystery that have been made over the centuries in several East Asian traditions. In Zen Buddhism, for example, gardens have long been held, in the words of one authority, to afford "a glimpse of this world as it appears to a Zen-enlightened sensibility".[41] This is a mysteriously emerging world, "something ineffable coming [to us] like *this*", as the great Zen master Dōgen put it.[42] Those words gesture towards an experience that is hard to articulate, but to which many gardeners attest. This is the sense that, in their work, there is a deep connection with the world of plants, creatures, stones, and seasons that is a 'gift', emergent from a source that is at once beyond the world yet totally intimate with it.[43]

Over the last few paragraphs, we have in effect answered the question of whether gardening really is a Way — a practice that is a form of authentic self-cultivation and in which the qualities it inspires are genuine virtues. In the East Asian traditions that concern us, a life is one of self-cultivation and virtue only if it is consonant with the way of things. We have seen that, within those traditions, good gardening is held to be a vehicle of implicit understanding of reality. The garden fosters a sense of interconnectedness, transience, spontaneity, and mystery. These are fundamental aspects either of the world of experience or of the source and ground of this world. To know these aspects is not a matter of assenting to a number of philosophical propositions, of signing up to a set of doctrines. It is, rather, to work and live with the kind of sensibility epitomized in the Way of the good gardener.

NATURE, HUMANITY, AND THE WAY OF THE GARDEN

The American composer and author John Cage recalled how, having explained to people the attractions of Zen Buddhism, some of them would say, "That's all very well, but it won't work for us, for it's Oriental."[44] Might it be similarly claimed that East Asian reflections on the Way of the garden are too remote from Western discourse to be fruitfully drawn upon? There are significant differences, certainly, in the contexts and assumptions of the two discourses, some of which stand in the way of dialogue. For example, Daoist and Buddhist doctrines concerning the connection between the moral and cosmic orders — 'correlative thinking', say, or the theory of karmic effects — will have little resonance for

people educated in contemporary physics and biology. One should, moreover, resist the temptation to explain away such doctrines, to treat them as merely figurative or only symbolic in intent. That said, it is important to view them within a framework of thought, concerning the establishment of harmony between human existence and the natural world, aspects of which should not offend contemporary science.

Other distinctive components of East Asian reflections on gardens and nature, far from inviting the sort of negative response John Cage recollects, might surely encourage reconsideration of tendencies in Western thinking. A striking difference, briefly noted earlier, is the absence in the East Asian discourse of the 'wilderness' ideal that has been so prominent in European and American environmental philosophy. In China and Japan, the garden has never been a 'problem' — a place that, since it bears the obvious mark of human intervention in nature, needs to be justified. One American lecturer recalls how his students were disappointed and angered to hear that Daoist hermits would employ effort and artistry in order to transform their natural surroundings. For these students, he remarks, "a true nature lover would simply leave nature alone." And this sentiment, as he rightly points out, betrays a "strictly disjunctive view of the relation between 'nature' and 'culture'" that has never had traction in East Asian thought.[45]

It is true that, in recent times, many Western writers have themselves criticized a long-entrenched tendency of 'opposing' human beings to the natural world. But their point, very generally, has been a reductionist one to the effect that men and women are 'really' nothing but a species of animal, subject to the same natural laws as animals are, and sharing with them the great bulk of their DNA composition. This has never been the point of Buddhists, Daoists, and Confucians, who reject a culture/nature dichotomy. In fact, they have tended to emphasize the respects in which human beings are distinguished from all other beings — not least, in their capacity to question and care about their relationship to these other beings. These respects are undeniably there, irrespective of data about DNA and a common subjection of all things to the fundamental laws of nature.

In East Asian traditions, the basis for challenging the dichotomy of nature and culture is entirely different. It is hinted at in Zhuangzi's remark that it is impossible, in any sphere of activity, to separate out what is "done by the human" and what is done by the non-human, by 'heaven', or nature.[46] It is made more explicit in a remark I quoted earlier that refers to a "dialectic" of "cooperation between humans and the natural world". Elsewhere I have labeled this relationship between culture and nature "co-dependence".[47] The term refers to a relationship between human creative effort and the way the natural world is experienced. Each, I have argued, is dependent on the other. There can be no creative effort except in the light of a way of experiencing natural things. Equally, any way

Figure 4/ A fusion of human artifice and nature. Moon Bridge, West Lake Hangzhou, China. Photograph by Neil Morgan.

in which nature is experienced is a function, in part, of our creative practices in relation to nature.

Co-dependence is paradigmatically exemplified and expressed by gardening. What the gardener does cannot help but shape an experience of nature, just as the latter is bound to impact on what he or she does. What the stone is experienced as requesting will decide where it is placed in the garden, and where it is placed will in turn invite an experience of the garden as a whole and of the natural environment beyond its boundaries. There is an apt visual metaphor for the fusion between human artifice and nature in the moon-bridge that is a feature of many Asian gardens [Figure 4]. Above the stream there is the man-made creation, in stone or wood; beneath the bridge is its reflection in the water of the stream. Together, and looked at from an appropriate angle, the bridge and its natural reflection form a perfect circle.

If we are to appreciate the force of rejecting the familiar dualism of artifice and nature, it is important to recognize that it belongs to a network of dichotomies that have structured ideas about humanity and nature in Western traditions of philosophy, religion, and science. Others in this network include sharp contrasts between the aesthetic and both the moral and the religious; between knowledge and both virtue and emotion; between theory and practice; and between social responsibility and private pleasure. In this essay, we have seen how each of these contrasts is softened or recalibrated within East Asian traditions. It is not that there is a blunt denial of a distinction between, say, questions about duty and ones about beauty, or between theoretical understanding and practical skills. Rather, the terms of such distinctions are treated as abstractions, convenient for certain purposes, from a more integrated vision of human life.

It is in the notion of a Way — the Way of the garden, especially — that one finds the terms of these contrasts elided and an integrated vision of life expressed. On my desk is a book on the arts of Japan in which a photo of a bridge leading into a Shinto sacred garden is used to illustrate a "'religio-aesthetic' tradition" — one that is as marked in Buddhism as it is in Shinto — where religious and aesthetic sensibilities can only be artificially prized apart.[48] Earlier we noted how the private pleasures of Chinese literati in their secluded gardens are inseparable from virtues of friendship and respect that extend beyond the garden to the wider world of social relationships. Understanding aspects of reality that include the transience of phenomena and the mystery of their source is manifested less in the utterances of scholars and poets than in mindful engagement with the plants, creatures, and elements that come together in a garden.

I could go on, but the point is made that in the Way of the garden the dualisms central to Western conceptions of humanity and its relationship to the world are abandoned in favor of more nuanced connections. It is here that the main value of the East Asian Way of the garden is to be found. The 'gardener of the cosmos', to recall our opening metaphor, is not a messianic figure at the head of the charge 'to save the planet'. He or she is someone whose own life and whose relationship to the natural environment are modeled on those of the good gardener. This is a man or woman whose engagement with the living world cultivates sensibility to beauty, bodily grace and discipline, spontaneity, and other virtues that enable lives to flourish, and understanding of the way, and of the mystery, of things.

The final word on the bequest of the good gardener as a model for humanity I leave to a poet we heard from earlier, Cheng Hsieh. He invited his readers, recall, to "regard the universe as a garden". This, he explains, will lead to "the enjoyment of life": indeed, it is a vision that, fully embraced, will "enable all beings to live according to their nature". "Great indeed", the poet concludes, "is such happiness."[49]

NOTES

1/ Nietzsche, Friedrich, *The Genealogy of Morals* III. 6, and Preface to *The Birth of Tragedy*, in *Basic Writings of Nietzsche*, Walter Kaufmann trans., New York: Modern Library, 1968, pp. 31, 539.

2/ Miller, James, *Daoism: A Short Introduction*, Oxford: Oneworld, 2003, pp. 45–46.

3/ Cited in Jean C. Cooper, *An Illustrated Introduction to Daoism*, Bloomington, IN: World Wisdom, 2010, p. 129.

4/ Shunmyo Masuno, *The Modern Japanese Garden*, Michael Freeman and Michiko Rico Nosé intro., London: Mitchell Beazley, 2002, p. 14.

5/ Carter, Robert E., *The Japanese Arts and Self-Cultivation*, Albany, NY: SUNY Press, 2007, p. 3.

6/ Davey, H. E., *The Japanese Way of the Artist*, Berkeley, CA: Stone Bridge, Kindle Ed., 2012, loc. 72; Yuriko Saito, "Japanese Aesthetics", *Encyclopedia of Aesthetics*, vol. 2, Michael Kelly ed., New York: Oxford University Press, 1999, p. 551.

7/ *The Great Learning* (*Da Xue*), *A Sourcebook in Chinese Philosophy*, Wing-Tsit Chan trans., Princeton, NJ: Princeton University Press, 1963, p. 90.

8/ Kirkland, Russell, *Taoism: The Enduring Tradition*, New York: Routledge, 2004, p. 33; Schipper, Kristofer, *The Taoist Body*, Berkeley, CA: University of California Press, 1993, p. xiv.

9/ *The Great Learning*, pp. 92–94.

10/ Pilgrim, Richard B., *Buddhism and the Arts of Japan*, Chambersburg, PA.: Anima, 1993, p. 10.

11/ *The Analects of Confucius*, Roger Ames and Henry Rosemont trans., New York: Ballantine, 1999, p. 88; *Hsün Tzu: Basic Writings*, Burton Watson trans., New York: Columbia University Press, 1963, p. 91; *Zhuangzi: The Essential Writings*, Brook Ziporyn trans., Indianapolis, IN.: Hackett, 2009, p. 68.

12/ *Chuang-Tzu: The Inner Chapters*, A. C. Graham trans., Indianapolis, IN: Hackett, 2001, p. 157.

13/ *The Analects of Confucius*, Introduction, p. 56.

14/ Sokyo Ono, *Shinto: The Kami Way*, Tokyo: Tuttle, 1962, Kindle Ed., loc. 433.

15/ Kasulis, Thomas P., *Shinto: The Way Home*, Honolulu: University of Hawai'i Press, 2004, pp. 32, 36.

16/ Cited in François Berthier, *Reading Zen in the Rocks*, Chicago: University of Chicago Press, 2000, p. 136.

17/ Meyer, Jeffrey, "Salvation in the garden: Daoism and Ecology", *Daoism and Ecology*, N. Girardot, J. Miller, and Xiaogan Liu eds., Boston, MA: Harvard University Press, 2001, p. 223.

18/ *Sakuteiki: Visions of the Japanese Garden*, Jiro Takei and Marc P. Keane trans., Boston, MA: Tuttle, 2001, p. 4.

19/ On Sima Guang, see Maggie Keswick, *The Chinese Garden*, London: Academy, 1980, pp. 84ff.; on Chen Fuyao, see Joseph Cho Wang, *The Chinese Garden*, Hong Kong: Oxford University Press, 1998, pp. 23ff.

20/ Schipper, *The Taoist Body*, p. 139.

21/ *Illustrations for Designing Mountain, Water, and Hillside Field Landscapes*, David E. Slawson, *Secret Teachings in the Art of Japanese Gardens*, Tokyo: Kodansha, 1991, §63.

22/ Wang Bi and Wing-Tsit Chan, quoted in Wang Keping trans., *The Classic of the* Dao: *A New Investigation*, Beijing: Foreign Languages Press, 1998, p. 87.

23/ *Daodejing: A Complete Translation and Commentary*, H-G. Moeller trans., Chicago: Open Court, 2007, p.149; *Zhuangzi: The Essential Writings*, p. 38.

24/ See Zhuang Yue and Wang Qiheng, "The Poetics of Dwelling a Garden: A Confucian Mode of Being", *Teaching Landscape with Architecture*, A. Laffage and Y. Nussaume eds., Paris: Editions de la Villette, 2009.

25/ See Wang, *The Chinese Garden*, pp. 58–59.

26/ *One Robe, One Bowl: The Zen Poetry of Ryōkan*, John Stevens trans., New York: Weatherhill, 1977, p. 48.

27/ In Keswick, *The Chinese Garden*, p.194.

28/ In Horace Walpole's actual words, Kent "leaped the fence, and saw that all Nature was a garden", cited in John Dixon Hunt and Peter Willis, *The Genius of the Place: The English Landscape Garden 1620–1820*, Boston, MA: MIT Press, 1988, p. 313.

29/ Ji Cheng, *The Craft of Gardens*, Alison Hardie trans., New Haven: Yale University Press, 1988, p. 39.

30/ See Kristofer Schipper, "Daoist Ecology: The Inner Transformation. A Study of the Early Daoist Ecclesia", *Daoism and Ecology*, pp. 79–93.

31/ *The Book of Lieh-tzu*, A. C. Graham trans., New York: Columbia University Press, 1990, pp. 43, 55, 179.

32/ Quoted from the *Spring and Autumn Annals* in Fung Yu-Lan, *A Short History of Chinese Philosophy*, New York: Free Press, 1966, p. 18.

33/ *Mencius*, D. C. Lau trans., London: Penguin, 1970, pp. 99–100.

34/ Chi-Tim Lai, "The Daoist Concept of Central Harmony in the *Scripture of Great Peace*: Human Responsibility for the Maladies of Nature", *Daoism and Ecology*, p. 96.

35/ Schipper, *The Daoist Body*, p. 139.

36/ Zhang Zhou, quoted in Jean C. Cooper, *An Illustrated Introduction to Taoism*, p. 122.

37/ Hearn, Lafcadio, *Kokoro: Japanese Inner Life Hints*, Public Domain e-book, 2005, loc. 268.

38/ *The Classic of the* Dao, Wang Keping trans., Chapter 25, p. 231.

39/ Nishida Kitarō, *Last Writings: Nothingness and the Religious Worldview*, D. Dilworth trans., Honolulu: University of Hawai'i Press, 1987, p. 111.

40/ Herrigel, Gustie L., *Zen in the Art of Flower Arrangement*, London: Souvenir, 1999, p. 119.

41/ Yuriko Saito, "Japanese Gardens: The Art of Improving Nature", *Chanoyou Quarterly*, 1996, no. 83, p. 59.

42/ Dōgen Zenji, *Shobogenzo*, vol. 2, G. Nishijama and C. Cross trans., London: Windbell, 1996, p. 3.

43/ For fuller accounts of gardens and mystery, see David E. Cooper, *A Philosophy of Gardens*, Oxford: Oxford University Press, 2006, and *Convergence with Nature: A Daoist Perspective*, Dartington: Green Books, 2012.

44/ Cage, John, *Silence: Lectures and Writings*, London: Boyars, 2009, p. 143.

45/ LaFargue, Michael, "'Nature' as Part of Human Culture in Daoism", *Daoism and Ecology*, p. 47.

46/ *Zhuangzi: The Essential Writings*, Chapter 6.

47/ See David E. Cooper, *A Philosophy of Gardens* and "Gardens and the Way of Things", *Earth Perfect? Nature, Utopia and the Garden*, Annette Giesecke and Naomi Jacobs eds., London: Black Dog Publishing, 2012, pp. 20–33.

48/ Pilgrim, *Buddhism and the Arts of Japan*, p. 2.

49/ Quoted in Jean C. Cooper, *An Illustrated Introduction to Taoism*, p. 128.

50 /FRANKLIN GINN

ECHOES OF HISTORY FROM PŪTARINGAMOTU, A NEW ZEALAND SWAMP FOREST

Pūtaringamotu is the Māori name for a small forest on New Zealand's South Island. The name means 'place of an echo'. Inspired by the name, this essay is concerned with the echoes that can be heard from this place, commonly known as Riccarton Bush, and what these echoes can tell us about nature, loss, and recovery. Listening closely, the essay discerns echoes of the past: the dying words of a hard-nosed Scottish farmer; the rustle of oak leaves; the squeal of trapped possums; the desire of settler culture to erase colonial sins; subjugated and resurgent Indigenous identity — echoes from beyond history, too: the promise of science to eternalize ecology. And as Pūtaringamotu faces an uncertain future, the forest reverberates with the echoes of possible extinction.[1]

1842

They paddled their canoes up the Ōtākaro river, avoiding patches of swamp and the few thick forests that dotted the plains. Where the river shallowed out their canoes scraped gravel; they hauled themselves along by grasping flax plants at the river's edge. The eight-mile journey from the coast took all afternoon. When they finally arrived, William Deans looked across the land in the fading summer sun. The scene was as he had imagined: a grove of trees of about 200 acres; a small stream; low, sandy hummocks. If not exactly beautiful the land certainly had potential. William's companions — a carpenter together with his wife and their three children, and another couple with their three children — had followed him to the far side of the world. By leaving Scotland for New Zealand's South Island these companions entrusted their livelihoods, and perhaps their lives, to their collective farming savvy. The group's hope, at the same time practical and

revolutionary, was that the land, once "laid out in moderate sized paddocks, and sown down with English grasses", would increase in "value amazingly".[2] William Deans and his brother John, who joined the group in late 1842, called the place Riccarton, after their home in Scotland.

William was a tough, independent-minded Scot, who though destined for a career in law was lured by the promise of breaking new land and the independence emigrating might offer him. Three years previously William had purchased land orders and sailed to the far end of the earth — New Zealand's North Island. There, dissatisfied with the marshy, ferny, and

Figure 1/ Riccarton, the residence of John Deans Esq., 2 February 1851. J. E. Fitzgerald watercolor. Canterbury Museum, New Zealand.

hilly land available, and frustrated by colonial bureaucracy, William had struck out alone. Ingratiating himself with local Māori just beyond Wellington, at Wairarapa, he followed a lead south to the great plains of Te Waipounamu (the South Island), a shifting mosaic of water, grass, and tree.[3] Ngāi Tahu, the largest Māori tribe on the South island, knew the Bush where the Deans settled as Pūtaringamotu, the 'place of an echo'. The name's origins are unclear. Perhaps it was an echo of forests lost, a testament to the low swamp forest that once peppered the lowlands. Or perhaps the name originated from a curious quirk of sound which meant, it was said, that you could press your ear to the ground in the Bush and feel the vibrations of approaching creatures. For Ngāi Tahu, a complex social system governed the use and management of these lowlands through an ethic of *kaitiakitanga* (guardianship), or the long-term duty to care for the spiritual, physical, and ecological well-being of a place.[4] From the small forests quail, kererū (native pigeon), woodhen, and kākā (a flightless parrot) were harvested; Māori fished shrimp and eels from the nearby river. Such activities were undertaken throughout an island-wide network of food-gathering places, or *mahinga kai*, according to seasonally optimal harvest times.

Local Ngāi Tahu elders knew a good deal when they saw it. If the Deans brothers wanted to pay for access to the resources of Pūtaringamotu, then that could be negotiated. The rent was set at £8 a year for some 72,000 acres around Pūtaringamotu, the contract to last 21 years. Such rental agreements were traditionally gestures of reciprocity — as much about the relationship involved as the economic worth of the land — and for the first few years there was a yearly feast on pigs, potatoes, sugar, flour, and rice on "rent day".[5] In common with other early European arrivals to New Zealand, the Deans seemed to appreciate Ngāi Tahu's rights over the islands. Indeed, local Māori seemed to get on well with these Scots: the brothers wrote repeatedly in their letters home of the "very good terms" they shared with their landlords. According to *utu*, or 'reciprocity', the Deans and the local sub-tribe were tied together, just as each was tied to the land.

During the first year the Deans built a timber-framed house, hacking great gouges from the forest, and when native pigeons flocked to feed on the berries of the tall kahikatea trees (white pine, *Dacrydium dacridiodes*) of the Bush, the brothers shot them as fast as they "could recharge their guns" [Figure 1].[6] They planted fruit trees, oak, ash, gorse, thorn hedges for shelter, and grasses for pasture. The next year they set up a stockade and imported 61 cows, 43 sheep, and a few horses. The Deans embarked on the long, slow labor of draining swamps and improving their lands, working to "reclaim them and make them useful or beautiful as a garden".[7] By the late 1840s the surveyor and theodolite (surveying instrument) had arrived, and the New Zealand Company began to carve up swamp and hill into planned, geometric settlement. During protracted negotiations, complicated by the Deans' early

Figure 2/ Jane Deans. Canterbury Museum, New Zealand.

arrival on the South Island and their lack of formal ownership, it seemed at times that the brothers would lose everything. Eventually, though, the Deans bought 400 acres from the Crown in 1848. The Bush, then down to about 55 acres in size, was dissected: half left to the Deans, half given over to the new settlers in Christchurch, the emerging town a couple of miles east.

William died at sea in 1851, drowned along with the sheep he was bringing back to Riccarton. In 1852 his brother, John, returned briefly to Scotland to marry a tough Presbyterian woman, Jane McIlraith [Figure 2]. Unfortunately, John Deans contracted tuberculosis on his return to Riccarton. On his deathbed a few years later in 1854, he implored Jane to make sure that "what remained of Riccarton Bush should be preserved forever".[8] His motivations remain unclear. The Deans were social climbers, ready to secure their place in the city's founding mythology. Their early plantings of orchard and oak paid social as well as financial dividends: they had received dignitaries in their picturesque garden, and had successfully cultivated an image as the city's 'first pioneers'. Did John imagine that their home, a picture of how — through diligent labor and Calvinist obstinacy — they had 'improved' swampy grassland by turning it into a productive landscape, would one day be surrounded by suburban sprawl, and that, perhaps, the land's value might escalate accordingly?[9] Or was it the attachment to a small corner of the earth that claimed John's labor and ultimately, his life? Or was it a love of trees? The brothers' letters home are full of talk of trees — not in adoration or in homage, but of their practical uses, their differing grains, the way different species met wind and rain: the Deans knew their trees, that much we can say. Jane, who guarded this death bed legend as fiercely as she did Riccarton Bush, was clear: this was an early, enlightened impulse to save what was left of a fast-vanishing nature.

A TIME OF NOSTALGIA

In common with islands elsewhere, evolutionary time moved rapidly in New Zealand. Those shaky islands broke from the Gondwana supercontinent around 80 million years ago, and their isolation in the South Pacific and the absence of mammals encouraged flightless birds, insects, and reptiles to evolve and fill unusual ecological niches; gigantism and longevity were marked. 80 percent of New Zealand's plant species, and even some entire plant orders, and 25 percent of its bird species are endemic. Weird species persist: the tuatara, for example, is the last remaining member of the ancient group of reptiles, Sphenodontia, while all three of New Zealand's frog species are among the oldest on earth. Of course, long before the Deans joined a wave of settlers making their new home in New Zealand in the mid-nineteenth century, the islands had been discovered — the last great landmass found by humans. By 500 CE Polynesian peoples had explored the Pacific and established a flourishing network of communities linked by inter-island 'sea-paths'. From there they set out to the extremities of the Polynesian triangle: Hawai'i in 600, Rapa Nui in 690, and finally New Zealand in 1200.[10] Cut off from the rest of Polynesia after landfall, the arrivals developed their own, Māori, culture. They spread rapidly across the New Zealand islands, thanks to their ingenuity in capitalizing on available food sources: moa, giant flightless birds, and fur seals weighing around 200 kilograms apiece were easy prey. 14 bird species were made extinct during Māori times, more than the total number of extinctions in the previous 11,000 years; and forest cover was reduced from 75–80 percent of the total land area of New Zealand at the time of Māori arrival to only 50 percent by European settlement.[11] Māori introduced animals and plants to New Zealand, the kumara (sweet potato) having long-lasting impact, and the kiore (Polynesian rat) reaching plague proportions.[12] Once easy food sources were exhausted (and moa extinct), Māori became "hunter-gardeners".[13] Tribes specialized in gathering, trading, and gift-exchanging all sorts

of resources: salt fish, mutton birds, pigs, sweet potato, ducks, eels, flax, *pounamu* (greenstone), seaweeds, cod, shellfish, shrimp, seals, penguins, pigeons, carvings, *waka* (canoes), eggs, or bark. Harvesting was done according to season and reciprocal ties of access and rights to resources, neither of which were firmly tied to territory, but governed through a highly complex system of prestige, access, and resource management.[14] This period of New Zealand's history has been typified as one in which Māori spent the first 500 years taking the land apart and the next 500 years learning how to put it back together.[15]

For Māori the forest was multiple, its meaning and uses — its very 'being' — manifold. Trees were one descendant of Tāne, god of the standing forest; forests were animated by spiritual presence. Trees could be cut down for carving, construction, and land clearance. Forests could be fought over. Equally, they could be preserved, treasured *mahinga kai* (food gathering places), or sacred *taonga* (treasure, valued object). But for European settlers the metric was simpler: forest was to be chopped down, swamps drained, plains divided and turned to pasture, and the wilderness improved into a productive landscape. As the surveyor Charles Hursthouse wrote of the South Island,

> The cultivation of a new country materially improves the climate. Damp and dripping forests, exhaling pestilent vapours from rank and rotten vegetation, falls before the axe; and air and light get in; and sunshine ripening goodly plants. Fen and marsh and swamp, the bittern's dank domain, fertile only in miasma, are drained; and the plough converts them into wholesome plains of fruit, and grain, and grass.[16]

While Ngāi Tahu saw the lowlands of the South Island as a useful and shifting landscape, replete with spiritual and practical significance, the Deans and other European settlers saw an empty land that invited labor and industry.

The British signed the Treaty of Waitangi with Māori chiefs in 1840, which opened the gates for mass settlement.[17] Aided by dubious land purchases — the terms of which the Crown systematically violated — adverts of a 'Britain of the South', and assisted passage, the European population grew from 2,000 in 1840 to 500,000 by 1890.[18] Wetlands were drained (670,000 hectares reduced to 100,000 today) and forests further cleared (cover fell from 50 percent to today's 25 percent).[19] Europeans were accompanied by nonhuman settlers, too: rats, stoats, grasses, gorse, weeds, bunnies, bees, and birds of all kinds. These cosmopolitan creatures of Empire didn't always behave as they should, exceeding the desires and aims of those who introduced them, and creating a new, mixed island ecology.[20] Of the some 850 mammal, bird, amphibian, reptile, and mollusc species made extinct by humans since 1500, 72 percent were on islands.[21] This was because the very ecological traits that produce high biodiversity in places like New Zealand also make their ecological communities vulnerable: low population density, slow life history or low fecundity, and small geographical range all made island species vulnerable to invasive species and to the hybrid ecologies that emerged through imperialism.

Victorian racial hierarchies were confused by Māori. How had such a supposedly 'primitive' race out-smarted the British in successive military engagements (1840s and 1860s)? Darwin nevertheless despised their "crude savagery" and put them on a rung of civilization just above Tierra del Fuegians; Walter Buller, New Zealand conservationist and anthropologist, placed Māori above Indians but just below the Irish.[22] All turn of the century commentators agreed, though, that Māori were a dying race. By the end of the nineteenth century, as the last great old kauri (*Agathis australis*) fell, as swamps were drained and the forests emptied of birdsong, many commentators saw New Zealand's indigenous inhabitants — nonhuman and human alike — as receding into the past. The Māori population declined to less than 50,000 in 1890, in part due to their separation from *mahinga kai* through illegal land British purchases, with one elder lamenting that "the tuis [native bird] and all other birds are gone, and the roots of the *kauru* [food from the cabbage tree, *Cordyline australis*] and the fern have been destroyed."[23] For Europeans, these changes confirmed racial hierarchy. Conservationist Elsdon Best wrote that

> a people settling in a forest country must destroy the forest or it will conquer them. The forest is conservative, repressive, making not for culture of advancement.... Someday a civilised tribe, from open lands, happens along, and hews down that forest. The Children of Tane, human and arboreal alike, disappear, and the place knows them never again.[24]

For Best, to wander around what was left of the forests was to wander around a primitive, haunted landscape: its people — whom he called children of Tāne, god of the standing forest — gone, their *taonga* (treasure, valued object) displayed in museums and toured round Europe as fine emblems of the country's unique past.[25]

Even as landscape improvement relegated indigenous people, flora, and fauna to the past, nature was being resuscitated as part of an incipient eco-nationalist identity. Early twentieth-century writers celebrated the native bush scenery, the unique birdlife, as well as sublime wilderness, and began to elevate these to symbols of an emerging nation. As one botanist put it, "These remarkable forms of plant and animal life, which are distinguishing marks of our country, and have world-wide fame, as amongst our most precious possessions, are passing away, little by little, and day by day, no serious effort having been made to preserve them."[26] By 1905 there were two national parks, five reserves, and three bird sanctuaries dedicated to the preservation of New Zealand's nature. Through the actions of local societies and private individuals, over 214,000 acres had been set aside in Scenic Reserves by 1914 — though such conservation measures focused largely on 'unproductive' Māori land.[27] Nostalgia was the main motive for early conservation, which was benevolent and backward looking. Clearly, while productive of an emerging eco-nationalist sentiment, such conservation measures descended from the same imperial processes that sought to locate, contain, and separate the *tangata whenua* (people of the land, all Māori) from their customary ties to land and the flows of Papatūānuku (Mother Earth).

CONSERVING RICCARTON BUSH

By the early twentieth century Pūtaringamotu was in trouble [Figure 3]. Not only was the forest now part of a growing 'Garden City' of broad avenues and parks lined with poplar, elm, and oak — Christchurch — but it bordered domestic gardens populated with Australian, Eurasian, and American plants. Now that the Deans family had fulfilled their evangelical mission to tame Pūtaringamotu, they could "look back in grateful pride on the fruits of the labour and capital spent in reclaiming the wilderness".[28] The Bush was no longer a resource to fuel the future but a yardstick by which to measure how far the settler family had come. To protect the Bush, Jane Deans planted hardy exotics — including poplar, elm, and oak — as nursery trees to protect native seedlings against strong winds. The unintended result, however, only confirmed Darwinist views of fragile native plants falling before a more vigorous,

Figure 3/ Aerial Oblique of Riccarton Bush, 1924. W. G. Wiegel, Department of Lands and Survey.

invasive European flora, as she recorded that, "The planted trees have done well, but the result has not been what was desired; for, instead of protecting the young native trees, they have smothered them out, in summer by their shade, and in winter with fallen leaves."[29] As well as planting fast-growing species that thrive on disturbance, like ash, Jane Deans also collected firewood, rather than let branches decay, and thus helped exotic grasses grow on the forest floor. These early conservation impulses showed just how little the settlers understood of the ecology on which they capitalized.

A more scientific plan for the Bush came from the English-born botanist, Leonard Cockayne. An expert in New Zealand's flora, he specialized in the plants that lived on New Zealand's wind-swept, sub-Antarctic, outlying islands. At his home on the coast to the east of Riccarton Bush, Cockayne obsessively tended his experimental garden, Tarata, where he tried to grow swamp, rock, river-bed, forest, scrub, lowland, and mountain plants in their own micro-climates. Cockayne advocated "eradicating foreign growths" from the Bush. He also wanted to deny access to the uneducated masses, arguing that "probably a good many people are not aware that the New Zealand native forest will not stand daylight, nor the footprint of man or beast. The moment either approaches it decays."[30] Botanists would re-seed the Bush with native plants according to "the best scientific evidence procurable" and finally "let the Bush severely alone" so that it became "for us and for our descendants a source of justifiable pride and highest pleasure".[31] Cockayne's vision for Pūtaringamotu left no doubt: there would be no harvesting kererū, no taking eels from the stream (they had in any case been replaced by trout), no chopping timber. In short, nature, in Riccarton Bush, could only be spoken for by the benevolent hand of Western botanists — its plants were too fragile, Māori too close to nature, and local people too uneducated [Figure 4].

Figure 4/ Riccarton Bush, 1934. W. A. Taylor Collection, Canterbury Museum, New Zealand.

Practicality and beauty trumped ecology in the early preservation of Pūtaringamotu, however. The forest was gifted to the city in 1914 when Jane Deans died (the city refused to pay the family for it), and the Riccarton Bush Trust (including representatives of the city authorities and the Deans family, though not Ngāi Tahu), established to ensure John Deans' dying wish that the forest be preserved, was upheld. In 1972 the government published an assessment of scenic reserves and concluded that Riccarton Bush "in a biological sense at best just escapes being poor, at worst bad".[32] The Bush had been managed in much the same way as the English-style parklands that comprised the city's other urban green spaces. Lawns had been seeded within the Bush to produce the effect of open English woodland. Mowing these lawns damaged kahikatea roots, prevented native species from establishing a scrub layer, and led to the extinction of several species of native shrub.[33] Open lawns also provided ample opportunity for invasive and fast-growing weeds like ivy, iris, and elderberry. Leaf litter and plant debris, which play important roles in seed regeneration and moisture levels, were collected and burnt. In addition, encroaching urbanization encouraged informal paths through the trees and dumping of household refuse, both vectors for exotic weeds. Finally, a lowered water table left the forest in a water deficit.[34] Overall then, by the 1970s the Bush was a "mess" of native trees and exotic weeds and in a "dreadful state".[35] Hope remained, however, in the form of a dense core of kahikatea in the centre.

ETERNALIZING ECOLOGY

Kahikatea trees, as the late ecologist and writer Geoff Park pointed out, "resonate with paradox".[36] They are an ancient species, evolutionary holdovers from the Jurassic when their seeds were spread not by kererū or blackbirds, but by pterodactyls. These tall, thin trees reach up to 200 feet and congregate in groves, where their buttress roots mingle and intertwine. They are long-lived, too. At the heart of Pūtaringamotu stands a group of kahikatea, the oldest of which is over 600 years old. Yet kahikatea inhabit ephemeral ground that is frequently flooded: river and land patch-working even as the trees grow old and die in their same spot.

Against a future of slow decline and the eventual death of Pūtaringamotu's kahikatea, some members of the Riccarton Bush Trust articulated a different vision. Enthused by the nascent science and craft of ecological restoration, ecologist Brian Molloy joined the Trust in 1974 and proposed a radical plan to save this "priceless remnant" and transform it into a "rally point around which the remaining crumbs of our natural history will be gathered up and protected".[37] Molloy's vision, in essence, was to take these kahikatea trees, an echo

Figure 5/ Growth in vegetation at the eastern edge of the Bush, 1978. Courtesy of Riccarton Bush Trust.

Figure 6/ Growth in vegetation at the eastern edge of the Bush, 1982. Courtesy of Riccarton Bush Trust.

of history, and to revitalize and eternalize their ecology. The plan combined restoration, reconciliation (a desire to re-connect Christchurch urbanites to their swampy past), and an appeal to local boosterism. Molloy recommended restricting public access, discontinuing mowing, leaving debris and leaf litter in situ, removing systematically invasive exotics, repressing weeds and pests, and hiring an experienced ranger. Molloy wished to ensure that the Bush could last forever, not stretching forward into the future, but rather being re-placed in the 'no-time' of an undisturbed ecosystem.

The oak trees planted by the Deans were by now extremely large and inhibiting native regeneration. Symbolically, the obvious presence of large, exotic trees bordering the Bush called into question its meaning as "the last surviving area of native white pine swamp". The slow growth of these oak trees, these "foreigners in the unique bush area" as Molloy put it, had blurred colonial (exotic) and indigenous (native) spaces for nature, creating an unsatisfactory hybrid landscape.[38] They were for the chop. Predictably, locals objected to their removal. For many, these most English of trees were symbols of "beauty, strength and permanence": oaks were the "agents through which modernity, progress, the erasure of the colonial past [were] articulated".[39] The Trust responded to critics by reiterating the uniqueness of the Bush, its remnant status and the need to preserve it for future generations: "I am absolutely certain this is going to benefit, not this generation, but generations in years to come." Molloy pointed out that the kahikatea in the Bush were older than the oaks by about 500 years, and with hundreds of years of life left, "in the long run they are more important than any exotic tree".[40] The kahikatea embodied an incontestable pre-colonial nature beyond politics or dissent.

Like any good gardener, Molloy and the other ecologists knew they couldn't do the work of restoration

Figure 7/ Bushranger in the plant nursery, date unknown. Courtesy of Riccarton Bush Trust.

themselves. Nor was mere protection sufficient. Their role, rather, was to create the right conditions to enable native flora to flourish. They felled oak trees, erected fences, closed paths, stopped mowing grass, left debris to rot in situ. From 1975 onwards, thousands of seedlings were raised in a nursery established on site. This plant nursery used seed only from within the Bush, or from the nearby Port Hills if none were available. Ribbonwood, kohuhu, lemonwood, cabbage tree, and karamu seedlings were cultivated intensively in raised beds and under cloches before being planted back into the Bush. At its peak the nursery had over 7,000 bagged trees of 29 different species on site in three growing stages. Controversy at the removal of oak trees faded as seedlings grew and the fast-growing edge-of-forest trees "stilled the voices of protest" [Figures 5, 6, 7].

Ironically, the restoration project was attempting to restore a swamp forest without any swamp. Pre-colony, the Waimakariri river created a braided, flood-plain mosaic, with rich alluvial soils supporting podocarp forest. But the urbanization of Christchurch lowered the water table within the city and left the damp-loving kahikatea and its wetland ecology vulnerable to drought. In 2000, the Trust deployed a $NZ 170,000 irrigation network to deliver water direct to the Bush. Molloy recalled that "on a hot summer day with huge drain on topsoil moisture I used to see ferns and mahoe gone limp. You don't see that any more.... You hit it with the irrigation pipes before a crisis." It remains, however, "hard to monitor the health of the place scientifically", according to bush ranger John Moore. Irrigation is more a question of instinct and feeling, of close observation of how plants behave. Through craft and embodied, embedded understanding of plants as much as through science, Molloy and the others involved in regenerating the Bush were drawn into a relationship of care with the trees of Pūtaringamotu.[41]

To protect this fragile plant community the Trust installed a two meter high predator-proof fence in 2004 [Figure 8]. The fence excludes pests like cats, possums, and rats. It is made of tight wire mesh with an underground skirt to prevent digging pests and a curved top to keep out superior climbers.[42] When the fence was installed, the ranger laid traps and poison to eliminate remaining rats, hedgehogs, and possums (cats were encouraged to climb out, but the fence's design prevented them climbing back in), creating a "mainland island".[43] The danger to the Bush now lies not with unruly naturalized pests, but with humans who fail to appreciate their indigenous nature: "the biggest threat now is likely to be a person; some joker with a bag of possums or something."[44] The fence seals the Bush from local, everyday life and serves as a "reminder that people of Christchurch should treat Riccarton

_ Figure 8/ Predator proof fence, 2005. Photograph by Franklin Ginn. _

Bush as a precious national, perhaps, international, treasure, rather than as a pretty pace for a picnic or a shortcut to the Riccarton shops".[45] In the past, the edge of the forest was a fertile hunting ground for bird, eel, and timber — both for Māori and for the Deans. By contrast, today the fence fixes the Bush in space: outside the fence is manicured lawn and suburban sprawl; inside is a caged, primaeval nature. The fence also embodies an enduring irony of colonialism: that a settler culture, born of movement and migration, should be so pathologically distrustful of movement that it expends such great energy seeking to order and enclose.[46]

Ecology in New Zealand has seemingly become a neutral terrain on which national identity can rest. As the national government have noted:

> New Zealand's biological world is the inspiration for our national icons — the kiwi, silver fern and koru. As New Zealanders, we are shaped by these symbols of our natural environment and our relationship to it — whether by cabbage trees or kahikatea forest, weta or whitebait. We would be impoverished kiwis indeed if our national icons went the way of the huia and the moa [two extinct birds].[47]

Such precious cargo, of course, needs protection: New Zealand is ring-fenced by biosecurity and quarantine controls at harbors and airports to the tune of around £36 million a year, while the Department of Conservation spends over £50 million managing New Zealand's natural heritage, including the suppression of invasive species such as opossums or Japanese knotweed.[48] On a smaller scale, the Riccarton Bush fence protects its fragile ecosystem. But as well as implying spatial division, such restoration efforts imply a temporal boundary, too.[49] For restoration is measured against a pre-colonial nature that has escaped contamination by Eurasian plants and animals: even as any return to that state is acknowledged to be impossible, it is still yearned after. Physically and symbolically, New Zealand eco-nationalist sentiment and its associated conservation practices articulate a desire to contain, atone for, and perhaps one day reverse the damage done by the colonial founders. Trust ecologist Brian Molloy captures popular sentiment when he describes the Bush as a local treasure "that has survived through two cultural periods ... the last in line of a series of temperate forests that periodically occupied the site of Christchurch over hundreds of thousands of years between successive ice ages. In this respect it stands as a constant reminder of the city's past."[50] Having survived two cultural periods — a long history of Māori (largely sustainable) use and British settler (largely unsustainable) exploitation — the Bush, Molloy implies, no longer exists in any cultural period. Rather, science has now secured it safely within the timeless and universal realm of 'Nature'. Furthermore, by standing as a "constant reminder of the city's past" that reaches back over "hundreds of thousands of years", the Bush projects this static nature back in time, extending the totalizing logic of ecology and conservation to encompass pre-human history, Māori settlement, and misguided imperial exploitation: these become "buried epistemologies" in the body of nature, such that "what counts as nature today is often constituted within, and informed by, the legacies of colonialism".[51] The fence, therefore, firmly fixes Pūtaringamotu out of time altogether in an attempt to erase the colonial and to fend off death and extinction indefinitely.

POST-COLONIAL FUTURES

When the Crown purchased the Canterbury Plains—including Pūtaringamotu—in 1848, they promised that Ngāi Tahu would retain customary access to their *mahinga kai* (food-gathering places), their *taonga* (treasure, valued object), and their sacred sites. This never happened. The first protest was made by a Ngāi Tahu elder in 1849, and the tribe continued campaigning for restitution for 140 years, consistently arguing that "water, fisheries and *mahinga kai* resources are Ngāi Tabu *taonga*, as are their cultural and spiritual values [and] they remain Tribal property".[52] After much struggle, the tribe signed one of the largest Indigenous settlements ever reached with the Crown in 1997.[53] The Waitanigi Tribunal, set up to consider land grievances for all Māori, concluded that the Crown had "acted unconscionably and in repeated breach of the principles of the Treaty of Waitangi in its dealings with Ngāi Tahu", and that it "failed to set aside adequate lands for Ngāi Tahu's use, and to provide adequate economic and social resources".[54] A wide-ranging settlement saw Ngāi Tahu reclaim their authority or ownership over many of their former lands, from government forests, to urban commercial properties, and airports, as well as a cash settlement to enable the tribe to re-establish its economic base. Although Pūtaringamotu was one of the 3,000 *mahinga kai* mentioned in Ngāi Tahu's submission to the Tribunal, in the end the tribe prioritized more important seasonal food-gathering places, and thus Pūtaringamotu was not included in the settlement process.

Alongside the Waitangi restitution process, mainstream conservation has increasingly incorporated or at least considered Māori knowledge of biodiversity.[55] Since 1987, state actors must consider Māori ancestral relations and cultural values in any resource management decision.[56] And increasingly strident Māori voices have regained customary rights such as mutton birding or harvesting kererū (native pigeon), while concepts like *tiakanga* (protocols), *tapu* (prohibitions, sacred), *rāhui* (temporary restrictions) and *kaitiakitanga* (guardianship) have entered mainstream conservation in New Zealand.[57]

The Riccarton Bush Trust has reintroduced several native animals, including tree weta (large insects), while the population of native birds such as fantails, robins, and pigeons has grown as predators have been eliminated. The Bush has also been used as a *crèche* to train young captive-bred kiwi (the iconic, flightless, and vulnerable birds) in foraging before release into the wild. This is part of a move to contribute to wider conservation goals, educate the public about their precious indigenous fauna, and 'complete' the restoration of the Bush. Since Ngāi Tahu has no place on the Riccarton Bush Trust board, the tribe has no formal management input, although legislation requires that they be consulted on native bird relocations and management. While the Riccarton Bush Trust may enjoy healthy informal relations with Ngāi Tahu, they believe that Western ecological knowledge is the best approach. According to Trust ecologist Brian Molloy, "It's part of the protocols to talk to Māori about relocating native birds, which we will do of course—we have a good relationship. But I'm not really sure of the point in this case—they'd probably only end up wanting to eat them."[58] This off-hand remark betrays unease at a Māori world-view of interrelationship with and sustainable exploitation of nature. Across a series of New Zealand sites, scholars have noted the tendency to circumscribe Māori practices within mainstream conservation practices so that Western science remains sovereign.[59] Much of the conservation movement remains opposed to the idea of Māori *kaitiakitanga* (guardianship) over conservation resources; for example, one leading conservation movement reacted with hostility to a limited move to give one local tribe harvesting rights over kiekie (*Freycinetia banksii*), a climbing plant used for many important cultural purposes, like weaving *tukutuku* (decorative latticework). They called the transfer of permits to Ngāti Rakaipaaka (the local tribe) "a dangerous and unfortunate precedent which will open the floodgates to unsustainable harvesting of threatened species".[60] Conservation, here, is treated as a technical matter of governing nature, not as a question of power over land. Moreover, mainstream conservation, even as it attends to Māori authority over resources or Indigenous management practices, circumscribes such practices with a dominant Western preservationist ethos.

Of course, regardless of human desires, or the historical unfolding of post-colonial politics, the trees and creatures that make their homes in Pūtaringamotu live on. The kahikatea of the Bush are reproductively isolated from their kin; they are living in what ecologists call extinction debt, or the inevitable, if delayed, death of the ecological community due to events in the past.[61] Since urbanization and agriculture have overwritten the shifting, forest swamp mosaic of pre-settlement times, this surviving remnant will eventually die without help or intervention: hence the irrigation and the fence. While the Trust has seeded kahikatea in the less dense parts of the Bush and around its perimeter, for its longer-term survival the forest needs to expand its population beyond the fenced-off enclosure.[62] This is a dream of renewal as much as it is practical ecology, for to replace the mature kahikatea that comprise the heart of the forest remnant will take hundreds of years.

At the same time, there is growing interest in recruiting domestic garden owners into conservation to increase biodiversity — in this case, the genetic diversity of Pūtaringamotu forest remnant — and to reconnect urban dwellers to the responsibilities and joys of environmental stewardship.[63] Kahikatea seeds are spread by birds around urban Christchurch — and exotic blackbirds are as happy to do so as native kererū. Where these seedlings land determines their chances of success: most garden owners cannot identify junior kahikatea (their form is quite different to the more familiar adult version), most people will dig out self-seeding species, and although half of local gardeners claim they would be prepared to plant Bush species, it is unclear what would change their behaviors.[64]

Nevertheless, the spread of kahikatea seed belies the notion of a native remnant isolated from all processes of renewal [Figure 9]. Rather, the seedlings' movement marks an adaptive and vital arboreal agency, and shows trees surpassing their construction as museum pieces or timeless remnants. This movement of life, this impulse of kahikatea to re-colonize suburban Christchurch, is one that can be suppressed or encouraged by gardeners, and suppressed or encouraged by the way the city council maintains its greenspace. Kahikatea are as capable of becoming weedy as they are of embodying pre-colonial purity. These trees must therefore be understood in terms of the intensity of the relations through which they grow into being, rather than simply their natural form. Within the Bush, the trees grow into and constitute a set of beings grasping towards a future, with ecologists, legislation, and mythology firmly allied to support that future. Outside the Bush, the trees face the harder challenge not simply of moving out across the urban landscape, but of weaving other people into their emerging lifeworld, of creating a new pattern of respect and intensity around their growing bark.[65] Thus the spread of kahikatea through urban space becomes less a question of containing life in its proper place, but rather one of differentiating "good circulations" of matter and life from bad [Figure 10].[66]

THE TEMPORALITIES OF A MULTI-SPECIES LANDSCAPE

Walking through Pūtaringamotu today you can see lichen, mosses, and liverworts clinging to rock and tree, you can smell a damp layer of leaf litter — all good indicators of healthy forest humidity. Kahikateas' moisture-loving buttress roots entwine into a mass of lower limbs: individual trees can be hard to distinguish. When you reach the forest's central grove, your eyes are drawn up through the canopy, skywards. To walk through Pūtaringamotu today is to do much more than experience a swamp forest, however. To walk through Pūtaringamotu is to walk through a landscape of multiple temporality.

For European settlers the Bush stood in a receding past. The creatures of the Bush were finite resources caught up in a forward rush of time: an improving impulse in which native biota receded as quickly as progress could sweep across plains and pull down trees. But turn-of-the-century settler guilt, nostalgia, and a desire for colonial distinction halted — in some places — the onward rush of progress. The Bush was preserved as a romantic gesture to a vanishing past. Such desire reached its scientific high point with attempts to eternalize bush ecology, to fix nature out of historical time, reaching unendingly into the future — though this vision is undercut

Figure 9/ Kahikatea on both sides of the predator proof fence, 2005. Photograph by Franklin Ginn.

—— **Figure 10/** Riccarton Bush from the air, 2011. Becker Fraser Photos. Photographs relating to the Canterbury earthquakes of 2010 and 2011. ——

by the continued need to protect the Bush and the constant warning of the Bush's vulnerability, which the fence embodies. These two temporalities — nostalgic longing for a decaying remnant of the past and the secular-scientific no-time of ecology — are paradigmatic of Western conservation. They blend together and take substance in sanctuaries, reserves, and wilderness parks, yet such spaces for nature merely end up confirming a will to enclose life and magnanimity in the face of destruction. This brew of science and reverence, once potent, no longer sustains a compelling narrative for the future, for it leaves us strolling through little patches of the earth that are "deteriorating, *tapu* [sacred], tiny, with no room for mistakes".[67]

Fortunately Pūtaringamotu still echoes with other histories. When governed by Ngāi Tahu, Riccarton Bush was made through intimate material and spiritual flows, and known through *whakapapa* (genealogy): from Papatūānuku

(Earth Mother), through Tāne, god of the standing forest, through its nonhuman inhabitants and visitors, and to humans, in a great, reversible chain of being animated by *mauri* (life force). Although in Māori cosmology such connections "between places, people, animals, plants, stars and gods [stretch] back to the beginning of creation", there is no promise of eternal nature, but rather an unfolding, reciprocal beat of time in which lives — of humans, nonhumans, and spirits — animate landscape.[68] But Indigenous voices should not be seen as echoes of past innocence lost.[69] Resurgent Indigenous voices can remind the visitor to Riccarton Bush that the *tangata whenua*, the people of the land, claim their rights over territory still and that they might have something to say about living with precious other species beyond parcelling pieces of land.[70] For Māori the relationship between human and nonhuman is reciprocal: "It is wrong to think that we humans act as 'kaitiaki' [a complex term inadequately

—— Figure 11/ *Kahikatea 1, Bones,* Karen Crisp. One of six images in her *Kahikatea Series,* 2007. Image reproduced by permission of Karen Crisp. ——

translated as 'guardian'] of nature — that is a Pākehā [Western] view. The earth kaitiaki's us; what we must do is respect and nurture the kaitiakitanga of Papatūānuku."[71] In other words, it is not that humans should simply garden well in the conventional sense of 'planting, tending plants, and harvesting or culling', but that humans should view 'gardening' as the guardianship of Papatūānuku (Earth Mother) and all those other nonhumans to which we are linked by genealogy and land. As the Māori biologist Mere Roberts points out, Māori understandings of land, life, and nature offer alternate ways to relate the ontological and the ethical. Might it be possible for a new environmental ethic to take shape not around 'our' own desires, but around kahikatea trees? This requires us to approach these trees as vital beings with a life force of their own. The multiple temporalities of Pūtaringamotu are written

into these trees' bark, their roots, their seeds, and their leaves: the decline of native birds and the arrival of exotic species that eat and spread their seed shape the trees' chances of reproduction; charcoal burns from underbrush fire linger for years after the event; roots delve deeper, seeking moisture as suburban sprawl lowers the water table. The big kahikatea trees have lived for hundreds of years, and seem to warp time around them, marking Pūtaringamotu through their temporal endurance. More than that, kahikatea have been formed through deep time by multiple interactions with multiple others — with reptiles and birds, with micro-organisms that return their biomass to earth: they are "embodied knots of multispecies time".[72] Some time ago, one of the large, old kahikatea became unstable and had to be felled. When the ranger dissected its body, no one could count the tree's annual growth rings: no accurate historical record could be discerned, for the archive of these trees' endurance is written in a language that is not like ours. Such trees warp time around them not only by channelling echoes of the past, but also by reverberating with echoes from the possible future. Elsewhere, long-standing groves of kahikatea — even those isolated by Eurasian grasses or farmland — might be the bones around which a future biogeography will form, where echoes from the future are not solely of extinction and loss to come, but of other, more hopeful ways to live together [Figure 11].

Environmentalists like to think that, whatever their particular allegiances, they share some appreciation of the vitality of ecological community. Sensing this vitality and the possibilities of its extinction, the environmentalist mantra goes, urges us to "reconnect": to find or re-find what it means to be fully embedded in more-than-human lifeworlds. If Riccarton Bush offers a mere simulacrum of such embeddedness (not walking through a swamp forest, but walking through a 'swamp forest'), then it is nonetheless valuable in firing our imaginations, enjoining us to ask what a settler ethic of reciprocity to the land might look like. But to what do we seek to reconnect? To what do we return? There is no pre-settled nature to return to, no transcendent nature to gaze upon, for nature must be made-up or constructed: Pūtaringamotu is an historical patchwork woven of multiple pasts, not an innocent lure. If co-flourishing is the name of the game, then the game doesn't benefit from a unitary temporality in which nature is a mere measure of humanity's sin and redemption.[73] Through which of the temporalities of Pūtaringamotu should we walk when we attempt to 'reconnect' with its nature, be it in person or through the narrative prosthetic I have offered here? All of them and others, too. In the end, to walk through Riccarton Bush is not to immerse yourself in a singular, powerfully affecting present, but to hear the echoes of your own desire, and the desires of all those others that echo through history. And if you put your ear close enough to the ground, you might hear echoes from the future, too.

NOTES

1/ This essay is composed from several sources: the extensive correspondence between John and William Deans and their family back in Scotland; Jane Deans' diaries and published memoirs; the Riccarton Bush Trust archive; coverage in the *Christchurch Press*; walking interviews in 2005 with staff, in particular ecologist Brian Molloy and ranger John Moore.

2/ Deans, John, "Letter, 8 December 1849", *Pioneers on Port Cooper Plains*, John Deans ed., Christchurch: Simpson and Williams, 1964, p. 56.

3/ More specifically the immediate area was under the guardianship of Ngāi Tuahuriri, a *hapu*, or sub-tribe of Ngāi Tahu; Evison, Harry, "Pūtaringamotu: The Land: Māori and European", *Riccarton Bush: Pūtaringamotu, Natural History and Management*, Brian Molloy ed., Christchurch: Riccarton Bush Trust, 1995, p. 12.

4/ Waitangi Tribunal, *Ngāi Tahu Land Report*, Wellington: Department of Justice, 1992; Young, David, *Our Islands, Our Selves: A History of Conservation in New Zealand*, Dunedin: University of Otago Press, 2004. Māori definitions from P. M. Ryan, *The Reed Dictionary of Modern Māori*, Wellington, New Zealand: Wright and Carman, 1997.

5/ Deans, John, ed., *Pioneers of Canterbury: Deans Letters 1840–1854*, Dunedin: Reed, 1937; Deans, Jane, "Canterbury Past and Present", *New Zealand Country Journal*, vol. 6, no. 6, 1882, pp. 381–392.

6/ Deans, William, "Letter, 6 October 1843", *Pioneers on Port Cooper Plains*, p. 24.

7/ Deans, Jane, "Letter, 16 December 1887", *Pioneers of Canterbury*, p. 37.

8/ Cited in Gordon Ogilvie, *Pioneers of the Plains: the Deans of Canterbury*, Christchurch: Shoal Bay Press, 1997, p. 245.

9/ New Zealand took measures earlier than most other colonies through the 1874 Forest Bill, which protected native forests thanks to a core of committed conservationists. See www.envirohistorynz.com/2009/12/10/were-the-scottish-greener, accessed October 2013; and Graeme Wynn, "Pioneers, Politicians and the Conservation of Forests in Early New Zealand", *Journal of Historical Geography*, vol. 5, no. 2, 1979, pp. 171–188.

10/ Salmond, Anne, *Between Worlds: Early Exchanges Between Māori and Europeans, 1773–1815*, Auckland: Penguin. The exact date of arrival is unclear, but is generally thought to be between 900 and 1200 CE.

11/ Wilson, Kerry-Jane, *Flight of the Huia: Ecology and Conservation of New Zealand's Frogs, Reptiles, Birds and Mammals*, Christchurch: Canterbury University Press, 1997.

12/ Wilson, *Flight of the Huia*.

13/ Belich, James, *Making Peoples: a History of the New Zealanders from Polynesian Settlement to the End of the Nineteenth Century*, Honolulu: University of Hawaii Press, 1996.

14/ Tau, Te Maire, "Ngāi Tahu and the Canterbury Landscape: A Broad Context", *Southern Capital: Christchurch, Towards a City Biography 1850-2000*, John Cookson and Graeme Dunstall eds., Christchurch: Canterbury University Press, 2000, pp. 41–59.

15/ O'Regan, Tipene, "The Ngāi Tahu Claim", *Waitangi: Māori and Pakeha Perspectives on the Treaty of Waitangi*, Ian Hugh Kawharu ed., Auckland: Oxford University Press, 1989, pp. 234–262.

16/ Hursthouse, Charles, *New Zealand, or Zealandia, the Britain of the South*, London: Edward Stanford), 1857, p. 69, cited in Geoff Park, *Theatre Country: Essays on Landscape and Whenua*, Wellington: Victoria University Press, 2006, p. 180.

17/ The Treaty of Waitangi was signed between the British Crown and various Māori chiefs in 1840. The Treaty recognized Māori *rangatiratanga* (full exercise or expression of chiefly power) over their land and gave them status as British subjects, as well as the Crown's right to govern and settle New Zealand. The Treaty had two translations, English and Māori, with unfortunate mistranslations (between governance and sovereignty, and between authority over land and ownership of property).

18/ King, Michael, *The Penguin History of New Zealand*, Auckland: Penguin, 2003.

19/ Park, Geoff, "'Swamps Which Might Doubtless Easily Be Drained': Swamp Drainage and its Impact on the Indigenous", *Environmental Histories of New Zealand*, Eric Pawson and Trevor Brooking eds., Auckland: Oxford University Press, 2002, pp. 151–165.

20/ Ginn, Franklin, "Extension, Subversion, Containment: Eco-nationalism and (post)Colonial Nature in Aotearoa New Zealand", *Transactions of the Institute of British Geographers*, vol. 33, no. 3, 2008, pp. 335–353; Clark, Nigel, "The Demon-seed: Bioinvasion as the Unsettling of Environmental Cosmopolitanism", *Theory, Culture & Society*, vol. 19, no. 1–2, 2002, pp. 101–125.

21/ Baillie, Jonathon, et al., *Global Species Assessment*, Gland: IUCN, 2004.

22/ Park, *Theatre Country*.

23/ Tau, Te Maire, Anake Goodall, David Palmer, and Raldihia Tau, *Te Whakatau Kaupapa: Ngāi Tahu Resource Management Strategy for the Canterbury Region*, Wellington: Aoraki Press, 1990, pp. 4–22.

24/ Best, Elsdon, "Māori Forest Lore: Being Some Account of Native Forest Lore and Woodcraft, as also of many Myths, Rites, Customs and Superstitions Connected with the Flora and Fauna of the Tuhore or Urewera District — Part One", *Transactions and Proceedings of the New Zealand Institute*, vol. 41, 1907, pp. 185–256, cited in Park, *Theatre Country*, p. 90.

25/ McCarthy, Conal, *Exhibiting Māori: A History of Colonial Cultures of Display*, Oxford and New York: Berg, 2007.

26/ Cockayne, Leonard, "Riccarton Bush: Its History and Its Future", *Christchurch Press*, 15 May 1905, pp. 14–15.

27/ The 1903 Scenery Preservation Act was drafted to secure picturesque exemplars of indigenous landscape, Young, *Our Islands*.

28/ Deans, Jane, "Letter, 16 December 1887", *Letters to my Grandchildren*, Christchurch: Wyatt and Wilson, p. 36.

29/ Deans, Jane, *Letters to my Grandchildren*, p. 392.

30/ Cockayne, "Riccarton Bush: Its History and its Future", p. 8.

31/ Cockayne, "Riccarton Bush: Its History and its Future", p. 8.

32/ Kelly, G. C., *Scenic Reserves of Canterbury: A Provisional Account of Scenic and Allied Reserves and Selected Similar Places of the Canterbury Land District, Biological Survey of Reserves, Report Two*, Wellington: Department of Lands and Survey, p. 247.

33/ Molloy, *Riccarton Bush: Pūtaringamotu*.

34/ Molloy, Brian, "The History and Management of Riccarton Bush", *Journal of the Royal New Zealand Institute of Horticulture*, vol. 3, no. 1, 2000, pp. 13–18.

35/ Molloy, interview, January 2005.

36/ Park, Geoff, *Ngā Uruora: Ecology and History in a New Zealand Landscape*, Wellington: Victoria University Press, 1995, p. 38.

37/ Molloy, Brian, and Les Brown, "Vegetation History", *Riccarton Bush: Putaringamotu*, pp. 85–115.

38/ Molloy, Brian, *Christchurch Press*, 6 June 1974.

39/ Rival, Laura, ed., *The Social Life of Trees: Anthropological Perspectives on Tree Symbolism*, Oxford and New York: Berg, 1998, p 13; Cloke, Paul, and Eric Pawson, "Memorial trees and treescape memories", *Environment and Planning D: Society and Space*, vol. 26, no. 1, 2008, pp. 107–122.

40/ Molloy, Brian, *Christchurch Press*, 3 July 1979.

41/ Atchison, Jennifer, and Lesley Head, "Eradicating bodies in invasive plant management", *Environment and Planning D: Society and Space*, vol. 31, no. 6, 2013, pp. 951–968; Jones, Owain, and Paul Cloke, *Tree Cultures: The Place of Trees and Trees in Their Place*, Oxford and New York: Berg, 2002, p. 8.

42/ Fuller, Michael, *Some Thoughts on Predator Exclusion Fences*, Wellington: Karori Wildlife Sanctuary, 2003.

43/ There remains some debate about the efficiency of such predator proofed mainland islands, but they are effective on small scales; Alan Saunders and David Norton, "Ecological restoration at Mainland Islands in New Zealand", *Biological Conservation* vol. 99, 2001, pp. 109–119.

44/ Molloy, interview.

45/ Rooney, Derrick, "Riccarton Bush", *Christchurch Press*, 5 December 2002, p. 14.

46/ Carter, Paul, *The Road to Botany Bay: An Exploration of Landscape and History*, Chicago: University of Chicago Press, 1997.

47/ Department of Conservation, Ministry for the Environment, and Ministry of Agriculture and Fisheries, *The New Zealand Biodiversity Strategy*, Wellington: New Zealand, 2000, p. 3.

48/ Barker, Kezia, "Biosecure Citizenship: Politicising Symbiotic Associations and the Construction of Biological Threat", *Transactions of the Institute of British Geographers*, vol. 35, no. 3, 2010, pp. 350–363.

49/ Head, Lesley, "Decentring 1788: Beyond Biotic Nativeness", *Geographical Research*, vol. 50, no. 2, 2012, pp. 166–178.

50/ Molloy and Brown, "Vegetation History", pp. 85–115, p. 114.

51/ Braun, Bruce, "Buried Epistemologies: The Politics of Nature in (post)Colonial British Columbia", *Annals of the Associated American Geographers*, vol. 87, no.1, 1997, pp. 3–31, p. 5.

52/ Tau, et al., *Te Whakatau Kaupapa: Ngāi Tahu Resource Management Strategy for the Canterbury Region*, part 2. 5.

53/ Since 1975 the Waitangi Tribunal has arbitrated disputes between Māori and the Crown. The Tribunal from 1985 was empowered to investigate historic breaches by the Crown of the Treaty of Waitangi, signed by Māori chiefs and the British Crown in 1840. The Ngāi Tahu claim discussed in this essay was one of the largest cases considered by the Tribunal.

54/ *The Ngāi Tahu Claims Settlement Act 1998*, http://www.legislation. govt.nz/act/public/1998/0097/latest/whole.html, last accessed October 2013, part 6. 2.

55/ Jull, Peter, "The Politics of Sustainable Development: Reconciliation in Indigenous Hinterlands", *Indigenous People: Resource Management and Global Rights*, Svein Jentoft, Hilary Minde, and Ragnar Nilsen eds., Delft: Eburon, 2003, pp. 21–44.

56/ Wheen, Nicola, "A History of New Zealand Environmental Law", *Environmental Histories of New Zealand*, Eric Pawson and Tom Brooking eds., Auckland: Oxford University Press, 2002, pp. 261–274.

57/ Kawharu, Merata, ed., *Whenua: Managing Our Resources*, Auckland: Reed, 2002.

58/ Molloy, interview.

59/ Roberts, Mere, Waerete Norman, et al., "Kaitiaitanga: Māori Perspectives on Conservation", *Pacific Conservation Biology*, vol. 2, no. 1, 1995, pp. 7–20; Coombes, Brad, Jay Johnson, and Richard

Howitt, "Indigenous Geographies I: Mere Resource Conflicts? The Complexities in Indigenous Land and Environmental Claims", *Progress in Human Geography*, vol. 36, no. 6, 2012, pp. 810–821.

60/ Cited in Brad Coombes, "Postcolonial Conservation and Kiekie Harvests at Morere New Zealand: Abstracting Indigenous Knowledge from Indigenous Polities", *Geographical Research*, vol. 45, no. 2, 2007, p. 191. Similar sentiments are expressed in joint river management too: See Amanda Thomas, "Indigenous More-Than-Humanisms: Relational Ethics for Rivers in Aotearoa New Zealand", *Environmental Humanities*, forthcoming.

61/ For another island story see Genese Marie Sodikoff, "The Time of Living Dead Species: Extinction Debt and Futurity in Madagascar", *Debt: Ethics, the Environment, and the Economy*, Merry Wiesner-Hanks and Peter Paik eds., Bloomington: Indiana University Press, 2013, pp. 140–226.

62/ Doody, Brendan, Jon Sullivan, Colin Meurk, Glenn Stewart, and Harvey Perkins, "Urban Realities: The Contribution of Residential Gardens to the Conservation of Urban Forest Remnants", *Biodiversity and Conservation*, vol. 19, no. 5, 2010, pp. 1385–1400.

63/ Cook, Elizabeth, Sharon Hall, and Larson Kell, "Residential Landscapes as Socio-ecological Systems: A Synthesis of Multi-scalar Interactions Between People and their Home Environment", *Urban Ecosystems*, vol. 15, no. 1, 2012, pp. 19–52; Ginn, Franklin, and Rob Francis, "Urban Greening and Sustaining Urban Natures in London", *Sustainable London? The Future of a Global City*, Rob Imrie and Loretta Lees eds., Bristol: Policy Press, 2014.

64/ Doody, et al., *Urban Realities*.

65/ Ginn, Franklin, "Jakob von Uexküll Beyond Bubbles: On Umwelt and Biophilosophy", *Science as Culture*, vol. 23, no. 1, 2014, pp. 129–134.

66/ Hinchliffe, Steve, John Allen, Stephanie Lavau, Nick Bingham, and Simon Carter, "Biosecurity and the topologies of infected life: From borderlines to borderlands", *Transactions of the Institute of British Geographers*, vol. 38, no. 4, 2013, pp. 531–543.

67/ Park, *Ngā Uruora*, p. 222; Marris, Emma, *Rambunctious Garden: Saving Nature in a Post-Wild World*, New York: Bloomsbury, 2011.

68/ Waitangi Tribunal, *Report on the Crown's Foreshore and Seabed Policy*, Wellington: Legislation Direct, p. 2.

69/ Johnson, Jay T., and Brian Murton, "Re/Placing Native Science: Indigenous Voices in Contemporary Constructions of Nature", *Geographical Research*, vol. 45, no. 2, 2007, pp. 121–129.

70/ Panelli, Ruth, "Social Geographies: Encounters with Indigenous and More-Than-White/Anglo Geographies", *Progress in Human Geography*, vol. 32, no. 6, 2008, pp. 801–811; Coombes, Johnson, and Howitt, "Indigenous Geographies I: Mere Resource Conflicts?".

71/ Roberts, Mere, Waerete Norman, et al., "Kaitiaitanga: Māori Perspectives on Conservation", *Pacific Conservation Biology*, vol. 2, no. 1, 1995, pp. 7–20, p. 14.

72/ Rose, Deborah Bird, "Multispecies Knots of Ethical Time", *Environmental Philosophy*, vol. 9, no. 1, 2012, 127–140, p. 136, after Donna Haraway, *When Species Meet*, Minneapolis, MN: University of Minnesota Press, 2008.

73/ Haraway, *When Species Meet*.

64 /SUSAN WILLIS

JOHN MUIR'S SOJOURN IN BONAVENTURE CEMETERY

On September 1, 1867, just two years after the Civil War, John Muir set out on a remarkable cross-country trek that would take him from Louisville, Kentucky, through Tennessee and Georgia, across Florida and on to Cuba. He carried few belongings — a map, a flower press, the Bible, Milton's *Paradise Lost*, a collection of Robert Burns' poetry, his journal, and possibly some spare socks, although clothing is never mentioned [Figures 1, 2]. He relied on the hospitality of strangers, but often slept in nature, and seems to have subsisted on bread. He was 29 years old and the journey would be his life's turning point — marked at its commencement as a dramatic break from all he had done before, and defined at its conclusion as the moment when he would fully commit himself to the life of a naturalist.

To read the now published journal of *A Thousand Mile Walk to the Gulf* is to encounter an experience of nature that cannot be ours.[1] For Muir, nature is not defined first and foremost as an image and then secondarily discovered as a reality. This is not to say that Muir was not familiar with images. Indeed, he was an accomplished illustrator. But to trace a tree or plant with eye and pencil is very different from the act of photographing it and requires an intimate, almost tactile connection with nature's living forms. By contrast, the image has become our primary access to nature, certainly ever since Ansel Adams made his starkly pristine photographs of natural landscapes. Nevertheless, just ten years after his trek to the Gulf, Muir would find himself guiding artists into the Sierra Nevada. Their landscape paintings defined the incipient stage of a process aimed at translating California's wilderness into consumable images. It's a democratizing process, as critic and philosopher Walter Benjamin argued, with respect to the way film and photography brought art to the masses.[2] But the outcome — one that Benjamin did not foresee — is a society's wholesale development of the faculties for appreciating and reading *images* at the expense of foreclosing the mental, sensory, and physical capacities necessary for engaging *nature*.

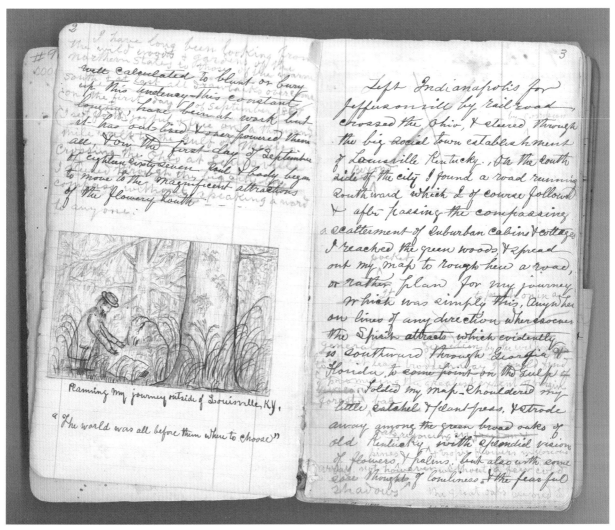

───── **Figure 2/** Planning my journey. John Muir, journal illustration, July 1867–February 1868, "The Thousand Mile Walk from Kentucky to Florida ─────
and Cuba". John Muir Papers, Holt-Atherton Special Collections, University of the Pacific Library. © 1984 Muir-Hanna Trust.

Simply put, once we've come to accept the BBC documentary *The Living Planet*'s 'high def' rendition of nature, can we see the world as anything but a less successful image?

Muir apprehended the actual journey in terms very different from the way such an undertaking would be characterized today. He did not set out to purposefully test his endurance as many of today's elite athletes might choose a comparable distance. One such athlete, Dianne Van Deren, recently ran the thousand mile Mountain-to-Sea Trail from Clingman's Dome in Tennessee to Jockey's Ridge on North Carolina's Outer Banks — her time: 22 days, five hours, and three minutes. She slept a mere three hours per night, wore most of the skin off her feet, and was probably more aware of her calorie-starved body than of the surrounding

countryside. Nor was Muir's hike a politically motivated one such as Granny D's cross-country pilgrimage, a walk in excess of 3,200 miles across the continental United States that she undertook at age 88 to campaign against 'soft' money in politics. Although Muir would later champion conservation and spearhead the creation of America's first National Parks, his walk to the Gulf was in no way comparable to all the walk, bike, and run-a-thons currently deployed to raise awareness and money to combat health and social ills. Additionally, Muir's undertaking was never conceived to garner fame or following. Such is the difference between his personal journal, which wasn't even published until after his death, and our propensity today to live and conceptualize every activity as the raw material for our social media. To understand Muir's

Figure 3/ Bonaventure Cemetery, Savannah, Georgia. Photograph by Mat Marrash.

journey is to ask how we can go into nature without tweeting, blogging, or 'YouTubing' ourselves in it.

BOTANIZING

If Muir were asked to define his journey, he would simply say he was "botanizing".[3] What botanizing meant for Muir includes, but is not restricted to, collecting, studying, and cataloguing plant taxonomies. Indeed, botanizing offers a way to think outside of our impoverished, consumer-driven sense of nature. On the grandest scale, botanizing means witnessing first hand the transitions in landscape and ecologies that the act of trekking overland articulates. Our own experience of topographic change is usually from inside a car hurtling at 70 mph on a mind-numbing Interstate. Botanizing may have been ploddingly slow, but unlike the tunnel vision framed by a car's windshield, it was punctuated by eye-opening sights of wonder. Muir's every step might reveal a "splendid palmetto", a "gorgeous sunset", or a "magnificent grass".[4]

Additionally, botanizing meant stepping out of the world defined by labor. As a farm boy, Muir certainly knew the rigors of work — the dawn to dusk toil of clearing virgin forest, digging a 90-foot well by hand, plowing the stiff soil with yokes of oxen, planting wheat, corn, and potatoes by the acres, and then harvesting, "cradling (the wheat) in the long sweaty dog-days, raking and binding, stacking, thrashing".[5] What's most remarkable is that Muir also knew carpentry, mechanics, and physics. Stealing time from sleep, he awoke in the pre-dawn hours to invent and construct clocks, barometers, thermometers, a mechanical reading desk, and a machine for getting a person out of bed. He exhibited some of these at the Wisconsin State Fair, where acclaim led to various industrial jobs and, eventually, admission to the state university. It's possible that Muir might have continued to develop as a machinist and inventor had not an industrial accident almost blinded him. What is certain is that weeks after recovering his sight and strength, Muir set out on his thousand-mile journey.

By comparison to the work of farm or industry, botanizing is effort wholly disconnected from labor. And it conforms with its own temporality, dictated neither by the clock time of industrial labor nor the exigencies of sustenance on the farm. If botanizing and farm labor have anything in common it is a regard for the nocturnal and diurnal divisions of the day; but they do so for very different purposes. Where the farm regulates the lives of plants and animals according to the farmer's needs, botanizing allows the observer to approximate the ways that plants and animals live the alternation between light and dark.

Muir's freedom from the dictates of 'clock time' shaped his subsequent rambles in the Sierra Nevada. Recounting one such journey in the late fall, he describes his return to Yosemite Valley, where he would spend the winter, from the high country

where he had been surveying glaciers. The descent took him from alpine meadows, over mountain passes, down through autumnal forests, and finally into the valley, where he quipped that he had arrived "in due time — which, with me, is any time".[6] The remark dramatically juxtaposes Muir as a man who lives in sync with the temporality of walking, the freezing and thawing of water, the changes in terrain, and with the group of artists who await his return. Unlike the naturalist, the artists have a schedule, and they desperately want to fit Muir into it as their guide into the high country. Winter is closing in and the artists want to procure picturesque examples of mountain scenery before the deep snow falls. Thus, even the time of art is associated with quantifiable production.

Finally, and most interesting, botanizing means blurring the boundary between the human and non-human denizens of the natural world — both plant and animal. With infrequent human contact, Muir was wholly embraced by nature. Is it any wonder, then, that he felt himself "greeted" at every turn by a tree, insect, or animal? Is it out of the ordinary that birds are characterized as "scolding or asking angry questions", or that plants described as strangers to Muir might be caught "looking him full in the face"?[7] Indeed, the journey is a trek through anthropomorphism. The banks of a river are "luxuriantly peopled with rare and lovely flowers", while flocks of pelicans and herons conjure an "assembling of feathered people".[8] If we read Muir's propensity to personify nature's species as either quaint or childish, we miss the profound connection Muir felt with nature. Botanizing his way through Appalachia, the Piedmont, and into the swamps of Florida, Muir uses anthropomorphism to express commonality with plants and animals. They are approachable, knowable. They may be new — even strange — but they are never 'other'.

BONAVENTURE

Many who read *A Thousand Mile Walk to the Gulf* agree that there is one singularly meaningful place in the journey where all that came before and all that will follow pivot upon a set of significant observations and meditations. This is the week that Muir spent in Bonaventure Cemetery just outside Savannah, Georgia [Figure 3]. The circumstance of his sojourn in the cemetery is meaningful in itself. Having depleted his habitually meager funds, Muir was awaiting the arrival of a money package that his brother was to have sent. With no money left, Muir slept in the cemetery, subsisted on crackers, and each day journeyed back to the city only to discover that his funds had not yet arrived.

At the time of Muir's visit, Bonaventure was separated from Savannah by some four miles and was situated on a bluff overlooking the Wilmington River. Unlike the city's older Colonial Park Cemetery, nestled in the city's midst, Bonaventure occupied a place of remove, not only beyond the city, but also beyond its adjacent cultivated fields. And unlike Colonial Park Cemetery, which at the time of Muir's visit was already home to 700 victims of the yellow fever outbreak of 1820, Bonaventure was thinly populated. Thus, both spatially and demographically, the city and the cemetery were polar opposites—set at opposite ends of a continuum that defined the trajectory of Muir's day. Waking each morning in the cemetery to birdsong and the happy anticipation of his money package, Muir traveled to the city only to have his hopeful expectations crushed. Thus, cemetery and city designate opposite points in a landscape that is both physical and emotional—their only seeming connection, the road between them upon which Muir undertook his daily transit.

That said, the difference between city and cemetery is not absolute. Indeed, the two sites that we perceive as polar opposites tend, on closer inspection, to collapse into each other. Significantly, this dynamic of identifying categories in opposition so as to undo their polarization will define Muir's narrative as a whole and come to be identified with his conceptualization of nature—most specifically, the place of humans with respect to plants and animals. Thus, Muir's description of his sojourn in Bonaventure Cemetery is key to deciphering the narrative as the discursive form of botanizing.

Bonaventure is where Muir's forward trajectory of 25 miles a day falls into limbo. By comparison to the days spent trekking, Bonaventure anchors the trekker in stasis. But Bonaventure is not a fallow island in time. Instead, it's the privileged place where everything that Muir would have previously remarked sequentially as an aspect of his journey, comes together as a concentration of apparent opposites whose polarization will prove to be false. The name of the cemetery offers a case in point. Said in Italian, *B(u)ona-ventura* (from the Latin *bona ventura*, 'good fortune, good things to come') voices the wish for a pleasant journey. Is it ironic, then, that Bonaventure designates the last resting place for those who will no longer travel? Journey or stasis? Adventure or climax? Muir's sojourn in Bonaventure unites resting place with journey. Neither fallow nor static, the cemetery offers a landscape for exploration. Neither grim nor ghostly, the cemetery is *bon(us)*—a good and fortuitous place.

History is one of the forces that works to erode the polarization between the city as a community of the living and Bonaventure, the community of the dead. Even though Muir undertakes his trek just two years after the end of the Civil War, his narrative avoids direct reference to history and the scars of the recent past that would have been evident in some of the southern portions of his journey. Rather, history seeps in as an unrecognized feature of Muir's observations. Such is the case soon after he arrived in Savannah and realized that he would have to stay until his funds arrived. Unable to pay for lodging, Muir set out in search of a place

to pass the night. Wandering beyond the city's limits, he came to a terrain of dunes and tall grasses. The air was dank. Muir began to be aware that this abandoned landscape was frequented by numbers of "idle negroes".[9] Fearing misadventure, Muir recalled that earlier in the day he had chanced upon the cemetery whose avenue of welcoming oaks now seemed a propitious omen. Thus, Muir decided to return to Bonaventure: "There, thought I, is an ideal place for a penniless wanderer."[10]

Though Muir's thoughts don't return to the "idle negroes", his subsequent account of Bonaventure suggests his implied understanding of why they might be casting about in an apparent wasteland on the outside of the city. According to Muir, Bonaventure had a previous incarnation as a plantation whose grounds could well have been worked by the now "idle negroes". Its great house in ruins, the fields no longer productive, Bonaventure fell to the city, which, itself, had only just been spared General Sherman's scorched earth campaign that cut a swath of destruction from Atlanta to the city's gates. The "idle negroes", the ruined manor house—these gave scant physical evidence of all that the war had obliterated—fields burned, livestock appropriated and carried off.

That Muir was attuned to history becomes clear when his money package finally arrived, some seven days after his arrival in Savannah. Famished, he stumbled out of the post office, money in hand, and happened upon a black woman selling gingerbread. This he eagerly purchased, and "walked rejoicing and munching along the street".[11] Elated over his liberation from the ordeal of hunger, Muir exclaimed, "Thus my 'marching through Georgia' terminated handsomely in a jubilee of bread."[12] Here, Muir borrows the word 'jubilee' from the black woman's historical vocabulary, to capture the joy of his freedom from hunger with a word that she would use to celebrate her emancipation from slavery. And, in the same sentence, he ironically summons Sherman's march of destruction to antithetically characterize his own light-footed transit as a botanist.

Besides history, nature is the most significant force that collapses all that we perceive as opposites into communalities. Muir's first lesson in botany offers a case in point. During a stint at the State University in Wisconsin, Muir obliged a fellow student bent on demonstrating his skills as a teacher. The student picked a flower from a locust tree and asked Muir to tell what family the tree belonged to. At that time Muir knew nothing about botany, but he ventured that the flower resembled a pea flower. The student seized upon Muir's answer and proceeded to show him how all the particulars of the flower—its stamens and pistils, its petals and seeds—were exactly like those of the pea flower. The one might be a "big thorny hardwood tree" and the other "a weak, clinging, struggling herb", but together they bespeak a "unity with boundless variety".[13]

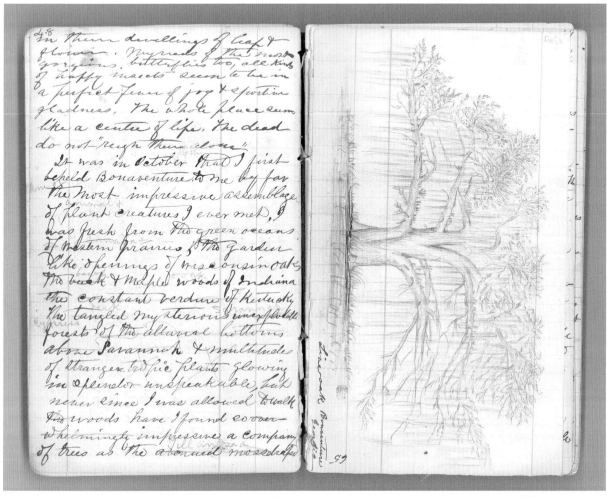

—— **Figure 4/** Live oak, Bonaventure, Georgia. John Muir, journal illustration, July 1867–February 1868, "The Thousand Mile Walk from Kentucky ——
to Florida and Cuba". John Muir Papers, Holt-Atherton Special Collections, University of the Pacific Library. © 1984 Muir-Hanna Trust.

It is, thus, not gratuitous that Muir commenced his sojourn in Bonaventure in the "gloaming", that brief, but special period when daylight seeps into the gathering darkness and the night absorbs the day.[14] The gloaming, like the locust flower, underscores unity where we are wont to see distinction. For what is the antithesis between night and day when both are plotted as durational periods in the earth's rotation that also includes their waning, the one into the other, the gloaming?

In the spirit of the gloaming and preparing to spend his first night in the cemetery, Muir turned his thoughts to life and death. As he would have seen it, history provided the stroke that felled the manor house, but it's nature that pulled it down with the force of gravity, and it's nature's process of decay that reduced the manor to the base materials of earth. Speaking from the perspective of nature, Muir chastised those who might fear the cemetery and admonished, "The dead do not reign there."[15] Instead, "The rippling of living waters, the song of birds, the joyous confidence of flowers, the calm un-disturbable grandeur of the oaks, mark this place of graves as one of the Lord's most favored abodes of life and light."[16] Buoyed by the "beautiful blendings and communions of death and life" that have been his experience throughout nature, Muir looked forward to a night of "rest and peace" in the cemetery [Figure 4].[17]

In later years, Muir's explorations of the mountains of California and Alaska often brought him face-to-face with death — and in a more abrupt manner than he had encountered it in the cemetery. In these instances, he was not unsusceptible to fear. Indeed, his ascent of Mt Ritter offers a memorable example. It was late in the season, the mountain had never been climbed, and ice slickened the foreboding

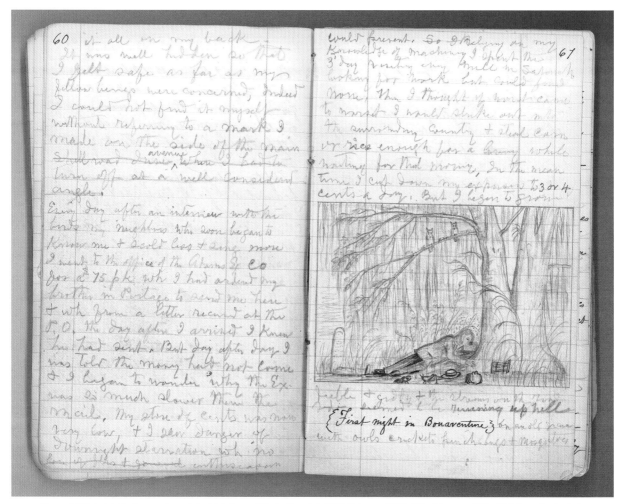

Figure 5/ First night in Bonaventure. John Muir, journal illustration, July 1867–February 1868, "The Thousand Mile Walk from Kentucky to Florida and Cuba". John Muir Papers, Holt-Atherton Special Collections, University of the Pacific Library. © 1984 Muir-Hanna Trust.

and sheer rock-face of Ritter's peak. Struggling to find foot and hand-holds, and knowing that he had climbed to a point where it would be harder to go back than to continue, Muir was brought to a "dead stop" with arms outspread, clinging close to the face of the rock, unable to move hand or foot either up or down.[18] In his own words, "My doom appeared fixed. I must fall. There would be a moment of bewilderment, and then a lifeless rumble down the one general precipice to the glacier below."[19] Death would come with the finality of an inert stone dropped off the side of the mountain.

A breathtakingly similar fate seemed to await Muir during a trek across glaciers in Alaska. Again, the conditions were inauspicious — night coming on, a storm gathering, and Muir, alone but for a small dog, was stranded on a glacier island that was severed from the larger mass of ice by formidable crevasses. His only hope was a knife-thin bridge of ice that

spanned a 50-foot wide crevasse. But to attain the bridge, Muir would have to chip footholds down the side of the glacier to the point of the bridge's attachment. On the brink of attempting the descent to the bridge, Muir spoke words of encouragement to the little dog, who would have to accomplish the same feat:

> 'Hush your fears, my boy,' I said, 'we will get across safe, though it is not going to be easy. No right way is easy in this rough world. We must risk our lives to save them. At the worst we can only slip, and then how grand a grave we will have, and by and by our nice bones will do good in the terminal moraine.'[20]

In both instances, Muir reckons his death with a detachment that puts aside emotion and the anticipation of the physical pain that one would most certainly feel when falling off a mountain or into a crevasse. These he overleaps to instead imagine his body having already become one with the rocks of the earth. What's striking is that Muir's absolute detachment is what enables him to rally his concentration and resolve. With renewed vigor and almost machine-like precision he accomplished the ascent of Ritter and the ice bridge crossing — and he managed to coax the little dog across as well.

A good many of Muir's accounts are apt to be read as adventure yarns. After all, on another occasion he decided that the best place to experience a gale force wind was at the top of a 100-foot wind whipped pine. But to read for adventure risks overlooking the philosophical meditation at the heart of Muir's narrations. The elation Muir felt at the top of Ritter was not simply the thrill of a man who beat death, as it would be in a story of adventure. Rather, for Muir elation represents the summation of knowing that the body always connects life to death — the living bone to the glacial moraine. And in nature, neither bone nor stone is truly dead because both will mill and churn in the earth's relentless process of wearing and building.

Process is also evident in Bonaventure Cemetery where it drives nature to fuse with its opposite: art. For what is a cemetery but a work of art — a garden whose design and execution, albeit performed in living species, nevertheless embodies art rather than nature. But unlike the well-tended gardens in Savannah that Muir perused during his daily trips to the post office, Bonaventure is a garden actively being reshaped by nature. The process is ongoing and the indices of art and nature often fuse. Thus, the avenue of oaks, the garden's most obvious design feature, have long been host to streaming tendrils of moss, whose symbiotic relationship with the oaks reworks the trees' structure and sturdiness with a mantle of billowing softness [Figure 5]. What's more, the main branches of the oaks reach out across the driveway, "embowering" it in such a way as to make the spheres of art and nature indistinguishable.[21] Indeed, the very branches have become gardens, adorned with "ferns, grasses, and flowers", whose roots have found purchase in the trees' bark and canopy.[22] Thus, nature and art produce symbiotic symmetries: nature sprouts from the cultivated tree, and the trees grow beyond the limits of their design to envelop the cemetery's driveway in nature's embrace.

The graves, too, have been contrived as works of art. Treated like flower beds, each is planted with the same unerring precision. According to Muir, "There is generally a magnolia at the head near the strictly erect marble, a rose bush or two at the foot, and some violets and showy exotics along the sides or on the top."[23] But, here too, nature's host of airborne seeds have intervened to sow configurations of grasses that trace the patterns of natural forces and disrupt the intentional design. Finally, and with the same measure of glee that he felt for the weeds amongst the exotics, Muir details the patient corruption

of rust on the neatly wrought metalwork that fences many of the gravesites.

Some hundred years later, conservationist and writer Rachel Carson similarly sought to demonstrate the collapsing of boundaries, although in a very different environment. Carson explored the shore with an eye to understanding whether land and sea actually comprise distinct and mutually exclusive worlds. Where Muir considered the opposition between night and day, death and life, art and nature, Carson saw the shore as a vital laboratory where land and sea fuse in accordance with the ebb and flow of the tides. Her essay, "The Marginal World", describes the edges of the sea as "an elusive and indefinable boundary", whose life forms have evolved to inhabit a changeful and dual environment.[24] To the casual eye, the shore may seem a barren, tide-washed beach. To Carson, who poked into its crannies, fissures, and grains of sand, the shore teemed with life.

In her explorations, one place stood out for its magical erasure of boundaries: a cave, which only "the lowest of the year's low tides" would reveal to a terrestrial visitor.[25] This cave was particularly fascinating because it contained a tidal pool. Crouching and gazing into the cave, Carson remarked that all the animals and plants that clung to the roof of the cave were reflected on the surface of the pool, where they appeared to mingle with the creatures that carpeted the bottom of the pool. Thus were land and sea fused and held together by the surface tension of the water. The optical illusion gives figural expression to Carson's broader understanding of a 'marginal world' as a place that resists the imposition of boundaries and distinctions. Similarly, when Muir 'delves' the rust and considers the symbiosis of art and nature, he 'plumbs' the same marginal world to discover life's processes of change and adaptation.

An important consideration is where Muir positions himself as a man passing through, observing, and engaging with nature. Waking on his first morning in the cemetery, he is surprised to discover that while sleeping he had pillowed his head on a grave mound. His reference to a pillow is key to understanding the cultural and specifically domestic filter that inflects much of Muir's thinking about nature. He is no Bear Grills of the TV program "Man vs. Wild", who parachutes into remote wilderness settings and survives by eating grubs, cactus pulp, or turtle eggs. Indeed, Muir never conceived of himself as being in a wilderness, even though a considerable portion of his trek was through uninhabited terrain. Nor did he consider his journey as a test of survival, even though his food supply was never plentiful. This is because the construction of nature is very different from wilderness. And for Muir, nature is home.

Indeed, after spending his first night in the rough, Muir decided to fashion himself a "nest" in a sparkleberry thicket. In so doing, he put himself on a par with the birds, his "neighbors", who also inhabited the thicket and sang him awake each morning.[26] Actually, Muir's nest was more of a hut. Selecting a spot where four bushes would conveniently provide the four corners of his abode, he bent their tops together, then overlaid them with rushes to produce a sheltering roof. Then, to cushion his sleep, he spread a deep blanket of moss on the ground. In the end, his hut "was about four or five feet long by about three or four in width".[27] Muir so identified himself and his comfort with his hut that each night after yet another unfruitful journey to the city, he described himself returning to his "graveyard home" [Figure 6].[28]

HEIMLICH

Muir's use of the word 'home' conjures Freud's distinction between *heimlich* and *umheimlich*. Writing on the uncanny, Freud explains that the uncanny is unsettling precisely because it is not familiar. It lacks the hominess associated with the *heimlich*.[29] For Muir, the thicket — indeed, all of nature — is imbued with hominess and, thus, can be comforting and sustaining.

Many years after his trek to the Gulf, while climbing in California's Sierra Nevada, Muir would recapture the at-homeness in nature that he first experienced in Bonaventure Cemetery. The landscape couldn't have been more starkly imposing. As he described it, "Rugged spurs, and moraines, and huge, projecting buttresses began to shut me in."[30] But they failed to exert a chilling effect because, as Muir succinctly put it, "going to the mountains is like going home".[31] Then, to clarify, he appears to echo Freud's sentiment, "We always find that the strangest objects in these fountain wilds are in some degree familiar, and we look upon them with a vague sense of having seen them before."[32]

However, lest we interpret Muir's at-homeness in the cemetery to an appropriation of nature to human social ends, we should bear in mind that Muir is quick to contrast his abode in the thicket with the structures people have built over the gravesites. Apparently, the dead are averse to rain, for each grave sprouts a peaked and shingled roof, supported on corner posts like a house. The architecture of a house may serve to connect the living with their departed family members who can be seen as having a roof over their heads, albeit not the family's roof. However, as Muir would have seen it, the separation from nature that architecture evokes shrouds death in fear and loss. The natural connection between life and death — something that ought to be familiar — is denied and replaced by its opposite. Thus does death become a source of the uncanny.

Muir's at-homeness in nature is not confined to his bivouac in the thicket, but conditions his characterization of the larger world. A forested area constitutes "a company of trees".[33] More than a simple group, the trees offer the companionship of their numbers. Similarly, Muir perceives the live oaks as not entirely different from himself. They, too, have arms — "strong

evergreen arms".[34] They, too, have heads — "broad, spreading, leafy heads".[35] This is not to suggest that Muir has inducted the oaks into the human world. Rather, in recognizing a commonality of form, he affirms a living bond between life's human and floral expressions.

The hominess of nature takes on a truly domestic note when Muir deepens his contemplation of the oaks and describes their complement of draped and trailing moss as vegetal "skeins".[36] Here, Muir imports a reminiscence of homespun domestic production into the natural growth pattern of the moss. It's a reference he repeats when, lying on his back and gazing up through the overlapping configuration of leaves, he discovers a "broderie" in the pattern of the leaves and filtering light.[37] Notably, Muir summons those aspects of rural homestead labor — knitting and embroidery — that lend beauty to daily toil. He is not comparing the pattern of leaves to freshly turned soil or the trailing moss to winnowed furrows. It's not the farm he conflates with nature to make it familiar, but the home.

Summing up his impression of Bonaventure, Muir defines the cemetery as "one of the most impressive assemblages of animal and plant creatures I have ever met".[38] The word 'assemblage' suggests a form of agency — a force, if not an intent, whereby myriad plants and animals have been brought together. This echoes his notion that the trees in Bonaventure form a 'company'. But, here, the assemblage includes animals as well as plants. What's more, both are categorized as "creatures" — a word we commonly apply to pets, insects, even human babies, but never to plants. How might the oaks, the moss, the grasses, and flowers be conceived as creatures? For Muir, the commonality may well reside in the etymological derivation of creature in the Latin *creatus*, the root form of 'creation'. Indeed, for Muir all life forms share and express the plenitude of creation. All have been brought into existence and evince a harmony that Muir would call divine. From this perspective, Muir, himself, is a creature; and as such, he can 'meet' the animals and plants, and be accepted into their company.

As a naturalist, Muir fully knew the biological distinction between plants and animals. And as a man of science, he had an extensive knowledge of plant taxonomy. What's remarkable is that for Muir science is not at odds with a vision of nature as a divine totality that does not set humankind outside of itself; but instead includes humans as one life form among many. Or as Muir put it, "Nature's object in making animals and plants [is] first of all the happiness of each one of them, not the creation of all for the happiness of one."[39]

Thus, when Muir ascribes human qualities like happiness to plants and goes on to describe flowers as "confident" or the oaks as "calm", his personification of nature does not sever the plant from its botanical reality and cause it to be assimilated to the human, as we might say that Mickey

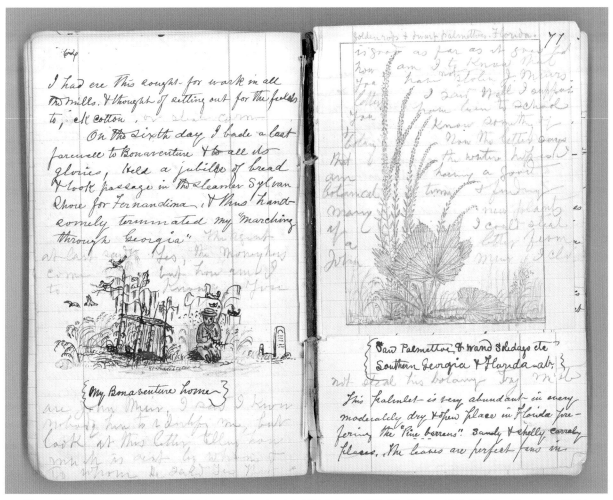

Figure 6/ My Bonaventure home. John Muir, journal illustration, July 1867–February 1868, "The Thousand Mile Walk from Kentucky to Florida and Cuba". John Muir Papers, Holt-Atherton Special Collections, University of the Pacific Library. © 1984 Muir-Hanna Trust.

Mouse leaves off being a mouse and becomes a human with mouse features.[40] Rather, because Muir does not see himself outside of nature, he can conceive of a quality like confidence being absorbed by the plant so that 'confidence' becomes an integral part of its nature. The flower is confident in the same way as it might also be fragrant.

Some hundred years after Muir's sojourn in Bonaventure Cemetery, author Annie Dillard wrote of her own sojourn in nature, *Pilgrim at Tinker Creek*. Following Muir's reasoning, Dillard maintains that to be in nature one must be wholly and purely in the present. She goes on to explain that while we can direct consciousness to the experience of nature, self-consciousness intervenes to "unplug" our connection with nature.[41] As she puts it, "So long as I lose myself in a tree, … I can scent its leafy breath or estimate its broad feet of lumber, I can draw its fruits, or boil tea on its branches,…. But the

second I become aware of myself at any of these activities…. The tree vanishes."[42]

What's interesting about Muir's relationship with nature is the absence of a self. He never, as Dillard puts it, catches himself "looking over [his] own shoulder" and reflecting on what it means to be John Muir doing what he's doing.[43] This is not to suggest that Muir is any less a subject. But the absence of self does have consequences on how he perceives and interacts with the natural world. As a subject unburdened of self and all the baggage that accrues to the self, like ego-defined wants and desires, Muir conceptualizes a world wherein plants and animals can also be subjects and present themselves as such. Additionally, a world depleted of self and comprised of myriad and diverse subjects casts into doubt the category of object. If a flower looks us in the face and greets us, can we, then, think of it as an object? Doesn't the fact of a greeting put us in communication as two subjects who meet each other in a charmed present that exists only so long as self and object are held at bay?

CASSIOPE

Muir's *Thousand Mile Walk to the Gulf* may capture a young trekker's exuberance and a young writer's less than polished style, but the sense of nature that Muir conveys in that account will continue to inform all his subsequent travels and writings. Witness his description of a flower that he happened upon some ten years later while climbing in the mountains of California:

> In this so-called 'land of desolation,' I met cassiope, growing in fringes among the battered rocks. Her blossoms had faded long ago, but they were still clinging with happy memories to the evergreen sprays, and still so beautiful as to thrill every fiber of one's being. Winter and summer, you may hear her voice, the low, sweet melody of her purple bells. No evangel among all the mountain plants speaks Nature's love more plainly than cassiope. Where she dwells, the redemption of the coldest solitude is complete. The Very rocks and glaciers seem to feel her presence,....[44]

Here, the fusion of femininity and flower is so complete that it's hard to tell where the one supplants the other. Named for the beautiful, but vain queen of Ethiopia in Greek mythology, cassiope also has a twofold presence. On the flower side of her being, she displays blooms (now faded) and evergreen foliage. And as a feminine presence, she conveys happy memories, her beauty thrills, she has a low, melodious voice, and she speaks of love. But not just any love; for cassiope is the redeemer, who takes root amongst the battered rocks to convey nature's love to a harsh landscape.

It's tempting to read Muir's description as an allegory of Christianity, wherein God sends a messenger, who is cast into a land of desolation and hardship, but whose love brings transformative redemption into the bleak and barren world. The problem with such a reading is that for Muir, nature and God are so completely fused that it's impossible to distinguish which one allegorizes the other. Is this a story of a flower that tells us about Christ? Or does the story of Christ tell us about the flower? Can there be a knife blade so thin as to slice between nature and God?

The answer may reside in what Muir calls "the first garden", the Biblical Eden.[45] At the conclusion of his walk to the Gulf, Muir closes his journal with a meditation on the journey as a whole and what it has meant. Here, his thoughts turn to the way religious doctrine puts mankind at the center of creation with the entire non-human world existing 'for us'. Vexed, he offers a litany of our anthropocentric point of view:

> … whales are storehouses of oil for us, to help out the stars in lighting our dark ways until the discovery of the Pennsylvania oil wells. Among plants, hemp, to say nothing of the cereals, is a case of evident destination for ships' rigging, wrapping packages, and hanging the wicked. Cotton is another plain case of clothing. Iron was made for hammers and ploughs, and lead for bullets; all intended for us.[46]

But what, Muir asks, of all the "man-eating animals" whose purpose is to devour us — and what, too, of mosquitoes, flies, and other "noxious insects"?[47] Are these the work of Satan? Are they the legacy of our fall from grace? our exile from Eden? Muir's answer is to posit a nature whose perfect totality excludes the Biblical Garden and all it presumes. The world, once rid of anthropocentrism, becomes a magical place where even rocks can experience things we can't begin to fathom. As Muir puts it,

> Plants are credited with but dim and uncertain sensation, and minerals with positively none at all. But why may not even a mineral arrangement of matter be endowed with sensation of a kind that we in our blind exclusive perfection can have no manner of communication with?[48]

For Muir, nature and creation are synonymous and divine. Is it not, then, ironic that one of the books Muir took pains to carry the thousand miles of his walk was Milton's *Paradise Lost*?

Lest we imagine Muir's vision died with him or was peculiar to his fusion of nature with the divine, we have only to read America's foremost Buddhist poet of nature, Gary Snyder. His poem "Mother Earth: Her Whales" charts the degradation and destruction of the earth and asks the same question Muir asked at the conclusion of his journey, "IS man most precious of all things?"[49]

In answer, the poet calls upon "The People" to rise up against the polluting, war-mongering forces that have plundered the earth. Again, echoing Muir, Snyder summons the people,

> Solidarity. The People
> Standing Tree People!
> Flying Bird People!
>
> Swimming Sea People!
> Four-legged, two-legged, people![50]

To know nature, as did John Muir, is to see humans simply as creatures among many, distinguished only by the number of our legs.

NOTES

1/ Muir, John, *A Thousand Mile Walk to the Gulf,* Memphis: General Books. 2009.

2/ Benjamin, Walter, "The Work of Art in the Age of Mechanical Reproduction", *Illuminations: Essays and Reflections*, New York: Schocken, 1969.

3/ Muir, *Thousand Mile Walk*, p. 2.

4/ Muir, *Thousand Mile Walk*, pp. 38 and 25.

5/ Muir, John, *Nature Writings*, New York: Library of America, 1997, p. 107.

6/ Muir, *Nature Writings*, pp. 345–346.

7/ Muir, *Thousand Mile Walk,* pp. 33 and 25.

8/ Muir, *Thousand Mile Walk,* pp. 16–17 and 52.

9/ Muir, *Thousand Mile Walk*, p. 31.

10/ Muir, *Thousand Mile Walk*, p. 31

11/ Muir, *Thousand Mile Walk*, p. 34.

12/ Muir, *Thousand Mile Walk*, p. 34.

13/ Muir, *Nature Writings*, pp. 138–139.

14/ Muir, *Thousand Milk Walk*, p. 31.

15/ Muir, *Thousand Milk Walk*, p. 30.

16/ Muir, *Thousand Milk Walk*, p. 30.

17/ Muir, *Thousand Milk Walk*, pp. 30 and 31.

18/ Muir, *Nature Writings,* p. 355.

19/ Muir, *Nature Writings,* p. 355.

20/ Muir, *Nature Writings,* p. 567.

21/ Muir, *Thousand Mile Walk*, p. 30.

22/ Muir, *Thousand Mile Walk*, p. 30.

23/ Muir, *Thousand Mile Walk*, p. 31.

24/ Carson, Rachel, "The Marginal World", *By the Light of the Glow-Worm Lamp,* Alberto Manguel ed., Memphis: Da Capo Press, 1998, p. 151.

25/ Carson, "The Marginal World", p. 152.

26/ Muir, *Thousand Mile Walk*, p. 32.

27/ Muir, *Thousand Mile Walk*, p. 32.

28/ Muir, *Thousand Mile Walk*, p. 32.

29/ Freud, Sigmund, "The Uncanny", *The Uncanny*, David McLintock trans., London: Penguin, 2003, pp. 123–162.

30/ Muir, *Nature Writings*, p. 352.

31/ Muir, *Nature Writings*, p. 352.

32/ Muir, *Nature Writings*, p. 352.

33/ Muir, *Thousand Mile Walk*, p. 30.

34/ Muir, *Thousand Mile Walk*, p. 30.

35/ Muir, *Thousand Mile Walk*, p. 30.

36/ Muir, *Thousand Mile Walk*, p. 30.

37/ Muir, *Thousand Mile Walk*, p. 32.

38/ Muir, *Thousand Mile Walk*, p. 30.

39/ Muir, *Thousand Mile Walk*, p. 54.

40/ Muir, *Thousand Mile Walk,* p. 30.

41/ Dillard, Annie, *Pilgrim at Tinker Creek,* New York: Harper Perennial, 1999, p. 82.

42/ Dillard, *Tinker Creek*, p. 82.

43/ Dillard, *Tinker Creek*, p. 82.

44/ Muir, *Nature Writings,* p. 351.

45/ Muir, *Thousand Mile Walk,* p. 54.

46/ Muir, *Thousand Mile Walk*, p. 53.

47/ Muir, *Thousand Mile Walk*, p. 53.

48/ Muir, *Thousand Mile Walk*, p. 54.

49/ Snyder, Gary, "Mother Earth: Her Whales", *Turtle Island*, New York: New Directions, 1974, p. 48.

50/ Snyder, "Mother Earth", p. 48.

2

POLITICS

OF

PLANTS

78 /ANNETTE GIESECKE

THE GOOD GARDENER AND IDEAL GARDENS OF STATE

Figure 1/ The Good Gardener: *Washington as Farmer at Mount Vernon*, 1851, Junius Brutus Stearns (American, 1810–1885), oil on canvas. Virginia Museum of Fine Arts, Richmond. Gift of Edgar William and Bernice Chrysler Garbish. Photo: Katherine Wetzel @ Virginia Museum of Fine Arts.

Then, as the British forces were preparing their ferocious onslaught, Washington brushed aside his generals and his military maps, sat in the flicker of candlelight with his quill and wrote a long letter to his estate manager and cousin Lund Washington at Mount Vernon, his plantation in Virginia. As the city braced itself, Washington pondered the voluptuous blossom of the rhododendron, the sculptural flowers of mountain laurel and the perfect pink of crab apple. These 'clever kind[s] of Trees (especially flowering ones),' he instructed, should be planted in two groves by either side of his house.[1]

Horticultural musings might seem an egregiously misguided and ill-timed indulgence in the face of deepest peril. But George Washington's vision for an orderly planting solely of native species mirrored his vision for an independent, 'indigenous' social order.[2] In equating the garden with the state — or the state with a garden — and its 'governor' with a 'good gardener', Washington, whether consciously or subconsciously, followed a tradition already millennia old in the Western world [Figure 1]. The Western tradition, in turn, owed much to Near Eastern traditions that were older still — those of ancient Persia, Mesopotamia, and Egypt.

It is no coincidence that in historical retrospectives and assessments Washington, one of America's Founding Fathers, is so often compared to Augustus Caesar, father of the new Roman state (*pater patriae*). Both would cast themselves (or be cast) as gardeners, if ultimately of a very different sort.

ROMAN PARADISE

The first *de facto* emperor in a country intolerant of monarchy, Augustus had to tread with care. In the year 509 BCE, Lucius Junius Brutus had led the effort to overthrow Rome's kings and establish a republic. His descendant Marcus Junius Brutus joined others to wield the dagger that claimed the life of Augustus' adoptive father Julius Caesar, regarded by the aristocracy as a dangerous, would-be king. Upon Caesar's death, two rivals emerged to govern Rome: Caesar's lieutenant Marcus Antonius (Mark Antony) and Caesar's son Octavian. A naval battle near the city of Actium (31 BCE) in Greece would settle this rivalry. Here Octavian, with Marcus Agrippa at the command of his fleet, defeated the combined forces of Antony and his exotic paramour, Queen Cleopatra of Egypt. Capitalizing on the fact that he had put an end to decades of a civil war so intense and bloody that it threatened to irreparably rend the fabric of Roman society, Octavian — now called Augustus — promoted himself as author of a new era of universal peace, the *Pax Romana*.[3] Under the auspices of her First Citizen, as Augustus styled himself, Rome as well as her empire, which extended from the Atlantic in the west

Figure 2/ "Augustus Bevilaqua". Bust of Augustus (reigned 31 BCE–14 CE). The Emperor wears a wreath of oak, the *corona civica*, which was bestowed on him by the Senate in 27 BCE for preserving the lives of Rome's citizens, now safe after decades of civil war. Photograph by Renate Kühling. Courtesy of the Staatliche Antikensammlungen und Glyptothek München.

to the Euphrates in the east, would experience a Golden Age of harmony and plenty, founded on piety and the agrarian values of old. And the Republic, now stripped of all its cancers, would be restored to its hallowed, primitive, pristine state. All this Augustus adeptly promoted through the appropriation of an elaborate botanical mythology [Figure 2].[4]

Chief among the plants closely associated with Augustus were the palm and laurel, together with the ficus, myrtle, and rose. The palm, symbolizing victory, had close ties with Apollo, god of healing, light, and prophecy. It was a palm tree that the goddess Leto gripped in the throes of parturition, while giving birth to Apollo and his twin sister Artemis, protector of animals and goddess of the hunt. Apollo was also the Sun god, and his warming rays were the source of life. This was the god recognized by Augustus as his personal protector. According to the historian Suetonius (c. 69–122 CE), "when a palm tree sprang up between the crevices of the pavement before [Augustus'] house, he had it transplanted to the inner court" of the Temple to Apollo — not coincidentally located right next door — and "took great pains to make it grow".[5] As has been remarked, "He had good reason, for the palm tree

———— **Figure 3/** Paradisiacal Augustan garden. Fresco from the Villa of Livia at Prima Porta, detail, c. 20 BCE. Museo Nazionale, Palazzo Massimo. ————
Photograph by Annette Giesecke, su concessione del Ministerio per i Beni e le Attività Culturali–Soprintendenza Speciale
per i Beni Archeologici di Roma.

was verdant proof … that Augustus was the son of Apollo, the rightful heir of the Divine Julius Caesar, and the living assurance of Rome's rebirth."[6]

A similar message was sent by the famous pair of laurel trees planted in front of the Emperor's door on the occasion when he was given the name Augustus ('exalted one') by the Senate in thanks for 'restoring' the Republic. The laurel had a manifold significance.[7] As a purifying herb it was an apt symbol for the healer of the once-ailing Roman state. Its boughs were traditionally used to crown Roman generals, Augustus among them, in triumph. And the laurel, like the palm, had close associations with Apollo. Indeed, no plant was more sacred to that god than the laurel, called *daphne* in Greek after the nymph who bore that name. The story of Apollo's unrequited but unending love for Daphne is a favorite among the myths of Classical antiquity. The lovely nymph, distressed at the god's relentless pursuit, asked her divine father for salvation. Her wish was granted, and she escaped the god's advances by transforming into a laurel tree. Loving her even in this form, the god made the laurel his emblematic tree. Boughs of laurel

graced his head, and a laurel tree grew in the inner sanctum of his famous temple at Delphi. Here Apollo's priestess chewed leaves of laurel to induce the psychic trance whereby she could communicate with the god on behalf of the pilgrims who, for centuries, came from far and wide to learn what the future might bring.

The fragrant myrtle and rose, on the other hand, were associated not with Apollo but with Venus, goddess of sexual love.[8] The most highly valued and most extensively cultivated flower in antiquity, the rose was said to have sprung from the sand, suffusing the earth with color, when Venus, born from the waves, emerged from the sea and stepped onto dry land. Before the Graces came to clothe the newly born goddess in robes of divine splendor, she sought shelter behind a myrtle bush. Thereafter, rose and myrtle, planted around her temples and worn in garlands by her celebrants, would remain symbols of the goddess and her powers. As goddess of procreation, Venus was viewed as mother of all life, mistress of gardens, and mother, in particular, of the Trojan hero Aeneas, from whom Augustus himself traced direct descent.

Aeneas, the mythic originator of the future Roman state, had ties not only with rose and myrtle but also with ficus, another of Augustus' favored plants.[9] It was under a ficus that infants Romulus and Remus, among Aeneas' most illustrious descendants, were discovered by the she-wolf who suckled them; the twins had been cast into the Tiber river upon the orders of the king, their own uncle, who justifiably feared that they would one day claim his stolen throne. Consciously linking past with present, Augustus refurbished the hallowed, ficus-shaded wolf's den that had housed the infant founders of Rome. This den, the so-called Lupercal, was located in the Forum just at the foot of the Palatine Hill. From a public, political perspective, the Forum was the most highly charged and visible location in Rome.

In the private sphere, Augustus was known for decorating his own villas "not so much with handsome statues and pictures as with terraces [and] groves".[10] One of the most elaborate Augustan usages of botanical symbolism appears in a house that entered imperial holdings via the emperor's wife, Livia. A gardener in her own right, Livia was said to have introduced new varieties of fig and laurel, thus adding to her husband's metaphorically-loaded botanical repertoire. The so-called House of Livia at Prima Porta, located 15 kilometres north of Rome, enjoyed views down the Tiber valley to the City — a borrowed landscape — and as was typical of Roman villas of the time, incorporated lavish gardens, including a famed grove of laurel. In this villa, too, all four walls of a subterranean dining 'grotto' opened — by sleight of painterly hand — onto a lush, animated, paradisiacal garden teeming with plant and bird life [Figure 3].[11] In the painted garden grow a wide variety of plants, including spruce, cypress, ilex, palm, pine, laurel, quince, box, arbutus, myrtle, oleander, viburnum, fern, ivy, pomegranate, oak, acanthus, iris, chamomile, chrysanthemum, poppy, rose, violet, and daisy. At first glance the whole is a chaotic botanical mélange, but closer inspection reveals an organic degree of control, a harmonizing rhythm. Not only is the wild garden triply-bounded by wicker fence, wall, and close-shorn verdant walk (punctuated by sparse clumps of ivy, fern, or violet), but one plant emerges as dominant within the apparent chaos of the copse: recurring both as tree and shrub, the laurel, Augustus' and Apollo's favored plant, anchors the composition.

Needless to say, this is no ordinary garden. Not only is there a perfect balance of 'wild' nature and nature tamed, but — miraculously — plants flower and produce fruit with no regard to seasonality. And, every plant is symbolically loaded, suggestive of Augustan peace and prosperity.[12] For example, the quince and pomegranate were standard symbols of fertility; both were sacred to Venus, the Near Eastern nature/mother goddess Cybele, and Juno, patron goddess of women as wives and mothers. The pomegranate, together with the poppy, had ties with Ceres, goddess of the harvest, too; it was this fruit that had sealed the fate of Ceres' daughter Persephone as Hades' reluctant queen. The venerable oak, meanwhile, was sacred to Jupiter, king of the gods and guarantor of civic order; the acanthus to Apollo; and violets, pine, and ivy to Bacchus, god of the vintage and wine, and also, importantly, the god responsible for all burgeoning plant growth. By implication, the entire Roman pantheon collaborated in the design of this painted garden, which so vividly demonstrated the fruitful, paradisiacal rebirth of the Roman state.

The Prima Porta garden fresco and its message are complemented by a host of other Augustan monuments, central among them the Ara Pacis. This Altar of Peace was dedicated in the year 9 BCE to celebrate the peace brought to the Roman Empire by Augustus' military victories. The monumental altar — more precisely, an altar enclosed by a precinct wall, all raised above ground level — was ornamented, inside and out, with carving in relief. Interior panels bore renderings of garlands, heavy with foliage and the varied produce of the imperial 'garden', while exterior panels featured Romulus and Remus, Rome's founders; pious Aeneas, progenitor of the Roman race; the fecund Earth personified; Augustus in the garb of priest, accompanied by his family; and, below these peopled scenes, an exuberant garden in which some 90 species of flora — variously signifying fertility, rebirth, good fortune, and healing — have been identified [Figure 4].[13] Predominant among this sculpted garden's plants are spiraling acanthus and laurel, Apollo's favorites, entwined with Bacchus' life-asserting vine. Here, too, Venus makes her munificent tutelage known through the presence of roses and swans, majestic birds sacred also to Apollo.

As in the House of Livia's painted garden, the fertility and prosperity of the Roman state is everywhere manifest, along with the underlying order upon which that prosperity so

Figure 4/ Spiraling flora, Ara Pacis Augustae (Augustan Altar of Peace), detail, dedicated 9 BCE, Rome. Photograph by Annette Giesecke, su concessione del Ministerio per i Beni e le Attività Culturali–Soprintendenza Speciale per i Beni Archeologici di Roma.

heavily relied. Augustus was a good warrior; the establishment of peace depended on his military prowess. Significantly, the altar was constructed on the Campus Martius, the Field of Mars, that long had been the exercise ground of the Roman army. But Mars himself, the god of war, was also a god of agriculture, protector of the crops. Interestingly enough, the best known of Augustus' likenesses, the statue that presents the cuirass-clad emperor as commander of the Roman army, was found in the grounds of the Prima Porta villa that harbored the painted paradise. Thus, Augustus' prowess as warrior and his skill as gardener were intertwined. The Princeps was a second Cincinnatus, summoned from the plow to assume the office first of consul and then of dictator of the Roman state.[14] Indeed, Vergil's poem on farming, the *Georgics*, should be viewed as a guide not for every or any Roman citizen-farmer, but for Augustus specifically, as gardener of the Roman state. His moral stewardship would ensure the agricultural munificence both of Italy and of all the Empire.

CYRUS THE GREAT AND THE BIRTH OF PARADISE

Augustan botanical propaganda did not spring from a vacuum. It was at once deeply rooted in traditional Roman values — such as those espoused by the elder Cato who famously equated the "good man" with the "good farmer" — and redolent of the wisdom and traditions of the Near East, where gardening had long been considered a statesmanly activity.[15] In ancient Persia, for instance, the King certainly presented himself as good warrior and good hunter, but his role as good gardener was equally critical. He could, and *should*, himself engage in planting and cultivation, thus ensuring the prosperity of the kingdom's fields.

Improbably lush oases in what could be a most inhospitable climate, Persian royal gardens testified not only to their creators' wonder-working ability, evidencing the favor and collaboration of the gods, but also to their ability to nourish and sustain the lands beneath their sway despite unfavorable natural conditions.[16] Inherently ephemeral, these gardens' plantings have not survived, but literary descriptions tell of beautiful parks containing glistening streams and sun-drenched meadows, interspersed with pavilions, exquisitely adorned. The gardens contained hunting parks and orchards heavy with fruit, drifts of fragrant rose and jasmine, as well as shady allées in which the royals and their entourage could stroll. The precious bones of such a garden have been found at the heart of an ancient palatial complex at Pasargadae in what is now Iran. Pasargadae, a 300-hectare 'garden city', was

the first dynastic capital of the Achaemenid Empire. It was founded in the sixth century BCE — five centuries prior to Caesar Augustus — by Cyrus II the Great in Pars, homeland of the Persians [Figure 5].

Cyrus' complex personal mythology paints him as gardener of the state from the moment of his birth. One origin tale is recorded by Greek historian Herodotus (c. 480–425 BCE).[17] Before Cyrus' birth, his grandfather, king of Media, awoke with a prophetic dream in which a grapevine growing from his daughter's body overran first Media, then the world. The dream's meaning was unequivocal: the child would conquer first Media and then the entire earth. To prevent this outcome, the infant Cyrus was left to die in the mountains, but rescued and raised by shepherds, he lived to fulfill the prophecy. That this tale bears striking similarity to the tale of Romulus and Remus, founders of Rome, is no coincidence. In a very different tale, the first century BCE author Nicolaos of Damascus (incorporating material from Ctesias, a Greek who became physician to the Achaemenid court), suggested that Cyrus was the son of a poor Persian and that he infiltrated the royal household by becoming first the king's gardener and then his cupbearer. In actual fact, Cyrus was the son of the Persian king Cambyses I and Mandane, a daughter of the Median king Astyages.

In any event, his destiny as ascendant gardener sealed, Cyrus led the Persian tribes to conquer the ancient kingdoms of the Near East. One by one they fell: Media, Lydia, Elam, and Babylonia, which at that time controlled Assyria. Of the great kingdoms, only Egypt eluded his grasp, though he paved the way for its conquest at the hands of his son, Cambyses II. In the space of just two decades, the Persians became masters of an area that stretched from India to eastern Greece, leaving Cyrus, in his own words, "king of the universe, the great king, the powerful king, king of Babylon, king of Sumer and Akkad, king of the four quarters of the world".[18]

More astounding, perhaps, than the unprecedented size and ethnic diversity of the empire forged by Cyrus and his successors is the fact that it endured for more than two centuries in relative peace. While the empire's size attests to Cyrus' skill as a military tactician, its longevity attests to his remarkable qualities as statesman. Indeed, in stark contrast to the "barbarous and cruel" Assyro-Babylonian kings, Cyrus is remembered for an unprecedented tolerance for the laws, traditions, and religions of his subject peoples.[19] His own nation called him 'father'; the priests of Babylon recognized him as liberator, appointed and guided by their god Marduk; and Jewish literature presents Cyrus as a chosen ally of Yahweh, a messiah. In his benevolence, he had decreed the exiled Jews' return from Babylon to Jerusalem, the rebuilding at his own expense of the Temple of God, and the restoration of the sanctuary's treasures that had been pilfered by the Babylonian Nebuchadnezzar [Figure 6].

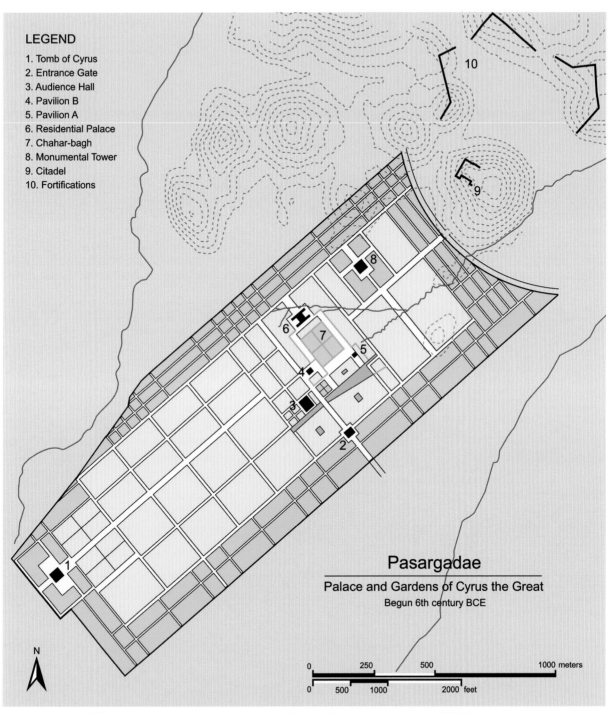

LEGEND

1. Tomb of Cyrus
2. Entrance Gate
3. Audience Hall
4. Pavilion B
5. Pavilion A
6. Residential Palace
7. Chahar-bagh
8. Monumental Tower
9. Citadel
10. Fortifications

Pasargadae

Palace and Gardens of Cyrus the Great

Begun 6th century BCE

N

Figure 5/ Pasargadae, plan of the palace and gardens of Cyrus the Great, begun sixth century BCE, Marv-Dasht plain, Iran. Plan by Annette Giesecke and Stephanie Bryan after Farzin Rezaeian, *Recreating Pasargadae*, Canada: Sunrise Visual Innovations Ltd., 2012 p. 39; Christophe Benech, Rémy Boucharlat, and Sébastien Gondet, "Organisation et aménagement de l'espace à Pasargades, Reconnaissances archéologiques de surface, 2003–2008", *Arta*, vol. 3, 2012, p. 3; and David Stronach, "The Garden as Political Statement: Some Case Studies from the Near East in the First Millennium B.C.", *Bulletin of the Asia Institute*, N. S. vol. 4, 1990, p. 175.

Figure 6/ *Cyrus Restoring the Vessels of the Temple,* illustration from *The Holy Bible,* illustrated by Gustave Doré (1832–1883), engraving realized by Doré's assistant Adolphe François Pannemaker (1822–1900), 1866. Private Collection, The Bridgeman Art Library.

Cyrus' new empire required a suitable capital from which the benevolent king could both assert world dominion and underscore his Persian heritage. Cyrus chose a location on the great plain of Marv-Dasht, east of the Zagros Mountains and watered by the Pulvar River. This was the territory of the Pasargadae, the tribe to which belonged the clan of the Achaemenidae, from whom Cyrus claimed descent. The territory shared the name of the tribe. According to the Greek geographer Strabo (c. 65 BCE–35 CE), it was here that Cyrus had defeated Astyages, King of Media, in a definitive battle to which the palace would serve as eternal memorial. [20]

Visitors coming for the first time to this resonant place would, indeed, have experienced something wondrous, an architecture and land art entirely new. Dignitaries from all of Cyrus' far-flung empire arrived, laden with gifts of fabrics, jewels, incense, ornate weaponry, vessels crafted from precious metals, exotic fruits, and botanical specimens — "the most valuable productions of their country, whether the fruits of the earth, or animals bred there, or manufactures of their own arts", as the Greek author Xenophon (c. 430–354 BCE) reports.[21] Here, weary from their travels, they found an oasis of

improbable magnitude and lushness in this desert landscape. A complex of palatial structures punctuated a verdant park with their glistening white.[22] Visitors came first upon a freestanding monumental gateway, at that time unique in that it was not embedded in a defensive circuit wall. Its message was unmistakable: the great king had nothing to fear from any adversary, animal or human. In his rule, all the gods and all of Nature were complicit. Next the visitors proceeded along a tree-shaded avenue and crossed a bridge over a manmade lake, another most unexpected sight, and made their way to the Audience Hall. This Hall was the palace that presumably served as the primary public venue for the king and court. A few hundred meters north-east of the Audience Hall, at the heart of Pasargadae's royal park, lay a four-fold garden, its boundaries defined by a system of water channels constructed of finely cut limestone. The garden, a microcosm of the World quartered by the waters of Creation, would have been planted with both native plants and specimens representative of the extent of Cyrus' empire, all arranged in symmetrical, geometric patterns.[23] Among the trees, one imagines, were fruit-bearing apple, pomegranate, almond, citrus, sour cherry, olive, and date palm, together with cypress, which symbolized eternal life and provided welcome swaths of shade. Around the trees was planted a carpet of sweet-scented rose, jasmine, and lily, interspersed in their seasons with brightly colored tulips, ranunculi, poppies, iris, and fragrant native grasses. Grapes very likely could be found clinging in great clusters to arbors or small garden pavilions. At the garden's north-western end was the great king's residential palace. His

Figure 7/ Ruins of the Residential Palace of Cyrus the Great, Pasargadae, Iran. The palace faces the *chahar-bagh,* a four-part rectangular garden outlined by channels of finely cut stone. Photograph courtesy of Farzin Rezaiean.

Figure 8/ Apple allée, view from within the *chahar-bagh* of Cyrus the Great, Pasargadae, Iran. Reconstruction concept and design by Annette Giesecke and Donald Dunham, rendering by Don Cowan.

Figure 9/ Stylistic hybrid mirroring the Persian Empire's diversity, Tomb of Cyrus the Great, Pasargadae, Iran. Photograph © Julian Chichester, The Bridgeman Art Library.

exterior throne was strategically aligned with the garden's central axis, affording him an exquisite view. Cyrus' garden with its crystalline palace pavilions, its plethora of scents and tapestry of colors, and its soothing, cooling, gently flowing waters had been designed to engage all the senses [Figures 7, 8]. This earliest of the imperial Persian *paridaeza* or paradises, as the Greeks and Romans would call them, may have been the physical model for the Biblical and Qur'anic Eden, the primordial paradise lost and eternally longed for. It appears also to have been the first *chahar-bagh*, that four-fold garden from which the Islamic garden would claim direct descent.[24] At Pasargadae, Cyrus' garden architects had adhered to the principles of collaboration and synthesis that guided the king's

governance so successfully.[25] Skilled Ionian (Eastern Greek) and Lydian masons left their mark on the fine stonework that characterized the palaces and water channels. Fragmentary remains of relief and other sculpture bear unmistakable traces of Egyptian, Babylonian, and Assyrian influences. In departure from the frontality then typifying design in the Near East, the palatial structures fused architectural forms traditional in ancient Iran with the Greek dipteral temple, which had on its exterior a double row of columns affording visual interest on all sides. Standing at a distance from the site's other major structures was Cyrus' tomb, which Alexander the Great famously visited two centuries later to pay homage to the Great King [Figure 9]. This iconic monument, a gabled tomb resting on a high plinth, quite remarkably has remained substantially undamaged over 25 centuries. As the second-century Roman historian Arrian reported, "round it had been planted a grove of all sorts of trees; the grove was irrigated, and deep grass had grown in the meadow".[26] Like the other structures on the site, the tomb was a hybrid of vernacular styles, and ultimately a creation uniquely conforming to Cyrus' vision. Indeed, the entire garden complex was manifestly the result of an elaborate master plan, unprecedented in scale, that oriented all the major palatial structures towards the *chahar-bagh*.

KEEPER OF THE TREE OF LIFE

In arid climates, vegetation, as well as the water necessary to sustain it, was held to be divine. Herein lies the origin of the religio-mythical tradition of the Tree of Life, the *axis mundi* or center of the universe that connects the earth with both sky and underworld and is nourished by the Waters of Creation.[27] It is a male entity that penetrates the fecund goddess Earth and is capable, with its fruit, of providing sustenance. Evident in cultures across the globe, the Tree of Life is strongly represented in the artifacts and texts of ancient Mesopotamia, from where, one may infer, it reached the Persians. Mesopotamian sources reveal that in order to ensure the prosperity of his people and the region over which he held sway, the king was charged with this tree's keeping, thus sustaining the divinity that inhabited it. And as the tree's keeper, he might himself embody the tree's powers. The planting of sacred groves in temple precincts and the furnishing of palace grounds with garden spaces thus become actions all the more resonant. Whether planted next to a temple or in a palace context, a tree or any other vegetation had both sacred and utilitarian significance, for the two dimensions were inextricably entwined. It follows logically that the garden and garden efforts would accrue political significance as well, being symbolic of the state and the manner in which it was governed or looked after by the gardener-king.

There was a long line of Mesopotamian gardener-kings in whose footsteps Cyrus would later follow.[28] Among them were the Babylonian king Adad-shuma-usur (reigned c. 1218–1189 BCE), a relatively shadowy figure whose palace gardens are attested in inscriptional evidence, and the Assyrian Tiglath-Pilesar I (reigned c. 1115–1077 BCE). The latter's annals boast of his concern for the prosperity of his land and people, which he assured by the annexation of new territories, the expansion of cultivated land, and the importation and planting of exotic trees. "Plows I did harness throughout the whole of the land of Assyria and I heaped up more heaps of grain than my forefathers did", the annals declare, adding:

> Cedar, boxwood, Kanish-oak from the lands over which I gained control — those trees which none of the previous kings my forefathers had planted — I took and I planted them in the orchards of my lands. Rare orchard fruits, which did not exist in my land, I took and filled the orchards of Assyria [with them].

Thus the king transformed Assyrian lands from a wilderness into a well-watered paradisiacal garden. For his own enjoyment, he stated, "I planted a garden for my lordly leisure."[29] Such leisure showed that he had eradicated all threats of human foe or hostile Nature.

Similar sentiments were echoed and amplified by a host of others, among them Assurnasirpal II (reigned c. 883–859 BCE) [Figure 10]. On the occasion of the opening of his new palace at Nimrud in the year 879, he recorded an extraordinary horticultural achievement: "I excavated a canal from the Upper Zab River, cutting through a mountain at its peak. I named it 'Canal of Abundance'. I irrigated the pasturelands beside the Tigris River [and] I planted gardens in its vicinity with fruit trees

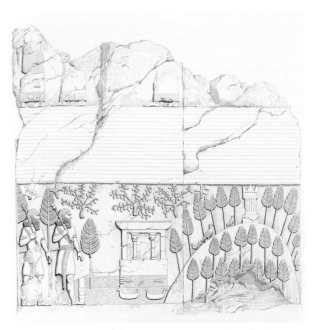

Figure 11/ A park like unto Mount Amanus planted with "all the spice trees of the Hittite land" and with a body of water at the foot of the mountain. Drawing of a relief depicting the garden of Sargon II (reigned c. 722–705 BCE) at Khorsabad, Iraq. Plate 114, Paul Émile Botta and Eugène Flandin, *Monument de Ninive, vol. II: Architecture et sculpture*, Paris: Imprimerie Nationale, 1849. Image courtesy Universitätsbibliothek Heidelberg.

Figure 10/ King Assurnasirpal II, appearing twice, to either side of the Tree of Life. Gypsum wall panel, relief. Neo-Assyrian (c. 865–860 BCE), North West Palace, Room B Panel 23, Nimrud, Iraq. British Museum inv. BM124531. Photograph courtesy The Trustees of the British Museum.

of every kind."[30] In his palatial garden, he planted trees, cuttings, and seeds collected from all the lands through which he had traveled in the course of his campaigns. Some 41 plant species are referenced, including cedar, cypress, box, juniper, myrtle, date palm, ebony, olive, oak, tamarisk, almond, terebinth, ash, fir, pomegranate, apricot, pine, pear, quince, fig, grapes, plum, mint, sycamore, and frankincense. "Canal-water came flowing down from above through the gardens", he continued; "the paths are full of scent, the waterfalls [sparkle] like the stars of heaven in the garden of pleasure. The pomegranate trees, which are clothed with clusters of fruit like vines, enrich the breezes in this garden of delight." So ample was the produce of this garden, that the king could "gather fruit continuously in the garden of joys like a squirrel".[31]

This proud gardener-king's successors included Sargon II (reigned c. 722–705 BCE), who constructed at Khorsabad a new capital with "a park like unto Mount Amanus … laid out by its side" — a marvel in this flat landscape — and in which were gathered "all the spice trees of the Hittite land" and "the fruit trees of every mountain" [Figure 11].[32] This Amanus, a symbol of the king's conquest of Hittite territories, is a mountain range in what is now south-central Turkey. Sargon II's son Sennacherib (reigned c. 704–681 BCE) followed suit, constructing not far from his own palace "a great park like unto Mount Amanus", another garden requiring no small amount of engineering in order to sculpt the land. Later, at Babylon, rose the fabled Hanging Gardens of Nebuchadnezzar II (reigned c. 604–562 BCE) [Figure 12]. The authorship and location of these gardens, deemed one of the seven canonical wonders of the ancient world, have long been a matter of dispute, a surprising fact in view of the unstinting praise heaped upon them by the authors of Classical antiquity.[33] Among the fullest descriptions is that of Diodorus of Sicily (c. 90–30 BCE), a Greek historian who was a contemporary of Julius Caesar. Diodorus wrote that the Hanging Garden was built by an unspecified king "to please one of his concubines; for she, they say, being a Persian by race and longing for the meadows of her mountains, asked the king to imitate, through the artifice of a planted garden, the distinctive landscape of Persia". A lengthy description follows:

The park extended 4 plethra on each side, and since the approach to the garden sloped like a hillside and the several parts of the structure rose from one another tier on tier, the appearance of the whole resembled that of a theatre. When the ascending terraces had been built, there had been constructed beneath them galleries which carried the entire weight of the planted garden and rose little by little one above the other along the approach; and the uppermost gallery, which was 50 cubits high, bore the highest surface of the park, which was made level with the circuit wall of the battlements of the city. Furthermore, the walls, which had been constructed at great expense, were 22 feet thick, while the passage-way between each two walls was 10 feet wide. The roofs of the galleries were covered over with beams of stone 16 feet long, inclusive of the overlap, and 4 feet wide. The roof above these beams had first a layer of reeds laid in great quantities of bitumen, over this two courses of baked brick bonded by cement, and as a third layer a covering of lead, to the

—— **Figure 12/** *Babylon taken by the army of Cyrus the Great*; Nebuchadnezzar's Hanging Gardens loom large behind the palatial ziggurat. ——
From *Cassell's Illustrated Family Bible*, c. 1870. Private Collection, image © Look and Learn, The Bridgeman Art Library.

end that the moisture from the soil might not penetrate beneath. On all this again earth had been piled to a depth sufficient for the roots of the largest trees; and the ground, when leveled off, was thickly planted with trees of every kind that, by their great size or any other charm, could give pleasure to the beholder.

Strabo joined Diodorus in commenting on the garden's wondrous watering mechanism: "The ascent to the uppermost terrace is made by a stairway, and alongside these stairs there were screws, through which the water was continually drawn up into the garden from the Euphrates by those appointed for the purpose."[34] Whether or not he was motivated by a desire to comfort a homesick consort or concubine — assuming that Nebuchadnezzar was responsible for the garden's construction — it would be impossible to discount as a factor the desire to emulate and out-do his Assyrian predecessors, particularly as Babylon had been their vassal state.

GUARDIAN OF THE SACRED WATERS

The Pasargadae garden, then, was both heir to and culmination of a long tradition of Mesopotamian royal gardens that reflected their creator's skill as gardener of the state and also, by showcasing specimens from throughout conquered lands, exhibited the extent of his sovereignty. Amply demonstrated by descriptions and illustrations of the various gardens, this fact is underlined by distinct echoes of Mesopotamian lore in the legends surrounding Cyrus' origins and ascent to the throne.

Among the earliest known accounts of a Mesopotamian ruler's rise to kingship is that of Sargon of Akkad (ruled c. 2334–2279 BCE). Sargon, the story goes, was born to non-royal parents and cast adrift in a basket in the river Tigris:

> Sargon, the mighty king, king of Agade, am I.
> My mother was a high-priestess, my father I knew not.
> The brother(s) of my father loved the hills.
> My city is Azupiranu, which is situated on the banks of the Euphrates. My mother, the high-priestess, conceived me, in secret she bore me. She set me in a basket of rushes, with bitumen she sealed my lid.
> She cast me into the river which rose not (over) me.
> The river bore me up and carried me to Akki, the drawer of water. Akki, the drawer of water, lifted me out as he dipped his e[w]er.
> Akki, the drawer of water, [took me] as his son (and) reared me.

Sargon's foster-father, "Akki, the drawer of water", then appointed Sargon "as his gardener".[35] Sargon thus was a gardener, learning skills that put him in good stead, before he became a king charged with feeding all his people.

This tale of a foundling rising to king's estate became a topos in the Fertile Crescent's folk history and was appropriately transferred, among others, to Cyrus — hence the tale preserved by Herodotus recounted above. Interestingly enough, Romulus and Remus, those famous ancestors of the Roman emperor Augustus and of the entire Roman race, would also be assimilated to this tradition. Like Sargon they had been set adrift as infants in the very river that later would sustain the state; in their case, the river was the Tiber.[36]

Mythologizing aside, Cyrus certainly embodied the aspect of the gardener-king tradition that entailed guardianship of the sacred, life-sustaining waters. To this, Pasargadae's

Figure 13/ Osiris, guardian of the sacred waters. Papyrus from the Book of the Dead of Nakht: Nakht (a royal scribe and army overseer) and his wife worshipping Osiris in their garden. From Thebes, Egypt. Late Eighteenth Dynasty, c. 1350–1300 BCE. British Museum, London. Photograph © The Trustees of the British Museum, Art Resource, NY.

—— **Figure 14/** Mortuary temples of Queen Hatshepsut (foreground, reigned c. 1475–1458 BCE), and of Menuhotep II (reigned c. 2055–2004 BCE), Deir el-Bahari, Egypt. De Agostini Picture Library, G. Sioen, The Bridgeman Art Library.

—— **Figure 15/** Reconstruction of the mortuary temple and garden of Menuhotep II (left) and of Hatshepsut (right), Deir el-Bahari, Egypt. Color lithograph, Italian. Private Collection, De Agostini Picture Library, The Bridgeman Art Library.

elaborate water features attest, as does the fact that Cyrus and his successors increased the productivity of territories in the empire by improving irrigation. Existing canal systems were repaired and enlarged, as in Babylon, and other areas were for the first time assured a reliable supply of water via *qanats*, gently sloping underground canals that conducted water over long distances without evaporation, and by jubes or *jouies*, open channels distributing water between rows of plants.[37]

As new lord of Mesopotamia, Cyrus logically had become heritor of that region's ever-evolving, folk-historical traditions and diverse emblems of kingship, including guardianship of plants and waters. It would be remiss, however, to discount the influence of Egypt on Cyrus' self-fashioning as gardener-king and the symbolism of his Pasargadae gardens. In particular, it is worth noting the links between pharaoh and water. Just as Mesopotamian kings had critical associations with the Tigris and Euphrates, so the kings of Egypt were closely aligned with the Nile, whose annual flooding brought a rich, dark, life-giving mud.

The Nile itself, the Egyptians believed, owed its fertility to the fact that the god Osiris' severed male member resided in its waters. Osiris, the god of vegetation as well as lord of the afterlife and resurrection, personified the cycle of life and death that was so dramatically enacted in the natural world by the Nile's annual flooding [Figure 13]. Egyptian pharaohs were living counterparts of this god, who lay buried beneath the Mound of Creation. According to the account of cosmic origins, which must have been inspired by the Nile's flooding, the Mound of Creation was a fertile island that arose from the chaotic, primeval waters of Nun. Underscoring the identity of pharaoh and Osiris, royal temple-tombs mimicked and perpetuated that originary mound, securing the regent's status of best gardener, solely equipped to feed

his people — in this life and in the life beyond. The garden, in turn, represented both a fertile, prospering Egypt and the felicitous hereafter.[38]

Among the now iconic pharaonic mortuary temples are those of Menuhotep II (reigned c. 2055–2004 BCE) and Queen Hatshepsut (reigned c. 1475–1458 BCE) at Deir el-Bahari, and that of Ramses III (reigned c. 1187–1156 BCE) at Medinet Habu, all three monuments being on the west bank of the Nile opposite the city of Luxor. Menuhotep's pyramidal temple rose in terraces from the foot of Deir el-Bahari's spectacular cliffs, and its base was a walled grove of trees. Sycamore figs were planted in rows on either side of the avenue leading to a ceremonial ramp that served as the structure's main access; on either side of these were rows of tamarisk. A carved temple plan suggests the inevitable presence also of a pool. More than half a millennium later, Queen Hatshepsut ordered her architect Senmut to build her mortuary temple alongside that of Menuhotep [Figures 14, 15]. While including a sacred grove, terraces, and pools like its neighbor, Hatshepsut's temple departed from previous models; its design reflected its patron's strong political motivations, for she wished to establish her unprecedented right as female successor to the throne. Deviating from the strictly pyramidal model, her 'mountain' temple has the appearance more of a grand garden villa, its planted terraces ascending the cliffs' formidable face. Indeed, this temple was to serve also as an earthly palace for the Sun God, Amun-Re, who resided in Punt. Of her expedition to Punt, which is variously identified as the Somali coast and the Arabian Peninsula, the Queen reported:

Trees were taken up in God's Land, and set in the ground in Egypt … for the king of the gods. They were brought bearing incense therein for (giving of themselves) ointment for the divine limbs, which I owe to the Lord of the Gods ... he commanded me to establish a Punt in his house, to plant the trees of God's Land beside his temple, in his garden.[39]

Thus the temple mimicked that region's terraces of myrrh.

In the case of Ramses III's temple-tomb, the pharaoh's own words make explicit the associations with the Mound of Creation and its watery origins:

> I made ... an august house of millions of years, abiding on the mountain of 'Lord of Life,' ... built of sandstone, grit stone, and black granite; the doors of electrum and copper in beaten work. Its towers were of stone, towering to heaven, and carved with the graver's tool.... I built a wall around it, established with labor, having ramps and towers of sandstone. I dug a lake before it, flooded with Nun (celestial water), planted with trees and vegetation like the Northland (the Delta).[40]

Fewer Egyptian palatial remains are extant than those of temples, but as the functions and identities of these became blurred, with temples functioning as ceremonial royal residences, similarities are to be expected. Furthermore, both temple and palace, abodes of divinity and royalty, shared an origin in the 'ordinary' dwelling house with its enclosed fore-court and its plantings and water features as elaborate as the householder's means allowed.[41] In the case of kings responsible for the order and abundance of life-sustaining growth, these gardens were correspondingly profuse. Thus, for instance, Akhenaten's (Amenhotep IV) palaces at Tell el-Amarna boasted a series of courtyard gardens containing pools and water channels surrounded by shrubs, trees, and flowers. The plantings, in turn, were mimicked on painted pavements that portrayed fish and ducks in lotus-filled pools, surrounded by ornamental grasses and flowering shrubs [Figure 16]. Frescoes decorating the palaces' walls also depicted gardens; here too were pools, stands of papyrus, and birds flitting through banks of reeds. Not only paint transformed flat surfaces into gardens: in this, the regent's house — conceived of as a micro-Cosmos — columns, transformed into sacred papyrus and lotus, 'grew' from the fertile earth towards the heavens.

It must be stressed that in antiquity, as now, the kingdoms of the Near East shared certain fundamental traditions, and the passage of ideas through trade and other forms of contact was fluid and on-going. In Mesopotamia, as in Egypt, can be found the notion of the sacred mountain: hence the ziggurats of Sumer as well as the afore-mentioned royal mountain parks. Nor were Assurnasirpal II and Sargon II by any stretch alone in gathering the bounty of their extensive empires in their gardens. This is amply demonstrated in the Festival Temple of the pharaoh Tuthmosis III (reigned c. 1458–1425 BCE) at Karnak. Here the walls of a special room, which may have contained a planted garden as well, were decorated with the diverse plant, animal, and bird species that the pharaoh had collected in the course of his expeditions in Syria and Palestine.[42] Both Egyptian and Mesopotamian royal gardens, then, must have contained the ideological seeds from which would spring Cyrus the Great's imperial garden.

BRIDGING EAST AND WEST

That Cyrus' gardens at Pasargadae were influential from the moment of their creation cannot be doubted. Just how the ideas encapsulated in them reached the West — Rome specifically — is a most interesting tale of empires lost and won. To borrow a verse from the Roman poet Horace (65–8 BCE), it is also a tale of captured or subjugated peoples captivating their conquerors in turn, via the magnetism of their cultures.[43] Already a symbolically resonant 'artifact' entrenched in parts of the Near East, the paradise, a royal pleasure garden and hunting park, was spread still more widely by the Persians with the creation and expansion of their empire. Cyrus the Great, as Xenophon reports, ordered his provincial governors, the satraps, to establish paradises; the satraps would have been all too eager to follow the Great King's lead in this regard.[44] In fact, according to Xenophon, it appears to have been characteristic of the Persian kings to take care "that there [were] paradises, as they call them, full of all the good and beautiful things that the soil will produce ... in all the districts [they] reside[d] in and visit[ed]".[45] Paradises did, in fact, exist in each satrapy. Among the numerous satrapal paradises was that of Tissaphernes (c. 445–395 BCE) at Sardis in Lydia. The Greek historian Plutarch (c. 45–120 CE) describes this as "the most beautiful of his parks, containing salubrious streams and meadows, where he had built pavilions, and places of retirement royally and exquisitely adorned".

That Greeks were exposed to and admired the paradises of the Persian kings, as well as the ideologies underlying them, is demonstrated vividly in a passage from Xenophon's *Oeconomicus* (*Treatise on Household Management*) in which the author's mouthpiece, Socrates, describes the Spartan general Lysander's visit to the paradise garden of the Persian prince Cyrus the Younger (c. 423–401 BCE) at Sardis:

> Lysander admired the beauty of the trees in it, the accuracy of the spacing, the straightness of the rows, the regularity of the angles and the multitude of the sweet scents that clung round them as they walked; and for the wonder of these things he cried, 'Cyrus, I really do admire all these lovely things, but I am far more impressed with your agent's skill in measuring and arranging everything so exactly.' Cyrus was delighted to hear this and said: 'Well, Lysander, the whole of the measurement and arrangement is my own work, and I did some of the planting

myself.' 'What's that you say, Cyrus?' exclaimed Lysander looking at him and marking the beauty and perfume of this robes, and the splendor of his necklaces and bangles and other jewels that he was wearing: 'Did you really plant part of this with your own hands?' 'Does that surprise you, Lysander?' asked Cyrus in reply: 'I swear by the Sun-god that I never yet sat down to dinner when in sound health, without first working hard at some task of war or agriculture, or exerting myself somehow.'[46]

While Xenophon's vignette is certainly laudatory, it is important to note that the author's intent was not to praise the paradise garden as a source of sensory delight, but first and foremost to draw attention to the Persian king's complementary blend of military prowess and agronomic acumen. In so far as the kings possessed these attributes, they could serve as models for an ideal Greek citizenry. For in the Classical Period (fifth century BCE) to the time of Alexander's conquests, the citizens of Greek city states other than Sparta were largely farmers, who would be called upon to defend their own land and that of

their fellow citizens. There were no monarchs in this period and no pleasure gardens. The gardens of Classical Greece were primarily utilitarian: orchards and fields of grain, vegetables, herbs, or flowers. They also took the form of groves planted specifically to provide shade in public places, to honor a divinity, or to appease one's beloved dead.[47]

The ideal Greek garden, the mainstay of the ideal *polis* (an autonomous city and its sustaining countryside), was not a reflection of an individual's super-human ability to manipulate a hostile Nature and transform her into a bounteous Eden. The *polis* was exemplified by Athens and based on an anthropocentric model sketched by Homer in the *Iliad* and *Odyssey*.[48] In this model, humans — a collective — and human works are central. Nature, potentially threatening even when tamed by gardening, was forced to the urban periphery outside the city walls, everywhere and with greatest effort held in check [Figure 17]. But by no means were garden and gardening disdained, for thereon the city and civilization depended. Thus in the *Odyssey*, a foundational utopian work, Odysseus, the hero, returns to his island state from Troy to find his homeland in complete

Figure 16/ Painted garden: birds and papyrus, fragment of a painted pavement from the Maru Aten, a hallowed garden precinct of Pharaoh Akhenaten (Amenhotep IV) at Tell el Amarna, c. 1353–1337 BCE. Egypt, Eighteenth Dynasty. Painted gypsum, Egyptian Museum, Cairo, Egypt. De Agostini Picture Library, A. Dagli Orti, The Bridgeman Art Library.

disorder. He returns to new times in need of a new, enlightened, 'democratic' social order. Monarchy is a thing of the past. Having gleaned invaluable information in the course of his decade-long wanderings, Odysseus will create a new society, a city-state. Importantly, his first step is to restore his ancestral garden and its fallen wall.[49] The garden is unequivocally the new city's foundation, and the good gardener is defined by his ability to keep nature closely in check and subservient to humankind.

If Greeks of the Classical Period eschewed the luxury (as they saw it) of the Eastern monarchs and embraced only the productive aspect of the paradise garden and the work ethic of its gardener, things were rather different with Macedon's Alexander the Great, who between 336 and 323 BCE made himself master of the vast Persian Empire. Alexander spread the language and culture of Greece throughout his new empire, but, like Cyrus, whose empire he now controlled, he appears to have recognized and fostered the local traditions of conquered peoples. Doubtless having visited myriad paradise gardens beyond that of Cyrus at Pasargadae in the course of his epic travels, Alexander died wracked with fever, deriving what comforts he could from the Babylonian paradise in which he lay.[50] Having inherited administration of their deceased commander's empire, Alexander's generals and the dynasties they established also inherited the Persian satrapal estates and palaces, together with their paradises; in their hands, the physical features of these estates would be blended with architectural forms of Greece, such as theater and gymnasium.[51] One such palatial hybrid was the *basileia* (palace) of the Ptolemies in Alexandria. This royal property,

which reportedly covered a quarter of the total area of the city, contained not only a palace complex nestled in spacious parks but also a theater, a *palaestra* (exercise ground), a gymnasium, botanical and zoological gardens, a number of temples and sanctuaries, and the famous Museion, a cultural institution dedicated to furthering the arts and academic pursuits, with its great Library.

Beginning in the second century BCE, Rome bit-by-bit absorbed Alexander's former empire. The Romans, who tended to be conservative and traditionally minded, were troubled to some extent by Eastern royal luxury. Nevertheless, they found the lure of the garden's delights irresistible. Among those who fell under the spell of the Eastern garden's enticements was the infamous, profligate general Lucullus (118–57/56 BCE). Upon his return to Rome from his Eastern campaigns, Lucullus began building garden villas in Rome and elsewhere in Italy.[52] His villas and their grounds contained hunting parks, aviaries, and elaborately-engineered fishponds — supplied with fresh water by a channel dug through a mountain to the sea — that earned him the moniker 'Xerxes in a toga'. The Xerxes referenced here was none other than the Persian king (reigned 486–465 BCE) who, in an extravagant engineering effort, had dug a tunnel through the Mount Athos peninsula to facilitate his invading fleet's passage to Greece.

Lucullus was not alone in his villa-building efforts. Commencing in the latter half of the second century BCE and gaining momentum in the first, there was an explosion of villa construction.[53] Wealthy Romans were quick to realize both the pleasurable and the politically advantageous aspects of such estates and their lavish gardens. The more elaborate the estates and the more equipped with masterpieces — the more, too, that they echoed the wonders of the East, which was steadily being absorbed into the Roman Empire — the greater was the esteem in which one was held by one's elite peers and the greater one's chances of political advancement. These villa gardens and their accoutrements became so popular and desirable that they were emulated by small householders, as is evidenced by the ubiquity of ornamental gardens in the houses of Herculaneum and Pompeii. In these town houses, the Nile, 'Babylonian' hanging gardens, and Persian hunting parks were all reproduced on a scale suited to the setting.

Importantly, however, these Roman gardens, both large and small, did not represent the 'state' in microcosm, being vehicles instead for their owners' personal gain. The same was true of the public gardens, equipped with a theater, shaded walks, and pools, that Pompey the Great established in Rome (55 BCE), as well as of the gardens of Julius Caesar, which were opened in his lifetime to the public and bequeathed to the Roman people upon his death in 44 BCE — in Pompey's garden. The first Roman gardens that were symbols of the state and mirrors of their creator's skill in governance were those of Augustus — the painted, the sculpted, and the

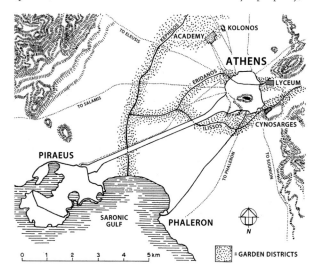

Figure 17/ Nature kept to the urban periphery: Athens and its garden districts in the fifth century BCE. Map after M. Carroll-Spillecke, *ΚΗΠΟΣ: Der antike griechische Garten*, Munich: Deutscher Kunstverlag, 1989, p. 29, fig. 10. Rendering by Michael Monahan.

—— **Figure 18/** The Emperor Augustus wearing a crown of laurel: creator of an enduring garden state. *Maecenas Presenting the Liberal Arts* ——
to the Emperor Augustus, c. 1745, oil on canvas, Tiepolo, Giovanni Battista (Giambattista) (1696–1770). Hermitage, St Petersburg, Russia,
The Bridgeman Art Library.

planted. For later Romans, the challenge remained how to stay pure and pious farmers at heart while at the same time coveting and re-creating the splendors of the Eastern pleasure park. Thus Roman villas featured expansive decorative plantings but, at the same time, maintained a productive agricultural core. The balance of piety and luxury was difficult to maintain, and no other did this more adeptly than the emperor Augustus had done [Figure 18]. His nostalgic garden-state was progressive enough to withstand the pressures of five centuries.

NOTES ——————————————————

1/ Wulf, Andrea, *Founding Gardeners: The Revolutionary Generation, Nature and the Shaping of the American Nation*, New York: Vintage, 2011, p. 14.

2/ Wulf, *Founding Gardeners*, p. 14.

3/ See Werner Eck, *The Age of Augustus*, second ed., D. L. Schneider and R. Daniel trans., Malden, MA and Oxford: Blackwell, 2007; Karl Galinsky, *Augustan Culture*, Princeton: Princeton University Press, 1996; Andrew Wallace-Hadrill, *Augustan Rome*, London: Bristol Classical Press, 1993; and Paul Zanker, *The Power of Images in the Age of Augustus*, Alan Shapiro trans., Ann Arbor, MI: University of Michigan Press, 1990.

4/ See, for example, David Castriota, *The Ara Pacis Augustae and the Imagery of Abundance in Later Greek and Early Roman Imperial Art*, Princeton: Princeton University Press, 1995; and Barbara A. Kellum, "The Construction of Landscape in Augustan Rome: The Garden Room at the Villa *ad Gallinas*", *The Art Bulletin*, vol. 76, no. 2, 1994, pp. 211–224.

5/ Suetonius, "The Deified Augustus", *The Lives of the Caesars*, J. C. Rolfe trans., Cambridge, MA: Harvard University Press, 1979, p. 263 (92.1).

6/ Kellum, "Construction of Landscape", p. 211.

7/ See Annette Giesecke, *The Mythology of Plants: Botanical Lore from Ancient Greece and Rome*, Los Angeles: The J. Paul Getty Museum, 2014, pp. 32–39.

8/ Giesecke, *Mythology of Plants*, pp. 21–23.

9/ See Annette Giesecke, *The Epic City: Urbanism, Utopia, and the Garden in Ancient Greece and Rome*, Cambridge, MA: Harvard University Press, 2007, p. 151.

10/ Suetonius, "The Deified Augustus", p. 237 (72. 3).

11/ See Mabel Gabriel, *Livia's Garden Room at Prima Porta*, New York: New York University Press, 1955; and Salvatore Settis, *La Villa di Livia: le pareti ingannevoli*, Milan: Electa, 2008.

12/ For the symbolism of individual plants, see Castriota, *Ara Pacis*, and Giesecke, *Mythology of Plants*, both passim.

13/ Caneva, Giulia, *Il Codice Botanico di Augusto, Roma-Ara Pacis* (*The Augustus Botanical Code, Rome—Ara Pacis*), Rome: Gangemi Editore, 2010 (text in Italian and English).

14/ For a full discussion of Cincinnatus and the ideals he represented, see Michael J. Hillyard, *Cincinnatus and the Citizen-Servant Ideal*, Philadelphia: Xlibris, 2001.

15/ Marcus Cato, "On Agriculture", *Cato & Varro: De Re Rustica*, W. D. Hooper and H. B. Ash trans., Cambridge, MA: Harvard University Press, 1979, p. 3 (pref., line 2).

16/ The vast literature on ancient Persian gardens includes: Penelope Hobhouse, *Gardens of Persia*, London: Kales Press, 2004; Mohammad Gharipour, *Persian Gardens and Pavilions: Reflections in History, Poetry and the Arts*, London: I. B. Tauris, 2013; Medhi Khansari, M. Reza Moghtader, and Minouch Yavari, *The Persian Garden: Echoes of Paradise*, Washington, DC: Mage Publishers, 2004; Elizabeth B. Moynihan, *Paradise as Garden in Persia and Mughal India*, New York: George Braziller, 1979; and Donald Newton Wilber, *Persian Gardens and Garden Pavilions*, second ed., Washington, DC: Dumbarton Oaks, 1979.

17/ Cyrus' origin tales are summarized in Pierre Briant, *From Cyrus to Alexander: A History of the Persian Empire*, Peter T. Daniels trans., Winona Lake, IN: Eisenbrauns, 2002, pp. 14–16; and Robert Drews, "Sargon, Cyrus, and Mesopotamian Folk History", *Journal of Near Eastern Studies*, vol. 33, no. 4, Oct., 1974, pp. 387–393.

18/ This quotation is from the Cyrus Cylinder in the collection of the British Museum. For the Cylinder's full text, see Irving Finkel, "Translation of the Cyrus Cylinder", *Cyrus the Great: An Ancient Iranian King*, Touraj Daryaee ed., Santa Monica, CA: Afshar Publishing, pp. 78–84, and for the cited words, p. 80.

19/ Briant, *Cyrus to Alexander*, p. 47.

20/ *The Geography of Strabo*, vol. 3, H. C. Hamilton, Esq. and W. Falconer trans., London: George Bell & Sons, 1903, p. 134 (15.3.8).

21/ Briant, *Cyrus to Alexander*, p. 395; and Xenophon, *Cyropaedia*, Walter Miller trans., London: W. Heinemann, 1914, (VIII.6.23), digitized by Perseus.org.

22/ For descriptions of the site and its structures, see David Stronach, "Cyrus and Pasargadae", *Cyrus the Great: An Ancient Iranian King*; and Farzin Rezaeian ed., *Recreating Pasargadae*, Canada: Sunrise

Visual Innovations Ltd., 2012. The classic archaeological publication of the site is David Stronach, *Pasargadae: A Report on the Excavations Conducted by the British Institute of Persian Studies from 1961 to 1963*, Oxford: Clarendon Press, 1978. See also Rémy Boucharlat, "Pasargadae", *Iran*, vol. 40, 2002, pp. 279–282; and Christophe Benech, Rémy Boucharlat, and Sébastien Gondet, "Organisation et aménagement de l'espace à Pasargades, Reconnaissances archéologiques de surface, 2003–2008", *Arta*, vol. 3, 2012, pp. 1–37.

23/ For the author's recreation of the gardens, see Annette Giesecke, "Outside In and Inside Out: Paradise in the Ancient Roman House", *Earth Perfect? Nature, Utopia, and the Garden*, Annette Giesecke and Naomi Jacobs eds., London: Black Dog Publishing, 2012, p. 130.

24/ Stronach, David, "The Garden as a Political Statement: Some Case Studies from the Near East in the First Millennium B.C.", *Bulletin of the Asia Institute*, N. S. vol. 4, 1990, p. 178.

25/ See John Boardman, *Persia and the West: An Archaeological Investigation of the Genesis of Achaemenid Art*, London: Thames & Hudson, 2000, pp. 19–84; as well as David Stronach, "The Building Program of Cyrus the Great at Pasargadae and the Date of the Fall of Sardis", and Mohammad Hassan Talebian, "Persia and Greece: The Role of Cultural Interactions in the Architecture of Persepolis-Pasargadae", both in *Ancient Greece and Ancient Iran: Cross-Cultural Encounters*, Seyed Mohammad, Reza Darbandi, and Antigoni Zournatzi eds., Athens: National Hellenic Research Association, 2008, pp. 149–173 and 175–193, respectively.

26/ "Anabasis of Alexander", *Arrian: Volume II*, E. I. Robson trans., Cambridge, MA: Harvard University Press, 1933, p. 195 (6.29.4–5).

27/ See Geo Widengren, *The King and the Tree of Life in Ancient Near Eastern Religion*, Uppsala: A.-B. Lundequistska Bokhandeln, 1951.

28/ Stronach, "Garden as Political Statement", pp. 171–174.

29/ Green, Douglas J., *I Undertook Great Works: The Ideology of Domestic Achievements in West Semitic Royal Inscriptions*, Tübingen: Mohr Siebeck, 2010, pp. 48, 50, 51.

30/ Green, *I Undertook Great Works*, p. 54.

31/ Stronach, "Garden as Political Statement", p. 477.

32/ Green, *I Undertook Great Works*, p. 59.

33/ See Stephanie Dalley, *The Mystery of the Hanging Garden of Babylon: An Elusive World Wonder Traced*, Oxford: Oxford University Press, 2013; as well as Timothy Potts' review of Dalley's book, "Looking for the Hanging Gardens", *The New York Review of Books*, 26 September 2013, http://www.nybooks.com/articles/archives/2013/sep/26/looking-hanging-gardens-babylon/.

34/ Diodorus Siculus, *Library of History* (II.10) and Strabo, *Geography* (XVI.1.5), as cited in Dalley, *Mystery of the Hanging Gardens*, pp. 31, 32.

35/ Drews, "Sargon, Cyrus, and Mesopotamian Folk History", p. 389.

36/ As was said of Cyrus, too, a bitch cared for the infants Romulus and Remus: Cyrus' surrogate mother was a woman called Kyno (Greek, 'she-dog'); that of Romulus and Remus was the fabled she-wolf or, alternatively, a prostitute named Lupa (Latin, 'wolf'). See *Herodotus: Volume I*, A. D. Godley trans., Cambridge, MA: Harvard University Press, 1981, p. 143 (I.110).

37/ Moynihan, *Paradise as Garden*, pp. 25–27.

38/ On the gardens of Egypt and their symbolism, See J.-C. Hugonot, "Ägyptishe Gärten", *Der Garten von der Antike bus zum Mittelalter*, M. Carroll-Spilleke ed., Mainz am Rhein: Verlag Philipp von Zabern, 1992; Earl Baldwin Smith, *Egyptian Architecture as Cultural Expression*, Watkins Glen, NY: American Life Foundation, 1968; Alix Wilkinson, *The Garden in Ancient Egypt*, London: The Rubicon Press, 1998.

39/ Quoted in Wilkinson, *The Garden in Ancient Egypt*, p. 83.

40/ Quoted in Smith, *Egyptian Architecture*, p. 141.

41/ Smith, *Egyptian Architecture*, passim, on the relation between houses, temples, and palaces.

42/ See Stephen Forbes, "Enquiry into Plants: Nature, Utopia, and the Botanic Garden", *Earth Perfect?*, pp. 224–225.

43/ "Graecia capta ferum victorem cepit et artis / intulit agresti Latio" (Horace, *Epistles*, II.1.156–157). Captive Greece took captive her savage conqueror and introduced her arts into uncouth Latium.

44/ Xenophon, *Cyropaedia*, (VIII.6.12).

45/ Xenophon, "Oeconomicus", *Xenophon: Memorabilia, Oeconomicus, Symposium, Apology*, E. C. Marchant trans., Cambridge, MA: Harvard University Press, 1923, pp. 395–397 (IV.13); Briant, *Cyrus to Alexander*, p. 233; Plutarch, "Alcibiades", *Plutarch's Lives*, vol. 4, Bernadotte Perrin trans., Cambridge, MA: Harvard University Press, 1959, p. 69 (24.5).

46/ Xenophon, "Oeconomicus", pp. 399–402 (IV.20–25).

47/ See Maureen Carroll-Spillecke, *ΚΗΠΟΣ: Der antike griechische Garten*, Munich: Deutscher Kunstverlag, 1989; and Robin Osborne, "Classical Greek Gardens: Between Farm and Paradise", *Garden History. Methods and Approaches*. Dumbarton Oaks Colloquium on the history of landscape architecture XIII, J. Dixon Hunt ed., Washington, DC: Dumbarton Oaks Research Library and Collection, 1992, pp. 373–391.

48/ Giesecke, *The Epic City*, pp. xi–78.

49/ Homer, *The Odyssey*, vol. II, A. T. Murray trans., Cambridge, MA: Harvard University Press, 1980, p. 419 (24.222–225).

50/ Arrian, "Anabasis of Alexander", pp. 289–293 (VII.25).

51/ See, for example, Jan N. Bremmer, *The Rise and Fall of the Afterlife*, London: Routledge, 2002, pp. 109–119; and Inge Nielsen, "Types of Gardens", *A Cultural History of Gardens in Antiquity*, K. Gleason ed., London: Bloomsbury, 2013, pp. 56–57.

52/ See Arthur Keaveney, *Lucullus: A Life*, London: Routledge, 1992, pp. 143–165.

53/ See Giesecke, "Outside In", pp. 118–135.

/WILLIAM RUBEL

CULTIVATING EDENIC HARMONY: THE EARLY MODERN BRITISH KITCHEN GARDEN 1600–1830

That Man no Happiness might want,
Which Earth to her first Master could afford;
He did a Garden for him plant,
By the quick hand of his Omnipotent Word.
As the chief Help and Joy of Humane Life,
He gave him the first Gift; first, even before a Wife.[1]

In 1600, Queen Elizabeth I was in the last years of her reign. London was growing rapidly and had just reached a population of a quarter of a million. Shakespeare had written *Romeo and Juliet* but not *Othello*. Modern science and industry were taking on the forms we recognize today. The Spanish Armada had recently been defeated. England was 20 years away from establishing a permanent settlement in North America. For the affluent these were good times, indeed, and although the path wasn't always smooth, England was on its way to becoming the first industrialized nation and a colonial power on a colossal scale.

Then, as now, food played an important social role amongst those fortunate enough to eat for pleasure. Prior to railways and reliable all-weather roads, easily damaged and perishable fruits and vegetables had to be produced locally. In London, high quality produce was grown in nearby gardens whose purpose it was to supply the city's markets. These gardens were centers of agricultural innovation.[2] In the countryside, from small household to large landed estates, it was primarily a garden near the house that provided each household with vegetables, culinary herbs, medicinal plants or 'simples', and fresh fruit.

The tradition of the walled kitchen garden that serves large country houses is of ancient origin. It is this walled garden of the elite, particularly those over half an acre, that is the subject of this essay. It is in these gardens, and especially those that were acres in size and thus backed by a fortune, that the social forces transforming the culture at large were at work pushing the boundaries of horticultural possibilities.

The English walled kitchen gardens of 1600 were, by any measure, already extraordinarily productive and a pleasure to visit. Technical innovations to extend season such as heated walls and heated greenhouses were just beginning to be adopted.[3] Walled kitchen gardens were laid out on principles of symmetry with thought given to how the garden looked when viewed by visitors. In season, as they had been for centuries, the kitchen gardens were both production gardens and lyrical spaces that could be appreciated in their own right [Figure 1]. Just as the small ships of the Elizabethan era presaged the much larger ones that would project English power 200 years later, so the kitchen garden of 1600, productive and beautiful as it was, underwent substantive development in the following two centuries.

London's population continued to grow. It topped one million inhabitants by 1800 and was now the largest city in the world. For the elite, the continued growth of London meant that their country houses were of increasing importance to them as places of retreat. As the English elite became more numerous and wealthier, they invested heavily in their kitchen gardens. All of the factors that were intensifying the economic development of England were applied to their kitchen gardens with this impulse: the explicit dream of recreating an Eden in their own property. It took generations of gardeners, starting with the gardens of 1600, but by the end of the eighteenth century it was always spring, as in Eden, somewhere in the kitchen garden. Production of even the most delicate greens was year-round. The seasons were overcome through horticultural skill.

In modern terms, because of their size and productivity, the large kitchen gardens would be classed as small farms; but in terms of design and conception they were gardens, not walled fields. The kitchen garden was worked with a spade, which is the gardener's tool, and never with the farmer's plow. By the early decades of the eighteenth century, in the more elaborate kitchen gardens the network of paths could be as complex as that of the pleasure garden. Batty Langley

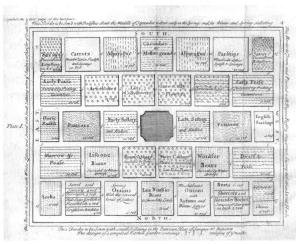

Figure 2/ Battey Langley, Plate I, *Border to be Sown with Small Salleting, New Principles of Gardening*, London, 1728. Courtesy Botanicus Digital Library, Missouri Botanical Garden.

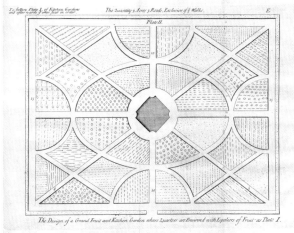

Figure 3/ Battey Langley, *The Design of a Grand Fruit and Kitchen Garden, New Principles of Gardening*, London, 1728. Courtesy Botanicus Digital Library, Missouri Botanical Garden.

(1696–1751), a creative and influential writer on garden design, offers a series of plates for designing kitchen gardens in *New Principles of Gardening* (1728).[4] His published designs are for walled gardens ranging from three-quarters of an acre to three acres. They offer the classic kitchen garden mix of vegetables and espaliered fruit trees. The comparatively prosaic first plate illustrates how different wall aspects were used to favor salad plants during the four seasons and displays the diversity of crops sown; it is in the following plates with their central water features and curved paths and beds that he shows us the level of imagination that many will have brought to the design of their kitchen garden [Figures 2, 3].[5]

Figure 1/ Georg Strauch, *The Nuremburg Residence and Garden of Magdalene Pairin*, 1626–1711, German. Courtesy The J. Paul Getty Museum Open Content Program.

While, on the one hand, the walled gardens were 'production farms', as Langley's more elaborate designs show, gardens were very clearly intended to be strolled through by the gardens' owner. The more complex designs suggest that guests were expected to be impressed by such gardens' similarity to intricately laid-out pleasure gardens. Even simpler kitchen gardens, like those resembling the one illustrated by Georg Strauch in Figure 1, were conceived as more than a utilitarian production facility. This was purposeful. The period commentary on the Biblical Garden of Eden story that explicitly inspired much of the garden literature assumed it to have been a pleasant place to stroll, as well as a place that produced food. The 1835 summation of Early Modern gardening by the great Scottish botanist, gardener, and garden designer John Loudon (1773–1843) confirms that elaborately designed kitchen gardens were a norm by the end of the period discussed in this essay in both general layout and in details.[6] Ironically, Loudon published his monumental work on kitchen gardens just as social forces, including an integrated railway system, broke the isolation of the country-house and hence the need for such elaborate gardens. Also, inevitably, fashions change.

EDENIC BOUNTY

Early British cookbooks are notorious for the paucity of their vegetable recipes. Based on cookbook recipes alone one would never guess at the complexity of the Early Modern kitchen garden. With few exceptions — *Aceteria* (1699) and *Adam's Luxury and Eve's Cookery: Or, the Kitchen-garden Displayed* (1744) being the two most notable — an analysis of recipes does not support the thesis that the Early Modern kitchen garden was exceptional, much less Edenic. Vegetables seem to have been prepared in ways that were thought of as common and thus not worth recording. They were served as salads, boiled and dressed with butter, used as garnishes, and incorporated in soups or other dishes, but for the most part the cooking methods and links between method and vegetable variety were sufficiently understood by period readers to require little notation. Our own cookbook literature has similar lacunae. The basic green salad is rarely included in a cookbook. Parsnip recipes are few and far between despite the piles of parsnips in the grocery. In America, the ever-popular and oft eaten peanut butter and jelly sandwich is impossible to deduce as a popular food from the cookbook literature. Only an analysis involving the sale of peanut butter in groceries would suggest its cultural importance, and then only from other indirect evidence. Similarly, one of the better ways of understanding the importance of vegetables in the Early Modern Britain is through a look at the capital and labor investment put into the kitchen garden.

The best direct association between kitchen and garden is provided by the produce lists organized by season published in period cookbooks such as Hannah Glasse's popular *The Art of Cookery Made Plain and Easy* (1748) and Martha Bradley's *The British Housewife*, that were published around the same time. Both women wrote for a general audience. The following is what Bradley says the British cook should expect to have available from her kitchen garden in January c. 1760 [Figure 4]:

> Greens and Roots in Season in January are Cabbages and Savoys, Carrots, Parsneps, Turneps, Potatoes, Leeks, Onions, Garlick, and Shallots; also Beets and Borecole, and Cellery,

— **Figure 4/** John Parkinson, *Horse Raddish, Goatsbeard and Alliums,* — *Paradisi in Sole Paradisus Terrestris,* London, 1629. Courtesy Botanicus Digital Library, Missouri Botanical Garden.

and Endive: Thefe are in the common Ground. From Hot-Beds there are Lettuces, and young Salleting, as Creffes, Turnep, Radifh, young Mint: And there will be Afperagus upon the Beds made in November; there are alfo Skirrets the white and red, and purple Brocoli, Salsify and Scorzonera, Sorrel, Parsley, Sage, Thyme, and Winter Savory. There are also Coleworts, and Sprouts from the Cabbage and Savoy Stalks; and Finally Cardoons, Spinach, Leaves of the white and red Beets for Soops and other Uses; and Mushrooms.[7]

While Bradley's list of 37 named vegetables is impressive as written, it is certainly not complete. For example, cauliflowers are not mentioned amongst the brassicas, but it is known that around Christmas time, as these began to flower, the practice was to move them into greenhouses.[8]

Demands of the kitchen drove the garden work schedule and pushed agricultural innovation. As an example, this is Steven Switzer (1682–1745), an important early eighteenth-century horticulturalist and writer, on planting cauliflowers: "But as cooks, in the dressing and garniture of their dishes, desire to have as many different kinds of boil'd sallet as they can, for variety sake, this fifth sowing [mid-March collyflower] should not be omitted."[9]

Bradley references greens suitable for delicate salads by way of a few examples of potentially dozens of plants that might be used for salads.[10] She doesn't specify cultivars, but there were multiple cultivars of many plant species available to the gardener, supplied by numerous seedsmen, so readers are likely to have assumed that they might plant multiple cultivars of many of the vegetables listed [Figure 5]. Today's agricultural system favors economies of scale over multiple varieties. But in these bespoke gardens dug by hand, and implicitly managed in consultation with the kitchen to whose door the produce was delivered, there was no advantage to planting all one kind of anything.

The variety of produce, which can fairly be described as Edenic, was further augmented through the way plants were utilized for food. Today, we tend to identify a single point in a vegetable's lifecycle as the edible stage. In contrast, during the Early Modern period many plants were utilized as food through multiple life stages. For example, the radish was used at three points in its lifecycle. Its tiny leaves were picked when still tender, its bulbous root was harvested as we do, and its seedpods were pickled. Thus, while we tend to read 'radish' as a single food, period readers will have understood Bradley to mean three very different foods. Bradley's January list includes the side shoots from cabbages which she calls "sprouts". For cabbages to produce sprouts they will have been left to bolt rather than having been fully harvested in the heading stage. Cabbage sprouts are like small broccoli spears.

In addition to the substantial number of vegetables, Bradley lists 21 varieties of pear and 19 varieties of apple as

Figure 5/ John Parkinson, *Cabbages and Coleworts, Paradisi in Sole Paradisus Terrestris*, London, 1629. Courtesy Botanicus Digital Library, Missouri Botanical Garden.

available fresh in January. Imagine walking into a grocery with 20 varieties each of apple and pear! She also assumes the availability of almonds, medlars, and grapes. The vast variety of vegetables and fruits consumed in the dead of winter will have satisfied the demand of the rich for a table that reflected the bounty of a Terrestrial Paradise. Even by the standards of contemporary urban retail options in wealthy cities like New York or London, cities that draw on an international supply chain, the depth and breadth of specie selection (Edenic variety) and length of season over which fruits and vegetables were grown (Edenic weather) is striking [Figure 6].

Figure 6/ Joachim von Sandrart, *Woman with Fruit*, c. 1644, German. Courtesy The J. Paul Getty Museum Open Content Program.

EDENIC ENGLAND

That England was a special place, and specifically that it had something of the Edenic about it, was a common idea in the seventeenth and eighteenth centuries. Shakespeare articulated this idea in *Richard II* when he referenced England as "This other Eden, demi-paradise."[11] It is notable that several of the writers who were central to the accelerated development of the kitchen garden, amongst them diarist, polymath, and agricultural writer, John Evelyn (1620–1706), describe a history of gardening in which gardens in general and kitchen gardens in particular are the product of post-exile yearning for Eden itself:

> When Almighty [God] had exiled our Fore-fathers out of Paradise, the memorie of that delicious place was not yet so far obliterated, but that their early attempts sufficiently discover'd how unhappy they were to live without a Garden.[12]

To aspire to recreate an Eden within Edenic England fit with a spirit of the time. Also, the idea of being inspired to actual action by a belief in the Terrestrial Paradise had an intellectual respectability then that it no longer has. In the pre-Darwinian, Biblically-based history of human development, it was Adam himself who transferred knowledge acquired in Eden to the post-exile world. John Parkinson (1567–1650), one of modern botany's foundational writers, highlights the God of Genesis as the source of botanical knowledge even as he solidifies the foundation of modern botany. Adam's deep understanding of useful plants was "inspired in him" by God near the moment of creation for the purpose of enabling Adam to name the plants accurately "according to their several natures":[13]

> And although Adam lost the place for his transgression, yet he lost not both the naturall knowledge, nor use of them: but that as God made the whole world, and all the Creatures therein for man, so he may use all things as well of pleasure as of necessity, to be helpes unto him to serve his God.[14]

Central to the innovations that made the kitchen gardens so productive was a focus on observation and empirical science. Parkinson did not defer to ancient texts for information. Rather, he observed plants he grew in a multi-acre botanic garden of his own. He and others looked to the plants around them as the primary source of botanical information.[15] This was part of the Early Modern shift of focus from a backward looking reliance on tradition to the embrace of empirical research. The fact that Parkinson and his peers literally thought that the plants they studied were Eden's diaspora may have hindered their ability to see evolution at work, but this belief also helped strengthen their resolve to understand and control

the plants of the kitchen garden. Parkinson might spend a lifetime studying nature and still only acquire a fraction of what he presumed Adam's knowledge to have been, but, according to his theology, one of the rewards of this study is that it offers each of us a direct path to celebrate and thus serve our Lord [Figure 7]. In this same vein, Frances Bacon (1561–1626) suggests studying both "the book of God's word" and "the Book of God's work".[16] Science and faith were not at odds with each other. Bacon was widely seen in his own time as an inspiration for the founding of the Royal Society, the first modern association composed of the leading scientists of the day. This model was copied throughout the world in the following centuries: the American Academy of Arts and Sciences, founded in 1780, is the American version of the Royal Society.[17] Before Darwin, the idea that in

—— **Figure 7/** John Parkinson, Title Page, *Paradisi in Sole Paradisus* —— *Terrestris*, London, 1629. Courtesy Botanicus Digital Library, Missouri Botanical Garden.

studying plants one reveals the Divine was a generally accepted tenet and will have been, to a greater or lesser degree, depending on personality and nuances of faith, consciously acknowledged by all gardeners.

John Evelyn, a founding member of the Royal Society, in his monumental unfinished work, *Elysium Britannicum or The Royal Gardens* (2001), only fully published a few years ago, is as clear as Parkinson that what we know about gardening began with Adam and that we, through our disciplined efforts, recover that knowledge through practice:[18]

> And though the rest of the World were to them but a Wildernesse, Adam instructed his Posteritie how to handle the Spade so dextrously, that in the process of tyme, men began, with the indulgence of heaven, to recover that by Arte and Industrie, which was before produced to them Spontaneously.[19]

The Garden of Eden offered a model that dovetailed perfectly with what, as a practical matter, was actually needed to create a garden that could provide the variety and quality of vegetables and fruits demanded by high status tables of the time. Believers imaged the Garden of Eden to be a well-watered place within the larger, more arid land of Eden. Just so, kitchen gardens often featured centrally located pools and even small canals to provide water for seedlings and when rain failed. In paintings,

Figure 8/ Boucicaut Master, *Adam and Eve in the Garden of Eden*, c. 1415. Courtesy J. Paul Getty Museum Open Content Program.

prints, and drawings Adam and Eve are often depicted within a walled garden, not unlike the kitchen gardens. The walled space was integral to the concept of the Terrestrial Paradise. The word itself, *paradise*, derives from the Persian term for a walled enclosure [Figure 8]. While a modern secular sense of Paradise may be something like a vacation with no end, Eden was a Paradise in which one did have to do some amount of work. As the King James' translation tells this part of the story, "And the LORD God took the man, and put him into the garden of Eden to dress it and to keep it...." While dressing and keeping a garden is work, it isn't the heavy labor of subsistence field farming; Adam and Eve's time was their own and they did not need to plow. They decided between them what was needful to be done and as long as they did what was required for the general upkeep of the place, then every day was a feast day. In contrast, Northern European field-based farms usually yield only one crop per year. The distinction between garden and farm was central to the Early Modern kitchen garden [Figure 9].

Following the logic of the story, the Early Modern concept of the Garden of Eden was a place of preternatural spring. January or July, there was always something wonderful to eat. This is implicit in the poetic first sentence of John Parkinson's *magnum opus*, *Theatrum Botanicim* (1640): "From a Paradise of pleasant Flowers I am fallen (Andam [sic.] like) to a world of profitable Herbes and plants."[20] Making sure that there was always a spot of spring within the kitchen garden, and thus always herbs and plants to profit from, drove garden innovation.

While we read Parkinson's evocation as poetry — a poetic reference to another poem — it helps to clarify the difference between our time and theirs to always keep in mind that, up until it was superseded by the theory of evolution, Genesis was the primary explanation for the origins of life and thus had a secular reality. Pre-Darwin, even the *Encyclopedia Britannica* included the Garden of Eden as a stop in their otherwise increasingly credible speculative early history of gardening.[21] Similarly, when John Evelyn speaks of the "memorie of that delicious place" in his own poetic introduction to the *Britannicum Elysium*, he is acknowledging within the lovely language a religious belief in Eden as having been a real place. In the year of publication of *On the Origin of Species* a writer for a Canadian scholarly journal refers to descriptions and speculations about Eden with the same tone one would use if Eden were a garden associated with a derelict great house that was undergoing restoration:

> From what we read of the garden of Eden, it seems to have been of a mixed character; and I think there is every reason to suppose, that in a considerable degree it resembled what we now term a kitchen garden and orchard, as we are told as much as that there was everything good for food.[22]

Figure 9/ John Constable, *Ploughing Scene in Suffolk*, 1824–1825, British. Courtesy Yale Center for British Art, Paul Mellon Collection.

THE SEARCH FOR EDEN TRANSFORMED

Perhaps there is no greater demonstration of the literalness with which the Garden of Eden was taken than the fact that European explorers, like Christopher Columbus, believed that finding the Terrestrial Paradise was actually possible. In the case of Columbus himself, he so believed in the existence of a Terrestrial Paradise and was so sure of its character (which included a mild climate) that when he encountered conditions he associated with it off the coast of South America, he was certain it was close by. Washington Irving, in his biography of Christopher Columbus, defends Columbus' sanity by offering extensive period intellectual context for Columbus' belief in the Terrestrial Paradise.[23] As a matter of historical fact — well presented by John Prest — when it finally became clear, after repeated failures, that the Garden of Eden was not going to be found, there was a shift in imagination from discovering the Earthly Paradise to reassembling the Garden in the context of what we now read as a modern science-based enterprise — the encyclopedic botanic garden.[24] This was the intellectual context in which John Parkinson and other Early Modern botanists and gardeners were working. The formative years for developing botanic gardens began in Zurich (1560) and ran for a little more than 100 years.[25]

Kitchen gardens can be thought of as a subset of the botanic garden even though kitchen gardeners were not systematic collectors, classifiers, and users of New World, African, and Asian edible plants. They were interested in what would grow and in what consumers of their produce thought good to eat. This said, within the limitations imposed on the garden by culinary taste and climate, the kitchen gardens tended towards expansive displays of variety of both species and cultivars. Plant lists found in agricultural and gardening books from the singular Elizabethan alchemist, entrepreneur, eccentric, and agriculturalist Sir Hugh Plat (1608) to Loudon (1835) suggest that kitchen gardens were regularly stocked with most European domesticated edible greens along with a few that also grew in the wild.[26] Plant lists included a substantive gathering of New World crops such as the pumpkin, *phaseolus* bean, and Jerusalem artichoke. Period seed catalogues support and even expand upon the gardening-authors' plant lists.[27] If recommended plantings were laid out systematically, as in a botanic garden, they would offer a credible essay on domesticated European edible plants and a foray into New World vegetables.

The gardening books were supported by works on botany, notably those of Gerard (1598, rev. 1633), John Parkinson (1629 and 1640), who has already been mentioned,

Figure 10/ Adriaen van Utrecht, *Still Life: Game, Vegetables, Fruit, Cackatoo*, 1650, Flemish.
Courtesy The J. Paul Getty Museum Open Content Program.

and the English edition of Tournefort (1719).[28] These works offered detailed information on edible plants, both domesticated and wild. They grew out of the tradition of herbals but are works of modern science. The illustrations from Gerard through Tournefort evolve from rough approximations of actual plants to precise engravings that could be used to illustrate a botanical text today. In terms of today's genre, they were more field guide than simple botanical text. In addition to taxonomy and nomenclature they often offered a history of the plant along with at least some medicinal and culinary usage. Kitchen gardening was also supported by an active trade in seeds and nursery plants.[29] In some senses the botany books functioned as an enhancement of the seedmen's lists. The seventeenth- and eighteenth-century seed trade was international, with large quantities of seeds imported to London seed merchants; thus the British garden plant inventory will have shared a core set of plants with Continental gardens, even if culinary usage may have meant different planting ratios and consumption patterns.[30]

EDENIC IDEAS AS A GARDENING MODEL

Eden was thought to be characterized by two distinct features: all the plants of creation and an idyllic climate. The virtually season-free bounty described by Martha Bradley in her cookbook and implied by gardening texts was achieved through purposeful experimentation and the conscious pushing of technical boundaries. In this period the idea that enough is never enough was a key part of a revolutionary spirit whose dynamism we still feel today. By the beginning of the reign of James I and the publication of Plat's *Floraes Paradise* (1608), gardeners had embraced the rapid improvement in garden technique as the norm.[31] By the early eighteenth century, practice had changed so radically that Switzer observes in the 1720s that gardeners from the past would not have known what to do, such had been the advances of the previous decades. By way of example, he mentions extended seasons and improvements in the quality of forced crops.[32] As there were already heated walls in Plat's time, as has been mentioned, his reference is to a sense that the accumulated menu of optimized growing methods amounted to something very different from the gardens of the past. John Ambercrombie, writing as Thomas Mawe in 1767, notes in the preface to his hugely popular work, *Everyman His Own Gardener*, "[W] orks of this kind can never be absolutely complete, owing to the many new discoveries which are every day making in the various parts of Europe."[33]

These gardens were driven to peaks of excellence through what proved to be a fortunate blending of faith, botanical science, horticultural innovation, and the all too human practice of conspicuous consumption. Anyone can feast on a goat, a sheep, an ox, or a hunted animal, and anyone can feast on tender greens in spring and fruits in season, but only in the Terrestrial Paradise could one live off of these botanical delicacies all year long [Figure 10]. The achievement of the Early Modern kitchen garden was that the preternatural spring of a supernatural garden was recreated in the inhospitable English climate.

Loudon, who worked for decades in elite English gardens, frames his monumental *Encyclopedia of Gardening* with two observations on vegetables and luxury. The first is the simple but not widely made observation that there is a level of consumption in which vegetables are a luxury: "The products of the kitchen-garden form important articles of human food for all ranks of society; and furnish the chief luxuries of the tables of the rich, and a main support of the families of the poor."[34] And his second observation, a corollary, though stated as a universal principle applying to rich and poor alike, is that the demand for vegetables as social display drives the huge intellectual, labor, and capital investments made in kitchen gardens by the wealthy: "Every man who does not limit the vegetable parts of his dinner to bread and potatoes, is a patron of gardening, by creating a demand for its production."[35]

The sumptuous display of plates, candles, finely cooked food, and wine on the tables of the rich in the eighteenth century signified high status, but it was the display of home-grown vegetables, salads, and fruit which confirmed this. The year-round appearance of seasonal greens and salads and out of season fresh fruit, either artificially grown or carefully stored until needed, revealed a table supplied by a terrestrial paradise. The people dining at such a table (and those who paid for the garden) will have seen themselves as having at least a peripheral part in the story of Adam and Eve [Figure 11]. It is also noteworthy that the system of table service during this period was one in which all of the many dishes — two dozen was not unusual — were placed on the table at the

Figure 11/ Jean-Siméon Chardin, *Still Life with Peaches, a Silver Goblet, Grapes, and Walnuts*, c. 1759–1760, French. Courtesy The J. Paul Getty Museum Open Content Program.

same time. Such a table setting emphasized the variety of garden produce on offer and thus supported a garden striving for Edenic variety. The cooks didn't necessarily need a lot of any one fruit or vegetable, as serving plates could differ from each other, for example, in the vegetable garnish that accompanied a roast.

THE MECHANICS OF EDENIC GARDENING

The wall-bound garden was a multi-layered space. While the walls were consistent with the iconography of the Terrestrial Paradise, it was the actual practice of kitchen gardening that set the garden land apart from the land that surrounded it in ways that were more profound than simply being a garden within a wall.

The walls had practical purposes. Principally, they kept animals out and created natural microclimates for fruit and vegetable production. Trees and vines set against the south-facing wall received significantly more heat than plants situated elsewhere. These walls also favored early peas. Cooler aspects, like north-facing walls, protected cool weather brassicas and lettuces from early bolting in summer.[36] The wall microclimate was sometimes further regulated through heating the walls. As previously noted, the building of interior flues within the perimeter walls was known from the end of the Elizabethan era; John Loudon thoroughly documents the practice at the end of the heyday of kitchen gardens.[37] Unmentioned in period texts, the high walls increased security, protecting valuable produce from theft.

Walking through a kitchen garden, one was in a space that both was and wasn't situated in the English countryside. Whatever the natural geology of the place, the soil in the kitchen garden was made homogenous down to at least three feet (one meter).[38] From the first detailed descriptions of kitchen gardening by the foundational authors of the gardening book genre, like Nicolas de Bonnefons (active 1650s), the conversion of the top meter or more into loamy topsoil was a key aspect of the gardening method.[39] The soil was initially deeply dug and well worked with manure and other composts; repeated top dressings of aged manure during the gardening year converted ordinary soil into soil of unparalleled fertility. The depth and degree of fertility set the kitchen garden apart from farmland, other parts of the country house garden, or any natural place: "It appears to be generally agreed on by practical men, that there ought to be between two and a half and four feet of good soil over the whole surface of the kitchen-garden. This depth will rarely be found to exist naturally."[40]

It is difficult today to recreate the soils of these gardens because they relied on an effectively unlimited supply of well-aged horse manure. In effect, the land of exile from Eden, which was the land of Cain that produces weeds and thistles that a farmer must fight to get out crops with a good yield, was replaced by the verdant soil of their imagined Eden. The gardener didn't work with the limitations of local geology; he replaced it with an idealized soil. Through the careful study of plant species and attention to each individual plant in the garden, gardening was, compared with farming, a bespoke business. Thus, ailing plants were given tonics in the form of manure teas produced from various barnyard animals, notably pigeon.[41]

Besides the manipulation of the soil, the manipulation of the season was central to the garden's Edenic character and key to its production of fruits and vegetables as signs of luxury. Substantial areas of the kitchen garden were set outside of time and place through systems that altered air and soil temperature. The heat or shelter offered by garden walls is almost a footnote to this aspect of the kitchen garden horticultural practice. The season-altering workhorse was the hot bed. Fermenting manure was piled up into beds approximately four feet high (120 cm) and five feet wide (150 cm). These steaming beds were cased with a few inches of dirt, and then covered with glass to better retain that heat and further augment it by capturing the sun's heat, as well. Hot beds were used extensively during the cold months, but were also used in the summer if there was a cold snap. Glass in the form of frames and cloches was used extensively throughout the garden. There was also often a heated greenhouse. If too much heat was a problem then plants were shaded with mats [Figure 12].

Thus, while the garden as a whole did not have the gentle climate of the imagined Eden, even on snowy winter days there were parts of the garden where it was spring. The gardens were also irrigated. There was often a deep pond or even a canal to bring water inside the garden for easy watering. The tender greens served to guests at country house dinners were always perfect, never wilted by frost or drought, nor were they ever scorched by the sun.

Given the excellent histories found in the herbals *cum* botany texts, period diners would have been well aware that they were eating produce that originated in many parts of the world: cardoons from Spain, broccoli from Italy, melons from France, French beans from the New World, and the occasional wild plant, like Alexander. The plethora of vegetables and fruits available through extended seasons defined the garden as an Edenic space in striking contrast to field agriculture with its single annual crop.

THE ORDERED GARDEN

The kitchen garden was a well-ordered space, both physically and temporally. As has been observed, even at their simplest, the garden designs of Switzer and Langley were garden-like rather than farm-like.[42] Beds were dug and worked by hand, so shape didn't matter. Symmetry was a guiding design principle. Defined pathways could be elaborate, with wider central pathways defining an axis off which straight or curved paths flowed [Figure 13]. As seen today at the *Potager du Rois* just outside the perimeter of Versailles Palace, espalier fruit trees might line sections of bedding. The garden-like appearance provided an aesthetic gloss to a highly technical gardening system.[43] The physical order, and in some cases the hidden complexity of the architectural space, was mirrored by no less concrete, if invisible, multi-dimensioned logistical planning.

The seasons imposed on the garden by England's geography established the overall structure to the work year.

Figure 12/ John Ambercrombie, Frontispiece, *Every Man His Own Gardener*, London, 1767.

A substantial portion of the physical work of the ongoing labor of gardening was the creation of microclimates, even on the scale of individual plants. Glass cloches were an integral part of the gardening system. As the ultimate point of the elite kitchen garden was to grow the maximum number of plants over the most extended season possible to a standard level of perfection, the gardeners had to know their plants so they could develop specie-specific systems for optimizing growth. Kitchen gardening crops weren't left to just grow. Chance was minimized. The scale and complexity of these gardens is hinted at in Ambercrombie's *Every Man His Own Gardener* (1767), a work that offers the most precisely detailed gardening information in a small format work. John Loudon's massive *An Encyclopædia of Gardening* (1835) codified the Early Modern practice at its highest point of development, just as the system began to disappear because changes in dining practice and urbanization altered the demand for kitchen garden produce and cheap transportation made it possible to buy what previously was more practical to grow oneself.

By the early eighteenth century, the scale and complexity of these gardens calls to mind a modern industrial enterprise. Thinking of the garden in terms of Eden, the ordering of the garden was a manifestation of human art modeling the divine, with the master gardener as the regulator of the garden universe. He oversaw the logistics of assembling fresh horse manure, composting it, and then moving around the tons required; deciding what was to be planted and then assembling the seeds and plants required (which included growing plants to save seeds as well as purchasing seeds and plants from diverse commercial sources); planning out the planting schedule for well over 100 vegetable crops; setting up hotbeds; regulating glass; regulating shade screens; managing heated walls and greenhouses; planting and transplanting seedlings to suit planned harvest schedules and kitchen demand; weeding; turning over and manuring beds in preparation for the next planting; managing top dressing and manure teas; watering; tool maintenance; inventory control for tools, glass, and frames; pruning of vines and trees; daily harvests; fine tuning production in consultation with the kitchen; and so much more. On top of what can be planned are the variations of 'normal' imposed over the entire garden by the vagaries of weather. An unseasonable cold snap or heat wave required a system-wide response in order to maintain plant health and production schedules.

Visible to the observer was the activity of a troop of laborers. Invisible but implicit were the budgets, account books, and clocklike scheduling of temporary and permanent labor that got plants to the point of harvest and then to the kitchen for use. As these gardens pushed the limits of what was possible with continuous advances from at least 1600 to the first decades of the nineteenth century, the gardens will have been understood as demonstrations of what human

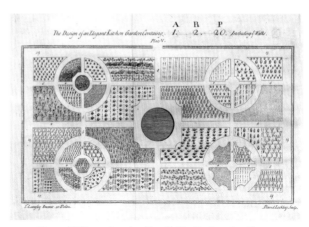

Figure 13/ Battey Langley, Plate V, *The Design of an Elegant Kitchen Garden, New principles of gardening*, London, 1728. Courtesy Botanicus Digital Library, Missouri Botanical Garden.

ingenuity can achieve through the study of nature and the application of capital and focused labor.

The fertility of Early Modern British kitchen gardens was, even by our contemporary standards, awe-inspiring. Though competition between owners of these gardens must have played a role in the more aggressive gardening practices — such as planting peas in succession beginning in late fall in the hopes of having the first spring peas — in its totality, the gardening effort was driven by visions that went beyond merely supplying the high status dining table.[44] These gardens exemplified the emerging culture that underpinned the Industrial Revolution: gardens are an early example of the effectiveness of empirical engineering and a demonstration of the radical improvements achievable through the accretion of small changes.

When judged by what they produced, the gardens were idealized spaces, actual Edenic places clawed back from an unforgiving earth through the single-minded application of knowledge and a belief in the possibility of creating, or recreating, a degree of perfection here on earth. But the gardens were situated within a modern state. There are other ways to look at the gardens, one that offers a less romanticized utopian vision.

THE GARDEN IN THIS WORLD

We cannot know what the first generations of people in the Fertile Crescent thought when it was widely understood that there was no turning back, that as a group they were now as domesticated by their bread grains, fig trees, and animals as their crops and animals were domesticated by them. By the time the Genesis stories were written down, thousands of years had passed since hunting and gathering had given way to farming. The story is wary of agriculture and its consequences. As an example of its negative attitude towards farming (as opposed to gardening), it offers Cain as the first farmer — but he was also the first murderer, the first to lie to his Lord, and the founder of Enoch, the first city (Genesis 4:17). In Jewish tradition, he was something of a warlord, a subjugator. The Early Modern gardening and botany texts don't engage with Cain. Even though the wealth of the men who paid for the gardens was based on the kinds of things Cain did, like farm large tracts of land, get people to work for him, and build urban spaces, the part of the Genesis story they identified with was a romanticized garden and Adam, the first gardener, after the Lord himself.

The story of Adam and Eve and the Garden of Eden, their easy-going ways within that Garden, and their subsequent fall from grace and exile to a hard scrabble land that more easily yielded weeds than food, offers a dramatic literary interpretation of the shift from hunting and gathering on common ground to farming a fixed plot of land [Figure 14]. It is a lovely story that the plants selected for the pleasure, kitchen, and simples gardens were Eden's diaspora, remnants of a natural world that existed before there were people, a world in harmony with itself, untouched except by the Creator. In that myth, which was the seventeenth- and eighteenth-century story as told in botany texts and gardening books, the study of plants brings us close to the greatest miracle of all, the creation of life on earth.

But the archaeobotanical evidence from Neolithic farming sites supports a different narrative.[45] The narrative supported by science is that the flowers of our gardens, the greens on our table, and the plants of the pharmacopeia

rest on a foundation of the disorder humans brought to the natural world through disruptive farming practices. A substantial number of our garden plants are descended from tiller weeds, the plethora of plants that were favored by Neolithic agriculture's annual tilling. It isn't from Eden that we get the wild strawberry, cress, cabbage, sorrel, mallow, violas, cornflower, and so many other familiar garden plants. Instead they are the inheritance of the Genesis Lord's curse that Adam and his descendants would henceforth have to live by farming, made especially onerous because a cursed soil will throw up thorns and thistles to hinder the plow and contaminate their grain harvests.

We don't know which thorny and thistly plants the Genesis poets were thinking of as they penned the Lord's curse, as there are so many prickly tiller weed candidates, but the story's emphasis on weediness and staple grain production (barley and wheat are the implied bread grains) skews the narrative away from the fact that so many of those weeds, including prickly ones, were useful food plants. As examples, the edible *Lactuca serriola* is the closest relative to the domesticated lettuce, *L. sativa L.*, and the most intractable of the thistles, one that could be imaged as being one with soil itself, *Cirsium arvens*, is an indomitable plant that sends out rhizomes meters deep and wide and thus welcomes being broken up and spread by the plow.[46] Even so, this difficult plant produces beautiful flowers and its several parts are edible. An Edenic plenty follows the plow and human-disturbed soils.

The break from hunting and gathering to farming was never as cut and dried as it seems today when viewed by urbanites with industrial agriculture as their reference point. Patience Grey's classic, *Honey from a Weed*, records late twentieth-century gathering practices in Southern Europe.[47] Gathering of plants outside the strictures of agriculture's monocultures was a common practice of the European poor during the Early Modern period. Today, South-East Asia, and in particular Isaan province, Thailand, still has a rich reservoir of agricultural practices illustrating the blurred lines between farming and gathering, including the tending of plants in the wild implied in the Genesis story.[48] The kitchen garden literally placed a wall between the domesticated and the wild. It made the garden private and thus imposed a hierarchy of access to the greens and fruits within its walls, whereas the practice of gathering wild greens from harvested fields, wasteland, and common land was inherently egalitarian.

Period writers on botany and gardening didn't understand the causal relationship between ancient farming practices and the wild progenitors of so many of their garden plants. However, the literature recognizes the existence of wild plants beyond the garden walls and sometimes suggests collecting in the wild. Nicolas de Bonnefons recommends collecting wild sorrel and Langley recommends gathering

Figure 15/ *Golding Constable's Kitchen Garden*, John Constable, c. 1815, British. Courtesy The Wolsey Art Gallery, Christchurch Mansion, Ipswich Museums.

Brooklime (*Veronica beccabunga*).[49] But what the literature's authors did not do is explicitly recognize the social and egalitarian activity of gathering greens in the wild. This is a practice we can assume they witnessed on their country walks, and that all those involved with kitchen gardens, even as owners, should have had at least some limited experience with recreational gathering of wild foods, like wild strawberries and field mushrooms.

A PRIVATE PARADISE

It is ironic that period gardening writers had the story of the kitchen garden all wrong. Their kitchen gardens weren't the progeny of the Garden of Eden but rather of the troubled history that began with Cain, a history with which they did not identify. As they liked to see it, they dropped into the garden with Adam, the gardener of common land, not as overseers of a labor force that worked for them on land they owned [Figure 15].

Jean-Jacques Rousseau (1712–1778) was one of the Enlightenment philosophers asking questions about how

humans got to where we are, what binds us together, and by what rights or laws, divine or human, just or unjust, are societies bound. Rousseau performed a thought experiment in which he imagined the beginning—the time before walls when all of the earth was a commons—and then asked the question, what was the lost nail that cost us our rights and freedoms?

> The first man who, after enclosing a plot of land, saw fit to say: 'This is mine', and found people who were simple enough to believe him, was the true founder of civil society. How many crimes, wars, murders, sufferings and horrors mankind would have been spared if someone had torn up the stakes or filled up the moat and cried to his fellows: 'Don't listen to this impostor; you are lost if you forget that the earth belongs to no one, and that its fruits are for all!'[50]

Rousseau was not original in his thinking, only perhaps more dramatic than some earlier writers. Amongst the ancients, Ovid (43 BCE–17/18 CE), among others, wrote about a Golden Age where land was common. To Evelyn, and the other seventeenth- and eighteenth-century authors of kitchen gardening books, the idea that the world had once belonged to all but now belonged to the rich who used it unfairly was familiar from Classical authors. At times during this period it was also the stuff of current events. The ferment of the English Civil War (1642–1651) engendered a great deal of talk about land use and land distribution. The writings of Gerrard Winstanley (1609–1676), best known as leader of the Diggers who briefly occupied common land with the purpose of growing food on it, were widely distributed in the 1640s and 1650s. They remain important documents in British political thought. In Winstanley's words, "The land which had been as common to all as the air or the sunlight was now marked out with the boundary lines of the wary surveyor."[51] Similarly, the walled-in and unpicked apples that poet Robert Frost would later celebrate in *Unharvested* are fruits imprisoned by property rights. Only the scent could be taken without unlawful trespass: "So smelling their sweetness would be no theft."[52]

While the owners could stroll their own kitchen gardens to graze on strawberries, peas, and tree fruits whenever they liked, the gardens were not open to the surrounding countryside. The Lord provides bounty for all, but the master of the Kitchen Garden provides bounty only for his own use.

GARDENING IN THE INDUSTRIAL REVOLUTION

The energy of the Industrial Revolution is in the Early Modern kitchen garden. It was a garden grounded in a myth handed down through the centuries, but it was itself destructive of tradition. Little by little the science, empirically-based improvements in gardening practice, and the logistical accomplishments of the garden merged into the larger skill set that created the Industrial Revolution. Industrialization destroyed the culture and eating habits that underpinned the gardens.

By the end of the eighteenth century, large aggressively managed gardens were always active. Even in winter these gardens were perceived as a scene for viewing. Thomas Whately, in a work on garden design, explicitly suggests siting the kitchen garden near the greenhouses in part because the work of the garden, even or perhaps especially in winter, affords a spectacle:

> The walk may also lead to the stoves, where the climate and the plants are always the same: and the kitchen garden should not be far off; for that is never quite destitute of produce, and

always an active scene; the appearance of business is alone engaging; and the occupations there are an earnest of the happier seasons to which they are preparative.[53]

As the head gardeners pushed back production dates and improved quality, the laboring core of the garden workers toiled in any weather it was possible to be out in. From the workers' perspective, advances in season-busting horticultural practice meant more work in the cold and wet. From their perspective, toil under a dull, wet winter sky was the inverse of the "happier seasons".

We are today familiar with the disparity between lovely things we can buy and the unlovely conditions of the people who made them for us. Then as now, the skills of the people who created things of value, in this case fabulous gardens, may not have been fully appreciated. There is evidence that the social status of the workers who achieved the horticultural successes was not high. Switzer suggests that the general gardener was on a par with "dog-boys" who worked in a "circle of labour and toil".[54] His contemporary, Batty Langley, implies that they were paid less than house servants: "I cannot but take the Liberty to say, that a good Gardener deserves a much greater Respect and Encouragement than that of Stewards, Butlers, &c. who oftentimes undeservedly possess a much larger Share thereof."[55]

While the Edenic vision remains implicit in the 1760s, the Industrial Revolution is truly afoot, and elite taste is democratizing; the spirit of the garden is becoming more overtly material, coarse, and technical. *Everyman His Own Gardener*, a masterpiece of the now common genre of the do-it-yourself manual, remained in print for more than 100 years. Its focus is personal achievement. The work is stripped of broader perspectives beyond the goal of having the most productive garden possible: "As it is the ambition of most gardeners to excel each other in the production of early cucumbers, all necessary preparations would be made this month [January] if not done before."[56]

Phillip Miller's reference to the entertainment value of so many workers beetling around the winter garden suggests both a pool of cheap labor and the open acceptance of ogling at, and even openly envying, purposefully displayed signs of wealth. In the culture of Jane Austen's early nineteenth-century novels, everyone knows exactly how much money everyone else has. At the same time as the garden developed the potentialities of the plants within, the men who worked the garden began their apprenticeships as teenagers with seven years servitude that some represented as "hard labour".[57] Alienation of labor is the hallmark of the post-Edenic fall. The workers labored rather than tended, and unlike Adam and Eve, they were not in control of their time. The plants and the enterprise itself were valued more highly than the labor that fostering these entailed.

GARDENER AS POTENTATE: POTENTATE AS GARDENER

The greatest of these kitchen gardens, the ones that most pushed the boundaries of the conceivable, were made possible by owners who had access to fortunes. Great or small, the well regulated kitchen garden seemed to offer lessons for life and even an analogue for what powerful men did in the exercise of their power. The good gardener is the good potentate; conversely the bad potentate is a bad gardener. Two of the foundational writers, John Evelyn and Switzer, cite the use of the garden as a source of wisdom in the ancient world.[58] Even to a great lord there was a recognized equality between a state, even an empire, and a garden.

> And it is of such Great Souls we have it recorded; That after they had perform'd the Noblest Exploits for the Publick, they sometimes changed their Scepters for the spade, and their Purple for they Gardiner's Apron. And of those, some [...] were Emperors, Kings, Consuls, Dictators, and Wise Statesmen; who amidst the most important Affairs, have quitted all their Pomp and Dignity in Exchange of this Learned Pleasure.[59]

Examples from the ancient world may well have enhanced many garden owners' sense of the value of gardening as a source of wisdom they could apply to the world at large. We can less speculatively look to Shakespeare for insights into the Early Modern acceptance of the idea of King as Gardener.

In *Richard II*, Richard's queen hears from a gardener whom she addresses as "Adam" that Bolingbroke had just murdered two of her close friends and captured her husband. Adam is the only character in the play to offer a comprehensive theory for Richard's fall. The critique this gardener-everyman offers of the failed king's rule can be understood as a common wisdom shared by the play's audience. The wisdom is based on the logic of Genesis: Adam, the first gardener after the Lord himself, derived all the experience he needed to succeed in the post-exile world from having tended the Garden of Eden. Here is what Shakespeare's Adam says:

> They are [dead]; and Bolingbroke
> Hath seized the wasteful king. O, what pity is it
> That he had not so trimm'd and dress'd his land
> As we this garden! We at time of year
> Do wound the bark, the skin of our fruit-trees,
> Lest, being over-proud in sap and blood,
> With too much riches it confound itself:

> Had he done so to great and growing men,
> They might have lived to bear and he to taste
> Their fruits of duty: superfluous branches
> We lop away, that bearing boughs may live:
> Had he done so, himself had borne the crown,
> Which waste of idle hours hath quite thrown down.[60]

On 2 May 1607, King James I, an admirer of Shakespeare, in an example of life imitating art, brings the Good Gardener as the guiding principle behind good governance to the center of an important speech to Parliament. James, who had recently ascended to the English crown following the death of Elizabeth I, was James I, King of England and James VI, King of Scotland. He wanted Parliament to unite the two sovereign states under the English crown, but Parliament wasn't enthusiastic. The classic image of the farmer in this period was a man broadcasting grains while striding over a field. This is the image James draws upon to open his talk: "It is the chiefest Comfort of the Sower, to sow his Seed in good Ground where there is Hope it may yield Fruit."[61]

The farmer must hope, because even the best prepared ground yields a poor crop if the rains come at the wrong time, or don't come at all. Flinging commands like seeds and expecting the best works only for autocrats surrounded by yes-men. In this case, the King was addressing a parliament filled with men whose hearts offered stony rather than good ground for his proposals. When you have to work with people, then, it is best to turn to gardening for guidance and this is what the King does. He turns to the wisdom offered by Shakespeare's common man, Adam, that the precepts of gardening are a more sure way for a King to achieve results. James I offers his Parliament compromise in these words: "I shall do but the Part of a good Gardener, to prune, to dress, and take away the Weeds and Brambles, that may hinder the springing and budding of this good Plant."[62]

Whether the kitchen garden be great or small, the lessons it teaches are lessons about life — don't put off, do what is needful today and reap the benefit tomorrow, pay attention to details, work with people as if they were plants, study them and listen to what they have to say, responding to each according to their nature and immediate need. The great gardens offered their affluent owners the model of a complex system of people and things operating according to a plan that consistently produced multiple products literally fit for a king's table. Even if the owner didn't actively participate in the management of the garden the agents he hired did.

The Garden of Eden story is a tricky analogy for one's garden, which is so obviously a human contrivance and not a natural God-given place. Even more crucially, these aristocratic gardeners are clearly not tending the garden themselves. But if the aspiration to recreate Eden didn't inspire owners to redistribute their land, it did offer them a justification to underpin the investment in the garden and its agricultural goals.

MODERN EDEN

The Lord himself was the first gardener, as many of the early gardening books point out. It is easy to imagine the mid-eighteenth-century owner of a large capital and labor intensive kitchen garden walking its paths with lordly pride while at the same time wishing that the rest of his enterprises could be managed so smoothly — a very different attitude from walking with the contentment of Adam, the actual gardener, for craft well done.

Great cultural achievements are usually judged by their results, not by an over-critical analysis of their creators or their motivations. These gardens are difficult to recreate. In a sense, they are a lost performance art. They achieved their goals with the same level of visual elegance and technical achievement that period artists and artisans brought to their works. Inspired by a poem, they were poems in a landscape animated by the intellectual and technical ferment that were the last centuries of the Early Modern.

In the late sixteenth and seventeenth centuries, the kitchen gardens were the focus of men like Plat, Parkinson, and Evelyn, who were recognized as leading scientists and innovative thinkers; in the first decades of the eighteenth century, garden development shifted to the influence of men like Swizter and Langley who had good foundations in botany and gardening as well as entrepreneurial drive; later in the eighteenth century, and into the nineteenth, gardening experts like Ambercrombie and Loudon, reflecting changes taking place in the culture at large, brought a focus on technology and technique to ever larger audiences in a language of how-to books that we easily recognize today. But such changes also brought the steam engine, the train, paved roads, urbanization, and a different way of eating, and thus the end of the garden as it had been, though it continued in simpler form well into the twentieth century.

The great kitchen gardens at the dawn of the reign of Victoria were heirs to the vision of Eden recreated through science, technology, and the huge dreams and energy of that era. As we are not gods and cannot will a garden to appear out of thin air, these may have been as close as we are likely ever to come to recreating Edenic bounty in the context of a sustainable ecology. Relying on local resources, notably locally produced fertilizers, they offered a continuous supply of perfect garden produce grown with skills that overcame problems of geography and climate to furnish tables set for the era's most discerning diners — and all grown just outside the kitchen door, even when snow lay heavy on the land.

But, importantly, these gardens and their bounty relied also on the uncelebrated toil of many — the children of Adam and of Cain. A serpent resides in every Eden.

NOTES

I would like to thank Malcolm Thick for sharing with me his library of early gardening books, for reading this essay, and for the generosity with which he shared his knowledge of Early Modern British kitchen and market gardens, and Jane Levi, whose critical and editorial suggestions through multiple drafts were always insightful.

1/ Evelyn, John, *Kalendarium*, London: George Huddleston, 1699, p. B4. The poem is written by Abraham Cowely.

2/ Thick, Malcolm, *Sir Hugh Plat, The Search for Useful Knowledge in Early Modern London*, Totness: Prospect Books, 2010.

3/ Thick, Malcolm, *The Neat House Gardens: Early Market Gardening Around London*, Totness: Prospect Books, 1998.

4/ Langley, Batty, *New Principles of Gardening*, London: A. Bettesworth and J. Battley, 1828.

5/ Langley, *New Principles*. Walled kitchen gardens shared characteristics with many commercial market gardens of the time — they also had neatly arranged beds and plots and narrow beds under walls to catch the sun. Samuel Pepys describes a visit to one such garden and his pleasure at walking between the neat rows of vegetables.

6/ Loudon, J. C., *An Encyclopædia of Gardening*, London: Longman, Rees, Orme, Brown, Green, and Longman, 1835.

7/ Bradley, Martha, *The British Housewife*, London: S. Crowder & H. Woodgate, 1746, p. 18.

8/ Switzer, Stephen, *The Practical Kitchen Gardiner*, London: Thomas Woodward, 1727, p. 123.

9/ Switzer, *The Practical Kitchen Gardiner*.

10/ Evelyn, John, *Acetaria. A Discourse of Sallets*, London: B. Tooke, 1699. *Acetaria*, with its scores of salad greens and flowers should probably be read as at least in part a experimental work intended to inspire gardeners and cooks to delve more deeply into salads. None of the plants suggested for salads are particularly exotic. Authors who mention small salletings, like Martha Bradley, seem to assume that personal preference will determine the actual choices.

11/ Shakespeare, William, *The Complete Works of William Shakespeare, Richard II*, vol. x, Henry Hudson ed., Boston: Ginn & Company, 1900, Act 2, Scene 1, p. 163.

12/ Evelyn, John, *Elysium Britannicum or the Royal Gardens*, Philadelphia: University of Pennsylvania, 2001, p. 29.

13/ Parkinson, John, *Paradisi in Sole, Paradisus*, London: H. Lownes and R. Young, 1629, epistle.

14/ Parkinson, *Paradisi in Sole*, epistle.

15/ Prest, John M., *The Garden of Eden, The Botanic Garden and the Re-Creation of Paradise*, New Haven: Yale University Press, 1981, p. 39.

16/ Bacon, Francis, *The Works of Francis Bacon, Baron of Verulam, Viscount St Alban, and Lord High Chancellor of England, in Five Volumes*, Printed for A. Millar in the Strand, 1765.

17/ Magner, L. N., *A History of the Life Sciences*, third ed., New York: M. Dekker, 2002, p. 120.

18/ Evelyn, *Elysium Britannicum*.

19/ Evelyn, *Elysium Britannicum*, p. 29

20/ Parkinson, *Theatrum Botanicum*, p. 1.

21/ *Encyclopaedia Britannica*, vol. 9, Edinburgh: Archibald Constable, 1823, p. 381.

22/ Hamilton, William, "Kitchen Gardens for Farmers", *The Canadian Agriculturist, and Journal of the Board of Agriculture of Upper Canada*, vol. 11, no. 1, 1859, p. 18.

23/ Irving, Washington, *History of the Life and Voyages of Christopher Columbus*, Philadelphia: Lea & Blanchard, for G. W. Gorton, 1841, p. 341.

24/ Prest, *The Garden of Eden*.

25/ Hill, Arthur, "The History and Functions of Botanic Gardens", *Annals of the Missouri Botanical Garden*, vol. 2, no. 1–2, 1915, p. 192.

26/ See in particular Langley, *New Principles*, and Loudon, *An Encyclopædia of Gardening*.

27/ Harvey, John, and Norman Jones Fletcher, *Early Gardening Catalogues*, Chichester: Phillimore, 1972.

28/ de Tournefort, Joseph Pitton, *The Compleat Herbal, Vol. I & 2*, London: R. Bonwicke, 1719.

29/ Harvey, *Early Gardening Catalogues*.

30/ Thirsk, Joan, *The Agrarian History of England and Wales*, vol. 5, Cambridge: Cambridge University Press, 1985, p. 527.

31/ Platt, Sir Hugh, *Floraes Paradise*, London: W. Leake, 1608.

32/ Switzer, *The Practical Kitchen Gardiner*, p. iii.

33/ Abercrombie, John, and Thomas Mawe, *Every Man His Own Gardener*, London: W. Griffin, 1767, n.p. Preface.

34/ Loudon, *An Encyclopædia of Gardening*, p. 732.

35/ Loudon, *An Encyclopædia of Gardening*, p. 732.

36/ Langley, *New Principles*, Plate I, 1828.

37/ Thick, *Sir Hugh Plat*, p. 50; Loudon, *An Encyclopædia of Gardening*, p. 732.

38/ This was also a feature of commercial London gardens at the time. It had the added advantage that crop rotations were not needed: Leonard Meager remarks that "their grounds are in a manner made new and fresh once in every two or three years, by dung and soil, and good trenching; so that their ground is as it were new and fresh for the same king of crops every year." Leonard Meager, *The English Gardener*, London, 1670, p. 165.

39/ de Bonnefons, Nicolas, *The French Gardiner, Instructing How to Cultivate All Sorts of Fruit Trees and Herbs for the Garden*, John Evelyn trans., London: J. C. for John Crooke, 1658.

40/ Loudon, *An Encyclopædia of Gardening*, p. 725. Loudon's work is full of technical details. The explanation of hot flues is just one of innumerable examples that could be cited.

41/ de Bonnefons, *The French Gardiner*.

42/ Langley, *New Principles*.

43/ Loudon, *An Encyclopædia of Gardening*, p. 732.

44/ Abercrombie, *Every Man His Own Gardener*, p. 360.

45/ See for example A. Kreuz, E. Marinova, E. Schafer, and J. Wiethold, "A Comparison of Early Neolithic Crop and Weed Assemblages from *Linearbankeramik* and Bulgarian Neoltithic Cultures, Differences and Similarities", *Vegetation History and Archeobotany*, v. 14, 2005, pp. 237–258; and C. Brombacher, "Archaeobotanical Investigations

of Late Neolithic Lakeshore Settlements Lake Biel, Switzerland", *Vegetable History Archeobotany*, vol. 6, 1997, pp. 167–186.

46/ Brombacher, "Archaeobotanical Investigations"; Kreuz, "A Comparison".

47/ Gray, Patience, *Honey from a Weed*, London: Prospect Books, 1986.

48/ Wester, Lyndon A., and Dina Chuensanguansat, "Adoption and Abandonment of Southeast Asian Food Plants", *Journal of Home & Consumer Horticulture*, vol. 1, no. 2–3, 1994.

49/ de Bonnefons, *The French Gardiner*; Langley, *New Principles*, part vii, p. 15.

50/ Rousseau, Jean-Jacques, *Discourse on the Origin of Inequality*, London: Penguin, 1984, p. 42.

51/ Ovid, *Metamorphoses, A New Verse Translation*, David Raeburn trans., London: Penguin, 2004, p. 10.

52/ Frost, Robert, *A Further Range*, London: Jonathan Cape, 1937, p. 58.

53/ Whately, Thomas, *Observations on Modern Gardening*, London: T. Payne, 1770, p. 255.

54/ Switzer, *The Practical Kitchen Gardiner*, pp. vi, iv.

55/ Langley, *New Principles*, p. 102.

56/ Abercrombie, *Every Man His Own Gardener*, p. 1.

57/ Hitt, Thomas, *A Treatise of Fruit-Trees*, London: T. Osborne, 1757, p. 140.

58/ Switzer, Stephen, *The Nobleman, Gentleman, and Gardener's Recreation*, London: B. Barker, 1715, p. 28.

59/ Evelyn, *Acetaria*, preface A7.

60/ Shakespeare, William, *The complete Works of William Shakespeare, Richard II*, vol. x, Henry Hudson ed., Boston: Ginn & Company, 1900, Act 3, Scene 4, p. 268.

61/ *Parliamentary History of England*, vol. 5, p. 207.

62/ *Parliamentary History of England*, vol. 5, p. 207.

114 /ANASTASIA DAY

THE INDUSTRIAL GARDENER: WORLD WAR II VICTORY GARDENERS AND THE FACTORY PARADIGM

In 1943, close to 21 million families planted seven million acres of victory gardens across the United States.[1] *Life* magazine reported with incredulity that "Every unprotected piece of ground was being dug up for victory gardens: in Boston's Copley Square and in the Portland (Ore.) Zoo, in Chicago's Arlington Racetrack and in the Wellesley College campus, in New York's Schwab estate and in the Naval Air Station at Olathe, Kan." The phenomenon cut across class, race, and other demographic axes, reaching the White House and public housing alike: "Everybody was busy tucking seeds to bed in the moist spring soil — movie stars, soldiers, admirals, airline hostesses, nuns and prisoners", the reporter noted.[2] A National Opinion Research Center poll reported that 61 percent of Americans planned to have a victory garden in 1944 — more than three-fifths of the population.[3] Over the course of the war, those Americans and others planted more than 50 million registered victory gardens.[4] Another NORC poll in 1944 found that 95 percent of Americans believed that victory gardens "helped increase the food supply last year", and that 77 percent of Americans believed they "helped a lot".[5] The facts confirm popular sentiment: in the previous year, victory gardens produced 42 percent of the total fresh produce for Americans.[6]

Despite its undisputed popularity and success, the Victory Garden Campaign is widely misunderstood, misremembered, and misconstrued. Victory gardening is often eulogized as a model for contemporary grassroots, organic, urban gardening, and other environmental movements; the campaign serves as namesake for enterprises ranging from actual gardening endeavors to hipster goat milk confectionary shops in New York City.[7] However, the Victory Garden Campaign was not a local food movement, an environmental crusade, a revival of folk knowledge of the earth, mere wartime boosterism, nor an occupation for housewives alone. It was the logical extension, rather than the antithesis, of the American narrative of progress. Not content with only industrializing and maximizing the corporate resources of the nation, America sought to rationalize home production of war materials as well. One war material that almost any American could home-manufacture was food [Figure 1]. Production was the primary function of victory gardens, fueled by science and industrial technology. The material impact of victory gardening was not merely a surprisingly impressive side effect of a morale-raising effort, but the very *raison d'être* of the Victory Garden Campaign.

MANUFACTURING WITH NATURE

A pervasive metaphor among the deluge of promotional materials for victory gardens is the factory: a model of efficient production of the most materials with the least waste possible. Far from a 'back-to-the-land' reversion to pre-technological practices necessitated by wartime privations, victory gardens constituted an intrusion of twentieth-century technological

Figure 1/ "War Gardens for Victory", 1942, color lithograph. Private Collection, © Galerie Bilderwelt, The Bridgeman Art Library.

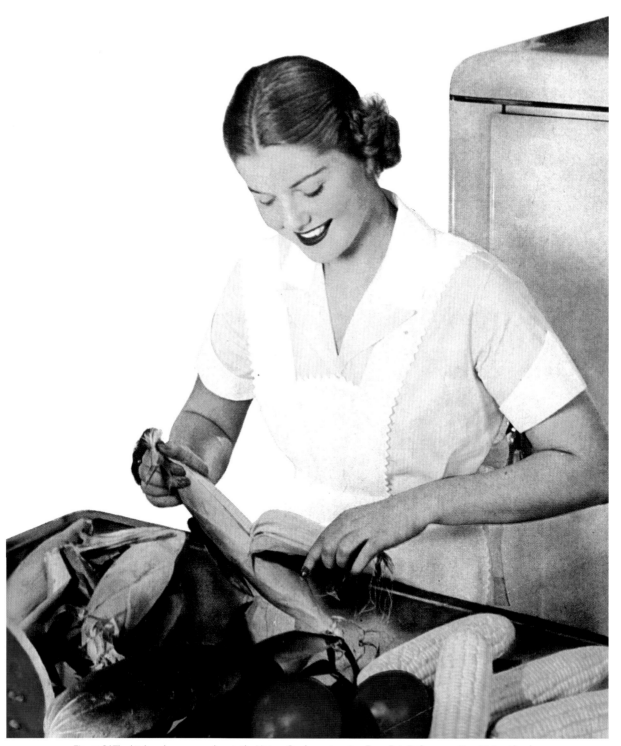

Figure 2/ The kitchen, her proper place in the Victory Garden enterprise. From E. L. D. Seymour, *Your Victory Garden*, Chicago: J. G. Ferguson, 1942, inside back cover.

advances in food production into the private sphere of the American citizen's backyard. The adoption of modern, "mechanistic" mindsets, as well as the application of scientific management (called Taylorism after its founding father, Frederick W. Taylor) and an industrial production ethos, shaped everything from physical plot design and cultivation practices, to standards of success as a gardener.[8] The factory analogy was particularly instantiated in the selection, treatment, and instruction of victory garden laborers. As a result, the mythic independence of the yeoman farmer was supplanted by dependence on scientific authority for instruction. Likewise, rationalized divisions of labor reinforced gender norms of home and workplace, and 'recreational' gardening turned into yet another war job for these garden workers.

A 1942 booklet entitled *Your Victory Garden* brings to the forefront this forgotten, or rather, unstudied, aspect of the Victory Garden Campaign. "Growing plants in a garden — any kind of plants — is actually a manufacturing process in which you and Nature go into partnership", the author wrote; "Like any manufacturing enterprise it calls for a 'factory', raw materials, tools and equipment, labor, and intelligent management; also an investment of some money, but more careful attention and continuing interest."[9] Rather than organic growth there was "manufacturing"; rather than soil, sunshine, and rain there were "raw materials". The goal of the endeavor was not sustenance, recreation, health, or house chores, though it might have entailed all those things, but rather a calculated "investment" in a business-like "enterprise". In terms of work, "labor and intelligent management" supplanted the homeowner and gardener. This same version of the victory garden conformed to standard gender roles of the time, within both house and factory; an illustration of an aproned woman shucking corn in a spotless kitchen is complemented by a photograph of "a typical home gardener surveying *his* handiwork", complete with masculine pipe [Figures 2, 3].[10] The message was clear: in order to be serious about production, a modern industrial mentality is necessary, and everyone needs to find his or her proper place in the "master machine" of the victory garden factory.[11]

World War II was a war of production, most of it American. Washington knew by 1938 "that any American involvement in another European war would be based on the strength of the United States economy and its potential for the production of military equipment, munitions, and logistical services" — well before the Lend-Lease Act of early 1941 cemented the primarily economic basis of America's involvement.[12] As Europe lost factories and farmland to the ravages of war, America produced enough goods to support the Allied forces in Europe, Asia, and the Pacific, as well as her own troops. In so doing, the American economy not only fully recovered from the Great Depression, but reached globally unprecedented heights: "The federal budget, about $9 billion

in 1939, rose to $100 billion in 1945. Under that impact, the gross national product, $91 billion in 1939, reached $166 billion in 1945. During the war, 17 million new jobs were created, the index of industrial production rose 96 percent, of transportation services 109 percent."[13] Over half of the total world manufacturing production during World War II occurred in the United States.[14] While the conversion of car factories to airplane assembly sites perhaps had a more dramatic effect on the popular mind, food was a vital component of this war by economic output. President Roosevelt even asserted in a speech to congress, "Food is as important as any other weapon in the successful prosecution of the war."[15] The Victory Garden Campaign was, in turn, a vital component of the nationwide drive for maximum food production.

The Victory Garden Campaign formally began on 19 December 1941 at a conference called by Secretary of Agriculture Claude R. Wickard in Washington D.C., less than two weeks after the attack on Pearl Harbor. The War Food Administration ultimately spearheaded the victory garden program, but a wide variety of government agencies were

Figure 3/ A typical victory gardener surveying his handiwork. From E. L. D. Seymour, *Your Victory Garden,* Chicago: J. G. Ferguson, 1942, back cover.

involved: the United States Department of Agriculture (USDA), the Cooperative Agricultural Colleges Extension Service, the Office of Civilian Defense and, inevitably, the Office of War Information. From this base, a large, bulky superstructure was quickly erected to organize from the national level down to town and county victory garden committees. In the private sector, the National Victory Garden Institute was at the forefront of the Victory Garden Campaign. The Institute focused on fostering the alliance between industry and government through shared war efforts, with a board full of figures representing the largest corporations in America, rather than experts in gardening and public policy.[16] In addition to the agencies and organizations already mentioned, countless private citizens and professional gardeners took it upon themselves to publish instructions for victory gardening.

AMERICAN GARDENING EXPERIENCE (OR LACK THEREOF), 1940

In the World War II battle of production, both industry and victory garden organizers struggled with the all-important 'labor problem'. While this phrase has often been used as a euphemism for unions and strikes, in World War II, patriotism, necessity, and new prosperity worked together to decrease striking; the dominant meaning of the phrase became management of under-qualified labor for maximum production.[17] As the male populace was drafted in increasing numbers and the demand for goods grew ever higher, industry had to adapt to colossal workforces of unskilled labor by phasing out the remaining skilled artisans.[18] The gardening movement had few artisans at the start, but found it similarly profitable to simply train skilled and unskilled alike rather than tailor materials and programming to these two different demographics. The need to train unskilled labor, while not seeking to turn it into skilled labor — which would require a large investment of time and resources — resulted in a middle ground of what Frederick Taylor referred to as "the ready-made, competent man.... It is only when we fully realize that our duty, as well as our opportunity, lies in systematically cooperating to train and to make this competent man, instead of in hunting for a man whom some one else has trained, that we shall be on the road to national efficiency."[19] Efficiency, of course, was vital for attaining maximum production, and neither efficiency nor production were feasible without well-instructed workforces, whether in a factory or in a garden. Gardeners no less than

their industrial counterparts struggled with "The Problem of Labor"; as one horticulturist lamented in *House & Gardens*, "All of us face it, gardeners as well as merchants and manufacturers. We shall have to get along with what we find."[20]

The first thing that organizers found was considerable horticultural ignorance among mid-twentieth-century Americans. On some level this is surprising; for most of American history, domestic food gardens had been a necessity. Ad copy from 1944 pointedly invoked this history: "Raising a garden was once an American habit. Let's revive it."[21] In early American pioneer life, women were delegated almost sole responsibility for garden food production, management, and preparation, while men dominated the production of market crops and the heavier outdoor labor. Nor was this true only on farming homesteads, but also in town homes where the men worked as artisans or merchants. At that time, women produced vegetables, herbs, and food products for the household's consumption. They kept down weeds and disease by mixing plant families in shared beds and rotating crops yearly, while insects were taken care of by free-roaming chickens — a method that would be called integrated pest management today. This gardening style grew from the folk-English system of gardens arranged in beds rather than rows, which were better suited for monoculture field production and machine harvester, tillers, and cultivators.[22] Although such elites as Thomas Jefferson in the United States and John Evelyn in England were emphasizing botany and plant soil composition during the colonial period, what took hold in seventeenth-century America was "the smaller garden of traditional Europe", rather than "the aristocratic, scientific craft of John Evelyn".[23]

Home gardens became increasingly unnecessary for the average American as the United States entered the second industrial revolution. Canned foods were among the first mass-produced goods leading this revolution, while the number of Americans living in cities increased rapidly. By 1920, the census reported that the majority of the population now resided in urban areas. Less yard space and the greater convenience of purchasing food contributed to a shift away from home food production in a rapidly urbanizing nation. As the 1940s commenters on the victory garden movement attest, by the time of World War I, gardening was already something of an arcane art for many Americans.

Indeed, the precedent of World War I 'war gardens' resonated only negatively with the American populace of World War II. Organized and funded largely through the efforts of Charles Lathrop Pack, the National War Garden Commission had not been founded until 1917. Its achievements amounted to a scant five million war gardens — scarcely more than would have been expected to be planted anyway on farms and in rural areas around the country.[24] This last minute effort reeked of desperation and panic. A note sounded not infrequently at the start of the WWII Victory Garden Campaign was one of conscious distance from the previous experience: "The mistakes that were made in garden activities during the last war should not be repeated. Many of us remember the hysteria and lack of understanding that ruled garden planting at that time."[25] The adults of World War II described despairingly how their parents had "rushed into the field with hardly any preparation for their heroic labors, beyond looking up Agriculture in the dictionary to see what it meant".[26] Gardening practice and knowledge only further declined in the interwar years: "Home vegetable gardens, as indicated by sales of packets of vegetable seeds, declined 50 percent from 1925 to 1941," one avid gardener noted.[27]

By the time of World War II, anecdotes made clear the loss of cultural knowledge. An army nurse testifying for the National Victory Garden Institute's 1944 conference about growing Victory Gardens in army hospitals gave a poignant example: "One case, a man had never seen vegetables grown — had no idea of how they grew. He had seen them in the market, on tables, but he did not know exactly how vegetables grew. One day he came to me and said, 'I am so thrilled! Have you seen the blossom on the eggplant?'"[28] Oral histories confirm that even in more mundane circumstances, gardening was a novelty for some: "we all grew vegetables in our small backyards for the first time in our lives", one interviewee recalled.[29] The impetus that convinced the urbanized American population to attempt gardening anew was a policy of maximum war production. Surprisingly, the amateur status of the would-be gardeners facilitated more than obstructed this policy's implementation.

In Frederick Taylor's words, solving this labor problem was "our duty, as well as our opportunity".[30] The lack of gardening experience created an opportunity for organizers of the Victory Garden Campaign to promote a vision of gardening based on the model of a factory; the *tabula rasa* of the masses of newly urbanized Americans allowed authorities to shape the discourse surrounding gardening in conformity with modern industrial practices and gender conventions alike. Accordingly, the Victory Garden Campaign organized itself around the spread of information. The USDA created a handbook for local victory garden leaders, emphasizing that "A great many people are eager to become victory gardeners, but they need information. This is really your job — information."[31] Some pamphlets even took the time to illustrate, label, and explain the functions of such commonplace tools as a spade or hoe. One such definition began, "Rakes are used for working the surface of the soil into a fine texture and for smoothing out small irregularities. They are also handy for collecting scattered stones, trash or other debris."[32] Meanwhile, government film productions presented comedic figures like entertainer Jimmy Durante, playing a hopelessly inept victory gardener who digs a six-foot hole for his radish seeds and puts mayonnaise rather than fertilizer on his tomatoes — not a far cry from practices officials noted in the populace.[33] The poet Ogden Nash wrote

a poem mocking this epidemic of ignorance and the attempts of the authorities to ameliorate it, concluding: "So don't ask me to tell a string bean from a soy bean / I can't even tell a girl bean from a boy bean."[34]

Anecdotes, poetic fancy, and impressions of admen and officials aside, it is hard to ascertain precisely how many Americans were really introduced to gardening for the first time during the war. Concrete estimations varied wildly. *Life* magazine proclaimed, "Six million new gardeners in 1942."[35] One year later, the chairman of the USDA's Victory Garden Committee boasted that, "a half or more of our Victory Gardeners [in 1943] were green, unskilled, and untried".[36] The Office of War Information staked the more modest claim that in 1943, a mere third of victory gardeners were beginners.[37] These statements, though inconsistent, still point to a perceived widespread dearth of gardening knowledge. Such ignorance solved what Taylor saw as one of the largest problems facing the implementation of scientific management and achieving maximum efficiency: facilitating the transition from old ways of work and production to new ways.[38] No old habits would contradict the latest edicts of soil scientists, and no folk wisdom clash with empirical findings. The ignorance of many Americans eliminated an obstacle to optimal production. Now modern "best practices" could be easily introduced.

AUTHORITY AND MANAGEMENT

Centralization of gardening knowledge in the hands of a few select authorities was important for the Victory Garden Campaign. It allowed for a reinvention of gardening — and even a rewriting of the collective memories of older gardening practices. While vegetable growing for daily consumption had historically been women's domain, now it was reconfigured as a historically male example of self-reliance: "The vegetable garden was once a feature of almost every American home.... To be sure of supply [of food], one grew his own", a male pamphleteer asserted.[39] M. L. Wilson, Director of Cooperative Extension Work and associated with both the War Food Administration and the USDA, took time to explicate Jefferson's scientific approach to gardening as if it defined early American practice. "Botany and its applied practice to gardening" constituted, in Jefferson's words, one of "the most valuable sciences." Given that "Jefferson wrote those words 130 years ago when scientific knowledge about plants and plant life was still in its elementary stage", this is only truer now, Wilson concluded: scientists must light the way.[40] According to the victory gardening rhetoric, growing your own food was a scientific, mechanical endeavor, and had never been anything else. The ideal victory gardener was firmly situated within a factitious historical tradition: male, rational, and informed not by experience, but by higher authorities wielding the scepter of science.

Vitally, this description suits not only the ideal victory gardener, but the ideal industrial worker as well, especially regarding the lack of reliance upon experience or prior knowledge. Henry Ford reputedly "declared that he would rather have operators with no experience at all; he wanted workers who had 'nothing to unlearn' and who would work just as they were told".[41] Unconditional deference to authority and obedience to instructions, in both the factory and the garden, were vital to making ignorance into an asset. One pamphlet noted, "Beginners often have better gardens than old-timers because they are conscientious in following advice given to them."[42] New gardeners needed to strictly follow the prescribed practices as enumerated by the local and national authorities: "The novice can have a successful garden if he will plan carefully, follow directions, and do the necessary work at the right time."[43] These practices were often codified into actual rules for ease of both understanding and compliance, especially by the national government [Figure 4]. The USDA helpfully reminded all the readers of *Life* magazine that "Good gardeners obey simple rules", at the top of their list of "the dozen 'don'ts'" of the USDA.[44]

As these rules indicate, the rise of scientific management elevated the importance of the process of production over the end product itself — a process guided by the latest informed and scientific consensus among authorities. The words 'proper', 'correct', and 'right' haunted amateur victory gardeners in their quest to achieve these ideals of horticultural practice. Indeed, Frank and Lillian Gilbreth (collaborators on the development of motion study as an engineering and management technique) and Frederick Taylor predicated their respective philosophies of scientific management upon the existence of "one best way". Frank Gilbreth phrased it succinctly in the opening of his famous *Motion Study* (1911): "the aim of motion study is to find and perpetuate the scheme of perfection". The first step of this process was naturally, "Discovering and classifying the best practice."[45]

These ideals were in turn predicated upon distance from unaided processes of nature and the substitution of human rationality and science in their stead. Left unharnessed and unimproved by science and technology, gardeners and gardens alike were wont to be inefficient and unproductive. A comedic article in *Life* illustrated this point all too clearly when discussing a monkey who tried his hand at victory gardening: "Cookie [the monkey] was an apt pupil, not in becoming a good gardener but in showing how most amateur gardeners behave. He dug earnestly, if without spirit. He tried new ways of using garden tools. He paused without provocation to refresh himself. Cookie's performance will seem painfully familiar to a great many victory gardeners." A monkey, here the incarnation of 'man' without the aid of science and

given over completely to his irrational instincts, was what any victory gardener could become without the guidance and enlightening influence of the correct authorities. The fine line between the ignorant human and the primate was made clear in the article's concluding sentiment: "It is easier to make a monkey out of a victory gardener than to make a victory gardener out of a monkey."[46] Luckily, gardeners were never to be left alone in their struggles for perfectly efficient production if it could be helped; a common tenet of the Victory Garden Campaign and of scientific management alike was the need for oversight.

GARDEN AS PANOPTICON

Supervision was the antidote to personal discretion, widely feared both in the factory and in the victory garden. Taylor had repeatedly emphasized the "substitution of science for rule of thumb" and for the "individual judgment of the workman".[47] This view clearly influenced the victory garden planners who sought to drive home to prospective gardeners that "It is very often unsafe ... to rely on common sense or ingenuity."[48] The stakes were simply too high to rely on the opinions of lay Americans; after all, this was war production, and every leaf of lettuce mattered. When instructing women on how to home-can the produce of victory gardens, Mrs. Helen Kendall from the Good Housekeeping Institute advised that promoters explain "not only what [the housewife] should do, but what will happen if she doesn't".[49] Catastrophic results could range from botulism, to wasted seeds and fertilizer, to the downfall of the free world — and all could be prevented by enlightened supervision.

Indeed, the calls for supervision in victory gardens often openly avowed that this was needed to protect the plants from gardeners themselves. They emphasized the need for "capable, experienced, guidance.... All possible protection should be given the crops, not only against insect and animal enemies and plant diseases, but also against careless, ignorant, or vandalistic humans."[50] More often than not, the gardeners themselves were construed as the greatest threat to a victory garden's success, even greater than the enemy Japanese Beetle. A local professor of horticulture noted that in Minneapolis, "It was found that not all garden enemies live around the plants [like insect pests]. There's the person who expects the lettuce to kill off the quack grass, which, of course, just doesn't happen. And there is the kind who piles his quack grass on the land next to his."[51] This emphasis on product over and above the gardener himself granted more responsibility to the supervisors; to the minds of the victory garden movement organizers, guidance could be directly responsible for a victory gardener's success or failure: "many an amateur Victory gardener might have lasted longer if he had professional guidance", they ruefully reflected.[52]

For such a diverse and popular movement, victory garden leaders were able to put into practice an impressive amount of this recommended supervision. Guidelines for company-employee victory gardens, community gardens, and school gardens alike stated that "better results can be attained through proper supervision and management."[53] The principle extended to backyard gardens in equal measure. The USDA advised local victory garden committees that "instructions and demonstrations on the ground by competent gardeners are always especially helpful" for such backyard gardeners. Accordingly, many prominent victory gardens were plotted in front of town halls and on public greens as demonstration and instruction sites.[54] Many communities sponsored victory gardening contests where participation entailed no less than two visits by a garden expert to the premises over the course of the growing season, such as in Ingham County, Michigan.[55] The nationally distributed contest materials provided by the National Victory Garden Institute encouraged just such a two-visit system of evaluation.[56]

PLANTS IN THE ASSEMBLY LINE

The factory metaphor was not confined to comparisons of gardeners to factory workers and organizers to foremen; victory gardeners also metaphorically served as foremen in their own right, making the plants in their gardens all workers on "a feed 'assembly line'".[57] Just as supervision of victory gardeners by authorities supposedly led to higher rates of gardener success, so too would oversight of plants lead to higher production rates: "The victory gardener has a big advantage over the commercial grower because he can keep a keen watch on almost every individual plant", an insect control guide noted.[58] The pervasive factory metaphor also applied to the question of worker selection, plant and human alike. Taylor had ardently espoused "the scientific selection of the workers" — e.g. those with high "personal coefficient".[59] With plant 'workers' especially, gardeners were encouraged to be highly selective. Accordingly, plants with the greatest aptitudes for success were recommended: "Plant standard, adapted varieties.... Don't waste space on freak novelties", gardeners were told.[60] The clear message was that selection should be guided not by intuition, but by the edicts of authorities; the USDA even put out an official list of vegetables and appropriate varieties of those vegetables for victory gardeners.[61] Failing that, the selection process should still be rationalized and quantified: "Which [vegetables] saved the most money, or points [for wartime rationing]? What vegetables should be eliminated in favor of others that are more productive?" gardeners were urged to ask themselves.[62]

Figure 4/ 7 Steps To Your Victory Garden. Office of War Information, undated. File "Food Fights for Freedom Master File: Victory Gardens". Box 8, NC-66, RG 208: Office of War Information. National Archives at College Park, College Park, MD. Declassified: NND 785042. In so far as they related to the war effort, Victory Garden materials were 'classified' by the government as sensitive materials.

The status of plants and gardeners alike as workers in these Victory vegetable factories even allowed for workers to be fired. Ordinances for community or company gardens inevitably included a provision "[t]hat whenever the Licensee fails to cultivate, operate or maintain this 'Victory Garden' properly, it shall be declared abandoned by the Director and the Licensee shall thereby lose all rights in this 'Victory Garden' including the growing crops".[63] Compliance was enforced for a host of codified workplace rules, such as "mimeographed instructions with reference to rules of conduct, hours of work, maintenance, obtaining help, and other things governing the use of the tract".[64] Violation of any of these constituted a breach of contract and could bring sanctions. Organizers also preemptively screened plot applicants and aspiring gardeners who might incur such disciplinary measures; they actively discouraged those who might be unsuited to the demands of such an important war job. Thus the garden patch and gardener alike could be found unfit for the war effort: "If now I am called upon to give advice to prospective gardeners who cannot find a sunny patch of ground, reasonably free from tree roots and really pestiferous weeds, my advice is 'Don't.' Incidentally, 'Don't' is also good advice for the potentially indolent", wrote one blunt editorialist.[65] Publicity campaigns aimed to "point out limitations such as poor soil and other factors that might make gardening inadvisable in certain areas or with certain individuals".[66] In so many words, authorities urged Americans to evaluate themselves and their resources for Taylor's "personal coefficient" of job aptitude before joining the victory garden labor force.

GENDER AT WORK

Laziness, shortage of time and resources, and lack of diligence could all render a victory gardener unfit, but gender was not a disqualifying attribute. "Not a single man, not a woman, not a single healthy child who can sow a seed or pull a weed can be spared from Victory Gardens", pamphlets reiterated.[67] This is not to say that gender was irrelevant to the Victory Garden Campaign. Rather, gender played an important role in structuring the labor policies of the victory garden workplace. Industrial precedent, traditional gendering of work, and conservative social forces all urged divisions of labor along gendered lines, and the majority of victory gardening materials were explicitly addressed to a male reader.

Men were presented as, and may well have been, both foreman and factory worker in the war plant of the family garden.[68] Certainly, males were the predominant embodiments of victory gardeners in popular discourse, as well as leaders in the factory labor system. An oft-cited advertisement from Calvert Distillers Corporation entitled "SALUTE TO A CLEAR-HEADED AMERICAN" presented itself as a tribute to the male victory gardener, baring his ripplingly masculine chest in

bas-relief.[69] Another stark visual equation of victory gardening with masculinity is a 1944 cartoon where a man is looking at his wall of mounted animal heads, hammer and nails in hand. His wife whispers, "Gerald is preparing a place for his victory garden trophies" [Figure 5].[70] The male typecasting of the victory gardener served to reflect his role as industrial worker and factory foreman within the discourse of garden-as-factory; Gerald with his trophy wall is commemorating his participation in one of the most basic goals of science, hunting, factories, and victory gardening alike: control of and profit from nature. This is why many images present the victory gardener as a white-collar worker; illustrations of victory gardeners as men at an architect's desk are plentiful.[71] The starkest example may be yet another cartoon, where two men in suits in a high-rise office building peer over an intricate blueprint, with a framed picture of a factory behind them. The blueprint they are examining, however, is not for another automobile factory but for a vegetable factory; "This is where I'm going to plant turnips", says one to the other [Figure 6].[72] Masculinity, hard rationality, and manipulation of the natural

"Gerald is preparing a place for his victory garden trophies"

——— **Figure 5/** Placing his victory garden trophies. Office of War ———
Information, "Mats Sent to OWI List", 14 February 1944. File "Food
Fights for Freedom Master File: Victory Gardens". Box 8, NC-66, RG 208:
Office of War Information. National Archives at College Park,
College Park, MD.

Figure 6/ Plans for the garden factory. Office of War Information, "Mats Sent to OWI List", 14 February 1944. File "Food Fights for Freedom Master File: Victory Gardens". Box 8, NC-66, RG 208: Office of War Information. National Archives at College Park, College Park, MD. Declassified: NND 785042.

rich kale, instead of petunias and geraniums", pamphlets urged.[74] The journals of wartime homemaker and housewife Dorothy Atkinson Robinson conform to such notions; while writing primarily about her flower beds and canning fruit preserves, she mentions her husband and a male neighbor as doing the work for, and knowing more about, the process of growing vegetables.[75]

Although the dominant rhetoric emphasized gendered divisions of labor keeping women within the "kitchen department" or elsewhere apart, women did occasionally get out on the floor, so to speak, and undertake heavier work — and even heavy machinery. In a company victory garden photo spread, Standard Stations Inc. proudly displayed a female employee behind the wheel of a tractor in the victory garden field, boasting that "It isn't for the camera's benefit — she runs the thing."[76] Rather than delegate women to merely working on flower beds and herb gardens, retailers sought to make it easy for women to work in industrially straight and efficient rows using modern machinery: "Another mail order company is offering a new hand cultivator called a 'krust-buster' which is light enough to be used by women and children", one promoter noted.[77]

Still, a strong current of conventional ideas about women and work persisted, perhaps by way of reaction to more 'liberal' views. Despite the historically private and domestic nature of gardens, the Victory Garden Campaign had turned backyard weeding into a wartime factory job, and women were ideally absent. One illustration of this sentiment, paradoxically, is the frivolous female in a photo-essay accompanying an article addressed explicitly and exclusively to a male-gendered victory gardener. "Mrs. William Wyatt, a

world are inextricably related not only in this comic, but also in the Victory Garden Campaign.

Women's roles in this greater scheme of specialized labor varied to a degree, but promotional materials almost inevitably upheld conservative gender notions. This distanced females from the primary act of production and allied them more closely with the secondary production of meals from raw food in the family division of labor. While males were primarily addressed in pamphlets on victory gardening itself, females were the primary intended audience for pamphlets about canning, food preservation, and menu planning to incorporate the fruits of the victory garden. Often, women constituted another department within the garden factory infrastructure; one pamphlet described "husband gardeners, who will need co-operation from the kitchen department" [Figure 7].[73] If not in the kitchen department, women's jobs were still invariably feminine in a traditional sense. They often were encouraged to garden under the guise of home decoration: "Window boxes will be just as decorative but far more useful, planted to feathery-foliaged carrots, radishes, and vitamin-

Figure 7/ Cooperation from the kitchen department. Housewife Preserving Tomatoes from Her Victory Garden, US Dept. of Agriculture Photo, 1944. Private Collection, J. T. Vintage, The Bridgeman Art Library.

pretty and practical housewife" wears a beruffled polka-dot and floral print apron with cute pumps — her white gloves, light colored dress, and white heels never accumulate dirt.[78] Properly married, identified only by her husband's name, and dressed both modestly and femininely, Mrs. William Wyatt served as the equivalent of bikini-clad babes stretched out on sports cars in ads today — except that Mrs. Wyatt was selling not sex, but comforting gender normativity in a changing world where 'Rosie the Riveter' threatened the monopoly of 'Susie Homemaker' [See also Figure 8].

HOW TO GARDEN

Regardless of gender, once on the job each worker needed to be as efficient as possible. The opinion of Frank Bunker Gilbreth that "there is no waste of any kind in the world that equals the waste from needless, ill-directed, and ineffective motions" can be seen in precise instructions given to gardeners on how to physically complete given tasks, ranging from hand cultivation to spading over sod, making furrows and sowing seed.[79] For example, *Popular Science* not only instructed its readers on the latest irrigation technology for the home, but also made sure to explain the most efficient use of basic garden tools to a constituency unfamiliar with their use: "Force the spade or fork deep into the earth…. To ease the task, stand so you can use the right knee and upper leg as a lever. Press upward with the knee, down on the handle with the hands."[80] Illustrations sometimes aided comprehension; two contrasting stick figures were accompanied by the caption, "Conserve your energy. The

"WE'RE JUST *MADE* FOR EACH OTHER…I WATER HIS VICTORY GARDEN, AND HE STAKES MY TOMATO PLANTS."

—— **Figure 8/** We're Just MADE for Each Other…. I Water His Victory —— Garden, and He Stakes My Tomato Plants, c. 1943–1943, Artworks and Mockups for Cartoons Promoting the War Effort and Original Sketches by Charles Alston, compiled c. 1942–1945, Office for Emergency Management, Records of the Office of War Information, 1926–1951, Record Group 208, National Archives at College Park, MD.

hoe isn't a golf club. Scraping the soil with short strokes is good practice."[81] Gilbreth would have called such standardized ways of performing tasks 'accidental' in origin rather than 'scientific' because the processes (most likely) were not developed in laboratory settings. However, the influence of his motion studies is evident in the sheer amount of instruction on how to physically complete tasks.

The influence of John Gilbreth and his spouse Lillian Gilbreth's *Fatigue Study* is also discernable. Rather than spade the garden for planting all at once, pamphlets often recommended breaking up the spading over multiple days, since, as the Gilbreths wrote, "Careful observation and records show that a little fatigue is easily overcome if proper rest is supplied immediately."[82] One encouraging article noted, "Many amateurs get fun by not completing every job, but by varying tasks. For example, cultivate four rows, hand-weed one, replant a row, and then go back to cultivating. Those in the know highly recommend a loaf and a cigarette every hour or so; and as the sweat pours off, one can say 'Look what I done!'"[83] The discovery that frequent, short breaks could increase productivity was a finding common to both Gilbreth and Taylor, and was notably incorporated into a ball-bearing factory's operations in a case study by Taylor.[84] However, skilled planning could eliminate the need for breaks by making sure that labor itself was already broken up into small periods of time. Gardeners were repeatedly urged to devote small periods of time to their victory patch each day, rather than engage in 'weekend gardening' and working long shifts at a time on weekly intervals.

Labor expenditures did require careful planning and calculation of input. Again and again, materials emphasized that any investment should be financially sound — the benefits should outweigh the costs on paper before any labor was expended. A victory gardener should be sure to get the full "value for the money and man or woman hours invested in your vegetable factory".[85] One eager gardener who shared his experiences in the magazine *American Home* hoped to inspire others with his good example of calculated labor use: "With about two hours of work per week until the end of June, my 200' of peas *should* give me an estimated 56 lbs."[86] Gardening materials emphasized that the work should be distributed regularly throughout the growing season (i.e. 'per week' labor measurements), and they helped sell the victory gardening pitch by citing precise labor demands. One pamphlet estimated that, "Once dug up (a day's hard work for a hired man) [a garden] can be tended by an average of seven or eight hours' work a week — more in spring, less as summer goes along."[87] It was also a vital part of good business practice to be keeping track of labor use, allowing for improved efficiency in following years. In Firestone and other massive company victory garden endeavors, "records of man and machine hours are also kept to determine cost of operations," just as they were within the walls of the actual factory.[88] Such

Figure 9/ Victory Garden Plots Free For Employees, c. 1942–1943. War Production Board, Compiled 1942–1943. Office for Emergency Management. Records of the War Production Board, 1918–1947, Record Group 179. National Archives at College Park, MD.

Rivera's 1932 studies of Ford's River Rouge automobile plant in Detroit made the factory a particularly visible icon of this quest.[89] Factories controlled people, time, space, and processes more precisely and on a larger scale than ever before. In times of war, more than any other, people seek precisely this sort of order. Furthermore, in World War II, faith in the unlimited power of science and technology to create and maintain such order was strong. Through the dominating factory metaphor and practices, divisions of labor upholding traditional values, and comforting chains of authority and instruction, war gardens could provide a backyard example of ordered production for laborers. But in fact, the gardens also provided a sense of satisfaction in creation that could never be found in line production.

The rhetoric of propaganda and prescriptive literature intentionally conflated labor practices in both types of 'war plants' promoted in American during World War II, but no amount of rhetoric could erase the fundamental differences between digging in the earth and assembling a B52 bomber. Working in a garden was not like working in a factory; the rational order and control that managers tried to exert over human labor forces could not be applied in the natural world as easily as on a factory floor. As one contemporary observer noted, "I suppose any man who has any kind of work is helping to create something; but he doesn't always have the satisfaction of knowing it. You can have all you want of it in a garden for a half-hour of labor daily invested."[90] In this sense, working in a garden — seeing the 'whole plant' through from seed to fruit — was fulfilling in a way that firing the same three rivets for countless planes was not. Production was not only the driving goal of victory gardeners, but ultimately the most fulfilling aspect of the gardening endeavor. Enforced dependence on authority for instruction couldn't erase the self-sufficiency gained in the act of production. Victory gardeners, though so carefully selected, prepared, supervised, and managed as part of a system of production, worked at least in part for "a sense of security and satisfaction which nothing else in this topsy-turvy world seems to give".[91]

calculations presupposed that victory-gardener-workers were disciplined, functioning either on-the-clock or off, with no grey zone in between. While gardeners might take breaks to increase productivity, leisurely and inefficient afternoons in the garden were not part of the job description. Recreation disappeared in the harsh calculating mentality of the factory model of production and labor use [Figure 9].

FRUITS OF THE GARDEN FACTORY

The goal that fundamentally connected American production efforts in factories and backyards alike was the quest to impose order and rationality. The factory metaphor was an integral part of a larger search for control and order over the world, both natural and otherwise. Artworks such as Diego

NOTES

1/ Gallup, George, *The Gallup Poll; Public Opinion 1935–1971*, vol. 1, 3 vols., first ed., New York, NY: Random House, 1972, p. 378.

2/ "Victory Gardens: They Are Springing up in Strange Nooks and Crannies All over U.S", *Life*, 3 May 1943, p. 29.

3/ Cantril, Hadley, and Mildred Strunk, *Public Opinion, 1935–1946*, Princeton, NJ: Princeton University Press, 1951, p. 996.

4/ Fox, Frank W., *Madison Avenue Goes to War: The Strange Military Career of American Advertising, 1941–45*. Provo, UT: Brigham Young University Press, 1975, p. 54.

5/ Cantril and Strunk, *Public Opinion, 1935–1946*. p. 996.

6/ National Victory Garden Institute, *Manual for Company-Employee Gardens*, New York: The Institute, 1944, p. 3.

7/ For an urban agriculture/local food movement in Vancouver, see "Victory

Gardens—Grow What You Eat!" 2013. [http://victorygardensvancouver.ca], accessed 5 June 2013. See also the website for this goat milk ice cream parlor: "Victory Garden—New York City". [http://victorygardennyc.com], accessed 5 June 2013.

8/ See Carolyn Merchant, The Death of Nature: Women, Ecology, and the Scientific Revolution, San Francisco: Harper & Row, 1980.

9/ Seymour, E. L. D., Your Victory Garden, Chicago: J. G. Ferguson, 1942, p. 12.

10/ Seymour, Your Victory Garden, Inside back cover and back cover itself. Italics added.

11/ I have borrowed the conception of factory as the "master machine" from Lindy Biggs, The Rational Factory: Architecture, Technology, and Work in America's Age of Mass Production, Baltimore: Johns Hopkins University Press, 1996, p. 2.

12/ Carew, Michael G., Becoming the Arsenal: The American Industrial Mobilization for World War II, 1938–1942, Lanham: University Press of America, 2010, p. 220.

13/ Blum, John Morton, V Was for Victory: Politics and American Culture During World War II, New York: Harcourt Brace Jovanovich, 1976, p. 91.

14/ Hooks, Gregory, Forging the Military-industrial Complex: World War II's Battle of the Potomac, Urbana: University of Illinois Press, 1991, p. 2.

15/ Roosevelt, Franklin D., "Message to Congress on the Food Program", 1 November 1943. Online through Gerhard Peters and John T. Woolley, The American Presidency Project, [http://www.presidency.ucsb.edu/ws/?pid=16337], accessed 28 May 2013. See especially Elizabeth Collingham, The Taste of War: World War II and the Battle for Food, New York: Penguin Press, 2012, p. 8.

16/ For example, William M. Jeffers, the President of Union Pacific Railroad Co., served as Chair. National Victory Garden Institute, Manual for Company-Employee Gardens, pp. 3, 38.

17/ On the decreased number of union strikes in the war, see the boasts of the chairman of the War Production Board: Donald Marr Nelson, Arsenal of Democracy, the Story of American War Production, New York: Harcourt, Brace and Co., 1946.

18/ See especially Carew, Becoming the Arsenal, pp.170–174.

19/ Taylor, Frederick Winslow, The Principles of Scientific Management, New York and London: Harper, 1911. p. 6.

20/ Wright, R., "This Year's Victory Gardens", House & Garden, vol. 83, March 1943, p. 55.

21/ War Campaigns Committee of the Central Council of National Retail Association, "Grow More in '44: Retailers War Program", American Retail Foundation, April 1944. File "Food Fights for Freedom Master File: Victory Gardens", Box 8, NC-66, RG 208: Office of War Information, National Archives at College Park, College Park, MD.

22/ Merchant, Carolyn, Ecological Revolutions: Nature, Gender, and Science in New England, Chapel Hill: University of North Carolina Press, 1989, p. 169.

23/ Tucker, David M., Kitchen Gardening in America: A History, Ames: Iowa State University Press, 1993, p. 25.

24/ Pack, Charles Lathrop, War Gardens Victorious, Philadelphia: J. B. Lippincott, 1919, p. 15. He did, however, coin the phrase 'Victory Garden'.

25/ Gabler, Earl R., "School Gardens for Victory", The Clearing House, vol. 16, no. 8, 1 April 1942, pp. 469–472, doi:10.2307/30177734, p. 649.

26/ Robbins, Leonard Harman, "15,000,000 Victory Gardens", New York Times Magazine, 23 August 1942, p. 15.

27/ Burdett, James H., Victory Garden Manual, Chicago and New York: Ziff-Davis Pub. Co.,1943, p. 4.

28/ Van Hosen, Mrs. Stephen J., "Gardening in an Army Hospital", in National Victory Garden Conference, "Report: National Victory Garden Conference. U. S. Department of Agriculture Auditorium, Washington, DC, November 28–29, 1944", War Food Administration, Extension Service, 1944, p. 23.

29/ Balcomb, Ruth D., "College Days Without Men", Women of the Homefront: World War II Recollections of 55 Americans, Pauline E. Parker ed., Mcfarland & Co. Inc., 2002, p. 39.

30/ Taylor, Principles of Scientific Management, p. 6.

31/ United States Department of Agriculture, Victory Garden: Leader's Handbook, Washington, DC: United States Department of Agriculture, 1943, p. 10.

32/ Everett, T. H., and Edgar J. Clissold, Victory Backyard Gardens: How to Grow Your Own Vegetables, Racine, WI: Whitman Publishing Co., 1942, p. 11.

33/ War Activities Committee, "V FOR VEGETABLES AND VICTORY FILM BULLETIN", Universal Newsreels, Release 296, 22 May 1944, in Universal Newsreels 296, Universal Pictures Company Inc., 1944. 19:34 mins.

34/ Nash, Ogden, "My Victory Garden", House & Garden, November 1943, p. 63.

35/ "Gardens for U.S. at War: Six Million Amateurs Work the Soil", Life, 30 May 1942, pp. 81–84.

36/ National Victory Garden Institute, "Gardening for Victory: A Digest of Proceedings of the National Victory Garden Conference", 1943. Folder "Victory Gardens", Box 229, Entry e-72, NC-148, RG 208: Office of War Information, National Archives at College Park, College Park, MD, p. 4.

37/ Office of War Information, Domestic Radio Bureau, "Summary of Radio Campaign", 31 February 1944. File "Food Fights for Freedom Master File: Victory Gardens", Box 8, NC-66, RG 208: Office of War Information, National Archives at College Park, College Park, MD.

38/ See Taylor, Principles of Scientific Management, p. 130.

39/ Burdett, Victory Garden Manual, p. 3.

40/ Wilson, M. L., "Gardening After Victory", Report: National Victory Garden Conference, p. 10.

41/ Biggs, The Rational Factory, p. 106.

42/ Platenius, Hans, Victory Garden Handbook, A Guide for Victory Gardeners in New York and Neighboring States, Ithaca, NY: Cornell University Press, 1943, p. 2.

43/ National Victory Garden Institute, Victory Gardens for Every Family, New York, NY: National Victory Garden Institute, 1943, p. 2.

44/ "Gardens for U.S. at War: Six Million Amateurs Work the Soil", p. 82.

45/ Gilbreth, Frank B., Motion Study: A Method for Increasing the Efficiency of the Workman, New York: D. Van Nostrand Company, 1911, p. v.

46/ "Speaking of Pictures ... These Show That Monkeys Are Not Good Gardeners", Life, 14 June 1943, p. 7.

47/ Taylor, Principles of Scientific Management, pp. 25, 114.

48/ United States Department of Agriculture, Substitutes for Scarce Materials, Washington, DC: US Department of Agriculture, 1944. p. 1.

49/ National Victory Garden Institute, "Gardening for Victory", p. 44.

50/ Seymour, E. L. D., *The New Garden Encyclopedia; A Complete, Practical and Convenient Guide to Every Detail of Gardening, Including Special Supplement for 1943 Victory Gardens*, New York: W.H. Wise & Co., 1943. p. 1366.

51/ Keen, Grace Graham, *Let's All Grow Vegetables*, Minneapolis: University of Minnesota, 1944, p. 74.

52/ National Victory Garden Conference, *Report*, p. 2.

53/ National Victory Garden Institute, *Manual*, p. 6.

54/ United States Department of Agriculture, *Substitutes for Scarce Materials*, p. 3.

55/ See Elizabeth Belen, "Report Of Ingham Country Victory Garden Committee (World War II)", 23 October 1945, Microfilm: USAIN state and local literature preservation project, Michigan; Reel 309, No. 9, Michigan State University Libraries, p. 6.

56/ National Victory Garden Institute, *Victory Garden Score Card*, New York, NY, 1943.

57/ Bailey, Ralph Sargent, "Plan Your Victory Garden for Three-Shift Production", *House Beautiful*, February 1944, p. 44.

58/ Curran, Charles Howard, *Insect Control in the Victory Garden*, New York: American Museum of Natural History, 1943, p. 3.

59/ Taylor, *Principles of Scientific Management*, p. 97.

60/ National Victory Garden Institute, *Victory Gardens for Every Family*, p. 4.

61/ "The Agriculture Department recommended list of vegetables to be grown by victory gardeners is based on high vitamin content varieties that are easy to grow", from "Victory Vitamins", *Business Week*, 9 January 1943.

62/ Wing, Andrew S., "Your 1945 Victory Garden", *Nature Magazine*, March 1945, p. 149.

63/ "Model Ordinances on Victory Gardens", *American City*, vol. 58, May 1943, p. 91.

64/ United States Department of Agriculture, *Substitutes for Scarce Materials*, p. 3.

65/ Bailey, David Washburn, "For Victory Your Garden Must Have Good Ground", *House Beautiful*, May 1942, p. 136.

66/ Helyar, F. G., "To Make Victory Gardens Victorious", *American City*, March 1943.

67/ War Advertising Council, "Uncle Sam Is Calling for More Victory Gardens in 1945", n.d. Folder "Victory Gardens", Box 13, NC- 66, RG 208: Office of War Information, National Archives at College Park, College Park, MD, p. 6.

68/ Bentley, *Eating for Victory*, p. 5.

69/ Calvert Distillers Corporation, "Salute to a Clear-Headed American", n.d. File "Food Fights for Freedom Master File: Victory Gardens", Box 8, NC-66, RG 208: Office of War Information, National Archives at College Park, College Park, MD.

70/ Office of War Information, "Mats Sent to OWI List", 14 February 1944. File "Food Fights for Freedom Master File: Victory Gardens", Box 8, NC-66, RG 208: Office of War Information, National Archives at College Park, College Park, MD.

71/ See, for example, the illustrations in Paul Maley, "Paper Work for My Second Victory Garden", *American Home*, March 1944.

72/ Office of War Information, "Mats Sent to OWI List".

73/ Burdett, *Your Victory Garden*, p. 8.

74/ Putnam, Jean-Marie and Lloyd C. Cosper, *Gardens for Victory*, first ed., New York, NY: Harcourt, Brace, and Company, 1942, p. 4.

75/ Robinson, Dorothy Atkinson, *It's All in the Family: A Diary of an American Housewife, Dec. 7, 1941–Dec. 1, 1942*. New York, NY: William Morrow & Co., 1943.

76/ Standard Stations Inc., "Standard Chevron", April 1944. Folder "Victory Gardens", Box 13, NC-66, RG 208: Office of War Information, National Archives at College Park, College Park, MD. p. 4. It is important to note that this photo appears explicitly within the context of victory gardening —not farming with the Women's Land Army, where women running tractors was not uncommon.

77/ Middleton, D. K., "Victory Gardening: OPA's New Rationing, 'Long War' Psychology Spur Backyard Farming Industry Helps Trend Along —Gardening Enthusiasts Are Better Arms Producers; The Seed Supple Is Adequate Victory Gardening Spurred by OPA's New Rationing, 'Long War' Feeling", *Wall Street Journal*, 8 February 1945. Hand cultivators are designed to work along rows, rather than in beds, and their popularity at the end of the twentieth century hastened the transition from bed to row gardening, imitating industrial agriculture more closely. See page 89 onward in Tucker, *Kitchen Gardening in America*.

78/ "Wartime Gardening: Amateurs Plan Their Private Crops", *Life*, 8 March 1943, p. 67.

79/ Gilbreth, Frank B., *Motion Study: A Method for Increasing the Efficiency of the Workman*, New York: D. Van Nostrand Company, 1911.

80/ Gast, Ross H., "Home Gardens for Victory", *Popular Science*, May 1943, p. 190.

81/ *Victory Gardens in Greater New York*, New York: Greater New York Victory Garden Council, 1943.

82/ Gilbreth, Frank Bunker, and Lillian Moller Gilbreth, *Fatigue Study, the Elimination of Humanity's Greatest Unnecessary Waste*, New York, Sturgis & Walton Company, 1916, p. 5.

83/ Everitt, C. Raymond, "Trouble I've Had: Or, Victory in the Garden", *The Atlantic*, May 1943, p. 117.

84/ Taylor, *Principles of Scientific Management*, p. 94.

85/ Alexander, J. G., "Your Victory Vitamin Garden", *Hygeia*, June 1943, p. 430.

86/ Maley, "Paper Work for My Second Victory Garden", p. 58.

87/ "Gardens for U.S. at War: Six Million Amateurs Work the Soil", p. 81.

88/ "Firestone Victory Gardens", *Recreation*, vol. 37, May 1943, pp. 93–94.

89/ Biggs, *The Rational Factory*, p. 163.

90/ Robbins, "15,000,000 Victory Gardens", p. 16.

91/ Lovell, Helen D., "It's Easy to Grow Your Own Seasoning Herbs in the Victory Garden", *House & Garden*, April 1942, p. 48.

128 /SHELLEY BOYD

"NATURE-ALTERING TOOLS": MARGARET ATWOOD AND THE POLITICS OF DIRT

When the Canadian novelist Margaret Atwood was asked to recount her earliest memory, she replied, "Digging in mud with a spoon, 1942."[1] This love for dirt, for tools, and for digging has been a common thread in her life as well as her writing, from the early poetry to the recently completed dystopian trilogy, the *Maddaddam* series. Throughout her career, Atwood has revealed the garden and its tools to be 'revolutionary technologies' that not only transformed humankind's relationship to the natural world thousands of years ago, but also carry the potential to alter our consciousness and make way for a more hopeful future. In Atwood's figurative garden shed, tools such as the shovel, the lawnmower, and the compost bin shape the literal and imaginative grounds through which we inhabit and perceive our worlds.

GARDEN TECHNOLOGIES: PAST, PRESENT, AND FUTURE KNOWLEDGE

Women throughout history have been associated with "utensils and implements", those low-tech objects used to care for the domestic.[2] Atwood herself is an inventor as well as a user of tools, including the LongPen, an electronic arm that operates as "a long-distance signing device", and a squirrel deterrent made "out of chicken wire and coat hangers, which spent years in development".[3] Despite what feminist scholars have noted to be an uneasy relationship between the feminine and the technological, Atwood, the LongPen visionary, remains reassuringly tied to the material world of nature, tending her garden through household odds and ends. She has observed

— **Figure 1/** Evelyn Blair seeding garden, Penhold area, Alberta, 1930. —
Photograph courtesy of Glenbow Archives.

Figure 2/ Cutting Weeds, W. D. Scott's Farm, Dundas, Ontario, July 1910. Photograph by William James Topley, Courtesy of Library and Archives Canada.

Figure 3/ Woman mowing the lawn, Kitimat, British Columbia, 12 June 1956. Photograph by Rosemary Gilliat Eaton, Courtesy of Library and Archives Canada.

that "a tool is for actualizing what we desire and defending against what we fear.... Human tool-makers always make tools that will help us get what we want, and what we want has not changed for thousands of years."[4] Indeed, some of the earliest garden tools — such as the dibble (or dibber), which dates back to 5000 BCE in the form of mammoth bones used for digging — can be readily purchased at garden shops today. Each of these tools serves an enduring desire not only for plentiful food but for a manageable nature [Figure 1].

Historically, garden implements and their related processes have been highly regarded. During the Renaissance, tools "would often be blessed along with farm animals in the hope of providing a bountiful harvest", and during the seventeenth century, blacksmiths forged custom-made items "to fit the strength and size of a gardener's hands".[5] In contrast, the industrial era adopted a mass-produced, one-size-fits-all approach and made fewer varieties of tools for specific tasks. One cannot help but wonder what was lost and gained as both tools and tool-making changed. Greater access to affordable, mass-produced tools means increased participation and, therefore, knowledge across the social spectrum.[6] But when efficiency takes precedence, familiar tools become outmoded. New ways of reducing human labor are invented, and gardeners are distanced from the plants they tend. It has been noted that "to know ... a tool, it is not enough simply to look at it" because "'reading' the axe yields a different kind of knowledge than using it".[7] If specific technologies provide distinct physical experiences of understanding and consciousness, then uniformity leads to a less particular, less intimate sense of the skills and work, and old tools become "mere accessories" valued for their "sculptural form".[8] After the the invention of the push lawn mower by Edwin Budling in 1830, scythes and shears that

were once used for cutting grass were set aside to be admired as decorative objects [Figures 2, 3]. The push mower itself was subsequently aestheticized, of course, once replaced by steam-powered and gasoline engines. Thus, rather than being abandoned entirely, some old technologies acquire a new cultural life associated with pleasure.[9] Tasks once thought essential, such as gardening or knitting, transform into leisure activities, where if the quaint tools of old are used, they serve as expressions of nostalgia. Similarly, modern food production and the supermarket industry relegate gardening (a millennia-old invention itself) to a creative pastime [Figure 4]. Atwood notes that today, the average "city dweller's relation to food

Figure 4/ One Man Cultivates Nine Rows at a Time, Sherrington, Quebec, between 1930–1960. Photograph courtesy of Library and Archives Canada.

is ... closer to the gathering-hunting model than to the horticultural-agricultural one.... The shopping experience is given all the trappings of a walk in a magic forest.... All you have to do is reach out your hand, as in the Golden Age."[10] The garden then becomes merely a kind of "pet", a space providing pleasure, but ultimately "completely marginal to [your] existence" in that you do not depend upon it for the necessities of life.[11]

Atwood's writing about near-future worlds and their garden technologies dramatizes this distancing effect. In *Oryx and Crake*, the first novel of her dystopian trilogy, old-fashioned cultivators are among the "obsolete words" that Jimmy recites for personal comfort: "*Dibble ... Breast Plough*".[12] Physical labor has become ancient history in a time when the Watson-Crick Institute's research division "Décor Botanicals" invents an algae-infused "Smart Wallpaper" that changes color in response to one's mood. No hand tools are needed here, as these genetically engineered 'gardens' grow according to interior design. The food industry has similarly been revolutionized through Happicuppa coffee beans that "ripen simultaneously" and are harvested by machines. In this world, human gardeners as well as manual tools are superfluous.

Atwood's futuristic account is not too distant from tendencies in our own world today. Indeed, the most prominent 'cultivating' device of the present day may be the computer. In her 2012 article "Atwoodville", Atwood analyzes the online game "Frontierville", which simulates a homestead, as an analogy for "our disintegrating relationship with nature".[13] Players make the land 'useful' by tidying debris and arranging their surroundings; they are virtual pioneers mimicking the labor of past eras [Figure 5]. Atwood admits that "Frontierville got a lot right" by representing "some of the conditions we need to maintain human life". Water, for instance, appears in the form of a decorative fountain. But the hard work of obtaining that water, cleaning it for human consumption, or distributing it for successful agriculture is entirely absent [Figure 6]. The virtual gardener is completely separated from the physical work and firsthand knowledge of turning the soil, and is immune to ecological checks and balances; "the population never outgrows the carrying capacity of the land".

Figure 5/ Mr. and Mrs. Samuel Mammel with their children in the family's vegetable garden, Hanna, Alberta, 1928. Photograph courtesy of Library and Archives Canada, C-063262.

Figure 6/ Water hauled in a tank for steam engines to water vegetable garden (by hand), Pendant d'Oreille area, Alberta, c. 1910. Photograph courtesy of Glenbow Archives.

Richard Louv has argued in *Last Child in the Woods* (a book Atwood includes on an online reading list for *The Year of the Flood*) that such distance from nature characterizes an entire generation of today's urban children, who suffer from "nature-deficit disorder", despite the many demonstrated benefits (physical, mental, spiritual) of close, regular contact with nature.[14] According to Louv, America has now entered a Third Frontier characterized by "electronic detachment" from the natural environment: food origins are not recognized; distinctions are blurred between humans, living creatures, and machines; and life is transformed into a commodity. This Third Frontier (eerily simulated in Frontierville) stands in stark contrast with both the First Frontier (the actual settlement of the wilderness which was completed during the nineteenth century) and the Second Frontier (the romanticized frontier of twentieth-century culture that included some lingering contact with rural America through family farms). The 'nature' experienced in a game like Frontierville extends this illusion of control and transcendence: a digital 'progression' of both nineteenth-century pioneers and twentieth-century homeowners tending their respective homesteads and yards.

In Atwood's view, the changes that accompany digital culture are ultimately tied to subtle shifts in consciousness. One of the biggest dangers is that "we will pave over ... too much of paradise, because we will have forgotten about it."[15] Peter H. Kahn, Jr's hypothesis of "environmental generational amnesia" (in *Technological Nature*) is clearly relevant here. This term suggests that generations formulate understandings "of what is environmentally normal based on the natural world encountered in childhood. With each generation the amount of environmental degradation increases, but each generation tends to take that ... condition as ... the [norm]."[16] Kahn describes an art installation similar to Frontierville called the "*Tele-garden*", where users tended an actual community garden through social media by directing a robotic arm, but engaged in little discussion about nature. The clicking mouse used to play Frontierville and the robotic arm of the *Tele-garden* are prime examples of Marshall McLuhan's theory of the mechanical "extensions" of man through "auto-amputation": human limbs and sensory abilities are effectively "turned off" and removed from doing the actual work.[17] Technology appears both independent and all-powerful because we neglect the socio-political dimensions through which technologies are formed and operate.[18] One hazard of the technologies of cultivation, then, is the creation of irresponsible gardeners who, in failing to self-reflect, neglect and abuse their former relationship with the soil, thereby altering their awareness of what it means to be human.

YOUR BEST TOOL

If technologies alone are not to blame for environmental degradation, but rather the human desires and values that (mis)direct the invention and use of tools, then what can be done to rectify society's nature deficit? And can the garden help in this reform? Atwood believes that respect for nature and its creatures "must have been part of our ancestral toolkit", but that this mode of thinking seems to have been forgotten or misplaced.[19] This concern is central to her *MaddAddam* trilogy. In this near-future dystopia, a few survivors deal with the aftermath of a plague engineered by the mad scientist Crake, who sought to replace dysfunctional humankind with a more perfect creature of his own design. Set against Crake and his kind are the eco-religious sect God's Gardeners, who model their lives according to a past vision of stewardship of the land, all the while preaching that the fall of man has been due in part to a descent into technology.[20] In *The Year of the Flood*, the second novel in the series, the God's Gardeners counter society's exploitative tendencies by preaching that "you create your world by your inner attitude". When the novel's protagonist Toby first joins the sect, she busies herself with gardening tasks (weeding, hauling dirt, identifying plants). Although Toby expresses doubt over the sect's teachings, the leader Adam One reassures her, "In some religions, faith precedes action.... In ours, action precedes faith." His suggestion — that by *doing*, one perceives anew — reminds us of the premise that "Technologies are not just objects but also the skills needed to use them. Daily life is saturated with tacit knowledge of tools and machines."[21] Toby considers the Gardeners' theories "remote" and "fanciful", yet she eventually excels at their practices, becoming adept with their tools, and by extension, their green and modest lifestyle.[22] She gathers supplies in preparation for the "waterless flood", and when the pandemic hits, she tends her garden, becoming a model of self-sufficiency. Later, when she leaves her shelter to search for a missing friend, she knows that "Tools are more important than food" and she packs a trowel "for digging roots", a pocket knife, and "[c]loth bags for wild edibles". Toby's adopted technological culture is highly integrated, attuned to the environment and to the Gardeners' moral teachings.

Relying upon her practical knowledge for subsistence, Toby stands in direct contrast with Snowman (previously known as Jimmy), the sole human survivor of the corporate Compounds featured in the first novel, *Oryx and Crake*. As a word person, Jimmy was never adept with tools, and as Snowman, he barely survives, relying on the post-human Crakers to deliver a single fish for his meager weekly sustenance. Rather than fending for himself by learning about his present environment, Snowman scavenges the remains of his former world, the RejoovenEsense Compound, naively believing that mass-produced food will be abundant: "Once they'd figured out what was going on, the Compound inhabitants dropped everything and fled. They wouldn't have stayed long enough to clean out the supermarkets.... He might unearth all sorts of things. Cherries preserved in brandy; dry-roasted peanuts; a precious can of imitation Spam.... A truckload of booze."[23] Jimmy's past lifestyle had been characterized by ease and rapid consumption; it was a veritable happy hour. In this world of plenty, tools were understood in a conventional way as extensions of human power over nature. Following the waterless flood, Jimmy/Snowman remains stuck in this mode of thinking even as he faces obsolescence.

In contrast, the God's Gardeners use tools in ways that acknowledge humanity's vulnerability and dependence on the earth. Rejecting the mainstream's culture of excess and environmental abuse, the God's Gardeners create their own eco-cult of carefully selected practices: they ban (for the most part) digital devices, prohibit shopping, conserve water through infrequent bathing, label exploitative products like paper sinful, and worship ecological 'saints' such as Rachel Carson, whose 1962 book *Silent Spring* prompted industries and backyard gardeners to reconsider their use of chemical pesticides and herbicides, such as DDT [Figure 7].

Choosing to live simply and apart from society, the Gardeners are the kind of counter-cultural group that gravitates toward "'low-tech' ideas ... because they empowe[r] individuals to select and construct their own technological systems".[24] For these environmentalists, ethical attitudes and moral choices are paramount to their technological culture and its survival. As Toby reminds herself while packing her tools, "Your best tool is your brain."[25]

The God's Gardeners teach their children to engage directly with nature, bestowing hands-on knowledge of ecology through foraging and gardening. Their "Wild Botanicals" class

Figure 7/ Car trunk full of garden chemicals, including a 45-gallon drum of banned DDT, during a pesticide pickup, Calgary, Alberta, June 1971. Photograph courtesy of Glenbow Archives.

Figure 8/ Children working in school garden plot, Yankee Valley, Alberta, August 1909. Photograph courtesy of Glenbow Archives.

educates students on how to identify plants and to appreciate that "food comes from the Earth", not the supermarket. In many ways, the sect attempts to create what Louv describes as the "Fourth Frontier": a curtailing of the Third Frontier's "electronic detachment" through the purposeful restoration of children's relationship with nature via education and access to parks and open terrain.[26] The God's Gardeners' survival education echoes the school garden movement, which grew in popularity throughout Canada (and elsewhere) from 1890 to 1930 in response to "'the rural problem'" of an "ever-increasing migration to the cities".[27] Many feared that agriculture would be abandoned unless country students received a relevant curriculum by doing (tending outdoor plots with tools) rather than studying textbooks in a classroom [Figure 8]. The objective was "maintaining the right order of society by creating citizens who knew their place": that place was on the farm, sustaining urban populations and Canada's economic wellbeing. The movement waned as Canadians moved down a path of 'progress': other industries (apart from agriculture) grew in economic importance, rural Canada became urbanized through technologies of the train, car, radio, and telephone, and social reform movements dissipated. For the God's Gardeners, who live surrounded by an over-populated, polluted world with little arable land, it is humanity as a whole, not simply migrating rural folk, that has lost its place. From the early decades of the twentieth century to the futuristic world of Atwood's novel, then, the use of the garden-as-educational-tool speaks to underlying anxieties regarding an ever-increasing distance between people and the land, a sense of weakened morality, and a misdirected economy ignorant of ecological consequences.

Despite their best efforts, the God's Gardeners appear ineffectual in reforming society at large. Atwood fully

appreciates that when it comes to solving environmental problems, gardening education is a target of ridicule and is often perceived as "extra, frilly, prissy, goody-goody".[28] Critics of Atwood's trilogy similarly suggest that the story warns against "a failure of the imagination": while it is important, on the one hand, to remember "our kinship with the natural world", on the other hand, we must remember that "ethical behaviour is something that requires practice and self-discipline".[29] Admittedly, the God's Gardeners contend with these shortcomings as their own teenage pupils mock their courses through clever nicknames: "Poop and Goop for violet biolet instruction" and "Guck and Muck for Compost-Pile Building".[30] Nonetheless, the garden persists as a site of learning because within its complex mixture of socio-cultural practices and the material environment, humans face their dependence on the earth, especially if they work to grow their own food and to benefit the larger ecology. The alternative to gardening's slow reform is Crake's radical solution of genetically engineering a 'greener' species, the Crakers. As Hannes Bergthaller notes, Crake's tactic is "to breed the wildness out of man, creating a species of human beings that will be congenitally unable to soil the planetary *oikos*" as they have been "permanently housebroken".[31] Although this strategy seems logical in Crake's mind, the Crakers are not exactly human. To be human is to be a tool-user, and Crake designs his "Paradice People" never to need tools and never to become "agriculturalists, hungry for land".[32] Atwood implies that either we relearn how to 'garden' as humble custodians who use tools and processes that guard against a purely instrumental view of nature, or we face extinction. According to Atwood, the debate over "our proper relationship with nature and how much we can or should exploit its resources" is "as old as our nature-altering tools", which prompts one to speculate: if humanity's present course requires a change in direction, what can be learned from the garden tools of the past, particularly as Atwood represents them?[33]

SURFACES AND DEPTHS: SHOVELS, LAWNMOWERS, ASTROTURF

Remarking on the need to reduce our energy consumption, Atwood suggests, "let's ban gas-powered leaf blowers. And throw in gas-powered lawn mowers.... I'd also say get a rake, but there would be a rebellion if I said that."[34] Admittedly, human nature is resistant to change; we want tools that do the work for us. Yet her suggestion holds merit: turning to the tools of old, not simply for pleasure and nostalgia, but

Figure 9/ Workmen paint the siding of a prefabricated house for war workers Mr. and Mrs. Harry Kalek while others roll out grass sod on the lawn, Vancouver, British Columbia, May 1944. Photograph by Harry Rowed, Courtesy of National Film Board of Canada. Photothèque, Library and Archives Canada.

for the historical lessons they impart may lead to different modes of engagement with the soil. Perhaps the most famous garden tools in Atwood's literary worlds are shovels used by nineteenth-century settlers looking to transform the wilderness. Many of her early poems explore this process. In "Progressive Insanities of a Pioneer" from *The Animals in That Country* (1968), the settler turns the soil, planting both himself and his vision: "He dug the soil in rows, / imposed himself with shovels / He asserted / into the furrows, I / am not random."[35] In "The Planters" from *The Journals of Susanna Moodie* (1970), pioneers weed their vegetable crop alongside the irregular forest — the straight rows an "illusion solid to them as a shovel".[36] In both poems, Atwood implicates this digging tool with levels of consciousness: the shovel makes tenable, albeit in a tenuous way, the materialization of an agrarian system and the settlers' delusional sense of control over their surroundings. For Atwood's early pioneers, the solidity of their beliefs is ultimately challenged through the earth. With shovels they dig and realize that "dirt is the future", but their settlement plans are utterly undone, for 'progress' leads not to technological domination, but to an unraveling mind. In contrast to Atwood's gothic depiction, actual kitchen gardens from frontier Canada were far more successful.[37] One possible explanation for this difference is that in her early work, "Atwood imposes ... a view of the land that comes from our own time, when urbanites tend to find any contact with the wilderness frightening."[38] Where the truly detached and ignorant relationship with nature exists is with modern-day city dwellers, settling a second frontier without ever lifting a shovel.

Atwood's poem "The City Planners" from *The Circle Game* (1966) features this fearful world of suburban 'homesteads' erected in rapid succession following the Second World War. Rows, not of vegetables, but of uniform houses line the streets. In this sterile landscape the topsoil is stripped clean with houses built on "clay-seas" or on ready-made lawns through the installation of sod [Figure 9].[39] The only audible sign of life is "the rational whine of power mower / cutting a straight swath in the discouraged grass".[40] The speaker yearns to see beyond the tightly controlled surface, where the benign plastic garden hose suddenly appears "poised in a vicious / coil". Here, the catalyst for disorder is not the wilderness, but the blindness of human nature itself, as reflected in an ill-conceived, mass-produced, artificial habitat. The poem conjures up Atwood's own childhood when her family moved to post-war Toronto with its newly built suburban wasteland. Eventually "a mountain of topsoil was delivered, and a lawn came into being", followed by the vegetable garden.[41] Her parents' edible yard (a continuation of their earlier Victory Garden) was not the norm; "Simple-minded abundance was the order of the day", especially with wartime food rationing having ended and supermarkets close at hand.[42] Vegetable gardening was regarded as unnecessary

as homeowners directed their energies towards replicating a popular lawn aesthetic.

In "The City Planners", the lawnmower's "rational whine" sounds the oxymoronic character of suburbia: paradisiacal in appearance, yet destructive and out of sync with the larger environment. The unappealing mechanical noise is that of modern 'progress' at work in the garden. Following the Second World War, the popularity of lawns made 'high-tech' gardening necessary; "[b]efore the invention of the hand-push mower, the rubber hose and sprinkler, pesticides, herbicides, and commercial fertilizer, and the introduction of appropriate lawn grasses, lawns as we know them today were impossible" [Figure 10].[43] Today, yard maintenance appears so complex and scientific under the direction of the chemical fertilizer industry, that some even refer to the lawn as "a large technological system".[44]

The lawn finds a 'natural' place in the futuristic world of *Oryx and Crake,* where residents of the enclosed Compounds drive golf carts through an artificial 'green' oasis. In keeping with the history of pleasure grounds, this landscape belongs to the social elite who live sheltered from climate change, as "Rockulators" (fake rocks) absorb and release moisture as "natural lawn regulators".[45] In contrast, at the under-valued, under-funded Martha Graham Academy where Jimmy studies, the lawns are "mud, either baked or liquid, depending on the season". Even in the days leading up to the pandemic, yard maintenance remained part of Compound life. In the aftermath, Snowman stumbles upon a notepad with a 'to do' list: scrawled at the top are the words "GET LAWN MOWED" followed by *"Call clinic...."* These references may seem anachronistic; surely grass could have been genetically engineered to never grow beyond a specified length. The lawn

Figure 10/ Bryant Flyer sprinkling the lawn, Canada, July 1899. Photograph courtesy of Library and Archives Canada.

is, however, in keeping with this culture where human desires reign. So powerful and everlasting is the lawn aesthetic that one environmental group, the Golfgreens Greenies (who grow cabbages along fairways), "still spray the grass".[46] Even from the greenest of hearts, the lawn ideal is difficult to dispel. Ultimately, the story of the lawn is about men's "use of power machinery and chemicals, the tools of war, to engage in a battle for supremacy with Mother Nature".[47] In *Oryx and Crake* this narrative endures, as lawnmower metaphors inform Snowman's vocabulary when he wishes he could "mow down" a group of pigoons that corner him.[48] More importantly, the impulse to create the perfect lawn — "to beat Mother Nature and produce artificial 'natural' beauty" —parallels the motivations of the RejoovenEsense bioengineers who design improved living creatures.[49] Lawnmowers and genetic engineering even appear strangely related when Crake unveils his newly created Paradice People. Crake mentions that one customized model has been formulated to eat "nothing but grass", to which Jimmy is incredulous: "Oh good.... Your baby can double as a lawn mower."[50]

Atwood both questions this landscape's cultural hold, and appreciates its changing status in a world of nature-altering tools. For instance, her 2013 Father's Day tweet plays with sentiments surrounding yard maintenance: "Hope all the dads and grandads had a #HappyFathersDay! Here, the celebration involved a scythe, a weed whip, and hey! It stopped raining!"[51] While nodding to the tradition of husbands and fathers mowing (down) the lawn, Atwood revises the convention by highlighting alternative practices. At her household, non-polluting, labor-intensive tools are among the implements of choice. Atwood is certainly aware of the ecological issues raised by lawns; she once referred to the front lawn as "a water-gobbling waste of space".[52] Nevertheless, she recently became a 'grassroots' supporter of the Back Campus Green, a group protesting the replacement of the University of Toronto's natural playing field with artificial turf for the 2015 Pan Am Games. Ironically, this large sward was in need of protection, as astroturf was promoted as a necessary progression for the downtown campus. The author's use of social media to protect her local landscape captured the attention of the *Globe and Mail* (a national newspaper), which reprinted one of her protests: "So, @UofTNews: as a soon-to-be dead alum w. $ to leave, am I annoyed by the anti-green plan? Y!"[53] Despite strong opposition and Atwood's high-profile advocacy, the University proceeded with the planned renovation. Fittingly, one editorial from the *National Post* quoted an English graduate student who called this push for artificial turf a form of "ecophobia": "There's this fear of grass and fear of mud. It's a bad sign when we are afraid of mud."[54] At one time, Atwood's nineteenth-century pioneers represented twentieth-century suburbanites' terror of the wilderness and preference for safe sterility. Now, actual twenty-first-century mega-city dwellers

raise the ante by eliminating all irregularities of "ruts, weeds and bare patches" that inevitably come with those fearsome 'natural' playing fields.

SELF-CONTROL THROUGH PEST CONTROL: SLUGS, ZOMBIES, HUMANS

Other implements in Atwood's shed combat disorder as an essential part of garden maintenance. Implements concerned with pest control make an appearance in the poem "Nothing New Here", where Atwood describes mice-ravaged roses outside "the cage" erected around the garden, and slugs breeding under the hay-mulch used to deter weeds between the rows of vegetables [Figure 11].[55] Though far from perfect, this "ragged space", the speaker observes, "still / gives what we eat".[56] The poem was inspired by Atwood and her partner Graeme Gibson's one-time Ontario farm, where, Atwood recalls, "every slug within a 10-mile radius headed for our garden"; these voracious pests were dealt with in a number of ways: targeted chicken predation, death by drowning in beer-laden saucers, the "rubber-boot-and-stone" method, and midnight raids conducted with flashlights and tin cans of kerosene.[57] Curiously, this slug-infested poem was quoted in a 1994 *Globe and Mail* column by an ecologist and environmental educator, as an example of the misdirected elimination of wild nature and the fight "to keep it back from the homestead plot".[58] In a Letter to the Editor the following week, Atwood noted that the lines from her poem had been taken out of

Figure 11/ Man picking radishes from a vegetable garden surrounded by a protective fence, Flin Flon, Manitoba, 28 June 1956. Photograph by Rosemary Gilliat Eaton, Courtesy of Library and Archives Canada.

context; if reading "with true environmentally-conscious sensitivity, the ecologist would have seen that this garden was an *organic* garden" — hence all the slugs.[59] This misreading brings to mind Kahn's theory of "environmental generational amnesia" and our diminishing ability to assess nature. Perhaps in this changing world of 'frontiers', poems are bound to be dramatically repurposed, as are tools. Indeed, Atwood opens her letter by stating that the *Globe and Mail* is an "excellent garden accessory — slugs prefer it to other papers". When it comes to repurposing, however, knowledge about an invention's original context and meaning affords insight for present and future uses. If the human desire for bountiful food has directed the invention of the garden and its tools, then perhaps it is not surprising that these same tools are required, in Atwood's literary worlds, to control our very selves.

In *The Happy Zombie Sunrise Home*, an apocalypse narrative Atwood co-authored with Naomi Alderman, Clio, a Toronto grandmother, contends with two pests: the inevitable slugs (which she manages with the product "Slug-Be-Gone") and the less predictable zombies. Having witnessed her neighbor's demise after the software-controlled barrier system surrounding his property crashes, Clio feels confident in her antiquated technology. Waging battle from her domestic home-front, Clio selects a varied arsenal: broken glass placed atop her garden wall; rhubarb stalks worn for their odor (a natural zombie-deterrent); a home-made rhubarb pie, which is only to be used as a last resort; and a range of tools, such as her three-pronged cultivator, four-tined fork, hoe, and potato gun. According to historians, "[h]unting weapons were the antecedents of the sharp tools the gardener always carried", and Atwood plays up this deadly versatility [Figure 12].[60] At the time of the narrative's serialization, she even tweeted a link to Lee Valley Tools' online catalogue (Canada's premier tool shop) with the line "At my fave garden supply: Useful anti #zombie tools!"[61] If gardening undertaken by women is supposed to be a leisure activity, then the repurposing of their tools as lethal weapons raises problematic associations with "'wildness' in all of its varied meanings, clearly out of place in the carefully controlled environment of suburbia".[62] Reflecting on the relationship between technology, gender, and race, sociologist Wairimu Njambi recounts the uneasiness of her Floridian neighbors with her own use of a machete. This tool she had used during her childhood in Kenya, but her neighbors associated it with masculinity, weaponry, and third world countries. Unlike Njambi — who "represents a disruption to the order of [her] exclusive community" of middle-class, white America — Atwood's Clio appears ordinary, even resourceful as she casually chops up zombies as fertilizer for her rhubarb. Using her tools against this new pest, she thinks of the living-dead as oddly vegetative: "their skulls are soft, more or less like pumpkins", their bodies, "squishy" like "over-ripe vegetable marrow".[63] Adapting her gardening routine to the

Figure 12/ Weapon or tool? Jim McLean, Irma, Alberta, 1912. Photograph courtesy of Glenbow Archives.

circumstances of this new frontier, the grandmother reveals that the nature that has run wild stems from imbalanced human-monsters created by, and out of, civilization. Brought on by a faulty health beverage, the zombie apocalypse plays on the familiar tropes of voracious appetites and mindless consumption gone awry. The zombies now embody the uncontrollability of the wilderness with its rampant growth and disturbing spread.

But it is important to note here that *human* characters (not just the living-dead) pose a threat comparable to insatiable garden pests hungry for vitality in Atwood's fictional worlds.

Figure 13/ Feeding our inner monster. Illustration by Vance Rodewalt, 20 November 1999. Image courtesy of Glenbow Archives.

In *The Year of the Flood*, Blanco (Toby's former boss who brutally preys on women) meets an end similar to that of Clio's zombies. When Blanco attacks the rooftop garden, the God's Gardeners defend themselves with a two-pronged fork, a plant-hydrator, bees, and the ethical (snail-related) practice of relocation. Later, Toby dispatches Blanco through an overdose of a poppy-infused painkiller, and drags his body to "the rooted-up earth of the flower bed".[64] The assumption that human appetites (for food, resources, immortality, sex) can forever grow and be satisfied ultimately feeds something monstrous in ourselves that must be addressed [Figure 13]. Likely this same realization informs Snowman's series of questions — "Why am I on this earth? How come I'm alone? Where's my Bride of Frankenstein?" — when he confronts his own abhorrent nature as the last remaining human following Crake's god-like experiment in mass extinction and species replacement.[65] Rather than striving for perpetual bounty and complete control over our surroundings, we must shift our attitudes and come back 'down to earth' by consciously reaching for tools that remind us of our limits. The arrogance of civilization surely prompts the zombie-ridden Clio to turn to the humble wisdom of her favorite book, *Mulch for the Mind: Down to Earth Jottings of Famous Horticulturalists*. One passage reads, "The whole of nature is a conjugation of the verb 'to eat', in the active and passive tense", serving as a reminder that humans are part of the food chain and will be eaten in turn.[66] Reflecting this sentiment, Atwood scholars note that humankind's indebtedness to nature is paramount to both *Oryx and Crake* and *The Year of the Flood*; without this realization, nature (or a mad scientist) will certainly correct the imbalance for us.[67] In this light, Atwood sees a powerful role for humankind's inventions, not as "soulless technological marvels [that will] save us", but rather as an embedded part of a responsibly-minded, material culture.[68]

COMPOSTING: REMEMBERING THE EARTH

Although rampant human desires can be detrimental to the garden, alternative scenarios are possible, and this brings us to Atwood's favorite tool: the compost bin. When asked as part of the LongPen interview what "[i]tem … [had] improved [her] life recently", Atwood replied, "a rotary compost maker that accelerates the decomposing process".[69] As the purposeful "mixture of various ingredients for fertilizing or enriching land", composting has a long history.[70] Some link it to the invention of gardening; others trace its shifting popularity depending on cultural practices and the advent of chemical fertilizers.[71] Atwood boasts a lifelong, highly literary relationship with compost. Describing her parents' northern vegetable patch, Atwood recalls that her father ferried via motorboat sacks of manure taken from a nearby logging camp: "it was dug in, along with … all the plant waste from the kitchen. This is perhaps when I learned to value such things as old potato peelings; I still can't discard one without a pang."[72] These childhood memories surely inform the short story "Unearthing Suite" (1983) where the writer-narrator declares, "My parents do not have houses, like other people. Instead they have *earths*."[73] The elderly couple's unconventional existence is foregrounded through their "dens": the Toronto garden, the one halfway up the province, and the northern hideaway. These nomads model a conscious dependence on, and active respect for, the earth that most of society seems to have let lapse through laziness and convenience. The writer-narrator notes her father's awareness "of the uses to which the earth is wrongly … put", and she confesses that while her parents grow their own food, she "creep[s] out to some sinful junk-food outlet or phone[s] up Pizza Pizza". Eventually, the parents' cultivation of multiple gardens prompts the reflection that "Gardening is not a rational act. What matters is the immersion of the hands in the earth, that ancient ceremony of which the Pope kissing the tarmac is merely a pallid vestigial remnant. In the spring, at the end of the day, you should smell like dirt." References to the Pope, immersion, and ceremony evoke reverence for the land, a near-baptism via the soil, as gardening infuses its tools and processes with systems of belief, imaginative impulse, and a seasonal mode of living that pays humble tribute to the earth.

The father of "Unearthing Suite" believes that the "proper activity" of mankind "is digging".[74] Not surprisingly, this occupation appears in Atwood's texts where composting facilitates a shift in consciousness. Compost brings individuals into direct contact with processes of decay and reconstitution, enabling them to remain 'grounded' in the material world and the human condition. Such is the purpose behind Atwood's poem "Digging", which provides a metaphor for an artist's philosophy and craft. Working the shovel in the compost so as to fertilize the melons, the speaker draws inspiration from the "archaeology of manure" (remnants of past breakfasts and animal bones) in order to "ward off anything / that is not a fact".[75] Refusing to spiral into the ether as artists and intellectuals are prone to do, this digging figure sees compost as the physical, imaginative connection to the daily realities of living and dying. The speaker uncovers an earthy spirituality through basic implements and materials: the shovel, the "temple to the goddess / of open mouths" (a cardboard box used to carry manure), and the "strict dogma" of half-buried rodent teeth. This dark reverence for dung and the quasi-religious insight it affords enter other Atwood poems where compost and soil are pivotal. The poem "All Bread", for instance, starkly declares the material interrelation of all things:

> All bread is made of wood,
> cow dung, packed brown moss,
> the bodies of dead animals, the teeth
> and backbones, what is left
> after the ravens. This dirt
> flows through the stems into the grain,
> into the arm....[76]

The poem speaks of something larger than us, not necessarily a divine creator, but an ecology of dirt in which everything is formed, as "Together / we eat this earth." While the lines resonate with early twentieth-century defenders of composting and the organicism movement, they also suggest a humble system of belief. The decay and growth of all living things provide our daily bread and a form of communion.[77] Digging in and acknowledging dirt bring about reconstituted modes of thinking, reordering the human spirit within a framework of humility. In the poem "Daybooks II", the section entitled "April, Radio, Planting, Easter" traces how earth "browns" the lover's feet, "thickens" his fingers, and "unfurls in [his] brain", just as it does in the tray of onion seedlings the speaker sets under a window.[78] The earth feeds the mind with new growth by literally opening up neurological pathways; the garden informs our ways of relating to the world through the most intimate materiality. Whereas the radio assaults the lovers with air waves that bring "wiry screams / and toy pain", the remedial 'technologies' of gardening (starting seedlings indoors) enable the earth to wash over them with a different kind of wave. The speaker observes, "We do not walk on the earth / but in it, wading / in that acid sea." Working in the springtime is a humble reminder of this couple's most fundamental connection to all things, bringing the possibility of tangible renewal in a modern world where suffering seems otherwise disembodied and unreal.

THE POLITICS OF DIRT

In "Unearthing Suite", the parents' gardening and the writer-narrator's creative process are paralleled as regenerative powers, since the story "celebrates the triumph of beginnings over endings".[79] Just as the parents create their "earths" for living, the writer-narrator forms her own imaginative dwelling through story: "the 'suite,' in this ongoing process, implying a form of eternal life". However, the revolutionary potential of this gardening process is spiritual only, not yet political. The combined images of compost, decay, and dirt merit further consideration as literal and figurative disruptions, as necessary precursors to social change. After all, compost results from the breaking down of a pre-existing order.

Mary Douglas, a key theorist of the sacred, finds ideas of pollution, defilement, and dirt to "relate to social life ... and a general view of social order".[80] For Douglas, "Where there is dirt there is a system. Dirt is the by-product of a systematic ordering and classification of matter, in so far as ordering involves rejecting inappropriate elements." This notion of 'dirt' is modeled most evocatively in "Unearthing Suite" through the mother's behavior and choices. As a young girl, the mother was expected to conduct herself with quiet feminine propriety, yet her first memory "is of sliding down a red clay bank in her delicate white post-Victorian pantaloons. She remembers the punishment, true, but she remembers better the lovely feeling of the mud."[81] This rebellious pleasure extends further when, as a young woman, she lived in Montreal's red-light district (another figuration of impurity), and when she later married her husband, whose research meant living in the wilderness and escaping a tidy domestic life of "antimacassars on the chairs". There is something to remaining 'grounded' — in this case, in touch with dirt and the unconventional — that enables the mother to see through and past modes of thinking that impose socially accepted (or 'clean') limitations on her behavior. Her association with the impure makes her an "anomaly", in Douglas' sense of the term, which implies the potential to "create a new pattern of reality" by unearthing and dwelling within other possible 'grounds' that satisfy her own personal inquisitiveness and testing of social norms.[82] This kind of solitary rebellion appears in other Atwood texts, but figures of 'dirt' are exceptional.[83] An individual may alter his or her preconceived notions, but as Douglas warns, "cultural categories are public matters" and "cannot so easily be subject to revision".[84]

In Atwood's recent speculative fiction, the politics of 'dirt' operate on a communal scale through the utopian vision of the God's Gardeners. Sect members embrace compost for its disruptive properties, just as they construct an alternative lifestyle, recruit members, spread their doctrine, and challenge the surrounding order of the Pleeblands and Compounds. A radical branch even cooperates with renegade Compound scientists, engaging in guerrilla gardening warfare by targeting the infrastructure and technologies of mainstream society. Microbes designed to consume asphalt are planted along highways, as are mice that have been formulated to attack cars. The objective of this "bioform resistance" is to breakdown the literal system and its values, reclaiming the earth as a commons so "the planet could repair itself. Before ... everything went extinct."[85] When anomalies disrupt existing cultural patterns, they are often ignored, physically controlled, condemned, or labelled as dangerous.[86] The God's Gardeners are met with all of these reactions. Residing in abandoned buildings and vacant lots, group members are denounced as "ecofreak[s]", "subversive ... fanatical greenies", and "fanatical greenie weirdo[s]".[87] Indeed, some of their practices, such as "slug and snail relocation", seem at once impractical and absurd; they would no doubt find Atwood's rubber-boot-and-stone method sacrilege.[88] Critics are typically unsure what to make of the sect. Bergthaller asserts that the Gardeners' way of life is "not ... a viable path to a sustainable future" and their religion is "patently silly".[89] Others observe that Atwood, an agnostic, creates a "tongue-in-cheek" portrayal of these religious extremists.[90] Certainly Atwood cannot share the Gardeners' conviction that all writing should be avoided. Nevertheless, the sect enables Atwood to capture the ways in which organizations that challenge the status quo (especially in terms of environmental stewardship) are often resisted with ridicule, social condemnation, and even regulatory intervention.

The God's Gardeners' preachings may be called "sweet but delusional", yet a closer look at their philosophy of compost reveals a radical politics that challenges mainstream values of growth, abundance, and consumerism.[91] At the heart of *The Year of the Flood* lie two competing systems and discourses of 'dirt'. On the one hand, the elite, corporate Compounds and lower-class Pleeblands adhere to a linear economy, where waste (including dead bodies) is tossed into the "garboil": an invention that transforms matter into petroleum for endless energy consumption and pollution. Here garbage consists of items that do not break down or are toxic, as Snowman observes when the Crakers gather debris: "A plastic BlyssPluss container, empty.... A computer mouse.... Sometimes they find tins of motor oil, caustic solvents, plastic bottles of bleach."[92] By contrast, the God's Gardeners create a cyclical economy, teaching their children that "There was no such thing as garbage, trash or dirt, only matter that hadn't been put to a proper use."[93] During "Young Bioneer scavenging day", members of the sect gather discarded materials from the Pleeblands. These Bioneers are 'pioneers' on the frontier of reclassifying waste material into something of living value. Hotel and restaurant soaps thrown out "by the shovelfull" are gathered and reconstituted into new slabs and sold at the Gardeners'

Tree of Life Natural Materials Exchange, just as discarded wine is fermented into vinegar for non-toxic household cleaner. Devoted to upholding a cyclical, organic economy, the God's Gardeners even refuse to use plastic toothbrushes, which symbolically would defile their bodies and beliefs.

Honoring 'dirt' and decay as central to life, the Gardeners counter the predominant culture where humans attempt to transcend the limits of their material world through advanced technologies. When working undercover at the AnooYoo Spa, Toby reflects that her customers fear "The whole *thing* thing. Nobody likes it, thought Toby — being a body, a thing. Nobody wants to be limited in that way. We'd rather have wings. Even the word *flesh* has a mushy sound to it." The elite go to extreme lengths to stop this inevitable decline. Epidermal replacements, such as the Fountain of Yooth Total Plunge, superficially remove clients from the lifecycle by perpetuating a youthful glow. This world is one of purity, where no visible signs or odors of 'dirt' are detectable: in other words, the earth and the body's inherent connection and return to it are erased. Remembering her childhood at the HelthWyzer Compound, Ren recalls that her mother always took her shopping, played golf, or would go "off to the AnooYoo Spa to get improvements done to herself, and then she'd come back smelling nice". Later, when Ren returns to the Compound as a teenager and is reunited with her father, she thinks he "smell[s] funny ... — like disinfectant", and she "miss[es] the leafy smells of the Gardeners". During her first night, Ren bathes in a clean white tub with "fake-flower bath essence" and is made to "feel dirty, and also stinky. I stank like earth — compost earth, before it's finished." To smell of compost is evidence of belonging to an alternative social order that ensures personal integration with the earth, as opposed to a culture of endless consumption, perpetual youth, and digital detachment. Toby similarly detects her new smell after escaping the Pleeblands and becoming a sect member: "At night, Toby breathed herself in. Her new self. Her skin smelled like honey and salt. And earth." These experiences suggest compost can be transformative, converting dirt into "a different kind of *cleanliness*, one that makes the organic processes visible".[94] The Gardeners' homes are organized to reflect these revised classifications of order and disorder. For instance, Ren recalls that only a curtain separated the violet biolet (a compost toilet) from the main living space: "The Gardeners said digestion was holy and there was nothing funny or terrible about the smells and noises that were part of the end product of the nutritional process."[95] Because the God's Gardeners reject consumerism and perpetual growth, they uphold a complete life (and digestive) cycle through their quotidian technologies. In this way, waste is literally observed and sensed so as to retain its place in human consciousness, culture, and identity. The most tangible expression of this rebellious social order, where dirt is clean and a humble reminder of one's own connection to the soil, is when Pilar's body is surreptitiously planted in a public park as natural fertilizer for an elderberry shrub. In direct contrast to the dominant society that views death as another means of profit, the God's Gardeners preach that bodies must be "broken down and returned to their elements to enrich the lives of other Creatures". Thus, the interment is referred to as "Pilar's composting".

Tackling the old definition of "dirt as matter out of place", the God's Gardeners work to give dirt its proper place as a central part of human existence and identity.[96] While they are ineffectual in changing consumer culture, their message nevertheless resonates when the latter's system terminates in the waterless flood and, most notably, in mounds of bodies subsumed in the earth by new plant growth. The consequence of not respecting compost (and by extension, dirt) as an intrinsic part of human culture is the eventual failure to recognize and respond to the disorder that society creates in its endless pursuit of vitality, economic growth, and material abundance. In *Oryx and Crake,* Snowman explains this scenario to the Crakers in his revised version of the creation myth, which he illustrates by way of a pail full of water mixed with a handful of dirt:

> 'There were too many people, and so the people were all mixed up with the dirt....' 'There', he says. 'Chaos. You can't drink it...'
> 'No!' a chorus.
> 'You can't eat it....'
> ...
> 'The people in the chaos were full of chaos themselves, and the chaos made them do bad things. They were killing other people all the time. And they were eating up all the Children of Oryx [the animals].... They ate them even when they weren't hungry.'
> ... 'And then Oryx said to Crake, *Let us get rid of the chaos.* And so Crake took the chaos, and he poured it away.' Snowman demonstrates sloshing the water off to the side, then turns the pail upside down. 'There. Empty. And this is how Crake did the Great Rearrangement and made the Great Emptiness. He cleared away the dirt, he cleared room....'
> 'For his children! For the Children of Crake!'
> 'Right. And for....'
> 'And for the Children of Oryx, as well!'[97]

Equating humans with dirt and disorder, Snowman's tale crystallizes the fact that an imbalanced culture will become absolutely the thing it tries to transcend. Despite advanced technologies facilitating desires, human culture is material and has limits. In the second volume of Atwood's trilogy, compost plays a transformative role by challenging the dominant social order. In the final novel, *MaddAddam*, Snowman's oral storytelling is followed by a written composition (coincidently, another definition of 'compost'). One of the Crakers learns to write and "create[s] a text ... that does not disappear in performance, but remains to be passed on and interpreted by future generations".[98] These narrative tools and processes imaginatively reshape the earth and its inhabitants in much the same way that Douglas' "dirt" (in the form of cultural anomalies and "ambiguous symbols") enters into "poetry and mythology, to enrich meaning or call attention to other levels of existence".[99] Bringing the past (the dead) forward in time through reinterpreted forms, storytelling offers the possibility of reconstitution: it breaks down what has come before, rearranges it, and hopefully provides insight for the future. In this way, storytelling, like composting, becomes a timeless tool.

TURNING THE EARTH, TRANSFORMING OURSELVES

Yesterday, planted shallots, onions. Today: potatoes ... maybe some peas, spinach, kale + lettuce? Risk-taking....
Margaret Atwood,
Twitter Post,
28 April 2013, 7:17 am.

When it comes to living in the earth as opposed to on it, the God's Gardeners and Atwood's many other cultivating figures reveal that it is illogical to think of the garden as external to our lives, as "a pet" we keep purely for pleasure.[100] The contents of Atwood's figurative garden shed — the shovel, scythe, Twitter feed, and compost bin — suggest that direct and humble engagement with our local, material worlds will help to counter our "environmental generational amnesia" as we grasp our inherent connection with the soil. This is not to say that old tools are necessarily better than the new. After all, the garden itself was an invention that led to new sets of problems: agriculture, displaced peoples, social stratification, taxation, and depleted soils. In the end, we must keep in mind that users, not technologies, are the real culprits. If we choose only to garden electronically, our skills, knowledge, and consciousness of the earth will be drastically curtailed. For a 'digging' writer like Atwood, to remain grounded means both questioning the status quo and actively remembering that "the real world ... is composed ... not of words but of drainpipes, holes in the ground, furiously multiplying weeds, hunks of granite."[101] The revolutionary tools of the future may be the most ordinary ones, as backyards, front yards, and rooftops become experimental grounds for greener realities. In the end, the story of the garden and its tools is ultimately the story of ourselves, our changing relationship with nature and the many 'frontiers' we have created and destroyed [Figure 14]. Only by engaging with the garden in ways that demand more from us — through physical labor working in tandem with mental toil — can we reach into the earth and rediscover ourselves.

NOTES

1/ I would like to thank Kwantlen Polytechnic University, the Office of Research and Scholarship, and the 0.6 percent Faculty PD fund, which enabled me to travel to the University of Delaware to present a preliminary version of this essay at the Earth Perfect? symposium in June 2013. For the quote see Rosanna Greenstreet, "Q&A: Margaret Atwood", *The Guardian*, 28 October 2011, *The Guardian*, Web, www.guardian.co.uk/lifestyle/2011/oct/28/margaret-atwood-q-a, accessed 23 May 2013.

2/ Wajcman, Judy, *Feminism Confronts Technology*, University Park: Pennsylvania State University Press, 1991, p. 89.

3/ Sangster, Heather, "Mother of Invention", *Belle*, fall 2006, p. 70.

4/ Atwood, Margaret, "The Art of the Matter", *The Globe and Mail*, 24 January 2004, A19, ProQuest, 25 April 2013, n.p.

5/ Slesin, Suzanne, Guillaume Pellerin, et al., *Garden Tools*, Everyday Things Series, New York: Abbeville Press, 1996, p. 14.

6/ See Rachel Maines, *Hedonizing Technologies*, Baltimore: John Hopkins University Press, 2009, p. 126.

7/ Nye, David E., *Technology Matters: Questions to Live With*, Cambridge, MA: MIT Press, 2006, p. 4.

Figure 14/ Pupils ready to work in school garden, Lang, Saskatchewan, c. 1917. Photograph courtesy of Glenbow Archives.

8/ Slesin, et al., *Garden Tools*, p. 14, 135; see p. 14 for the quote.

9/ Maines, *Hedonizing Technologies*, pp. 3, 122.

10/ Atwood, Margaret, "Victory Gardens", *Moving Targets: Writing with Intent, 1982–2004*, Toronto: Anansi Press, 2004, p. 354.

11/ Treib, Marc, "Power Plays: The Garden as Pet", *The Meaning of Gardens*, Mark Francis and Randolph T. Hester, Jr eds., Cambridge, MA: MIT Press, 1990, p. 87.

12/ Atwood, Margaret, *Oryx and Crake*, Toronto: Random House, 2003, pp. 316, 245, 218.

13/ Atwood, Margaret, "Atwoodville", *Alternatives Journal*, vol. 38, no. 1, 2012, pp. 28, 30.

14/ See the website, http://www.yearoftheflood.ca/ca/book/reading-list, which explicitly connects the reading list to the God's Gardeners'

philosophy; and Richard Louv, *Last Child in the Woods*, New York: Chapel Hill, 2008, pp. 3, 16, 19. For Louv's discussion of the successive frontiers see pp. 16–31.

15/ Atwood, "Atwoodville", p. 32.

16/ Kahn, Jr, Peter H., *Technological Nature: Adaptation and The Future of Human Life*, Cambridge, MA: MIT Press, 1994, p. xvii (for the quote) and ch. 10.

17/ McLuhan, Marshall, "The Gadget Lover", *Understanding Media: The Extensions of Man*, Cambridge, MA and London: MIT Press, 1994, pp. 42–43.

18/ Marx, Leo, "Technology: The Emergence of a Hazardous Concept", *Technology and Culture*, vol. 51, no. 3, July 2010, p. 577, *Project Muse*, DOI: 10.1253/tech.2010.0009.

19/ Atwood, "Atwoodville", p. 31.

20/ Atwood, Margaret, *The Year of the Flood*, Toronto: McClelland and Stewart, 2009, pp. 188, 315, 168.

21/ Nye, *Technology Matters*, p. 4.

22/ Atwood, *The Year of the Flood*, pp. 265, 363.

23/ Atwood, *Oryx and Crake*, pp. 184–186.

24/ Nye, *Technology Matters*, p. 104.

25/ Atwood, *The Year of the Flood*, pp. 363, 149.

26/ See Louv, *Last Child in the Woods*, Part VI: "Wonder Land: Opening the Fourth Frontier", pp. 235–287.

27/ von Baeyer, Edwinna, *Rhetoric and Roses: A History of Canadian Gardening*, Markham: Fitzhenry and Whiteside, 1984, pp. 36–37, 43, 64–65.

28/ Atwood, "Victory Gardens", p. 359. "Victory Gardens" originally appeared as the foreword to Elise Houghton's *A Breath of Fresh Air: Celebrating Nature and School Gardens*, Toronto: Sumach Pressnansi, 2003.

29/ Bergthaller, Hannes, "Housebreaking the Human Animal: Humanism and the Problem of Sustainability in Margaret Atwood's *Oryx and Crake* and *The Year of the Flood*", *English Studies*, vol. 91, no. 7, November 2010, p. 741, Academic Search Premier, accessed 27 April 2013.

30/ Atwood, *The Year of the Flood*, p. 176.

31/ Bergthaller, "Housebreaking", p. 735.

32/ Atwood, *Oryx and Crake*, p. 367.

33/ Atwood, "Atwoodville", p. 31.

34/ Tancock, Kat, "Interview with Author Margaret Atwood", *Canadian Living Magazine*, Web, 22 April 2013, n. p.

35/ Atwood, Margaret, "Progressive Insanities of a Pioneer", *Selected Poems*, Toronto: Oxford University Press, 1976, pp. 60–63, ll. 10–14. This poem was originally published in *The Animals in That Country*, 1968.

36/ Atwood, Margaret, "The Planters", *Selected Poems*, p. 84, l. 15. This poem was originally published in *The Journals of Susanna Moodie*, 1970.

37/ Atwood, "The Planters", l. 13. See chapter one in my book *Garden Plots: Canadian Women Writers and Their Literary Gardens*, Montreal and Kingston: McGill-Queen's University Press, 2013, for a discussion of the contents and form of Susanna Moodie's backwoods garden, which was an extensive adaptation of the English cottage garden tradition.

38/ Hatch, Robert, "Margaret Atwood, the Land, and Ecology", *Margaret Atwood: Works and Impact*, Reingard M. Nischik ed., Rochester: Camden House, 2000, p. 188.

39/ Atwood, Margaret, "The City Planners", *Selected Poems*, Toronto: Oxford University Press, 1976, pp. 10–11, l. 27. This poem was originally published in *The Circle Game*, 1966.

40/ Atwood, "The City Planners", ll. 11–12, 21–22.

41/ Atwood, Margaret, "A Garden Memoir", *Toronto Life Gardens*, spring/summer 1996, p. 73.

42/ Atwood, "Victory Gardens", p. 355.

43/ Jenkins, Virginia Scott, *The Lawn: A History of an American Obsession*, Washington and London: Smithsonian Institutional Press, 1994, pp. 9–10.

44/ Whitney, Kristoffer, "Living Lawns, Dying Waters: The Suburban Boom, Nitrogenous Fertilizers, and the Nonpoint Source Pollution Dilemma", *Technology and Culture*, vol. 51, no. 3, July 2010, pp. 653, *Project Muse*, DOI: 10.1353/tech.2010.0033.

45/ Atwood, *Oryx and Crake*, pp. 243, 226, 282.

46/ Atwood, *The Year of the Flood*, p. 141.

47/ Jenkins, *The Lawn*, p. 134.

48/ Atwood, *Oryx and Crake*, p. 325.

49/ Jenkins, *The Lawn*, p. 134.

50/ Atwood, *Oryx and Crake*, pp. 367–368.

51/ Atwood, Margaret, Twitter Post, 16 June 2013, 3.08 pm., http://twitter.com/MargaretAtwood.

52/ Atwood, "Victory Gardens", p. 359.

53/ Bradshaw, James, "Atwood Leads the Charge Against Fake Turf at U of T", *The Globe and Mail*, 14 March 2013, A6.

54/ Kuitenbrouwer, Peter, "U of T Battlefield: Natural or Artificial?", *National Post*, 5 June 2013, p. A8.

55/ Atwood, Margaret, "Nothing New Here", *Selected Poems II: Poems Selected and New 1976–1986*, Toronto: Oxford University Press, 1986, pp. 8–9, l. 14. This poem was originally published in *Two-Headed Poems*, 1978.

56/ Atwood, "Nothing New Here", l. 36, ll. 46–47.

57/ Atwood, "A Garden Memoir", p. 74.

58/ Schluter, Andrea, "Fifth Column: Outdoors", *The Globe and Mail*, 7 October 1994, p. A22. *ProQuest Historical Newspapers: The Globe and Mail* (1844–009), accessed 28 January 2013.

59/ Atwood, Margaret, "How Does Ms. Atwood's Garden Grow?", *The Globe and Mail*, 15 October 1994, p. D7. *ProQuest Historical Newspapers: The Globe and Mail* (1844–2009), accessed 28 January 2013.

60/ Slesin, et. al., *Garden Tools*, p. 99.

61/ Atwood, Margaret, Twitter Post, 25 October 2012, 6.00 am., http://twitter.com/MargaretAtwood.

62/ Njambi, Wairimu Ngaruiya, and Mellisa Putman Sprenkle, "Rethinking Masculinized Tools: Machetes, Women's Work, and Suburban Yard Maintenance," *NWSA Journal*, vol. 16, no. 2, summer 2004, pp. 123, 128, 124. *Project Muse*, DOI: 10.1253/nwsa.2004.0060.

63/ Atwood, Margaret, and Naomi Alderman, *The Happy Zombie Sunrise Home*, Wattpad, 2012, Web, ch.1, ch. 9. This online story is unpaginated.

64/ Atwood, *The Year of the Flood*, p. 384.

65/ Atwood, *Oryx and Crake*, p. 207.

66/ Atwood and Alderman, *The Happy Zombie Sunrise Home*, ch. 5.

67/ For a spiritual reading of humanity's ecological dilemma in Atwood, see Shannon Hengen, "Moral/Environmental Debt in *Payback* and *Oryx and Crake*", *Margaret Atwood: The Robber Bride, The Blind Assassin, Oryx and Crake*, J. Brooks Bouson ed., London and New York: Continuum International Publishing Group, 2010, pp. 129–140. For an evolutionary perspective, see Bergthaller, "Housebreaking", pp. 731–732

68/ Hengen, "Moral/Environmental Debt", p. 135.

69/ Sangster, "Mother of Invention", p. 70.

70/ "compost, n.1", OED Online, June 2013, Oxford University Press, http://www.oed.com/view/Entry/37811, accessed 29 July 2013.

71/ On the invention of gardening, see William E. Doolittle, "Gardens Are Us, We Are Nature: Transcending Antiquity and Modernity", *American Geographical Society*, vol. 94, no. 3, July 2004, p. 392, JSTOR, http://www.jstor.org/stable/30034280, accessed 25 March 2013. On the replacement of compost by chemical fertilizer, see William Bryant Logan, *The Tool Book*, New York, Workman Publishing, 1997, p. 209.

72/ Atwood, "A Garden Memoir", p. 73.

73/ Atwood, Margaret, "Unearthing Suite", *Bluebeard's Egg*, Toronto: McClelland and Stewart, 1983, p. 247. Emphasis added. Following are references to pp. 247, 243, and 255, respectively.

74/ Atwood, "Unearthing Suite", p. 254.

75/ Atwood, Margaret, "Digging", *Selected Poems*, Toronto: Oxford University Press, 1976, pp. 181–182, l. 22, ll. 33–34, 3, 29. This poem was originally published in *You Are Happy*, 1974.

76/ Atwood, Margaret, "All Bread", *Selected Poems II: Poems Selected and New 1976–1986*, Toronto: Oxford University Press, 1986, p. 52, ll.1–7, 28–29. This poem was originally published in *Two-Headed Poems*, 1978.

77/ Vogt, Kathleen, "Real and Imaginary Animals in the Poetry of Margaret Atwood", *Margaret Atwood: Vision and Forms*, Kathryn VanSpanckeren and Jan Garden Castro eds., Carbondale and Edwardsville: Southern Illinois University Press, 1988, p.177.

78/ Atwood, Margaret, "Daybooks II", *Selected Poems II: Poems Selected and New 1976–1986*, Toronto: Oxford University Press, 1986, pp. 43–47, sect. 13, l. 22, l. 23, l. 24, ll. 15–16, 28–30. This poem was originally published in *Two-Headed Poems*, 1978.

79/ Godard, Barbara, "Tales Within Tales: Margaret Atwood's Folk Narratives", *Canadian Literature*, vol. 109, summer 1986, Web, p. 72.

80/ Douglas, Mary, *Purity and Danger*, London and New York: Taylor & Francis, 2003, ebook, introduction, pp. 51, 147. Pagination changes in the ebook depending on font size and the vertical or horizontal position of the iPad, so I have included chapters as well as page numbers (for the horizontal view).

81/ Atwood, "Unearthing Suite", pp. 251, 252.

82/ Douglas, *Purity and Danger*, ch. 2, p. 157.

83/ In Atwood's first novel *The Edible Woman* (1969), the protagonist Marian stops eating in response to her consumer society and her engagement. At the same time, this normally tidy young woman enters a period of literal and figurative disorder. The novel also makes a brief reference to another woman who subverts social norms when she stops bathing for a year.

84/ Douglas, *Purity and Danger*, ch. 2, pp. 157–158.

85/ Atwood, *The Year of the Flood*, p. 333.

86/ Douglas, *Purity and Danger*, ch. 2, pp. 158–160.

87/ Atwood, *The Year of the Flood*, pp. 40, 266, 294.

88/ Atwood, *The Year of the Flood*, p. 217.

89/ Bergthaller, "Housebreaking the Human Animal", pp. 738–739.

90/ Bouson, J. Brooks, "'We're Using Up the Earth. It's Almost Gone': A Return to the Post-Apocalyptic Future in Margaret Atwood's The Year of the Flood", *The Journal of Commonwealth Literature*, vol. 46, no. 9, 2011, p. 17, Sage, DOI: 1177/0021989410395430.

91/ Atwood, *The Year of the Flood*, p. 103.

92/ Atwood, *Oryx and Crake*, p. 9.

93/ Atwood, *The Year of the Flood*, pp. 68–69, 216, 264, 65, 209, 101.

94/ Braham, William H., "Waste and Dirt: Notes on the Architecture of Compost", *Dirt*, Megan Born, Helen Furján, and Lily Jencks, with Phillip M. Crosby eds., Philadelphia and Cambridge, MA: PennDesign and MIT Press, 2012, p. 274. Emphasis added.

95/ Atwood, *The Year of the Flood*, pp. 63, 160, 184.

96/ Douglas, *Purity and Danger*, ch. 2, p. 147.

97/ Atwood, *Oryx and Crake*, p. 125.

98/ Scurr, Ruth, "A Score for Voices", *TLS*, 16 & 23 August 2013, pp. 3–4.

99/ Douglas, *Purity and Danger*, ch. 2, p. 161.

100/ Treib, "Power Plays: The Garden as Pet", p. 87.

101/ Atwood, "Unearthing Suite", p. 258.

GARDENING AS
SUBVERSIVE ART
/ LINDA WEINTRAUB

THE ART OF
GARDENING

148 /STEPHANIE N. BRYAN

THE SORCERESS' GARDEN: CIRCE AND MOUNT STEWART, NORTHERN IRELAND

We sought the grove of oaks; and there we found
Deep in the glades a place beautiful,
Built on a rising knoll with polished stones:
And there a mortal or a goddess sang....
/ Homer[1]

In 1744, Alexander Stewart, a successful businessman, purchased from Robert Colville an extensive landholding in County Down, Northern Ireland. The property included the manors of Comber and Newtownards, as well as the Templecrone demesne. Alexander called the estate Mount Pleasant; his son Robert, later the first Marquess of Londonderry, changed the name to Mount Stewart. Throughout the eighteenth and nineteenth centuries, the estate evolved as it passed through several generations of family who expanded the house, gardens, and landscape park. In 1915, Charles Stewart Henry inherited Mount Stewart and succeeded to the title of seventh Marquess of Londonderry. This provided his wife, Edith Helen, Lady Londonderry, the opportunity to transform the gardens at Mount Stewart, an endeavor that she undertook with great passion — and at great expense — for a span of nearly 40 years, until her death in 1959 [Figure 1].

Like many gardens throughout the United Kingdom, Lady Londonderry's gardens were comprised of exotic plants; indeed, Mount Stewart's mild microclimate was particularly well suited to sustaining plants collected from around the globe. And similar to other gardens of the period, the layout at Mount Stewart is a mixture of 'borrowings', particularly from Mediterranean sources. But the place has its own distinctive character reflecting the extraordinary personality of its creator. Because much of the atmosphere of the gardens derives from ephemeral and intangible qualities, it cannot be captured entirely on plan or fully understood through images. Rather, a close examination of Edith's correspondence, photo albums, published writings, and the nine garden journals

that she maintained from 1917 to 1959 taps into the intent and creative essence of her gardens. An exemplar of an early to mid-twentieth-century horticultural collection that also exhibits noteworthy imagination in its design, Edith's gardens at Mount Stewart stand apart because of her identification with the powerful literary figure of Circe the Sorceress. This association resulted in an eclectic and idiosyncratic landscape that continues to transport visitors to an unexpected realm in the midst of Northern Ireland. Themes of mythology, magic, and metamorphosis are evident throughout the gardens at Mount Stewart, which for Edith became a place of personal enchantment — in her own words, "a land of Heart's Desire".[2]

FIRST IMPRESSIONS AND MOTIVATIONS

The lonely island and the sounding beach
Answer with barks and howls, the scream of birds
Her uncontrollable, aching cry of love.
/ A. D. Hope[3]

During the 1910s, Edith first visited Mount Stewart with Charles, her husband of 11 years, while he recuperated from appendicitis. At the time, Charles' parents, Charles Vane-Tempest-Stewart and Lady Theresa Susey Helen, sixth Marquess and Marchioness of Londonderry, presided over the estate. The unfavorable circumstances of Edith's visit shaped her intial impression of Mount Stewart, and her writings from decades later reveal a dismal first impression of the house and grounds. In a 1935 article for the *Journal of the Royal Horticultural Society,* Edith recounted that Mount Stewart was "a dark and damp abode, with dank and dripping vegetation all round!"[4] Similarly, in 1956, she recalled it as "the dampest, darkest, and saddest place I had ever stayed in, in the winter.

Large Ilex trees almost touched the house in some places and sundry other big trees blocked out all light and air."[5] By contrast, Edith's mother-in-law, Theresa, had a very different opinion of the gardens, writing only a few years after Edith's stay:

> In January when we gain the shelter of the drive, the brilliant green of the grisileas and the grey green ilexes give a sense of warmth and comfort.... Snowdrops all planted round the stems of the trees and the deciduous trees look like ghosts mixing with the evergreens and the dark glossy leaves of the rhododendrons, with here and there a patch of brilliant colour, the early flowering scarlet which never fails to show buds and flowers in early January.[6]

Theresa described her gardens in a highly romanticized style for several pages, suggesting that she perceived them as an inviting place filled with beauty and delight.

In 1915, Theresa's husband died, causing her to change residences. As their only son, Charles inherited the family's status and immense wealth, which included Mount Stewart among other estates. Charles and Edith did not immediately move to Mount Stewart but rather remained at Londonderry House in London during World War I (WWI) while Charles served in France with the Royal Horse Guards,

which were part of the eighth Cavalry Brigade. After the war, Charles accepted a new post as the Minister for Education in the first Ulster Parliament, and so he and Edith moved to Mount Stewart because of its proximity to Belfast.

While Edith had tolerated her powerful and forceful mother-in-law, she did not particularly like her. Thus, Edith was compelled to make Mount Stewart into a place entirely of her own. It seems that Edith never would have felt at liberty to transform Wynyard, the family seat.[7] But upon arriving at Mount Stewart, she immediately removed "three beautiful Ilex trees on the south side of the house", those very trees that she had earlier described as blocking out the light. Not only the ilex trees were removed. As Edith would recount, "[in] planning the new formal gardens on the southern and western aspects, numerous other trees and shrubs and huge masses of Rhododendrons had to be felled and cleared, until at last the space intended for the gardens began to take shape".[8] Other motivations beyond personalizing the landscape drove her transformative efforts. While Edith saw the demobilization of the army after WWI as an opportunity to indulge her creative ambition at Mount Stewart, she also felt a sense of patriotic duty to provide employment to jobless war veterans. Further, Edith's endeavor to make the gardens and grounds "not only more cheerful and livable, but beautiful as well", was rooted to

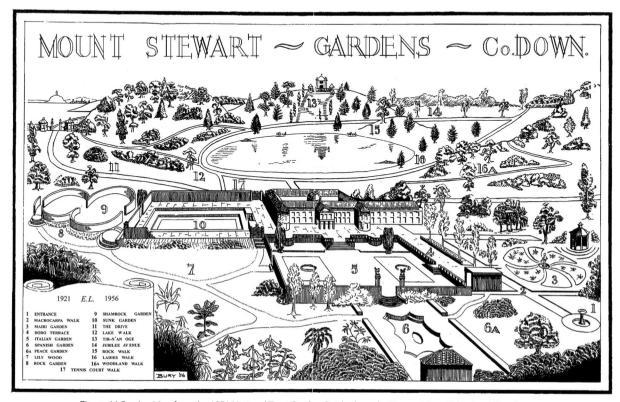

Figure 1/ Garden Map from the 1956 National Trust Garden Guide drawn by Viscount Bury, © National Trust Images.

some extent in her unfulfilled relationship with Charles.[9] By the time the couple moved to Mount Stewart, separation had become an integral part of their marriage. Charles was, in fact, absent most of the time due to political, social, and sporting engagements, in addition to extramarital love affairs.[10] Earlier in their marriage, Edith had summed up her feelings about the situation in a note that stated: "I feel like a bird with only one wing when you are away."[11]

Edith's correspondence suggests that her separation from Charles was almost unbearable during their early marriage, yet during WWI she had discovered two outlets from this reality that required great energy and organizing capabilities: she established and managed a volunteer force comprised of tens of thousands of women, known as the Women's Legion; and she formed a social group called the Ark, an eclectic mix

of personalities who gathered weekly at Londonderry House. Ark members were required to adopt the name of a real or mythological creature, often alluding to some aspect of the individual's personality. Because Edith attracted a circle of admirers through both the Women's Legion and Ark club, poet-friend Sir Edmund Gosse the 'Gos-hawk' christened her as 'Circe the Sorceress', a reference to the beguiling enchantress who waylaid the hero Odysseus in the course of his return voyage from Troy. It was a befitting character, for both Edith and Circe had alluring personalities that attracted many men. Nevertheless, as Edith passionately loved Charles, she repeatedly wrote to him: "I am convinced we shall be together some day, somewhere, always."[12] Thus, Edith also resembled Penelope, the faithful wife of Odysseus awaiting her hero's return home.

After the war, when the couple moved to Mount Stewart, Edith shifted her attention from the Women's Legion and the Ark to a new vehicle for expressing her power and creative energy: gardening [Figure 2]. She had previously shown interest in gardening at her other homes located in the colder parts of England and the far north of Scotland, but what had been a hobby evolved into a passion at Mount Stewart. Edith cultivated a sense of inner happiness through gardening, which became a spiritual act for her. At the beginning of one of her garden photo albums, she copied by hand a stanza from a poem by Dorothy Frances Gurney: "The kiss of sun for pardon / The song of the birds for mirth / One is nearer God's heart in a garden / Than anywhere else on earth." Although she did not repeat the entire poem, the last two lines read: "Where the angel of strength was the warden / And the soul of the world found ease."[13] While Edith's time at Mount Stewart was one of reconciliation with Charles, gardening certainly gave her great strength and ease amid her longstanding personal woes with him.

Figure 2/ Edith, Lady Londonderry, clearing firewood from the Lily Wood at Mount Stewart. Although Edith was an aristocrat, she did not hesitate to partake in the hard labor required to maintain her gardens. c. 1940, from family album. Courtesy of Lady Rose Lauritzen and the National Trust, B. Rutledge.

INFLUENCES ON THE DEVELOPMENT OF THE GARDENS

By your dwelling there, and so near
Plenty of life! Plenty of frivolity!
Will speedily make you forget,
And enjoy all earth's many vanities!
/ John Appleby[14]

The gardens at Mount Stewart would become a highly personalized amalgamation of diverse influences and inspirations. Edith found inspiration in sources including travel destinations, fond childhood memories, literature, and

Figure 3/ Balustrade on the Isolotto at Boboli Gardens. Photographer Charles Latham, originally published in *Country Life*, vol. XIX, 19 May 1906, p. 702. Courtesy of *Country Life*.

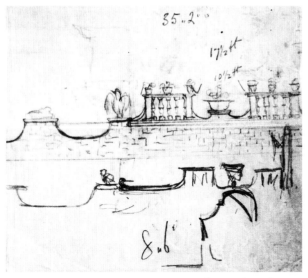

Figure 4/ Edith, Lady Londonderry's sketch for the balustrades that flank the eastern and western sides of the Italian Garden at Mount Stewart. Date unknown, from family collection. Courtesy of Lady Rose Lauritzen and the National Trust.

her Celtic heritage as well as the current gardening practices showcased in well-known publications that she kept in her sitting room. Many of the gardening books that she owned contain notations and placemarkers, while others hold loose sketches indicating the direct influences of these sources. A sense of Edith's influences may also be gleaned from her garden journals, which are largely comprised of plant orders, instructions, and documentation of design work, article clippings, photographs, correspondence, and miscellaneous notations.

Edith's Mediterranean travels, coupled with her well-read copy of the Arthur Thomas Bolton's *The Gardens of Italy*, infused a strong Italian influence into her designs. She derived the structure and organization of the herm statues at the southern end of her Italian Garden from the Upper Garden of the Villa Farnese at Caprarola. In addition, she fashioned the balustrades of the terraces that edge her Italian Garden after the ones at the Boboli Gardens in Florence [Figures 3, 4]. While such peripheral elements show the direct influence of Italian sources, the parterres that Edith centered in the space referenced the terraced gardens at her childhood home, Dunrobin Castle in Scotland.[15] Edith's great-grandfather, the second Duke of Sutherland, had Dunrobin's gardens laid out in an Italian Renaissance style by Sir Charles Barry, an English architect best known for his role in the rebuilding of London's Houses of Parliament in the nineteenth century. Perhaps Edith incorporated this design at Mount Stewart because it conjured fond memories from her past.

Edith also called upon her Scottish heritage and upbringing to entwine themes from Celtic folklore into her gardens. She delineated the Shamrock Garden with a trifoliate enclosure of clipped hedges. Atop the hedges, multiple topiaries depicted:

> a complete caricature of an ancient hunting scene supposed to represent the family of Stewart arriving for the chase: the arrival by boat in an ancient coracle in which they are all seated; the start; the hunt, in which the stag is haunched by an arrow shot from the bow of an intrepid amazon; the return journey with but a wretched hare, the devil having come to the rescue of the stag. The figures, with the exception of the coracle, which was copied from an ancient tombstone, were taken from Mary 1st of England's *Book of Hours*.[16]

The main feature inside the Shamrock Garden, however, was a large bed that formed "the left hand, the bloody hand of the McDonnell's, the direct ancestors of Frances Anne, Marchioness of Londonderry".[17] As the story goes, two rival Scottish clans raced from Scotland to Ireland, and whoever should touch Ireland first would possess the land. When McDonnell saw that he was losing the race, he cut off his left hand, threw it on the shore, and claimed the land. Celtic themes are evident elsewhere in the gardens, too, such as in the family burial grounds, which Edith aptly named Tír na nÓg — or "land of the forever young" — complete with a sculpture of the white stag, that, according to legend, accompanied spirits to this land.[18]

Edith also incorporated playful references to her friends and family. On a terrace adjacent to the Italian Garden, Edith commemorated certain members of her Ark club through cast-concrete sculptures of their 'assumed' characters. Four dodo birds that sit atop stone pillars represented her father,

— **Figure 5/** A Miniature of Noah. From *Queen Mary Psalter*, Royal 2 B. — VII, F. 7. England, c. 1310–1320. Courtesy of The British Library Board.

Lord Henry Chaplin, whom the *Westminster Gazette* satirized in 1895 for sitting in Parliament for such a long period. A sculpture of 'Charley the Cheetah' symbolized Charles, whose Ark name was a pun that referenced his rampant infidelity to Edith. Other statuary depicted Lt Col Cyril Hankey as 'Cyril the Squirrel', Lord Alister Levenson-Gower as 'Alister the Alligator', the Marquess of Dufferin as 'Freddy the Frog', and so forth. Edith positioned most of these pieces around a sculpture of the Ark. As in the case of the topiaries of the Shamrock Garden, she again based the design on illustrations in Mary I of England's *Book of Hours*, a religious book that, as a gift from her mother, held special significance for her [Figures 5, 6].[19]

It is more difficult to decode the inspiration and meaning of the herm statues in the Italian Garden adjacent to the Dodo Terrace [Figure 7]. The first depicts a feminine face, flanked by clusters of grapes, which could represent either Edith as Circe or one of Edith's enemies, a rival for her husband's attention.[20] On the second herm, the face has begun to metamorphose — now having goat-like pointed ears as well as eyes bulging and mouth gaping in alarm — while a pair of hands grasps a cup, perhaps filled with wine or the

very potion that occasioned the metamorphosis. Finally, the third herm depicts a fully transformed bestial face with a pair of cloven hooves draped over each shoulder. The slanted faces and exaggerated features of the herms resemble those from a Richard Dadd painting entitled *Bacchanalian Scene*, which British politician and art collector Philip Sassoon had given to Edith.[21] Tellingly, Dadd's painting was previously known as *Circe*; like the herm grouping, it depicts a feminine face alongside a satyr drinking from a golden cup.[22] To visitors unaware of Dadd's painting, the herms at Mount Stewart recall the sequence from Homer's *Odyssey*, where Circe used magic "philtres" to transform humans into swine.[23] While the significance of the orangutans sitting atop the herms is unknown, they perhaps represent another human to animal transformation. Overall, just as the gardens at Mount Stewart often served as a social setting for Edith's circle of family and friends, the herms were symbolic of her power and place in society.

Elsewhere in her gardens, Edith used mythological elements as biographical commentary. Alongside the loggia at the southern end of the Dodo Terrace and hidden from view, a sculpture of a fox reaching for a cluster of grapes alludes to the familiar allegory from Aesop's fables. The morality of the tale, which depicts a creature pretending not to care for something he wants but cannot obtain, would have appealed to Edith. Although she continuously desired her husband's time and attention, Edith eventually rationalized that Charles' philandering was an unalterable aspect of his personality. Thus, while creating her gardens, Edith underwent a profound transformation as she began to accept the situation by corresponding openly with Charles about his fleeting love interests. Edith gained great power by becoming Charles' friend as well as his wife; she became the one he

— **Figure 6/** The Dodo Terrace at Mount Stewart. c. 1925, — R. J. Welch. Courtesy of Lady Rose Lauritzen and the National Trust, B. Rutledge.

Figure 7/ Herm statues in the Italian Garden at Mount Stewart. Photographs by Stephanie N. Bryan, 2012.

turned to when his love affairs went awry and was the female figure that endured for the rest of his life.[24] Interestingly, this reconciliation between Edith and Charles reflected the metamorphosis in Homer's *Odyssey* when Circe and Odysseus surrendered the notion that one must have clear dominance over the other, and their male-female hostility turned into union and trust.[25]

EVOLUTION OF THE GARDENS

Around her fountain which flows...
Are flowers that no man knows.
/ T. S. Eliot[26]

Edith realized her ideas for the gardens at Mount Stewart largely during the 1920s.[27] She once explained,

No architect has been employed on the design and make of the gardens: whether for better or worse this must be left for visitors to decide. We are singularly happy with our gardener

Mr. T. Bolas who is able and willing to carry out designs from the roughest plans, and together he and I have worked out the designs, whether of buildings, walls, or flower-beds on the actual sites.[28]

Edith's own garden journals contain few plans or sketches, confirming that Thomas Bolas translated many of her ideas directly onto the ground. The gardens at Mount Stewart thus grew organically, without a master plan that would have visualized all of its components as a whole. As a result of Edith's nonlinear thought and design processes, the gardens at Mount Stewart do not emphasize layout.

Another of the gardens' characteristics, their ephemeral quality, resulted from widespread plantings of exotics. Because of Mount Stewart's location on the northern end of the Ards Peninsula in County Down, Northern Ireland, the landscape can host a variety of exotics: hardy, half-hardy, and tender shrubs and trees, in addition to herbaceous perennials [Figure 8]. Plant-hunter Frank Kingdon-Ward once explained, "In this favoured spot they grow faster than they do anywhere else, thus making nonsense of the collector's reports of their size in the field."[29] A mild marine microclimate distinguishes this area, as the Ards Peninsula separates Strangford Lough from the North Channel

Figure 8/ Aerial photograph from 1933 showing the location of Mount Stewart house and gardens (center) along Strangford Lough (solid area at the bottom). Photographer unknown. Courtesy of Lady Rose Lauritzen and the National Trust, B. Rutledge.

of the Irish Sea. Accordingly, rainfall is relatively modest, humidity is high, the annual temperature range is narrow, and hard winter frosts are infrequent. These conditions cause many nonnative plants, particularly those from southern hemispheric regions, to mature and then to decline rapidly.

Assisted in her endeavors by the climate, Edith — like other garden designers throughout the United Kingdom during the early and mid-twentieth century — filled her garden spaces with exotic plants, yet she carried the practice to unusual lengths. A 1922 visit to the gardens at Rostrevor House, which Sir John Ross-of-Bladensburg had created on the slopes of a sheltered hill overlooking Carlingford Lough in County Down, incited Edith's interest in exotic plants. She reminisced, "I shall never forget the wonder and amazement of that visit ... in which Sir John initiated me into the many

and marvelous trees, shrubs and plants from countries all over the world that could, with knowledge and skill, be grown" at Mount Stewart.[30] She continued to write about a terrible gaffe on that occasion when she remarked to Sir John, "I have never seen such shrubs before. It might be the gardens at Kew," and he exclaimed, "'Dear Lady Londonderry, never mention Kew to me again. I can grow things here that Kew has never heard of."[31] Subsequently, their friendship grew and Sir John Ross became Edith's gardening mentor, supplying her with "countless shrubs of all descriptions, seeds, and cuttings".[32]

Following in the footsteps of Sir John Ross, Edith acquired large quantities of rare and uncommon exotic plants from sources across the globe. A letter from head gardener Thomas Bolas described *Meconopsis violacea*, a particularly rare plant that Edith obtained from one of Frank Kingdon-

Ward's expeditions.[33] Once the seeds had been successfully cultivated at Mount Stewart, as Bolas recalled, "it took a horse and four wheeled lorry to remove the stock of plants from the Kitchen Garden into the woods, what a sight those hundreds of first plants really were."[34] Edith also sought fine specimens of shrubs and trees, and, in a letter dated 9 March 1926, Sir Herbert Maxwell referenced the "herculean labour in transporting huge rhododendrons" from overseas to Mount Stewart. By September that year, he wrote to Edith: "The lust for lilies is a contagious disease as deadly as rhododendronitis, from which you suffer incurably already."[35] Edith was indeed particularly fond of rhododendrons, and planted them in groups as large as 50 plants, where space allowed.[36] Ultimately, Edith's extensive exotic plant collection at Mount Stewart not only may have surpassed many other private gardens of the period like Bodnant, Rowallane, Hidcote, Great Dixter, or Sissinghurst, but rivaled the collections of the Royal Botanic Gardens in Edinburgh and Kew.[37]

While Edith had the money to finance plant expeditions, and the microclimate at Mount Stewart was favorable to many rare and uncommon exotic plants, her head gardener Thomas Bolas played a significant role in the shaping and flourishing of Edith's gardens. A highly skilled plantsman, Bolas had gained considerable experience from working at Mount Stewart during the former Lady Londonderry's tenure. He certainly possessed extensive knowledge of the microclimate and its nuances throughout the Mount Stewart landscape and thus contributed to the great success of cultivating many tender plants in the gardens, such as *Rhododendron fragrantissimum*, *Buddleja madagascariensis,* and *Acacia dealbata*, among others. Bolas would have known what type of location, whether in the open or protected against a wall, suited each particular plant so that it would have the best possible chance of thriving at Mount Stewart.

As is inevitably the case with gardens, those of Mount Stewart continued to evolve with the passage of time. Throughout the 1930s, Edith had continued acquiring rare plants from friends who shared similar gardening interests, plant catalogues, and nurserymen, and she continued to finance plant expeditions in foreign countries. During the Interwar period, the gardens served as a place of pleasure and indulgence for Edith and her family, as well as a social setting for friends. A vast change in purpose, however, defined the period during World War II, when the gardens became more utilitarian by mostly producing vegetables and fruits for consumption and flowers for local markets. Various efforts to revitalize the gardens then defined the years following the war, as management shifted toward determining new ways to economize during a time of financial uncertainty instigated by the post-war Labor Government. Accordingly, Edith sought adaptive management strategies to reduce labor costs and to regain knowledge lost after Thomas Bolas retired.

Edith believed it was important to "ensure that these Gardens should be permanently preserved and maintained in the future". Thus, she and Charles were determined that their youngest daughter, Lady Mairi, would inherit and care for the Irish estate. Charles passed away in 1949, and within a few years the National Trust of England, Wales, and Northern Ireland began to manage the gardens. Inevitably, during this transition period, some of the original planting schemes changed, and the gardens lost the exuberance that characterized them during the Interwar period. Then in 1959, after nearly a decade of attempting to revitalize the gardens, Edith passed away at the age of 80, and Lady Mairi continued to live at Mount Stewart until her death in 2009.

DESIGN CHARACTERISTICS

The senses steal, the soul and brain beguile
Till all seem merged in feeling....
/ Leigh Gordon Giltner [38]

During the 1920s and 1930s, Edith's gardens gave a strong impression of what might best be described as exuberance — an intangible quality she achieved by filling her planting beds with exotic plants that exhibited vibrant colors and intense fragrances, and by encouraging vigorous, almost unrestrained growth [Figure 9]. Indeed, the high degree of this exuberance is what most distinguished the gardens at Mount Stewart from others of the period. Edith preferred hot-colored flowers; crimsons, maroons, wines, oranges, fuchsias, magentas, and bronzes consistently dominated her rare plant

—— **Figure 9**/ View of the Sunk Garden from the Mount Stewart house. ——
Photographer unknown; originally published in *Country Life*, 12 October
1935. Courtesy of Lady Rose Lauritzen and *Country Life*.

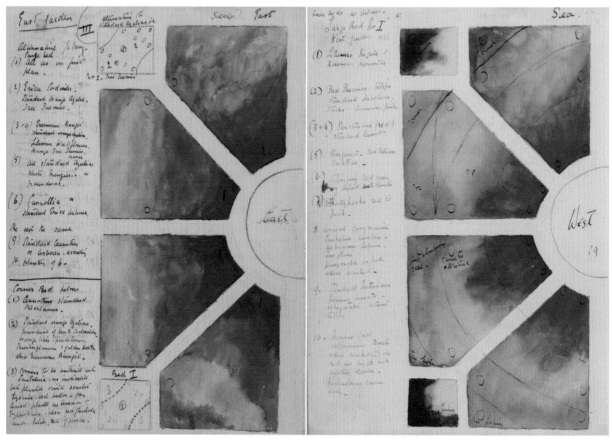

Figure 10/ Color schemes for the Italian Garden parterres painted by Edith, Lady Londonderry. East, at left, the colors resemble those of a sunrise; West, at right, a sunset. c. 1925. Courtesy of Lady Rose Lauritzen and the National Trust, B. Rutledge.

palette. She was careful not to place these selections haphazardly throughout the landscape; rather she experimented with many color combinations to achieve a dramatic display acceptable to her discerning eye.

In addition to vibrant colors, she highly valued intense fragrance in the landscape. She once remarked, "These gardens are gardens of sweet scents. However insignificant or humble the flower, if it has fragrance, an honoured place is reserved for it. For is not a garden of fragrant herbs a perpetual delight?"[39] Thus, she sought to acquire curiously fragrant plants, such as *Boronia serrulata*, which a representative from Stuart Low Company described in a letter as having "a haunting scent" and appealing "to people in a quite occult manner".[40] Edith meticulously recorded how such plants performed. The gardens at Mount Stewart can thus be characterized as a continual exercise in experimentation and improvement, a place reflecting the owner's high aesthetic and horticultural aspirations.

Edith strategized to extend the season of her exceptionally colorful and fragrant flowers by organizing

groupings that would create a succession of blooms. One way she achieved this was by using vines like clematis to grow over and through large bushes and standard trees. She explained, "The shrubs lend themselves to this dual purpose: not only are they lovely when in bloom themselves in spring and early summer, but they display a mass of colour [when the clematis bloom] during the late summer and autumn months."[41] Although Edith's selections and groupings bear some resemblance to the informal borders typical of cottage gardens, she practiced the technique on a much grander and more highly managed scale. Most British gardeners of the early to mid-nineteenth century had conventionally planted their parterres with carpet bedding (a patterned arrangement of low or clipped herbaceous and varicolored foliage plants), but by the late nineteenth century, modern gardeners began to fill their beds with floribunda roses and other hardy shrubs that were easier and less expensive to maintain. After Edith realized that large groupings of floribunda roses would not thrive in her gardens so close to the sea, she then attempted to create "a rich medley of plants of every kind" within her beds and borders.[42]

Edith's 1925 plans for the eastern and western parterres in the Italian Garden contained a great variety of plant types, such as annuals and carpeting plants, bulbs and herbaceous perennials, shrubs and trees. This variety gave the parterres a very informal and asymmetrical feeling. While these groupings were integrated with plants of a more formal appearance, such as rosemary trained onto tripods and azaleas shaped into standards, Edith heightened the sense of informality and asymmetry by selecting a different combination of plants for each individual bed within her parterres, rather than mirroring the same scheme throughout the beds. Furthermore, in the Italian Garden, she used a gradation of ruby red to pink set off by an edge of purple for the western parterre, while the eastern parterre exhibited a gradation of scarlet to orange complemented by an edge of blue and grey tones [Figure 10].

The combination of highly informal and asymmetrical planting schemes with a formal and symmetrical framework produced a very unusual and uncommon aesthetic, suggesting that Edith not only desired to break free from staid tradition, but gardened in her own distinct way without concern for criticism by her contemporaries.[43] Edith's parterres exuded a strong energy as her varied selections and arrangements of exotic plants almost burst forth from the edges and towered over her visitors and guests; they were filled with so many plants that the walking paths between some of the planting beds almost disappeared. Edith also encouraged plants suited to dry conditions to grow within the cracks and crevices that formed part of her design on terraces and in other paved areas within the gardens [Figure 11]. This exuberance spread into the surrounding walls, down the steps, and onto open spaces where daisies often intermingled with lawn [Figure 12].

Achieving this exuberant or 'natural' appearance with plants in a geometric framework required great proficiency on the part of the gardening staff. For example, the staff maintained a well-stocked nursery garden in order to propagate tender plants growing in the parterres. They tended multiple greenhouses, in addition to hot and cold frames.[44] In her garden journal, Edith suggested that her staff should keep plants in a reserve garden and not allow them to flower in order to obtain sufficient cuttings for the next year's stock.[45] The reserve garden also allowed staff to give areas within the main garden a boost of color or foliage as the season progressed. This process kept the parterres looking full for the greater part of the year. The ability to maintain this exuberant effect truly attested to the attention and skill of head gardener Thomas Bolas, who orchestrated the gardening team's efforts on a daily basis.

THE GARDENER AS SORCERESS

"Though shalt not 'scape me so," pronounced the dame,
"If plants have power, and spells be not a name."
/ Ovid[46]

The extraordinary exuberance of the plant collection at Mount Stewart lends the whole the appearance of a magical island, in turn suggesting an overarching mythological and literary inspiration. The key to understanding the distinct aesthetic of Edith's gardens lies in her identification with the mythological character of the sorceress goddess Circe. Although Edith's appellation of Circe originated during WWI, the connection

Figure 11/ The Shamrock Garden at Mount Stewart, c. 1925, R. J. Welch. Courtesy of Lady Rose Lauritzen and the National Trust, B. Rutledge.

Figure 12/ The Rock Garden at Mount Stewart, c. 1925, R. J. Welch. Courtesy of Lady Rose Lauritzen and the National Trust, B. Rutledge.

— **Figure 13/** Painting depicting Edith and her children as Circe and the Sirens in the gardens at Mount Stewart. Edmond Brock, *Circe and the Sirens*, 1926. Image © National Trust Images, B. Rutledge.

became increasingly significant during the Interwar period, as she fully embraced the persona when creating most of her garden spaces at Mount Stewart. In 1926, artist-friend Charles Edmund Brock painted a portrait of Edith as Circe dressed in a gauzy green gown and grasping a golden chalice [Figure 13]. She and her three daughters rest beside the loggia while the herm statues of the Italian Garden are visible in the distance.[47] Edith's correspondence also confirms her persisting identification with Circe. On Christmas Eve 1935, Sir Herbert Maxwell of Monreith affectionately wrote to her as "Circe *mavourneen* (my darling)" to offer gardening hints on the slow-growing *Eucryphia pinnatifolia*.[48] And on 19 June 1945, another friend, Charles Dunleath, addressed a letter regarding plant cuttings to "My dear Circe".[49]

Having gained much attention as society's queen in wartime London, Edith may have felt somewhat 'banished' when she and her husband first moved to Mount Stewart — a place that initially held negative associations for her and was relatively remote in its Northern Ireland location, a virtual 'island'. Similarly, Homer's Circe inhabited a remote island, the Island of Aiaia, where her house stood on divine ground in the midst of a clearing surrounded by a dense wood. Homer described Circe's house as *hiera dōmata*, a sacred place befitting a goddess, and, most unusually, the house is constructed of stone polished smooth on all sides — a labor-intensive building

material whose use in a society comprised only of women, such as that presided over by Circe, alludes to her high level of competence in realms customarily viewed as 'male'.[50] To Edith, the landscape at Mount Stewart similarly possessed an inherent sacredness. She explained, "There is a feeling of enchantment about the place, and indeed it is not hard to believe that in this most mystical land it is, even now as much, the magic island of gods and initiates as it was when the sacred fires flashed from its purple heath-covered, honey scented mountain tops and mysterious round towers on island and hill."[51] And like Circe's polished stones, Edith's lush plant arrangements reflected a high degree of labor and an exemplary level of management. Never entirely satisfied with her plant selections, she continually acquired new plants and rearranged the majority of groupings, which became increasingly complex throughout the years. The colors, fragrances, frequency of change, and complexity of Edith's plant selections and arrangements at Mount Stewart correlate with the mindset of her adopted persona of Circe, who symbolized passion, power, and metamorphosis.

With its house clad in dense vines and surrounded by exotic plants and statuary, Mount Stewart was undoubtedly bewitching to its visitors, and for Edith, gardening became a form of magic through which she could command the attention of her visitors with the vibrant colors, intense aromas, and overall abundance of her exotic plant collection. The plants also charmed Edith herself; whether or not she was aware of these physiological effects, the bold hues of reds and oranges ever-present throughout her gardens would have made her feel strong, energetic, passionate, and powerful.[52]

It is noteworthy that while the gardens were captured through conventional black and white photography during

—— **Figure 14/** Floodlit image of the eastern parterre of the Italian Garden at Mount Stewart. September 1934, from family album. Courtesy of Lady Rose Lauritzen and the National Trust, B. Rutledge.

Figure 15/ Floodlit image of the Italian Garden with the Spanish Garden in the distance at Mount Stewart. September 1934, from family album. Courtesy of Lady Rose Lauritzen and the National Trust, B. Rutledge.

their implementation stage, they were photographed in an entirely new manner c. 1934.[53] The method of floodlighting the garden at nighttime produced a theatrical effect, making the gardens resemble a setting for an ancient Greek drama [Figure 14]. The floodlit photography enhanced the gardens' exuberance and reinforced the importance of the Circe myth; the viewers cannot help but feel as though they have stumbled upon Circe's magical and mysterious realm, a clearing in the midst of a remote island [Figure 15]. These photographs show that the gardens of this period had reached a pinnacle of both creativity and upkeep. Edith had fulfilled her intent to contrive not only a garden that stimulated the senses, but a place that interpreted the Circe myth. Thus Edith's garden creation — whether a conscious concretion or subconscious expression of an order that was important to her — shows an exceptional degree of imagination.

Edith's gardening mentor, Sir Herbert Maxwell, recognized that her power and creative energy were the greatest sources of the magic at Mount Stewart. In a letter about the gardens dated 4 September 1933, he wrote to her, "You certainly fulfill the role of enchantress in all that you touch...."[54] Maxwell's quote not only referenced the continued metamorphosis of Edith's gardens but insinuated the degree to which her extraordinary personality and vision affected others. Following the previous owners of Mount Stewart, Edith felt that it was her "duty to endeavor to leave the place more beautiful and rich in the trees and shrubs than when it came into the orbit" of her life.[55] She felt that "Gardens are meant to be lived in and enjoyed and I hope they may long continue to be a source of pleasure to those who visit them, as they have been in the past."[56] And so her gardens, managed by the National Trust since the mid-1950s, continue to transform lives as

Figure 16/ The gardens at Mount Stewart, a continuing source of pleasure to those who visit them. Image © National Trust, Claire Takacs.

they have become a place where all generations can cultivate relationships with nature and with each other [Figure 16]. A quote from the Roman poet Horace (65–8 BCE), inscribed in a folly at Mount Stewart, foretold the charm Edith and others would discover in her gardens: *Ille terrarum mihi praeter omnes angulus ridet* — That corner of the world smiles to me beyond all others.[57]

NOTES

1/ Schomberg, George Augustus trans., *The Odyssey of Homer*, London: John Murray, 1879, p. 279.

2/ W. B. Yeats once visited Mount Stewart, according to a memoir by Edith, Marchioness of Londonderry, *Retrospect*, London: Frederick Muller Ltd., 1938, p. 204. Several lines from a play by W. B. Yeats appear in the preface of an article by Edith, Marchioness of Londonderry, "Mount Stewart: The Land of Heart's Desire", *Northern Ireland*, vol. 1, no. 8, 1926.

3/ Hope, A. D., "Circe", *The Wandering Islands*, Sydney: Edwards & Shaw, 1955, p. 39.

4/ Londonderry, Edith, Marchioness of, "The Gardens at Mount Stewart", *Journal of the Royal Horticultural Society*, vol. LX, no. 12, 1935, p. 520.

5/ Londonderry, Edith, Marchioness of, "Foreword", *Mount Stewart Garden Guide*, UK: National Trust, 1956, p. 5.

6/ From a transcription by Anne Casement, "Mount Stewart Garden Archives and Historical Survey 1917–1959, Part One", unpublished, n.d., pp. 13–15, the "Theresa, Lady Londonderry Papers", Public Records Office, Northern Ireland.

7/ I would like to acknowledge Frances Bailey, Project Curator at Mount Stewart, for this insight.

8/ Londonderry, "The Gardens at Mount Stewart", p. 520.

9/ Londonderry, "Foreword", *Mount Stewart Garden Guide*, p. 5.

10/ See Anne de Courcy, *Circe, The Life of Edith, Marchioness of Londonderry*, Great Britain: Sinclair-Stevenson, 1992, pp. 92–93.

11/ Quoted in de Courcy, *Circe*, p. 51.

12/ Quoted in de Courcy, *Circe*, p. 202.

13/ Gurney, Dorothy Frances, "God's Garden", *Poems*, London: Country Life, 1913, p. 1.

14/ Apple, John, "Le Circe's Story", *Le Circe and Other Poems*, London: Provost and Co., 1873, p. 39.

15/ Londonderry, "The Gardens at Mount Stewart", p. 521.

16/ Londonderry, "The Gardens at Mount Stewart", p. 521.

17/ Edith, Lady Londonderry, wrote this on page 40 of her journal entitled "Mount Stewart Garden Book No. 1 1922–1927", "Envelope B" of the manuscript archives at Mount Stewart.

18/ Londonderry, "The Gardens at Mount Stewart", p. 530.

19/ Edith obtained a copy of this book during Christmas 1912 from her mother. The volume contains various notations and marks by Edith.

20/ Edith presumably distrusted women because she felt in competition with them for Charles' attention.

21/ Again, I would like to credit Frances Bailey, Project Curator at Mount Stewart.

22/ Alderidge, Patricia, *Richard Dadd*, New York: St Martin's Press, 1974, p. 98.

23/ Schomberg, *The Odyssey of Homer*, p. 277.

24/ de Courcy, *Circe, The Life of Edith, Marchioness of Londonderry*, p. 94.

25/ Yarnall, Judith, *Transformations of Circe: The History of an Enchantress*, Urbana: University of Illinois Press, 1994, p. 21.

26/ Eliot, T. S. "Circe's Palace", *The Harvard Advocate*, vol. 86, no. 5, 1908.

27/ Casement, Anne, "Mount Stewart Garden Archives and Historical Survey 1917–1969 Part 2", unpub.,1999, pp. 1–2.

28/ Londonderry, "The Gardens at Mount Stewart," pp. 520–521.

29/ Kingdon-Ward, Frank, "The Rhododendrons at Mount Stewart", *The Gardeners' Chronicle*, 1954, p. 46.

30/ Londonderry, *Retrospect*.

31/ Londonderry, *Retrospect*.

32/ Londonderry, *Retrospect*.

33/ This plant was lost at Mount Stewart during World War II. A letter years later from Frank Kingdon-Ward suggests that Edith was the only person in the UK to successfully cultivate it from seed. Letter from Frank Kingdon-Ward to Edith, Lady Londonderry, 17 December 1949, the manuscript archives at Mount Stewart.

34/ Letter from Thomas Bolas to Edith, Lady Londonderry, 31 December 1949, the manuscript archives at Mount Stewart.

35/ Letters from Sir Herbert Maxwell to Edith, Lady Londonderry, 9 March 1926 and 16 September 1926. Both letters are saved within the pages of Edith, Lady Londonderry's ochre colored garden journal entitled "Mount Stewart Gardens 1927–1936", "Envelope D" of the manuscript archives at Mount Stewart.

36/ Porteous, Neil, Mike Buffin, and Phil Rollinson, "Mount Stewart Garden Conservation Management Plan 2011", unpub., p. 21.

37/ Edith frequently corresponded with both Royal Botanic Gardens regarding rare plants, and after World War II she received multiple requests to supply them with certain ones lost from their collections due to neglect during the war.

38/ Giltner, Leigh Gordon, "Circe", *The Path of Dreams: Poems*, Chicago: Fleming H. Revell Company, 1900, p. 55.

39/ Londonderry, Edith, Lady, "Mount Stewart", *The Gardener's Yearbook*: 1927, pp. 36–47.

40/ Letter from a representative of Stuart Low Company to Edith, Lady Londonderry, 11 April 1940. Edith, Lady Londonderry, saved the letter on page 6 of her brown leather hardback garden journal entitled "Garden 1935". This journal is located in "Envelope E" of the manuscript archives at Mount Stewart.

41/ Londonderry, "The Gardens at Mount Stewart", p. 525.

42/ Hellyer, A. G. L., "Fantasy in an Irish Garden", *Country Life*, London: 1969.

43/ In a letter to Edith dated 19 December 1925, Gertrude Jekyll wrote, "Looking at the photograph of the house front with the large flight of steps it looks as if the house ought to be relieved of the thick growth of Ivy that smothers the pediment and top of the portico and in fact the whole projection. That facade wants these architectural features unobscured, and to have the natural light and shade of all the part that stands out as intended by the architect.... I know you will let me make these remarks...." Historic photographs from the 1930s reveal that Edith instead maintained a heavy cover of vines on the south facade of the house.

44/ It is likely that when the gardens were at their peak before World War II, all of these greenhouses, if not more, would have been in constant use. In 1952, during the time when the gardens were transitioning to the National Trust, at least six frame houses were recorded by Patrick Woods, "Mount Stewart in 1952: A Horticultural Experience", *MOOREA: Journal of the Irish Garden Plant Society*, 2006, p. 15.

45/ Edith, Lady Londonderry, wrote this on page 143 of her blue marble covered garden journal entitled "Mount Stewart Garden Book No. 1, 1922–1927".

46/ Garth, Samuel trans., *Ovid's Metamorphoses*, vol. I, London: Suttaby, Evance, and Fox, 1812, p. 157.

47/ Edith's husband and son curiously are absent from the family portrait, although a bird and a goat may represent transformations of these masculine figures.

48/ Letter from Sir Herbert Maxwell to Edith, Lady Londonderry, 24 December 1935, tab "M" in the pages of Edith, Lady Londonderry's dark brown hardback journal entitled "Mount Stewart Gardens: 1937–", "Envelopes G and H" in the manuscript archives at Mount Stewart.

49/ Letter from Charles Dunleath to Edith, Lady Londonderry, 19 June 1945, the manuscript archives at Mount Stewart.

50/ Yarnall, *Transformations of Circe*, p. 11. See also Annette L. Giesecke, *The Epic City: Urbanism, Utopia, and the Garden in Ancient Greece and Rome*, Cambridge, MA: Harvard University Press, 2007, pp. 21–26.

51/ Londonderry, "Mount Stewart: The Land of Heart's Desire".

52/ These colors bear a strong association with Circe throughout literature. For example, "Straight Circe reddens with guilty shame, / And vows revenge for her rejected flame" appears in Garth, *Ovid's*, p. 149. In addition, when Aeneas sailed past Circe's island, "The sea was just reddening in the dawn", as translated by John Conington, *The Aeneid of Virgil*, New York: The MacMillan Company, 1917, p. 150.

53/ The A. R. Hogg Collection in the Ulster Museum has several floodlit photographs of the gardens. One of Edith, Lady Londonderry's photo albums entitled "House (exterior) and Gardens" contains many additional floodlit images that possibly could be the work of A. R. Hogg, but, unfortunately, are not attributed to any photographer.

54/ Letter from Sir Herbert Maxwell to Edith, Lady Londonderry, 4 September 1933. The letter can be found within the pages of Edith, Lady Londonderry's ochre colored garden journal entitled "Mount Stewart Gardens 1927–1936".

55/ Londonderry, "The Gardens at Mount Stewart", p. 531.

56/ Londonderry, "Foreword", *Mount Stewart Garden Guide*.

57/ Francis Turner, *Landscape in Poetry from Homer to Tennyson*, New York: The Macmillan Company, 1897, p. 53.

162 /ROBERT FINLEY

MARLENE CREATES' BOREAL POETRY GARDEN

As the crickets' soft autumn hum
is to us
so are we to the trees
as are they
to the rocks and the hills.
/ Gary Snyder[1]

These lines from Gary Snyder's "Little Songs for Gaia" do a good job precipitating that shift in perspective that can sometimes befall us when we look up into the vastness of space at the twinkling of long dead stars, their light still on its way to us millennia after the demise of the stars themselves — or down into the fossil record beneath our feet,

— **Figure1a/** Marlene Creates, *The High Tide as it acts upon an X,* — *England 1980*. Azo dye (Cibachrome) print, diptych, each 33 x 23 cm (13 x 9 in). Image courtesy of the artist.

— **Figure 1b/** Marlene Creates, *The High Tide as it acts upon an X,* — *England 1980*. Azo dye (Cibachrome) print, diptych, each 33 x 23 cm (13 x 9 in). Image courtesy of the artist.

where we might discover the location of our habitual Starbucks to have been a place of refreshment, a comfortable patio facing the sun, for well on 500 million years, our kin of one kind or another thus neighbored to us in time. Such moments of insight are hard to live with in a daily way, situating us, as they do, on that line, that giddy high wire that stretches from the recently established Ediacaran, when complex life forms first appear in the planet's fossil record, to our own time, in the now to be named (part boast, part *mea culpa*) Anthropocene era of human tenure.

Another way of evoking the same lift and flutter just under the heart, suggests Canada's great wilderness poet Don McKay, is to enact a metaphor for deep time attributed to the writer John McPhee: "This", McKay says, "calls for a beautiful assistant and a stage — real or imagined. Simply extend your arm, I say, and she (or it may be he, according to your imagination's preference) complies. Your shoulder, I say, is the big bang, and your fingertip is the present. Then I produce, with a flourish like Errol Flynn drawing his sword, a nail file. Carefully I file one stroke from her (his) middle fingernail, erasing hominids from the planet's history — not, some would say, such a bad idea."[2] Not so long have we been gardening here. But let us say you grasped and held such a perspective of your place in time and set the age of the rocks and trees themselves against your own tenure, or even the tenure of your species in the garden. How might you garden then?

Marlene Creates has been a major figure in Canadian land art for over 30 years. Her work has been centered for most of that time on photography, a medium with its own evocative relationship to time, slicing out, as it does, an instant in the flow of things to record and carry forward. This is a relationship she has complicated by the introduction into her installations of field work, text, quoted interviews, and site material, all toward cultivating a richer notion of our relationship to the physical world. In the last decade, however, in developing a major ongoing installation that is her six acres of forested property in Portugal Cove, just outside St John's, Newfoundland, she has made a deliberate move away from photographic representation and the gallery. Having distilled the role of the artist/guide, she takes us, actually takes us, to the place itself: her *Boreal Poetry Garden*. In many and important ways, including the literal, she has brought her practice home.[3]

I would like to introduce you to that Garden, in as much as I am able. But before we get there, I want to bring out some of the particular qualities of Marlene Creates' work as it has developed over the past few decades, as a way of identifying what we might call her 'gardening techniques' or the 'gardener's toolkit' that makes *The Boreal Poetry Garden* possible. These earlier works include her photographed exterior installations, or Landworks, of the 1980s, and her richly layered gallery assemblages of the 1990s.

— **Figure 2/** Marlene Creates, *Stone Ground Drawing: Wave Patterns,* — *Lake Nipissing 1986*. Granite boulders, 6.7 x 6.7 m (22 x 22 ft). Image courtesy of the artist.

LANDWORKS

The Landworks keep carefully to non-invasive land art principles: her installations are entirely provisional, lasting only a short while until they are disrupted by natural forces in the passage of time. In *The High Tide as it acts upon an X, England 1980*, for instance, the carefully aligned veins of quartz that cut through a selection of beach stones on a pebble strand in England are formed into an X, that human signifier, the X that 'marks the spot', and photographed [Figures 1a, 1b]. On returning to the site the next day Marlene finds and re-photographs the center stone that had suggested the arrangement initially. The others, of course, are by then jumbled into another, or into their natural order by the evening tide and the usual action of the waves on the shore. In *Stone Ground Drawing: Wave Patterns, Lake Nipissing 1986*, the pattern of the waves at the shore is echoed in the sand with an arrangement of granite boulders approximately 22 feet square [Figure 2]. This piece, or traces of it, will last longer than the pebbles on the beach, but the stones will eventually be carried off or covered over with sand by the waves working on that stretch of open shoreline. This piece, interestingly, garnered a fierce debate in the Canadian press, initiated by local residents who felt that the artist, funded by the public institution of the Canada Council for the Arts, had done nothing lasting, and so nothing worthwhile.

Because both the momentary human assembly of these sculptures and their imminent and ongoing reassembly by ordinary natural forces can be read in the photographs simultaneously, we gain from them a strong and, I would say, poignant sense of the artist's transitory presence and momentary intervention in the vaster scale of things: for instance, her delicate alignment of veins of quartz, on the one hand, and the long action of the waves and of the tidal

Figure 3/ Marlene Creates, *Paper and Water Lilies, Newfoundland 1982*. Azo dye (Cibachrome) print, 33 x 48 cm (13 x 19 in). Image courtesy of the artist.

round against a stretch of pebble beach, on the other. These works point to something in delight and astonishment, frame in wonder, for instance, the 'eternal' overlapping pattern of the waves. They also sketch with the very lightest and deftest of strokes a fleeting human presence, an instant of human attention, on the land. The photographs are their only relatively permanent trace, beyond the ongoing natural forces to which the works attend. "I sense quite strongly that I am a transient figure, both when I'm a traveler, and when I'm a dweller", says Marlene Creates.[4] And this sense of transience, of passing through, is the first quality in the kit of gardening tools that she brings to bear on *The Boreal Poetry Garden*.

In *Paper and Water Lilies, Newfoundland 1982*, we find the same framing attention of the sculpture, the same framing wonder, and the same marked transitoriness as well, underlining the transience of the hand at work [Figure 3]. That paper won't last long there in the water, it's clear. (And, indeed, the artist removed it after taking the photograph.) Here too a quality of lightness comes through, a lightness of touch: tricky getting the paper laid down like that so that it floats over the surface so evenly without disturbing the lilies or the lily pads themselves. Lightness of touch we might associate with a kind of sensitivity to fine detail, or, using the light, translucent paper here as an

example, to receptivity, or impressionability. The opposite of an imposition of form on nature, the piece is itself a form of attention, a way of attending to what is already there: its gesture seems to be directed more toward taking in an impression than to giving expression. "The paper represents me", says Marlene.[5] "My artworks are the result of what I find along the way — they are not acts of imagination. They are entirely dependent on the circumstances in the specific place at the exact time that I am there. My work comes from the act of paying attention and being receptive to whatever is there."[6] Let us say that 'impressionability' is another important thing to have in our gardener's toolkit.

Or consider *Sleeping Places, Newfoundland 1982*, a sequence of 25 black-and-white photographs which, together, make up one of the loveliest of these earlier works [Figure 4]. On a two-month tour around the island of Newfoundland (itself a place of family origin and return for her), the artist photographed the places in which she had slept outdoors while on her journey. A day of wind, a rainfall, and, as with deer beds or moose beds, the grass will spring back up and the place that these photographs trace will disappear, the mark of the artist's temporary presence erased. But these sculptural engagements with the land are intensified by an additional set of preoccupations beyond what we find in the stone and paper pieces. In these transitory testaments to a human presence on the land, these 'nests', the notion of land use comes into the work, the notion of space becoming place through human action. The land here is not only the subject of human attention and wonder; it is inhabited, if briefly, and put temporarily to human use. "The land is important to me, but even more important is the idea that it becomes a 'place' because someone has been there", says Marlene.[7] "What interests me is the interplay and reciprocity between people and places. I wonder, 'What is a place to me?' And, 'What am I to a place?' "[8] Curiosity about land use, about space becoming place 'because someone has been there' might be added to our kit as well.

MEMORY WORK

Through the 1990s, Marlene began working with assemblages of photographs, text, interview material, and samples of site material. Though photography remains key, these additional elements extend and deepen the dimension of time in the work. The pieces from this period take up the preoccupation with land use but are configured in such a way as to attend to 'use over time'. Their scope goes beyond natural forces acting on momentary and isolated interventions such as the artist's arrangement of stones on the beach or her temporary sleeping places; here the pieces try to gather in the relatively long interventions of other people in place, people who were at home in a place for a time. This emphasis signified a major shift in Marlene's work at that time: from a focus on her own experience in a place as a traveler, to the experiences of others, many of whom were living in, and speaking about, the place in which they had been born. This is work, memory work, most efficiently carried out by story, and Marlene begins to introduce text into the installations in the form of transcribed accounts and labeled memory maps.

In *Rosie Webb, Labrador 1988*, for instance, we have an assemblage which consists of a photograph of Rosie Webb [Figure 5]; a memory map drawn by her [Figure 5a]; a transcription of interview material in which she describes memories about the place that arose as she drew her memory map of it; a subsequent photograph by Marlene of the place described [Figure 5b]; and a material sample, a metonymic sample of that place, a square of the "blackberry sod" mentioned in the text. The text does what the photograph cannot do and

Figure 4/ Marlene Creates, excerpt from *Sleeping Places, Newfoundland 1982.*
Selenium-toned silver print, 27 x 39 cm (10.5 x 15.5 in). Image courtesy of the artist.

Figure 5a/ memory map drawn by Rosie Webb.
Excerpt from *Rosie Webb, Labrador 1988*. Pencil on paper, 22 x 28 cm
(8½ x 11 in). Image courtesy of the artist.

Figure 5/ Marlene Creates, *Rosie Webb, Labrador 1988*,
from the series *The Distance Between Two Points is Measured in
Memories, Labrador 1988*, assemblage of photographs, memory map
drawn by Rosie Webb, story, and blackberry sod. Collection: MacKenzie
Art Gallery, Regina. Image courtesy of the artist.

Figure 5b/ Marlene Creates. Excerpt from *Rosie Webb,
Labrador 1988*. 22 x 28 cm (8½ x 11 in). Selenium-toned silver print.
Image courtesy of the artist.

what the memory map cannot do by itself. It details a relationship between a person and the land over a period of time, an interplay and reciprocity between place and person:

> I had ten boys and one girl. I had fifteen altogether. Some of them is dead. I don't know how many grandchildren. I never counted. I stayed up there in Webb's Bay ever since I got married. When we got married there was only one house, his father's house. That old house is still up. Log house. Smokehouse and everything up there. Smokes char. Use what they call blackberry leaves. Cuts out square pieces of sod. It was a boat, half a boat. Just the top of a boat put on the ground. Old man's house here. Path up to our house. And Jim's house up here. Our house. And Ronald's. And Henry's little old house there. It's old that smokehouse. Way over a hundred years it must be now. Still uses it. Still good.[9]

"When we describe the land", says Marlene, " — or, more frequently, remember events that occurred at particular points on it — the natural landscape becomes a centre of meaning, and its geographical features are constituted in relation to our experiences on it. The land is not an abstract physical location, but a *place*, charged with personal significance, shaping the images we have of ourselves."[10]

Another example from the many assemblages Marlene constructed during this decade is *OUR COASTLINE IS NATURAL & SCENIC* from the *Language and Land Use, Newfoundland 1994* series [Figure 6]. Here we have an array of three photographs forming a panorama of the subject site, including, in the central image, the sign which gives the piece its title and which reads, in full: "OUR COASTLINE IS NATURAL & SCENIC... WHY

SPOIL THE LOOK? THANK YOU FOR NOT LITTERING."
The image on the left gives just a glimpse of the large, perhaps not so scenic tanks from an oil storage facility at the shore. These photographs are installed along with a handwritten text recounted from the artist's visit to the site and a material sample from the site in the form of some of the beach rocks mentioned in the text:

> 'This whole area', the curator at the nearby museum told me, 'they spread acres and acres of beach rocks for drying fish. The rocks, being round, leave air pockets between them', he explained, 'and of course the sun heats them up. It's a French technique that comes from Brittany. This place was first settled by the French in the 1600s. Just four miles away, there were English people and they used flakes for drying fish. Even where the oil tanks are, all that was what they called beaches. You see remnants of it everywhere and there's only one reason for the beach rocks to be there, it's because someone hauled them up there.' He continued. 'Most of the people who tended the fish were women. Women used to refer to it as working on the beaches. And down where the houses are, that was all beaches. There were no houses there then. All just a big mass of fish down around here, spread out on the beaches as far as the eye could see. The widows would be given preference to work on the beaches. They wore long black dresses and black sunbonnets. In those days there used to be quite a few widows because if there was a schooner lost with all hands, as high as twenty-six people could go down with it.' I met an elderly man who was taking a walk along the beach with his son and daughter-in-law. They were visiting from another part of Canada. The man told me his mother used to work all along here, supervising the fish-drying. 'She was boss of the beaches', he said.[11]

The assembled elements taken together can "evoke what is absent and unseen in a place", says Marlene; the historical scope of the texts is augmented by the insistent present tense of the photographs, and both text and image are ballasted by the presence of the sea-smoothed beach stones. "I put the photographs, the stories, and the found objects together in order to express something poetic, pointed, and sometimes humorous, but also something challenging — a devotion to the ineffable quality of places."[12] 'A devotion to the ineffable quality of places' might certainly be in our toolkit too.

Figure 6/ Marlene Creates, *OUR COASTLINE IS NATURAL & SCENIC*, from *Language and Land Use, Newfoundland 1994*. Assemblage of 3 b/w selenium-toned silver prints, each 41 x 51 cm (16 x 20 in); one handwritten text panel, pencil on matboard, 25 x 30 cm (10 x 12 in); and beach rocks from the site. Collection: Saint Mary's University Art Gallery, Halifax. Image courtesy of the artist.

Figures 7, 8, 9, 10, 11, 12/ Marlene Creates, *The Boreal Poetry Garden*. Images courtesy of the artist.

THE BOREAL POETRY GARDEN

Now, with this gardener's toolkit in hand — acknowledged transience, lightness of touch (reticence), impressionability, a devotion to the ineffable qualities of places, and attention to their multiple histories, let us make our way to *The Boreal Poetry Garden* [Figure 7]. *The Boreal Poetry Garden* is a live art event that takes place on the six acres of forested property where Marlene has lived for the past decade and which has been both the focus and the locus of her art practice for the past decade. The property is on the outskirts of the city of St John's on Newfoundland's Avalon Peninsula, which itself is located on the Atlantic edge of the largest biome on earth: the boreal forest, an ecosystem that makes up approximately one third of the world's vegetation with about three billion acres of hackmatack (larch), fir, spruce, alder, birch, poplar, and willow; moss and lichen; bog, brook, marsh, and pond.[13]

We arrive at the Garden on a cool summer evening and make our way up to the house with its campfire burning in welcome. Once everyone is assembled, about 25 of us, we accompany the artist on an hour-long walk along a network of paths through the woods by the Blast Hole Pond River. From time to time we stop — at a bend in the path, at the waterfall, at a rock face, beside a particular tree, or the stump of a blown down spruce no thicker than an old man's wrist, its surprising ring count indicated on a small marker: 108 years — and Marlene recites one of her site-specific poems. These, in her own words, "commemorate certain fleeting moments of my interaction with the land where I live", and they are recited or "published" only at the sites which gave rise to them in the first place.[14] In form, the poems tend toward a haiku or cinquain-like

concentration, reserve, and intense engagement with the natural world. As is especially apparent in the last example below, they also often engage with the rich local dialect and its names for things: *bawn*, or a meadow near a house or settlement; *livyers*, or the permanent early settlers of coastal Newfoundland as opposed to migratory fishermen from England.[15] Figures 8 through 12 following are photographs provided by the artist of the sites within the garden to which the quoted poems attend. Seasons may have come and gone since the memories the poems record were laid down:

Will I
trim off this branch
jutting in the new path?
The next pass, a yellow leaf brushes
my lips.

Deadfalls to chain saw;
logs to fire to warm feet;
ashes to flowers

Stillness,
like the moment
after the moose bolted,
clipped the turn: hoofbeats in the
footpath.

Rocks moved to grow potatoes
so many years ago,
moss.

The rattling brook path

To look at it now,
even if you could see
beneath the snowdrifts to the worn ground
between the bunchberries, starflowers,
creeping snowberry, moss,
knees of tree roots and
knuckles of rocks
hundreds of millions of years old,

still, you wouldn't see
the moose, the musicians,
the sailors, the curators,
the neighbours, the nephew,
the snowshoe hares,
the writers, the father, the artists,
the geologist, the anthropologist,
the brother, the mother,
the visitors from Victoria, Tasmania,
Kentucky and Kippens,
the niece, nor the naked boy running
after a dip in the rattling brook.

What I wish I could See
livyers from the cove
years ago
hauling water up the path
from the brook to the bawn,
where willow and fireweed
have since taken root in the furrows
of their vegetable gardens.

And as we wander, pause, and listen, the space of this fragment of a vast forest gradually becomes a place of particulars, and layered with meaning: not trees, but this tree, its yellow leaf brushing the artist's lips while path-clearing; not a woodland path, but this path, connecting the small river to the vegetable gardens it was used to water a generation ago; not a bend in the path, but this bend in the path where the moose bolted one summer afternoon; not blueberry bushes, but these bushes picked one day in August with a beloved young nephew [Figure 13]. This process of individuation has been taken up in other of Marlene's works stemming from her life at the Garden, for instance, in the ongoing photographic project, *Larch, Spruce, Fir, Birch, Hand*, in which she has undertaken to photograph the individual trees on the property that she has come to know, a relationship manifested by her hand held up to the tree trunks [Figure 14].

Apart from the creation of some of the paths through the wood by harvesting windfalls for the fire, no gardening has been done here beyond this: our own presence and these simple recitations that mark and inform the land with anecdote or story. Is it fair, then, to call it a garden? Donald Dunham, in his fine essay "Architecture *without* Nature?", gives us some useful parameters. A garden, he says, needs gardening:

> Without gardening, a garden cannot exist. All gardeners, bent uncomfortably over their plants and their ground, will tell you this. Gardens only exist as a result of continuous human intervention, whether that intervention involves carving space out of a dark forest, or appropriating an empty space found between buildings in the city.[16]

A garden needs gardening, or "care" as Robert Harrison calls it in his book, *Gardens: An Essay on the Human Condition*; a garden requires constant human care or attention:

Figure 13/ *The Boreal Poetry Garden.*
Photograph by Don McKay.

Figure 14/ Marlene Creates, excerpt from *Larch, Spruce, Fir, Birch, Hand, 2008* (ongoing since 2007). Selenium-toned silver print, 27 x 39 cm (10 ½ x 15 ½ in). Image courtesy of the artist.

A humanly created garden comes into being in and through time. It is planned by the gardener in advance, then it is seeded or cultivated accordingly, and in due time it yields its fruits or intended gratifications. Meanwhile the gardener is beset by new cares day in and day out. For like a story, a garden has its own developing plot, as it were, whose intrigues keep the caretaker under more or less constant pressure. The true gardener is always 'the constant gardener'.[17]

But what gardening goes on in *The Boreal Poetry Garden?* What manifestations of care? Not carrots. Not tilling the soil. Neither planting nor harvest. But could we not still say that there is a careful and potent kind of cultivation that takes place here? A continuous human intervention? A constant gardener? The word 'cultivate' leads back to the Indo-European root $k^w el$-, 'to revolve', 'circle', 'wheel', 'turn over', all of which meanings we can see in the action of the plow or the spade on soil: that turning over of rich garden soil, the first ritual gesture of the gardener, the gardener's invocation. But $k^w el$- carries with it other meanings useful to our understanding of *The Boreal Poetry*

Garden as a garden: 'to move around', 'sojourn', 'inhabit', and 'to dwell'. These are terms that imply place. And a garden, Dunham continues, requires 'place':

> By virtue of its sheer presence, a garden automatically activates a boundary condition. This boundary creates a specific site or place. Martin Heidegger wrote, 'A boundary is not that at which something stops but, as the Greeks recognized, the boundary is that, from which something begins its presencing [its being].' Without 'place' the garden is not a willful construction....[18]

Could we say that what gets 'turned over' in *The Boreal Poetry Garden* is story, that what gets planted are poems, that the gardening done there gets done with words? That the ritual readings of the poems in situ and the remembered events which they subscribe make the wood a locus of social meaning (the Garden's 'harvest'), and both neighbors us to it and fixes it in memory as a discrete place? That the attention, or care, that this activity betrays makes it a place apart?

A GOOD GARDENER?

If we can — if we can agree that *The Boreal Poetry Garden* is a place apart, defined inasmuch as it is subject to human care and cultivation, that is to say, a garden, I wonder if we could also say that it and its gardener are good? For myself, the first answer to this question is found in the fireweed that illuminates the circle in which the artist participates by attending to this six acres of land: "Deadfalls to chain saw;/ logs to fire to warm feet;/ ashes to flowers." But there is something more happening here, more than just the perfect circle the fireweed describes, more than the cultivation of the land through story, something reciprocal that the garden sets in motion and we bow to unawares, even as we take up the counters Marlene's poems offer us and fix the place in our memories: the Garden's secret gift. Shadows are lengthening now through the tangled slow growth of the northern forest, our own shadows lost among the standing and the fallen trees. Our presence here as evening falls; our collective exhalation, "Ah", as a poem closes; the speaking of the words themselves in place; the light exchange of our voices as we round our way back to the house and its fire — these disperse into the air around us just at dusk, in the last long inhalation of the trees before nightfall. Trees are made of air, of the carbon they breathe in and fix, and our momentary presence here, our words, our breath, are caught up and bound in the long slow vowel of their forming rings, a deep 'O' far below the cricket's hum of our hearing. We are gardened, too.

And more than we could ever know, this forest is our dwelling place, our very words greening into what's around us [Figure14].

NOTES

1/   Snyder, Gary, *Axe Handles,* San Francisco: North Point Press, 1983, p. 51.

2/   McKay, Don, "From Here to Infinity (or so)", *The Shell of the Tortoise,* Kentville, Nova Scotia: Gaspereau Press, 2011, pp. 127–128.

3/   This article develops ideas first introduced in my short review of Marlene Creates' *Boreal Poetry Garden* for the online review file of *Canadian Art,* September, 2011.

4/   Creates, Marlene, "Tuning and Being Tuned By a Patch of Boreal Forest: works from Blast Hole Pond Road, 2002 to the present", unpublished notes for a PowerPoint presentation for English 3845, Writing With Pictures (Department of English, Memorial University), at *The Boreal Poetry Garden,* 29 January 2013.

5/   Gibson Garvey, Susan, "The Specificity of Place", catalogue essay for *Marlene Creates: Landworks 1979–1991,* Memorial University of Newfoundland Art Gallery, 25 February to 11 April, 1993, p. 7.

6/   Creates, Marlene, artist statement, 1985, in Gibson Garvey, "The Specificity of Place", p. 18.

7/   Creates, Marlene, "Tuning and Being Tuned".

8/   Creates, Marlene, "Tuning and Being Tuned".

9/   Creates, Marlene, *The Distance Between Two Points is Measured in Memories, Labrador 1988,* North Vancouver: Presentation House Gallery, 1990, p. 17.

10/ Creates, Marlene, *Places of Presence: Newfoundland kin and ancestral land, Newfoundland 1989–91,* St John's: Killick Press, 1991, p. 5.

11/ Creates, Marlene, "OUR COASTLINE IS NATURAL & SCENIC," *Language and Land Use, Newfoundland 1994,* Halifax: Mount Saint Vincent University Art Gallery, 1998, p. 59.

12/ Creates, Marlene, in an interview with Joanne Marion, curator, The Medicine Hat Museum, Art Gallery & Archives for the July 2000 opening there of *Language and Land Use, Alberta 1993.*

13/ *The Boreal Poetry Garden* also has a virtual location well worth wandering through, at: http://marlenecreates.ca/virtualwalk/. At this site you can follow along the paths through the garden and listen to Marlene's recitations of a number of the poems. One key element of the gardener's toolkit which I have been at a loss as to how to set out in this essay will become immediately apparent to you as you view the site: the gardener's graciousness toward and high regard for the individual elements (plants, creatures, watercourses) in the garden around her.

14/ Creates, Marlene, http://www.marlenecreates.ca/works/2005boreal.html.

15/ Story, George M., W. J. Kirwin, and J. D. A Widdowson, *The Dictionary of Newfoundland English,* Toronto: University of Toronto Press, 1982.

16/ Dunham, Donald, "Architecture *without* Nature?", *Earth Perfect? Nature, Utopia, and the Garden,* Annette Giesecke and Naomi Jacobs eds., London: Black Dog Publishing, 2012, pp. 138–139.

17/ Harrison, Robert Pogue, *Gardens: An Essay on the Human Condition,* Chicago: University of Chicago Press, 2008, p. 7.

18/ Dunham, "Architecture *without* Nature?", p. 139.

172 /LINDA WEINTRAUB

GARDENING AS SUBVERSIVE ART

The categorical shift from 'garden' to 'garden as artwork' occurs when its creator consciously exceeds physical necessity by adding meaning. Some further intention or purpose is indicated. Some theme is expressed. As such, art gardens may produce flowers or vegetables, but they also convey social commentary, or deliver a political critique, or formulate ethical concerns, or model a preferred state. Thus, art gardens are always more than arrangements of botanical and geological specimens. They are settings replete with significance and expressiveness. These enriching qualities are acquired when their creators introduce references, metaphors, and commentary into their gardening methodologies and garden designs. Such devices invest these special gardens with drama, humor, irony, pity, indignation, and countless other forms of expression. Thus, art gardens are sites for interpreting, as well as for observing and tending.

Artists who garden tamper with many traditional components of their profession. Fundamentally, they exchange the predictable outcomes offered by inert studio media for the vagaries of germination, growth, and death. Unlike the calculated attributes of conventional art media, the genetically prescribed patterns of living media can never be fully anticipated. Living organisms function as willful, finicky, demanding collaborators, not compliant instruments. While all artists' efforts are circumscribed by the characteristics of their media, artist-gardeners cannot escape the inviolable rules of botanicals when composing their works. To enlist a living art medium necessitates deviation from a variety of artistic conventions. For instance, instead of occurring within controllable studio conditions, production becomes dependent upon seasons, climate, and weather, and cycles of the sun and moon. Aesthetic considerations are diverted from the artists' self-determining decisions to the functionality of shapes, colors, and sizes of a plant's anatomy. Meanwhile, exhibitions become arenas for ongoing dynamic transformation, not presentations of the culmination and refinement of the artist's creative process. Storage of such work requires conditions conducive to life, the opposite of the sterile and static architectural conditions that are typically required. Finally, instead of being offered a finite, portable material object, collectors encounter works of art that grow, have roots, require tending, may become sick, and will inevitably die.

SUBVERSIVE GARDEN ART

While some art gardens nourish the body and soothe the soul, the art gardens discussed in this essay transform the elemental act of planting a seed into an opportunity to promote radical causes. They constitute what George McKay, author of *Radical Gardening*, calls "horti-counterculture", a term intended to reverse the association of gardens with rest and repose, and align them with activism and opposition.[1] In an extended meditation on the etymologies of gardening terms, McKay notes that the element of danger suggested by 'a plot' (a scheme to accomplish some unlawful purpose) may seem incompatible with the innocent seeming 'plot' (a small piece of ground) where gardens typically are located. Likewise, the aggressive implication of 'propaganda' (communication designed to manipulate opinion) seems distant from the nurturing act of 'propagation' (reproduction through organic cultivation).[2] Furthermore, the uncompromising stance of 'radicals' who campaign for drastic political, economic, or social reforms hardly seems connected to the 'radicals' or root formations of a healthy plant. Yet many artists have set aside such common forms of protest as rallies and sabotage to exploit the contrary implications of plots, propaganda, and radicals. They campaign for drastic social reforms with their feet on the soil and their hands in it. As such, their work tends to deviate as far from conventional forms of protest as from conventional forms of art.

Artists' gardens become 'subversive' when they are designed to undermine an established condition, entity, or legally constituted authority. Gardening offers artists a powerful tool for 'waging' subversion, because entire social, political, spiritual, environmental, and ethical philosophies are imbedded in forms of human-induced biological productivity. But while these subversive actions are bent on destruction, they are not necessarily undertaken to harm or agitate. The destruction on the minds of most artist gardeners involves eradicating some detrimental behavior or unjust attitude. While a few assertively defy an institution or publicly shame a guilty party, most pursue uplifting utopian visions rather than aggressive treachery. These artist-gardeners advocate noble causes and enlightened principles. Nonetheless, their work is subversive because, by deviating from norms and tampering with the commonplace, they unsettle those with vested interests in the status quo. Their horticultural tactics seem to combine Henry David Thoreau's version of civil disobedience and Mahatma Gandhi's nonviolent resistance. Both of these lofty thinkers championed gentle tactics adopted by the multitudes to instigate sweeping social reforms.

Three forms of subversive offense are exemplified by the seven garden artworks presented in this essay. The first targets inequities based upon social and territorial exclusivity; the second exposes the detrimental effects of GMOs, lawns, and mono-agriculture; and the third combats endemic forms of social discrimination. The artists who created these works have all departed from studio sanctuaries in order to correct social maladies and initiate cultural reforms. To fulfill these missions they have replaced conventional forms of artistic expression with planting, tending, pruning, mulching, and harvesting. While some retain the garden's normal functions relating to food production and landscaping, and others explore the garden's metaphorical potential, all function as triggers to radical actions.

GREEN GUERRILLAS AND THE ATTACK ON PRIVATIZATION

The community gardening movement that emerged during the 1960s earned the adjective 'subversive' because, being founded on the principles of sharing and cooperation, it deviated from mainstream, capitalist culture. When the drive to resist privatization involves "the illicit cultivation of someone else's land", the subversive aspects of gardening escalate.[3] Such clandestine actions, known as 'guerrilla gardening', peacefully but emphatically defy capitalist societies' definition of 'capital' as privately owned material wealth. In the United States, such capital is sacrosanct — protected by the constitution, upheld by law, and reinforced by custom.

Guerrilla gardening, acts of planting that resist privatization, are unsanctioned and illegal. They typically take place on neglected ground in urban settings — road

Figure 1/ Liz Christy Community Garden, 1973, New York City. Photograph courtesy of Donald Loggins.

medians, sidewalks, untended flowerbeds, alleys, and vacant lots. Such orphaned plots, usually owned by a municipality or an apathetic landlord, are viewed by guerrilla gardeners as neglected assets that merit being transformed into verdant greenery. The first recorded use of the term 'guerrilla gardening' was in 1973 when Liz Christy (1950–1985) spearheaded an action to construct a garden in a derelict private lot described as "the ultimate slime spot in the City" [Figure 1].[4] Christy, an artist and graphic designer, enlisted friends and neighbors into her band of rebel gardeners, who became widely known as the Green Guerrillas. Their radical gardening procedures initially took the form of 'bombing' barren urban lots with 'seed grenades' they fabricated from balloons filled with seeds and fertilizer. In this manner they launched botanical invasions of property they did not own. Other clandestine activities included planting sunflower seeds in the center meridians of busy New York City streets and installing flower boxes on the window ledges of abandoned buildings.

Christy's initiative coincided with the actions of 1970s artists who banded together to issue searing institutional critiques concerning racism, sexism, anti-war sentiments, and other contested ideological principles. The Guerrilla Art Action Group (GAAG), for example, waged non-violent protests against the ethical failures of US culture and government. At the same time, the Art Workers Coalition staged symbolic revolts against the war in Vietnam, as well as public demonstrations supporting civil rights. The adjective 'guerrilla' describes their art actions because, like guerrilla fighters, they resisted the authorities through unconventional forms of warfare. The botanical focus of Christy's renegade art practice also coincided with other uses of living plant matter as an artistic medium, as evidenced by Alan Sonfist's "Time Landscape" (1978-ongoing), Helen and Newton Harrison's "Portable Orchard" (1972–1973), Charles Simond's "Growth House" (1974–1994), and Hans Haacke's "Directed Growth" (1972), to name a few.

Christy's Guerrillas contributed to this convergence of political action and art production when, in 1973, they undertook the massive task of cleaning up an abandoned lot owned by the city of Manhattan at the corner of Bowery and Houston Streets. At this time, due to urban riots and a financial crisis, large sections of New York City had been abandoned by landlords. The city government became the inadvertent owner of thousands of properties when owners defaulted on their taxes. Buildings crumbled, leaving empty lots that quickly became cluttered with litter and infested with vermin. Christy sought and ultimately received permission to remove the debris and transform the site into a garden oasis. The project took an entire year. 60 raised beds were constructed. Droppings from mounted police horses were hauled in for fertilizer. A Parks Department giveaway provided seeds.

The Green Guerrillas' radical engagement with gardens was not limited to the cultivation of plants. The group also cultivated the 'community' component of community gardening by helping others initiate public gardening projects in neighborhoods throughout the city. The Green Guerrillas conducted gardening workshops and organized plant giveaways. They also planted experimental plots to discover which plants were capable of thriving in hostile urban conditions, and they shared their garden produce with other inhabitants of the Bowery.

Christy's initiative is thus associated with two landmark 'firsts': New York City's first guerrilla gardening action and its first community garden. The garden did not remain an anomaly for long. It expanded into a movement when residents of other neighborhoods transformed their neighborhood wastelands into gardens. Indeed, even the City Parks Department joined the initiative in 1978 by offering plants, tools, horticultural expertise, and dollar-a-year leases to community groups who would cultivate vacant lots. The results were remarkable. As reporter Steve Brooks and ecologist Gerry Marten report,

> The Green Guerrillas interrupted the cycle [of decline]. They took one part of the eco-social system — a vacant lot — and changed it from an eyesore to an oasis. A virtuous cycle began. By cleaning out the lot, the gardeners removed a habitat for criminals. As their streets became safer, residents spent more time on them reducing crime further. As gardening strengthened the social bonds among neighbors, the neighborhood became safer still. Instead of moving out, people started moving in. Empty buildings became occupied. As the virtuous cycle gained momentum, the quality of life went up, and the former slum attracted more and more residents.[5]

Ironically, community gardens are often threatened by their own success, because as neighborhoods become more desirable, land becomes more valuable for private development and property tax revenues. These factors accounted for Mayor Rudolph Giuliani's move to revoke community garden leases in the 1980s. When indignant gardeners throughout the city's boroughs galvanized to resist the action, community gardeners once again became overtly and subversively political.

The Liz Christy Garden survives, thanks to public support. It exists today as a memorial to its activist founder and a testimonial to a guerrilla community garden movement. Maintenance is shared by volunteers. While its website promises visitors the opportunity to enjoy a pond inhabited by fish and turtles, a wildflower habitat, a grape arbor, numerous tree species, vegetable gardens, and flowering perennials, the project's significance as an art work lies in the values it promoted more than in the verdant environment it created. Christy's garden has entered the history of art as a model of how artists can facilitate participatory democracy and communal cooperation while perpetuating art's traditional role as an exemplar of humanity's shifting concerns.

While the cultural tenor has calmed in the intervening years, this form of radicalism has not dissipated with art. The examples that follow provide evidence that the role of gardening with fine art continues to thrive as a pragmatic solution to the escalating pressure to sustain human populations, as a poignant metaphor for social ills, and as a tool of protest.

THE HUMBLE GARDEN AS FINE ART

Gardens can demonstrate how to become self-sufficient by growing one's own food rather than relying on imported goods. Food production is a particularly urgent concern for Taiwan, because its citizens rely on imports for almost all of their food, and because the island is vulnerable to the rising sea levels that result from climate change. Mali Wu (b. 1957, Taiwan) tampered with many art conventions to create a vivid reminder of Taiwan's vulnerability. It took the form of a multi-station installation at the Taipei Museum of Fine Arts titled *Taipei Tomorrow as a Lake Again* (2008). Less than 500 years ago, Taipei was a lake. There was no city. Wu directed the art-viewers' attention toward urgent social issues by summoning a known

historic condition that predicts a probable future condition. As she explains, "I chose the title because Taipei could return to that state again. As operators, managers, and planners of this city, how should we deal with this issue?"[6]

Taipei Tomorrow consisted of three sections carefully sequenced to remind visitors of their dependence on plants. One took the form of interactive stations installed within the museum. This evolving presentation documented the entire project and presented evidence of the dire effects of global warming on Taiwan and Taipei. The magnitude of this disaster was evoked by titling this section "Green Ark", a reference to Noah's Ark. The alarm raised by this part of the installation laid the foundation for the workshops and actions that constituted the "Virescent Taipei" section. These introduced visitors to strategies for mitigating their insecurities by establishing agendas for urban development that could counter global warming: eco-building, a bike paradise, a farm city, etc. The use of the word 'virescent' (turning green) in the title suggests the possibility of replacing fear with resolution. The workshops' confidence-building strategy culminated in the outdoor gardens titled "Edible Landscape Taipei" [Figure 2]. Its centerpiece was a mobile kitchen garden on the terrace of the Museum, neatly planted with potatoes, peppermint, and other vegetables and herbs.[7] To divert people from mere visual stimulation and reintroduce utility into art, Wu invited exhibition visitors to harvest the crops. The plant groups she selected offered reliable

Figure 2/ Mali Wu, "Edible Landscape Taipei", 2008, Taipei Museum of Fine Arts. Photograph courtesy of the artist.

and robust reseedings that enable continuous production. Upside-down beverage crates served as convenient pathways between the beds.

By implication, if a garden could thrive on a paved museum terrace, one could also be constructed on the museum's roof and balcony, and on the terraces, roofs, and balconies of buildings throughout the city. The benefits abound. Constructing gardens in the empty spaces in Taipei would give people control over their food, eliminate the need for dangerous herbicides and pesticides, remove emissions associated with transporting food, lower the city's temperature, reduce air pollution, create a genial environment, and enable urbanites to experience botanical life.

Wu has lived in Taiwan throughout her life, except when enrolled at the Academy of Fine Arts in Düsseldorf. After graduating in 1985 she returned to Taiwan and quietly repudiated her formal art training:

> When I returned [to Taiwan] from Germany, I encountered a society robustly pursuing changes.... [T]he United States severed their diplomatic relations with us in 1978, and '87 was the lift of martial law. Seeing these historic moments became vital to my growing experience;... If art is a linguistic medium, I wondered, how could I articulate my concerns with it? Like most art students, we were dealing with subjects such as the medium or style in school, and the presentations of our works were too limited to art settings. This was a self-contained system, from education, to presentation, and circulation. With a desire to go beyond the limits of this structure, to break free from the art bubble, I experimented with the limits of the concept of art.[8]

Wu's pragmatic way of practicing art confronted museumgoers who might not have expected to encounter a warning about an impending climate crisis, or an admonition that each person must assume responsibility for the survival of life on Earth, or information about how to accomplish food security. Yet Wu's critical perspective ultimately transformed a woeful condition into a work of art that conveyed a positive, solution-based message. She describes her artistic vision as a "new energy capable of creating interconnectedness, a reality where the elements of the past conjugate and converge with the evolved facts of the present".[9]

If the word 'subversive' refers to disruptions of the norm, then Wu's garden certainly qualifies as subversive. Her installation asserts that survival in an era of impending climate change demands a complete overhaul of agriculture and art. Agriculture must shift from large-scale centralized production to localized subsistence farming, and artists must divert their professional utilization of resources, space, and time away from visual pleasures and apply them to survival strategies. Functionality and didacticism remain particularly troublesome forms of 'newness' in art. Like sentimentality in the 1970s and

beauty in the 1980s, they are frequently taken to disqualify art from popular and scholarly consideration. Wu's projects manifest these forms of 'newness'. Like many eco artists who adopt functional and didactic approaches, she eliminates utopian and dystopian extremes, and focuses instead upon optimistic strivings for improvement. Practical answers replace imaginings, emotions, and speculations. Even definitions of artistic 'success' shift because they are directed away from media attention and commercial value and toward measurable outcomes. While achievement remains a product of an artist's ingenuity, it now takes the form of strategic designs and tactical media. As such, the importance, meaning, and worth of such eco artworks are subject not to the individual 'likes' and 'dislikes' of the audience, but to objective criteria with predetermined purposes. For all these reasons, functional and didactic art can communicate to people who have little knowledge of art history and theory, who may not seek encounters with contemporary art, who may not possess cultivated visual sensibilities, and who may not even realize that the experience they are encountering is being offered as a work of art. Ironically, it is through such disruptions that artists assume the esteemed role of emissary of cultural change in an era of environmental crisis.

CONTESTATIONAL BIOLOGY

Gardening is designed to nourish living botanicals, enhance their vitality, increase their productivity, and defend them against their enemies. The unique feature of *Molecular Invasion* (2002), the gardening project conducted by members of the Critical Art Ensemble (CAE), is that perishing, not thriving, was the goal of the experimental garden they installed at the Corcoran Museum of Art in Washington, DC. The outcome of the 'bio-art' experiment carried out by Steve Kurtz, Steve Barnes, Hope Kurtz, and Beverley Schlee of CAE, collaborating with other artists, scientists, and Corcoran students, was not determined until the last day of the exhibition. Success as they defined it would be the death of the genetically modified corn, soy, and canola plants they had planted!

Up until this climactic conclusion, the sprouts that the artists planted had been meticulously cared for. They thrived in stylishly designed planters under grow lights [Figure 3]. Museum visitors were informed that some of the crops had been genetically modified to make them resistant to Monsanto's powerful herbicide RoundUp. Other plants served as the control group; their genetics had not been manipulated, so it was known that the herbicide sprays would be lethal to them. What was not known was whether a few impudent artists could sabotage the interventions of an agricultural corporate giant by eradicating the protections engineered into the genetically modified (GMO) plants' genes. Since monoculture,

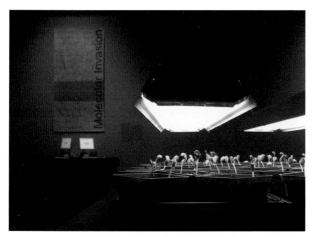

Figure 3/ Critical Art Ensemble, with Beatriz da Costa, Claire Pentecost, and students from the Corcoran School of Art. *Molecular Invasion* 2002, Installation view at the Corcoran, Washington, DC. Photograph courtesy of the artists.

by definition, only permits a single crop to grow on a plot of land, all competing species in the vicinity are classified as enemy weeds and exterminated.

RoundUp functions by inhibiting a specific enzyme that plants require to grow. After a single treatment, conventional plants die in a few days. But Monsanto's 'RoundUp Ready' crops can produce a resistant enzyme protecting them from the herbicide. The artists began their disruptive action by transforming the museum into a rebel 'garden laboratory'. When the plants were fully grown, the artists applied a non-toxic chemical disrupter, P5P, to the GMO crops in the hope that it would eradicate their herbicide resistance.[10] A few days later, CAE sprayed all the plants with RoundUp. Then everyone waited. Would the GMO plants survive or would they succumb to the herbicide despite their high-tech protections? The rogue molecular biology experiment was declared a great success when the genetically protected plants died alongside the plants in the control group. By demonstrating that genetic manipulations can be overcome, the experiment proved that a few indignant artists are capable of undermining the calculated manipulations of a corporate giant.

CAE explains that its goal is "to discover and create products for resource management that are harmonious with the ecosystems in which they function".[11] While this goal is probably shared by most gardeners, it is not shared by most industrial agricultural enterprises. CAE's term 'contestational biology' reveals the group's subversive intention. In pursuit of their benign vision, they aggressively combat the corporate underpinnings of genetic manipulations that challenge such harmonious management. Steven Kurtz, one of the group's founding members, comments, "We do protest the system.... We do not categorically condemn genetic modification."[12] The

part of the system that they protest is the pan-capitalism that "only fuels, strengthens, and expands the profit machine" by attempting to consolidate and control the world's food supply.[13] Traditional methods of contestation seemed insufficient to accomplish this imposing challenge. The artists asked themselves, "How can the new molecular/biochemical front be directly engaged as a means to disrupt profits? This is an area that is completely under-theorized, and is the subject matter of contestational biology."[14]

CAE acknowledges that the short-run benefits of GMOs enable farmers to easily eliminate weeds without harming their crops. Such efficiencies translate into lower consumer prices. Still, the artists are indignant about the worrisome unknowns associated with genetically altered foods. In an interview, Kurtz explained that GM seeds for RoundUp Ready crops are a product of advanced science research coalescing with strong profit motives. The corporate entity that benefits from this unsavory alliance is also responsible for testing the safety of its products. As a result, claims of safety made by such corporations and reinforced by their media agents are not responsibly critiqued before the products are marketed. The absence of objective studies fosters fears that genetically engineered foods, in combination with the intensive use of herbicides associated with cultivating GM crops, lowers nutritional value and antibiotic resistance, increases allergic reactions, contaminates ordinary crops, harms wildlife, and promotes the spread of 'super weeds' and pesticide-resistant insects.

Not content to denounce this "capital-driven technocracy", CAE conducts public experiments on these products to strip the industry of its immunity from democratic review.[15] Like most citizen uprisings, CAE's opposition depends upon cunning, not might. In the end, their strategy involves deploying 'fuzzy biological sabotage', which they define as nonaggressive actions that embolden the public to challenge corporate and scientific authorities. To encourage amateurs to resist centers of power, the artists offer three attack principles derived from military strategy. First, focus the attack on the weakest link in the system: CAE discovered a crack in the defense of corporate/science mergers. "Whenever a product is patented, including GMOs, all the information surrounding it is placed in the public domain. Scientists and the public can take that information and investigate it, replicate experiments, and publish their results."[16] Next, form accurate targeting systems to avoid collateral damage: CAE calculated that Monsanto would not sue the artists, because they would also have to sue the venerable art institution, part of the Smithsonian, that hosted the show. Because Monsanto's public image was already tarnished, the company would want to avoid more negative publicity. Kurtz explains that the Corcoran "provided an umbrella of legitimacy. Just try to get us now! It was like having Superman protecting you."[17] Finally, use the minimum amount of force necessary to accomplish an objective: CAE discovered that reversing GMO modifications did not require technically advanced processes, expensive laboratory equipment, or advanced degrees in science. The biochemical intervention it utilized was vitamin B-6, which can be purchased at any vitamin store. Thus, the process was simple enough and safe enough for artists to carry out publicly in a gallery setting before a large group of witnesses.

In sum, Kurtz explains the radical aspects of CAE's intervention by stating, "What was innovative was not our chemical process. The way we used it was innovative. We made the plant's strength its weakness. We used the process for political reasons: to train the public to become GMO industry watchdogs and to undermine the corporations' immunity from scrutiny."[18] This work introduced 'bio-hacking' for political purposes into the ever-expanding domain of art practice.

LAWNS VS.
EDIBLE ESTATES

The promise of combining the calm of the country with the advantages of the city has lured two out of three American families into suburbia. But where some see a green, secure refuge, critics see only the illusion of a pastoral idyll: assembly-line houses wrapped in aluminum siding, located on a monotonous grid of rectangular plots, and arranged along automobile thoroughfares providing access to work, shopping, and recreation. As variants of this model have colonized vast territories around most North American cities, housing developments replace forests, wetlands, and farmlands. As a result, 'nature' in suburbia is confined to parks, plazas, sports fields, bike trails, and endless expanses of lawn.

Environmental Protection Agency (EPA) statistics attest to the serious environmental problems associated with the roughly 20,000,000 acres planted as residential lawns in the US: 30 to 60 percent of urban fresh water is used for watering lawns; 67,000,000 pounds of synthetic pesticides are used on US lawns; 580,000,000 gallons of gasoline are used for lawnmowers.[19] Eco-terrorists like members of the Earth Liberation Front respond with direct destructive action. One of the 13 offensive actions attributed to the ELF in 2005 included an act of arson in Sammamish, Washington, targeted at new development located in a golf course subdivision. Police who investigated the incident discovered a paper condemning the rape of the Earth and claiming responsibility on behalf of ELF. It reads, "Where are all the trees? Burn, rapist, burn. E. L. F."[20] The group's strident stance is summed up in their proclamation, "We will not sit back as all that is natural and beautiful is destroyed."[21]

Eco artist Fritz Haeg shares ELF's indignation. His radical art is "an attack on the American front lawn and everything it has come to represent".[22] However, his protest against the suburban lawn's assault on vegetation takes the form of gentle persuasion rather than criminal action. He invites ordinary homeowners to join this crusade by replacing the ubiquitous suburban lawn with edible landscaping. His appeal is easily justified by the fact that emerald green carpets of grass, the pride of many homeowners, are compromised ecosystems.

To diminish the harmful consequences of lawn care, the EPA recommends watering at night to reduce evaporation, planting drought-tolerant species, using non-polluting pest controls, etc. But Haeg's scheme exceeds mere damage control. He is seeking a positive gain by taking advantage of the wasted ecological opportunities wherever single-family homes are built upon private lots. Sunshine and rain are horticultural treasures that suburbanites receive free of charge. Soil and its microorganisms in their yards are miracle workers capable of supporting growth processes. Haeg proposes a way for suburban environments and all their living occupants to maximize their benefit from these abundant resources. Instead of growing grass, grow food! Thus, Haeg offers homeowners the double advantage of revitalizing their front yards and escaping from "engineered fruits and vegetables wrapped in plastic and Styrofoam, cultivated not for taste, but for ease of transport, appearance and uniformity, then sprayed with chemicals to inhibit diseases and pests that thrive in an unbalanced ecosystem".[23]

Haeg describes his scheme, titled *Edible Estates*, as "a practical food-producing initiative, a place-responsive landscape design proposal, a scientific horticultural experiment, a conceptual land-art project, a defiant political statement, a community out-reach program and an act of radical gardening".[24] To amplify the installations' social agenda, Haeg carefully selects the locations of his *Edible Estates*. For example, the first edition of *Edible Estates* was established in the front yard of Stan and Priti Cox's suburban home in Salina, Kansas, the geographic center of the United States. The second edition partnered with the Foti family in Lakewood, California, an iconic 1950s housing development ten miles from Los Angeles. Lakewood is the nation's first post-war planned housing development. It is also the first to utilize assembly line production, which made it possible to churn out homes at the astonishing rate of 1,000 per month. Within three years, 17,500 homes were built on a former beet farm, adding 70,000 suburbanites to its rural population.

Since his program was initiated on Independence Day in 2005, Haeg has undertaken *Edible Estates* in nine regional districts around the United States [Figures 4a, 4b]. In each instance, one family living in a suburban neighborhood grants him permission to replace their entire front lawn with an edible garden. The artist works with local horticultural or agricultural research organizations to design a garden tailored to the conditions at each site and to the household's food preferences. Armed with this information, Haeg designs the garden and teaches the residents how to cultivate the fruits, vegetables, grains, and herbs he plants in their yards. All costs associated with establishing the garden for the first season are covered, typically through grants from a sponsoring cultural institution. In return, each participating family commits to maintaining the garden as long as they occupy the house. In so doing, they make a long-term pledge of defiance against suburban landscaping norms as well as industrial means of acquiring food. Fully complicit with the artist's agenda, these families engage in a non-essential form of radicalism originating in discontent, not necessity; they are surrounded by abundant supplies of food from conventional sources, but protest the objectionable aspects of industrial food production. Their front yards perpetually announce a crusade against the "the banal lifeless space of uniform grass in front of the house" and replace it with "the chaotic abundance of bio-diversity".[25] These home gardeners are doubly radical. First, by attending to their own nutritional needs, they are liberated from the oppressive regime of the mega-corporations that currently dominate food production; in this manner they resist the institutional takeover of their economic and practical lives. Secondly, instead of relying on anonymous foods produced in remote locations under conditions they cannot observe or control, they become intimately acquainted with their foods during growth, cultivation, and harvesting.

Yet the impact of each Edible Estate extends well beyond participating families. Haeg's lawn conversions not only take place in conspicuous public street settings, but they are also extensively documented, appearing ultimately on websites, books, brochures, and videos. Documentation of the first season's growth is displayed as a public exhibition in a local, sponsoring art institution. And in order to instigate a beneficial contagion of lawn replacements throughout each region beyond the closing dates of the exhibitions, Haeg also distributes a free booklet that lists local nurseries, itemizes regional fruits and vegetables and edible native plants, and provides a directory of local gardening resources. Haeg thus serves as the project's mastermind, administrator, educator, and public relations officer at once.

MONO-AGRICULTURE AND *LIVE DINING*

The Canadian artist Nicole Fournier (b. 1966, Montreal) gardens to subvert two venerable attitudes that characterize Western culture: that advances in 'culture' are measured by increases in humanity's ability to dominate 'nature', and that expediency is privileged over prudence. Fournier has engaged in a variety of performative 'environmental' actions in an effort to highlight the baneful effects of monoculture (which boosts yields and profits while contributing to environmental blight and depletion) and of processed foods (produced, as they are, far from where they are ultimately consumed, and subjected to industrial procedures and engineering manipulations). Her 2002 series of "Corn Field Performances" dramatized the potential dangers of GMO crops by drawing parallels between hair follicles in skin and corn plants in fields, and then walking through a mature GMO corn field wearing a full suit of protective gear. By 2004, she had shifted her focus from problems to solutions, and that is when she began experimenting with alternative agriculture systems, in particular the poly-agriculture system (polyculture) championed by permaculturist founder, Bill Mollison. A complete reversal of mono-agriculture, polyculture encourages multiple kinds of crops to coexist in the same space at the same time.

Figure 4/ Fritz Haeg, *Edible Estates garden #15*, Twin Cities, Minnesota, 2013. Estate owners: Catherine and John Schoenherr, Woodbury, Minnesota. Commissioned by Walker Art Center for "Fritz Haeg: At Home in the City". Established 24–26 May 2013. Photograph by Olga Ivanova, use courtesy of the artist.

It is the benefits of polyculture that Fournier pursues to this day.

Deploying her ample skills as an artist, polyagriculturist, activist, feminist, herbalist, and gardener, Fournier revises food practices from their points of origin in the earth to their destination in the mouths of eaters in the project that she calls *Live Dining*. While retaining the goal of maximizing productivity, Fournier deliberately exposes her plants to weeds, insects, birds, moles, rabbits, groundhogs, neighbors, harsh winds, etc. In fact, she welcomes these marauders, radically recalibrating the conventional concept of a thriving garden. In the process, Fournier opposes both conventional hobby food gardening and global, corporate, large-scale mono-agriculture (monoculture) with her subversive alternative, 'growing'.

One example of Fournier's *Live Dining* art practice exists as a community garden at Place Benoit, a rundown neighborhood in Montreal where low-rent apartment blocks have housed a succession of immigrants from the West Indies, India, Ukraine, and Italy since the 1950s [Figures 5a, 5b]. When Fournier joined the garden project in the fall of 2010, Issiaka Sanou, an urban agronomist, had already constructed raised beds for planting an area paved with asphalt and enclosed by three brick walls. The open side of this urban garden enclosure faced the neglected parking lot of an industrial park. But Fournier did not perceive urban blight there. Instead, she gazed happily upon the abundance and diversity of weeds growing in the spaces between the buildings and the asphalt. She was pleased to discover that "the building was falling apart. The asphalt was breaking apart. Nature was taking over."[26]

Sanou had intended to plant all the beds with only one crop — kiwis. When Fournier joined the initiative, the plan was expanded into an elaborate polyculture system by introducing three pre-industrial strategies for acquiring food: foraging, polyculturing, and rewilding. These primeval methods vitalize ecosystems by building soil, diversifying habitats, producing ecotones (the transitional area between two biomes), and increasing biodiversity.

Foraging, the direct procurement of edible plants that have grown without being cultivated, was humanity's sole means of acquiring these food staples for all but the last 10,000 of our five million year history. In foraging, harvesting proceeds without the need to plant, weed, and water. Now, the practice has all but disappeared. Shopping has replaced foraging as the primary method of obtaining fresh ingredients for meals. Though convenient, it imposes the requirement of earning money in order to eat. In Place Benoit, Fournier introduced impoverished urban residents to this practical means of acquiring food. Community members joined her in searching out robust and nutritious specimens of wild plants, guaranteed to be vigorous, in vacant lots and cracks in sidewalks. She taught them how to identify edible weeds that are typically eradicated with herbicides or yanked out by the roots. The participants then learned how to conduct harvesting as a mindful practice that would preserve the weeds' abilities to continue to thrive and reproduce after they were foraged. Fournier explains, "Beneficial weeds grow all around us. Foraging lets the wildness be."[27]

In the actual garden, Fournier allocated space for multiple kinds of vegetables. Then she added flowers and herbs, mixing perennials and annuals. Her commitment to diversity expanded to include 'enemy' plant species. At first, she sowed or transplanted only edible weeds. Later, her departure from conventional gardening and mono-agricultural protocols escalated into a betrayal when she welcomed into the garden weeds with no known nutritional or medicinal uses. She defends her action by stating that these are important "for ecosystem maintenance, for greening spaces, for human global food security".[28] Of course, the 'useless' weeds for the project could not be purchased from nurseries. Fournier acquired them by foraging in her own yard.

Figure 5/ Nicole Fournier, *Kiwi Box Live Dining*, 2010, Place Benoit community, St Laurent Borough of Montreal, integrated urban revitalization project. Photograph by Luc Bourgeois, use courtesy of the artist.

Fournier's maverick vision for urban gardening ultimately involves leaving space for wild things to grow according to their own inclinations. For the gardener, 'rewilding' entails suspending judgments about which plants are desirable and which are disagreeable. In fact, the wild species to which Fournier grants 'squatters' rights' are not only plants. She also welcomes mice, squirrels, pigeons, insects, and birds to make their homes in the garden, since animals are essential to self-perpetuating life systems. Most significantly, a commitment to rewilding prevents the artist/gardener from imposing her personal taste, controlling the appearance of her garden, or even choosing its components. Weeds sprout and grow without her involvement. Critters nibble and nest wherever they choose. This strategy is significant because, as Fournier notes, mono-agriculture's fixation with being in command parallels a broader cultural trend:

> Civilization is about control, controlling, managing, designing every aspect of human made environments, including plant and tree growth, and measuring, and monitoring scientifically with our inventions in technology, all aspects of human-environment relationships. There is no wildness left (hardly) in the city.[29]

People are another form of life that factors into the vagary of Fournier's *Live Dining* gardens: residents connect to the sources of their foods by participating in the cultivation and the harvest. They also prepare recipes with these foods. The culminating event of each project is the meal, a performance that occurs outdoors exactly where the plants grew. Fournier describes this manner of eating as the "touching of our physical organic environment, in the site of food growth, while dining, which includes touch, proximity, intimacy in exchange and production".[30] For example, the menu that was served at the opening of the so-called *Kiwi Box Live Dining* project in urban Benoit consisted of nettle soup and carrot soup seasoned with onions, yarrow, and basil, as well as salads made of tomato, lettuce, evening primrose petals, and yarrow.

Fournier characterizes these dining events as "a way to celebrate the creation of this green space for people, plant biodiversity and ecosystem development".[31] Such a celebration is an implicit attack on the 'mono' aspect of industrial food production. Fournier radicalizes the concept of diversity to welcome all zoological as well as botanical species living in the garden's environs. In addition, she disregards mono-agriculture's goal of maximizing short-term production by emphasizing instead the continued productivity of the ecosystem far into the future. Finally, Fournier eliminates the supply line between the foods' cultivation and their consumption. In all these ways, Fournier ethically and strategically reverses the biological disasters that are the unfortunate by-products of mono-agriculture's efficiency and productivity. Her work demonstrates how habitats can be vitalized even as they serve as sites for food production.

— **Figure 6/** Paul Harfleet, " Faggot!", 2013, Canary Wharf, London, — *The Pansy Project*, 2005–. Photograph courtesy of the artist.

THE PANSY PROJECT: ROOTING OUT HOMOPHOBIA

In an essay on gardening, it might be assumed that the word 'pansy' would refer only to the familiar flower with its distinctive purple tint and rounded velvety petals. Indeed, the British artist Paul Harfleet (b. 1970) has planted approximately 10,000 pansies as part of his ongoing *The Pansy Project*, initiated in 2005. However, he intends each of these flowers to also signify the pansy's colloquial meaning as a slur targeted at an effeminate male. Its synonyms are sissy, fag, and fairy.

Harfleet plants a single pansy on the piece of public land closest to a location where a homophobic attack has occurred [Figure 6]. This act extrapolates the practice, common in many cultures, of placing flowers at the scene of a crime or accident. He applies this ritual to a misfortune that is typically neglected or suppressed. The pansies serve as poignant markers of the hostile actions that members of the gay community frequently confront: harassments, taunts, stone throwings, beatings, and even murders. The fragile beauty of these subtle floral incursions evokes the anguish of a defenseless victim. Harfleet comments, "Floral tributes subtly augment the reading of a space that encourages a passer-by to ponder past events at a marked location, generally understood as a crime or accident; my particular intervention could encourage a passer-by to query the reason for my own ritualistic action."[32]

After Harfleet plants the pansy, he photographs it on location. Collections of these photographs comprise far more than wrenching memorials to individual victims. They also testify to the frequency of attacks against homosexuals, and indict societies that tolerate this abuse. The photographs are made public when exhibited in galleries and posted on *The Pansy Project* website. Harfleet refers to this collection as "a complex anthology of homophobic verbal abuse as experienced by gay people in towns and cities today".[33] The visual anthology is augmented by captions that repeat the offensive insults spewed by the attackers. Thus, each delicately beautiful image is accompanied by such chilling slurs as "Let's kill the bati-man!" "Fucking faggot." "What the fuck are you looking at? Faggot!" "Fuck off and die, faggot!" "Fucking Queer Comes." These affronts are accompanied by the location where the abuse occurred.

By contrast, on the sites of the assaults, there is no verbal marker of the hostility that provoked this action. The flower stands alone. These small alterations memorialize the aggressive events that took place there and confirm Harfleet's intention to comfort the victims, not retaliate against their assailants. He explains, "The memorialized locations primarily become a place where the participant has planted a pansy, not where an attack has occurred. This action adjusts the memory of each location which has the effect of overlaying the remembered event in the mind of the participants with a more positive association."[34] The process of planting, in itself, serves as a ceremony of mourning and grief. Harfleet comments, "The subtlety and elegiac quality of the flower was ideal for my requirements. The action of planting reinforced these qualities, as kneeling in the street and digging in the often-neglected hedgerows felt like a sorrowful act. The bowing heads of the flowers became mournful symbols of indignant acceptance."[35] This healing 'ritual' culminates after the planting is complete: "if you are planting a pansy for a loved one or yourself; this is the most emotive moment. I always take time to look at where the pansy is and contemplate what has happened at the location…. I consider this part of the process of letting go of the violence that occurred and literally moving on from it."[36]

Three separate hostile incidents on one summer's day in Manchester, England, in 2005 were the catalysts for this project. Harfleet planted a bloom to mark each of these personal homophobic attacks. Then he began to plant pansies to mark the anti-gay incidents suffered by others in the LGBT community. He also organized events to distribute pansies to others, inviting them to acknowledge, in this gentle manner, the personal assault they had suffered. As such, *The Pansy Project* encourages victims to move beyond retaliation or suppression and adopt a third alternative that victims of verbal abuse rarely consider: healing. "*The Pansy Project* acts as a formula which prevents the 'victim' from internalizing the incident, the strategy becomes a conceptual shield; a behavior that enables the experience to be processed via the public domain."[37]

The visual component of this project is as carefully shaped as its conceptual basis. Harfleet's training as a visual artist is apparent in the care he lavishes on the aesthetic components of his photographs. Invitations for others to contribute photographs of the pansies they have planted come with precise instructions:

> Although pansies are available in multiple tones and hues, restrict the color palette to pink, violet, purple, and blue because they are associated with gay culture.
> Avoid pansies that are a solid color and those that are dark because they are less photogenic.
> Maximize the metaphorical content of the image by pruning off all but a single blossom on each pansy plant.
> Since pansies are most beautiful in the spring, take your pictures at this time of year.
> Plant the pansy on public property such as tree pits, hedgerows, or car parks.
> Include some architectural feature or detail to identify the location in the photograph because that helps tell the story of the planting.

Harfleet's intention is "for the pansy to be the main focus of the picture", and as he remarks,

> this often takes some time to focus on the detail of the pansy…. The key to a successful picture seems to be to get on the ground. This is often the most exposing moment, and takes some bravery, lying on the ground of the street looks very odd to passersby, they may comment as they pass or ask questions of you. Given the nature of the activity and depending on the area I will either tell them exactly what I'm doing or just say I'm planting some flowers as a guerrilla gardener, this usually avoids the potential for confrontation….[38]

In defining his outdoor installations, Harfleet has modified the phrase, 'the thin red line' — a popular political phrase defining a point of no return, the precise instance when safety can no longer be guaranteed and defensive action must be undertaken. While altering the phrase's reference, his "thin pink line" nevertheless retains the red line's stern posture. One line of 2,000 planted pansies that led from the Manchester

Art Gallery to a nearby site of a homophobic murder was Harfleet's contribution to the Queerupnorth Festival in 2005. He augmented the work's impact by enlisting uniformed members of the local police to participate in the plantings. In this manner, these defenders of citizens' rights and safety declared their support of homosexuals against hostile acts of intolerance.

The Pansy Project has been embraced by the gay community worldwide. Harfleet has taken the initiative to demonstrate that members of the LGBT community everywhere confront homophobic bullying and aggression. He has planted pansies in London, Turkey, Berlin, Austria, New York, and other cities, transforming the heartening image of another common phrase, 'the world as your garden' into a disturbing sign of global bigotry.[39]

ETHNOPHOBIA, THE FEAR OF APPLES?

Susan Leibovitz Steinman's (b. 1943) lifelong commitment to economic and social justice was kindled by a convergence of early experiences. Her undergraduate degree in journalism taught her that "the difference between having an education and not is mostly the ability to research ... to find out what's happening and what your options are".[40] After graduation, her brief experience as a social worker in the South Bronx positioned her at an epicenter of social unrest in the turbulent years at the end of the 1960s. 20 years later, as a graduate student at the California College of Arts and Design, Steinman was introduced to art that took the form of an action, performance, or gesture, forms of art that were particularly effective for shaping relationships and social processes. Steinman explains how her political and social radicalism developed into an art practice:

> I was looking for a political issue that felt right for me to work with.... I learned that urban kids did not for the most part know where their food came from, and mostly had never experienced a food garden. I was also interested in bringing food and trees into the inner city ... that kids/people should not have to travel out to rural areas to see trees or farms, that food needed to be raised close to where people live inside the city. I was locavore before there was that term.[41]

Steinman's gardening interests took a political turn when she learned that Proposition 187 would appear on the ballot of her home state of California in 1994. Prop 187 established a state-run citizenship screening system and prohibited illegal aliens from receiving health care, public education, and other social services in the State. Section 1 of Proposition 187 states, "The People of California find and declare as follows: That they have suffered and are suffering economic hardship caused by the presence of illegal immigrants in this state. That they have suffered and are suffering personal injury and damage caused by the criminal conduct of illegal immigrants in this state. That they have a right to the protection of their government from any person or persons entering this country unlawfully." Activists on campuses, churches, and ethnic communities in California and across the country rose to protest the proposition. Steinman channeled her indignation into an artwork that took the form of a tidy apple orchard.

Urban Apple Orchard I, 1993–1995, was a San Francisco Public Art commission aimed at reviving the economy of a depressed neighborhood, which had many vacant stores and a large homeless population [Figure 7]. Steinman added a new element to that agenda by joining the campaign to protect immigrants in California. She chose the apple as her crop because it contributed a powerful symbol in defense of immigration. Because there are no native apple trees in America, every apple grown in America is an 'immigrant'. Thus, this popular icon of Americana exposed the folly of defining a 'true' American. As Steinman explains, "Early immigrants brought apple seeds with them when they came to this continent because apples were essential for making alcohol and sugar."[42] Today, apples are typically propagated by grafting, which limits diversity. But in the New World, the trees were planted from seeds, which accounts for the diverse varieties of wild apple trees throughout the country, mirroring the diverse varieties of human populations: "Each tree looked different. The apples tasted differently. They ripened differently. They stored differently."

The fruit featured in *Urban Apple Orchard* was so incontestably desirable that it disclosed the folly of rebuffing immigrants. Despite their alien origin, apples are recognized symbols of American prosperity and national pride. The phrase "for Mom and apple pie" was a morale-booster for American soldiers in World War II. The advertisement, "baseball, hot dogs, apple pie and Chevrolet" exploits this patriotic connection. Each of these positive associations confirms the benefits of welcoming aliens onto our shores and into our culture. Anyone can be 'as American as apple pie' without having been born in America. In all these ways the trees served as poignant symbols of how immigrants enrich their adopted country. Steinman conveyed this theme to viewers by mounting labels on the 12 potted apple trees, each a different variety. The labels bore the tree's American name, its Latin name, its country of origin, and the year it arrived on this continent. Thus, each testified to the contributions of the immigrants who brought that variety of apple.

Like her crop, the location of Steinman's orchard was carefully selected. It was constructed on the site of a freeway exit ramp that collapsed in the earthquake of 1989 and had not been restored. The collapse did not displease the neighbors, who had resented the fact that the elevated freeway had

Figure 7/ Susan Leibovitz Steinman, *Urban Apple Orchard*, 1994–1995, San Francisco. Photograph courtesy of the artist.

disrupted the community by splitting the neighborhood in half, creating slums, and blocking the sunlight. Steinman initiated a partnership with the San Francisco League of Urban Gardeners (SLUG). Together they trained six local homeless people who had been camping on the site to maintain the orchard and serve as its docents. In exchange, the workers received salaries paid from grant monies Steinman had received to support this participatory 'installation'. Workers also gained marketable landscaping skills that might enable them to find employment. In addition, children who had never left the adjacent urban neighborhoods benefited from Steinman's art intervention. These children had only encountered packaged food on shelves in the liquor stores. The orchard provided a unique opportunity to introduce them to live food production. Working with a local artist who ran a street-front art program for community children, Steinman taught the children to prepare the planters and document the trees' cultivation and growth photographically, thus formally themselves becoming artists.

Steinman describes herself as a guest/itinerant artist: "When I leave, the community owns the project, not me. Community-based ownership is critical to the collaboration, the design, the final artistic, ethical, ecological, social and economic intent of what it's all about."[43] After the installation was dismantled, Steinman donated the potted trees to the church across the street, a nearby park, and the local elementary school. Her work places Proposition 187 in a larger cultural context of immigration. She comments that even 'Native' Americans migrated here on foot, canoe, or kayak. Apples

and Native Americans prove that newcomers become 'naturalized' without being 'invasive'.[44] Steinman sums up her subversive orchard by commenting, "What made this country exciting is that we are a blend of so many people. Our human survival depends on cross-fertilization. I believe that biodiversity applies to humans as well as plants and other species. If you only marry your own kind, you will not have healthy stock." With these words, she justifies and complicates the connection that advertisers and politicians frequently exploit between apples, American prosperity, and national pride.

THE POWER OF PANSIES, LAWNS, VEGGIES, AND APPLES

Art remains a powerful expressive force even when produced by artists whose humble media consist of soil, compost, seeds, plants, and worms. And when these tangible components of gardens become art, they acquire the non-tangible power to be confrontational, or inspirational, or remedial. Liz Christy disobeyed private property protocols. Mali Wu rejects art's elitist and egocentric pretensions. Critical Art Ensemble defies corporate power. Nicole Fournier protests mono-agriculture. Fritz Haeg decries domestically-scaled waste and contamination.

Paul Harfleet and Susan Steinman challenge prejudice. In each case, the potential negativity of radical content is tempered by the tending and nurturing required to maintain botanical life. Thus, exotic apple trees, delicate pansies, and thriving vegetables provide inspiring examples of autonomous actions for progressive social and environmental reforms. When grafted to art, gardens become domains for visionary initiatives.

NOTES

1/ McKay, George, *Radical Gardening: Politics, Idealism, and Rebellion in the Garden*, London: Frances Lincoln Publishers, 2011, p. 6.

2/ McKay, *Radical Gardening*.

3/ Diepenhorst, Swantje, "Richard Reynolds About Guerrilla Gardening: Here is London's Guerilla Gardener No. 1", *Labkultur*, 28 May 2013, http://www.labkultur.tv/en/blog/richard-reynolds-about-guerrilla-gardening.

4/ Ferguson, Sarah, "A Brief History of Grassroots Greening on the Lower East Side", *The New Village Journal*, vol. 1: Community Revitalization, Oakland, CA., 2005, p. 83.

5/ Brooks, Steve, and Gerry Marten, "Models for Success in a Time of Crisis", June 2005, http://www.ecotippingpoints.org/our-stories/indepth/usa-new-york-community-garden-urban-renewal.html.

6/ Interview by Larry Shao.

7/ Mali worked with the Organization of Urban Re-s (OURs). It was her contribution to the 2008 Taipei Biennial.

8/ Wu, Mali, interviewed by Larry Shao, *Diaaalogue*, Asia Archive, November 2010. http://www.aaa.org.hk/Diaaalogue/Details/931.

9/ Wu, Mali, *N.paradoxa*, Katy Deepwell ed., online issue 5, November 1997, p. 46. Quote from press release, Mali Wu, *Scriptura*, Galleria Giorgio Persano, Turin.

10/ Vitamin B-6 exists in different forms. One, pyridoxal 5'-phosphate (PLP), serves a cofactor in many enzyme reactions.

11/ "Where is Critical Art Ensemble?" Artnet Questionnaire, *Artnet.com*, 21 March, 2007. http://www.artnet.com/magazineus/features/quest/quest3-20-07_detail.asp?picnum=4.

12/ Kurtz, Steve, correspondence with the author, 8 July 2011.

13/ Kurtz, Steve, *The Molecular Invasion*, vol. 7, Brooklyn, New York: Autonomedia, Artnet Books, 2009, Introduction, http://www.critical-art.net/books/molecular.

14/ Critical Art Ensemble, "Fuzzy Biological Sabotage", 2013, *The Molecular Invasion*, vol. 10, http://www.critical-art.net/MolecularInvasion.html.

15/ Critical Art Ensemble, "Fuzzy Biological Sabotage", 2013.

16/ Kurtz, interview with the author, 3 June 2011.

17/ Kurtz, interview with the author.

18/ Kurtz, interview with the author.

19/ *Wild Ones: Native Plants, Natural Landscapes*, Environmental Protection Agency, 26 June 2012, http://www.epa.gov/greenacres/wildones/handbk/wo8.html.

20/ "Timeline of Earth Liberation Front Actions", *Wikipedia*, 2007, http://en.wikipedia.org/wiki/Timeline_of_Earth_Liberation_Front_actions#2009

21/ "ELF Strikes Twice in 48 Hours Against Urban Sprawl in California and Michigan", Press Release, *Earth Liberation Front*, 4 June 2003, http://www.mindfully.org/Heritage/2003/ELF-Urban-Sprawl4jun03.htm.

22/ "*Edible Estates* Opening", *Machine Project*, September 2006, http://machineproject.com/archive/events/2006/09/29/edible-estates-opening/.

23/ "Our Food", *Edible Estates, Machine Project*, October 2006, http://machineproject.com/archive/news/2006/10/01/edible-estates-2/.

24/ http://machineproject.com/archive/news/2006/10/01/edible-estates-2/.

25/ www.fritzhaeg.com/wikidictionary/writing/full-frontal-gardening/.

26/ Fournier, Nicole, telephone interview with author, 31 March 2011.

27/ Fournier, Nicole, "Edible Plants in Urban Cracks", 23 May 2007, *Live Dining de Nicole Fournier*, http://livedining.blogspot.com/2007_05_25_archive.html.

28/ Fournier, Nicole, "Industrial Park Living Dining, 15 May, 2009—Update", http://industrialparklivedining.blogspot.com/2009/06/industrial-park-live-dining-2009-update.html.

29/ Fournier, Nicole, "Industrial Park Live Dining 2009–2011—Update", http://industrialparklivedining.blogspot.com/2009/06/industrial-park-live-dining-2009-update.html.

30/ Fournier, Nicole, "Background to Live Dining—2002 & 2004", http://livedining.blogspot.com/2007_06_20_archive.html.

31/ Fournier, "Industrial Park Live Dining 2009–2011—Update".

32/ Harfleet, Paul, Video interview, *The Pansy Project* website: http://www.thepansyproject.com/.

33/ Harfleet, Paul, artist's statement, *The Pansy Project* website: http://www.thepansyproject.com/page2.htm.

34/ Harfleet, Tom, quoted in McKay, George, *Radical Gardening: Politics, Idealism and Rebellion in the Garden*, London: Frances Lincoln Publisher, 2011, p. 147.

35/ Harfleet, *Pansy Project*, http://www.thepansyproject.com/.

36/ Harfleet, *Pansy Project*: http://www.thepansyproject.com/The%20Pansy%20Project%20Guidelines.pdf.

37/ Harfleet, *Pansy Project*, http://www.thepansyproject.com/page2.htm.

38/ Harfleet, *Pansy Project*, http://www.thepansyproject.com/The%20Pansy%20Project%20Guidelines.pdf.

39/ To suggest a location for a pansy planting, write to Paul Harfllet on Twitter @ThePansyProject, via Facebook, or through the blog: thepansyproject.blogspot.co.uk.

40/ Steinman, Susan, interview by the author, 9 August 2013.

41/ Steinman, Susan, in correspondence with the author, 21 September 2013.

42/ Steinman, interview by author.

43/ Steinman, Susan, quoted in Sue Spaid, *Green Acres: Artists Farming Fields, Greenhouses and Abandoned Lots*, Cincinnati: Contemporary Arts Center, 2012, p. 2013.

44/ Steinman, interview by author.

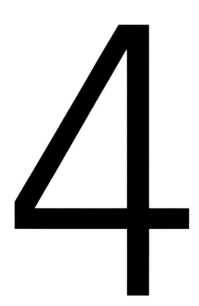

DWELLING IN THE GARDEN

188 /M. ELEN DEMING

GARDENS AND THE WORKING BODY IN THE BRITISH UTOPIAN PROJECT

The Garden City is a poignant chapter in the history of the British cultural imagination that has had a profound impact on the spatial constructions of twentieth-century cities. It also has affected the way the developed world regards the body at work in the domestic landscape. The character and transmission of this cultural motif — the gardener — has been remarkably elastic in the last century. Whether seen as the work of thrift, or consumerism, or citizenship, or family contentment, or even as the work of sustainability — the laboring body in the domestic garden nearly always signifies some form of social agenda. With the Garden City project as context, this essay examines the social agendas of British reformers just prior to World War I. By advocating for lower housing densities and larger domestic landscapes, these reformers changed the way working and middle-class families have physically experienced life at home for the past century and, possibly, for the next.

The idea of the Garden City began late in the nineteenth century when the romantic socialist utopia wooed, and won, the domestic revival project. In reaction against the shocking deterioration of the nation's physical health and social morale resulting from the rapid industrialization of British cities, well-to-do reformers established three objectives: the renaissance of English culture, the renewal of English social unity, and the regeneration of the English race. As a scheme intended to address all three challenges, the Garden City was inspired by the vast utopian possibilities presented both by empire and eugenics.

One of many reform movements of its time, the Garden City idea was nearly coterminous with the Arts and Crafts movement, an informal federation of art and design workers inspired by William Morris' passion for pre-industrial craft aesthetics. Another contemporary reform group was the Fabian Society, comprising a group of elite and middle-class socialists who advocated not for violent overthrow of the government but for the gradual infiltration of members to the ranks of government, there to transmute a socialist agenda into law.

The genesis of the Garden City thus carried the DNA of Victorian art, Ruskinian social theory, the Arts and Crafts movement, Fabian socialism, and liberal British housing reform legislation.

ORIGINS OF GARDEN CITY

Among other things, the Garden City was a radical socialist housing reform and economic development scheme that aimed to relocate large segments of the industrial infrastructure, along with its working population, into new settlements in abandoned rural districts. In building a network of new, self-sufficient industrial settlements, connected via the railway system to major regional capitals, the Garden City proposed to decentralize and rebalance England's industrial and agricultural spheres [Figure 1]. Here, workers were to have the best of both worlds — the 'marriage' of town and country. The idea of the Garden City thus extended well beyond a single settlement: it was intended as a sustainable social infrastructure designed for an entire nation.

Key to the success of the whole movement — and perhaps its 'Achilles' heel' as well — was that it could only work on land bought cheaply. The 'unearned increment' — that is, the appreciation in land values resulting from improvement — was to be the main source of shared prosperity, and anticipated growth would strategically offset the need for taxes ('rates'). Paradoxically, however, the very problem that the Garden City sought to correct — rural abandonment and devaluation — was the one condition that it required for its own survival. Shortly after World War I, the rapid gentrification of the British suburbs effectively blunted the socialist edge of the whole campaign. What remains of the Garden City today comprises two communities — Letchworth Garden City and Hampstead Garden Suburb — along with a widespread popular aspiration to live in a home with a garden.

Since the image of the domestic garden is such an essential and enduring motif in this campaign, it seems a bit surprising that gardens were barely mentioned in Ebenezer Howard's original utopian proposal of 1898. The manifesto, entitled *To-Morrow: A Peaceful Path to Real Reform,* laid out four basic parameters of the Garden City: a commonwealth established for collective ownership of all infrastructure and public land; a greenbelt surrounding the town; an average density of eight to 12 dwelling units per acre; and limits to growth for a projected population of 33,000. Internally, at least, the conceptual and logistical cornerstones of the Garden City concept appear to rely very little on the domestic garden. Nevertheless, garden imagery was imported and inscribed on this radical scheme by its advocates [Figure 2]. So what was the real role of the garden, where did it originate, and who overlaid it upon Howard's economic venture?

Despite widespread concern over the problems of rural depopulation and urban degeneracy, the Garden City attracted very few financial backers at first, and only a small market segment was likely to move from London to embrace such a risky real estate initiative. Selling the movement therefore depended on idealized rural imagery deployed by Garden City propagandists. Images of countryside, rural villages, and vernacular gardens were all highly charged symbols of the nation

Figure 2/ The importance of garden imagery. Unknown artist, *Old Cottages at Norton*, Letchworth Garden City, c. 1905–1908. Commercial postcard, 8 x 13 cm (3 x 5 in). Image courtesy First Garden City Heritage Museum, Letchworth.

at this time. In the broad visual discourse of Victorian socialism, gardens often functioned as a critique of capitalism and the city, a metaphor for social progress, and a wishful image representing the nation. And certainly the domestic garden was already understood by middle-class reformers (such as the architects of the Garden City) to be an integral part, the *sine qua non*, of a 'proper' English home. Lavish use of garden images thus made it possible to encode the Garden City as the symbol of England, *and* the site of an English social utopia, at the same time.

It must be emphasized that the 'Englishness' of English gardens is an "invented tradition", a term defined as "a set of practices, normally governed by overtly or tacitly accepted rules, and of a ritual or symbolic nature, which seek to inculcate certain values and norms of behaviour by repetition, which automatically implies continuity with the past".[1] While such 'traditions' may in fact be quite new, they only require an appropriate referent to manufacture a convincing sense of timelessness. The referent invoked to naturalize and thus legitimize the invented traditions of the Garden City was the English domestic landscape [Figure 3]. But why and when was the tradition of the English garden invented for the industrial classes?

In his seminal work on British cultural history, *The Country and the City* (1973), Raymond Williams offers a plausible explanation — the concept of the *structure of feeling*. In this watershed literary analysis, Williams shows us that the pastoral image of the English countryside was actually re-presented, re-oriented, and re-produced over many centuries. His thesis, that pastoral references to tradition and traditional values have no historical practices or period to which they are securely anchored, illustrates one of the main traits of myth-making, the loss of specific history.[2] In residual culture, "the backward reference has its own logic", according to Williams:

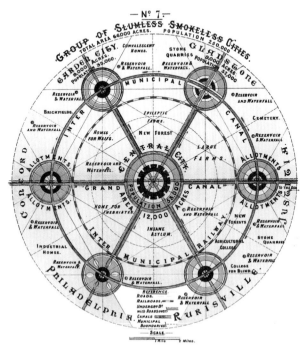

Figure 1/ Visualizing the Garden City. Ebenezer Howard, "Diagram No. 7: Group of Slumless Smokeless Cities". Original published in *Tomorrow: A Peaceful Path to Real Reform*, first ed., London: Swann Sonnenschein, 1898.

> [M]any old forms, old practices and old ways of feeling survived into periods in which the general direction of new development was clear and decisive. And then what seems an old order, a 'traditional' society, keeps appearing, reappearing, at bewilderingly various dates: in practice as an idea, to some extent based in experience, against which contemporary change can be measured. The *structure of feeling* within which this backward reference is to be understood is then not primarily a matter of historical explanation and analysis. What is really significant is this particular kind of reaction to the fact of change, and this has more real and more interesting social causes.[3]

To the extent that forms of gardens, cottages, and villages are made to participate in such an ideology of representation, as Williams notes, the "real and more interesting social causes" of the reactionary landscape deserve closer study. And as part of these causes, we must also recognize that nostalgia is an integral part of Modernism; as a "reaction to the fact of change", nostalgia serves as Williams' yardstick measuring the quality of that change. In Britain and Europe, both landscape and architecture (along with practically all other expressive art forms) were key participants in the negotiation of industrial Modernism. However, because nostalgic forms of gardens, cottages, and villages are so often deployed in period representation, we should be wary of assigning superficial meanings to recurring historical forms that persist through the social and environmental upheavals of industrial modernization. Instead, as Williams suggests, our goal ought to be "to explain, in related terms, both the persistence and the historicity of concepts".[4]

Given Williams' theory of the structure of feeling, the persistence of village-ness and garden-ness in the First Garden City at Letchworth suggests two things: there was at that time a compelling need to express traditional values ascribed to domestic landscapes, and the inscription of these values needs to be reconsidered in the context of broader twentieth-century social, political, and technological issues. The five vignettes outlined below help explain the persistence of the Garden City image in the twentieth century, and provoke reflection on the ways that society and domestic landscapes are mutually constructed.

VIGNETTE 1. THE ALLEGORY OF THE PICTURESQUE HAMLET

When the second edition of Howard's book was retitled *Garden Cities of To-Morrow*, the socialist illustrator Walter Crane — one of the Vice Presidents of the brand-new Garden City Association — was entrusted with the design for the frontispiece of the third printing (1902). This iconic image suddenly became a trademark of the campaign, remaining on the front cover of its official journal — *Garden Cities Association*, later *Garden Cities and Town Planning* — until after the end of World War I [Figure 4]. While some have blamed the later conservatism of the Garden City movement on Howard's title change, calling its "beguiling vagueness" the "enemy of his wider purposes", others believe Crane's retrogressive imagery revealed key tensions within the movement:[5]

> [T]he frontispiece of the new edition, by Walter Crane, reflected the degree to which the movement was prepared to look backward in a manner Howard never intended. Rather than evoke the futuristic diagrams that accompany Howard's text, Crane showed readers an enthroned medieval princess, holding aloft the model of a medieval city in her delicately medieval hand.[6]

If Crane was looking backward, almost everyone involved in the design of the project, *except* for Howard, was looking in the same direction. For this is no ordinary medieval princess: Crane has drawn an allegorical personification — a pre-Raphaelite version of the spirit of Nature, or England (or both). Even if the details of her dress, face, and other attributes are late Victorian confections, they suggest a strategic comparison with the allegorization of the Italian provinces in Cesare Ripa's *Iconologia* (1603) [Figure 5]. Medieval emblems and early Renaissance allegorizations were popular among Arts and Crafts enthusiasts in the late nineteenth century, and certainly would have been familiar to Crane. In *Iconologia*, the provinces were personified as female to represent nature and regional landscape; their various attributes (for example the walled city, staff, throne, wheat, fruit, and so on) represented secular virtues of good government, good husbandry, and the region's natural blessings. In Crane's allegory, a crowned woman dressed in richly embroidered robes holds a model city in her left hand; dense, walled, and architecturally diverse, it represents the pre-industrial ideal of *gemeinschaft* — the direct, organic life that many urban and aesthetic reformers hoped to foster.

Crane's imagery evokes a more comprehensive, synthetic reform campaign linking landscape to urbanism, art to labor, and collective feeling to social health and wellbeing. It is also intertextual, linking the cultural imagination of the English domestic revival to Victorian urban reform. Barry Parker (1867–1947) and Raymond Unwin (1863–1940), the young architects of the First Garden City at Letchworth, directly inherited Victorian aesthetic and social values from their forebears who included the giants of the Gothic

Figure 5/ Allegorization of the Italian provinces. Cesare Ripa, *Lombardia*, 1603. Woodcut published in *Iconologia overo Descrittione Dell'imagini Universali cavate dall'Antichità et da altri luoghi* (Rome).

Revival — architect and critic A. W. N. Pugin (1812–1852) and John Ruskin (1819–1900) — and artist/reformers such as William Morris (1834–1896) and Walter Crane (1845–1915), among others.

The artist and critic John Ruskin best articulates these values. Having adopted romanticized concepts of fourteenth-century labor and social formation, Ruskin's account of the moral codes of art and architecture in the essay "The Nature of Gothic" (1853) was aimed at a broad program of aesthetic and cultural reform.[7] His influential writings and lectures extended into many other fields — to landscape practices, urban design, radical politics, even labor reform and economics.[8] Significantly, in *Sesame and Lilies* (orig. pub. 1865), Ruskin advocated for a type of urban reform that could easily have been illustrated by the traditional hamlet held aloft by Crane's allegorical princess almost 40 years later. What was needed, he wrote, was:

> thorough sanitary and remedial action in the houses we have and then the building of more, strongly, beautifully, and in groups of limited extent, kept in proportion to their streams and walled round, so that there may be no festering and wretched suburb anywhere, but clean and busy street within and the open country without, with a belt of beautiful garden

Figure 4/ An enthroned medieval princess, holding aloft the model of a medieval city. Walter Crane, Title page for Ebenezer Howard, *Garden Cities of Tomorrow*, third ed., London: Swann Sonnenschein, 1902.

and orchard round the walls, so that from any part of the city perfectly fresh air and grass and sight of far horizon might be reachable in a few minutes walk. This [is] the final aim.[9]

This often-quoted passage precisely describes the visual model, the scale, and the spatial hygiene that would later be translated by Ebenezer Howard and the Garden City architects. While other architectural representations of organic social order had been tested much earlier in the nineteenth century, for instance in almshouse communities such as Blaise Hamlet (c. 1840), Standish Meacham has argued that the immediate predecessors of the Garden City — specifically the early model industrial villages at Port Sunlight (1888) and Bournville (1895) — were seminal works "that contributed significantly to a public understanding of what genuine English community might be".[10]

Ruskin's values were paralleled by the Fabian-style socialist understanding that landscape is not just an inherited resource, but is a laboriously constructed kind of machine, a means of production that performs services and returns wealth as a result of labor invested in it. As stated in the *Fabian Tracts* (1908), "Every farm or garden, every mine or quarry, is saturated with the effects of human labor. Capital is everywhere infused into and intermixed with land.... Who distinguishes from the farm the lanes, the hedges, the gates, the drains, the buildings, the farm-house?"[11] This remarkable insight foreshadows our more contemporary attitude towards domestic and urban landscape. Particularly in England, however, where the cultural landscape had been quite literally hand-constructed over slow millennia, this passage spoke to the awareness of landscape continuity, husbandry, and conservation. The socialist land ethic also expressed reaction to the hated seventeenth and eighteenth-century Enclosures Acts in England. In descending order, Fabian valuation of land-use types ranked residential gardens over cultivated tillage, then grazing and pasturage, and finally the despised hunting park over 'wastes' or nonarable land (which were deemed useless except, possibly, for hiking). In the socialist hierarchy of productive landscape, therefore, houses with gardens were favored as a concentrated form of capital yielding the highest social and material return on labor.

In Walter Crane's vision, the type of settlement Ruskin described was simply an enlargement upon other organic works of art that expressed the joys of collective feeling, joys he expressed in his socialist verse and decorative works [Figure 6]. On the other hand, Garden City architects Raymond Unwin and Barry Parker envisioned this structure of feeling as a kind of social ecology:

> The village was the expression of a small corporate life in which all the different units were personally in touch with each other, conscious of and frankly accepting their relations, and on the whole content with them. This relationship reveals itself in

Figure 6/ Joys of collective feeling. Walter Crane, *The City of Love*, 1891. Decorative header published in *Renascence: A Book of Verse*, London: Mathews at the Sign of the Bodley Head, 1891.

> the feeling of order which the view induces. Every building honestly confesses just what it is, and so falls into its place. The smallest cottage has its share of the village street on to which the manor house also fronts. It is content with that share and with its condition, and does not try to look like a villa.[12]

The social picturesqueness and class harmony that Unwin imagined in the traditional village was essential to promoting the visual rhetoric of the Garden City movement. While the first orthodox Garden City at Letchworth (begun in 1903) actually was an object lesson for socialist reform, we have seen that the traditional landscape imagery used to promote the settlement helped secure the confidence of more conservative British investors and homebuyers. By drawing upon the trope of the harmony of traditional class structure in the English hamlet, the designers were able to develop a special formal code for streets, cottages, and gardens — thus inventing a new tradition to illustrate the evolution of 'natural' corporate life into an experimental settlement.

VIGNETTE 2. THE NATION AS A GARDEN

To make the Garden City more recognizably English, the garden became both a means and an end in itself — for marketing the Garden City movement, certainly, and for winning hearts and minds. Perhaps the most important function of the garden was to stabilize a national narrative of domesticity. The ubiquity of the garden in the discourse of Victorian reform is evident in lectures, essays, art, and poems by Ruskin, Morris, Crane, and others, and all of them in one form or another use the term 'garden' as a utopian metaphor for Britain.

Clearly, the predations of nineteenth-century industrialism on the countryside caused such men considerable anguish. In *Sesame and Lilies* for instance, Ruskin excoriated the poor stewardship and greed that permitted private enterprise to dig a "coal shaft" in the middle of their children's "garden" simply to make a profit. "Yet this is what you are doing with all England", he scolded:

> The whole country is but a little garden, not more than enough for your children to run on the lawns of, if you would let them *all* run there. And this little garden you will turn into a furnace-ground, and fill with heaps of cinders, if you can; and those children of yours, not you, will suffer for it.[13]

William Morris also pays considerable homage to the English landscape in his utopian novel *News from Nowhere* (1890–1891). Making an autobiographical allusion to his own garden romances, the fictional protagonist (called William Guest) journeys from London to Morris' very own country retreat at Kelmscott Manor, which served as his home from 1871 until his death

in 1896. Morris regarded Kelmscott as an earthly paradise: a model of English domesticity that had maintained its timeless charm for centuries [Figure 7]. Built in two phases between 1570 and 1670, the house still occupies the sleepy floodplain of the upper Thames river. It has been noted that although the reference to Kelmscott as "Manor" has no historical justification, "it indicates the importance of the house to the neighbouring village, a small, quiet settlement of cottages and barns, built of the local Cotswold stone and slate and with a strong affinity to its landscape".[14] Morris wrote tenderly of his countryside retreat, "It has come to be to me the type … of the homes of harmless simple people not overburdened with the intricacies of life; and as others love the race of man through their lovers or their children, so I love the earth through that small space of it."[15]

In *News from Nowhere*, Morris' uses of the term 'garden' range from the descriptive to the metaphorical to the ideological — in representing a discrete space as well as

Figure 7/ An earthly paradise and model of English domesticity. Marie Spartali Stillman (1844–1927), *A Study of Kelmscott Manor*, c. 1904. Ink and watercolor heightened with bodycolor on Whatman board. Mark Samuels Lasner Collection, on loan to the University of Delaware Library. Image courtesy of Mark Samuels Lasner.

the entire countryside, 'garden' becomes a synecdoche for the nation. Interjecting Morris' own voice into the novel, the crusty historian Old Hammond explains how the utopian nation-state evolved:

> This is how we stand. England was once a country of clearings amongst the woods and wastes, with a few towns interspersed.... It then became a country of huge and foul workshops, and fouler gambling-dens, surrounded by an ill-kept, poverty-stricken farm, pillaged by the masters of the workshops. It is now a garden, where nothing is wasted and nothing is spoilt, with all the necessary dwellings, sheds and workshops, scattered up and down the country, all trim, and neat, and pretty.[16]

The motive for this new environmental order was principally moral — to avoid the *shame* of waste, of poverty, of misery; it was simply indecent for a great country to be so poorly stewarded. Morris' metaphorical invocation of England as a well-tended moral garden thus supplies a powerful referent for the meaning of the Garden City. He extends the revelation of the eighteenth-century poet of the picturesque, Horace Walpole (1717–1797), to utopian dimensions: all of (English) nature would now become a garden.

Amplifying the conditions of Morris' manor garden at Kelmscott to the scale of the regional or national landscape was a theme taken up and advanced by the architects of the Garden Cities campaign, and was explicitly stated by Raymond Unwin. Late in his life, after copying a portion of Morris' essay "Art and Beauty of the Earth", Unwin wrote: "We must turn this land from the grimy backyard of a workshop into a garden. If that seems difficult, I cannot help it: I only know that it is necessary."[17] If only it could take root and grow, the Garden City ideal offered some hope for Unwin and others that the entire nation might be tidied up and reorganized in a matrix of benevolent, productive, and above all, relentlessly hygienic gardens.

Certainly others had spoken of the 'marriage' of town and country well before Howard published his famous treatise, and there is a curiously conjugal theme running through the discourse of the Garden City movement. For instance, a passage in *News from Nowhere* describes the way the townspeople, liberated from their lives in the industrial city, "flocked into the country villages, and, so to say, flung themselves on the freed land ... and in a very little time the villages of England were more populous than they had been since the fourteenth century".[18] And in an 1894 lecture to the Ancoats Brotherhood (Manchester), Morris speaks of the socialist utopian garden city as a *heritage*:

> I want neither the towns to be the appendages of the country, nor the country of the town; I want the town to be impregnated with the beauty of the country and the country with the

intelligence and vivid life of the town. I want every homestead to be clean, orderly and tidy; a lovely house surrounded by acres and acres of garden. On the other hand, I want the town to be clean, orderly and tidy; in short, a garden with beautiful houses in it. Clearly, if I don't wish this, I must be a fool or a dullard; but I do more — I claim it as the due heritage of the latter ages of the world which have subdued nature, and can have for the asking.[19]

Arguing that never before in the history of England had there been such an "unholy, unnatural" and artificial separation between town and country, Morris and Howard imagined a re-union of these two worlds through a dialectical geography of impregnation. Comparing the attractive features of town and country to magnets, Howard makes the spatial eugenics of his plan perfectly explicit:

> neither the Town magnet nor the Country magnet represents the full purpose and plan of nature. Human society and the beauty of nature are meant to be enjoyed together. The two magnets must be made one. As man and woman by their varied gifts and faculties supplement each other, so should town and country.... Town and country *must be married*, and out of this joyous union will spring a new hope, a new life, a new civilization.[20]

VIGNETTE 3. LANDSCAPE, CLASS, AND THE CONTENTMENT OF LABOR

If the offspring of the romantic socialist utopia issuing from the marriage of town and country was the garden, surely it would need workers to cultivate it. The left-leaning community held the myth of agrarian labor very close to its heart, but domestic garden work might also supply the natural moral hygiene and 'manly' discipline that social conservatives sought for youth at risk in urban slums. Reformers commonly voiced a belief that through gardening, the poor and working classes could elevate themselves morally and materially, not to actually join the ranks of the bourgeoisie but perhaps at least to emulate their manners. However, there was a clear difference between the type of gardens that middle-class reformers wished for themselves — enchanted gardens of sensual repose and reverie, retreats from the foul industrial metropolis — and what they wished for their working-class brethren. In middle-class gardens, father hardly ever appeared, while for the working classes, reformers dreamed of productive gardens, in which children and *especially* father were busily occupied in healthy pursuits. The middle-class logic of social reform concluded that — for the working classes — a mature relationship with nature must be based on *work*.

Morris' own style of socialism celebrated rural practicality and husbandry, and love of local flavor; he linked the vernacular cottage garden and pre-industrial agrarianism closely to nationalist and reformist feeling. Agrarian landscapes therefore provided the site of the direct, maturing relationship with nature that Ruskin, Morris, Edward Carpenter, and other reformers approved. Crane's socialist political cartoons of the late 1880s and 1890s presented agrarian or garden labor as masculine, healthy, morally dignified, and politically righteous [Figure 8]. And both aesthetic socialism and the Arts and Crafts ideal were founded on the notion that productive labor should be satisfying. "It may be proved, with much certainty", Ruskin lectured, "that God intends no man to live in this world without working: but it seems to me no less evident that He intends every man to be happy in his work. It is written, 'in the sweat of thy brow', but it was never written, 'in the breaking of thine heart,' thou shalt eat bread."[21]

Ruskin himself invigorated the nineteenth-century utopian tradition, and he implemented (or financed) several concrete utopian demonstrations based on manual labor and gardening. Among other things, Ruskin believed that digging, i.e. gardening, was one of the universal attributes of humanity; it distinguished men from animals, and manual labor performed in the garden was a righteous Christian virtue. In 1871 Ruskin conceived a utopian 'pyramid scheme' for a global agrarian community called the Guild of St George, to demonstrate how agriculture could be revived.[22] Although this attempt ultimately failed, a farm near Sheffield was made available for a short time as a community garden, purportedly to give "employment to any workmen or workmen's children who like to come so far — for an hour's exercise — and furnishing model types of vegetable produce to the Sheffield markets".[23] Astonishingly, Ruskin believed that workmen would gladly walk all the way from Sheffield at the end of an already grueling ten- or 12-hour workday. As a mythic scene of contented and grateful labor, St George's farm is significant mainly for its strange wishfulness and the enormous pleasure that Ruskin took from it.

Stranger still is one of Raymond Unwin's lectures given in 1897 to the Sheffield Socialist Education League called "Gladdening Versus Shortening the Hours of Labour":

> [W]e see ... the picture of the ploughman spending his twelve hours [as opposed to ten hours by machine] in the open air in the company of his horses, of the birds and the beautiful landscape round. He has a long day, truly, but he has a healthy job. He loves his team.... He is proud of his straight furrow and spends a happy day.[24]

Figure 8/ Garden labor as masculine, healthy, morally dignified, and politically righteous. Walter Crane, *Socialism*, 1889. Cover designed for *Fabian Essays* (1889). Published in *Cartoons for the Cause: 1886–1896*, London: The Twentieth Century Press, 1896.

Twelve hours of plowing, even if 'gladdened' by the company of horses and birds, is still a backbreaking day; it is unlikely Unwin would have so 'gladly' undertaken it. And in his own exhortation to harness oneself to the utopian plow, Ruskin probably never really pictured himself in the traces. But the consistency of the myth of the contented laborer helps explain the rhetorical utility of the reform garden as emblematic of the place of the worker in the natural world — an essentially Georgic image that owes much to Vergil's pastoral tropes of the harvest cycles and the simple pleasures of peasants. It is then not so curious that reform gardens were thought to play a key role in the transformation of an essentially unskilled rural work force into industrial laborers — by symbolically returning them to the land.

VIGNETTE 4. GARDENS AND SPATIAL EUGENICS IN THE MODEL VILLAGE

Despite the added cost of land, invocations of a new kind of industrial worker reclaiming the fields of the lost medieval village contributed to a comforting image of Englishness. Even in an urban settlement, it could be argued that adding gardens to dwelling units was in effect a restoration of the peasant to the land. The political resonance of providing individual cottage gardens, rather than allotments, for industrial workers is manifest because as it fostered civic maturity, the cottage garden also was thought to be good for the soul. In the words of F. D. Maurice, a late Victorian social reformer, "small unit cultivation elicited moral values which fostered political independence", for the English working classes' independence could be guaranteed "when they are working upon ground attached to their homes, upon which they are not hirelings".[25]

Because many reformers assumed an industrial laborer would *enjoy* working at 'spade cultivation' in his precious leisure time, gardens were cheerfully programmed into progressive housing models and standards, beginning in 1888 with the planned industrial village of Port Sunlight. The first 'strand' of the Garden City movement, the model industrial villages of Port Sunlight (1888), Bournville (1895) and New Earswick (1902), were initiatives undertaken by benevolent industrialists. These villages followed the Enlightenment tradition of idealized site schemes that expressed hierarchical industrial relations. There is no doubt they were established fundamentally as a way of optimizing worker wellbeing and longevity, thus rewarding the manufacturer with improved returns of skill, productivity, and morale. They also reduced potential costs to the employer in terms of faulty workmanship, new employee training, quality control and surveillance, sick days, labor strikes, etc. This was plainly acknowledged in 1914, when the chocolate manufacturer Edward Cadbury (founder of Bournville) stated, "We have always believed that business efficiency and the welfare of employees are but different sides of the same problem."[26]

Meanwhile, the 1888 plan of Port Sunlight (headquarters of the Lever soapworks) devoted much of the interior acreage of blocks to allotment gardens, while front gardens were planted and tended by the company. At Bournville, the company 'assisted' residents in keeping up appearances in both front and back gardens attached to dwellings. The building code at Letchworth Garden City (1906 and later) stipulated that tenants were responsible for maintaining the interface between public sidewalks and the private garden. Relatively rapidly, then, the terms of residency in the Garden City meant that industrial workers were expected, in their spare time, to become gardeners as well [Figure 9].

This strategy was eventually borne out by countless other progressive industrial communities in England and Europe at large, where many members of a well-intentioned elite conceived of adding agrarian pursuits to industrial lives. Model French mining towns provide an evocative parallel to the Garden City; in the creation of a new kind of industrial laborer historians have called "the untiring little worker", the miner would return home from work at the end of the day to immediately "take up the spade or the watering-can" to maintain his bit of garden:

> He is not completely detached from the ground. He is not drowning among the proletariats of the suburb…. For the density of the workers' city, the mining town substitutes spatial extension; instead of concentration, it offers juxtaposition; instead of a jumbled mob, a collection of separate individuals. It disentangles, disperses, and redistributes their bodies; that is to say, it disaggregates the unwashed horde from the deeps, and then extracts from it an honest worker: the mining town insulates him, accommodates him, embeds him, acclimatizes him, assimilates him, and domesticates him…. There indeed, peacefully indulging in the cultivation of its small garden, a 'race of hooligans' patiently rehabilitates itself.[27]

As an experiment in the eugenics of the labor force, the Garden City may be subject to both the reasoning and the implied critique expressed here. In model industrial towns, as in the Garden Cities, space devoted to gardens was key for justifying reduced housing densities for the working classes. On the one hand, it could be argued, cottage gardens in model settlements were proposed as a spatial discipline, a way of separating workers from the city. On the other hand, and perhaps more important, it was a way of separating them from each other.

VIGNETTE 5. THE WORKING CLASS AND THE REGENERATION OF THE ENGLISH RACE

In tracing the relationship of Garden City to the Victorian and Edwardian cultural imagination before, during, and after it was constructed, we can begin to understand how multiple

Figure 9/ Workers tending to allotment gardens at Bournville, unknown photographer. Published in *Sixty Years of Planning: The Bournville Experiment*, Bournville, UK: Bournville Village Trust. n.d., c. 1942–1943.

political positions and popular emotions, both liberal and conservative, modern and scientific, seized upon the logic of Garden City as a concrete utopian program for urban social reform. The model villages served to galvanize the public's imagination and also to advance formal language and policies about urban design and domestic architecture. More importantly they focused positive attention on potential solutions to what had become a national health crisis.

By the turn of the twentieth century, the image and appeal of the Garden City concept had already been established by the industrial model villages at Bournville and Port Sunlight; "they were the communities that men and women first thought of when the terms 'garden city' and 'garden suburb' began to receive currency after 1900. That the first annual conference of the Garden City Association took place at Bournville (1901), and the second at Liverpool, near Port Sunlight (1902) was no coincidence."[28] The successful ten-year-old object lessons of the model industrial villages, liberalizing British housing laws, and the appearance of Ebenezer Howard's *To-morrow: A Peaceful Path to Real Reform*, galvanized a general mood of earnest

optimism at the landmark First Garden Cities Conference. Attended by a long list of hand-picked elites and liberal political luminaries, the conference was aimed at the highest levels of national liberal politics.[29]

At the 1901 conference, one of the early leaders of the movement, Aneurin Williams, voiced the fear that plagued the nation:

> the people who are constantly drawn to our great cities, and more especially to London, are not merely an average sample of the English race, but are the very pick of the English people, and those are the people whose children, in the course of one or two generations, are reduced to a comparatively degraded condition. It is not that a certain number of the average of our race are being destroyed, but the very best of our race are being destroyed by the conditions of our great cities.[30]

The physical welfare of the working classes had reached the level of an obsession among the founders and chroniclers of the Garden City, as they sought to demonstrate that reform gardens could be linked directly to the propagation of a healthier working-class stock. Using modern techniques such as empirical statistics, economic indicators, and personal interviews, social and medical scientists sought to measure the inner social and biological workings of the model community. According to carefully administered studies, the benefits of gardens and temperance in the model towns seemed to yield demonstrable results among the working-class population.[31] In addition to abstinence from liquor, strict codes of behavior, moral and otherwise, were to be maintained at all times.[32] The results of this increased public (and presumably private) sobriety, according to sociologist and public health advocate W. L. George (1908), were stunning, accompanied by sharply diminished rates of domestic violence and an increase in stable family relationships.[33] As George put it, "At Port Sunlight, where family feeling reigns supreme, the man is not driven out of his home by squalor, but prefers to dwell there in quietude and ease."[34]

Paralleling the development of the first Garden City (1904), data collected from 1900 to 1907 showed that, in terms of infant mortality, a ghastly problem in turn-of-the-century England, Port Sunlight's rates were exactly half (70 per 1,000) of Liverpool's, a city only four miles distant.[35] Similarly, the Port Sunlight birth rate (42 per 1,000) exceeded the highest county rate in England (35.5 per 1,000) by 20 percent. Compared with Liverpool children, George pointed out that, "The [height] standards of Port Sunlight children are exceeded only by first-rate middle-class schools."[36]

The political and national ramifications of such data were immediately apparent to the Garden City reformers. Following the Liberal landslide that voted William Lever (founder of Port Sunlight) into Parliament in 1906, the Royal Commissions on National Degeneration and the under-feeding of school children addressed widespread concerns about the physical degeneration of the English population. To some, Port Sunlight seemed to model a potential solution:

> These [data] will suffice to show what a physical revolution has been worked in the children of the people by good food, good housing, open spaces, exercise, and regular employment of the parents. It is not too much to call it a revolution, for we must look to the children to perpetuate in their descendants the improvement of the race.[37]

Moral feeling and social spirit in Port Sunlight was also, apparently, important to family fertility. "The results of the Port Sunlight régime" suggested that "[t]he Sunlighter, healthy and comparatively prosperous, has every inducement to marry early and bring up a large family; his life is centered round his home and its simple pleasures, so that a large and well-reared family becomes a normal part of his economy."[38] The emphasis on family size and child health in particular, may serve partly to explain why so many postcards of the early Garden City feature numbers of children and large family groups. Ralph Neville, then chairman of the Garden City Association, pointed out that living conditions in British cities had fallen below reasonable humanitarian standards:

> [P]hysical degradation is proceeding … at a very rapid rate; … nothing can prevent the ultimate decadence and destruction of the race if we do not see that the mass of the people lead lives which are consistent with physical development—(hear, hear)—because physical development is at the bottom of all things…. [Y]ou cannot have intellectual capacity unless you have sound conditions of hygiene as the basis of the life of your countrymen.[39]

Even more embarrassing, the physical health of Britain's working-class citizens was worse than those of her competitors in trade. Neville's indignation that the Germans were far better organized in their industries and physical training programs than the British, and that they had added five years to the average man's life span, is absolutely key to understanding the importance of the garden from the ruling elite's point of view. Although Neville understood that the Garden City proposal was first and foremost a social and economic imperative dealing with the twin issues of the overcrowding of cities and the shrinking population in the countryside, he did not hesitate to link the Garden City idea to popular imperialism as well:

> The question really is a national question, nay it is more than that, it is an Imperial question—(hear, hear). And it is a question of paramount importance to the Empire, because … the ultimate destiny of our Empire depends upon the character and the capacity of the citizens.[40]

Decentralizing industry, returning laborers to agrarian pursuits, and improving martial training, he thought, would go a long way toward solving the nation's problems. The Garden City aimed to address two of these three challenges directly, and without a national system of military conscription to train young males for national service, many believed the next best thing was to maintain an active agricultural work force.

It should be remembered that the emergence of the Garden City was exactly contemporaneous with the disastrous Boer War in South Africa (1899–1902, waged by the British Empire against the settlers of two independent Boer republics, the Orange Free State and the Transvaal Republic), during which the majority of volunteers reporting for Army conscription fell below minimum standards for fitness. This fact was clearly in the back of everyone's mind. Concluding his 1901 conference address on a dire note, Neville urged the assembled leaders and lawmakers to strive to attain decent living standards. The global supremacy of the British Empire depended on its working classes; and the militarism of his metaphor was not lost on the audience:

I believe fully in the capacity of the British race; we are sprung from a splendid stock, and I think we still have the energy and the stamina which would pull us through in any struggle with rivals ... [but] ever since the introduction of the factory system into this country we have been drawing upon the strength of our population as though its force was absolutely illimitable ... anybody who uses his eyes in going about the streets of our large towns cannot fail to see that the reckless draft upon the strength of the people has told its tale.

[I]f we fall below the physical standard of our rivals, our bolt is shot, and in the end we must fail before them. We have got to devise some means of putting our population in at least as good a condition, from the physical point of view, as that of Germany or America.[41]

According to the proceedings of the 1901 conference, Neville received a thunderous ovation. We can imagine that, at that moment, the ruling elite in England saw in the Garden City not a socialist experiment, but the answer to their prayers — something approaching a national plan for the regeneration of the working classes, the repopulation of the countryside, and the defense of empire, all at the same time.

FOURSQUARE OUR CITY: THE GOOD GARDENER AS ALLEGORY

Pictured as a simulacrum of the traditional English village, the Garden Cities idea linked the promise of a better future with an idealized past. Opportunities to inculcate social ideals in the Garden City were pursued through a wide variety of mechanisms, not only through the design of the domestic environment, but also through graphic representation and public spectacle, educational programs, and practical events like garden shows and contests. A banner entitled "Foursquare Our City" was designed by Edmund and Dorothea Hunter to represent the First Garden City at Letchworth at major public festivals and ceremonies, such as the May Festival of 1909 and the coronation pageant of King George V (successor to Edward VII) in 1910. The artists were silk-weavers and designers of textiles and wallpaper inspired by the ideas and practices of William Morris.[42] Their banner measured easily six feet square, executed in multicolored, silk-embroidered fabric stretched between two poles carried by marchers [Figure 10].[43]

The original source and motto for the banner imagery was a poem written for the inaugural issue of the local monthly. The received interpretation of the allegory was supplied somewhat later in 1909 by Hope Rea, an early resident of the First Garden City:[44]

The tree here symbolizes the town, a unity holding and vivifying its great variety, all making for amelioration.... Held within the arms of the branching tree lies a nest, with eggs, promise of who may say what hatching. Above, almost resting on the upper twigs, is a golden star, a star of indication, of leading, of hope. The field against which the tree is laid pictures the reality, in the plane of visible things, of which the tree is symbolical. The corn and the grass surround a faintly indicated city, whose towers and pinnacles are shown in a haze of distance, not yet reached, still the goal of endeavor, 'beautiful city of our dream' [from Binn's poem].

In its iconography, composition, and spirit, the 1909 coronation banner reflected a structure of feeling and a system of thought that saturated the cultural imagination of the Garden City pioneers. Not surprisingly, the icon of the flowering and fruiting tree so popular in the late nineteenth century preserves the romantic socialism of Morris and Crane, as well as the medieval iconology they loved. The tree celebrated the unity of life and the interdependence of all its constituents in the shelter of its providential branches. The distant city, Rea's "goal of endeavor", was girdled with fertile fields and modeled after the so-called 'city of dreaming spires' — the Oxford of Ruskin and Morris' day. The agrarian environment portrayed is straight from the *Georgics*, with typical attributes of labor in the foreground. The handles of a spade and a pitchfork, and the blades of a scythe and threshing tool were clearly visible at the roots of the tree — a subtle reminder of the socialist adage: "The only true wealth comes from productive labor" necessary to cultivate either the thriving garden or city.

More important, in public allegory such as "Foursquare Our City", citizens are vividly reminded of the "effort, self-sacrifice and unity necessary to the maintenance of a commonwealth".[45] We may also see how conceptual relationships between myths of community and expectations of nature may drive larger patterns and practices of consumption. Whenever both space and subject perform a "need" for each other, constructing and naturalizing both without understanding the origin of the need, we reproduce an ideology of landscape. The ideology of the garden was accomplished at the Garden City in ways historically specific, nuanced, and situated within the work of individual thought leaders and the cultures they influenced. However, the legacy of Garden City ideology lives on today in our own domestic landscapes. In the dominance of the single-family detached home, the politics of family values, and the garden as a proving ground for nationhood, it is still possible to see the good gardener as an enduring allegorical figure of political independence, moral virtue, strength, stamina, and civic stability.

Figure 10/ Design for a coronation banner for The First Garden City at Letchworth. Edmund Hunter, *Foursquare Our City*, 1904.
From Hope Rea, "Foursquare Our City", *The City: A Monthly Magazine Written and Produced at the First Garden City*, vol. I, no. 5, May 1909.
Image courtesy First Garden City Heritage Museum, Letchworth.

NOTES

1/ Hobsbawm, Eric, and Terence Ranger eds., *The Invention of Tradition*, Cambridge, UK: Cambridge University Press, 1983, p. 1.

2/ This insight is supported also by Roland Barthes, "Myth Today", *Mythologies* [1957], Annette Lavers trans., New York: Hill & Wang, 1972.

3/ Williams, Raymond, "Golden Ages", *The Country and the City*, New York: Oxford University Press, 1973, p. 35. Italics added by author.

4/ Williams, *The Country and the City*, p. 289.

5/ Ward, Stephen, *The Garden City: Past, Present, and Future*, London: E & F. N. Spon of Chapman & Hall, 1992, p. 4.

6/ Meacham, Standish, *Regaining Paradise: Englishness and the Early Garden City Movement*, New Haven and London: Yale University Press, 1999, pp. 68–69.

7/ Ruskin, John, "The Nature of Gothic", *The Stones of Venice*, Book Three [1851–1853], New York: Da Capo Press, 1960.

8/ Ruskin, John, *Unto This Last: Four Essays on the First Principles of Political Economy* [1862], Lloyd J. Hubenka ed., Lincoln: University of Nebraska Press, 1967.

9/ Ruskin, John, "Of Queen's Gardens", *Sesame and Lilies* [1865], London: J. M. Dent, 1907 reprint, pp. 183–184.

10/ Meacham, *Regaining Paradise*, p. 19.

11/ Fabian Society, "Capital and Land", seventh ed., revised [1888], 1908 reprint, *Fabian Tracts: Nos. 1 to 156, with a Tract Index and Catalogue Raisonné, 1884–1911,* London: The Fabian Office, 1911, pp. 4–5.

12/ Unwin, Raymond, and Barry Parker, *The Art of Building a Home,* London: Longmans, Green & Co., 1901, pp. 92–93.

13/ Ruskin, *Sesame and Lilies*, pp. 69–70.

14/ Insall, Donald W., "Kelmscott Manor and Its Repair", *Monumentum: The International Council of Monuments and Sites* (ICOMOS), no. 8 [1972], in *Art and Kelmscott*, Linda Parry ed., London: Society of Antiquaries, 1996, p. 106.

15/ Morris, William, *News from Nowhere: or An Epoch of Rest* [1891], Krishan Kumar ed., New York: Cambridge University Press, 1995, p. 211.

16/ Morris, *News from Nowhere*, p. 75.

17/ Creese, Walter, *Search for Environment: The Garden City Before and After*, second ed., Baltimore: Johns Hopkins, 1992, p. 148.

18/ Morris, *News from Nowhere*, p. 74.

19/ Mackail, J. W., *The Life of William Morris*, vol. 2 [1899], New York: Dover Press, 1995, pp. 305–306. According to Mackail, Morris' lecture was called "Town and Country".

20/ Howard, Ebenezer, *Garden Cities of Tomorrow*, second ed., [1902], Cambridge, MA: The MIT Press, reprint 1965, p. 18.

21/ Ruskin, John, *Pre-Raphaelitism*, new ed., London: Smith, Elder and Co., 1862, p. 5.

22/ Armytage, W. H. G., *Heavens Below: Utopian Experiments in England 1560–1950,* London: Routledge and Kegan Paul, 1961, p. 291. See also M. E. Spence, "The Guild of St George: Ruskin's Attempt to Translate His Ideas into Practice", *Bulletin of the John Rylands Library*, vol. XL, 1957, pp. 147–210.

23/ Armytage, *Heavens Below*, pp. 293, 298. See also *The Works of John Ruskin*, vol. XXIX, E. T. Cook and Alexander Wedderburn eds., London: George Allen & Sons, 1905, p. 98. See also "Report of the St George's Guild", Cook and Wedderburn eds., *Works*, vol. XXX, p. 303.

24/ Meacham, *Regaining Paradise*, p. 83.

25/ Darley, Gillian, "The English Cottage Garden", *The Architecture of Western Gardens*, Monique Mosser and Georges Teyssot eds., Cambridge, MA: MIT Press, 1991, pp. 425–426.

26/ Swenarton, Mark, *Homes Fit For Heroes: The Politics and Architecture of Early State Housing in Britain,* London: Heinemann Educational Books, 1981, p. 6. Swenarton cites Edward Cadbury, "Scientific Management", *The Sociological Review*, vol. VII, no. 2, 1914, p. 106.

27/ Murard, Lion, and Patrick Zylberman, *Le Petit Travailleur Infatigable: Villes-Usines, Habitat et Intimités au XIXe Siècle*, second ed., Paris: Recherches, 1980, pp. 20–21. Translation by the author.

28/ Meacham, *Regaining Paradise*, p. 43.

29/ Garden City Association, *Report of Proceedings of the Garden City Conference at Bournville: 1901*, London: Council of The Garden City Association, 77 Chancery Lane, WC, pp. 4–5.

30/ Garden City Association, *Proceedings 1901*, p. 14.

31/ George, W.L., *Labour and Housing at Port Sunlight,* London: Alston Rivers, 1909, pp. 42–43.

32/ George, *Labour*, pp. 80, 82.

33/ George, *Labour*, pp. 144–145.

34/ George, *Labour*, p. 146.

35/ George, *Labour*, pp. 152–154.

36/ George, *Labour*, p. 158.

37/ George, *Labour*, pp. 154, 160.

38/ George, *Labour*, pp. 160–162, 164.

39/ Garden City Association, *Proceedings 1901*, p. 9.

40/ Garden City Association, *Proceedings 1901*, pp. 9–10.

41/ Garden City Association, *Proceedings 1901*, pp. 10–11.

42/ According to Hester Bury, the Hunters founded the St Edmundsbury Weaving Works in Haslemere in 1901, moved to Letchworth Garden City shortly after the town was founded, and remained from 1908 until the late 1920s. See Hester Bury, *Alec B. Hunter: Textile Designer & Craftsman*, exhibition catalog, Braintree: Warner & Sons, Ltd., 1979, pp. 3–4.

43/ The original banner has been conserved for the First Garden City Heritage Museum, Letchworth.

44/ Binns, Henry Bryan, "The Building", *The City*, vol. 1, no. 1, January 1909, reprinted in A. W. Brunt, *The Pageant of Letchworth: 1903–1914.* Letchworth Garden City, 1942. Also see Hope Rea, "Foursquare Our City", *The City: A Monthly Magazine written and Produced at the First Garden City*, vol. 1, no. 5, May 1909, pp. 102–103.

45/ Sargent, Irene, "Comments Upon Mr. Shean's 'Mural Painting'...", *The Craftsman*, vol. 7, no. 1 (October), 1904, p. 29.

202 /KATHLEEN JOHN-ALDER

IAN MCHARG: LANDSCAPE, NATURE, PROGRESS, MYTH

Throughout the inhabited world, in all times and under every circumstance, myths of man have flourished.
/ Joseph Campbell, *The Hero with a Thousand Faces*[1]

Modernity rests upon a myth of progress.[2] In the early twentieth century, avant-garde architects, combining visions of utopia with an equally strong fascination with machines, found this myth in factories, airplanes, ocean liners, automobiles, and rationally organized, infinitely expandable cities. Flush with excitement and youthful bravado, they embraced the twin dreams of speed and mass production embodied by these forms, and charted an exhilarating path towards the future, which they believed would alleviate poverty, promote social welfare, and support personal freedom. By the mid-twentieth century, however, a new generation of designers began to question this myth of progress, finding its vision of factories, cars, and the city to be widely out of sync with current reality [Figure 1].

One of the most famous of these critiques was *Design with Nature*, published in 1969 by the landscape architect and urban planner Ian McHarg. This critically acclaimed, best-selling publication challenged the vocabulary of mechanical forms favored by the architectural avant-garde. McHarg offered instead an equally ambitious vision of progress that championed natural processes and a localized reading of the land. McHarg's myth of progress, like that of his modernist predecessors, relied upon science and technology. Like them, he understood that science and technology provided valuable insights worthy of emulation. But he deviated from his progenitors in believing that the clearest, and best, benefit of science and technology was not that it allowed designers to project a glorious utopian future, but that it provided designers with the knowledge of how past actions had shaped the existing structure of the land.

McHarg argued that each landscape had its own story —a unique tale of physical, biological, and cultural evolution

"written on the place and upon its inhabitants". To understand the nuances of this intricately tangled narrative it was necessary to go back in time and "begin at the beginning".[3] Taking this concept of origins to an extreme level of abstraction, he devised a painstaking classification system that collated multiple layers of information. To ensure scientific veracity, the procedure always followed the same hierarchical order: geology, climate, physiography, soils, plants, animals, and land use.[4] In *Design with Nature*, site-specific case studies demonstrated the methodology, and visually intricate maps displayed the results [Figure 2].

McHarg's overlay system has long been considered his supreme professional achievement.[5] But the true genius

Figure 1/ Photographs of the contemporary city. From McHarg, *Design with Nature*. © 1992 by John Wiley & Sons, Inc. Reprinted by permission John Wiley & Sons, Inc.

of *Design with Nature* is not McHarg's deployment of science and technology to delineate the developmental structure of the landscape; rather, it is the way McHarg interweaves the story of the land with the story of his life. More than 45 years later, long after the book's science and methodology have been superseded, this narrative still resonates. McHarg could tell a good story, and he understood the power of iconic imagery.

SITUATING THE MYTH OF PROGRESS

Getting into harmony and tune with the universe and staying there is the principal function of mythology.
/ Joseph Campbell, *Transformations of Myth Through Time*[6]

Design with Nature was written toward the end of a period of unprecedented wealth, technological development, and social opportunity in the United States. Yet, this prosperity was shadowed by a growing awareness of physical fragmentation and social alienation. As the religious historian Robert Ellwood observed, the "earlier myths of prosperity beloved of modernist thought", which had proclaimed "a world of democracy, of ever-expanding scientific knowledge, of humming factories and ... even space flights to other worlds", were in doubt

following the apocalyptic horror of Hiroshima and Nagasaki, revelations of the health consequences of industrial pollution, and the moral ambiguity of Korea and Vietnam. One of the most intense reactions to this loss of faith was the rediscovery of ancient myths and mythic heroes, which, Ellwood argued, re-instilled a much-needed sense of wonder back into the everyday world.[7]

Social critic and historian Lewis Mumford, McHarg's intellectual mentor and author of *Design with Nature*'s introduction, described the sense of crisis as follows: "The difficulty is that our machine technology and our scientific methodology have reached a high pitch of perfection at a moment when our culture, particularly those [aspects of it] that shape the human personality — religion, ethics, education, and the arts — have become inoperative." Mumford followed this remark, which he made during his summation of the 1956 conference *Man's Role in Changing the Face of the Earth*, with the observation that "objective order has gone hand in hand with subjective disorder and formlessness", and the despairing comment that society had forgotten "the art of shaping whole human beings, immunized to pathological temptations".[8]

Mumford clearly felt that much of what he saw was symptomatic of the decay of modern life and the human personality. To help guide society toward a more robust future, he called for a rediscovery of history so that people could reconnect with their cultural roots and learn from the past. Mumford tied this rediscovery to "lived experience", or the self-discovery made possible by environments that provide escape from everyday pressures and routines. He repeatedly claimed that such physical and psychological enrichment allowed people to reflect upon the meaning of their lives and their surroundings. He also claimed it fostered a new set of values that countered the authoritarian tendencies of technology, and thus helped society redirect its energies away from harm. Interweaving human destiny into his argument Mumford wrote: "We cannot make sensible plans for the future without doing justice to the threads and fibers that run through every past stage of man's development." According to Mumford, a clear understanding of history would allow modern society to direct the cosmic energies (nuclear power) at its disposal to the correct purposes.

Even though Mumford spent considerable time detailing how modern society could benefit from the past, for the most part he avoided nostalgia. Instead, he sought systems of organization and patterns of behavior grounded in the characteristics of place, conceived within the context of contemporary urban dialogues, and played out with insights provided by science and technology. It is also important to note that Mumford, like many of his peers, believed humanity's unique consciousness gave it the right to control nature. But in order to exercise that control, humanity had to learn to exercise control over itself. As Mumford warned, this

Figure 3/ Adobe Guardians, Acoma, New Mexico (left); Apollo Moon Rocket (right). From McHarg, *Design with Nature*.
© 1992 by John Wiley & Sons, Inc. Reprinted by permission John Wiley & Sons, Inc.

goal would be achieved only if "the reductive techniques of contemporary science" were supplemented "with more holistic methods geared toward the revelation of life's intricate interdependence".[9] In other words, what we see around us depends upon the experiences through which we see it, and science, while valuable, is only one approach to knowledge and understanding.

One of the main attributes of Mumford's argument is his passionate belief in individual artistic and social liberty, which he pits against the material excess and social conformity of mass society. These ideas are perhaps best expressed in *The Golden Day: A Study in American Experience and Culture*, written in 1926. Here Mumford argues that modern progress, as seen through the eyes of the country's great writers, was not necessarily directed toward desirable ends. Indeed, his grand survey of American literature indicates a country overly concerned with personal comfort, acquisition, and domination. The result was a debased society captivated by machines. Mumford was drawn to writers, like Herman Melville, who

could imaginatively translate the physical reality of their lives into adventurous tales of "destiny, fate, and free-will". He likewise celebrated the nature essayists Ralph Waldo Emerson and Henry David Thoreau, and the 'people's poet' Walt Whitman for their ability to transform the mundane into the mythic. Five years later Mumford would reprise this theme in *The Brown Decades: A Study of Arts in America*. This text calls attention to Thoreau's ability to systematically observe, "touch", and "taste" the land, but it also stresses conservation and design. Mumford praised the geographer George Perkins Marsh for denouncing profligate resource extraction, and he applauded the urban parks of the landscape architects Frederick Law Olmsted and Charles Eliot, Jr. As this litany of individuals suggests, Mumford cast a wide net so that he could, in his words, gather into his concept of creativity "all that is vital in the practical in life, all that is intelligible in science, all that is relevant in social heritage".[10] Many of Mumford's ideas would be echoed and developed in McHarg's work.

THE NATURALIST

McHarg's avatar of creative individualism was the "Naturalist", a quirky mix of scientist-poet, pioneer-explorer, astronaut-steward, and shaman-mystic who found meaning "in the earth, and its processes" and devised rules of behavior in tune with "the way of things".[11] The name he chose was no doubt a nod both to the epic flights of the Apollo space program, images of which figure prominently in *Design with Nature*, and to McHarg's sponsor and publisher The Natural History Press, a subsidiary of The American Museum of Natural History in New York [Figure 3].[12]

The Naturalist's name and traits signal McHarg's desire to embrace the heroic legacy of exploration and discovery that figures prominently in the annals of environmentalism, as notably embodied by the famed nineteenth-century naturalist Alexander von Humboldt (1769–1859). This voyager to distant lands observed and recorded the natural events he saw, and in the process learned fundamental truths about the land and our interactions with it.

The first two volumes of Humboldt's the *Cosmos: A Description of the Universe*, written in 1845 and 1847 respectively, are of note in this regard for the way they interweave adventurous tales of Humboldt's life with scientific tales of discovery.[13] Considered masterpieces of natural history, these volumes' promotion of empirical observation, as well as their repudiation of any science that merely sanctioned pre-existing belief systems, established a genre of thinking and writing that would influence Emerson, Thoreau, Marsh—and through them, first Mumford and then McHarg.[14] Volume I of *Cosmos* details the beauty, harmony, and order of natural phenomena. As Humboldt guides his listeners up the slopes of active volcanoes, down tropical rivers, and to the farthest reaches of the Siberian tundra, he slowly weaves a synoptic vision of life on earth that draws inspiration from the sky above and the ground below. Subjects include the movement of the planets, sunspots, electromagnetism, volcanoes, and the geographic distribution of plants and animals. Volume II is a history of science that explains how the earth and its people assumed their present form, with the hope that this knowledge would excite a pure love of nature.

It was exactly this dual perspective, this ability to combine empirical reality with poetic imagination, that Mumford would praise in the introduction to *Design with Nature* when he called attention to McHarg's power of observation and his ability to look at "nature and human activity from an external vantage point" and to see "from within, as a participant and actor, bringing to the cold, dry, colorless world of science ... vivid color and passion, emotions, feelings, sensitivities, erotic and esthetics delights".[15] McHarg's argument includes carefully selected photographs and life-experiences designed to establish both the truth of his position and the errors of his peers. McHarg, like Mumford himself, had a specific agenda, and he was prepared to do whatever it took to make people believe it.

What *Design with Nature* does, then, is redefine the progressive myth of modernity using an idiosyncratic notion of objectivity that combines utopian idealism, empirical observation, systematic organization, social criticism, the adventurous history of nineteenth-century environmentalism, spectacular current events, and scenes from McHarg's life. Here, McHarg, like his fictional naturalist, is the mythic hero grappling with the complexity of the world — the participant-observer who is lured from home by adventure, undergoes a supreme ordeal, and receives a gift of knowledge which he brings back to his home and the everyday world. As outlined by the mid-twentieth century mythologist Joseph Campbell in *Myths to Live By*, such gifts of knowledge awaken "a sense of awe and gratitude in relation to the mystery and dimension of the universe", offer this image "in accord with the knowledge of the time", validate the norms of a "specific social order", and guide "people, stage by stage, in health, strength and harmony, through the foreseeable course of a useful life".[16]

THE WORLD OF APPEARANCE AND THE MEANING OF FORM

The material of myth is the material of our life, the material of our body, and the material of our environment, and a living, vital mythology deals with these in terms that are appropriate to the nature of knowledge of the time.

/ Joseph Campbell, *Transformations of Myth Through Time*[17]

The roots of McHarg's environmental odyssey are found in the city of his childhood — the industrial port of Glasgow, Scotland. In the 1920s and 1930s, the decades of McHarg's youth, the economy of Glasgow centered on shipbuilding and transatlantic trade. McHarg's family lived on the periphery of the city, a location that enabled easy access to both the urban center and the surrounding countryside.

In the opening chapter of *Design with Nature*, McHarg places himself midway between these worlds: "I spent my childhood and adolescence squarely between two diametrically different environments, the poles of man and nature."[18] He then describes these two settings and offers two choices. But

Figure 4/ Photographs of Glasgow and the surrounding countryside. From McHarg, *Design with Nature*.
© 1992 by John Wiley & Sons, Inc. Reprinted by permission John Wiley & Sons, Inc.

the images from the *Glasgow Herald* that McHarg selects to illustrate the city of his youth — one a dark, dank tenement courtyard and the other a village nestled in a sunny mountain valley — indicate there really was not much of a choice [Figure 4]. The path to the city offered the young McHarg the excitement of the theater, dances, circus, concerts, art galleries, bagpipe parades, soccer matches, the railroad station, and the christening of the Queen Mary. Yet to him these adventures were just "interludes in a grey impression of gloom and dreary ugliness". Emphasizing the worst, and giving his readers good reason to side with his call for more verdant cities, McHarg refers to the culturally stimulating but utilitarian Glasgow as a wasteland, "a sandstone excrement cemented with smoke and grime. Each night its pall on the eastern horizon was lit by the flames of blast furnaces, a Turner fantasy made real."[19] In contrast, here is McHarg's description of his country walk:

> ... the other path was always exhilarating and joy could be found in small events, the certainty of a still trout seen in the shadow of a bridge, the salmon jumping or a stag glimpsed fleetingly, the lambing, climbing through the clouds to the sunlight above, a cap full of wild strawberries or blackberries, men back from the Spanish Civil War at the firepot or a lift from an American in a Packard convertible.[20]

Unlike the awe-inspiring yet terrifying city, the country landscape is intimate, inviting, and full of light and life. Adding to the enjoyment is an unexpected mix of the exotic, with references to a wider world of adventure that includes tales of war and a flashy American convertible. These references are possibly allusions to McHarg's service during World War II and his student years at Harvard, which included an excursion across the United States in a convertible. More critically, McHarg's intellectual appreciation of the landscape relates to his intuitive response to its sensory delights.

McHarg's account transforms this pleasant walk into a life-altering experience that is both domestic and transcendent:

> The burn had familiar steppingstones, overhangs where small trout and red-breasted minnows lived, shaded by reeds, osiers and willows. Whitewashed stone farmhouses sat squarely with their outbuildings and old trees marked the ridges.... It was a myriad place. Its gem was Peel Glen, for most of the year an unremarkable woodland, mainly beech, deep shadowed and silent, but in Spring it was transformed. As you entered its shade there was no quick surprise — only slowly did the radiance of light from the carpet of bluebells enter and suffuse the consciousness.[21]

In this passage, a simple childhood memory of a village woodlot becomes a testament to the wonder of being. Joseph Campbell called this "mythic" way of thinking and seeing the ultimate system of order — a perceptual merger "known to the mind and beheld by the eye, as an epiphany of such kind that when lightning flashes, or a setting sun ignites the sky, or a deer is seen standing altered, the exclamation 'Ah!' may be uttered as a recognition of divinity" [Figure 5].[22] Additional tales of trials behind enemy lines during World War II and a battle with tuberculosis in a flyspecked hospital complete the story of McHarg's early adventures. Epiphany comes with a quiet respite in an Italian hillside village away from the horrifying noise, smell, and spectacle of war, and a journey to the summit of a lofty mountain where McHarg discovers the healing balm of sunlight, fresh air, and good food in a Swiss sanitarium.

But before he allows us to leave these romantic tales of adversity and triumph, McHarg brings the dream crashing down around us. He describes his return to Peel Glen as an adult, after having faced and overcome the challenges of war, Harvard, and tuberculosis. Expecting that time and experience would shrink his childhood memories, he instead discovers that Peel Glen had vanished. The ephemeral beauty of its bluebells had been sacrificed for post-war housing. While he notes that cheap and affordable housing was clearly needed after years of depression and the war, McHarg finds the land diminished and enduring damage done. The reader is left with the knowledge that the myth of modernity is all about life: the world we live in and how it shapes what we do, see, and feel. More immediately, these stories ask us to step back for a moment from everyday tasks and the comfort of what we are culturally trained to appreciate, and to question our motives. This perspective was the gift that McHarg brought back from his youthful adventures and gave to his readers in hopes that they, like he, could live in health, strength, and harmony through the foreseeable course of a useful life.

THE METAPHOR OF THE SUN

Our mythology now, therefore, is to be of infinite space and its light, which is without as well as within. Like moths, we are caught in the spell of its allure, flying to it outward, to the moon and beyond, and flying to it, also, inward.

/ Joseph Campbell, *Myths to Live By*[23]

There is another narrative strain in *Design with Nature* — another facet of McHarg's myth of progress — that likewise builds upon his cherished memory of Peel Glen and its bluebells. In this narrative, McHarg's exploration of memory and place is linked to the enlightenment that he found in the scientific knowledge of sunlight and its transformation by plants; this story, like his childhood adventures in the city and countryside, explores how the way we see and experience

Figure 5/ An image of the forest. From McHarg, *Design with Nature*. © 1992 by John Wiley & Sons, Inc.
Reprinted by permission John Wiley & Sons, Inc.

Figure 6/ Front and rear cover images from the first edition of *Design with Nature*. © 1992 by John Wiley & Sons, Inc. Reprinted by permission John Wiley & Sons, Inc.

the world shapes our outlook and actions. The dramatic photographs of the sun and earth that appear on the front and back cover of the first edition of *Design with Nature* symbolize this tale's cosmic epiphany [Figure 6]. As literal representations of the flow of energy from the sun to the earth, the images capture the fleeting materiality of this bond and transform it into a vision of eternity, unity, and harmony. As statements of McHarg's "personal testaments to the sun, moon and stars", the images of the sun and earth symbolized "a phenomenal universe, participating in the timeless yearning that is evolution, vivid expressions of time past, essential partners in survival and with us now in the creation of the future".[24] As a metaphor for modernity, the photographic juxtaposition of the sun and earth was, for McHarg, the ultimate expression of the mid-century ecological zeitgeist.

The image of the sun came from a show on sunspots at The American Museum of Natural History's Hayden Planetarium. The barely perceptible city skyline at the base of the sun is actually the stainless-steel trim around the base of the dome over the 750-seat auditorium.[25] The dome served as the display screen for a state-of-the-art Zeiss II projector [Figure 7]. Sky shows projected on its curved surface recapitulated the developmental history of the earth, beginning with its stellar origins. The shows were designed to complement the evolutionary narrative of the natural history displays in the main exhibition halls of the Museum.[26] More generally, planetarium sky shows were theatrical tableaus that projected a collective and optimistic vision of human destiny. In these

productions, the planet Earth literally became a biblical ark on an epic journey through a boundless cosmic sea. Travelers who embarked on this voyage had no control over their destination, but if they sat back and attentively observed the mythic narrative unfolding on the ceiling above their heads, they would ultimately discover a better world.[27] Meanwhile, the image of the earth on the back cover was taken in November 1967 by a NASA (ATS) weather satellite. A year

Figure 7/ Hayden Planetarium Zeiss II projector. Image # 121987 and Image # 325246, American Museum of Natural History Library.

before the publication of *Design with Nature*, the image had appeared on the front cover of *The Whole Earth Catalogue*, a counter-culture catalogue that peddled the tools of modern technology as a means to re-establish an organic connection to the land.[28]

McHarg's cosmic journey had begun in 1957, shortly after he assumed leadership of the Department of Landscape Architecture at the University of Pennsylvania and while he was assisting the architect Louis Kahn to select a site for the Research Institute for Advanced Studies (RIAS). A chance encounter with one of the institute's scientists opened McHarg's eyes to a vital, but hidden dimension of the landscape, which changed the way he read the land and perceived humanity's relationship to it. Established in 1955, RIAS was the research arm of the Glen L. Martin Company (now Lockheed Martin). Emulating the cosmic explorations of the nineteenth-century natural historians, its mission was to "observe the phenomena of nature", to "support investigations in search of underlying knowledge of these phenomena", and to apply this knowledge toward "the improvement and welfare of mankind" [Figure 8].[29] Areas of specialization included high-tech aeronautic materials, spacecraft guidance control, and chlorophyll research. Dr. Bessel Kok, an expert on photosynthesis, was the head of the division that studied chlorophyll. He and his team were instrumental in unraveling the molecule's energy conversion pathway [Figure 9].[30] The practical application of this work involved the potential use of algae as a food and energy source in manned space exploration. This is how McHarg's encounter with Kok appears in *Design with Nature*:

> Some years ago I spent a most instructive winter with Louis Kahn, searching for the appropriate site for a prospective temple of science. I learned much from my travels with this most perceptive architect, but my knowledge was even more enlarged by an encounter with a member of the research organization... his task was to send an astronaut to the moon with the least possible baggage.... The experimental design required a plywood capsule, a fluorescent tube representing the sun, some air, water, algae growing in water, some bacteria and man.[31]

McHarg goes on to note how the experiment marked a conceptual turning point in his thinking and his career. Plants were not just "benign" and "beautiful"; their ability to capture the energy of sunlight and store it in a useable form—negentropy—was "indispensible". Indeed, "All life", he wrote, "except for a few minor exceptions, was entirely dependent upon the plant and photosynthesis" [Figure 10].[32]

Waxing poetic, and totally entranced by the notion that light and material, as embodied by the plant, were one and the same, he states: "Suddenly I had an image of a green world, half turned toward the sun, leaves cupped to its light, encapsulating through their templates, into their beings, this

Figure 8/ Research Institute of Advanced Studies promotional material. Courtesy of the Glen L. Martin Maryland Aviation Museum.

Figure 9/ Dr. Bessel Kok using a differential spectrometer to measure photosynthesis in situ. Courtesy of the Glen L. Martin Maryland Aviation Museum.

modified and ordered sunlight."[33] He then launches into a history of life on Earth that includes energy flows and eons of material recycling. Lightning strikes; volcanoes erupt; hydrogen, oxygen and carbon combine; and DNA coils upward into plants and animals [Figure 11]. McHarg follows this remark with a vision of the grey and brown centers of our cities, as they appear from space, magically transformed into the green, life-giving organelles of plant cells. An electron micrograph of a diatom and a cross-section of a leaf reinforce this point.

These images, with their orderly yet fluid arrangement of cells and organelles, represent the beneficial mutualism between built form and natural processes that McHarg envisioned for modern cities and painstakingly detailed in his overlay methodology. Their shape and structure also make it easy for the reader to imagine the earth as simply a larger, albeit more complex and sustainable version of the RIAS algae experiments [Figure 12].

As McHarg delves deeper into technical details, his language becomes more urgent and poetic. Attempting to touch the ineffable quality of these cold, hard facts, he steps beyond the empirical, and like Humboldt, discovers a chain of connection that links all of nature. Here the earth is part of the sun; we are part of the earth, and the earth is part of us. An image of infinity opens up. Science joins divinity and we grow plant-like from this womb. Once we understand that we are inextricably tied to everything else, McHarg explains, our vision will clear and we will cross into "another realm" where we will leave "behind innocence and ignorance" and finally perceive "our allies and ourselves".[34] The knowledge and feelings from his childhood thus grow and deepen in accord with insights provided by science and technology.

BOTANY AND THE CHAIN OF BEING

McHarg's exaltation of plants follows a path blazed by Patrick Geddes (1854–1932), the Scottish polymath whose work also influenced the social criticism of Mumford. Though Geddes is best known as an urban planner and author of *Cities in Evolution*, he began his career as a botanist, and he wrote a long and detailed account of the work of the physicist and molecular physiologist Jagadish Chandra Bose.[35] Bose invented the crescograph, a recording device that borrowed techniques used by animal physiologists in their study of muscle movement, to measure a plant's response to external stimuli. Bose sought to demonstrate a commonality in response between plants and animals at the molecular level, and thus a common heritage uniting all of life. Even though he was castigated for suggesting that plants have "feelings", his work did elucidate the principle of phototropism, or the fact that plants direct their growth toward light, and thus bend and move in response to ambient environmental conditions. Geddes' treatise on Bose ties these experiments in light and movement to chlorophyll and

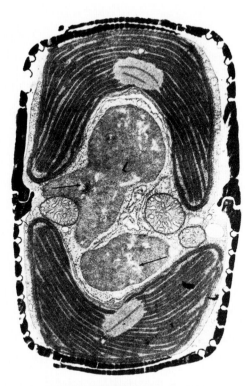

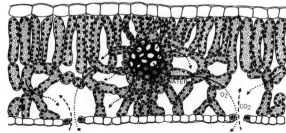

photosynthesis. More critically, Geddes himself had earlier studied the physiology of one-celled organisms under the auspices of the famed nineteenth-century naturalist Thomas Henry Huxley.[36] While looking through a microscope, Geddes discovered chlorophyll in the cells of primitive forms of animal life. His observations of these chlorophyll-containing animals, like those observations of plant movement made by Bose, caused Geddes to question the categorical boundaries separating plants from animals, and to envision evolution in terms of cooperation rather than struggle.[37]

Geddes, like McHarg, used his knowledge of plant physiology to highlight the critical importance of plants in the development of life on Earth and, thus, the development of human culture. Or, to put it another way, Geddes, like McHarg, was not just fascinated by the mechanics of plant physiology; he transformed the mutually beneficial biological processes he observed into the basis for a planning approach that he believed would restore metabolic order and vitality to urban communities.

50 years before McHarg praised the form and function of leaves in *Design with Nature* and then used this knowledge to invent a central role for plants in his urban renewal schemes, Geddes had made a similar observation and articulated a similar urban vision in a 1919 valedictory address to students at University College Dundee in Scotland, titled "Biology and its Social Bearings: How a Botanist Looks at the World".[38]

Figure 12/ A diatom and leaf cross-section. From McHarg, *Design with Nature*. © 1992 by John Wiley & Sons, Inc. Reprinted by permission John Wiley & Sons, Inc.

Speaking from a lectern surrounded by plants, Geddes posed a question that is remarkably similar to observations later made by McHarg:

> How many people think twice about a leaf? Yet the leaf is the chief product and phenomenon of Life: this is a green world, with animals comparatively few and small, and all dependent upon leaves. By leaves we live. Some people have strange ideas that they live by money. They think energy is generated by the circulation of coins. Whereas the world is mainly a vast leaf-colony, growing on and forming a leafy soil, not a mere mineral mass; we live not by the jingling of our coins, but by the fullness of our harvests.[39]

Turning from economics to education, Geddes' next remarks again prefigure McHarg, and in particular his adventures in the countryside: "Set the child observing Nature, not with labeled and codified lessons, but with its own treasures and beauty feasts — as of stones, minerals, crystals, of living fishes and butterflies, of wild flowers, fruits and seeds!"[40] Geddes then urges his audience to live this dream. In rapid succession, he admonishes them to follow his footsteps; become intellectual truants; witness the cosmic beauty of the "sunset and sunrise, and the moon and the stars, the wonders of the winds, cloud, rain, the beauty of woods" and in this manner discover the true beginning of the natural sciences. More practically, and reflecting his personal concern for the urban environment, he tells the students that it does make a difference if they follow his example and plant a garden in the heart of an urban slum.[41] To do so will require effort and will, like the fitful recovery of an invalid, take time; but the results will be miraculous:

> True town-planning begins with thus simply amending the surroundings of people.... It grows from small gardens to semi-public ones like this [garden at the college], and thence to parks and boulevards, and so to better houses for all upon their course or beyond it. This is, indeed, the way planning has actually grown: even the magnificent circles and avenues of Paris are but the outcomes of clearing the forest.[42]

To help capture the deep roots of his ideas, including their convoluted association with observation, intuition, and memory, Geddes outlines a great chain of being that entwines the external mechanics of energy flows and nutrient recycling with the internal circuitry of mental creativity. But Geddes' true genius, as noted by Mumford, relates to the way he combined the evolutionary view of life that he had learned under Huxley with his scientific investigations of cell metabolism, and then transformed these colorless facts into a cooperative vision of human development.[43] This, as Mumford also observed, allowed Geddes to turn the mechanistic paradigm of the industrial city into a biological metaphor.[44] Critical for this discussion is the fact that Geddes replaced technological efficiency with the "perfect health of the leaf and flower".[45]

Geddes' objective — the gift of knowledge he sought to bequeath — was an education that gave "everyone the outlook of the artist".[46] Geddes wanted his students to see past the dry analytics of laboratory science and poetically envision the ways in which they are literally and figuratively part of the land they inhabit. Like McHarg after him, Geddes used his life, and his personal and professional experiences, as a guide. In the Dundee address, his avatar of social enlightenment was the doctor-artist, an inspired diagnostician whose herbal remedies revitalize the everyday so that:

> Life like a dome of many-coloured glass
> Stains the white-radiance of eternity.[47]

Geddes embodied these ideas in the Outlook Tower, a museum of optical instruments located in Edinburgh, Scotland that he bought at auction and developed into an urban research institute. The Tower functioned as an interactive museum of cultural and natural history. Tours began at the top with the view from the parapet. Moving down through the building, visitors discovered the wonders of Scotland, Language, Europe, and the World. Both the name of the Outlook Tower and its geographic floor sequence illustrated Geddes' belief that learning begins from the local and moves outward.[48] The "Language" level related this learning pattern to Geddes' assertion that the stories people tell cultivate imaginative forms of self-discovery that unite rather than divide. According to Geddes, the Tower promoted "learning through living". In *Cities in Evolution*, he claimed that this type of participatory engagement "seeks to see as far as may be to recognize and

ARBOR SAECULORUM

———— **Figure 13/** The *"Arbor Saeculorum"* from *The Evergreen/* ————
A Northern Seasonal I, published in 1895 by Patrick Geddes and
Colleagues. Courtesy University of Strathclyde Library, Department of
Archives and Special Collections.

Figure 14/ Preliminary cover for *Design with Nature*. Courtesy of The Architectural Archives, The University of Pennsylvania.

utilize all points of view", whether city, countryside, or a distant land.[49]

To illustrate the unitary nature of his vision of physical and social growth, Geddes designed a stained-glass window for the Tower called the "*arbor saeculorum*", tree of life [Figure 13]. The colorful glass suffused outward views with poetic vibrancy, while the symbolic tree of life took Geddes' forward-thinking vision back to a doctrine of common origins related to the empirical study of plant morphogenesis carried out by the writer and poet-scientist Johann Wolfgang von Goethe (1749–1832).[50] Goethe argued that there was a primordial morphology — the leaf — from which all other plant forms had developed, and he sought to understand how and why this metamorphosis occurred.[51] Goethe's morphological inquiry into plant life influenced Alexander von Humboldt's transect studies of plant distribution. In like manner, Geddes would posit an archetypal pattern underlying all extant urban forms, which he would then illustrate in transect form as a stream corridor that flowed from the mountains to the sea and encompassed all of the plants, animals, human occupations, and settlement patterns along its banks.[52]

In his Dundee address, Geddes argued that his synoptic vision of life, much like the view of the city and countryside made possible by the camera obscura situated atop the Tower, opens the eyes and mind, allowing "hands to work wonders" and people to draw "fresh symbols" from Nature's "endless beauties".[53] Perhaps best of all — and as

McHarg would later illustrate in a proposed cover for *Design with Nature* in which the hands of the designer hover over collaged images of the city and countryside — this vision of urban planning reaches out, rediscovers, and brings back to life, all those things that modern society had lost, ignored, or devalued [Figure 14].

CODA

There is, however, another odyssey entwined within McHarg's personal narrative of sunlight — a story of progress entangled in a Faustian exchange, which indicates that the scientific and technical wonders he beheld at RIAS were less benign than they seem. Instead of a tale of mutual cooperation, this is a story of mutually assured destruction. Bessel Kok's algae experiment, renamed GIPSE, finally made it to space as the piggyback payload of an intercontinental ballistic missile [Figure 15].[54]

The personal narrative in *Design with Nature* is finally, then, a parable about the deceptiveness of appearance. Whether or not we accept all of his argument or his warning

Figure 15/ Preparation of the Gravity Independent Photosynthetic Gas Exchanger (GIPSE) for launch aboard an Air Force Atlas ICBM Missile. Courtesy of the Glen L. Martin Maryland Aviation Museum.

that humanity's path may not be identical to natural order, the quest McHarg undertakes and the discoveries he makes are intended to reveal the moral beauty beneath the surface of everyday experience. Progress is about not just doing better, but being better. Yet, as the shadowy silhouette of the city at the base of the sun on the cover of *Design with Nature* reminds us — like the ghostly shadows reflected on the wall of Plato's cave — the reality that McHarg perceives and promotes is much more complex than it at first appears, and a fine line exists between the sacred and profane in any myth of progress.

NOTES

1/ Campbell, Joseph, *The Hero with a Thousand Faces,* New York: Pantheon Books, 1949, p. 1.

2/ For the purpose of this essay 'myth' refers to an exaggerated or idealized conception of a person, place, or thing. See http://oxforddictionaries.com/us/definition/american_english/myth. 'Modern' refers to design approaches that break with the past, and 'modernity' refers to times, places or things being other and better than what had gone before. See *New Keywords: A Revised Vocabulary of Culture and Society*, Tony Bennett, Lawrence Grossberg, and Meghan Morris eds., Malden, MA: Blackwell Publishing, 2009, p. 220.

3/ McHarg, Ian, "An Ecological Method for Landscape Architecture", *The Subversive Science: Essays Toward an Ecology of Man*, Paul Shepard and Daniel McKinley eds., Boston: Houghton Mifflin Company, 1969, pp. 328–332.

4/ See Raymond K. Belknap and John G. Furtado, *Three Approaches to Environmental Resource Analysis*, Washington DC: The Conservation Foundation, 1967, pp. 59–75.

5/ See Carl Steinitz, Paul Parker, and Lawrie Jordan, "Hand-Drawn Overlays: Their History and Prospective Uses," *Landscape Architecture* vol. 66, September 1976, pp. 444–455; Anne Whiston Spirn, "Ian McHarg, Landscape Architecture, and Environmentalism", *Environmentalism in Landscape Architecture*, Michel Conan ed., Washington, DC: Dumbarton Oaks Research and Library Collection, 2000, pp. 97–114; and Forster Ndubisi, *Ecological Planning: A Historical Approach*, Baltimore: Johns Hopkins University Press, 2002.

6/ Campbell, Joseph, *Transformations of Myth Through Time*, New York: Harper Perennial, 1990, p. 1.

7/ Ellwood, Robert, *The Politics of Myth: A Study of C. G. Jung, Mircea Eliade, and Joseph Campbell*, Albany: State University of New York Press, 1999, pp. 16–21.

8/ Mumford, Lewis, "Prospect", *Man's Role in Changing the Face of the Earth*, William L. Thomas Jr. ed., Chicago: University of Chicago Press, 1956, pp. 1142–1149. Mumford, the geographer Carl Sauer, and the zoologist Marston Bates were co-chairs of the conference, which was dedicated to the work of geographer George Perkins Marsh.

9/ McHarg, *Design with Nature*, p. vii.

10/ Mumford, Lewis, *Golden Day*, New York: Boni & Liveright, 1926, pp. 146, 166.

11/ McHarg, Ian, *Design with Nature*, New York: The Natural History Press, 1969, pp.123–125.

12/ See McHarg, *Design with Nature*, copyright page. Founded in 1869, the mission of the American Museum of Natural History is to discover, interpret, and disseminate—through scientific research and education—knowledge about human cultures, the natural world, and the universe. See http://www.amnh.org/about-us/history/history-1869-1900, and http://www.amnh.org/about-us/mission-statement.

13/ Humboldt, Alexander von, *Cosmos: A Sketch of the Physical Description of the Universe Vol. I*, E. C. Otté trans., New York: Harper & Brothers Publishers, 1872; Humboldt, Alexander von, *Cosmos: A Sketch of the Physical Description of the Universe Vol. II*, E. C. Otté trans., New York: Harper & Brothers Publishers, 1873. See also Laura Dawson Walls, *The Passage to Cosmos: Alexander von Humboldt and the Shaping of America*, Chicago: University of Chicago Press, 2009.

14/ See also Ian L. McHarg, *A Quest for Life*, New York: John Wiley & Sons, Inc., 1996, pp. 155–162. The present essay traces an intellectual lineage extending from Humboldt to the natural historian Charles Darwin, and through Darwin to Thomas Henry Huxley, Patrick Geddes, Lewis Mumford, and finally McHarg. A second lineage extends from the poet-scientist J. W. von Goethe through Humboldt and the geographer Elisée Reclus, and then to Geddes and McHarg.

15/ McHarg, *Design with Nature*, p. viii.

16/ Campbell, Joseph, *Myths to Live By*, New York: Penguin Compass, 1972, 1993, pp. 214–215.

17/ Campbell, Joseph, *Transformations of Myth Through Time*, pp. 1.

18/ McHarg, *Design with Nature*, p. 1.

19/ McHarg, *Design with Nature*, p. 2.

20/ McHarg, *Design with Nature*, p. 2.

21/ McHarg, *Design with Nature*, p. 3.

22/ Campbell, Joseph, *The Inner Reaches of Outer Space: Metaphor as Myth and as Religion*, Novato, California: New World Library, 1986, 2002, pp. xx–xxi.

23/ Campbell, *Myths to Live By*, p. 266.

24/ McHarg, *Design with Nature*, p. 5.

25/ Photographic Archives, The American Museum of Natural History, New York.

26/ See PLACE MATTERS, a joint project of City Lore and the Municipal Art Society — Hayden Planetarium: http://www.placematters.net/node/1781.

27/ Marché, Jordan, *Theaters of Time and Space: American Planetaria, 1930–1970*, New Brunswick: Rutgers University Press, 2005, pp. 43–44.

28/ *The Last Whole Earth Catalogue*, New York: Random House, 1971,1974, p.1. See also http://www.wholeearth.com/issue-electronic-edition.php?iss=1010.

29/ Harwood, William B., *Raise Heaven and Earth: The Story of Martin Marietta People and Their Pioneering Achievements*, New York: Simon & Schuster, 1993, p. 283.

30/ Research Institute of Advanced Studies, Annual Reports, 1957, 1958, 1959, 1960, 1961, courtesy of The Glen L. Martin Maryland Aviation Museum.

31/ McHarg, *Design with Nature*, p. 44.

32/ McHarg, *Design with Nature*, p. 44.

33/ McHarg, *Design with Nature*, p. 53.

34/ McHarg, *Design with Nature*, p. 53.

35/ Geddes, Patrick, *An Indian Pioneer of Science: The Life and Work of Sir Jagadis C. Bose*, New York: Longmans, Green and Co., 1920.

36/ Stalley, Marshall, *Patrick Geddes: Spokesman for Man and the Environment*, New Brunswick, NJ: Rutgers University Press, 1972, pp. 8–10.

37/ Stalley, *Patrick Geddes*, p. 8. See also Volker M. Welter, *Biopolis: Patrick Geddes and the City of Life*, Cambridge, MA: The MIT Press, 2003, p. 11.

38/ See http://www.dundee.ac.uk/archives/geddes.htm.

39/ Defries, Amelia, *The Interpreter Geddes: The Man and his Gospel*, New York: Boni & Liveright, 1928, p. 175.

40/ Defries, *The Interpreter Geddes*, p. 186.

41/ Defries, *The Interpreter Geddes*, p. 185.

42/ Defries, *The Interpreter Geddes*, p. 179.

43/ Welter, *Biopolis*, pp. 88–99.

44/ Williams, Rosalind, "Lewis Mumford as a Historian of Technology in *Technics and Civilization*", *Lewis Mumford: Public Intellectual*, Thomas P. Hughes and Agatha C. Hughes eds., New York: Oxford University Press, 1990, p. 46.

45/ Defries, *The Interpreter Geddes*, p. 178.

46/ Defries, *The Interpreter Geddes*, p. 173.

47/ Defries, *The Interpreter Geddes*, p. 185. The lines of poetry are from "Adonaïs: An Elegy on the Death of John Keats" by Percy Bysshe Shelley.

48/ Wheeler, Keith, *From Goethe to Geddes and the Search for Environmental Understanding*, South Croyden: Proceedings Croyden Natural History and Science Society Ltd., May 1972, p. 410–428.

49/ Geddes, Patrick, *Cities in Evolution*, London: Williams & Norgate, Ltd., 1915 & 1949, pp. 111–115. See also Stalley, *Patrick Geddes*, p. 348.

50/ Welter, *Biopolis*, p. 95.

51/ von Goethe, J. W., *An Attempt to Interpret the Metamorphosis of Plants*, Agnes Arbor trans., United States: Chronica Botanica Company, 1946, pp. 69–115.

52/ Wheeler, *From Goethe to Geddes*, pp. 410–428.

53/ Defries, *The Interpreter Geddes*, p. 176.

54/ News Bureau Martin Company: A Division of the Martin Marietta Company, Press Release, GIPSE Release No. 3342_3163, courtesy of The Glen L. Martin Maryland Aviation Museum.

/VOLKER M. WELTER

FROM THE LANDSCAPE OF WAR TO THE OPEN ORDER OF THE KAUFMANN HOUSE: RICHARD NEUTRA AND THE EXPERIENCE OF THE GREAT WAR

"Wer spricht von Siegen? Überstehn ist alles."
(Who speaks of victory? Survival is everything.)
/ Rainer Maria Rilke, *Requiem*, 1908

In 1946, a decade after hiring Frank Lloyd Wright to design Fallingwater, the Pennsylvania weekend home that would become an icon of American architecture, Edgar Kaufmann, Sr retained the services of Richard Neutra to design a house for him at Palm Springs in the California desert [Figure 1]. While visiting the Kaufmann desert house with a group of students, I was asked about an intriguing architectural detail: angular metal gaskets that were mounted as weather seals on the edges of the guest bedrooms' doors.[1] When the doors are closed, the metal strips interlock with others fixed inside the doorframes. When the floor-to-ceiling windows are shut as well, the guest rooms are no longer parts of a continuous environment that encompassed house and garden as well as the wider landscape, but interior spaces hermetically sealed off from the exterior. This makes sense, considering that these doors open directly onto a passageway that is bordered on its opposite side not by a solid wall but only by a series of vertical aluminum louvers mounted on a low parapet. These louvers, which pivot on a vertical axis, may offer protection against some of the winds blowing down from Mount Jacinto behind the house, but not against the desert sands.

Viewed as a whole, the structures that comprise the Kaufmann House appear as a harmonious merger between architecture and nature; the two intertwine so closely that it is nearly impossible to draw a dividing line between the natural and the architectural environment. On the level of architectural detail, however, the doors' metal seals establish a firm barrier between inside and outside, revealing that the relationship between the natural world and the human-made one is a hierarchical order: architecture is an artificial addition to the site that creates spaces for humans in a constant state of defensive alert with regard to their surroundings.

Such a realization may appear at odds with the prevalent conception of Neutra's architecture as a manifestation of the architect's belief in the cosmos as a continuum and of humanity's ineffable place not 'apart from' but 'a part of' nature — suggesting harmony rather than dissent. It appears at odds as well with Neutra's opinion that his generation "more than any before, [was] attracted by nature, landscape, and the out-of-doors".[2] Indeed, Neutra, a proponent of the 'natural garden' — plantings based on nature's cues — was a skilled horticulturist and landscape architect, having worked both in the nursery trade and in the office of the Swiss landscape architect Gustav Ammann. It was Ammann, he later wrote, who "intensified my understanding that architecture was a production intimately interwoven with nature and the landscape in which it was inserted".[3] In Neutra's work, the architecture may be viewed as an integral part of an overall landscape design. Yet the simultaneously defensive or adversarial character of his architecture is not only manifest, it is fully comprehensible in light of Neutra's life experiences. In fact, the close relationship between humans, architecture, and the natural environment that characterizes much of Neutra's mid-twentieth-century architecture was influenced by his military service during the Great War, which placed Neutra into the mountains of the Balkans, a harsh and hostile environment in its own right, especially during winter, but then infinitely made worse by the military use of the land.[4] Thus for a prolonged period at the outset of his architectural career — his architecture studies and military service closely intermeshed between 1910 and 1918 — Neutra experienced nature as a malevolent rather than a benevolent force.[5]

NEUTRA AT WAR

Neutra was 22 years old when the Great War began and 26 when it ended in 1918 [Figure 2]. His military files have not survived, but his duty as a young officer of the Austrian-Hungarian Imperial army can be reconstructed from other sources.[6] His autobiography *Life and Shape* provides some information.[7] Although broadly correct with regard to chronology, the text is occasionally difficult to verify, as it freely mixes recollections with retrospective reflections. Watercolors and sketches produced during the war offer additional information regarding Neutra's whereabouts, as some are inscribed with locations and approximate dates. In addition, from early December 1915 until the end of April 1916, Neutra kept a war diary.[8] This essay draws primarily on the diary, a single, small volume into which Neutra wrote in German, mostly using a pencil. Some entries are written with the book resting on a firm surface like a table top; in others, the impressions on the pages are faint, as if noted while supporting the diary on a soft surface such as one's thigh. The war diary reveals that once Neutra was a soldier, his visual comprehension of his surroundings changed: landscapes once perceived as remote backdrops to human action were viewed as 'enclosing' environments in which one needed to survive.

Figure 1/ Richard Neutra, Kaufmann House, Palm Springs, CA, 1946. Distant view of the west elevation rising from behind rocks and boulders. Reproduction courtesy of Dion Neutra, Architect ©. Photograph © J. Paul Getty Trust. Julius Shulman Photography Archive, Research Library at the Getty Research Institute (2004.R.10).

Figure 2/ Richard Neutra (seated in center) with fellow soldiers in front of a fieldstone shelter on Mount Glumina to the east of Trebinje, Herzegovina, not dated. Image courtesy of Richard and Dion Neutra Collection, Archives-Special Collections, College of Environmental Design, California State Polytechnic University, Pomona, CA.

From a European perspective, the Mediterranean war theater was on the margins of the conflict, and the stretch from southern Herzegovina to Montenegro and northern Albania, where Neutra spent a large part of his active duty, was of even lesser importance.[9] The Austrian-Hungarian Army's *Militärschematismen*, regularly-published volumes listing office holders according to their military units and ranks, record the official stages of Neutra's military career. He was a member of the *Feldkanonenregiment* (FKR, Field Artillery Regiment) Nr 12, which, in turn, was part of the fortieth *Honvédinfanteriedivision* (Hungarian Infantry Division), stationed in Budapest.[10] The loss of his personnel records means that we do not know in which of the five battalions of FKR 12 he served, nor do we have details of the events leading to his military decorations.[11] Thomas Hines, Neutra's major biographer, argues that the relative quietness of the front between Herzegovina, in 1914

part of Austria-Hungary, and Montenegro, an ally of Serbia, meant that Neutra's war experience was mainly one of "illness and transience, … [and] of trial"; "the only armed combat Neutra saw was with Slavic partisans in Albania and Montenegro", and "the most painful aspect of the war for Neutra was witnessing the misery of the uprooted civilian population".[12] While Neutra's service was certainly much less intense over longer periods than that of those soldiers stationed in trenches at the Western Front, a closer investigation of the time Neutra spent on the Balkans unveils a more complex picture of his duties and his experiences.

Neutra's service as a soldier can be broadly divided into four periods. The first began just before the Great War and lasted until almost the end of 1915. The second period coincides with Neutra's participation in the Austrian-Hungarian offensive against Montenegro from the end of 1915 until the fall of the kingdom about a month later. During the third period, from around the end of January 1916 to the end of April 1916, Neutra was a member of the occupying forces of Montenegro. By the end of this time Neutra was in Cilli (Celje), Slovenia, on his way back to Vienna. At some point during the occupation, which included extensive travels into Albania, Neutra contracted malaria. Repeated outbreaks of the disease characterized the fourth period, which began with the temporary return to Vienna and ended together with the war in late 1918. This period is the least well documented, but in any case lies outside of Neutra's experiences of active military service in the war zone.

When the assassination of the Austrian Crown Prince and his wife on 28 June 1914 triggered the Great War, Neutra was already on his way to the garrison town of Trebinje in the south of Herzegovina to fulfill his peacetime duty of about four weeks of service every other year [Figure 3].[13] Located close to the border with Montenegro, Trebinje was part of a series of fortresses and military ports, like Sarajevo, Mostar, Bilica, and Cattaro, which formed the southern defense of the Austrian-Hungarian territory. Around Trebinje a network of smaller forts existed, some without permanent military personnel. Neutra was ordered to man Fort Kravica, "a desolate, neglected spot, a building with four ancient 70-mm field guns standing, forlorn and out of order, at the side of an emplacement under construction" which was "the farthest south … halfway to the border of Montenegro".[14] Occasionally, Neutra was called back to Trebinje, for example, when he participated in offensives into the territory of Montenegro. In late August 1914, he relocated temporarily to an old Turkish military post high above the Adriatic port of Gruz (Gravosa) adjacent to Dubrovnik (Ragusa). His orders were to prevent a possible landing of the joint French-British Mediterranean navies traveling up the Adriatic Sea — and this with a single horse-drawn field gun, 27 pieces of ammunition, and a small group of men.[15] Later, Neutra returned to the same spot for a second stint of duty, now as "first officer of a more regular field battery", indicating that provision of military equipment had improved with his rise in rank.[16]

The wit and irony with which Neutra describes this task in his memoirs mask serious concerns. The opening entries of Neutra's war diary repeatedly refer to difficulties arising from outdated equipment, shortages of material and ammunition that hindered adequate training, exercises dominated by harsh commanders, lack of provisions, and communication issues arising from the ethnic diversity of the soldiers of the Austrian-Hungarian empire who did not all share a common language.[17]

Neutra's perception of the enemy was shaped by his awareness of an imbalance between modern weaponry and more traditional techniques of warfare. The commanding, but exposed mountaintop position of Fort Kravica was juxtaposed with "a savage guerrilla-trained enemy", which, in the night,

burned down farm buildings and "frontier hamlets".[18] When the barbed wire defenses around his company's position were supplemented with wired dynamite charges, Neutra wondered — at least in retrospect — about their effectiveness against enemies who were "mountaineers of Montenegro, who had knives with which to cut our throats, pistols, guns, and matches".[19] Neutra's doubts were not limited only to the drawbacks of stationary weapons and defenses that aimed at keeping the enemy at distance versus more flexible, moveable, simpler weapons which required attackers to get close to their targets. He also noted that the former did not work well in the topography of Montenegro. When the dynamite charges went off during night, it was impossible to tell if this was caused by animals or spying enemies. A new searchlight may have flooded the foreground with bright light but also gave away the location of their position.[20] Accordingly, the landscape that crept right up to the small outpost was Neutra's main concern. His gaze remained fixed on that immediate danger zone from which a partisan attack might emerge.

The second period of Neutra's war service was dominated by Austria-Hungary's decision to conquer the kingdom of Montenegro after defeating Serbia by the end of November 1915.[21] The attack began on 8 January 1916, and ended on 26 January, when Montenegro surrendered; to occupy all major towns took until the end of the month.[22] Neutra was part of a broad western move into Montenegro; the garrison of Trebinje was ordered to march towards the city of Nikšić, from where all inessential troops were then to proceed south towards

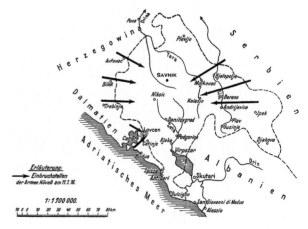

—— **Figure 3/** Map of the Austrian-Hungarian and German attack on ——
Montenegro in early 1916. Neutra was stationed near Trebinje, from where he moved towards Nikšić (center). The approximate location of Šavnik, the destination of Neutra's mountain march on 30 January 1916, has been added to this map. Image from Immanuel Friedrich, *Serbiens und Montenegros Untergang: ein Beitrag zur Geschichte des Weltkrieges*, Berlin: E. S. Mittler & Sohn, 1917, map nr. 8. Courtesy of E. S. Mittler & Sohn, Hamburg.

the city of Podgorica.[23] On 6 January, various units left the fortress of Trebinje. Among them was the artillery battery of a Captain Endlicher to which Neutra belonged, according to the many diary entries recording his disagreements with "Hpt. E". Neutra marched across the mountainous winter landscape with faster moving infantry, but traveled back and forth between the first units and the slower progressing battery of guns. The latter reached Nikšić only on 28 January.[24]

In the time leading up to the invasion, Neutra observed numerous inefficiencies and a lack of planning. On 2 January, he noted that astonishingly many soldiers were occupied with non-military tasks like repairing the horse-drawn light carriages of local dignitaries. He expressed surprise about Captain Endlicher's statement that ammunition would not be taken along. Neutra's more systematic way of preparing for the invasion, as recorded in the pages of his diary, culminated in a four page list that addressed numerous logistical issues including the all important calculation of the number of animals required to carry a daily supply of 80 liters of wine.[25]

More existential concerns surfaced along the way. When occupying a position near Pecine West, Neutra studied the terrain and concluded that their position was potentially exposed to enemy fire directed at them from flanking positions. He recommended that traverses should be created to the right of their location. A second diary entry later the same day states that, thanks to this precaution, only four people were wounded when the enemy fire hit as he had anticipated.[26] During this period, reflections about inadequate weapons again gave way to 'strategic' concerns — in this case, adapting to the quickly varying situations while moving in large numbers into enemy territory.

During the third period Neutra was a member of the forces that, without encountering much military resistance, occupied Montenegro. He writes about endless travels across Montenegro, mostly in order to fetch captured Montenegrin artillery guns from high up in the mountains, to transport ammunition, to organize supplies, and to obtain vehicles and animals as means of transport. One particular journey provides an exemplary instance of Neutra's close interaction with the natural environment at this time. On 30 January 1916, Neutra received orders at 3:30 am to march with 34 soldiers and 25 horses towards Šavnik, a small town 55 kilometers north-east of Nikšić [Figure 3]. His task was to fetch captured mountain guns. The group went first to Luvnok, 13 kilometers away, and then to Gvozd, 14 kilometers and an ascent of up to 1,570 meters away. The next leg was 31 kilometers long to Šavnik while descending 750 meters. On 31 January, the transportation of the guns back to Nikšić began, though Neutra himself traveled on to Bokovica to inspect more guns. While this village was only ten kilometers away, it meant climbing 800 meters through a frozen waterfall.[27] Neutra describes the journey from Gvozd to Šavnik as follows:

Then upwards to a height of 1570 meters. Forests of beeches and oaks, pastures, in between grotesque rock promontories and gigantic snow drifts. By noon time in Gvozd. From then onwards the path was completely snowed in. Descent of 700 meters. Heroic landscape. Rocks, hundreds of meters tall, snow filled *Dolines* [sinkholes], inclines of up to forty degrees, footpaths across expanses of snow, numerous cadavers of dead horses. Beech forests, wild fruit trees, greenish, soaked humus soil. Finally, 300 meters below, a small town, quite similar to our own towns, at a river fork deep down at the bottom of a valley: Šavnik. Difficult final descent.[28]

It is instructive to compare Neutra's observations of a mountainous scene on the island of Corsica, where he visited at the turn of 1913 to 1914:

A very soft breeze carries with it a scent, a barely noticeable, tender, fine fragrance that becomes far more concentrated on the streets further down and might originate, I think, from the ashen hillsides full of burned bushes: a scent as of a fairytale coffee made from figs. Usually rarely noticed, it is the sole sensation here under the sky's blue dome. The rocky precipices to the right of the middle ground, in the direction of Nice, show a play of shadows that seem to follow the layering of the rock and, complementing the violet of the burned hillsides, are of roughly the same or a slightly lesser tonal value than the sky.... They seem to float in azure.[29]

In contrast to the verbal staccato of the landscape of war, the peacetime landscape is captured in a colorful, painterly mode. There are many similar entries in the diaries Neutra kept while traveling in Italy and along the Adriatic Eastern Mediterranean during 1913.[30]

It is true that even in the war diary, entries of comparative painterly qualities can be found. In February 1916, for example, Neutra observes that, "At the center of the city of Nikšić lies a large square cattle market, which is bordered by the better stores." He continues:

One street cuts across longitudinally; two streets frame the shorter ends. Trees of medium age define its borders, and now in the evening a single lit petroleum gaslight sheds its soft greenish light over the curb onto the cobblestones of the sidewalks. One side of the square displays one-story buildings having reasonably steep roofs of the same height, each building painted in a different color. Along the opposite, longer side, single-story and two-story buildings alternate.[31]

Neutra effortlessly integrated the local war-scarred population into this picturesque scene of a quaint town square almost as if the image needed some human staffage: "Small, weak children, very pregnant women, old people, sick people carry the most sorry household goods — with lamentation or in sorrowful resignation — out into the night."[32] Regardless if painted with words or brush strokes, Neutra's observations portray him as a sympathetic observer of a country and its citizens during war.

Here the images remain wedded to a painterly point of view; Neutra's perspective is that of an observer who confronts scenery in a manner similar to that of a painter in front of both landscape and canvas. Yet to identify these impressions as the essence of Neutra's war experience is to miss the qualitatively new perception of space that is captured in the extract from Neutra's march to Šavnik.[33] In that entry the landscape is a surrounding space into which Neutra is immersed and of which he takes measure primarily with regard to physical characteristics that may hinder or help his traversing it in pursuit of both the accomplishment of his mission and his own survival. There appear to be no examples of this kind of immersive environment in the pre-war travel diaries, but more instances of this experience of space are recorded in Neutra's war diary.[34] Later, this immersive perception of space, rooted in the war experience, would become a source of Neutra's novel approach to architecture.

LANDSCAPES OF WAR

The precarious positions of individual soldiers in the landscape of war are central to many accounts of the Great War. Yet the particular environments described typically appear as part of the accidental circumstances into which men were thrown rather than those consciously reflected upon.[35] A rare exception is the essay "The Landscape of War" (1917), in which the Gestalt psychologist Kurt Lewin reflected (while recovering from battlefield wounds) on the spaces of a battlefield from the perspective of an individual soldier — in his case as a field artilleryman — and the fundamental changes in the perception of both details and characteristics of a landscape that the war brought about.

The essay opens with the difference between seeing a hill as a distinct spatial form rising upwards from below a flat plain and the same hill perceived primarily as a continuation of that plain, a "bump in the ground" or a "planar form" (Flächengestalt).[36] The former perception constitutes the phenomenological truth about the hill; the latter, indicates the view of a soldier gauging the formation of the land with regard to possibilities of military maneuvers and enemy positions on the crest or, increasingly common in modern warfare, the rear slope of a hill.[37] The soldier's perspective offers a more integrated view of the landscape, but the gain in coherence is paid for with a loss of comprehensiveness. The peacetime landscape is "round, without front and back" and offering space

that is infinitely larger than what is immediately visible, which depends on topography and the laws of optical perception.[38] The landscape of war is no longer limitless, as it is "bounded" and appears "to be directed". "Up 'ahead'" was the border zone, a stretch of land leading to the foremost frontline, from which point onwards it ran parallel to the front.[39] It was overlaid by a danger zone that comprised random danger points and islands of danger like snipers' and artillery's target areas. The latter were often found far back in the hinterland at a great distance from the front; Lewin points out that the active war zone could encompass anything between two and ten kilometers.[40] In part, battles were being conducted across ever broader and deeper areas as the result of the use of more powerful weapons and, correspondingly, new military tactics.

Over the nineteenth century, rapid advances in weapons technology improved the range, power, and accuracy of weapons like rifles and artillery guns. One tactical response was the creation of new battle orders, most notably the substitution of "'open order' deployment for 'close order' formations", which after much trial and error culminated during the Great War in the German army's concept of elastic defense.[41] This was the last stage of the gradual dissolution of formal battle orders, a process that expanded the battlefield and revolutionized the position of individual soldiers within it. In earlier centuries, Western armies mostly fought "shoulder-to-shoulder ... in tightly packed formations". Conspicuously dressed in colorful uniforms, "soldiers marched lockstep and loaded and discharged their weapons in unison" at an enemy who responded with like action.[42] Modern weapons increasingly rendered formal battle orders obsolete, not least because a mass of soldiers in formation was an obvious target. The alternative was to place "soldiers on the battlefield ... farther apart from one another than had been custom for most of recorded history".[43] Implementing such insights in appropriate tactics involved a prolonged seesawing between traditionalists and visionaries within almost any army that fought a war during the decades flanking 1900.[44]

The military historian John A. English calls "open-order tactics" the "decentralization of infantry".[45] Skirmishing, the most extreme form of such order, appealed as the best way to counter the effects of modern weaponry, but caused concerns regarding command and control of the more widely dispersed soldiers. More moderate tactical reforms tried to combine new and old methods. Regardless, most versions of open-order tactics shared certain characteristics. Among them was the re-organization of armies into smaller entities, especially at the bottom of the command hierarchy, where soldiers form small units. These now became even smaller and more numerous in order to gain greater flexibility for action. At the same time, battlefields expanded in width and depth. Strictly linear arrangement and densely packed single trenches at the front lines were superseded by staggered, overlapping, and widely-spaced lines, nodes, and positions for both defense

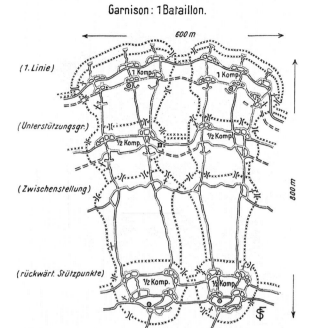

Garnison: 1 Bataillon.

600 m

(1. Linie)

1 Komp.

1 Komp.

(Unterstützungsgr.)

½ Komp.   ½ Komp.

(Zwischenstellung)

800 m

(rückwärt. Stützpunkte)

½ Komp.   ½ Komp.

Zeichen:

Feuergraben	eingedecktes Flankier. Geschütz
Scheingraben	Gefechtsunterstand d. Komp. Führers
Laufgraben	Gefechtsunterstand d. Batls. Führers
Laufgr. mit Schützenauftritt	Drahthindernisse
Laufgr. mit Schützenauftr. auf beid. Seiten	Lücken im Hindernis
Masch. Gewehr	Horchposten

Figure 4/ Beginnings of the extended, open order battlefield which in this example from Belloy, France, covers an area of 800 meters by 600 meters. Image from Friedrich Seeßelberg, *Der Stellungskrieg 1914–1918 auf Grund amtlicher Quellen und unter Mitwirkung namhafter Fachmänner technisch, taktisch und staatswissenschaftlich dargestellt*, Berlin: E. S. Mittler & Sohn, 1926, p. 221. Courtesy of E. S. Mittler & Sohn, Hamburg.

and attack, dispersing equipment and soldiers over a broader area and further apart within trenches in order to minimize losses [Figure 4].

Consequently, the modern battlefield became emptier, and soldiers had to learn to fight differently. They had to maneuver more, scan the landscape for even the slightest cover offered by topography and nature, crawl and hug the ground while moving forwards or backwards. All of these activities imposed close physical contact with nature.[46] To defend terrain required that soldiers be alone or in small groups in the foremost trenches, in hidden machine gun positions, or in shell holes that sometimes were converted into sophisticated tactical positions.[47] Once the German army had perfected their elastic defense, which was defined as thinly populated front lines that "temporarily evade the annihilating [artillery] fire — if possible by moving forward as far as the entanglements

— followed by a rapid attack by the reserves", small-scale attacks and raids were conducted in units of just a few soldiers (*Stoßtruppen*).[48] Moreover, elastic defense matched the fast-paced character of the space of the battlefield, as both gaining terrain and holding on to it were no longer ends in themselves but means to achieve larger strategic goals.

As previously noted, Neutra did not serve at the Western Front, one of the fiercest war theaters. Yet as contemporary sources point out, the war conducted in the mountainous regions of the Alps and the Western Mountain Barrier of the Balkans was second only to the Western Front with regard to the demands it put on soldiers.[49] War in a mountainous terrain spatially expanded the battlefield even more than on flat land, as the geological situation often only allowed for positions that were separated by distance and height, and foremost trenches that were just short, unconnected segments.[50] According to William Balck, German general lieutenant and author of studies of modern tactics,

Figure 5/ Austrian troops climbing a steep mountain during the Great War. Central News photograph. Image from Douglas Wilson Johnson, *Topography and Strategy in the War*, New York: Henry Holt, 1917, facing page 78.

mountain war was harder because it was both a struggle with the enemy and a "fight against nature". The latter was a consequence of the topography, the addition of height to distance, and the unpredictable swings of the weather. In addition, "troops had to learn a different way of ... breathing" as the geographical conditions forced soldiers to interact more intensely on a physio-psychological level with the environment [Figure 5].[51]

In short, the modern battlefield, especially the open order, demanded a new type of soldier. Mass psychology ensured the forward movement of shoulder-to-shoulder formations because individual soldiers could hide within the larger group that created the illusion of invisibility and invulnerability. The open order, however, required soldiers "who were self-reliant and selfless and possessed of both loyalty and initiative". In addition, they had to rapidly judge topographical, tactical, and other situations in order to adjust to fast-changing circumstances, even when cut off from the chain of command. These demands stood in sharp contrast to the sensibilities of emerging modern societies, since "men raised in the increasingly predictable and orderly environments of nineteenth-century towns and villages could not be expected to be at home on the empty battlefield".[52] For some individual soldiers, meanwhile, the latter may have constituted the ultimate modern space, surroundings in which they could experience themselves as individuals in an environment that was theirs to master.

UMWELT, THE ENVIRONMENT SURROUNDING HUMAN BEINGS

The new soldier in the open-order battlefield, Lewin traversing the landscape of war, and Neutra immersed in the mountains of Montenegro — they all employ a gaze radiating outward from a position central to their larger surroundings: their *Umwelt*. This German word combines the word '*Welt*' (world) with the prefix '*um*', which in this case signifies something that wraps around something else. Accordingly, *Umwelt* is the world that surrounds a subject or object at its center.

This *Umwelt* conception harks back to nineteenth-century psychology and biology. Early psychologists like Wilhelm Wundt, whose physio-psychology Neutra appreciated, were concerned with the physiological reactions of the human body to external stimuli. Thus a relationship between human beings and the environment was set up that placed the former at the center of the latter. A sketch in one of the books by physicist and philosopher Ernst Mach illustrates this nicely [Figure 6]. It shows a man whose gaze wanders outward from the eye,

Figur 1.

Figure 6/ Man surveying his *Umwelt*. From Ernst Mach, *Beiträge zur Analyse der Empfindungen*, Jena: Gustav Fischer, 1886, p. 14.

past the tip of his mustache, down his body, along his lower limbs, then across an interior filled with bookshelves, and, leaving the architectural space, through a window into the wider surroundings.[53] This human-centered worldview was confined neither to psychologists and physicists, nor, indeed, to German writers.

Already in the late 1870s, Thomas Huxley pointed out that to grasp the world required viewing it from the inside rather than looking at the globe from the outside, as if it were an object separate from the viewer.[54] A little over half a century later, philosopher Edmund Husserl argued that the earth is best comprehended by adding up impressions of the environment obtained by a series of individuals, each at the center of a smaller sliver of space bordered by that viewer's individual horizon.[55]

The most prominent formulation of such a view from the inside out onto the world came from Jakob von Uexküll, who coined the term *Umwelt* in order to distinguish it from *Umgebung* (surroundings).[56] Animal organisms, including human beings, exist in the same *Umgebung*, the objective world that surrounds them as 'a given', to paraphrase the German word. Within this larger entity, individual organisms live within their own *Umwelt*. This is subjective, as it is created in the interplay between the organism's needs — projected outwards into the environment via sensory organs — and the stimulations that the *Umwelt* provides for these organs. Sending signals and receiving stimuli are interactive acts, which bind organism and *Umwelt* in a feedback loop.[57]

Thus by the time Neutra studied architecture and served in the war, contemporary psychologists, scientists, and philosophers had envisioned *Umwelt* as a concept of space that was universal, even if non-Cartesian — and objective, even though based on subjective observations and perceptions. Most importantly, it did not confine individuals to abstract, geometrical space — comparable to the 'Vitruvian man' caught in a tight framework of circle and square — but envisioned them at the heart of a sensory environment.

Throughout his career, Neutra always emphasized the importance of a physiognomic reading of a landscape when pondering a site and a new design. This approach has roots in his fascination with the nexus between human perception and humans' physio-psychological responses to their surroundings, a legacy that harks back to his reading Wundt's *Grundzüge der physiologischen Psychologie* (*Principles of Physiological Psychology*) as a student.[58] As an architecture student, Neutra was spatially aware and perhaps pre-destined to enjoy a fine-grained perception of the environment. Yet the landscape of war made all of Neutra's preexisting knowledge about space tangible in a far more existential manner. Now he was forced to 'read' landscapes in order to survive.

FROM THE LANDSCAPE OF WAR TO THE OPEN ORDER OF THE KAUFMANN HOUSE

There are at least three 'defensive' attitudes towards the natural environment, presumably resulting from Neutra's experiences of the Great War, that reverberate through the spaces of the Kaufmann House. First, the environment of war was best mastered with an active approach that relied on human interventions into the landscape. Military installations, temporary and permanent, were inserted into the landscape in locations determined by strategy and tactics. If necessary, they were placed apart from each other, thus circumscribing the ground in-between as friendly, but contested territory. Second, nature was not benevolent. Instead, the existence of a soldier was intimately tied to a malevolent natural environment, even though that malevolence was to a significant degree human-induced rather than inherent. Third, self-preservation in the landscape of war, if anything other than accidental, required deliberate,

continuous, and close physio-psychological engagement with the environment, drawing on all senses in order to track changes in the terrain, weather, and other circumstances.

When Neutra arrived in California in early 1925, he was finally in a position to design his version of the utopian promises of architectural Modernism. He was closely acquainted with the visionary aspirations of the Modern Movement. From October 1920 onwards, he had lived and worked in Berlin, then one, if not *the* center for Modern architecture's drive to order anew the entire surroundings of contemporary society. Conceptually, projects from Neutra's early time in California continued that Modernist longing for a new, well-ordered world to be created by tackling the rational redesign of cities; proposing urban apartments, prefabricated housing, and social building types; and reinvigorating domestic architecture with structural and spatial innovations.[59] Neutra's experiments with the plans of houses were, however, still mostly confined within a tightly controlled volume.[60] Formally, horizontal windows and stucco bands, flat roofs, and structures and window frames made of steel dominated in his projects and thus contributed to the emerging language of international Modernist architecture. A good example from this period is the Miller House (1937), Neutra's first commission in Palm Springs. While large expanses of glass, a screen porch, and an adjacent reflecting pool open the house to views of the desert, the volume remains cubic and contained; in fact, the composition has been compared to Pueblo architecture.[61]

According to Esther McCoy, Neutra's California œuvre falls into two distinct periods. The first began around 1927, while the second dates to the design of the Nesbitt house in Los Angeles, on which Neutra worked from 1941 to 1942.[62] This period coincided with the Second World War, which (from an American perspective) had come much closer to home, especially to the West Coast, when Japanese forces attacked Pearl Harbor, Hawaii, on 7 December 1941, leading the US to enter the war the next day.

Neutra called the Nesbitt home a "war house" in which "life [was] reduced to simplicity".[63] Wartime rationing of building materials determined that brick and wood were used, which may have simplified the construction, yet the plan was anything but simple. Rather, with another world war menacing the US, Neutra's designs acquired a new complexity, which was innovative while harking back to his own experiences of the Great War.

The Nesbitt house achieved "a new kind of transparency" by juxtaposing a glass entrance with floor-to-ceiling windows on opposing sides of the same space [Figure 7].[64] Part of this openness was the arrangement of the interior spaces into pavilions — a larger one for the main living areas and a smaller one to serve as guest quarters or an office — which were connected by walkways under projecting roofs and pergolas but otherwise open to the surroundings.[65] The plan pulls

Figure 7/ Richard Neutra, Nesbitt House, Los Angeles, CA, 1941–1942. View of the main pavilion, seen from the garden side, the all-glass entrance into the house in the middle ground to the left. Reproduction courtesy of Dion Neutra, Architect ©. Photograph © J. Paul Getty Trust. Julius Shulman Photography Archive, Research Library at the Getty Research Institute (2004.R.10).

architecturally-defined rooms apart to form smaller units without creating two stand-alone buildings, and links these units with walkways. This distribution of the architectural components expanded the house's space in a manner comparable, though on a much smaller scale, to the Great War's transformation of ever larger slices of territory into potential battlegrounds through the dispersal of military installations and the use of further reaching weapon systems.

On an extended, open-order modern battlefield even an experienced soldier was at times hard pressed to precisely locate the dividing line between friendly and enemy territory. Similarly, at the Nesbitt house it is not easy to decide the exact line separating inside and outside, a task made more difficult by a brick wall that runs along the front of the main house

[Figure 8]. The wall, which has a low planter at its front, spans the distance between the pavilions, while open walkways on either side of it link them. The wall adds depth to the house's facade and its height evokes a breastwork underneath a sheltering roof overhang, like a fortification providing protection to one who fires over it from a standing position. Yet Neutra's intention was not to build houses that evoked military installations and shelter-like spaces. Rather, as the Kaufmann House illustrates, the goal was to offer safe homes in hostile environments.

Although built after the Second World War had ended, the Kaufmann House, too, was a product of the war, as building restrictions were still in place and about to be tightened when construction started.[66] The house continued

Figure 8/ Richard Neutra, Nesbitt House, Los Angeles, CA, 1941–1942. View of the front facade, with the brick wall linking the two pavilions on the left and the entrance into the main pavilion in the background to the left. Reproduction courtesy of Dion Neutra, Architect ©. Photograph © J. Paul Getty Trust. Julius Shulman Photography Archive, Research Library at the Getty Research Institute (2004.R.10).

the pavilion theme and transformed Neutra's "unusually relaxed" floor plans from the early 1940s into an open order arrangement, to borrow the military-historical term [Figure 9].[67] The pinwheel plan comprises four wings with the main entrance and adjacent garage, the servants' quarters, the guest rooms, and the master bedroom at their respective ends. An outlying small building for mechanical services extends the plan well past the master bedroom wing. And an additional pavilion sits on top of the main house, accommodating a sun- and lookout deck that was roofed over and partially shielded by vertical aluminum louvers.

The large living room with its fireplace appears to be the center of the house. Yet the architectural details counter the impression of a central hearth as a focus towards which both architecture and domestic life can gravitate (as they do, by contrast, in the open plan living quarters that Frank Lloyd Wright had designed from the turn of the century onwards). Instead, the reflections of the polished terrazzo floor in the Palm Springs house remind occupants that the house "*sat upon* the desert", and the visibly thin facing stone of the fireplace is too insubstantial in format and pattern to evoke protective coziness.[68] Neutra's plan merges traditional inside and outside spaces — and all transitions between the two — into a spatial continuum. Within that continuum, units of rooms like the guest rooms, built-in and freely distributed moveable furniture, and architectural and landscape objects like the swimming pool, a water channel, and outdoor terraces (equipped with underfloor heating and cooling) are arranged in a way that requires the occupants to maneuver around and between these elements when traversing the space.

Consequently, almost everywhere within the environment of the Kaufmann House, the occupant is placed into the open order of modern space without, however, being exposed to the dangers of the modern battlefield. Situating his subject into such an exposed, but now safe position might suggest that Neutra was re-enacting his own positions, and consequent need for prospect and refuge, in the dangerous landscapes of the Great War. Neutra was, however, more interested in the potential of the Kaufmann House as a prototype than in any therapeutic effect it might offer for past trauma. The house exemplified how "to extend the habitable area of the planet into places not yet inhabited and thus unendowed with any tradition of civilized design". Rather than being merely a masterpiece of regional Modernism, its intended reach was universal; Neutra projected that "there will be many other examples necessary in the jungles of the upper Amazonas [sic] or Congo, the Arctic regions, the arid sand wastes of Arabia."[69] Nonetheless, the language here of exploration, if not conquest, of unforgiving physical environments is inextricably linked to the notion of a 'malevolent nature' and, accordingly, reflects the second 'defensive' attitude gained by Neutra through his war experience.

When Neutra published *Wie baut Amerika?* (*How Does America Build?*) in 1927, the last image at the bottom of the final page shows "the primitive desert landscape to the north of the Oasis hotel in Palm Springs".[70] This desert photograph, which is similar to the one included in Figure 9, thus presents the Colorado Desert, one of the most challenging natural environments in California, as the ultimate destination of Modern architecture's efforts. If the camera had moved westward it would have captured the area where the spurs of Mount Jacinto meet the desert and where the Kaufmann House would later rise in a landscape visually recalling the Karst of the Balkans.

The Great War had introduced modern technology and buildings in the form of artillery gun positions, defensive structures, and other installations into the landscape. Whatever topographic and geographical circumstances the fighting armies faced in the mountains and valleys of the Alps and the Balkans, engineering skills could overcome them [Figure 10]. Friedrich Seeßelberg — architect, soldier on the Western front, and author of a 1926 study of the built environment of the battlefield — provides numerous examples of mountain tops and slopes reengineered according to military needs, including, for example, multi-story barracks for soldiers built into subterranean limestone caverns naturally occurring in the Karst.[71] Neutra's fascination with human settlements in hostile natural environments relied equally strongly on modern technology in order to overcome the challenges set by nature. Writing about the Kaufmann House, he states:

> A building is frankly and clearly an artefact [sic], a construct transported in many shop-fabricated parts over long distances into the midst of such rugged aridity. It is as little local as the much needed water which is piped to its site over many miles. The lawns and the blooming shrubs around this dwelling are imports just like its aluminum and plate glass.

Military installations tried to blend into the land, hoping that detection would be impossible or at least delayed; the modern house's relationship with its environment is more complex:

> A desert house cannot be 'rooted' in the soil to 'grow out of it' ... the building nevertheless fuses profoundly with its setting, partakes in its events, emphasizes its character. The structure exhibits no spectacular pseudo dynamics of its own, but with a serenity of truly human planning assimilates itself to the dynamics of the place from hot radiation to hectic sandstorms and the nightly cold under the starry sky.[72]

This quote invites another comparison with Frank Lloyd Wright, in particular with Fallingwater, the other Kaufmann House that, exemplifying an organic approach to architecture, nestles deeply into nature. The important difference between both houses is not their architecture but the concept of nature underlying their designs. Neutra does not mention nature in the quote above (or in the source text), indicating that the Kaufmann House and its setting were not conceived of holistically, in accordance with the transcendentalist concept of nature that informed the organic school of American architecture. Instead, Neutra references mostly factual environmental changes in temperature and air movement. This points to a view of nature as physical terrain upon which to site a building. Elsewhere, Neutra strengthens this impression: "Once upon a time the natural landscape had a face as familiar to man as that of his mate" — but this face had been threatened by human activities as soon as humans began changing the surface of the earth; civilization eventually destroyed it.[73] All that was left for individuals in the modern world was to read nature's physical, physiological, and physiognomic forms.[74] This approach made it possible to build in the most extreme landscapes, even on the moon with an environment formed in prehistoric time and which, in addition, had no cultural past to which architecture could refer.[75] Nature unencumbered by cultural references and memories thus leaves situational responses to sense stimuli originating from within a person's surroundings as the only

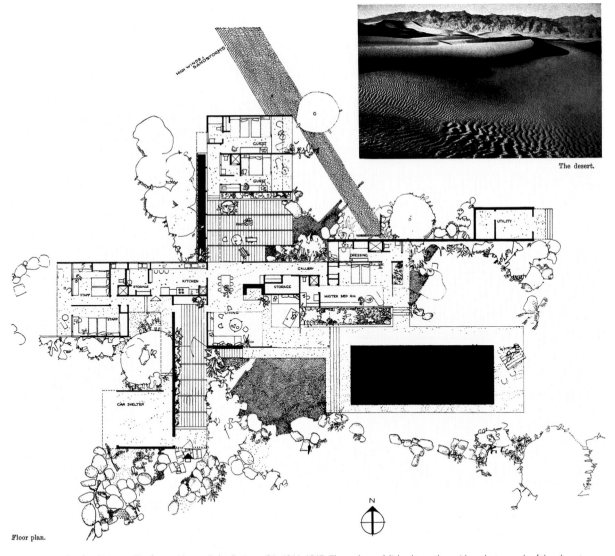

The desert.

Floor plan.

— Figure 9/ Richard Neutra, Kaufmann House, Palm Springs, CA, 1946–1947. Floor plan published together with a photograph of the desert —
similar to the one that Neutra included as the last illustration on the final page of *Wie baut Amerika?* (1927). From Richard Neutra, *Bauten und Projekte*, Zürich: Girsberger, 1955, p. 74. Reproduction courtesy of Dion Neutra, Architect ©.

means of comprehending the environment. This brings back physio-psychology, the third 'defensive' aspect of Neutra's experience of the Great War.

As Neutra explains in a section in *Survival Through Design*, mastering one's position in the open order of modern space was a deliberate act of physio-psychological interaction with the environment that comprised at least four stages.[76] Composed in the first person and relying on the language of perceptional psychology, the short passage is remarkable as it draws on events from the time of the Great War — apparently recalled by the Second World War, in the course of which the book was compiled — while envisioning how to negotiate a site in the design process in terms of a series of impulses and (re)actions.[77]

Neutra defines the first of these, the "*Orientation Response*", as readying himself for "acting to gain a position so that I can be fully aware of a particular event which I must face". Subsequently, he raises his head and body indicating that he might be surveying a dangerous situation, as when occupying a lonesome outpost surrounded by partisan fighters, while actually determining a site for a building. The following "*Defense Response*", offers two options, both involving structures. One is termed, "Escape"; some structure, perhaps a trench, has apparently collapsed, for Neutra ideally envisions himself "not surrounded by an obstructing enclosure or any other obstacles impeding escape". The other, "Protection", is more 'constructive'; in this case Neutra expresses the desire to be "well surrounded by an enclosure to shelter me safely". He next lists the "*Control Response*", which also involves alternatives. Here the architect, perhaps ultimately envisioning a well-laid-out, practically arranged modern interior, projects a circumstance in which "everything that I might want to use is handy", that "none of it seem to be out of reach". Yet the preceding sentence — "I desire ... to have full control of my limbs and of all objects or tools" — points equally to the moment when a soldier checks his own body for injuries after a blast. Finally, there is the "*Precision Response*", which continues the process of gaining increasing control of the environment, for Neutra has "succeeded in eliminating all vagueness, all blurred uncertainty from my sensuously accessible surroundings or from their impressions on me... everything ... is well in focus and defined".[78] These four 'responses' constitute a process that requires perpetual exchange between sensory stimulation and the corresponding reaction. Individual human beings thus exist at the center of an Uexküllian *Umwelt*, or as Neutra states elsewhere, "Man is always in the middle of something — this ineluctable presence, enveloping and permeating our lives, is called environment.... It determines who we are, how we feel and what our outlook is."[79]

Accordingly, the Kaufmann House is conceived as a human-made *Umwelt* providing a variety of spatial situations (enclosed, half-enclosed, open, covered, exposed, etc.) that place the occupant either inside, outside, or in transitional

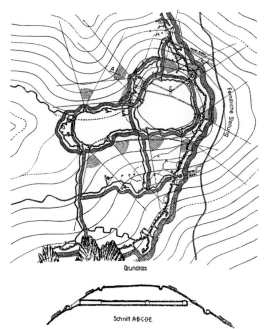

Figure 10/ Plan and section of a mountain top re-engineered into extended, open-order military installation above and below ground. Hatched bands indicate barbed wire, hatched angles show areas covered by machine guns. The enemy position is to the right of the continuous black line drawn from top to bottom. Image from Friedrich Seeßelberg, *Der Stellungskrieg 1914–1918 auf Grund amtlicher Quellen und unter Mitwirkung namhafter Fachmänner technisch, taktisch und staatswissenschaftlich dargestellt*, Berlin: E. S. Mittler & Sohn, 1926, p. 187. Courtesy of E. S. Mittler & Sohn, Hamburg.

zones. Within each setting, means of control (windows, curtains, aluminum louvers, heating and cooling elements in the terrace floors, water, etc.) offer numerous possibilities to vary the kind and degree of sense stimulation, depending on individual and environmental circumstances.[80] In one of the bathrooms off the master bedroom, for example, Neutra placed a mirror perpendicular to a large window above a low storage cabinet [Figure 11]. This put the inhabitant into a state of visual alertness when looking at a picture puzzle that oscillates between reflection and reality, while unconsciously also scanning the middle ground (or danger zone) surrounding the house (conceptually, one's 'military position').

Humans may have been placed at the center of the open order of modern space, yet they still required protection and isolation — as the interlocking metal gaskets of the guest room doors, with which this essay began, indicate. Further,

—— **Figure 11/** Richard Neutra, Kaufmann House, Palm Springs, CA, 1946–1947. View from one of the bathrooms adjacent to the master bedroom. ——
The mirror is on the right side of the image, the glass corner further beyond encloses the living room. Reproduction courtesy Dion Neutra, Architect
©. Photograph © J. Paul Getty Trust. Julius Shulman Photography Archive, Research Library at the Getty Research Institute (2004.R.10).

deep inside the Kaufmann House, Neutra provided for yet another, hidden shelter. Tucked away behind the other bathroom adjacent to the master bedroom, and accessible only through a small dressing area, is a private den. Located off the geometric middle of the plan, the room is nevertheless the center of house. It was fitted with a desk, a day bed, and, originally, a teletype machine with which Mr. Kaufmann conducted business remotely.[81]

Similar to the view of March's sketch of a man surveying his *Umwelt*, the room's sole window invites one to look over a sequence of indoor, outdoor, and transitional spaces [Figure 12]. Among them are, to the left, the living area with the door into the servants' quarter and the corner of the upstairs pavilion; straight ahead, the heated and covered terrace next to the guest rooms; and beyond the aluminum louvers and water channel in front of those rooms, the outdoor patio followed by the desert leading up to the mountain. Returning once more to the landscape of war, within the open-order floor plan this room recalls a dugout from where to strategically observe the one point where the highly differentiated environmental settings that the house offers most visibly intersect. The gaze from the little shelter onto that important junction is a permanent reminder that a person's survival at the center of his or her *Umwelt* requires constant caution and care.

The experiences of the Great War became an important source that, during the time of another world war, influenced Neutra's radical re-envisioning of Modern architecture. The open-order floor plan of the Kaufmann House gives a new meaning to the Modernist credo of designing from the inside out. Rather than outwardly expressing an inner essence or function of a building misunderstood as either an organism or a machine, Neutra designed from the perspective of a person at the center of his plans outward toward the latter's *Umwelt*. It would appear that the sudden emergence of the open plan in the aftermath of the Great War had closer links to many Modernist architects' firsthand experiences of the hostile landscapes of war and the open order of the modern battlefield than thus far known to us.

Figure 12/ Richard Neutra, Kaufmann House, Palm Springs, CA, 1946–1947. View from the den next to the master bedroom across the patio with aluminum louvers at the far end into the desert landscape and the mountains behind the house. From Richard Neutra, *Bauten und Projekte*, Zürich: Girsberger, 1955, p. 77. Reproduction courtesy Dion Neutra, Architect ©.

NOTES ─────────

1/ Many thanks to the owner of the Kaufmann house for making this visit possible.

2/ Neutra, Richard, "Landscaping — A New Issue", *Contemporary Landscape Architecture and its Sources*, exhibition catalogue, San Francisco: San Francisco Museum of Art, 1937, p. 21.

3/ See Johannes Stoffler, "Pflanzenverwendung auf Transatlantisch. Richard Neutra als Gartengestalter", *Topiaria Helvetica*, 2012, pp. 28–38. The quote is from page 29.

4/ In the context of the Great War and Modern architecture, historians have to date looked primarily at the importance of air warfare on Modern architecture's gaze at space and at architects who as pacifists resisted the war. The different experiences of those architects who

actively fought in the battlefields still await analysis. My focus on Neutra's participation in the war as one influence on his mid-twentieth-century architecture offers an exemplary case study of how the Great War may have shaped the development of the works of a Modern architect. See Christopher Asendorf, *Super Constellation. Flugzeug und Raumrevolution. Die Wirkung der Luftfahrt auf Kunst und Kultur der Moderne*, Vienna: Springer, 1997; David Leatherbarrow, *Uncommon Ground. Architecture, Technology, and Topography*, Cambridge, MA: MIT Press, 2000, chapter 1. Bruno Taut is a good example of the second category. See Iain Boyd Whyte, *Bruno Taut and the Architecture of Activism*, Cambridge: Cambridge University Press, 1982. Erich Mendelsohn is an exception. The importance of his wartime sketches for his post-war architecture is recognized, though little of his military service is known except for the different war time letters included in the German and English editions of selections of his correspondence. See Erich Mendelsohn, "Gedanken zur neuen Architektur [Im Feld 1914–17]", in "Erich Mendelsohn. Bauten und Skizzen", *Wasmuths Monatshefte für Baukunst*, vol. 8, 1924, p. 3; Oskar Beyer ed., *Briefe eines Architekten*, Munich: Prestel, 1961; Beyer, Oskar ed., *Eric Mendelsohn: letters of an architect*, Geoffrey Strachan trans., Nikolaus Pevsner intro., London: Abelard-Schuman, 1967.

5/ Neutra's peace time military service lasted from 1910 to 1911, his active war service from 1914–1918. He studied architecture from 1911–1912 to 1913–11914, and again 1917–1918 when he was on special leave. (Hines, Thomas S., *Richard Neutra and the Search for Modern*

Architecture, New York: Oxford University Press, 1982, p. 20). Scholarship on Neutra has argued for the important influences that he absorbed from both California and cognate disciplines. Most recently, the analytical focus has rested on Freudian psychoanalysis; other approaches concentrated on psychology and consumer culture, physio-psychology, the Southern Californian environment, and, especially in the earliest publications, nature in the most general sense. See for example: Sylvia Lavin, *Form Follows Libido. Architecture and Richard Neutra in a Psychoanalytic Culture*, Cambridge, MA: MIT Press, 2004; Todd Cronan, "'Danger in the Smallest Dose': Richard Neutra's Design Theory", *Design and Culture* 3, issue 2, 2011, pp. 165–182; Sandy Isenstadt, "Richard Neutra and the Psychology of Architectural Consumption", *Anxious Modernisms: Experimentation in Postwar Architectural Culture*, Sarah Williams Goldhagen and Réjèan Legault eds., Cambridge, MA: MIT Press, 2001, pp. 97–117; Leatherbarrow, *Uncommon Ground*, chapter 2; David Leatherbarrow, *Topographical Stories: Studies in Landscape and Architecture*, Philadelphia: University of Pennsylvania Press, 2004, chapters 2 and 3; Barbara Lamprecht, *Richard Neutra 1892–1970: Survival Through Design*, Cologne: Taschen, 2006; *L'Architecture d'aujourd'hui* 16, no. 6, May–June 1946, American Edition [special issue on Neutra]; Museu de Arte de São Paulo, Brasil, *Neutra Residências*, São Paulo: Todtman & Cia., 1951.

6/ Letter Hadtörténelmi Levéltár és Irattár (Hungarian War Archive), Budapest, Hungary, to author, 3 March 2011.

7/ Neutra, Richard, *Life and Shape* [1962], Los Angeles: Atara Press, 2009.

8/ Neutra, Richard, Diary, vol. 4, 1915–1916, Richard and Dion Neutra Papers, Department of Special Collections, Charles E. Young Research Library, University of California at Los Angeles. All translations from the Neutra diaries and other German language books are mine, except where otherwise noted.

9/ Hickey, Michael, *The First World War, Vol. 4, The Mediterranean Front 1914–1923*, New York: Routledge, 2003, p. 7.

10/ In 1914 Neutra was a *Kadett* with *Feldkanonenregiment* (FKR) Nr. 12; in 1916 *Leutnant der Reserve* with *Feldhaubitzenregiment* Nr. 31; in 1918 *Oberleutnant* with *Feldartillerieregiment* (FAR) Nr. 131, decorated with the *Karl-Truppen-Kreuz* and a *Bronzene Militärverdienstmedaille mit Schwertern*. Letter, Österreichisches Staatsarchiv, Abteilung Kriegsarchiv, Wien, to author, 17 February 2011. The three regiments were the same unit which was renumbered twice during re-organizations of the Austrian-Hungarian army. See Georg Sobička, *Gliederung und Entwicklung der Batterien der österreichisch-ungarischen Feld- und Gebirgsartillerie im Weltkriege 1914–1918*, Vienna: Karl Harbauer, 1920, p. 6.

11/ Letter Hadtörténelmi Levéltár és Irattár, Hungarian War Archive, Budapest, Hungary, to author, 3 March 2011. With regard to Neutra's medals see Johann Stolzer and Christian Steeb eds., *Österreichs Orden vom Mittelalter bis zur Gegenwart*, Graz: Akademische Druck u. Verlaganstalt, 1996, pp. 244–245, 238–240.

12/ Hines, *Neutra*, p. 25.

13/ Neutra, *Life*, p. 100.

14/ Neutra, *Life*, p. 106.

15/ Neutra, *Life*, pp. 109–115.

16/ Neutra, *Life*, p. 115.

17/ Neutra, Diary, vol. 4, 1915–1916, entries for 12/9/1915, 12/11/1915, 12/13/1915, pp. 1–3 (see note 8).

18/ Neutra, *Life*, p. 106.

19/ Neutra, *Life*, p. 107.

20/ Neutra, *Life*, p. 107.

21/ Friedrich, Immanuel, *Serbiens und Montenegros Untergang: ein Beitrag zur Geschichte des Weltkrieges*, Berlin: E. S. Mittler & Sohn, 1917, pp. 52–56, 65–69; Glaise-Horstenau, Edmund, ed., *Österreich-Ungarns letzter Krieg*, vol. III, *Das Kriegsjahr 1915 von der Einnahme von Brest-Litowsk bis zur Jahreswende*, Wien: Verlag der Militärwissenschaftlichen Mitteilungen, 1932, pp. 187–337.

22/ Friedrich, *Serbiens und Montenegros Untergang*, pp. 68–69.

23/ Glaise-Horstenau, Edmund, ed., *Österreich-Ungarns letzter Krieg*, vol. IV, *Das Kriegsjahr 1916, erster Teil: die Ereignisse von Jänner bis Ende Juli*, Wien: Verlag der Militärwissenschaftlichen Mitteilungen, 1933, p. 33.

24/ Neutra, Diary, vol. 4, 1915–1916, entries 1/8/1916 (p. 19), 1/12/1916 (p. 22), 1/5/1916 (p. 15), 1/26/1916 (p. 30); 1/30/1916 (p. 35) (see note 8).

25/ Neutra, Diary, vol. 4, 1915–1916, entries 1/2/1916 (pp. 9–10), 1/5/1916 (p. 13), 1/5/1916 (pp. 14–17) (see note 8).

26/ Neutra, Diary, vol. 4, 1915–1916, entries 1/8/1916, 10 am (p. 19), 1/8/1916, 6:45 pm (p. 20) (see note 8).

27/ Neutra, Diary, vol. 4, 1915–1916, entries 1/30/1916 (pp. 35–40), 2/1/1916 (pp 40–44) (see note 8).

28/ Neutra, Diary, vol. 4, 1915–1916, entries 1/30/1916 (p. 37) (see note 8).

29/ Neutra, Diary, vol. 2, 1912–1917, pp. 124–125 (see note 8).

30/ The later journey included visits to places which Neutra would see again as a soldier, for example Ragusa, Gravosa, and Cattaro.

31/ Neutra, Diary, vol. 4, 1915–1916, entry 2/7/1916 (pp. 48–49) (see note 8).

32/ Neutra, Diary, vol. 4, 1915–1916, entry 2/7/1916 (p. 49) (see note 8), translation from Hines, *Neutra*, p. 25.

33/ For example, Hines, *Neutra*, p. 25.

34/ Neutra, Diary, vol. 4, 1915–1916, entries 1/26/1916 (pp. 31–32), 1/31/1916 (pp. 39–40), 2/1/1916 (pp. 40–41) (see note 8).

35/ For an environmental history of the Great War, see William Kelleher Storey, *The First World War: A Concise Global History*, Plymouth, UK: Rowman & Littlefield, 2009.

36/ Lewin, Kurt, "The Landscape of War" [1917], Jonathan Blower trans., Volker M. Welter intro., *Art in Translation*, vol.1, issue 2, 2009, p. 201, italics in original.

37/ English, John A., and Bruce I. Gudmundsson, *On Infantry*, rev. ed., Westport, CT: Praeger, 1994, pp. 26–27.

38/ Lewin, "Landscape", pp. 201–202.

39/ Lewin, "Landscape", pp. 201–202, italics in original.

40/ Lewin, "Landscape", p. 202.

41/ English and Gudmundsson, *Infantry*, p. 1; and William Balck, *Entwickelung der Taktik im Weltkriege*, second ed., Berlin: R. Eisenschmidt, 1922, p. 120; English and Gudmundsson, *Infantry*, chapters 1–2. The following relies also on John A. English, *A Perspective on Infantry*, New York: Praeger, 1981.

42/ Xerxa, Donald A., "*Enduring Battle*: An Interview with Christopher H. Hamner", *Historically Speaking*, vol. 13, January 2012, p. 12.

43/ English and Gudmundsson, *Infantry*, p. 1.

44/ Balck, *Taktik*, p. 8. English and Gudmundsson, *Infantry*, p. 3.

45/ English, *Perspective*, p. 4; chapter 1 "An Epoch-Making Change. The Decentralization of Infantry Tactics", pp. 1–36.

46/ Balck, *Taktik*, pp. 9, 52–53.

47/ Seeßelberg, Friedrich, *Der Stellungskrieg 1914–1918 auf Grund amtlicher Quellen und unter Mitwirkung namhafter Fachmänner technisch, taktisch und staatswissenschaftlich dargestellt*, Berlin: E. S. Mittler & Sohn, 1926, pp. 173–181.

48/ Balck, *Taktik*, p. 120, also English and Gudmundsson, *Infantry*, p. 21.

49/ Balck, *Taktik*, pp. 164–172; Seeßelberg, *Stellungskrieg*, pp. 183–197; Johnson, Douglas Wilson, *Topography and Strategy in the War*, New York: Henry Holt, 1917, pp. 144–176; Johnson, Douglas Wilson, *Battlefields of the World War: Western and Southern Fronts. A Study in Military Geography*, New York: Oxford University Press, 1921, pp. 605–632.

50/ Seeßelberg, *Stellungskrieg*, pp. 185–186.

51/ Balck, *Taktik*, p. 165.

52/ English and Gudmundsson, *Infantry*, p. 21.

53/ Mach, Ernst, *Contributions to the Analysis of Sensations*, C. M. Williams trans., Chicago: Open Court Publishing, 1897, p. 16.

54/ Huxley, Thomas H., *Physiography: An Introduction to the Study of Nature*, New York: D. Appleton, 1878, p. vii.

55/ Husserl, Edmud, "Foundational Investigations of the Phenomenological Origin of the Spatiality of Nature: The Originary Ark, the Earth, Does not Move", Fred Kersten trans., Leonard Lawlor rev., *Husserl at the Limits of Phenomenology. Including Texts by Edmund Husserl*, Maurice Merleau-Ponty ed., Evanston, IL: Northwestern University Press, 2002, pp. 117–118.

56/ In the following I rely on Brett Buchanan, *Onto-Ethologies. The Animal Environments of Uexküll, Heidegger, Merleau-Ponty, and Deleuze*, New York: SUNY Press, 2008, pp. 21–28.

57/ Uexküll, Jakob von, *Theoretische Biologie*, Berlin: J. Springer, 1928, second ed., p. 228.

58/ Wundt, Wilhelm, *Grundzüge der physiologischen Psychologie*, Leipzig: Wilhelm Engelmann, 1874.

59/ For example: Rush City Reformed, 1925–1930; Jardinette Apartments, Los Angeles, 1927; Diatom Series, 1925–1930; Corona School, Bell, CA, 1935; Lovell Health House, Los Angeles, 1927–1929; VDL Research House, Los Angeles, 1932.

60/ McCoy, Esther, *Richard Neutra*, New York: George Braziller, 1960, p. 13.

61/ Lamprecht, *Neutra*, p. 44.

62/ McCoy, *Neutra*, pp. 12, 16.

63/ Neutra in Lamprecht, *Neutra*, p. 51.

64/ McCoy, *Neutra*, p. 16.

65/ McCoy, *Neutra*, p. 16.

66/ Hines, *Neutra*, p. 201.

67/ McCoy, *Neutra*, p. 13.

68/ Hines, *Neutra*, p. 205.

69/ "Desert House Richard Neutra architect", *Arts & Architecture*, vol. 66, no. 7, June 1949, p. 30.

70/ Neutra, Richard, *Wie baut Amerika?*, Stuttgart: Julius Hoffmann, 1927, p. 77.

71/ Seeßelberg, *Stellungskrieg*, pp. 183–197.

72/ "Desert House Richard Neutra architect", p. 32.

73/ Neutra, Richard, *Mystery and Realities of the Site*, Scarsdale, NY: Morgan & Morgan, 1951, p. 9.

74/ Neutra, *Mystery*, pp. 9–12.

75/ Neutra, *Mystery*, p. 8.

76/ Neutra, Richard, *Survival Through Design*, New York: Oxford University Press, 1954, p. 332.

77/ Hines, *Neutra*, pp. 193–194.

78/ Neutra, *Survival*, p. 332, italics in original.

79/ Marlin, William ed., *Nature Near, Late Essays of Richard Neutra*, Santa Barbara: Capra Press, 1989, p. 5

80/ Leatherbarrow discusses the "thermal passage" of humidity and temperature inside and outside of Neutra's buildings. See Leatherbarrow, *Topographical Stories*, pp. 103–106.

81/ Boesiger, W., ed., *Richard Neutra, Buildings and Projects*, Zurich: Girsberger, 1955, p. 77.

234 /DONALD DUNHAM

THE GOOD ARCHITECT?

*The good architect awakens early in the day to determine
the position of the rising sun. From this observation
and subsequent observations throughout the day, the
week, the month, and then the year, the good architect
has a working knowledge of the sun's position in the sky.
Passive solar design is, of course, one of the fundamental
guiding principles for the making of all good buildings:
it ensures an economical and ample source of daylight,
as well as heat from the sun on a cold day and shade from
the sun on a hot day. After all, aren't good buildings
what the good architect seeks?*[1]

*What's more important, the house we build or the tree
from which it came?*

THE DYSTOPIAN GARDEN?

The image stays in your mind: human beings clamber over
and through a mountain of trash. They are extremely focused
and busy, all seemingly part of a group identified by their
fluorescent green safety vests [Figure 1]. On closer inspection,
they are picking through garbage with deliberative speed and
placing their finds into large sacks. Scavenging birds circle
just above their heads. The noise of heavy machinery used to
compact and spread out the trash in the landfill can be heard,
but no odor is perceived. We are voyeurs at a safe distance —
we are watching Lucy Walker's award-winning, Oscar-nominated,
2010 documentary *Waste Land*. The film was shot in the one
of the world's largest open-air landfills, Jardim Gramacho in
the city of Duque de Caxias, on the outskirts of Rio de Janeiro.[2]
Over a three-year period, Walker documented artist Vik Muniz
as he photographed the Jardim Gramacho waste pickers or
catadores. The *catadores* are highly organized and efficient
professional collectors of recyclables, each specializing in a
particular material. With the pickers' permission and help,
Muniz creates their portraits on the floor of his studio at
a monumental scale, using recycled objects from Jardim
Gramacho. Then he captures the resultant assemblage in
a photograph. The film follows Muniz and Tião, one of the
catadores, to London where the photographs are exhibited
and auctioned; the substantial sum of money made from the
sale of the artworks is given to the *catadores* with the hope
of improving their lives and the community surrounding
Jardim Gramacho.

How strange that a landscape filled with human
flotsam and jetsam, no longer wanted or useful, would be
described as a *jardim* — a garden. Perhaps this appellation
reflects the 'garden's' shifting topographical and kaleidoscopic
beauty or the fact that Jardim Gramacho was established in the
1970s on the site of a former natural garden, an ecologically-
sensitive wetland near Brazil's Guanabara Bay. More likely
it was the locals' satiric way of turning an ecological and
neighborhood catastrophe into a bearable (and somewhat
profitable — at least for the professional recyclers and their
families) way to cope with the smells and pollution as well as
the community's proximal association with a public dump.
But like all gardens, Jardim Gramacho was inherently ephemeral,
and its life as a depository of material culture would come to
an end. Environmental concerns regarding waste contamination
forced Jardim Gramacho to close in June 2012 after 34 years
as a vast receptacle for consumer excess: over 300 acres
comprising 12 layers of detritus, each measuring about 15 feet
deep. Plans now call for methane gas to be harvested from the

Figure 1/ The Jardim Gramacho gardeners hard at work.
Photograph by Fabio Ghivelder, courtesy of Vik Muniz Studio.

Figure 2/ The Barcelona Pavilion replica. A new Dawn. Photographs by Donald Dunham.

estimated 60 million tons of trash and converted into energy. Interestingly, the *catadores* prolonged the life of the landfill by removing materials that ultimately would have filled Jardim Gramacho to capacity much sooner. Ironically enough, when the methane supply is exhausted, Jardim Gramacho will be turned into a park.[3]

LESS EXCESS?

Build, Baby, Build![4]

Buildings account for 39% of CO_2 emissions in the United States. Buildings consume 72% of the electricity load in the US. 15 million new buildings [in the U.S.] are projected to be constructed by 2015.[5]

The average diameter of the American-manufactured dinner plate has increased by almost 23%, from 9.6 inches to 11.8 inches since 1900.[6]

In 1928, German architect Mies van der Rohe won the commission to design the German National Pavilion for the 1929 Barcelona International Exposition. The actual building was seen in the flesh by very few people; most were exposed to it only through photographs and plan, until a replica was completed in 1986 [Figure 2].[7] More than just a political stage set for the extremely frangible Weimar Republic, the Pavilion was the physical manifestation of Modernism. After Frank Lloyd Wright's Fallingwater in Western Pennsylvania, the Barcelona Pavilion is arguably the most influential twentieth-century Modernist 'house', even though it was never a home. In the Pavilion, transparency abounds, as does the material lushness of opaque walls that modulate a dialogue between gridded space and structure. Two horizontal planes in an established hierarchy of dominance cantilever dramatically at every opportunity and are linked by a common wall. Two rectangular water gardens of different dimensions

and proportions, one internal, one external, balance the structure's asymmetrical plan. The building is open, having no conventional doors, and is largely empty save for a large rug and several 'Barcelona' chairs, ottomans, and tables. There is no other furniture. The architecture's sole humanizing presence, a figurative piece by sculptor Georg Kolbe titled *Alba* (Dawn), is placed in a corner of the smaller, interior water court [Figure 2]. A great deal has been written about the Barcelona Pavilion — a remarkable thing for a simple architectural gesture that opened 26 May 1929 and closed upon the conclusion of the Exposition less than a year later, on 15 January 1930.[8] Shortly thereafter, the Pavilion was dismantled and the building's salvageable materials were shipped back to Germany to be either incorporated into other buildings or lost. Only the foundation, and the indelible imaginal imprint of the building's aesthetic, would remain. The replica would be built directly upon the ghost of the original building.

Mention of Mies van der Rohe generally conjures the saying "less is more". Although he may never actually have uttered these words, it is certainly the case that beginning with the Wolf House in Gubin, Germany (built 1925–1927) his work, exhibited an architectural expression that could only be described as sparing.[9] The Wolf House, though more of a volumetric exercise than the planar, visually agile Barcelona Pavilion, suggests a stylistic direction in architecture that is entirely about visual and tectonic economy. Mies did not invent this language; humans have a long history of mechanical ingenuity and economy (think lever, wheel, axle/cantilever, arch, dome). But the early twentieth century was ripe with architectural inventions that enabled engineering and architecture to find new economies based on the function of form, and Mies was one of the premier practitioners of this economic architecture.

However, the best exemplification of genuine architectural economy may be the work of the less known German architect Konrad Wachsmann (1901–1980).[10] Wachsmann began his career as an apprentice cabinetmaker

Figure 3/ Zygodactylous: Wachsmann's super-hangar. Image courtesy of the Akademie der Künste, Berlin, Konrad-Wachsmann-Archiv. Photograph by Harry Callahan.

before studying at the arts-and-crafts schools of Berlin and Dresden and at the Berlin Academy of Arts. In 1929, working for timber-frame housing manufacturer Unamck Prefabricated Building Company, Wachsmann would design a modest summer house in Caputh, Brandenburg, Germany, for Albert Einstein. The acclaim that Wachsmann gleaned from this commission afforded him the opportunity to become self-employed as an architect. In 1938, with the help of Einstein, Wachsmann emigrated to the United States, where together with fellow German expat and friend Walter Gropius, he designed an industrialized prefabricated housing system, the "Packaged House".[11]

The design of the unassertive but very livable Packaged House was based on a standardized system of panels, each about 40 inches wide and 100 inches high. Yielding very little waste in production, the all-wood Douglas Fir 'sandwich' panels formed walls, floor, ceiling, and roof. What was particularly unique, however, was the panel-joining system that Wachsmann developed: complex yet simple-to-use X-shaped wedge connectors locked the panels together without nails, screws, or bolts. This system, which Wachsmann would patent in 1942 after he and Gropius had cordially dissolved their collaboration, was a precise and ingenious technological solution that allowed for great economy in terms of material savings and construction time, as well as the possibility of an endless variation of plan configurations. Eager to test the Packaged House concept,

Wachsmann formed the General Panel Corporation in 1941. The company would build a full-scale prototype in 1943 in Somerville, Massachusetts, before being acquired by the Celotex Corporation in 1946 and moving to Burbank, California. General Panel would produce about 200 houses total from the factory in Southern California — formerly a Lockheed aircraft plant for fighter jets — before going bankrupt in 1952.

Differing views on technology may have contributed to the split between Wachsmann and Gropius. Gropius, founder of the Bauhaus and one of the major forces of the 'International Style', was a longtime figure in the lingering debate about the dominance of art or technology in the making of architecture. While Wachsmann saw technology, not art, as architecture's guiding principle, Gropius advocated an inseparable union between the two. Accordingly, the work of the two architects that followed their collaboration on the Packaged House proceeded in entirely different directions. In 1939–1940 Gropius, together with Marcel Breuer, would design the Frank House, a work that could be described as the polar opposite of the Packaged House. Here the richness of material in form and texture describes a shift away from the 1926 building that Gropius had designed for the Bauhaus School in Dessau, Germany, which was a far purer expression of architecture *as* technology. The Frank House, by contrast, is a humanizing effort to soften the notions of machine-made or machine-like design. Consequently, it is everything the Packaged House is not: an expensive display of material, form, and excess. Multiple levels of indoor and outdoor living space include 13 bathrooms and an indoor swimming pool; the floor plan, totaling 17,000 square feet, is almost 17 times larger than the three-bedroom standard Packaged House. The Frank House is a poignant expression of form (and excess!) that dominates the manicured landscape in which it is sited. Here, object trumps its frame. This grandiose shift away from a correspondence between art, technology, and context, has largely defined the residential building industry, especially in the United States to the present day.[12]

Gropius and Breuer would go on to have distinguished careers in the United States, both as professors at Harvard University's Graduate School of Design and as architects. In their final design collaboration, they set new standards for federal housing design with the Aluminum City Terrace, a modest Alcoa Aluminum factory workers' housing project in New Kensington, Pennsylvania. Unlike the Frank House, Aluminum City was closely aligned with the utopian social tenets of Modernism. Their later work — including Breuer's expressive Whitney Museum and Gropius's projects as principal and mentor of The Architects' Collaborative (TAC) — remained for the most part Modern in style, but lacking the Modernist social agenda.

Wachsmann, after the failure of the Packaged House enterprise, accepted a position at the Illinois Institute of Technology (IIT) in Chicago from 1949 to 1964. He then returned to the Los Angeles area as director of the Building Institute of the University of Southern California from 1964 to 1974. The work that Wachsmann produced during these periods of academic support is of greatest interest, less for its technological flamboyance and rigor than for the sheer minimalism of the composition that ultimately informs the relationship between object and landscape. This work offers a paradigm for the recession of architecture into more environmentally responsible, elegant, and less physically dominant forms.

Mies and others had paved the way for architects to think about mechanisms by which to pare down spatial delineation visually (e.g. planarity, transparency, and stereotomy and filigree). Wachsmann not only went further with tectonic and visual play, but — in a vanishing act of supreme indifference to the still intact International Style — pursued form through pure technology. Between 1950 and 1953, Wachsmann had designed a system for constructing large aircraft hangars with prefabricated components for the US Air Force, which needed service hangars for its B-52 aircraft [Figure 3]. These space-frame megastructures, which were never built, recall great nineteenth-century ironworks such as the Forth Bridge (1882–1889) near Edinburgh, Scotland, by Sir Benjamin Baker; C.-L.-F. Dutert's Galerie des Machines, Paris (1889); and countless monumental train sheds such as London's St Pancras Station (1863–1876). However, unlike these more grounded works,

Wachsmann's epic shed appears to float, blurring the boundaries between landscape, horizon, sky, and building. This project undoubtedly informed Tomoo Fukuda, Koji Kamiya, and Kenzo Tange's 1970 Festival Plaza at Expo '70, in Osaka, Japan. At the invitation of Tange, Wachsmann organized a 1955 seminar in Tokyo which would result in the design of a light-weight space frame structure — unclothed, a dead-ringer for Festival Plaza, and clothed, eerily reminiscent of Mies van Rohe's 1956 Crown Hall at IIT.[13] Notable beyond the lightness of structure, reminiscent of Gustave Eiffel's trussed bridges and Paris tower, is the gentle manner in which Wachsmann's aircraft hangar engages the earth itself. Photographs and drawings of the model show groupings of bird-like zygodactyl feet, clearly too small for the massive wing-like structure that hovers above — yet somehow they manage to convincingly support the hangar's filigree 'skeleton'.

Of course, Wachsmann was not working in a vacuum; as director of architecture at IIT, Mies certainly had a major influence on Wachsmann's long-span work. Large "universal space" projects had consumed Mies, beginning in 1939 with his designs for the Armour Institute of Technology (AIT) campus plan.[14] In his theoretical projects, however, Wachsmann was able to transcend Mies' desire to incorporate architectural materiality into the clear-span armature by focusing on pure structural form. Also during this time, Wachsmann became consumed with even more serious structural economy in the form of a single, universal structural element that "could be used in building construction for every conceivable purpose".[15] The result, a three-legged 'wishbone-like' member called "Grapevine", potentially could reduce a building's mass and layered architectonic complexity to almost unheard of dimensions [Figure 4].

But it was one of Wachsmann's last works, the unbuilt California City Civic Center, 1966–1970, that exemplified the greatest degree of architectural minimalism. Here 'less' became less and less and less [Figure 5]. The proposed building in California's Mojave Desert, 65 miles from Death Valley, demonstrates less material, less structural and architectural contact with the ground, and less visual competition with the landscape, all the while maintaining a commanding yet unselfish presence. One of the earliest Modernist land-form prototypes, the California City Civic Center comprises a roof membrane of paper-thin dimensions, suspended by a series of high-tension cables and trusswork; there are no vertical supports apart from the bermed cable abutments 16 feet beyond the roof edge. Imagine the Barcelona Pavilion without walls or columns, with only the thin horizontal roof plane remaining. At California City, the roof provides shade while allowing cooling desert winds to pass under its cover; the Civic Center's enclosed spaces are set below the ground surface level, helping to moderate air temperatures for the comfort of the building's users. Hereby, the desert landscape surrounding the

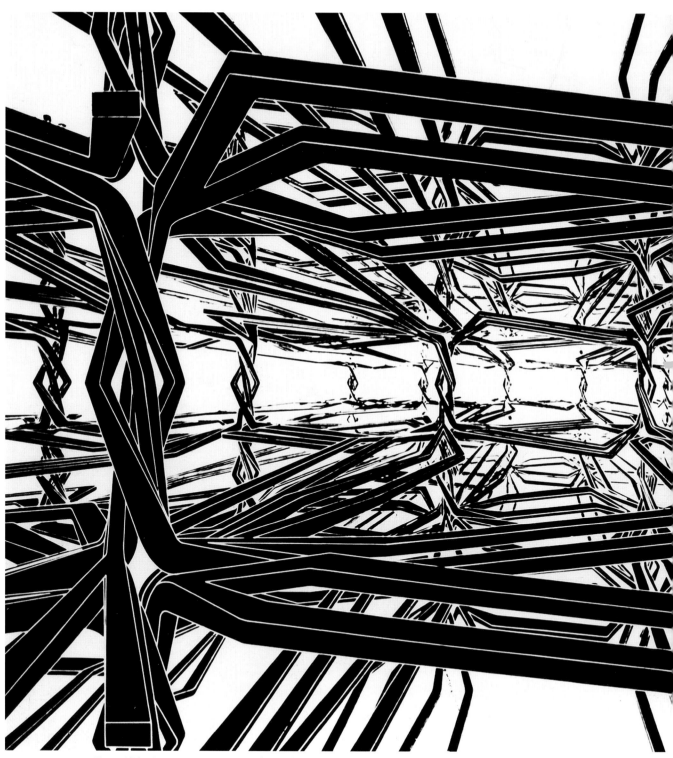

Figure 4/ The Grapevine: no connectors along with serious structural, architectural, and material economy.
Image courtesy of the Akademie der Künste, Berlin, Konrad-Wachsmann-Archiv.

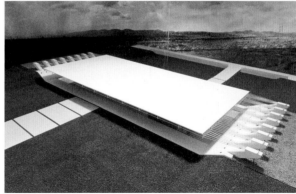

Figure 5/ California City Civic Center.
The CCCC has no supporting columns or walls. Image courtesy of
the Akademie der Künste, Berlin, Konrad-Wachsmann-Archiv.

Civic Center assumes visual control, and unlike Frank Lloyd
Wright's Falling Water, the structure allows the natural garden
to dominate completely. While certainly an overwhelming
display of virtuoso techno-play on Wachsmann's part, this is
genuine architectural cultivation, entirely unaffected by the
style of excess.

A CLUMSY PARADOX?

*Perhaps we may like our city just as it is. We may even
like the slums.*[16]

*The city is in trouble. What can save it, architecture
or trees?*

Don't worry. Be happy.[17]

The city has long been humans' answer to the problem of how
best to live, but it is a fragile construct. Based on complex and
varying social arrangements as well as the often transitory
three-dimensional infrastructural and architectural assemblies
that provide comfort and shelter, the city exists through sheer
human willpower. But as a method of organizing human
socio-spatial meanderings, the city has proven more robust,
more versatile, and more intriguing than alternative living
arrangements in managing large populations and their incumbent
economies. As early as the ancient Greek *polis*, a walled center
provided an 'ideal' harbor for a population apprehensive of
'wild Nature' — that which lies beyond the enclosure — while at
the same time attempting to dominate that which was feared.[18]
There, the center of the city-state featured the *agora*, the
market place and civic center, and the temple. As a Western

urban planning paradigm, the *polis* has endured through the Medieval city and into the present. Once architects discovered structural engineering and the benefits of the steel frame in the nineteenth century, the city was able to develop building density more radically in its center, the place of maximum economic profit. But the modern counterpart of the *polis* has become a capitalist engineering showcase that is less about ideal living and more about working to support heavily branded profit-driven enterprises and their attendant lack of largesse.

The great arched, domed, and buttressed structures built in the last 2,000 years employed structural technology that is still in use today. But the limited technology employed to build them often made their erection require a century or more of labor. Eventually, a city's center might offer one or two visible landmarks to the horizon, while a more modest center of commerce would complement the epicenter. Ultimately, the city would expand from its core, spilling beyond its defensive walls and no longer able to fit within these walls without building vertically. Vertical building was always a luxury few could afford. The tallest of the great Gothic churches at 530 feet, Ulmer Münster began construction in 1377 and was not completed until 513 years later in 1890. But the Eiffel Tower, completed in 1889, which reached a height of just over 1,000 feet, took only 26 months to build. The Empire State Building in New York City, completed in 1931, was Earth's tallest, human-made freestanding structure for almost 40 years: its construction took just under 15 months.

Here lies the problem: while the typical, rapidly-growing city may contain an assemblage of interesting structures and urban spaces, it is not sustainable. Reaching well beyond the historical center, the city is too large and too wasteful, proudly and unashamedly sitting upon Earth's terrain like a gaudy tablecloth spread over a beautiful table surface that is rich with the history of its use — stained, scratched, and uneven. Radiating out beyond the center, the usual urban problems abound: declining public schools, decaying housing stock, infrastructural deterioration, crime, racial and social divisiveness, limited food access, lack of open space, poor air quality, traffic congestion, and anything and everything else. The suburb, the standard escape from the city, will soon be engulfed by it, but the city's critics have yet to provide a reasonable alternative. Numerous visionary strategies for alleviating current urban difficulties have been proposed — for example Buckminster Fuller's 1965 redux of the Great Pyramids, *Tetrahedral City*; Superstudio's 1969 piece, *Continuous Monument*; Paolo Soleri's call to "miniaturize or die"; and the more recent proposals that these have spawned. But the city remains an unsustainable Ancient/Medieval strategy for human survival — at least for surviving 'well'.[19] In fact, Stanford Kwinter suggests, "although the city has disappeared, it is nevertheless here to stay — a clumsy paradox".[20]

This is not to say that visionary proposals will not provide actual blueprints from which to build additions or renovations to existing cities or new plans for hopelessly 'sinking' cities like New Orleans. The members of MVRDV, a Dutch urban research-oriented architectural practice, have for some time advocated new city strategies; their motivation is not in thrill-seeking forms or plan geometries but rather a genuine desire to save their own sinking homeland. Their thesis, FARMAX, proposes to "[compress] a population vertically and horizontally so as to give that population more space".[21] In zoning lingo, FAR is shorthand for 'floor area ratio', i.e. the ratio

Figure 6/ Aqua Tower. Dense urban living for those who can afford it and are not afraid of heights. Photograph by Donald Dunham.

of the total floor area of a building to the size of the land or parcel on which the building is built. In most cities, the FAR varies, but is highly regulated, limiting building floor area via limits to height and building bulk as well as setback requirements to insure population density control, daylight access for adjoining properties, or aesthetic conformity. MVRDV believes that all of these considerations can be successfully addressed if the FAR is pushed to the MAX or maximum; in other words, bigger, taller, more dense buildings able to accommodate more people on a given piece of ground.

  FARMAX also means more sustainable and energy-efficient structures. It is no secret that larger buildings within the city grid require less external infrastructure. A development of a thousand suburban houses requires miles of streets; miles of water supply, energy, telecommunication, and sewer lines; acres of impervious surfaces that contribute to stormwater runoff; and transportation systems (the car being primary) to move the population to jobs, schools, and recreation areas. Compare this with a typical urban high-rise residential structure such as the Aqua Tower, an 82-story, mixed-use, residential skyscraper in downtown Chicago, Illinois [Figure 6]. Designed by architect Jeanne Gang, this building occupies roughly one city block and includes restaurants, a large convenience store, gardens, gazebos, swimming pools, and a running track. With nearly 1,000 residential units comprising apartments, condominiums, and hotel rooms, the building's population rivals that of a suburban or even urban residential community, all in the space of one block. Unfortunately, these prototypes are available only to those who can afford to live in them.

  Furthermore, such high-rise schemes still bear the stigma of numerous twentieth-century failures. The difficulty of social interactions, the lack of ground-level urban amenities, distance from parks or other open spaces, and the casting of large shadows have all contributed to a knee-jerk reaction against the idea of placing communities, neighborhoods, and families hundreds of feet above the Earth's surface. J. G. Ballard's 1975 novel *High-Rise* reinforces this notion of the inhumanity of living stacked one upon another, upon another.[22] Playing on conventional fears of high-rise communities, Ballard envisions the worst: both the building and the residents' fragile social contracts begin to deteriorate, and the whole becomes a nightmarish dystopia. By contrast, in *The Death and Life of Great American Cities* (1961), Jane Jacobs successfully argued in defense of dense, mixed-use urban neighborhoods, as opposed to a more horizontal low-density suburban model.[23] For Jacobs, the culprit is not density but rather the form and resulting social arrangements of urban renewal policies of the mid-twentieth century, which devastated long-standing neighborhoods and generated barren and foreboding urban spaces.

  Despite the fact that many high-rise residential buildings continue to be built in the antiquated mold of their twentieth-century urban prototypes — some more successful

— Figure 7/ Personal freedom, diversity, flexibility, and neighborhoods: Torre Huerta Sociopolis, vertical village, MVRDV. Dense urban living for everyone else (and not afraid of heights). Image courtesy of MVRDV.

than others, with success usually calibrated by the relative affluence of the residents — architects like MVRDV see a new version of high-rise, high-density living as the only way forward. With FARMAX as a manifesto, MVRDV and their academic think-tank The Why Factory go much further than Aqua Tower or other urban residential towers. In fact, rather than appeal to the traditional forces that dominate the crafting of the built environment, MVRDV markets to a broader audience in the hope of having their message heard. Recognizing the failure of massive tower blocks characterized by repetitive International-style facades and lifeless floor plans, MVRDV proposes a "Block Attack": "vertical villages", places that promote "personal freedom, diversity, flexibility and neighborhoods" [Figure 7].[24]

  It would be silly to assume that the city as we know it can continue as a model urban planning typology able to serve the needs of the world's emerging populations. Information technology, service systems, and transportation innovations are rapidly making the city a relic in its own time. The city is dying as it transforms into a new form; in an act of autocannibalism, the new city is a new place defined not by a name but by its multitude of brands. Deyan Sudjic describes this dying/new city as a "100 mile" city where many cities are now connected to other cities that are themselves connected to others; these 100-mile human encampments encompass geographically expansive areas populated by 10, 20, 30, or more millions of people.[25] Los Angeles, for instance, is defined not as a particular place by its historical center but rather as a complex array of interlinked systems. The question, "where are you going?", is now answered by: http://disneyworld.disney.go.com/wdw/special/flashPages/index?id=GoogleEarthPage ("I'm gonna go to Disney World!").[26]

  In the rethinking of cities, perhaps no architect has embraced popular culture(s) so actively as another Dutch architect, Rem Koolhaas, and his firm, the Office for Metropolitan Architecture (OMA). Koolhaas and his Harvard University think-tank, Project on the City, have adopted a strategy for city planning that allows cultural behaviors to direct the impulses that reveal urban forms, frameworks, and discourses. Whether driven by the global economy of 'shop till you drop', by density, or by size (small, medium, large, or extra-large), Koolhaas accepts the city as a place (opportunity?) that must transcend conventional urban planning and design tropes. In strategizing plans for Beijing's future, Koolhaas considered the ancient city's historical value, and acknowledged preservation and performance as essential to the development and form of the contemporary city. Rethinking the modern notions of preservation, OMA regards the future Beijing as a garden. A good gardener considers the temporal nature of plants, sun, and soil, fully aware that such observation is both part of the gardener's curatorial process and part of his or her pleasure. Gardening is perhaps the most 'realistic' or at least fundamental relationship any human can have with Earth. Any farmer knows that the thought of preserving a garden or field in its original form for time immemorial is about as feasible as keeping Yosemite National Park physically intact, keeping the giant sequoias permanently alive or the iconic waterfalls cascading at peak flows all year long. 'Preservation' or more correctly, 'heritage' — an idea originating in the aftermath of the French Revolution — is a relatively recent concept in human history. The goal of keeping and maintaining artifacts in their original condition for other than pragmatic reasons may be an alien notion to most people. Treating the ineffaceable city as a garden is more alien still. However, what OMA has, in fact, suggested for Beijing is a strategy whereby urban preservation, analogous to farming crop rotation, is congruent with existing city planning practices:

> The most visionary approach to preservation would be to use it in a prospective rather than retrospective way by declaring different areas of the city to be preserved for different periods of time. Instead of a temporal monolith — a permanent center and

an ever changing periphery, the city will be defined and enriched by planned phase differences between its parts. The contrast between past and present will become more relative — 'older and newer' will share a permanent interface. It means new architecture will not limit its contributions to the periphery, but that construction can take place — visions articulated — in the center, where it counts. It also means that new architecture could appear anywhere, and that new 'building' would be distributed instead of concentrated in predictable 'extensions'.[27]

Epic top-down theoretical proposals are hardly the only sustainable and worthwhile models for the city. Far from it. At the bottom-up micro scale, everyday urban 'citizen-farmers' cultivate new ideas and put them into practice. For example, the environmental group White Roof Project sets out to "help solve big environmental problems one rooftop, one block, one city at a time".[28] They act upon research showing that to paint one percent of the world's urban surfaces white (rooftops and pavement) could reduce CO_2 emissions by 130 gigatons over the next 50 to 100 years.[29] Similarly, 'official' and unofficial guerrilla gardeners practice the "illicit cultivation of someone else's land", motivated by dissatisfaction with the current urban status quo:

> Most of us live in cities and have no garden of our own. We demand more from this planet than it has the space and resources to offer. Guerrilla gardening is a battle for resources, a battle against scarcity of land, environmental abuse and wasted opportunities. It is also a fight for freedom of expression and for community cohesion. It is a battle in which bullets are replaced with flowers (most of the time).[30]

Figure 8/ Planting the town red: City Lounge, St Gallen, Switzerland. Photograph by Thomas Mayer.

Figure 9/ BIG Mountain: as in the case of Jardim Gramacho, human activity buzzes around and atop a mountain of trash. Images courtesy of BIG.

These and other forms of innovation are generally found first in cities, where the opportunities to organize and test ideas are more numerous. City agencies, neighborhood activist groups (NAGs!), individuals, students, and others have all implemented schemes ranging from new public and alternative transportation systems, to recycling programs, to safer streets for children walking to and from schools in neighborhoods plagued by violence.[31] One particularly striking example, the result of a public competition, is architect Carlos Martinez and artist Pipilotti Rist's 2005 granulated red-rubber garden, City Lounge, in St Gallen, Switzerland. Here typical sidewalks and streets are transformed into a public living room [Figure 8]. Such 'light-green' community-centered joint efforts will always be needed, as no large-scale city prototype could ever satisfy the complex and ever-changing needs of human societies.

Another urban effort, on a much larger scale, recalls the Jardim Gramacho mountain of trash: a 'mountain' created by the Danish architectural firm BIG, Amager Bakke (Amager Hill) will be one of the largest waste-to-energy facilities in Northern Europe [Figure 9]. Located in an industrial area of Copenhagen, Amager Bakke features a year-round public ski slope on its rooftop. BIG (Bjarke Ingels Group), led by architect Bjarke Ingels, has employed the 'mountain' typology in past projects as well. These large pyramidal 'landform' structures are far kinder or more humane to us 'ground dwellers' than the tower, for they are more akin to familiar, natural geological formations.[32] This socio-sustainable project will ensure a more efficient use of garbage while at the same time creating a new, public urban space and providing an array of recreational activities in a dense (and topologically challenged) city.

But unless we are content with the city's dominance over the suburb, the village, the garden, and even possibly nature, the city cannot be the final answer in our quest for an ideal system of habitation. To whom should we entrust the designs for human habitation on the planet? To the 'good' architect who continues to plan new streets for cars, new buildings to fill the spaces between the streets, and a few open spaces for trees and wildlife, if and where permissible? Is building a few select structures for an elite few in the rambling contemporary city a viable paradigm for the future? If not, what should the good architect do?

An even bigger question here is: what is the fundamental reason for humans' concern about the future? Whose future are we thinking of? How many generations of our children's children's children are we willing to lose sleep over? At what point will we let go of the deep future and think only of next week, tomorrow, now? Are we afraid of being the generation remembered for not worrying about planet Earth and its survivors 1,000 years hence? Will we be accountable? Why worry? Be happy.

THE LAST GARDEN?

It is unlikely that beavers got the idea of building dams by watching human dam-builders at work.[33]

More gardens or more museums — in the end what has greater value?

Through the millennia, the architect or 'chief builder' (from the ancient Greek *arkhitekton*, *arkhi-*, chief + *tekton*, builder), has attempted to find the ideal solution for myriad design problems ranging from bridges to fortresses, from tunnels to towers and towns. Generally the architect will apply experience and information gleaned by on-site observation to make the best possible design for a proposed structure. Always aware of the sun's position in the sky, the climate, the prevailing seasonal winds, the slope of the ground, and the composition of the soil, the architect desires to make something well, in order to successfully repel the unpredictable actions of nature (including other humans!) — actions that often thwart human ambitions.

Indeed, architects and 'builders' have long yearned for a form of paradise. Their quest is manifested in the buildings, towns, and cities designed both by trained specialists and by intended users, "people with a common heritage acting under a community of experience".[34] In fact, this latter group, the anonymous producers of architecture, have been responsible for a majority of the buildings constructed on the planet. As Bernard Rudofsky writes in *Architecture Without Architects*, vernacular architecture "serves its purpose to perfection".[35] Of course, these solutions arose over long periods of persistent trial and error, during which the performative aspect of architecture trumped 'building style' in forging a durable, sustainable relationship between nature and architecture. As Rudofsky points out:

> There is much to learn from architecture before it became an expert's art. The untutored builders in space and time — the protagonists of this show — demonstrate an admirable talent for fitting their buildings into the natural surroundings. Instead of trying to 'conquer' nature, as we do, they welcome the vagaries of climate and the challenge of topography. Whereas we find flat, featureless country most to our liking (any flaws in the terrain are easily erased by the application of a bulldozer), more sophisticated people are attracted by rugged country. In fact, they do not hesitate to seek out the most complicated configurations in the landscape. The most sanguine of them have been known to choose veritable eyries for their building sites — Machu Picchu, Monte Alban, the craggy bastions for the monks' republic on Mount Athos, to mention only some familiar ones.[36]

Is it possible that the good architect's strategy may be found at the confluence of nature's imperatives or 'will' and our submission thereto ?

New Zealand could be described as Earth's last garden. This country of varied and extreme landscapes went untouched by other land forms for more than 50 million years.[37] Separated from other continents by great oceans, and solely occupied by coastal mammals and birds — including the Moa, a flightless bird that stood more than twice the height of an average person — it was the last land mass of size to remain uninhabited by humans. Migrant Polynesians landed in New Zealand less than 800 years ago, arriving from either the Cook Islands or Tahiti. Adapting to the rugged terrain, the settlers became known as Māori, "natural"; the Māori describe themselves as *tangata whenua*, "people of the land". New Zealand, which they called Aotearoa, "land of the long white cloud", is topographically defined by severe mountain peaks, plateaus, glaciers, and fiords. It owes much of its varied topography to volcanic activity and dramatic tectonic uplifts of land that continue today.

Within this landscape of supervolcanos, fertile coastal plains, and ancient forests, the air "is still as close as can be found, anywhere in the world, to what air was like before humankind came along".[38] In this land two distinct cultures have clashed and at other times harmonized in a fine balance between respect for cultural traditions, Polynesian and European, and respect for the island's sensitive ecology. Of course, New Zealanders — both the predominantly European *Pākehā* and the *tangata whenua* — have blundered and bobbled since the islands were first inhabited: there was wanton extermination of indigenous birds such as the Moa as well as out-of-control bush-burn clearing that led to the destruction of native forests and animal habitats. Old habits die hard, and remnants of post-European environmental destruction continue to this day.[39] But surprisingly for a compact and remote country, New Zealand quickly adopted a culture of pragmatic environmentalism that, for better or worse, has served as a model for the world. This environmental strategy is assisted by a relatively small population density ratio, the use of building materials suited to the generally temperate climate, and construction constraints arising from portability limitations in a country that is isolated both externally and internally.[40] Over the years, homegrown resources have been closely monitored and valued. Excess and opulence are not readily visible, nor do they overtly occupy public consciousness. Further, the many small towns that lie outside the main cities often appear to be nothing more than improvised camps or bivouacs, suggesting a frontier sturdiness that is well suited to the dramatic terrain. This is not a population that appears 'dug-in' to its environment for the long haul. Instead, the observer is presented with a 'snapshot' of determined people living off the land, perhaps even luxury-camping for the night. This is not a bad thing.

It is here that architect Ian Athfield has long taken a stand against the established culture of building *against* nature. Instead, Athfield has demonstrated an architecture that submits to nature, and that, in fact, allows the forces of nature to shape, transform, and ultimately consume a structure, if that is the desired result. Athfield's constructions, while more studied and deliberate than the average New Zealand building, seemingly capture the essence of the Kiwi lifestyle, culture, and ethos. Although often demonstrating the characteristics of the bivouac, the structures are remarkably connected to place, specifically to the New Zealand landscape. Ath, as he is known to friends, collaborators, and others, follows no discernable architectural style. Employing an assortment of traditional and modern tectonic methods and styles — containing echoes of the whitewashed houses of Santorini, the sculptural play of Antonio Gaudi, the discipline of Mies van der Rohe, and New Zealand's simple colonial vernacular — Athfield has ultimately defined an indigenous New Zealand architecture that is closely attuned to the spirit of place or *genius loci*.

In his own house in Wellington, NZ, which doubles as his office, Ath has in essence created a village [Figure 10]. Begun in 1965, the meandering complex cascades down a steep hillside; the organic assemblage of juxtaposed forms is still a work in progress. More than 40 people work there, while at any given time 25 or more people live within the composition. Informally hugging the hillside, the structure has been a full-scale working architectural laboratory and social experiment. Much of the building was done by Athfield himself. What is most interesting here is the unfinished nature of the House and Office, the haphazardness of the plan, and,

at one time, the casual intrusion of plant creepers into the interior spaces. The House and Office function in many ways as a habitable 'ruin' or garden; his work has been described as "composed in a tenuous quest for a plastic union with the New Zealand landscape".[41]

This insightful characterization of Athfield's prolific body of work is best embodied by his 1980–1981 Buck House, a private family home on the Te Mata Estate vineyard in the Hawke's Bay region of New Zealand's North Island [Figure 11]. One of the country's oldest wineries, Te Mata was planted in 1892 and prospered well into the twentieth century. However, by the mid-1970s the vineyard had hit hard times. New owners John Buck and Michael Morris began the process of resuscitating the vineyard and commissioned Athfield to design a house on the land. As one looks up from the bottom of the vineyard at the stark whiteness of Ath's signature plasticity, vertical and horizontal thrusts intermingle with the architectural nuances of roof gables, hips, and dormers. This house within the vines bears some similarity to Richard Meier's 1973 Douglas House on Lake Michigan in the United States, where an all-white composition offers a bold contrast

Figure 10/ Ath's Home and Office: the organic assemblage of juxtapositional forms is still a work in progress. Photograph by Stephen Hough.

to the nature that surrounds it. The Buck House, however, is a New Zealand building that shares the social aptitude and organic assembly of the House and Office but, at the same time, is more controlled, seemingly begging for more permanence within the volatile (and volcanic!), unpredictable New Zealand landscape. In large part this is achieved through the intersection of the rows of grapevines and the contrasting stark white architectural composition. The parallel rows seem to merge with the structure, appearing to continue through the house uninterrupted—the building seemingly locked into place with the viticultural garden. Incidentally, since the completion of the Buck House in 1980, Te Mata vineyard has produced some of the best red wines in New Zealand.

THE GOOD ARCHITECT?

We need to face the fact that there may not even be architects in thirty years.[42]

When asked by Field Marshall Rommel whether the house was already built or if he had built it himself, Malaparte replied "I bought the house as it stood. And pointing with a sweeping gesture to the sheer cliff of Matromania, the three gigantic rocks of the Faraglioni, the Sorrento peninsula, the islands of the Sirens, the distant blue of the Amalfi coastline, and the remote golden glimmer of the Paestum shores, I said: 'I designed the scenery'."[43]

Building, making, and fashioning, are all forms of gardening, for all known materials come from the Earth itself. Through human manipulation (technology), these materials can become bricks, ball-point pens, tablet computers, chairs, jet planes, or skyscrapers. Humans discovered that the garden provides the perfect opportunity, place, and methods for engaging and accommodating nature, which is often considered the antagonist in the human quest to survive. The garden is neutral ground. All constructions, regardless of scale, category, or sub-category, are gardening efforts. In the end, beyond the allegory, we all garden—some of us subconsciously, others deliberately—but most of us try to produce some kind of 'green' effect (however fumbling in our endeavor), whether through watering, tilling, farming, recycling, picking up our trash, or giving to Greenpeace. Architects have a long history of fumbling well. In the first century BCE, Vitruvius instructed architects to investigate the land so as to ensure a "healthy site" on which to build a city.[44] In *The Ten Books of Architecture*, 1485, Leon Batista Alberti described the ideal garden and house; Tony Garnier's Cité Industrielle, 1904, and Frank Lloyd Wright's Broadacre City, 1932,

Figure 11/ A tenuous quest for a plastic union with the New Zealand landscape. Buck House within the vines. Phtograph by Andrew Caldwell.

both unrealized projects for an ideal city, are liberally framed by trees and gardens.[45] More recently, architect and theorist Christopher Alexander provided a complete set of instructions in *A Pattern Language* both for connecting buildings to the earth and for landscaping and gardening in and around the house and town.[46] Many architects willingly engage Earth's terrain in a studied and highly responsible, sustainable manner, and many are in fact avid gardeners. Mies van der Rohe worked closely with landscape architect Alfred Caldwell during his Chicago days — Caldwell was also on the faculty at IIT and guided Mies on numerous projects to ensure "good roses and good vegetables".[47] Richard Neutra, known for visually seamless integration of exterior to interior, was not only a trained architect but also a landscape architect and horticulturist.

Currently, many architects seem to understand the need for sustainable building. Unfortunately, architecture is a profession that usually requires paying clients — paying clients for whom the value of sustainable building may be as a profitable commodity. Building owners may ask architects to attach any manner of 'eco-bling' to their skyscrapers, stadiums, and houses to value-up their investment. Meanwhile, a small handful of good architects march steadfastly to the drumbeat of 'less is more' as a guiding principle. Among them is Australian architect Glenn Murcutt, who over the course of the past 40-plus years has produced a succession of small houses and civic buildings that categorize him as a gardener *par excellence*. In his Magney House at Bingie Point, New South Wales, Murcutt demonstrates a profound opulence of minimalist design: seemingly as lightweight as a tent, the house is 'passively' heated and cooled through the use of retractable, external, slatted aluminum blinds and bottom-hung vents to promote cross-ventilation [Figure 12]. A 'butterfly' roof extends the length of the longitudinal plan. By inverting the more traditional gable roof, Murcutt's design allows more daylight into the house at every opportunity and easily captures rainfall into the roof 'valley'; at each end of the house, massive downspouts are fed by outboard rain gutters that project from this valley. The intention is clear: to harvest water. And beneath the house are rainwater storage tanks. Like every good gardener, this good architect understands the importance of sun and water.

Not every building that incorporates good garden practice is necessarily good, as is also the case with buildings incorporating performative add-on technologies that foster energy efficiency, i.e. geothermal or 'clean energy' systems for heating and cooling.[48] Thermodynamic efficiency is always paramount in this discussion, but thermodynamic efficiency

Figure 12/ Magney House: Like every good gardener, the good architect understands the importance of sun and water.
Photograph by Chad Dao.

Figure 13/ As provocateur of the built environment, the good architect is a gardener first: "The Basic House is a habitable volume; foldable, inflatable, and reversible; an almost immaterial house that self inflates with body heat or from the heat of the sun; so simple and versatile that it protects us from the cold and from the heat when reversed; so light that it floats and moreover, it folds up and fits into your pocket. Having everything without having almost anything. Basic House is not a product, rather a concept of extreme reduction. I was impressed with sustainability theorist Ezio Manzini's statement that 'Design's role in the future will be to make poverty attractive.' It is evident that the saturation of products in 'developed societies' doesn't mean a sign of progress, rather it is becoming a threat for the planet. If a house is kept in a pocket it is obvious that it can contain anything and breaks with our lifestyle based on consumption of products." Martín Azúa, 1999. Photographs by Daniel Riera.

is not a toy to be pulled out of the toy box when designing buildings that have no business being on this planet in the first place. Heating and cooling large spaces like shopping malls, movie theaters, and indoor sport complexes during off-hours really makes no sense, regardless of how 'efficient' the building might be. The question remains: can humans adopt a new paradigm? Can we really shift our attention away from an economy driven by 'want' to an economy driven by actual need? Perhaps the good architect exists somewhere at the intersection of architectural form, public want, and public need, though at the moment architectural pedagogy and praxis lean toward 'sustainability as toy' versus 'sustainability as ideal'. The aesthetics of sustainability should be invisible. Sustainability is about density, compact spatial geometries, and a desire to produce less with less. Less with less *is more*.

Landform building exercises and biomimetic strategies will no doubt enable us to do 'less with less'. Stan Allen, who defines landforms as a mash-up between architecture, landscape, and ecology, believes that landform architecture surpasses bio-architecture (which seeks to "make architecture more lifelike") in the creation of good buildings by favoring building program and process over imitations of natural forms.[49] The resultant constructions are seen as viable architectural tactics in the sense of responsible interventions in the landscape. Landforming and complementary organically-rooted bio-form exercises may be environmentally sound and visually interesting; however, if reduced to mere stylistic exercises, they may well disguise the elephant in the room.[50]

So why do so many humans care so passionately about the Earth? The 'dark-green' action-centric environmental 'movement', Earth First! serves a mission of "protecting wilderness" on the grounds that "that life of the Earth comes first"; their "actions are tied to Deep Ecology, the spiritual and visceral recognition of the intrinsic, sacred value of every living thing".[51] Deep Ecology, credited to philosopher Arne Næss, holds that the vast catalogue of Earth's life forms cannot be ranked in importance — a perspective that could be considered antihumanist. However, gardens and their architectures are, of course, very pro-human regardless of their eco-bias. This raises the question of just who the 'good humans' are. Are they gentle backyard gardeners, or Earth First!ers, or people simply hoping to save the 'here and now'?[52] In the end, what is more important to preserve, Earth or technology? Is Technology the new Earth? While technology is probably a good bet for some (in terms of long-term human survival), for others caught between the economies of consumerism, political maneuvering, natural disasters, and war, a technology-driven future is dangerously limited. While the unbuilt often holds the promise of betterment, building no longer necessarily brings to fruition the hope of creating a better place. Should we, therefore, build only where housing and centers for healthcare, education, recreation, and commerce, together with their supporting infrastructures, are lacking? Should architects tend to the abundance of plants already in the garden, helping to grow and maintain them, rather than clearing, tilling, and planting new fields? Is it possible that architecture is part of the garden rather than the other way around?[53]

Perhaps the good architect, a builder of propositions and a provocateur of the built environment, is, in fact, a gardener first [Figure 13]. Perhaps the good architect dreams most deeply not of buildings, but of the Earth.

NOTES

1/ These words are my own; however, the first known prescriptive voice regarding the importance of the sun in architecture comes from the Roman architect Vitruvius. See Vitruvius, *On Architecture, Books I–V,* vol. 1, Frank Granger ed. and trans., Cambridge, MA: Harvard University Press, 1931, p. 31, and *On Architecture, Books VI–X,* pp. 11–45. One of the first contemporary architects to address the importance of the sun in the built environment was Ralph Knowles. See Ralph Knowles, *Sun Rhythm Form,* Cambridge, MA: MIT Press, 1982. Ian McHarg wrote in his 1969 landmark work *Design with Nature,* that "This book is a personal testament to the power and importance of the sun, moon, and the stars, the changing seasons, seedtime and harvest, clouds, rain and rivers, the oceans and the forests, the creatures and the herbs." See Ian McHarg, *Design with Nature,* Garden City: Doubleday, 1971, p. 5.

2/ See http://www.wastelandmovie.com/.

3/ See http://usatoday30.usatoday.com/news/world/story/2012-06-03/rio-de-janeiro-jardim-gramacho-dump-closing/55352142/1.

4/ Driver, Nina, and Ilaina Jonas, "In bustling Houston, it's a case of 'Build, baby, build!'", Reuters, 2013, http://www.reuters.com/article/2013/08/25/us-houston-skyscrapers-idUSBRE97O06C20130825. The article substantiates this: "There are some 56 office buildings totaling at least 11 million square feet under construction in and around Houston, according to real estate services firm CBRE Group Inc. That is equivalent to 190 football fields."

5/ For this and other environmental projections, see www.usgbc.org/ShowFile.aspx?DocumentID=5033.

6/ Vanittersum, Koert, and Brian Wansink, "Plate Size and Color Suggestibility: The Delboeuf Illusion's Bias on Serving and Eating Behavior", *Journal of Consumer Research,* vol. 39, August, 2011. http://bear.warrington.ufl.edu/williams/MAR_3503/MAR_3503_Home_files/Van%20Ittersum%20%26%20Wansink%20-%20Plate%20Size%20and%20Color.pdf.

7/ Parts of this discussion of the Barcelona Pavilion are derived from my essay "Beyond the Red Curtain: Less is More Utopia" in *Utopian Studies,* vol. 25, no. 1, 2014, pp. 163–164.

8/ Dodds, George, *Building Desire: On the Barcelona Pavilion,* Oxfordshire: Routledge, 2005, p. 69.

9/ The motto "Less is more" is first found in print in C. M. Wieland, "Neujahrswunsch", in *Der Deutsche Merkur (The German Mercury),* a literary publication also published and edited by Wieland: "Minder ist oft mehr" [Less is often more], *Der Deutsche Merkur, 5 Bd.,* 1774, http://www.ub.uni-bielefeld.de/diglib/aufkl/teutmerk/teutmerk.htm. It also appears in "Andrea del Sarto", 1855, a poem by Robert Browning: "Well, less is more, Lucrezia: I am judged," http://rpo.library.utoronto.

ca/poems/andrea-del-sarto. Popular and academic sources cite Mies as having said 'less is more' — even going so far as to indicate that the aphorism appeared in the article "On Restraint in Design", *New York Herald Tribune,* 28 June 1959; however, I have been unable to verify the citation. Beyond this, there is virtually no documented evidence of Mies' use of the phrase 'less is more' other than the anecdotal. The earliest attribution of "less is more" to Mies may well be Philip Johnson's: "As in architecture, he has always been guided by his personal motto 'less is more'", *Mies van der Rohe,* Boston: New York Graphic Society, 1978 [1947], p. 49. Mies himself wrote, "The maximum effect with the minimum expenditure of means", Ludwig Mies van der Rohe, "Working Theses", 1923, in Ulrich Conrads, *Programs and Manifestoes on Twentieth Century Architecture,* Michael Bullock trans., Cambridge, MA: MIT Press, 1994 [1964], p. 74.

10/ For a survey of Wachsmann's work, see *Konrad Wachsmann: Toward Industrialization of Building,* catalog of an exhibition of the work of Wachsmann, Los Angeles: University of Southern California, 1971. Also see *Home Delivery: Fabricating the Modern Dwelling,* Barry Bergdoll and Peter Christensen eds., New York: The Museum of Modern Art, 2008.

11/ Joseph Hudnut, Dean of the Graduate School of Design at Harvard University, suggested the name, the "Packaged House". See Gilbert Herbert, *The Dream of the Factory-Made House: Walter Gropius and Konrad Wachsmann,* Cambridge, MA: The MIT Press, 1984, p. 249 and passim.

12/ See Sandy Isenstadt, *The Modern American House: Spaciousness and Middle Class Identity,* Cambridge: Cambridge University Press, 2006.

13/ Wachsmann, Konrad, *The Turning Point of Building: Structure and Design,* New York: Reinhold, 1961, pp. 208–216. For a thorough discussion of space-frame structures including their history (probably the earliest examples of space-frame structures were developed by telephone inventor Alexander Graham Bell), see John Chilton, *Space Grid Structures,* Oxford: Architectural Press, 2000.

14/ Lambert, Phyllis, ed., *Mies in America,* New York: Abrams, 2001, p. 423.

15/ Wachsmann, *The Turning Point of Building,* p. 194.

16/ Caldwell, Alfred, "Atomic Bombs and City Planning", *Alfred Caldwell: The Life and Work of a Prairie School Landscape Architect,* Dennis Domer ed., Baltimore: The John Hopkins University Press, 1997, p. 177.

17/ "Don't Worry, Be Happy" is a song by musician Bobby McFerrin, released in September 1988. The song's title is taken from a famous quote of the Indian mystic and sage Meher Baba (1894–1969).

18/ Giesecke, Annette, *The Epic City: Urbanism, Utopia, and the Garden in Ancient Greece and Rome,* Cambridge, MA: Harvard University Press, 2007, pp. 73–78.

19/ For an examination of visionary cities over the past 100 years or so, see *Utopia Forever: Visions of Architecture and Urbanism,* Robert Klanten and Lukas Feireiss eds., Berlin: Gestalten, 2011. Felicity Scott in *Achitecture or Techno-utopia: Politics after Modernism* defines the efforts of the late Modernist visionaries as "end-games". Modernism as a social and stylistic architectural movement was declared "dead" on 15 July 1972 at 3:32 pm by Charles Jenks upon the destruction of Pruitt-Igoe housing in St Louis, Missouri: see Charles Jencks, *The*

Language of Post-modern Architecture, New York: Rizzoli, 1977, p. 9. Paolo Soleri can be credited with formalizing the return to an ideology that "smaller is better." His iconic book *Arcology* begins, "This book is about miniaturization." The full text, "Miniaturize or die (has been the key rule for incipient life)" is found on page 2. Paolo Soleri, *Arcology: The City in the Image of Man,* Cambridge, MA: The MIT Press, 1969.

20/ Kwinter, Sanford, *Requiem for the City at the End of the Millennium,* Barcelona: Actar, 2010, p. 92.

21/ Maas, Winy, and Jacob van Rijs eds., *FARMAX: Excursions on Density,* Rotterdam: 010 Publishers, 1998, p. 1.

22/ Ballard, J. G., *High-Rise,* New York: Holt, Rinehart and Winston, 1975.

23/ Jacobs, Jane, *The Death and Life of Great American Cities,* New York: Random House, 1961.

24/ MVRDV and The Why Factory, *The Vertical Village,* Rotterdam: NAi Publishers, 2012, pp. 4–10.

25/ Sudjic, Deyan, *The 100 Mile City,* London: Flamingo/Harper Collins, 1992.

26/ "I'm going to Disney World!" and "I'm going to Disneyland!" are advertising slogans used by the Walt Disney Company to promote their theme parks in Florida and California. The campaign was launched following Super Bowl XXI on 25 January 1987 with a television commercial featuring New York Giants football team quarterback Phil Simms shouting the phrase upon the team's victory after being asked by an unseen person "What are you going to do next?"

27/ Koolaas, Rem ed., *Content,* Cologne: Taschen, 2004, p. 465.

28/ See http://whiteroofproject.org/.

29/ Lawrence Berkeley National Laboratory, Heat Island Group: http://heatisland.lbl.gov/. The white roof effort could, however, have less positive consequences. Scientists at Arizona State University estimated that painting all the rooftops white in the United States' metropolitan area of Phoenix and Tucson, Arizona could reduce annual rainfall by 4 percent. See http://iopscience.iop.org/1748-9326/7/3/034026.

30/ Reynolds, Richard, *On Guerrilla Gardening: A Handbook for Gardening Without Boundaries,* London: Bloomsbury, 2008, p. 5.

31/ See Safe Passage Chicago: http://www.cps.edu/Programs/Wellness_and_transportation/Safetyandsecurity/safepassage.

32/ See Stan Allen and Marc McQuade eds., *Landform Building: Architecture's New Terrain,* Baden: Lars Müller Publishers, 2011.

33/ Rudofsky, Bernard, *Architecture Without Architects: A Short Introduction to Non-Pedigreed Architecture,* New York: Doubleday, 1964, preface, p. 3.

34/ Pietro Belluschi, quoted in Rudofsky, *Architecture Without Architects,* preface, p. 4.

35/ Rudofsky, *Architecture Without Architects,* caption to Figure 1.

36/ Rudofsky, *Architecture Without Architects,* preface, p. 4.

37/ *The Oxford Illustrated History of New Zealand,* Keith Sinclair ed., Oxford: Oxford University Press, 1990, p. 2.

38/ Park, Geoff, *Ngā Uruora: The Groves of Life: Ecology and History in a New Zealand Landscape,* Wellington: Victoria University Press, 1995, p. 330.

39/ For a thorough discussion on the current state of New Zealand environmentalism, see Geoff Park, *Ngā Uruora-The Groves of Life.*

40/ Perhaps the first 'flat-pack' building material, corrugated iron, was invented in 1829. It paved the way for sustainable, pre-fabricated industrialized building in the far reaches of the world. Strong, light, and compact, 'corrugated' had been instrumental to colonial farming and land settlement, especially in Australia and New Zealand. One can surmise that corrugated helped to prevent the complete deforestation of native trees such as kauri, matai, totara, and rimu in New Zealand. See Adam Mornement and Simon Holloway, *Corrugated Iron: Building on the Frontier,* New York: Norton, 2007.

41/ Russel Walden, quoted in Clarence Aasen, "The Architecture of Ian Athfield", *World Architecture Review,* vol. 93, no. 4, Shenzhen, 1993, p. 21.

42/ Kwinter, *Requiem for the City,* p. 91.

43/ Curzio Malaparte in Marida Talamona, *Casa Malaparte,* New York: Princeton Architectural Press, 1992, p. 42. Malaparte did not buy the house; its authorship has always been in doubt, but most agree the principal designer was Malaparte. Construction began in 1938 based on a plan by architect Adalberto Libera and was largely complete by 1942, though the design had deviated from the plan. The spectacular house and site are located on an isolated rock promontory on Capri's eastern edge.

44/ Vitruvius, *On Architecture, Books I–V,* vol. 1, pp. 17–21.

45/ See Leon Battista Alberti, *The Ten Books of Architecture, The 1755 Leoni Edition,* Mineola: Dover, 1986, pp. 192–194. For a discussion of Garnier's and Wright's very green industrialized utopian visions, see Hanno-Walter Kruft, *A History of Architectural Theory From Vitruvius to the Present,* New York: Princeton Architectural Press, 1994.

46/ Alexander, Christopher, et al., *A Pattern Language: Towns, Buildings, Construction,* New York: Oxford University Press, 1977, pp. 790–825.

47/ Girot, Christophe, "Mies as Gardener", *Pamphlet,* Zürich: ETH, 2011, p. 7.

48/ For a lively critique of the current 'greening' phenomenon, See Ozzie Zehner, *Green Illusions: The Dirty Secrets of Clean Energy and the Future of Environmentalism,* Lincoln: University of Nebraska Press, 2012.

49/ Allen, Stan, "From the Biological to the Geological", Stan Allen and Marc McQuade eds., *Landform Building: Architecture's New Terrain,* Baden: Lars Müller Publishers, 2011, p. 20.

50/ For more examples and another take on landforms, see Aaron Betsky, *Landscapers, Building with the Land,* New York: Thames & Hudson, 2002. See also Michael Pawlyn, *Biomimicry in Architecture,* London: RIBA Publishing, 2011, especially notes 3 and 4 regarding the elephant.

51/ See http://www.earthfirst.org/ and http://earthfirstjournal.org/.

52/ The Earth First! motto is "No Compromise in the Defense of Mother Earth", http://www.earthfirst.org/.

53/ For a discussion on the relationship of architecture to nature and the garden, see Donald Dunham, "Architecture *Without* Nature?", *Earth Perfect: Nature, Utopia, and the Garden,* Annette Giesecke and Naomi Jacobs eds., London: Black Dog Publishing, 2012, pp. 136–155.

5

CULTIVATING HOPE

254 /EMMA MARRIS

GARDENING THE EARTH WITH JOY

Is the world a garden? Was it in the past? Will it be in the future? Consider the Garden of Eden. The Edenic narrative of the fall from grace is often invoked in conservationist discourse, for the Garden of Eden is many things that conservationists value; it is lush, green, and biodiverse — and, there are hardly any people in it. Yet for many North American conservationists, from John Muir to Edward Abbey and Micheal Soulé, the ideal state is not the garden, but the wilderness.

In both the popular mind and the law, wilderness has two distinct properties: it is primeval or unchanged from the past, and it has not been meddled with. A true wilderness is both unchanged and unmanaged, as the legal definition of wilderness in the United States — the Wilderness Act of 1964 — declares:

> A wilderness, in contrast with those areas where man and his own works dominate the landscape, is hereby recognized as an area where the earth and its community of life are untrammeled by man, where man himself is a visitor who does not remain.[1]

The problem is that it is not possible to have both lack of management and lack of change at the same time in 2013. If a place looks like it used to, someone is managing it: removing exotic plants, patrolling for poachers, controlling fire, and so on. And if it is truly unmanaged, it begins to look unfamiliar, with exotic species encroaching and an ecology changing in response to a changing climate.

I therefore challenge the concept of 'pristine wilderness' as an empty category and — more importantly — as a poor central organizing principle for nature conservation. If we want people to love nature, but we define it so narrowly that most of it is gone or going fast, we aren't going to get a lot of people signing up for an essentially symbolic defense of a lost cause. Few people want to join an environmentalism that is nothing more than hospice nursing. In fact, there is quite a bit of nature left to love on our highly humanized planet.

NO EDEN?

When Europeans arrived in North America, Australia, the Pacific Islands, and similar places, they assumed that these places were pretty much unchanged since the Flood. The people living there were dismissed as ineffectual in the face of nature, making

no more modification to their habitats than the animals. Until the 1970s, and in many cases much later, ecologists and conservationists accepted the instant of European colonization as the contaminating event that marked the departure from the 'baseline' — the correct and morally superior state for an ecosystem.

But, paleoecology, archaeology, and ecological history are increasingly showing us that the places we thought were pristine were already seriously altered.[2] Right up until the devastating waves of disease that followed Europeans — and sometimes even preceded them — the millions of people in these places were busy living in cities, overseeing large-scale agriculture, and managing the land. They had complex hunting rules, including 'no take' zones and seasons. They performed controlled burns and even planted useful species. And further back in time, more than 10,000 years ago, people were almost certainly responsible for a suite of extinctions of massive animals around the world, from mastodons to giant ground sloths to American camels to enormous wombat cousins in Australia [Figure 1]. These extinctions did more than just remove large species. In the absence of their grazing, their predation, and their interactions with other species, everything else shifted. Grasslands became forests; tree species moved ranges. We can see these fascinating changes by looking at fossil pollen records. Furthermore, we didn't just remove species, we also created new forms of species and even whole new species by domesticating them, creating corn from teosinte and cattle from aurochs.

The only conclusion that can be drawn from this evidence of ancient and modern change and human influence is that there was no Garden of Eden. There was no day before we messed things up. In North America, people have been changing the landscape since the day they arrived; and the day before that, most of the continent was covered in a sheet of ice — probably not a reasonable conservation goal. Nor is it possible to model what would have happened as the ice sheet retreated had *Homo sapiens* decided not to hazard the trek across the Bering Land Bridge. Ecosystems are inherently dynamic all by themselves. Despite the popular notion of the 'balance of nature' and 'timeless' ecosystems, a combination of non-human-caused climate changes, evolution, and pure luck (which ecologists term 'stochastic factors') means that few ecosystems persist for longer than 10,000 years without major compositional change.[3] And that's without any people

Figure 1/ Hominids hunting mammoths during the Pleistocene, an epoch that lasted from around 2.5 million to 11,000 years ago. The mammoth was a large mammal that ranged across North America, Europe, and Asia. It is depicted in cave drawings being hunted by early humans. Image courtesy of the Natural History Museum, London, Science Photo Library.

in the picture at all. Restoring the Earth to an unknowable alternative reality is neither feasible nor sensible. Today, even in places where no human has ever set foot, climate change puts the kibosh for good on the notion of a pristine wilderness. Everything is changed, everything will change further, and the toothpaste isn't going back into the tube.

As this reality has become clearer and clearer, conservation has felt a bit at sea, and the past five or ten years have been marked by a continuing conversation in its many sub-fields and groups about what clear, compelling goal could possibly replace 'put it back' as a unifying rallying cry. The old goal was handy and neat. Any other goal we might have, be it beauty or 'ecosystem services' or species preservation, was always best served by just putting things back the way they used to be. Now we need to somehow agree on a goal or many goals for every site and then figure out how to move forward toward those goals in an uncertain and changing world, despite our limited knowledge. The more the climate changes, the more species move around, the more land use changes, the harder it becomes to hold sites to past states. Clinging to historical baselines begins to be not only intellectually problematic, but exorbitantly expensive — and even dangerous, as it may make ecosystems more fragile in the face of intense challenges like drought or fire.

SHAMEFUL GARDENING

Consider Yellowstone National Park, where park culture and guidance documents like the *Leopold Report* of 1963 have meant that most park management aims to freeze it as it was in 1872, the year it became a park.[4] Today, more and more fiddling is required to make the park look un-fiddled-with. Non-native trout are fished out; native trout thrown back. Seed from whitebark pine that are resistant to the insidious bark beetle are being collected with a view towards breeding resistant trees for planting. Park workers weed [Figure 2]:

By 2010, approximately 70 park staff and over 100 volunteers were involved in invasive plant control and surveyed a total of 20,291 acres in the park. Of the 4,600 acres that were found to have nonnative vegetation, 105 acres were treated, including 9 acres that were treated twice. By 2011, permanent and seasonal resource management operations staff were spending 36% of their work hours on nonnative plant management, with most of that time used to pull or spray weeds.

/ "Invasive Vegetation Management Plan, Environmental Assessment", 21 February 2013.

Figure 2/ Youth Conservation Corps members carry away invasive plants that they removed at Yellowstone National Park. Photograph by Rachel Cudmore, the National Park Service.

And they cull:

> Yellowstone bison are managed towards an end-of-the-winter guideline of 3,000 animals. Managers at Yellowstone National Park also want to progress towards equal abundance in the central and northern breeding herds, an equal proportion of males to females, and an age structure of about 70% adults and 30% juveniles.... To progress towards desired conditions in terms of abundance and age, herd, and sex structure, we recommend the harvest of 25 adult male bison from the central herd in the western management area (Hebgen basin) and the harvest or culling of 425 bison (400 adult females and 25 adult males) from the northern management area (Gardiner basin) during winter 2013.
>
> / "Managing the Abundance of Yellowstone Bison, winter 2013", Chris Geremia, P. J. White, Rick Wallen, John Treanor, and Doug Blanton, 7 August 2012.

And they cut down trees to avoid undesirable fires, taking care that the results don't look too tidy:

> Initially, following treatment, a developed area will appear more groomed with the trees being more uniformly spaced. However over time, windthrow, regeneration and the accumulation of other forest debris will result in a less managed appearance.
>
> / "Yellowstone National Park Structure Protection and Firefighter Safety Hazard Fuels Management Guidelines" (An addendum to the *Yellowstone National Park Fire Management Plan*).

This is gardening to create the appearance of wilderness. Secret gardening. Shameful gardening.

I call for a psychological change. As conservationists, we should do two things. First, we should accept that we can only garden a very small percentage of the Earth to look just as it did at some historical point about which we are culturally nostalgic, as we are doing with Yellowstone. Many other protected areas and working landscapes will have to be managed to other goals. Second, we should embrace the gardening we are already doing as an acceptable and sensible strategy, not as an unpleasant last-ditch attempt to save that which is passing away. That is, we should garden not reluctantly, but with joy.

GARDENING HUMBLY

We may have to move species to new places to help them survive climate change. Let us do that with joy. We may have to add new species to undertake the roles — seed pollination, seed dispersal, and so on — of extinct species. Let us do that with joy. We may have to use working landscapes, like timber plantations or agricultural areas, as our canvases to create biodiverse landscapes. Let us do that with joy. Let us take up our spades and seeds and transportation crates and garden with joy.

You may object that the role of the gardener is insufficiently humble for such a joyous endeavor, that it implies mastery. But as any avid gardener will tell you, mastery is neither achievable nor desirable when working with nature. One coaxes plants and the land towards a goal, rather than dictating. Weeds never surrender; beloved plants die; birds turn up their noses at the expensive seed mix; slugs dine on our lettuces. Gardening humbles us every day with our incomplete understanding of the mind-bogglingly complex web of relations in our backyards. Global gardening humbles us on a massive scale. Changing an ecosystem is not like rearranging the furniture in an apartment. It is more like an unending collaboration or romance with a mysterious, unknowable network of interrelationships. We will never know the wolf, no matter how often we radio-collar her or knock her out with tranquilizer darts. We will never even know the potted palm.

And that's why good global gardening includes a large amount of doing nothing. In a world completely shaped by human actions, not intervening is a kind of intervention. It is leaving the windows wide open and letting climate change, regional land use change, and species movements blow in. In some places, choosing the intervention of not intervening will be morally prohibited, because it will mean extinction for one or more species. But in other places, we will want to choose non-intervention because we will learn so much from how nature adapts to our changing world. In 'novel ecosystems', places where humans have changed things radically but are not actively managing, we will see new ecosystems form, new relationships emerge between species. And these strange, novel ecosystems will very likely show us what will be robust and hardy in the mixed-up, climate-changed future. Our wild gardens will teach us what to plant.

Perhaps the best example of the conscious, humble gardening I am describing is a project in the Seychelles. There was a cinnamon forestry in these remote islands, and cinnamon trees (*Cinnamomum verum*) naturalized and took over a huge area. The initial, more traditional impulse was to remove them, but this turned out to be a bad idea. When the trees were removed from large areas, other non-natives sprang up in their place. The natives didn't have a chance. And researchers discovered that native birds would go hungry without the cinnamon fruits to eat. So Christoph Kueffer and his colleagues from the Swiss Federal Institute of Technology, in Zurich, played with taking out just one or two cinnamon trees and planting a few natives in the gap [Figure 3]. This strategy worked. The right mix turned out to be: accept the presence of the non-native forest, be thankful for the service it provides in the form of fruit for native birds, but plant in plugs of natives to ensure their continued presence on the islands.[5]

As the home gardener knows, sometimes the best way to proceed is to let the volunteers lead the way, rather than rip them out on principle because they do not belong. Thus gardening means not bending nature to our will and our preferences, but caring for all species in a rapidly changing world. This gardening is like stewardship, but with the acknowledgment that active intervention will be required to do the job. We have to get down on our knees and get our hands dirty. We garden with a view towards not merely protecting what is left, but making more. We want more big animals. More green. More connectivity. More diversity. More birdsong.

The Garden of Eden story says that the world was a garden and fell to become a wilderness. The North American conservation story says that the world was a wilderness and fell to become a garden. I say that the world is a garden now, has been a garden for thousands of years, and will be a garden for the foreseeable future. Now we must ask ourselves what kind of garden we want, and what kind of gardeners we will be. I think we should be humble and deferential in the face of the grand complexity of nature. We must garden carefully to make room for every species, but we should, when and where we can, let the garden go a bit wild and learn from how nature gardens herself.

Figure 3/ Seychelles Restoration Project. An actively restored patch of native vegetation in a cinnamon-dominated forest: stump of cut cinnamon tree in the foreground, replanted endemic palm saplings (and other endemic plant species) in the center, and dense cinnamon vegetation in the background. Photograph by Eva Schumacher.

How do we become these ideal gardeners? We must improve our biological and ecological knowledge, so our interventions can be more effective. We must have more master gardeners and more restoration ecologists (though we can debate whether the term 'restoration' is still appropriate). But we must also create a culture of dirty hands. We must not so venerate the tiny scraps of museum-style 'wilderness' in protected areas that we are afraid to touch them. It will not do to stand by with our hands in our pockets as species go extinct thanks to the forces that we have unleashed. Thus we must let our children play in nature and get off the paths. We must let them collect and pick and plant and touch and hunt and fish and build forts [Figure 4]. We can create safe spaces for them to do this, from the 'nature playground' at school to designated areas in parks. We human beings are meddlers by nature. Instead of denying this nature, we should practice it and learn how to harness it for the good of all species.

Get off the path, where you can. Collect some leaves and snail shells. Add some native or rare plants to your garden. Think about adding some natives from a zone or two south of you; as the climate changes, they may well flourish. Band together with your neighbors and create habitat for pollinators and migrating bugs and birds. Think about how you can improve things rather than just beat back destruction. Garden with joy.

NOTES ————————————————————————

1/ Marris, Emma, *Rambunctious Garden*, New York: Bloomsbury, 2011, p. 25.

2/ Marris, *Rambunctious Garden*.

3/ Jackson, Stephen T., "Vegetation, Environment, and Time: The Origination and Termination of Ecosystems", *Journal of Vegetation Science*, vol. 17, 2006, pp. 549–557.

4/ Marris, Emma, "The End of the Wild", http://www.nature.com/news/2011/110112/full/469150a.html.

5/ Kueffer, Christoph, et al., "Managing successional trajectories in alien-dominated, novel ecosystems by facilitating seedling regeneration: A case study", *Biological Conservation*, vol. 143, no. 7, 2010, pp. 1792–1802.

Figure 4/ We must let our children play in nature and get off the paths. We must let them collect and pick and plant and touch and hunt and fish and build forts. Photograph courtesy of Emma Marris.

260 /RICK DARKE

THE ACCIDENTAL LANDSCAPE

BLIND TO ORDER?

Any fool with a shovel and an eye for a straight line can create order. It takes a good gardener to appreciate order where none is apparent.

The human psyche readily recognizes order in straight lines and grids, in fixed-radius curves, in symmetry and uniformity. The capacity to impose order is equated with the power to control, and the ability to maintain order is valued as a confirmation of dominance. Together these tendencies result in an approach to landscape design and gardening that typically values the static over the dynamic and the predictable over the unpredictable. Design narratives are often equally risk-averse and a-contextual, derived from practiced ideologies rather than drawn from the contradictory nature of place. The unfortunate effect is that instead of revealing inherent order, design too frequently conceals it. We become blind to order.

In scientific contexts, where both the order and the immense complexity of dynamic natural systems are givens, the word 'chaos' is associated with the difficulty of predicting long-term future behavior rather than with an absence of order. In popular contexts, on the other hand, chaos denotes a state of confusion and absence of order. In actuality, chaos describes the

Figure 1/ Locally indigenous waterlilies float on the reflective surface of a century-old impoundment built for cranberry production at Whitesbog, near the center of what is now the New Jersey Pinelands National Reserve.

point at which our powers of observation fail to recognize the underlying order and our intellect fails to accept the unseen.

Art is no stranger to the complexity of obscure order, accepted on faith and celebrated for its beautiful influence. In reaction to the homogenizing effects of standardized design and culture, a growing global aesthetic elevates the irregular and the spontaneous. In the landscape, patinated elements whose aura is derived from associated character or has developed from unscripted interaction are increasingly in fashion — largely because they embody process.

THE APPEARANCE OF ACCIDENT

In the garden, the idea of working synergistically with the partly unpredictable nature of complex systems isn't new, but it is timely. We're growing nearer to accepting that an approach to design and management dedicated to complete control is not only expensive and impractical: in terms of global resource management, it is unsupportable. The visionary English gardener William Robinson (1838–1935) sensed this more than a century ago. His groundbreaking work, *The Wild Garden* (1870), introduced the concept of managed wildness in designed landscapes, and promoted an aesthetic embracing patterns that result from dynamic interaction.[1] Though this aesthetic is increasingly evident in modern landscapes from Chicago's Millennium Park to New York's High Line, Robinson was running contrary to the ordered formality of his Victorian era. After searching for the perfect epigram to open *The Wild Garden*, he settled on the following words from Sydney Smith (1771–1845), an Oxford-educated Anglican minister and moral philosopher celebrated for his wit and wisdom:

> I went to stay at a very grand and beautiful place in the country where the grounds are said to be laid out with consummate taste. For the first three or four days I was enchanted. It seemed so much better than nature that I began to wish the earth had been laid out according to the latest principles of improvement. In three days' time I was tired to death; a thistle, a heap of dead bushes, anything that wore the appearance of accident and want of intention was quite a relief. I used to escape from the made grounds and walk upon the adjacent goose common, where the cart ruts, gravel pits, bumps, coarse ungentlemanlike grass, and all the varieties produced by neglect were a thousand times more gratifying.

In one deceptively complex paragraph Smith rejects the ordered superficiality of the "made grounds" and opts for the intrigue of the utilitarian landscape. Functional but not beautiful in any formal sense, it's a place where diversity is inadvertently conserved by neglect. Smith has an eye for the beauty of

Figure 2/ Cranberry production at Whitesbog, c. 1920. Image courtesy Whitesbog Preservation Trust.

Figure 3/ Waterlilies, rushes, blueberries, and pines ordered by hydrology.

Figure 4/ The arrangement of grasses and shrubs reflects the site's hydrology.

process, and an imagination provoked by the subtler order that is preserved by want of intention. He writes not of accident but of the appearance of accident, knowing full well that the order of this landscape is rich by chance.

This essay employs a non-linear assemblage of images to provoke inquiry and point to the beautiful, meaningful, functional character of places where order is superficially masked by apparent disorder, disarray, dishevelment, messiness, or other characteristics antithetical to neatness and simplicity. Like most accidents, these so-called accidental landscapes are anything but accidental. Though inadvertent, unintentional, and unexpected, they are the authentic results of myriad interactions within complex cultural-ecological systems. Accidental landscapes are rich with intrigue and possibility because they are full of chance. They are rich with diversity because they harbor the autonomy that sustains ever-evolving life. The accidental landscape is worthy of observation because it has so much to teach good gardeners about the intentional preservation of living process.

Figure 6/ View from a Bluebell Railway coach window.

Such accidental order is evident in the area surrounding Whitesbog village, near Browns Mills in the heart of the New Jersey pine barrens [Figures 1–4]. Now largely protected by the Pinelands National Reserve, the million-acre region was originally referred to as a 'barrens' because its acid, sandy conditions were unsuited to traditional upland agriculture. Despite this, the indigenous plant and animal diversity is so unique that the Pinelands has been recognized as an International Biosphere Reserve.

Beyond the pitch pines and the buildings, the landscape is organized into clearly defined areas bordered by sand roads [Figure 2]. The lighter areas are cranberry bogs and the darker areas are impoundments of water used for wet-harvesting the berries in early autumn. In the early twentieth century, J. J. White's operation was one of the largest cranberry and blueberry producers in the state. The village has since become an historic site within Brendan T. Byrne State Forest, and many of the oldest bogs are out of

production. These derelict bogs and impoundments have inadvertently become some of the best places to observe a great diversity of indigenous pine barrens flora and fauna. Remnant landforms created by century-old agricultural engineering now present huge areas of open and edge habitat, especially along dike roads and the margins of impoundments. The linear patterns of vegetation evident in Figures 3 and 4 illustrate this. In Figure 3, shallow open water in the foreground is populated by the white fragrant waterlily, *Nymphaea odorata*. From mid-ground to far edge the water becomes more shallow, and soft rush, *Juncus effusus,* dominates. A hedge-like line of highbush blueberry shrubs occupies the moist but not inundated far edge. The forest of pitch pines, *Pinus rigida*, begins just beyond the moist edge, on higher dry sandy ground. The order of the vegetation is primarily the result of the varied yet ordered hydrology created by previous agricultural use. Similarly, Figure 4 shows the narrow strip adjacent to the dike road populated by moisture-tolerant staggerbush, *Lyonia mariana* (orange-red), and sweet pepperbush, *Clethra alnifolia* (yellow), near the wet edge, and drought-tolerant little bluestem, *Schizachyrium scoparium*, along the dry edge of the road. The pattern in Figure 1 might appear random; however, the water in the foreground is shallow enough to provide ideal conditions for the waterlilies, whereas the water beyond is too deep. The density of the waterlilies is ordered by the depth of the water. Though the order can be traced to common origin, the materials and meaning of this landscape have evolved with time and process. From the perspective of a gardener or an artist, the Monet-like drifts of waterlilies are beautiful and desirable. To a cranberry grower intent on keeping impoundments clear and functional, they are merely weeds capable of clogging the system. Whitesbog's unintentional gardens, evolved from utility, illustrate the principles advocated by William Robinson. ●

Figure 5/ Gravetye Manor in West Sussex.

In 1885 William Robinson purchased Gravetye Manor built in the sixteenth century by a local iron-maker [Figure 5]. Surrounded by extensive West Sussex forests, farmland, and meadows, the estate provided Robinson the opportunity to experiment with his wild gardening concepts. Though his gardens at Gravetye included formal elements nearest the manor, Robinson's successful naturalization of diverse native and exotic species has proved to be his most original and enduring work. Robinson was comfortable establishing populations of plants he believed were adapted to local conditions, then intervening only as deemed necessary in the processes he'd set in motion. Many of his plantings survive more than a century later.

A number of *plein air* artists painted Gravetye at Robinson's invitation. Among them, Henry Moon (1857–1905) devoted his attention to working landscapes and wilder parts of the estate. His *Evening Light Through Warrens Wood* (1903) [Figure 7], celebrates the accidental landscape, depicting Robinson's naturalized daffodils while allowing cart ruts to take center stage. Near the end of his life Robinson reflected on his work, writing:

> As to the origin of my ideas of the Wild Garden, I think they first occurred to me along the banks of the Southern Railway between East Grinstead and West Hoathly. Sometimes when I went through the station I had a pocketful of seeds or some bush or plant which I used to scatter about, usually forgetting all about them afterwards but most certainly they all came up again.

The Bluebell Railway still runs historic steam locomotives on this route, and on a recent journey I couldn't resist wondering, as I looked out the window, whether any of the wildflowers growing in the accidental landscape adjacent to the tracks could be traced to William Robinson's pockets [Figure 6].

In 2003, exactly a century after Moon's painting at Gravetye, New Jersey artist Michael Doyle painted a different accidental landscape [Figure 8]. Doyle's scene owes its origin to a power line right-of-way, opened and maintained to safeguard the high voltage transmission lines. Such clearings create edge habitat that is colonized by opportunistic vegetation and animals, both indigenous and introduced. It's doubtful that the utility company would anticipate that the clearing, the resultant vegetation, and the architecture of the transmission towers would create a composition worthy of being painted by someone with the eye to recognize its unintentional beauty and meaning.

Doyle's painting demonstrates a modern sensibility, celebrating what now comprises rural character despite the powerful presence of the tower. Like Moon, Doyle does not attempt to hide the utilitarian aspects of the landscape, or to mask evidence of machinery. In both paintings, utilitarian activity introduces elements that create readily apparent

Figure 7/ *Evening Light Through Warrens Wood*, 1903, Henry Moon. Image use courtesy Peter Herbert and Gravetye Manor.

Figure 8/ *Untitled*, 2003, Michael Doyle.

Figure 9/ Naturalized California poppies turn a disused Chilean railroad right of way into a garden.

visual order and focus, while the whole of the scene reflects the response of autonomous living elements and processes.

Accidental landscapes that have evolved in the aftermath of utilitarian human activity are often gardenesque, or at least have garden-like elements. While traveling in Chile in October 2007 to study indigenous grasses and to photograph designed spaces, I observed a particularly arresting landscape: a recently abandoned railroad line about three hours south of Santiago [Figure 9]. When the railroad was operational, the tracks and right-of-way would have been regularly cleared with herbicides. Shortly after the spraying stopped, the sunny, open conditions provided ideal habitat for California poppies, millions of which now add their color to miles of disused trackage. The state flower of California, this species, *Eschsholzia californica*, occurred from Washington south to Baja California and east to Nevada, Arizona, and New Mexico prior to human intervention. It was introduced to Chile over a century ago, both intentionally, as a garden plant, and unintentionally, along with alfalfa seeds imported from California. Since then it has become widely naturalized, especially in landscapes cleared or otherwise modified by human activity. Many of the spontaneous populations appear to be larger and more reproductively successful than those in their original North American habitats.

The accidental landscape isn't always pretty, but it is always meaningful. Two photos taken from the top of Absecon Lighthouse in Atlantic City, New Jersey, in October 2005, show what are variously called 'desire lines', 'desire paths', or 'paths of desire' [Figures 10, 11]. Built in 1857, the lighthouse was once surrounded by a vibrant community of sturdy brick and frame homes, shops, and churches. Though the lighthouse has been carefully restored, the neighborhood has been reduced to a Detroit-like pattern of abandoned lots and occasional houses. The absence of obstructing buildings enables pedestrians and bicyclists to take direct routes, and the precise order of their paths is revealed by patterns etched into the spontaneous vegetation covering the dry, sandy soil. The patterns are reminiscent of the contrived geometries of classical gardens, whose paths often go nowhere directly and are there merely to provide an opportunity for strolling and contemplation. These un-irrigated, unmanaged, austere Atlantic City paths possess a different drama born of utility and different desires.

Comprised of spontaneously regenerating vegetation and the faunal community it supports, the 'green' component of accidental landscapes often develops at a rapid pace. Designed by the architectural firm of Warren & Wetmore, Asbury Park's Casino was considered a jewel of the New Jersey boardwalk when constructed in 1929–1930. Mismanagement caused the roof to begin failing a half-century later, and by July 2000 the interior had become a virtual garden [Figure 12].

It is too easy to make judgments about the toxicity or viability of accidental landscapes. The living systems they include, especially the novel ones, are complex and often contradictory. In September 2010 while walking a shallow stretch of south-eastern Pennsylvania's White Clay Creek with a small camera in hand, I happened upon a green heron fishing from a fallen tree [Figure 13]. Contemplating the health of the creek's ecology, I took this as a positive sign. I ventured a

Figure 12/ The Casino, Asbury Park, New Jersey.

Figure 10/ Paths of desire photographed from the top of Absecon Lighthouse in Atlantic City, New Jersey.

Figure 13/ Green heron, White Clay Creek, Pennsylvania.

Figure 11/ A broader view from atop the lighthouse.

hundred yards further downstream and what appeared to be an unusual rock protruding above the surface caught my eye [Figure 14]. Closer inspection revealed the rock to be a mineral-encrusted gasoline engine still mounted on a submerged rotary lawn mower. Looking closer yet, I saw something moving inside the rusted-open gas tank. It turned out to be a rather large crayfish [Figure 15]. When I walked upstream a half hour later, the crayfish was still inside the tank.

Musing lightly on what conclusions might be drawn, I framed a range of possibilities: the creek ecology is healthy despite the presence of the mower; it's OK to dump old gasoline lawn mowers in a local creek, since they provide habitat for local wildlife as they rust; a rusted out gas tank of a submerged lawn mower can provide shelter for indigenous crayfish. Only the last is correct since only it is limited to direct observation. Despite my initial dismay at finding the mower, I felt compelled to accept what I observed as proof of possibility. When I walked the same section of the creek a week later after heavy rain and

Figures 14, 15/ Lawn mower engine resembles a rock; Crayfish in lawn mower gas tank.

flooding, the mower was gone. I wondered if the crayfish had found a suitable replacement.

At a quick glance, the adjacent image [Figure 16] might be mistaken for an elegant conservatory with subtropical plantings, but it is in fact the ruins of New Zealand's first Portland cement works. The vegetation on the site is entirely accidental — it is all self-sown — and is a mix of endemic, indigenous, and exotic species. The cabbage tree, *Cordyline australis*, at center, is endemic to New Zealand, occuring without human intervention only in New Zealand. It typically inhabits forest margins, riverbanks, swamps, and other open sunny areas, and is estimated to have been evolving since the Miocene era, approximately 15 million years ago. Long a part of New Zealand's human culture, cabbage trees were utilized by the Māori for food and fiber. The species has been widely introduced to other parts of the globe by humans. Cabbage trees are planted outdoors in mild climates and in greenhouses and conservatories in colder regions.

The cement works dates to the 1880s, when Glasgow immigrant Nathaniel Wilson began the first commercial manufacture of Portland cement in the southern hemisphere. Situated adjacent to the Mahurangi River in Warkworth, north of Auckland, the works produced cement and hydrated lime until its closure in 1929. The derelict state of the structures is not due entirely to time and weather. During the Second World War the site was used for demolition exercises by the New Zealand Home Guard and American military forces. The end result is an accidental landscape that juxtaposes dramatic post-industrial ruins with a wide range of native and naturalized vegetation, including lawn-like grassy cover on many of the moist open sunny areas [Figure 17].

The original vegetation of the Mahurangi River drainage was primarily forest. Since the late nineteenth century, many of the lowland areas have been used for grazing, along with plantation forestry primarily devoted to Monterey pine, *Pinus radiata*. A species endemic to the central coast of

Figure 16/ A self-sown cabbage tree, *Cordyline australis*, graces the Mahurangi Cement Works ruins north of Auckland, New Zealand.

Figure 17/ The sculptural quality of the cement works ruins adds to the appeal of this accidental landscape.

California and Mexico, Monterey pine has become thoroughly naturalized in the Mahurangi region, and the cement works ruins include many specimens of all sizes. When photographing the site in August 2007, I was captivated by one especially grand tree that seemed to have become one with the works [Figure 18]. The huge flare of its trunk and roots equally embraced bricks, cement chunks, and boulders. A cave-like opening just below a sign warning visitors to "stay well clear" of dangerous conditions was enticing. The scene bore an uncanny resemblance to Arthur Rackham's *The Little People's Market* of 1915 [Figure 19]. Rackham (1867–1939) was an English book illustrator revered for his uniquely imaginative contributions to whimsical children's books and mythologies intended for adult readers. Employing an exquisitely detailed style, Rackham pictured fantastical landscapes often inhabited

Figure 18/ A self-sown Monterey pine, *Pinus radiata*, at the Mahurangi ruin.

Figure 19/ *The Little People's Market* by Arthur Rackham.

Figure 20/ An accidental allée of trees nearly 30 m (100 ft) tall grow in the former Pomeroy and Newark railroad right of way.

by gnomes, fairies, and other creatures from mythology, folklore, and fable. Typical of many Rackham landscapes beloved by children and adults, *The Little People's Market* is not beautiful in any conventional sense, and in this aspect it is similar to many accidental landscapes such as the Mahurangi Cement Works. Rackham's fantasy is unapologetic in its celebration of process. Trees, roots, even the terrain itself clearly bear the marks of wear and tear, use and abuse, of diminishment and regeneration. *The Little People's Market* also suggests an outsider's landscape — vibrant and functional, yet separate from the ordered townscape nearby. Rackham hints that there's a lot going on in the accidental landscape that inhabits the periphery of the conventional.

EVIDENCE OF ORDER

———— **Figure 21/** New York ferns flank a pedestrian path below ————
woodlands that have regenerated along the former Pomeroy and
Newark railroad.

The accidental landscape resulting from the abandonment of the Pomeroy and Newark railroad offers evidence of order at both immense and intimate scales. Completed in 1873, the line originally ran from the town of Pomeroy, on the Pennsylvania Railroad's Main Line south through Newark, Delaware, and south-east to Delaware City. Passenger service ceased in 1928 and freight operation was almost completely abandoned by 1940. The tracks ran through woods, farms, and pastures, and crossed the White Clay Creek multiple times on bridges primarily supported by mortared stoneworks. While operational, the railroad kept the tracks and adjacent right-of-way clear of vegetation. In the 70-plus years since the trains stopped running, the line has become habitat for diverse flora and fauna, both indigenous and introduced. At the time of abandonment, many of the exotic tree species now widely naturalized in the region, such as tree of heaven, *Ailanthus altissima*, and Norway maple, *Acer platanoides*, were relatively uncommon. In their absence, indigenous species were the first to take advantage of the opportunity provided by the disused right of way. Trees including American beech, *Fagus grandifolia*, multiple oaks including white oak, *Quercus alba*, red oak, *Quercus rubra*, tuliptree, *Liriodendron tulipifera*, sycamore, *Platanus occidentalis*, and others established themselves and turned many sections of the former railroad into grand allées now nearly 100 feet in height. Photographed from a low-flying helicopter, these dramatic allées seem as though they must have been planted [Figure 20]. Certainly the deliberate establishment of such ordered plantings would require considerable effort and resources, as proved by similar allées in formal gardens.

The neat, ordered appearance of New York fern-lined pedestrian paths running in place of the tracks tells of ever-changing dynamics [Figure 21]. This fern species, *Thelypteris novaboracensis*, is locally indigenous. However, its occurrence in such large sweeps is the combined result of the original clearing for the railroad and its subsequent abandonment, plus the burgeoning population of white tailed deer. Increasing in density as human populations appropriate traditional habitat and eliminate traditional predators, the deer devour much of the ground layer vegetation and leave the ferns, which they find unpalatable. Human foot traffic along the rail trail is sufficient to eliminate fern growth directly in the path.

Close observation of vegetation on one of the line's remaining stone bridge supports offers evidence of order at a more intimate scale [Figure 22]. Colorful graffiti initially caught my eye in October 2005, and I then noticed a few ebony spleenworts, *Asplenium platyneuron*, growing between stones on the vertical surface. One of the larger ferns was partly covered with blue paint, and I wondered if it would survive [Figure 23]. I decided to find out, and made a promise to myself to document changes with photographs. Skipping to November 2007, the same fern had not only survived — it was thriving [Figure 24]. The obvious question was: why is this species growing in what seems such a challenging environmental niche? Like most spleenworts, *Asplenium platyneuron* tolerates highly alkaline conditions and often occurs on limestone rock outcrops and other exposed sites. It prefers evenly moist conditions but can withstand long dry periods. Within the White Clay Creek watershed, many of the spleenwort's former ground-level habitats are now dominated by introduced exotics, particularly Japanese stilt grass, *Microstegium vimineum*. Although the spleenwort is no longer competitive in its traditional niche, the increasingly exposed joints between the stonework now provide viable alternative habitat. Accumulating organic matter creates a growing medium, and lime leaching from the mortar creates alkaline conditions favorable to the spleenwort. The railroad's engineers were intent only on supporting the tracks. Little

Figure 22/ A graffiti-enhanced Pomeroy bridge support.

Figure 23/ Ebony spleenwort freshly painted, October 2005.

Figure 24/ The same plant in November 2007.

did they know their deteriorating work would accidentally become preferred habitat for indigenous ferns.

Returning in October 2012, I found the original spleenwort to be larger than ever and accompanied by dozens of equally healthy new individuals [Figure 25]. Though at a casual glance the spleenworts on the wall might appear randomly positioned, in fact they are highly ordered. All are aligned with joints in the stone.

Earlier in July 2012, I'd noticed ripe wineberries, *Rubus phoenicolasius*, on pendant branches a few yards from the spleenworts [Figure 26]. A group of young children on a natural history outing from a nearby urban school happened by, led by an instructor. After overcoming their initial hesitation I enticed them to sample the wineberries, which they correctly observed taste a lot like raspberries but are not as sweet. I explained that though wineberries were originally from eastern Asia, the species was introduced to North America more than a century ago as an ornamental plant and for hybridizing with commercial raspberries. Now widely naturalized, it is, for many intents and purposes, an integral part of the New World flora.

THE AUTHENTICITY OF AUTONOMY

In his 2006 article for the *Journal of Landscape Architecture* titled "Intentions for the Unintentional: Spontaneous Vegetation as the Basis for Innovative Planting Design in Urban Areas", horticultural ecologist Norbert Kühn begins by saying that spontaneous vegetation occurs without cost, is authentic, and is appropriate to site conditions.[2] In an age when debate about the correctness of natives versus exotics is rife with conflict, it is important not to overlook Kühn's points. The spontaneous plants that grow in accidental landscapes represent the ultimate in sustainable vegetation in that no resources have been consumed in their establishment or maintenance. They are authentic because they are the direct result of autonomous living processes: no intervention has been necessary to establish them, and they wouldn't be thriving unless their needs were being met by conditions on site. Whether spontaneous plants represent ideal vegetation is a matter of judgment. If the ideal is simply to cover a site with vegetation that provides ecosystem services such as cooling, groundwater recharge, carbon sequestration, shelter, and limited sustenance for indigenous fauna, all without commitment of resources, then spontaneous vegetation could be judged ideal. If the ideal is to provide sustenance for indigenous insect and animal specialists that feed only on plants with which they've co-evolved, spontaneous vegetation may be judged the opposite of ideal. Most accidental landscapes are the direct or indirect result of inadvertent or deliberate environmental

Figure 25/ The same spleenwort population in October 2012.

Figure 26/ Wineberries ripe and edible in July 2012.

Figure 27/ Callery pears increasingly dominate a Delaware roadside.

manipulation by humans. They are characterized by complex biological dynamics and a high degree of flux. The novel, evolving processes and biological relationships common to accidental landscapes may not always be ideal; however, the knowledge and resources needed to stop or reverse them on a vast scale do not exist. To recognize and maximize the functionality of accidental landscapes is likely to prove a more achievable and productive goal.

The origin of a great many accidental landscapes can be traced to the introduction of the automobile and its subsequent influence. Figure 27 illustrates an accidental landscape adjacent to the I-95 highway corridor in Delaware. Third or fourth generation woodlands comprised primarily of indigenous species were cleared decades ago during construction of the highway. In subsequent years, Department of Transportation crews used periodic mowing to eliminate spontaneous woody regrowth and to maintain an herbaceous groundcover. This practice was expensive, and the resulting vegetation produced few ecosystem services. As part of a DelDOT project to reduce resource consumption, increase visual appeal, and enhance habitat functionality, mowing was generally suspended. Since then, maintenance cost has been cut dramatically, and the site's appearance and environmental functionality have been significantly enhanced. Though the majority of species spontaneously colonizing the site are regionally indigenous, the exotic Callery pear, *Pyrus calleryana*, is increasingly dominating the site. Originally introduced as an ornamental, Callery pear has escaped from cultivation and is widely naturalized. It thrives in the Mid-Atlantic region without irrigation, fertilization, or pesticides, its fruits are eaten by birds, and its fall color rivals the best of indigenous trees. It is proving so well adapted to conditions on disturbed sites such as the roadside right-of-way that it is capable of producing near monocultures in the course of a few decades. Comprehensive management plans and techniques for maintaining an acceptable balance of Callery pears and more diverse, desirable vegetation have yet to evolve.

Leo Marx's landmark 1964 book *The Machine in the Garden: Technology and the Pastoral Ideal in America* is still relevant for any good gardener interested in contemplating the inherent contradiction between the ideal of what is often referred to as unspoiled Nature and the ideal of better living through technology. Rather than lamenting changes in landscape and human culture wrought by transportation technology, Marx suggests that we would benefit by accepting that "our inherited symbols of order and beauty have been divested of meaning" and by embracing "new symbols of possibility".[3] The 'pastoral' increasingly resides only in memory. The ever-evolving landscape of technology embodies the present. In this spirit I explore old automobile junkyards whenever the opportunity arises, observing and photographing today's Nature.

_____ **Figures 28, 29/** An oriole nest hangs from branches of gray birches; A gray birch emerges from a 1958 Cadillac in a Connecticut junkyard. _____

The two photos above [Figures 28, 29] illustrate the visual and intellectual tension to be enjoyed in a typical overgrown junkyard. I photographed this yard near Waterbury, Connecticut, in late winter, 2008. Look only at Figure 28 and you see the characteristic nest of an oriole suspended from the branches of indigenous gray birches, *Betula populifolia*. Figure 29 shows the immediate context. The birches are part of the spontaneous regrowth in the yard. They are equally authentic whether holding an oriole nest or threading through the front bumper of a 1958 Cadillac.

Ed Lucke's junkyard in south-eastern Pennsylvania is an authentically accidental landscape: a woodland smash palace where oxidation and spontaneous vegetation have resulted in a garden-like car park. The three years I've observed and photographed it have prompted many questions. For example, in terms a residential gardener might use, what would be the ideal foundation planting for a 1951 Lincoln, and what shrub would thrive with minimal care in the engine compartment? Empirical evidence at the yard suggests, respectively, white snakeroot, *Eupatorium rugosum*, and Japanese barberry, *Berberis thunbergii* [Figure 30]. The delaminating safety glass in a 1938 Studebaker Commander reminded me that we inhabit a delaminating landscape in which long-bonded layers are being prized apart by wind, rain, and us [Figure 31]. Our future will reflect how we choose to manage these layers.

To one immersed in such an accidental landscape, the notion of Nature seems quaint and outdated. I grew up knowing Nature as a near-sentient Other that was inclined to benign behavior — except when it wasn't. The problem with the conventional construct is that it is based upon a dichotomy: Man and Nature, or Us and Everything Else. It's difficult to clearly envision our role and responsibility if we are always above or separate from the rest. In his 1980 essay *Ideas of Nature*, Raymond Williams suggested Nature is "a singular name for the real multiplicity of things and living processes".[4] We're all in it, and I can live with that.

_____ **Figure 30/** White snakeroot dominates the ground layer around a _____ 1951 Lincoln while Japanese barberry inhabits the engine compartment.

FOR WANT OF INTENTION

Reminiscent of New York's High Line before it was redesigned, the 9th Street Branch of Philadelphia's Reading Viaduct floats above streets and flows between buildings. After trains stopped running in 1981 a spontaneous forest took root [Figure 32]. Chinese native empress trees, *Pawlownia tomentosa*, dominated, having naturalized in the area from seed pods imported long ago as packing material.

I began photographing the viaduct in 2004 with my friend Paul van Meter, who believed it could become a High Line-like space for Philadelphia. The Viaduct's ownership cleared the vegetation in late 2006, using chainsaws and herbicides to

Figure 31/ A black oak with a 1938 Studebaker.

Figure 32/ Reading Viaduct, 9th Street Branch, May 2006.

Figure 33/ Reading Viaduct, 9th Street Branch, October 2011.

discourage a growing homeless population. The landscape was lifeless, and we avoided it for a few years. Returning in 2010, we were stunned to find that the Viaduct had regenerated into an unintentional meadow garden. Butterflies flitted as flowers bloomed and set seed [Figures 33, 34, 35]. It provided powerful insight to the resiliency of the accidental landscape.

INTENTIONS FOR THE UNINTENTIONAL

On the night of 14 November 1940 incendiary bombs reduced Coventry, England's fourteenth-century cathedral to a burned-out shell with only the bell tower intact. The London Blitz could hardly be called accidental, yet the Coventry Cathedral landscape today is not entirely unintentional. Standing next to a new cathedral, the ruins have been preserved and the landscape turned inside out [Figures 36, 37]. In what was once the cathedral interior, plantings evoking the spontaneous vegetation that took root after the war grow, while occasional seedlings take advantage of nooks and crannies exposed to the elements.

While such deliberate, controlled plantings lack the authenticity or autonomy of spontaneous vegetation, they can be highly effective at evoking the appearance, mood, and history of truly accidental landscapes. New York's High Line park is a wildly successful example of intricately designed and highly managed plantings re-creating a sense of the spontaneous landscape that served as impetus and inspiration. Relatively few

Figure 34/ A buckeye in grass on the Reading Viaduct, October 2011.

Figure 35/ A variegated fritillary on an aster on the Viaduct, October 2011.

———— **Figures 36, 37/** Plants grow in what was once the interior of the Coventry Cathedral; The ruins of Coventry Cathedral view from the bell tower. ————

———— **Figures 38, 39/** Landschaftspark Duisburg-Nord in Germany's Ruhr Valley combines authentic spontaneous vegetation with new plantings; ————
A woodland edge comprised entirely of spontaneous growth.

———————— **Figure 40/** Spontaneous growth at left adjacent to ————————
ordered plantings at right.

of the High Line's current plant species were part of the original spontaneous vegetation: the majority are plausible substitutes.

There are many unresolved questions regarding the practicality of conserving spontaneous vegetation when accidental landscapes become public parks and gardens. Post-industrial sites in Germany demonstrate some of the possibilities. Situated north of Duisburg in the heavily industrialized Ruhr District, the 200-hectare Landschaftspark Duisburg-Nord was once home to a Thyssen blast furnace complex [Figures 38–44]. Begun in 1901, it produced pig iron until operations ceased in 1985. Peter Latz's 1991 re-design made a top priority of conserving and celebrating the site's industrial, cultural, and biological history. Spontaneous vegetation has been maintained in place, offering visual interest, cooling the site, and enhancing habitat value [Figures 39, 40, 41]. New plantings, instead of attempting to evoke wildness, were installed for unapologetically ornamental or functional purposes [Figures 38, 42, 43]. The formal order of these plantings provides dramatic contrast with the textures and patterns of wild growth and the aging industrial structures. Soils polluted when the furnace was in operation have been allowed to remain to be cleansed by phytoremediation [Figure 44]. Furnace buildings have been adapted for multiple visitor services, including a transformer room that is now a restaurant and pub. Despite the relatively un-manicured aesthetic, the park is visited by hundreds of thousands each year.

ADDITION BY REDUCTION

Can you imagine creating functional woodland and meadow spaces within an accidental landscape without doing any planting at all? A project at Carrie Furnaces near Pittsburgh, Pennsylvania, is testing the idea. Built in 1907, Carrie Furnaces

no. 6 and 7 are the only non-operative blast furnaces in the Pittsburg District to remain standing. Rare examples of pre-Second World War iron-making technology, the furnaces tower 92 feet over the Monongahela River [Figure 45]. At its peak the Carrie produced over 1,000 tons of iron per day, but the furnaces have been silent since 1978. Designated a National Historic Landmark in 2006, the furnaces are destined to become the core cultural attraction within the proposed Homestead Works National Park. Rivers of Steel Heritage Corporation has been working on stabilizing the site, establishing a museum, and developing related programs focused on the role of Carrie Furnaces in the region's iron and steelmaking industry.

I began studying and photographing the site in 2006, attracted by the visual power of its industrial architecture and especially by the extensive regenerative woody and herbaceous vegetation surrounding and partially enveloping the furnaces [Figure 46]. Acres of open sunny ground are covered with

—— **Figures 41, 42/** Spontaneous growth is conserved at the edge of new plantings; New plantings create a formally ordered space within wildness. ——

—— **Figures 43, 44/** Unapologetically ornamental planting provides contrast; Soil remediation is accomplished with formally ordered plantings. ——

meadow-like masses of native and exotic grasses and flowering forbs that have established themselves since the site has been idle. The mix includes little bluestem, ravenna grass, butterfly milkweed, multiple goldenrod species, St Johnswort, vibrantly blue-flowered viper's bugloss [Figure 48], and an unusual thoroughwort, *Eupatorium altissimum* [Figure 46], which also occurred on the High Line prior to reconstruction. Multiple sumac species, cottonwoods, and sycamores dominate the shrub and tree growth [Figure 49]. Though much of the vegetation needed to be eliminated to prevent damage to the historic structures, in many areas it added to the appeal of the site by providing flower and foliage color, relief from summer heat, and habitat for insects and animals. Rivers of Steel's tours and programs had been expanding beyond industrial history to include more recent cultural layers of the Carrie Furnaces. Art tours focused on the site's often beautiful graffiti attracted new audiences who then became curious about the iron and steel legacy [Figure 47].

With this in mind I began working in 2013 with Ron Baraff, Rivers of Steel's Director of Museum Collections, and Rick Rowlands, a steel industry expert helping with stabilization, on a project to add a biological component to site management and programing. Naming the project "Addition by Reduction", we set out to enhance the beauty and functionality of the site's vegetation by selective removal. We began this editing process by taking inventory on foot and from high vantage points on the furnaces, then determining where to mow or cut. Figure 50 shows the results of less than three hours work and two gallons of gas, employing a vintage Ford tractor to create pathways and a circular green 'room' that now provides a shaded space where tour groups can gather while viewing the furnaces.

The following month Ron and I were near the top of the furnace when a red-tailed hawk flew closely past. Then a bald eagle passed in a different direction. I watched the big bird until it landed in trees at the periphery of the site, then scrambled

Figures 45, 46/ Carrie Furnaces tower 28 m (92 ft) over the Monongahela River; Spontaneous meadows and woodlands in early September.

Figures 47, 48/ Graffiti enlivens an elevated track and derelict engine; Blue *Echium vulgare* blooms in mid-June.

Figure 49/ View to spontaneous woodlands from atop the furnace.

Figure 51/ A bald eagle takes flight at Carrie Furnaces.

down to see if I could get a photograph. I arrived just in time to catch the eagle again taking flight [Figure 51]. The episode proved that the Carrie Furnaces site is still very much alive, though in an entirely different way than when it began. It reminded me of the resilience of autonomous living communities, and I couldn't help thinking that to witness the wildlands of the future, we only need to look toward the accidental landscapes of today.

NOTES

All photography is by Rick Darke except Figure 2.

1/ Robinson, William, *The Wild Garden*, London: John Murray, 1870, p.i.

2/ Kühn, Norbert, "Intentions for the Unintentional: Spontaneous Vegetation as the Basis for Innovative Planting Design in Urban Areas", *Journal of Landscape Architecture*, Autumn 2006, pp. 46–53.

3/ Marx, Leo, *The Machine in the Garden: Technology and the Pastoral Ideal in America*, New York: Oxford University Press, 1964, pp. 364–365.

4/ Williams, Raymond, *Ideas of Nature* in *Problems of Materialism and Culture*, London: Verso, 1980, pp. 68–69.

Figure 50/ Paths and a green garden 'room' are created by editing.

280 /STEVEN BROWN

AGRIVATED ASSAULT: FROM GUERRILLA GARDENING TO THE AGE OF ECOLOGY

The ambition for something better than what will simply do translates across every language, nation, and era — well, almost every era. As the catastrophic energy of the twentieth century spills over into our own, even the most starry-eyed optimist today might second-guess his Zodiac. But minor revolutions abound. As chicken runs, beehives, and compost piles infiltrate the manufactured lawndoms of suburbia, and urban renewal projects like New York City's High Line reclaim defunct transit corridors for recreation, ecology strengthens its grip on the public imagination.[1] But change is slow, very slow, and if major revolutions are to come, legislative reform must aspire to something more creative than park subsidies and neatly arbored sidewalks.

"The imagination", John Dewey once argued, "endures because, while at first strange with respect to us, it is enduringly familiar with respect to the nature of things."[2] Thoreau knew this too. "To conceive of [nature]", he said, "with a total apprehension I must for the thousandth time approach it as something totally strange."[3] In the spirit of Dewey and Thoreau, I ask myself what strangeness characterizes our Age, if ours is indeed what environmental historian Donald Worster calls the Age of Ecology.[4] I take a walk toward Boston, a couple miles out from my apartment. I'm Don Quixote, ready to meet a giant wind turbine on the horizon. But no such luck. I see only Delta and American Airlines hoisting upward from Logan. I note one or two solar panels along the way — more like discarded Polaroids than sun farms. The word 'undeveloped' comes to mind and turns into a refrain as I pass abandoned construction lots.

I suppose I'm looking for what cultural historian Leo Marx called the "middle landscape" — that compromise between the garden and the machine, between country and city, that Marx and others like him believed we would have achieved by now.[5] I'm beginning to realize just how strange the concept of middle landscape really must be — how difficult to envision. How does a whole community expand the "circle of its imagination" (to borrow a phrase from Ralph Waldo Emerson) to include the unfamiliar?[6] And how can this be done within decades, not geological epochs? At this point, we know that the kind of environmental change needed far exceeds the capacity of conservationist policy and conservative planning. We've tilted the machine. The rules have changed. In the face of cataclysmic and irrefutable environmental disasters — the nuclear devastations at Chernobyl and Fukushima, the BP oil spill near Louisiana's Gulf Coast, and Big Coal's contamination of West Virginia's drinking water — radical environmental policy reform measures are now the only measures worth consideration. But those kinds of ideas, the hard-to-imagine ideas, exist at the peripheries of the larger debate.

Therefore, my walk takes a detour. I stray from strictly disciplinary thoroughfares, trespassing into fields of urban design, environmental and protest history, and literature, to reconcile environmental pioneering with the need for new symbols of ecological progress in a country whose aesthetic idols still derive from pastoral notions of the frontier. Then again, 'new' symbols are not exactly what we need, for the staying power of any symbol depends on the historical compost in which it has matured. I'm looking for an image like the middle landscape, an image rooted adequately enough in American history to be widely recognizable, but expandable enough to exceed the limits of its historical baggage, its injustices and flaws. A slew of such images may exist, but one in particular resonates with my love of a good walk: the figure of Johnny Appleseed, America's original guerrilla gardener [Figure 1].

To characterize the importance of Appleseed, the larger part of this essay homes in on the history, aesthetics, and labor of the self-proclaimed guerrilla gardener who attends to landscapes abjured by city authorities or hoarded by absentee landlords. Plant without permission and without precedent! — this is the guerrilla's call to arms, one that gets a little louder with every irreparable meltdown and every irreversible spill.

Guerrilla gardening, historically, has acted in response to some difficult questions: How do neighborhoods negotiate the roadblocks of state legislation against ecological development? How do nonprofits garner the financial support of a political system determined to keep in place familiar industries of exploitation? How can the public get involved effectively, beyond joining high-fee organizations and signing endless and too often pointless petitions? These are just some of the more tedious and aggravating concerns. But they are enough to bind the hands of those with the resources needed to meet head-on the challenge of creating the middle landscape.

HEAD-ON

What many have called the most energy efficient commercial building in America opened on Earth Day, 2013, in Seattle's Capitol Hill. The Bullitt Center is a 50,000 square foot, six-story, zero-waste complex built to accommodate both business and residential needs [Figure 2]. It is an incredible feat of eco-engineering, not just for the example it sets for the community but for what it asks of its community. Each occupant meets a rigorous energy budget, sacrificing (if one can call solar energy, rainwater recycling, and automatic window ventilation sacrifices) some of the conveniences of traditional apartment living. Even allowing for sacrifice, design can do only so much. If this 'living' building truly lives, it is because of assimilation rather than sacrifice, as a hermit crab animates its shell.[7]

But can it catch on? "If this building is alone five years from now", worries Bullitt Center Foundation CEO, Dennis Hayes, "then it's just been a complete waste."[8] The Bullitt Center, after all, is not utopian fantasy realized. It's the product of intense cooperative reform between city government, its political constituents, and the general public. But outdated and inefficient building codes, not just in Seattle but all over America, make sustainable building, and consequently the cultivation of urban ecology, practically illegal. Organizations like OCEAN (Online Code Environment and Advocacy Network), BCAP (Building Codes Assistance Project), and the AGC (Associated General Contractors) decipher reams of cryptic, outdated code in order to fashion toolkits for city developers. Unfortunately, energy efficiency is optional in the United States. Many state governments choose not to legislate the

Figure 1/ A group of Girl Scouts with Johnny Appleseed historical marker, Richland County, Ohio, c. 1950–1959.
Photograph courtesy of the Ohio Historical Society.

Figure 2/ A 50,000 square foot, six-story, zero-waste complex: The Bullitt Center, Seattle, Washington. Photograph courtesy of Nic Lehoux.

modest efficiency goals drafted by organizations like the Energy Efficient Codes Coalition. Therefore architects are often held hostage by political fiat.[9]

If simply constructing an energy efficient building is difficult, imagine the impatience of futurist architect Mitchel Joachim. Joachim got his start with the late urban designer William J. Mitchell. Together they created the MIT City Car, an emission-free, 200 mpg, all-electric vehicle that weighs less than 1,000 pounds.[10] The City Car was designed for dense urban environments. Scaling up those designs, Joachim cofounded Terreform One, an open-source, nonprofit, urban ecology think tank. Terreform One facilitates architectural design for an economically diversified consumer base — in other words, not just rich corporations or private firms. From jetpacks to passenger blimps, from collapsible cars to waste-imbibing fungus towers, from homes mobilized by caterpillar tracks to tree hotels, Joachim's team re-envisions the urban landscape in such a way that only nature itself, to recall Dewey, would find familiar.[11]

In 2010, Nick Kaloterakis sketched a concept design for Joachim's Eco-City [Figure 3].[12] At a glance, the entire landscape cuts a crystalline figure. Smooth, metallic balloons dot the troposphere. People bubble to work or to the store à la Glinda, the Good Witch of the North. Innumerable acres of photovoltaic farms on the city's roof space simulate an emerald facade. Geothermal and wind utilities reinforce the grid. And instead of a cathedral or bank tower, the central feature of this city is a waste-to-energy plant, the city's systole and diastole, its ecological showpiece. I call the left half of the image the *arbor resartus*, tree retailored. Here nothing as prominent as

the waste-to-energy plant stands out. But Terreform One's *Fab Tree Hab* project zooms in on ground-level mechanics. What looks to be an unexceptional, leafy canopy doubles as the awning of a pleached suburb. Pleaching, as most gardeners know, is the art of grafting plants to scaffolds and shaping them into fences, topiaries, or as the case may be, condos [Figure 4]. Like the Bullitt Center, Joachim's tree houses require a completely different approach to home maintenance. Instead of washing windows and siding, you have to know if your tree has beetles, if it needs water, or if the soil is too acidic [Figure 5]. Joachim explains the ins and outs:

> The trunks of inosculate, or self-grafting, trees, such as Elm, Live Oak, and Dogwood, are the load-bearing structure, and the branches form a continuous lattice frame for the walls and roof. Weaved along the exterior is a dense protective layer of vines, interspersed with soil pockets and growing plants. Prefab scaffolds cut from 3D computer files control the plant growth in the early stages. On the interior, a clay and straw composite insulates and blocks moisture, and a final layer of smooth clay is applied like a plaster to dually provide comfort and aesthetics. Existing homes built with cob (clay & straw composite) demonstrate the feasibility, longevity, and livability of the material as a construction material. In essence, the tree trunks of this design provide the structure for an extruded ecosystem, whose growth is embraced over time. Living examples of pleached structures include the Red Alder bench by Richard Reames, 'Sycamore Tower' by Axel Erlandson.[13]

The sheer magnitude of these projects reminds us that the clock is ticking. Whether the future of sustainable architecture aligns itself with Joachim's ecological Oz, or something less conspicuous, like Ebenezer Howard's Garden City with its agricultural greenbelts and open air markets, tomorrow's

Figure 3/ A sketch of Terreform One's Eco-topia. Nick Kaloterakis, *The Urban Remodeler*. Image courtesy of the artist.

———— **Figure 4/** A pleached suburb: *Fab Tree Hab* 1. Rendering by Mitchell Joachim, Lara Greden, Javier Arbona, and Melanie Fessel. ————
Image courtesy of Mitchell Joachim.

———— **Figure 5/** *Fab Tree Hab*, Living Graft Prefab Structure: "Our dwelling is composed with 100% living nutrients. Here traditional anthropocentric ————
doctrines are overturned and human life is subsumed within the terrestrial environs. Home, in this sense, becomes indistinct and fits itself
symbiotically into the surrounding ecosystem. This home concept is intended to replace the outdated design solutions at Habitat for Humanity. We
propose a method to grow homes from native trees. A living structure is grafted into shape with prefabricated Computer Numeric Controlled (CNC)
reusable scaffolds. Therefore, we enable dwellings to be fully integrated into an ecological community." Mitchell Joachim, Terreform One, 2014.
Rendering by Mitchell Joachim, Lara Greden, Javier Arbona, and Melanie Fessel. Image courtesy of Mitchell Joachim.

sustainable metropolis has 'No Trespass' written all over it. Even an optimist like Joachim hesitates to predict specific dates for the completion of his cities. "Once we heard about cell phones", he says, "it was seven years before we started dropping the landline ... it took about 15 years before you could buy a hybrid car on every lot. It takes around 40 years to produce a large shift in the way buildings are constructed. Entire cities? It's 100, 150 years."[14]

150 years? CO_2 emissions reached 400 ppm in 2013 for the first time in human history. To have another 150 years would be an impossible luxury. At this point, it's cold comfort to talk about cities of the future. So where do we begin?

DIGGING FOR UTOPIA

"It is always too early, or too late", argues Harvard professor Homi Bahba, "to talk about 'cities of the future'."[15] To look at the problem from the point of view of Bullitt Center founder Dennis Hayes, earliness and lateness have nothing to do with chronology. Architectural time evokes a helix of policy and building codes that speed up or slow down in proportion to the amount of red tape. Between early and late, between old policy and new, we step into the clearing called the present, perhaps the only usable notion of time in the Age of Ecology. While Hayes, Joachim, and others participate in the democratic system for reform, guerrilla gardeners work in those areas where policy has yet to be solidified.

Take graffiti, for instance. Paint a smiley face on someone else's "wall, fence, building, sign, rock, monument, grave stone", etc., and risk a three-year stint in state prison, a two-year house arrest, a fine of $1,500, or 500 hours of community service. Both the act and the consequences are pretty clearly defined.[16] But what if, instead of spray paint, I mix some buttermilk with moss puree and use it to paint an ox on a neglected public fence [Figure 6]? After a few weeks of gentle misting and negligible upkeep, the milky smudges vegetate, maturing into a green image reminiscent of Lascaux. Does my ox confound the legalese of damage and defacement, especially when the material used grows freely on sidewalks, brick walls, and fence posts? The real issue, of course, is property, and not just any property: properties forsaken by the city or its owners — places historically enticing to the guerrilla gardener.

Not surprisingly, the term 'guerrilla' originally became affiliated with gardening in New York City. In 1973, a young painter and her green-thumbed entourage scattered vegetable seeds in vacant, run-down lots around her neighborhood. The painter's name was Liz Christy. She and her friends called themselves Green Guerrillas because they knowingly littered on private property with their legumes. Christy's efforts, it must be said, came at an opportune moment. Given the poor

Figure 6/ Sustainable, eco-sensitive graffiti. Janelle Gunther, *Moss Bull*, buttermilk and moss puree. Photograph courtesy of the artist.

Figure 7/ Adam Purple cultivating his Garden of Eden, 1984. Lower East Side, New York City. Photograph by Stephen Barker.

economic state in which many parts of NYC found itself in the 1970s, any public work that beautified the city at no cost to itself might have thrived. In any case, Christy's garden gained favorable attention by local media, and not long afterwards, the city threw in its support legally, incorporating the plot as a community garden.[17]

Legal validation of gardens like Christy's is unique. Most guerrillas are denied the blessing of their municipality, most notably, David Wilkie, aka Adam Purple [Figure 7]. Purple's activism overlaps the same decade as Christy's. At the time, he lived in the Lower East Side of Manhattan, where children played in the garbage below his window. Recalling his own childhood outside of Independence, Missouri, among the "ducks and chickens and frogs", Adam Purple began to clear the trash and debris and to transform the lot into a garden.[18]

Later, Adam Purple would be evicted from his home (though technically he squatted there), but for many years he remained a visible icon, eccentrically regal in his purple jumpsuit, favoring a certain poet's beard and no less observant of the same poet's creed: "For every atom belonging to me as good belongs to you."[19] Adam Purple labored with local volunteers, bicycling manure in from Central Park and recycling nearby rubble into pathways and fencing for the garden. The city continued demolishing the buildings surrounding what Adam Purple called the Garden of Eden, apropos of his own *nom de guerre* [Figure 8]. But he wasn't just recycling wasteland. The scene became a living parable. In his mind, the garden expanded like the rings of a tree, knocking down the sprawl of condemned tenements and growing the core of the community.[20] Sadly, the city bulldozed Eden (loss being a fate to which Edens, by definition, succumb) despite backing from local TV and radio, despite the many and lengthy petitions, and despite the protests organized by those who had personally improved the land — property which, in the hands of the city, had become a threat to their children.

It would be naïve to use a word like 'failure' to describe the eventual destruction of Adam Purple's Eden. In its day, the garden attracted locals of all ages. Resident diggers, sowers,

pruners, and harvesters reaped compensations no paycheck could dignify. In the ensuing battle against the machines, the gardeners summoned a strange courage, strange at least by patriotic or cinematic standards. They stood by the four inches of topsoil they had rescued from oblivion, they stood surrounded by crumbling apartment complexes and destitution on par with Steinbeck's Joads, they stood alongside sunflowers, walnut trees, cornstalks, and raspberries, and, whether they knew it or not, by taking their stand, they joined in solidarity with guerrilla gardeners going back to the seventeenth century and beyond.

GUERRILLA GARDENING'S ROOTS

During the English Civil War, England's commons harbored and sustained those who could not or would not labor for the landed aristocracy. Self-reliant craftsmen set up shop in the forests. Squatters occupied the wastes. Itinerant merchants depended on the stability of unenclosed land. Crown and

Figure 8/ Adam Purple's Garden of Eden, 1982. Photograph by Stephen Barker.

Church stigmatized these people as lawless vagabonds, what in today's Occupy parlance we might call 'the 99 percent'. Privatization of the commons became a way to curtail vagrancy (of course, colonial exile was also an option). But equal access to land was a right etched into the hearts of both secular and religious Englishmen and women. In fact, given sectarian resistance to the privatization of the commons, one might argue that land remained one of the few things that bridged religious and secular values. Ranters, Seekers, Quakers, and Levellers all renounced celestial orthodoxy for terrestrial divinity. God bestrode the human heart, and the heart thrived in the world.[21]

Exemplary among these dissenters were the Diggers. The Diggers took their cue from Gerrard Winstanley, a religious nonconformist with sympathies we might liken to those of New England's Transcendentalists — namely, a sacred regard for nature and self-reliance. Though often depicted wearing the cleric's severe and eclipsing hat, Winstanley shared none of the Puritans' intolerance toward alternative thinkers, so long as the alternative had nothing to do with private property. He committed himself to humanity but, like poet Walt Whitman, took off his hat "to nothing known or unknown or to any man or number of men".[22] When Parliament threatened to sell off the commons in order to pay wartime debts, Winstanley resisted. Why should he, or anyone else who had quartered soldiers during the war, relinquish what he'd helped to preserve? In his pamphlets, Winstanley declared independence from the tyranny of all landlords. "Every freeman", he said, "shall have a freedom in the earth, to plant or build, to fetch from the store-houses anything he wants, and shall enjoy the fruits of his labours without restraint from any", and most importantly, "he shall not pay rent to any landlord."[23]

Winstanley didn't just talk the talk. When Surrey's landlords overran St George's Hill with their sheep and cattle herds, preventing public access to the commons, Winstanley organized a public dig. The action first evolved into something like an agricultural sit-in but eventually blossomed into a small community. Like Adam Purple's nonviolent protest against New York's wrecking crew, the Diggers gardened in vain against the landed elite. The lords of the surrounding estates harassed and filed suit against the Diggers. And when legal methods proved inadequate, they employed more violent tactics. The Digger communities were burned and destroyed, their women and children beaten severely.[24]

Winstanley's venture lasted only 12 and a half months. But environmental history owes much to the Diggers' legacy. Nineteenth-century back-to-the-landers and single-taxers drew inspiration from Winstanley's values. In 1966, inhabitants of San Francisco's Haight-Ashbury district appropriated the Digger name, as did the Diggers of Hyde Park. Many others followed, including, more recently, a Londoner named Richard Reynolds, founder of GuerrillaGardening.org and leading advocate for guerrilla gardening in the twenty-first century.[25]

ILLICIT FLOWER BOXES

Reynolds, a resident of Central London's Elephant & Castle junction, began his crusade in 2004 by reviving the dead flower boxes outside his apartment complex. Because no one seemed to care much about the state of these boxes, it came as some surprise to Reynolds when, after he tidied things up, the apartments' administrative authorities rendered the garden to its previous state of disrepair. A legal struggle ensued. Though I cannot imagine what the objections might have been, Reynolds insisted he would shoulder the cost of maintenance himself. Ultimately, management granted Reynolds permission to cultivate the site legally, which, Reynolds claims, is the ambition of all guerrilla gardeners.

But had permission been asked at the start, management doubtlessly would have refused.[26] Why? Who knows? But the experience emboldened Reynolds to adopt social heresies akin to Winstanley's: "I do not wait for permission to become a gardener", Reynolds says, "but dig wherever I see horticultural potential. I do not just tend existing gardens but create them from neglected space. I, and thousands of people like me, step out from home to garden land we do not own. We see opportunities all around us. Vacant lots flourish as urban oases, roadside verges dazzle with flowers and crops are harvested from land that was assumed to be fruitless." Guerrilla gardening is, put plainly, "the illicit cultivation of someone else's land".[27] Newly motivated and determined, Reynolds launched his guerrilla gardening website to help organize gardeners from all over the world to perform their midnight raids on urban wasteland.

THE MAN WHO PLANTED TREES

The guerrilla gardener, though committed to political reform and environmental justice, operates with an expectation of loss. I can think of no better example to explain just what I mean than Jean Giono's influential short story, "The Man Who Planted Trees" (L'homme qui plantait des arbres). Giono's tale recounts the life and works of a wandering agrarian, Elzeard Bouffier. The title is its own spoiler. Bouffier totes a sack of acorns across the Alpes de Haute Provence and its surrounding wastelands, leaving saplings in his prodigious wake. Plotwise, that's it. But to make matters somewhat more improbable, Bouffier plants his oaks in the shadows of the World Wars, dropping seeds while airplanes drop bombs. Many of Bouffier's trees burn at the altars of Ares. Nature, no less ruthless, cannibalizes her fare share as well. Bouffier's labor meets resistance on all sides. Nevertheless, he plants on, not ignorant of his losses but anticipating them.

If a crisis is to be found in Giono's story, it must have more to do with "illicit cultivation" than the loss of any trees. The narrator asks Bouffier if the land is his: "He said it wasn't. Did he know who the owner was? No, he didn't. He thought it must be common land, or perhaps it belonged to people who weren't interested in it. He wasn't interested in who they were."[28] By the end of his life, enough of Bouffier's seeds survive to reforest miles and miles of barren valley, attracting homesteaders to a *trompe l'oeil* of wilderness.

If the plot of Giono's story walks too fine a line between protest literature and allegory, consider the story's context: the technology of war obscured, indeed made totally invisible, by pastoral narrative. Time, in the invisible sphere of weapons and weapons development, progresses arithmetically, one bomb at a time, perhaps in a million different factories, but still at increments of one, since the bombs cannot reproduce themselves. The bombs drop arithmetically also. This kind of linear progression suggests its own goals. To reach point B from point A in the fastest time, all obstacles preventing a straight line of motion must go.[29] Earlier, I characterized progress and time for urban designers as matters of policy. In this scheme, progress and time maintain shared interests in the perpetuation of environmental disaster.

Now imagine if Bouffier had planted his trees along the bombardier's flight line or a line easily targeted by any machine advancing in linear fashion from target to target. The loss would have been swift and comprehensive: total rather than marginal. But progress and time for the guerrilla gardener are geometric rather than arithmetic, expansive rather than linear. Bouffier lives and works in the wasteland, off the highway and common lines of transport. The oaks he plants, unlike the bombs, have a reproduction value independent of his own labor. They proliferate themselves. In the wake of Bouffier's plantings, the forest grows not just forward but backward and outward, upward and downward. In the event of hurricanes, floods, fires, or insects, the biological factory keeps churning out seeds and leaves. Something will survive.

Slow forest succession complicates matters. Giono's story spans a lifetime. In that same period, several wars come and go. But if we bear in mind that this is only one person working with one species of tree (though Bouffier does experiment with others), we might imagine the impact of a hundred guerrilla gardeners armed with a plethora of species, adding to geometrical growth the advantage of dimensions.

But why study the life of fictional characters like Bouffier? Because real Bouffiers exist. In 2006, Indian conservationist and octogenarian, Bhausaheb Santuji Thorat, inspired by Giono's story, began planting millions of trees in the arid *tehsil* region outside of Mumbai. "I set myself a target of planting 10 million trees a month", says Thorat, "but I couldn't have done it alone. So I decided to get the people of Sangamner with me. That's how I exceeded the target by over

four times." In one year, Thorat and his community planted 90 million seeds over 49,000 acres. Like Bouffier, Thorat experienced loss. Drought and insects plagued the nurseries. Only an estimated ten to 12 percent of the trees survived.[30] But that slim wedge of cultivation did much to revitalize both the land and the community's optimism. Reynolds' flower box comes back to mind. What are a few sabotaged geraniums to the billion tree movement they inspire?

Thorat's commitment resonates with Nobel Peace Prize recipient Wangari Maathai's efforts in Kenya. Maathai, founder of the Green Belt Movement, responded to Kenya's deforestation and its consequence, rampant malnutrition, with a movement among women to empower themselves and their community by planting trees. Together, they planted over 47 million trees across Kenya against opposition from a ruthlessly misogynistic and antidemocratic government.[31] Eventually, the Green Belt guerrillas seduced a larger, international audience, inspiring the United Nations Environment Programme (UNEP) to develop a Billion Tree Campaign. Thorat and Maathai are just two prominent examples of how illicit cultivation can impact social climates by reclaiming natural environments. There are many other examples, including a figure at the forefront of American history who straddles the dividing line between fact and fiction: John Chapman, better known as Johnny Appleseed.

JOHNNY APPLESEED: ANTI-HERO OR WILDERNESS-SAINT?

Sometime between 1792 and 1796, John Chapman and his half brother Nathanial waved goodbye to the Connecticut River Valley and set out for the Great Unknown of the Ohio Wilderness on foot — actually, on bare feet. We know very little about his motivations, but being one of several siblings fighting for room to breathe in a small house may have expedited his escape. Post-Revolutionary America was also a mess economically. Congress had recalled all of its paper money, dropping the circulation value down to zero. Farming families, such as Chapman's, suffered most from the downturn. Then there is Chapman's religious fervor. He would later become a devoted Swedenborgian, but the initial allure of "religious individualism and romantic dreams" out there in the untainted territories might have called him from hearth and home. And as at least one historian argues, we can't discount the incentive of cheap land.[32]

Whatever the reason, Chapman's real story doesn't quite live up to Disney's animated sing-along. This barefoot, seed-bombing, homeless peripatetic is the antihero to America's lauded wilderness saints: backwoodsmen like Cooper's Natty

Bumppo or Davy Crockett and Daniel Boone; the larger than life, Paul Bunyan; the perpetual man-child, Rip Van Winkle; the Yankee oracle, Jack Downing; and the boatsmen of Twain's Mississippi adventures [Figure 9].

Chapman's nomadic gardening habits imply a more radical lifestyle than his legend would have us believe. To explain, we have to revisit the itinerant merchants and squatters mentioned earlier. Wandering families in preindustrial society proved difficult for kings to manage, which is to say, difficult to tax. In order to make the Chapmans of the world "legible", as historian James Scott puts it, the landed elites mapped local residents. Enter linear progress. By deforesting the commons and shaping them into quantifiable grids, the elites prevented self-sustaining farmers and craftsmen from using the wilderness to disappear. Authorities now monitored labor and enforced royal decree with less friction. Armies mobilized more efficiently through the grids. Add to these adjustments a few bureaucratic details, like fixing surnames as matters of public record, and the modern urban infrastructure is born.[33]

Chapman shared in the patriotic zeal one would expect from a generation of young Americans only a handful of birthdays removed from the nation's independence. He was not anti-statist by today's measure. But he did live off the map, calling home wherever he laid his cast iron hat. Nomadic life was not uncommon on the frontier. But few braved the winters, risked starvation, or bared themselves to ambush by Indians for very long if they could help it. Frontierspeople explored with purpose: to develop land and settle. And at first glance, this seems like Chapman's ambition too, given his early business investments.

In the mid-1790s, Chapman arrived at Warren, Pennsylvania, and was hired by a land agent of the Holland Land Company as a surveyor or speculator — an ironic role for one who defied all customs regarding private property and often exchanged labor in lieu of cash.[34] Chapman, like the fictional Bouffier, never settled. But if Chapman had wanted to succeed in the land business, he would have had to substantiate himself by proving ownership of some kind of estate, whether large or small. To prove ownership, you had to plant yourself in one spot. You had to be seen, and your land had to be 'improved', i.e., made recognizable. Chapman, however, remained hieroglyphic, planting only his trees and moving along. Historian Howard Means elaborates:

> If John Chapman was only one of many nurserymen trying to make a living at the edge of the known world of commerce, his approach to the business couldn't have been more original. Of overhead, he had none so long as he slept outside, as he most often did, and dined on the grains and nuts and berries the fields and forest had to offer. Capital costs were near zero, too: an ax for felling, a scythe for mowing, a grub hoe for planting.... Chapman left the nurseries to survive on their

own. Transportation costs didn't count, since he seemed compelled to walk in any event.[35]

Almost everything about Chapman turned the American Dream upside down, not least of all his pacifism. I've never heard of anyone else dousing his fire at night to prevent a mosquito's suicide. Chapman wouldn't even graft his orchards because he couldn't stand the thought of injuring the saplings. So he planted from seed, though it may have meant bitter, if not inedible, apples. Compare this Saint Francis-like empathy to the cruelties of other American wilderness heroes: Leatherstocking, for instance, who measures his He-Manliness by his marksmanship; or Bunyan who fells entire forests with a flex of his terrible bicep; or any of the Indian fighters who scalp their way into the hearts of fainting damsels.

Though Chapman did own land, his relationship to it was largely usufruct. He kept no one out and rarely kept himself in. He was a bricoleur, a vagabond, a patriotic anarchist, and a model guerrilla gardener, cultivating land without expanding territory.

MERELY HORTICULTURAL ANTICS?

— **Figure 9/** Johnny Appleseed, America's original guerrilla gardener. — Illustration of Johnny Appleseed planting seeds, from "Stories of Ohio" by William Dean Howells, 1897. Image courtesy of the Ohio Historical Society.

With the example of Bouffier and his avatars, I've moved away from the urban environments that prompted this essay. I provide these contexts for guerrilla gardening to emphasize the political significance of what otherwise might be dismissed as the antics of horticultural hipsters. The illicit cultivation of land is only part of the story. So too is the war against poverty, resistance to government surveillance, establishment of health and safety, advancement of minority rights, growth of community, accessibility to education, priority of empathy and tolerance, and the ongoing justification of art. These illicit cultivations bewilder — overtake with wilderness — the machines of linear progress. The guerrilla gardener, in essence, unmaps both her environment and herself. Only in this way can the necessary space be cultivated for the middle landscape of the future.

NOTES

1/ For links to more High Line ventures, see Vanessa Quirk, "The 4 Coolest High Line Inspired Projects", *Huffpost Arts & Culture*, 21 July 2012, http://www.huffingtonpost.com/2012/07/21/high-line-projects_n_1676139.html.

2/ Dewey, John, *Art as Experience*, New York: Perigee Books, 1980, p. 269.

3/ *The Writings of Henry David Thoreau*, http://thoreau.library.ucsb.edu/writings_journals_pdfs/J15f4-f6.pdf.

4/ Worster, Donald, *Nature's Economy: A History of Ecological Ideas*, second ed., Cambridge, UK: Cambridge University Press, 1994.

5/ Marx, Leo, *The Machine in the Garden: Technology and the Pastoral Ideal in America*, New York: Oxford University Press, 1964.

6/ Emerson, Ralph Waldo, "Circles", *The Essential Writings of Ralph Waldo Emerson*, Brooks Atkinson ed., New York: Modern Library, 2000.

7/ *Bullitt Center: A Project of the Bullitt Center Foundation*, http://bullittcenter.org.

8/ *Living Proof*: http://bullittcenter.org/news/blog/new-video-living-proof.

9/ Specific efficiency policies have not been issued in the US at the Federal level since 2007. Individual states and cities act on code revision independently. To see what building codes and policies your city has adopted, visit your city's website, or check out the US Department of Energy's Building Energy Codes Program to see what codes your state has adopted: http://www.energycodes.gov/adoption/states. For more info, See ASA.ORG (Alliance to Save Energy) and ICCSAFE.ORG (International Code Council). And for a brief summary of how these organizations draft, sponsor, and enact policy, read Katherine Salant's short article in the *Washington Post*, "Energy Efficiency Codes Mean Lower Utility Bills, but Not All Builders Are Sold", http://www.washingtonpost.com/wp-dyn/content/article/2010/05/14/AR2010051400355.html.

10/ "City Car", *Changing Places*, http://cp.media.mit.edu/research/54-citycar.

11/ *Terreform1: Architecture Group for Smart City Design, Ecological Planning, and Art*, http://terreform.org.

12/ Bradley, John, "Environmental Visionaries: The Urban Remodeler", *POPSCI*, last modified 23 June 2010, http://www.popsci.com/node/46221.

13/ *Mitchell Joachim: Terreform One*, http://www.archinode.com/fab-tree-hab-1.html.

14/ Joachim, Mitchell, "Ecotopia and Eco-Cities", lecture given at the European Graduate School, 2012, http://www.youtube.com/watch?v=6sRe8msqa90.

15/ Bhabha, Homi, "Mumbai on My Mind: Some Thoughts on Sustainability", *Ecological Urbanism*, Mohsen Mostafavi and Gareth Doherty eds., Zürich: Lars Müller Publishers, 2013, p. 78.

16/ "Graffiti", MGL c.266, s.126A-126B, *Massachusetts Trial Court Law Libraries*, last updated 26 August 2013, http://www.lawlib.state.ma.us/subject/popname/popnamed-k.html#g.

17/ *Liz Christy Community Garden*, http://www.lizchristygarden.us.

18/ *Adam Purple and the Garden of Eden*, dir. Amy Brost, 2011, http://www.youtube.com/watch?v=-VfBvdzgQxY.

19/ Whitman, Walt, "Song of Myself", *Leaves of Grass*, 150th Anniversary Edition, David S. Reynolds ed., New York: Oxford University Press, 2005.

20/ *Adam Purple and the Garden of Eden*, dir. Amy Brost, 2011, http://www.youtube.com/watch?v=-VfBvdzgQxY.

21/ Hill, Christopher, *The World Turned Upside Down: Radical Ideas during the English Revolution*, London: Penguin Books, 1991.

22/ Whitman, *Leaves of Grass*, preface, vii; Hill, *The World Turned Upside Down*, p. 113: "Landowners in the area round St George's Hill were more disturbed by the digging than the Council of State or General Fairfax, who had a series of amicable conversations with Winstanley — despite the latter's refusal to remove his hat to a 'fellow creature'."

23/ Winstanley, Gerrard, "The Law of Freedom in a Platform" (1662). http://www.bilderberg.org/land/lawofree.htm.

24/ Gurney, John, *Gerrard Winstanley: The Digger's Life and Legacy*, London: Pluto Press, 2013, pp. 83–84.

25/ Gurney, pp. 120–121.

26/ "Richard Reynolds at TEDxNewham", *TED: Ideas Worth Spreading*, added 1 July 2013, http://tedxtalks.ted.com/video/Richard-Reynolds-at-TEDxNewham.

27/ Reynolds, Richard, *On Guerrilla Gardening: A Handbook for Gardening without Boundaries*, New York: Bloomsbury, 2008, pp. 15–16.

28/ Giono, Jean, *The Man Who Planted Trees*, London: Harvill Press, 1995, p. 16.

29/ Virilio, Paul, *Speed and Politics*, Mark Polizzotti trans., Los Angeles: Semiotext(e), 2006. Virilio coined the word 'dromology' to account for the way in which wars drive history and time. Dromology is literally the science of speed.

30/ Contractor, Huned, "Seeds of Revolution", *harmonyindia.org*, December 2008, http://www.harmonyindia.org/hportal/VirtualPageView.jsp?page_id=8252&index1=0.

31/ "Wangari Maathai's Legacy", *The Green Belt Movement*, http://www.greenbeltmovement.org.

32/ Means, Howard, *Johnny Appleseed: The Man, the Myth, the American Story*, New York: Simon & Schuster, 2011, pp. 51–60.

33/ Scott, James C., *Seeing Like a State: How Certain Schemes to Improve the Human Condition Have Failed*, New Haven: Yale University Press, 1998.

34/ Means, *Johnny Appleseed*, pp. 65, 70.

35/ Means, *Johnny Appleseed*, p. 89.

290 /MARGARET MORTON

THE GARDENS OF THOSE CALLED 'HOMELESS'

I built a tent around a park bench. I have a garden outside. I've got a place. I've got a garden.
/ Nathaniel Hunter, Tompkins Square Park, New York City

In 1989, when my documentation of New York City's homeless communities began, there were more homeless New Yorkers than at any time since the Great Depression. 25,000 homeless poor sought beds in city shelters each night. Thousands more slept outside. As the situation worsened, a startling phenomenon occurred: homeless people began to scavenge building materials from the streets to improvise housing for themselves. These encampments, not seen on such a scale since the Hoovervilles of the 1930s, multiplied in Manhattan's public parks, vacant lots, along riverfronts, beneath bridges, and deep within underground tunnels. Clusters of dwellings frequently evolved into small villages, underscoring the need for a sense of security and community.

Figure 1/ Nathaniel's Garden. All photographs in this essay by Margaret Morton.

NATHANIEL

The largest of these was in Tompkins Square Park in Manhattan's East Village, where 150 homeless people had set up tents by the late 1980s. Nathaniel Hunter, who was nicknamed 'The Mayor' of the Park for his advocacy on behalf of the other homeless residents, built the largest tent in the Park. He also made a garden [Figure 1].

Nathaniel assembled his garden from a collection of found objects, nestled in a bed of dried leaves and twigs.

> Two or three big sunflowers came up there from seeds. I had a praying mantis there. I found it on the other side of the fence, caught him, and put him in a cage. I would bring him out to play in the garden in the daytime. At night I would put him on a stick and put him back in his cage and keep him in my tent.

The Tompkins Square Park homeless community was evicted by police in December 1989. The men and women fled the park with whatever they could carry, or watched, powerless, while their possessions were destroyed. Many made their way back. 18 months later, a phalanx of police in riot gear routed the homeless community from the park and closed it for renovation. When the park reopened two years later, a curfew was imposed.

After the park was cleared by police, many of the homeless women and men resettled a few blocks east in abandoned vacant lots, barren since the arsons of the mid-1970s when landlords had their own buildings torched to collect the insurance money.

PEPE AND HECTOR

Other encampments survived for several years and gradually expanded into more permanent settlements. In the late 1980s 12 homeless men and two women assembled plywood houses in a vacant lot on East Fourth Street. They had come to New York from the villages of Puerto Rico — young men and women with dreams of a better life. Soon they discovered low pay, illness, and bad luck. 30 years later they were unemployed and homeless, but not without the will to survive. They cleared debris from the deserted lot, scavenged building material in the early morning hours, and constructed plywood houses along a central path. In spite of, or perhaps because of, their unfortunate circumstances, residents continually embellished their homes with additions that stirred memories of places they had left behind. Interior courtyards, painted rock gardens, and open porches recalled their childhood homes in Puerto Rico. Salsa music filled the air.

Pepe Otero took over a friend's three-walled shack. "I arrived in 1990. When I took over, this was nothing, only this room. I was living in Tompkins Square Park for six months. I made my tent there with plastic bags. It was up to me to keep

Figure 2/ Pepe and Pepito.

my surroundings clean." Pepe set to work to expand the shack and make it his home. First, he repaired the roof.

> It was so low. I had to push it up, two inches more. I put in a new beam, this one in the center. It had so many leaks, leaking all over. I added the awning. I've improved it. And I'm going to improve it some more — try to make it better for next winter.

Pepe's improvements included a tool room, which served not only to safeguard his tools and building materials, but provided a workshop where he could earn money repairing lamps, radios, and cassette players for people who lived in the surrounding tenements.

Pepe added metal window grates cut from shopping carts to protect his home from vandalism by local gangs who cut through the lot. He built a front porch and enclosed it with a fence of discarded plastic bakery trays and framed his entrance with bedposts that he had found in the trash. "I'm going to make the porch look better. I'm going to make it [whistles] in the summer time ... to sit outside."

The following spring, Pepe paved the path in front of his home with marble tiles that had been discarded from an apartment renovation a block away. With the help of his friend, Pepito, Pepe dug holes for fence posts and covered the walkway with a *marquesina* [Figure 2]. "In Puerto Rico we have things like that." The roofed walkway also connected his house to a vegetable garden, which he walled with a double tier of plastic bread trays. Pepe tended his garden and harvested squash and string beans that he shared with other members of the community [Figure 3].

Figure 3/ Harvest.

Over four years, Pepe worked tirelessly to transform his plywood shack into a five-room home. "My house, in Puerto Rico, it was beautiful. A big house with a balcony. And so many rooms." During the winter months, he planned new building projects.

> The tool room is still unfinished. Too cold now. I'd like to finish the kitchen. Then I'm going to start a bathroom — soon as the weather gets a little warmer — if I'm still alive.

Pepe's neighbor, Hector Amezquita, who was nicknamed 'Guineo' for his love of bananas, built a house for himself on the same vacant lot. Hector added a painted rock garden and enclosed a courtyard that recalled his childhood home in Puerto Rico. When he found a sign along the path that read BUSHVILLE — this was 1992 — he added it to his courtyard fence, followed by an inflated palm tree and a salvaged garden statue that he had found in the trash [Figure 4]. Hector's private courtyard was his refuge, where he enjoyed quiet mornings reading the daily Spanish newspaper.

The following summer, Hector extended his plantings of bugbane to both sides of the entrance. He kept his plants alive by carrying water in buckets from a fire hydrant on Avenue D, as there was no water supply on the lot. In August, Hector added a roof over the courtyard for shade, but kept it open to catch the breezes. He attached a clothespin wheel to refrigerator shelving to form a decorative flower atop his courtyard-garden fence [Figure 5].

In late autumn, Hector completely enclosed his courtyard and added a roof to prepare his house for the impending cold. "I have to think of something to keep this place warm," he said. "The porch roof is not ready for winter. I have to make it better." When winter came, Hector moved his cooking fire indoors and painted his walls to better display his collections of found sculpture and musical instruments.

> This is my work. I can't work here. I can't work there. This is something I've got to do with my life. I figure if I don't do something here, my mind will die. I started like a poor person, but now I feel better, now I feel comfortable. This is the first time I do something for myself. I am on to fifty-five. Too much for me. For me, it's like a hundred.

The following spring, Hector did a second planting, surrounded by a string fence tied to four corner posts [Figure 6]. He decorated his house with small animal heads and a plastic pineapple. That same summer, workmen renovated the

Figure 5/ Clothespin Flower.

Figure 6/ Second Planting.

abandoned apartment building directly behind his home. Hector's home could be easily observed from the restored windows, which had been bricked shut for several years. The new tenants, low-income families, complained about the homeless community, which they viewed from the windows of their freshly painted apartments.

Figure 4/ Rock Garden.

Figure 7/ Destroyed.

Figure 8/ "Away, away, folks."

Despite its look of permanence, the homeless community could not endure. The residents had been warned of impending eviction, but had made no preparations because they had nowhere else to go. Early on a cold December morning, the bulldozers arrived. People quickly gathered their belongings. The noise of the heavy equipment was deafening. Massive shovels entered the lot and wrenched the small houses from their foundations [Figure 7]. First Hector Amezquita's house, then Pepe Otero's five-room home. The bulldozers held the small houses high, then hurled them to the ground. In moments, the community was destroyed. Everyone scattered, seeking temporary shelter in doorways, abandoned cars, or with friends, while their homes fell splintered, piles of refuse once again.

JAMES, MARIA, AND ANNA

Five blocks north, James Heyward assembled a garden on a vacant lot to protect his tent from demolition and to frighten away intruders. He found rocks on the lot, broken bricks on a nearby construction site, and salvaged enamel paint from the trash of a nearby car repair shop. Before painting images on the rocks, James washed, then sanded, painted, and sanded them again until the surface was smooth.

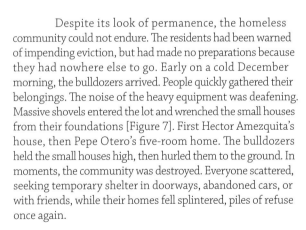

We have the number one tent and the number one garden. Every morning we clean and rake our yard. Every time you walk by here, you see it clean. We have a lady head with a knife in it and there's a gun pointing at her. That's for a reason. People know that means trouble. Away, away, folks. Even the cop, he knows what it means. And we leave it outside at nighttime, and nobody touches it [Figure 8].

Two blocks from James Heyward's garden, behind a high chain link fence on East Eleventh Street, a forest of ailanthus obscures a curious scene. The only entrance was blocked by a sign that warned: YOU SHALL BE DEALT WITH [Figure 9]. It was necessary to remove the sign and crawl through a narrow opening, over which a frayed metal wire, barely visible, was strung three feet from the pavement.

Inside, there were more than a hundred stuffed animals and dolls [Figures 10, 11]. The stuffed animals had been exposed to the elements for so long that they were hardened like cement. The plants were both living and plastic. The dolls were nestled among the stuffed animals, and the animals were arranged in such a way that they seemed to be watching over the dolls. But on closer observation, it became evident that although the stuffed animals had been left completely intact, the dolls were often maimed. Heads and arms, wrenched from bodies, were left detached.

The lyrical play of light and shadow through the trees in this sanctuary for stuffed animals seemed dissonant with the dolls' severed heads and limbs. Both of the gardeners were recluses. Maria lived alone in the crumbling, abandoned five-story building adjacent to the lot, which was labeled as unsafe for occupancy. Anna lived in a tenement across the

Figure 9/ Entrance.

street. Both women had come to Manhattan from Eastern Europe after World War II.

JIMMY

Jimmy carved an oval pond from the hard dirt of a sun-baked lot on the Lower East Side. He lined the pond with black plastic garbage bags and filled it with water from a nearby fire hydrant.

He bordered the pond with fragments of brick and stone from the rubble of an abandoned building and stocked it with goldfish that flickered in the sunlight. Streaks of orange would suddenly break the water's surface, then disappear. He told me that teenage boys would come into the lot and steal his goldfish or just leave them on the edge to die, but that he always replaced them with what little money he got from recycling cans. In the back of the lot, Jimmy grew corn and

Figure 10/ Curious Scene.

Figure 11/ Nestled.

Figure 12/ Jimmy's Fishpond.

tomatoes and slept in a small tent. Leaning back in his chair, he recalled his boyhood home in South Carolina: sunlight filtering through lace curtains, a piano in the parlor, and a house overlooking a pond [Figure 12].

When I returned eight days later, bringing photographs and a tape recorder, Jimmy, his fishpond, the tent, and the garden were gone. It seemed as though his idyllic setting had never existed. Two homeless men, who lived along the sidewalk outside of the fence, told me that a bulldozer had arrived with no warning and that Jimmy, highly distraught from the demolition of his home and beloved fishpond, had wandered the neighborhood for a few days, then disappeared.

IVAN, SHAFT, AND LISA

In Chinatown, a homeless community known as The Hill was assembled on a empty lot that borders the Canal Street off-ramp of the Manhattan Bridge. Bypassed by a steady stream of traffic from Brooklyn, The Hill gained renown for its highly visible homeless encampment and unusual dwellings.

After Ivan moved onto the Hill, he quickly transformed his makeshift lean-to into a more permanent home. He paved a walkway, hung decorations, and planted a tiny garden [Figure 13]. When Shaft and Lisa later took over his house, they raised the roof up four inches and started selling Christmas wreaths, which they had assembled from

found bits of discarded evergreen and ribbon, to the truck drivers who were constantly stuck in traffic on the Manhattan Bridge. They kept Ivan's walkway, but his garden disappeared. Shaft and Lisa defined a front lawn from discarded wall-to-wall carpeting that they found along the street. Their addition of this semi-public space extended their boundaries within the community that they could claim as their own. After Shaft added a Dutch door and some outdoor furniture, Sammy, a neighbor, complained, "This place is starting to look like Queens!"

MR. LEE

The most curious home on the Hill was that of Mr. Lee, who had arrived at the encampment without a word in 1989, carrying his possessions in a burlap sack. He soon astonished his neighbors by constructing a house without sawing a board or pounding a nail. Instead, his house was bound together with knots. Bright yellow plastic straps wrapped his soft rounded hut, binding old mattresses and bedsprings into walls [Figure 14]. The exterior was festooned with red bakery ribbons, paper lanterns, and castoff calendars that celebrated the Chinese New Year. Oranges, Chinese symbols of prosperity, had hardened in the bitter cold and hung from straps like ornaments.

Mr. Lee's life revolved around the ongoing creation and re-creation of his home. The majestic cluster of fruit perched atop his roof was in fact a teddy bear, which he had

Figure 13/ More Permanence: paved walkway, decorations, and a tiny garden.

Figure 14/ Mr. Lee's Garden.

Figure 15/ Majestic Cluster.

found on the street, bound tightly with knots, and skillfully transformed [Figure 15]. Each day at dawn, when Mr. Lee left the Hill, he placed a stone against a door that he had made from discarded loading palettes, then further secured it with more of his elaborate knots. Mr. Lee slowly wandered the streets of Chinatown with two burlap rice sacks slung over his shoulder, pausing to collect bits of cloth and cord left by the morning delivery trucks. In the early evening Mr. Lee returned and, with great ceremony, tied his new treasures to the exterior of his hut.

At five o'clock in the morning, on 29 May 1992, an arsonist, seeking revenge on another resident, set fire to Mr. Lee's home. He died in the blaze. A neighbor, who also had lost his home in the fire and barely survived, erected a memorial to Mr. Lee. YI-PO-LI. HE WAS ONE OF US.

ANGELO

A massive concrete pier stretches out into the Hudson River at West Forty-Fourth Street. To the south, sightseeing boats arrive and depart on the hour. To the north, tourists swarm over the Intrepid, a World War II aircraft carrier. The seven men on the wharf seem oblivious to these activities, as they go about their work, building their homes.

Angelo Aldi's hut had two small gardens, planted with children's toys and guarded by a driftwood snake [Figures 16, 17]. A hand-painted wooden sign, ALDI, marked the entrance to his four-foot-high home. Angelo bent low to enter. A taller visitor crawled on hands and knees. The interior

mysteriously seemed to expand. There was a bed, a dresser, a writing desk with a lamp, a basket filled with clothes, a collection of toys, framed photographs on the walls, an American flag, and a handmade calendar on which Angelo marked off the days.

BERNARD

The most longstanding of the homeless communities in Manhattan survived for over 23 years in an abandoned railroad tunnel stretching for two and a half miles under Manhattan's Riverside Park. Those who arrived first moved into pre-existing concrete structures that had been used by the railroad workers until the freight service went bankrupt in the early 1970s. When Bernard Isaac arrived in the early 1980s, he took over a concrete room deep into the tunnel. He carefully handpicked other homeless people to share his secret hiding place, and by the late 1980s his camp had grown to 17 men and women. Those who arrived later built plywood shanties for themselves, which they clustered beneath air vents, where shafts of daylight punctuated the darkness. When summer breezes carried seeds from the park's plants and trees through these openings to the tracks below, sometimes they would sprout. Bernard nurtured the young shoots as best he could and watered them until they took root.

Once the weather really gets warm, certain seeds will drop through the grate from up top and things sprout over here.

Figure 16/ Wharf Garden.

Figure 17/ Planted with Toys.

Figure 18/ Underground Garden.

This area has always had plant life. We even had some tomato plants. It will be interesting to see what comes up this spring. I guess you saw the melon seeds over there. I always throw the seeds of the watermelon on the mound. Some of them sprout and the vines grow down the hill. They always end up dying, but whatever. It's just good to see something green under here. That's why I do it all the time.

At night Bernard searched the streets of the Upper West Side where residents and restaurant workers had left trash along the streets for garbage collection. There he would find foodstuffs to cook on his grill and plants to add his underground garden [Figures 18, 19] .

I had a couple of fruit trees, but I didn't protect them in the wintertime and they died. It was either an orange or a lemon

Figure 19/ The Good Gardener: leaving something behind....

tree that survived up until the middle of December. The first
heavy snowstorm killed it, but it was amazing.

Bernard had already lived in the tunnel for 11 winters.

I envision that when I leave here I'm going to leave something
behind. I'd like to leave something like a plant or tree behind,
then one day return here and say, 'Look how my tree has grown.'

304 /CONTRIBUTORS

THE GOOD GARDENER?

EDITORS

ANNETTE GIESECKE is Professor of Classics at the University of Delaware. With a background in the art and literature of the classical world, she has written on a variety of subjects ranging from Epicurean philosophy and the poetry of Homer and Vergil to the history and meaning of gardens in classical antiquity. She is author of *The Mythology of Plants: Botanical Lore from Ancient Greece and Rome*, and *The Epic City: Urbanism, Utopia, and the Garden in Ancient Greece and Rome*. With Naomi Jacobs, she is editor of and contributor to *Earth Perfect? Nature, Utopia, and the Garden*.

NAOMI JACOBS is Professor of English at the University of Maine and past President of the Society for Utopian Studies. A member of the Editorial Committees for the journal *Utopian Studies* and the Ralahine Utopian Studies book series, she is the author of *The Character of Truth: Historical Figures in Contemporary Fiction* as well as of many articles on utopian and dystopian writers of the nineteenth and twentieth centuries, including William Morris, George Orwell, Ursula K. Le Guin, and Octavia Butler.

CONTRIBUTORS

Raised on the arid Saskatchewan prairies, **SHELLEY BOYD** is a transplant in the verdant west coast of British Columbia where she is a Canadian literature specialist at Kwantlen Polytechnic University. Her book *Garden Plots: Canadian Women Writers and Their Literary Gardens* examines the relationship between gardening and writing from pioneer domestic manuals to contemporary poetry.

STEVEN BROWN is a poet, photography critic, and literary scholar. He is currently a PhD candidate in Harvard's American Studies program, finishing a dissertation on 'aesthetics of waste' in early American art and literature. His recent publications include a book of poems, *To the Wheatlight of June*; an essay on contemporary photography in *Eyemazing: The New Collectible Photography*; and an essay on the Spanish painter, Dino Valls, in the monograph *Ex Picturis II*.

STEPHANIE BRYAN is a landscape historian, printmaker, and photographer from Atlanta, Georgia. In 2012, she was

awarded the Damaris Horan Prize in Landscape History by the Royal Oak Foundation, enabling her to travel to Northern Ireland to research Lady Londonderry's gardens at Mount Stewart. Her artistic endeavors include a series of intaglio prints of Italian Renaissance villas and a photographic documentation of suburban developments in Georgia abandoned after the recent economic downturn.

Professor of Philosophy Emeritus at Durham University, England, **DAVID E. COOPER** has written widely on aesthetics and Asian philosophy. His authored books include *A Philosophy of Gardens* and *Convergence with Nature: A Daoist Perspective*. David now divides his time between writing and his work as the Secretary of the charity, Project Sri Lanka.

RICK DARKE is design consultant, photographer, and author of numerous books. His work is grounded in an observational ethic that blends art, ecology, and cultural geography in the design and stewardship of living landscapes. Rick's projects include parks, post-industrial sites, transportation corridors, corporate and collegiate campuses, conservation developments, and botanic gardens. For more information, see www.rickdarke.com.

ANASTASIA DAY is a PhD Fellow in the Hagley Program for the History of Industrialization at the University of Delaware. Her research interests include gender, consumption, technology, and at the heart of these themes, the environment.

M. ELEN DEMING is Professor of Landscape Architecture at the University of Illinois, Urbana-Champaign, where she teaches design studio, landscape history, and research design. From 1993 to 2008, she taught at the SUNY College of Environmental Science and Forestry in Syracuse. Former editor of *Landscape Journal* (2002 to 2009), she also co-authored the book *Landscape Architecture Research: Inquiry/Strategy/Design*.

Architect and theorist **DONALD DUNHAM** is Assistant Professor in the College of Architecture and the Built Environment at Philadelphia University. His published work, which focuses on the utopian impulse in architecture, includes "Modulating a Dialogue between Architecture and Nature" in *The New American Dream*, "Architecture *Without* Nature?" in *Earth Perfect?*, and "Beyond the Red Curtain: Less is More Utopia" in the journal *Utopian Studies*.

ROBERT FINLEY keeps his own boreal gardens in Nova Scotia and Newfoundland where he teaches literature and creative writing at the Memorial University of Newfoundland. He is the author of *The Accidental Indies*, and (collaboratively) of *A Ragged Pen: Essays on Poetry and Memory,* books that are, in some sense, about gardens too.

Director at the Botanic Gardens of Adelaide, **STEPHEN FORBES** views botanic gardens as an institutional framework to address contemporary challenges in plant conservation and environmental reconciliation. He has promoted plant-based solutions to urban environmental and social issues through sustainable landscapes, green infrastructure, and community capacity building. An advocate of exploring applications of Traditional Ecological Knowledge, he chairs the South Australian Environment Department's Aboriginal Reconciliation Committee.

FRANKLIN GINN is a lecturer in Human Geography at the University of Edinburgh. His research focuses on more-than-human geographies. He has published on domestic garden cultures, and is currently completing a book, *Domestic Wild*. His current research explores cultures of apocalypse and the Anthropocene, and as part of an AHRC-funded project, religious responses to climate ethics.

KATHLEEN JOHN-ALDER is an Assistant Professor in the Department of Landscape Architecture at Rutgers University. Her research explores the transformative role of ecology and environmentalism in mid-twentieth century landscape design. Kathleen was awarded a Dumbarton Oaks Fellowship in 2013, and the Landscape History Chapter of the American Society of Architectural Historians essay award in 2014.

LEANNE LIDDLE has rich practical experience within the arid environment of Central Australia. She has worked to support greater understanding of the contribution Aboriginal people can and do make to protecting and sustaining native flora and fauna in the twenty-first century. An Arrernte woman from Central Australia, Leanne works with some of the world's experts in fire use and knowledge from the Anangu Pitjantjatjara Yankunytjatjara Lands. She is Manager, APY Lands & West Coast for the South Australian Premiers Department.

Author of *Rambunctious Garden*, **EMMA MARRIS** is a writer based in Klamath Falls, Oregon. She writes about the environment, evolution, energy, agriculture, and more. Her goal is to find and tell the stories that help us understand how humanity and other species on the planet may flourish, how to move towards a greener, wilder, happier, and more equal future. Emma's work has appeared in *Conservation*, *Slate*, *Nature Medicine*, *OnEarth*, and *Nature*.

MARGARET MORTON is photographer/author of *Transitory Gardens, Uprooted Lives*, co-authored with Diana Balmori; *The Tunnel: The Underground Homeless of New York City*; *Fragile Dwelling; Glass House*; and, most recently, *Cities of the Dead: The Ancestral Cemeteries of Kyrgyzstan*. She is Professor of Art at The Cooper Union in New York City.

Writer **WILLIAM RUBEL** lives in Santa Cruz, California. His focus is traditional foodways with an emphasis on culinary history. William is the author of *The Magic of Fire: Hearth Cooking: One Hundred Recipes for Fireplace and Campfire* and *Bread, a global history*.

LINDA WEINTRAUB currently teaches, curates, writes about, and creates art situated at the intersection of ecology and environmentalism. Her most recent book, *TO LIFE! Eco Art in Pursuit of a Sustainable Planet*, establishes the principles she enacts on a homestead in upstate New York where she lives sustainably and raises animals, fruits, and vegetables.

VOLKER M. WELTER is an architectural historian who has studied and worked in Germany, Scotland, and England. He is Professor at the Department of History of Art and Architecture, University of California at Santa Barbara, teaching Californian and European modern architectural history. His latest book is *Ernst L. Freud, Architect: The Case of the Modern Bourgeois Home*.

Having recently completed a collectively authored book on Las Vegas, **SUSAN WILLIS** is dedicating herself to the restorative powers of nature and the all but forgotten work of America's nature writers. Susan teaches courses on Literature and Culture at Duke University, and to explore the intersection of nature and culture, she operates an organic farm specializing in seasonal vegetables and goat milk products.

Artifice books on architecture
10A Acton Street   t. +44 (0)207 713 5097
London WC1X 9NG   f. +44 (0)207 713 8682

sales@artificebooksonline.com
www.artificebooksonline.com

All opinions expressed within this publication are those of the authors and not necessarily of the publisher.

Designed by Rachel Pfleger at Artifice books on architecture.
Edited by Annette Giesecke and Naomi Jacobs.
British Library Cataloguing-in-Publication Data.
A CIP record for this book is available from the British Library.

ISBN 978 1 908967 45 9

Artifice books on architecture is an environmentally responsible company. *The Good Gardener?: Nature, Humanity, and the Garden* is printed on sustainably sourced paper.

Front cover/ *Adam and Eve*, Albrecht Dürer, Nüremburg, 1504. Adam holding a branch of the Tree of Life and Eve the fruit of the Tree of Knowledge. Engraving on paper, bequeathed by Miss Alice G. E. Carthew, Victoria and Albert Museum, London. Photograph © Victoria and Albert Museum.

Back cover/ *Bernard*, fruit trees in the underground garden, New York City. Photograph by Margaret Morton.

The Good Gardener?: Nature, Humanity, and the Garden is a companion to *Earth Perfect?: Nature, Utopia, and the Garden* ISBN 978 1 907317 75 0, also edited by Annette Giesecke and Naomi Jacobs.